£1 — 1-50.

THE SPORTSPAGES
ALMANAC 1990

THE COMPLETE SPORTING FACTBOOK

**Matthew Engel and
Ian Morrison**

D0996014

SPORTS PAGES
SIMON & SCHUSTER

A SPORTSPAGES BOOK

First published in Great Britain by
Simon and Schuster Ltd in 1989

Copyright © Matthew Engel and Ian Morrison 1989

This book is copyright under the Berne Convention.
No reproduction without permission.
All rights reserved.

SPORTSPAGES
The Specialist Sports Bookshop
Caxton Way
94-96 Charing Cross Road
London WC2H 0JG

Simon & Schuster Ltd
West Garden Place
Kendal Street
London W2 2AQ

Simon & Schuster of Australia Pty Ltd
Sydney

British Library Cataloguing-in-Publication Data available
ISBN 0-671-65314-8

Typeset by Learning Curve, Watford
Printed and bound in Great Britain
by Billing & Sons, Worcester

CONTENTS

INTRODUCTION   v
ABBREVIATIONS   vi
THE THINGS THEY DID   vii
THE THINGS THEY SAID   viii
STARS OF THE '80s   xi
THE GUIDE TO 1990   xiii
AMERICAN FOOTBALL   1
ANGLING   6
ARCHERY   7
ASSOCIATION FOOTBALL   8
ATHLETICS   48
AUSTRALIAN RULES FOOTBALL   64
BADMINTON   65
BASEBALL   68
BASKETBALL   72
BILLIARDS   76
BOWLS   78
BOXING   81
CANOEING   97
COMMONWEALTH GAMES   100
CRICKET   116
CROQUET   153
CYCLING   154
DARTS   161
EQUESTRIANISM   162
FENCING   166
GAELIC SPORTS   168
GOLF   170
GREYHOUND RACING   189
GYMNASTICS   190
HOCKEY   194
HORSE RACING   196

ICE HOCKEY	219
JUDO	221
LACROSSE	223
MODERN PENTATHLON	224
MOTOR CYCLING	225
MOTOR RACING, AND RALLYING	229
NETBALL	237
ORIENTEERING	238
POLO	239
RACKETS	240
REAL TENNIS	240
ROWING	241
RUGBY LEAGUE	245
RUGBY UNION	251
SHOOTING	262
SHOW JUMPING *(see EQUESTRIANISM)*	
SKIING *(see WINTER SPORTS)*	
SNOOKER	264
SPEEDWAY	269
SQUASH	271
SWIMMING	273
TABLE TENNIS	282
TENNIS	285
VOLLEYBALL	301
WATER SKIING	302
WEIGHTLIFTING	303
WINTER SPORTS	305
WRESTLING	312
YACHTING	316
MISCELLANY	319
OBITUARY	320
THE GUIDE TO 1890	323

INTRODUCTION

In The Sportspages Bookshop in London it is possible to find a volume called *The Neuromechanical Basis of Kinesiology*. This is exceptionally useful if you want to find out about the relationship between position, velocity and acceleration of a triple-turning dive with one-and-a-half backward somersaults.

No? Then what about *The Art of Gymnastics on the Moving Horse?* Or *43 Years of Stirling Albion?* What there never has been is a straightforward reference book on the sporting year, aimed at all kinesiologists, moving-horse-gymnasts and Stirling Albion supporters and also everyone else who watches sport, argues about it and occasionally wants their memory refreshed.

So this is it. Who won the FA Cup, in 1989 or any other year? What won the Derby? What was Gooch's average in the Test series? Who were the most successful football and cricket teams of the 80s? What happened involving a cow and a cricket ball in Devon last summer? How did a man, his wife and his dog all get sent off a rugby field? Who won the world sidecar championship in 1952? (Look that one up.) *The Sportspages Almanac* does not only deal in the obvious.

This book includes a list of 1989 results in each sport followed by a list of past champions. Where appropriate, there are records and fixtures for 1990. There is a review of the year for the major sports, and a wide selection of quotes. We have tried to include everything that is important and a fair amount of the trivial and the downright irrelevant. The results run from January 1 1989, except in those cases like soccer where seasons do not start and finish so conveniently. Subsequent Sportspages years will run from roughly October to September. This first edition will, of course, eventually be priceless.

Starting an almanac like this is always fraught (ask Mr Wisden or Mr Rothman) and there are bound to be mistakes somewhere. We just pray they are trivial ones. We ask that you point them out to us – but gently – so they can be corrected for the 1991 edition. (There is a special health warning about the fixtures; they are always liable to change.) We would also be grateful for any suggestions for inclusions in the next edition plus any cuttings, oddities and quotes, particularly those from local and overseas newspapers that are harder to monitor.

The words are mine; the statistics are almost all Ian's. I am extremely grateful for his exceptional hard work and even temper, nearly all the time. We would both like to thank all the sporting officials who went to so much trouble to be helpful. They are too numerous to mention; it would be much easier to mention the three organisations which were downright obstructive, and next year I reckon we will.

We would also like to thank John Gaustad, Vivien Green, Clyde Hunter, Richard Wigmore, Tony Short, Clare Sychrava and Philippa McEwan for helping to drag the book, kicking and screaming, into the world; Ann Morrison and Clare Braithwaite for their special support; John Trachim for his brilliant detective work on the fixtures; and also Jeremy Alexander, Mike Austin, Mike Averis and everyone else on the *Guardian* sports desk, Simon Barnes, Steve Barnett, John Campbell, Leslie Cranfield, Robert Eastaway, Keith Elliott, Chris Fear, Reg Hayter, Norman de Mesquita, Gerald Mortimer, Andrew Nickolds, Pat Rowley, John Samuel, Geoff Slattery, Alex Spink, Patrick Sullivan, John Vinicombe, Barrie Weekes, Mike Weiss and Micky Wood.

There are also mentions for Adrian and Pat Mills of Scott's Bar, Santa Ponsa, Majorca, who provided Ian with his fuel; and my cat, who has learned how to walk across a computer keyboard in such a way that he can delete an entire chapter, a trick I could not manage even after reading the manual.

Matthew Engel
c/o Simon and Schuster, West Garden Place, Kendal St., London W2 2AQ

ABBREVIATIONS

List of abbreviations for countries commonly used in this book.

Alb	Albania	Jer	Jersey
Alg	Algeria	Ken	Kenya
Arg	Argentina	Kuw	Kuwait
Aus	Australia	Lie	Liechtenstein
Aut	Austria	Lux	Luxembourg
Bah	Bahamas	Mal	Malta
Bar	Barbados	Mex	Mexico
Bel	Belgium	Mon	Mongolia
Ber	Bermuda	Mor	Morocco
Boh	Bohemia	NI	Northern Ireland
Bol	Bolivia	Nic	Nicaragua
Bra	Brazil	Nig	Nigeria
Bul	Bulgaria	NKo	North Korea
Bur	Burma	Nor	Norway
Cam	Cameroon	NRo	Northern Rhodesia
Can	Canada	NZ	New Zealand
Chi	Chile	Pak	Pakistan
Chn	China	Pan	Panama
Col	Colombia	Par	Paraguay
Cub	Cuba	Per	Peru
Cyp	Cyprus	Phi	Philippines
Cze	Czechoslovakia	Pol	Poland
Den	Denmark	Por	Portugal
Dji	Djibouti	PR	Puerto Rico
Dom	Dominican Republic	Rho	Rhodesia
Ecu	Ecuador	Rom	Romania
Egy	Egypt	SA	South Africa
Eng	England	Sco	Scotland
Est	Estonia	Sen	Senegal
Eth	Ethiopia	Sin	Singapore
Fij	Fiji	SKo	South Korea
Fin	Finland	Som	Somalia
Fra	France	Spa	Spain
FRG	West Germany	Sri	Sri Lanka
GB	Great Britain	SRo	Southern Rhodesia
GDR	East Germany	Sud	Sudan
Ger	Germany	Sur	Surinam
Gha	Ghana	SVi	St Vincent
Gre	Greece	Swe	Sweden
Gue	Guernsey	Swi	Switzerland
Guy	Guyana	Syr	Syria
Hai	Haiti	Tai	Taiwan
Haw	Hawaii	Tan	Tanzania
HK	Hong Kong	Tha	Thailand
Hol	The Netherlands	Tri	Trinidad & Tobago
Hun	Hungary	Tun	Tunisia
Ice	Iceland	Tur	Turkey
Ina	Indonesia	UAR	United Arab Emirates
Ind	India	Uga	Uganda
IOM	Isle of Man	Uru	Uruguay
Ire	Republic of Ireland	US	United States
Irn	Iran	USSR	Soviet Union
Irq	Iraq	Ven	Venezuela
Isr	Israel	VI	Virgin Islands
Ita	Italy	Wal	Wales
Jam	Jamaica	Yug	Yugoslavia
Jap	Japan	Zai	Zaire
		Zam	Zambia
		Zim	Zimbabwe

THE THINGS THEY DID

Most of the great sporting triumphs of 1989 are mentioned in the chapters relating to the individual sports either in the reviews of each season or amongst the statistics. Pressure of space prevented the inclusion of every piece of news and some are simply impossible to classify. So here The Sportspages Almanac salutes . . .

For instant expertise: Lucy MacSwiney of Chester who won the world women's paragliding championship in Austria only a year after taking up the sport.

For assistance to wounded national pride: The Coq and Boules team from the City of London who beat the representatives of the French Embassy in the *Evening Standard* Boules Championship in Battersea Park.

For professional endeavour: Larry Nixon of Bee Branch, Arkansas, who won 208,000 dollars in a year for bass fishing.

For helpful information: Dr Jukn Sztajzel (sic), a doctor at the University Hospital of Geneva, who did the first scientific research into sex and athletic performance. He announced that sex two hours before sport produced increased heartbeat and thus lower endurance, but sex 10 hours or more beforehand had no effect. The study was prompted by the 1986 soccer World Cup when the Germans were forbidden to sleep with the wives, but the French were not.

For enterprise: Nick Akers (former Commonwealth Games representative of the Cayman Islands) and his brother Chris who formed an Island Games Foundation to include 500 islands ranging from Britain to various specks in the ocean. Guam, Malta, Lord Howe Island (off Australia) and Nantucket Island off Massachusetts all expressed interest. It is thought Britain might be stronger than these rivals at most sports, though perhaps not cricket.

For optimism: The EEC Commission, which proposed that Beethoven's Ode to Joy should be played instead of the national anthems whenever an EEC athlete won a gold medal at the 1992 Olympics.

For indomitability: Wang Ching Chang, 94, of Taiwan, who won over-89 age group gold medals in javelin, shot putt, 100 metres (23.15 secs) and 200 metres (52.33 secs) at the World Veterans' Championship in Eugene, Oregon. He gave the credit to a diet high in vitamins, traditional Chinese medicine and beans. The maximum opposition in each of his events was one: 90-year-old Herbert Kirk of Montana.

For gentle giantism: Andrea Roussimuff, a professional wrestler who headlocked a cameraman after a bout at Cedar Rapids, Iowa. Roussimuff is 7ft 4in and 38 stone. "We had to fit him in the patrol car sideways," said one of the 10 policemen sent to arrest him.

For honest enthusiasm: The ladies of Christchurch, New Zealand who organised a cake stall to help defray the projected £10 million deficit of the 1990 Commonwealth Games.

For misplaced enthusiasm: Myiesha Bradford of Richmond, California, who allegedly shot and paralysed her 38-year-old husband Alvin because she was angry that he rolled a gutter ball and lost a ten pin bowling match.

For lack of enthusiasm: The adult population of Dumfries and Galloway, only 31 per cent of whom participate in sport, compared to 52 per cent of the next lowest Scottish region and 62 per cent of the most active, Tayside.

For refusal to be bullshitted: The Samburu tribesman from Kenya who appeared in an Adidas commercial mouthing their slogan "Just do it". Lee Cronk, an anthropologist at the University of Cincinnati, pointed out that what he really said was "I don't want these. Give me big shoes."

THE THINGS THEY SAID

"I think we'll all be glad to see the back of 1989."
Anonymous soccer manager, Dec 31 1988

"In the 60s music was the mode, the most important means of communication; that's where the highest values of the race were being articulated. I don't think that's the case today. I think today it's sports – that's where our most intense imagination is invited to manifest itself. The sports figures in America are much more attractive, much more interesting and their lives are much more dangerous than the rock figures. They are in the traditional heroic mode."
Leonard Cohen

"I will never denounce apartheid."
Zola Budd, Dec 31 1988

"I do not support any political system that entrenches the superiority of one race over another." *Zola Budd, Jan 3 1989*

"I've always wanted to play for the Lions and I'll always regret it if I don't."
Jonathan Davies on rumours that he might sign for Widnes, Jan 3

"I think the time is right for me to go."
Jonathan Davies, signing for Widnes, Jan 5

"Brian Clough said yesterday that he regretted throwirg punches at fans who invaded the pitch a.ter his side's home win against Queen's Park Rangers on Wednesday."
Daily Telegraph, Jan 20

"If I catch spectators on my pitch in future I know exactly what I'll do. They'll get another clip round the ear'ole."
Brian Clough, The Sun, Jan 20

"Stockport County have made steady gains this season and there is growing optimism that Asa Hartford will guide them out of the bottom division for the first time in 21 years come 1990."
The Times, Mar 22

"Stockport today sacked player-manager Asa Hartford."
Evening Standard, Mar 22

"I've done the work. I've come to collect."
Lloyd Honeyghan, Feb 1, before he fought Marlon Starling

"I think Lloyd needs a nice, long rest and a heart-searching conversation with himself."
Mickey Duff, Honeyghan's manager, Feb 4, after he fought Marlon Starling

"It's like a one-two, one-two on one leg, a one-two, one-two on the other leg with three hops at the end."
Cincinnati Bengals player Ickey Woods describing the Ickey Shuffle before the Superbowl

"It's an offshoot of the Shuffle and we call it the Woo Woo. We call it the Woo Woo because when we shake our fingers we say Woo Woo."
Ickey Woods describing the Woo Woo

"The media hype does not turn me on. I'm not here to be a movie star. I can live without cameras in my face and the same dumb questions. It's a pain to repeat everything three or four times."
Ickey Woods after a solid week describing the Ickey Shuffle and the Woo Woo

"He is entered in the Champion Hurdle, but I think that's clutching at straws."
Trainer Toby Balding on his horse Beech Road
"We did quietly fancy him."
Toby Balding, after Beech Road won the Champion Hurdle

"Cricket's golden boy is back. And David Gower predicted a golden summer for England when his appointment as the fifth Test captain in 11 months was confirmed at Lord's yesterday."
Daily Mail, Apr 6

"Mr Edward Dexter and Mr David Gower – an apology: In common with all other newspapers, we recently published a number of articles about the prospects for the England cricket team under such headlines as "LORD TED'S TEST TONIC" and "IT'S SUPER ENGLAND AS WONDER GOWER RETURNS IN TRIUMPH" . . . The passage

"Make no mistake – Dave and Ted will stuff the Aussies this summer. Border's boys can XXXX off back down under." may in particular have given rise to the unintentional inference that we in some way believed that Mr Dexter and Mr Gower would somehow play a part in a revival of England's cricketing fortunes . . . We apologise to all English cricket-lovers for any distress that may have been caused by our earlier articles, which we now unreservedly withdraw."

Private Eye, Jun 23

THE MICKEY MOUSE SHOW – the *Sun*; GET OUT NOW! – *Daily Mirror*; NO PRIDE. .NO GUTS. .NO GOOD – *Daily Mirror*; ENGLAND MUST AXE PATHETIC PUPPETS – *Daily Star*.

"The press should examine its conscience. If you print headlines of abuse, you get abusive behaviour."

Jon Holmes, David Gower's agent.

"Young men who indulge in football hooliganism wish to portray a macho image so they are not likely to go to a football match in drag, are they?"

Lord Stoddart of Swindon proposing an amendment exempting women from soccer ID cards.

"Five Newport County supporters were arrested after they turned up at Kidderminster Harriers game in drag. About 150 visiting fans arrived in the town but 40 went to the Oxfam shop and bought women's clothes. 'I don't know whether this is a new style or what it is,' said Superintendent Peter Picken."

Worcester Evening News

"Martin Luther King took us to the mountain top and showed us the promised land. I want to take us to the bank."

Don King, boxing promoter

"One day he will asphyxiate by the force of his own exhaust"

Carmen Graciano, trainer, on King

"In the European Cup final, AC Milan gave a display no British side could hope to match . . . and the 97,000 supporters were also there just to enjoy themselves. NO lager louts. NO obscene chants. NO pitch invasion. NO violence."

Leader in The Sun, May 26

"Who says soccer violence is only a British problem? A Spanish riot cop clubs an Italian fan as violence hits the European Cup final."

Caption in Today, May 26

"I just don't have the desire to hurt people any more."

Donny Lalonde, Canadian light-heavyweight, announcing his retirement.

"It's disgusting. It's a false premise . . . I'm seriously thinking of suing this guy."

Donald Trump, owner of the hotel where Lalonde was due to fight.

"Graham Gooch, to my utter amazement, has again been entrusted with the England captaincy."

Ted Dexter, Sunday Mirror, Aug 21 1988

"Things are very different now."

Ted Dexter, making Graham Gooch England captain, Sep 7 1989

"I still remember the thrill of checking the Littlewoods coupon discovering I'd got the eight draws up and winning 30 shillings."

Cardinal Basil Hume, Archbishop of Westminster

"If there isn't something which reflects the qualities of cricket in Heaven, should I ever get there, I'd feel it was a bit of a let-down."

Dr Robert Runcie, Archbishop of Canterbury

"There was a show on about oversexed people and things like this . . . they were calling it a disease. I feel that's exactly what has happened – that a disease was overtaking Wade Boggs and it just did for four years."

Wade Boggs of the Boston Red Sox, embroiled in a $12 million palimony suit

"They were talking about banning me out of baseball because I've got a temper. I got to go to a psychiatrist because I got mad. Here's a guy who says he's a sex fiend. Now who needs the psychiatrist?"

Dennis "Oil Can" Boyd, Boggs's team-mate

"I believe I have learned to look at things more carefully. I am trying hard to evaluate people these days instead of criticising."

John McEnroe

"Your job is to call the score instead of fucking it up."

John McEnroe to umpire John Frame

"Sport isn't about cash. It's about dignity, fair play and being what we used to mean by a sportsman. Money will ruin sport."

Harry Carpenter

"Some say the monetary spiral must cease. I say it will not."

Mark McCormack

"Although it was great fun at the time, I believe that Stephen Potter's writings gave the greatest single shove in the decline of standards of sportsmanship and behaviour generally, by making cheating seem comical. Things have never improved since then."

Letter to The Times from John N. Harris of London W11

"We are England. We are England. No one likes us. We don't care."

Soccer supporters' chant heard in Stockholm

"My words constitute an appeal to Heaven, begging whomever is in charge there to bring about, with the greatest possible despatch, the end of ALL international sporting events, productive as they now are of nothing but cheating, drug-taking, money-grubbing, racial hatred, political statements, advertising, hooliganism, envy, litter, selfishness, vanity, corruption, intolerance, defamation, sexual excess, robbery, drunkenness and, from time to time, murder. (And if I were to dwell on the spectators as well I would need to construct an entirely new thesaurus of condemnation.)"

Bernard Levin, The Times

"Sport is like life with the volume up. The friendships are a little tighter, the laughter's a little louder and the nights are a little bit longer sometimes – like they will be tonight when I'm trying to figure out what happened."

Mike Reid, golfer, after losing the PGA

STARS OF THE 80s

World Sportsman of the Decade: Diego Maradona

World Sportswoman of the Decade: Martina Navratilova

British Sportsman of the Decade: Sebastian Coe

British Sportswoman of the Decade: Virginia Leng

B ecause the first Sportspages Almanac coincides with the end of the 1980s, there are — scattered throughout this book – various charts showing the most successful performers of the decade: the top cricket team, the top soccer team and so on.

Not everything can be measured, though. So we asked 26 leading British sports writers and editors to name their top sports performers of the 1980s. They had to name 1, 2 and 3 in each of four categories; three points were awarded for first place, two for second, one for third.

In each category, victory turned out to be fairly clear-cut, spectacularly so for Navratilova and Coe. Carl Lewis staged a late sprint towards Maradona, but hardly anyone placed him second or third. There was one nice statistical coincidence: the two great rivals Nick Faldo and Sandy Lyle finished level in their section; the same almost happened with Tessa Sanderson and Fatima Whitbread before Sanderson inched ahead. A magnum of champagne goes to James Mossop of the *Sunday Express* for best reflecting the popular will.

In a separate competition, customers of the Sportspages bookshop were asked to guess the results of the journalists' vote. The magnum of champagne for this goes to Mark Houghton of London E3. There are runners-up prizes (a copy of this volume) for R.B. Lonkhurst, N.D. Brown, H.H. Elias, Nic Jones and S. King. Thanks to everyone who took part. All ideas for next year's poll gratefully considered.

WORLD SPORTSMAN OF THE 80s

			1st 3 pts	2nd 2 pts	3rd 1pt	
1	DIEGO MARADONA	(Soccer)	4	8	3	31
2	Carl Lewis	(Athletics)	7	1	–	23
3	Ed Moses	(Athletics)	3	4	2	19
4	Severiano Ballesteros	(Golf)	2	3	3	15
5	Sugar Ray Leonard	(Boxing)	2	2	2	12
6	Sebastian Coe	(Athletics)	2	1	1	9
7	Alain Prost	(Motor Racing)	1	–	5	8
8	Mike Tyson	(Boxing)	–	3	1	7
9	Greg LeMond	(Cycling)	1	–	1	4
10=	Wayne Gretzky	(Ice Hockey)	1	–	–	3
	Ben Johnson	(Athletics)	1	–	–	3
	Jahangir Khan	(Squash)	1	–	–	3
	Mark McCormack	(Money)	1	–	–	3
	John McEnroe	(Tennis)	–	1	1	3
15=	Bernard Hinault	(Cycling)	–	–	2	2
	Magic Johnson	(Basketball)	–	1	–	2
	Walter Payton	(US Football)	–	1	–	2
	Ingemar Stenmark	(Skiing)	–	1	–	2
19=	Serge Blanco	(Rugby Union)	–	–	1	1
	Imran Khan	(Cricket)	–	–	1	1
	Joe Montana	(US Football)	–	–	1	1
	Viv Richards	(Cricket)	–	–	1	1
	Naim Suleymanoglu	(Weightlifting)	–	–	1	1

WORLD SPORTSWOMAN OF THE 80s

			1st 3 pts	2nd 2 pts	3rd 1 pt	
1	MARTINA NAVRATILOVA	(Tennis)	16	3	1	55
2	Katarina Witt	(Ice Skating)	3	4	4	21
3	Florence Griffith-Joyner	(Athletics)	3	4	1	18
4	Ingrid Kristiansen	(Athletics)	2	3	2	14
5=	Heike Drechsler	(Athletics)	–	2	2	6
	Nancy Lopez	(Golf)	–	2	2	6
7=	Chris Evert	(Tennis)	1	1	–	5
	Steffi Graf	(Tennis)	1	–	2	5
	Marita Koch	(Athletics)	–	2	1	5
10=	Grete Waitz	(Athletics)	–	1	2	4
	Maria Walliser	(Skiing)	–	1	2	4
12=	Mary Decker-Slaney	(Athletics)	–	1	1	3
	Susan Devoy	(Squash)	–	1	1	3
14=	Virginia Leng	(Equestrian)	–	1	–	2
	Jeannie Longo	(Cycling)	–	–	2	2
16=	Kristin Otto	(Swimming)	–	–	1	1
	Cao Yan Hua	(Table Tennis)	–	–	1	1
	Vreni Schneider	(Skiing)	–	–	1	1

BRITISH SPORTSMAN OF THE 80s

			1st 3 pts	2nd 2 pts	3rd 1 pt	
1	SEBASTIAN COE	(Athletics)	15	3	2	53
2	Ian Botham	(Cricket)	3	6	2	23
3	Daley Thompson	(Athletics)	1	3	4	13
4	Kenny Dalglish	(Soccer)	1	2	4	11
5	Steve Davis	(Snooker)	–	4	1	9
6	Malcolm Cooper	(Shooting)	1	2	1	8
7=	Nick Faldo	(Golf)	1	1	–	5
	Sandy Lyle	(Golf)	–	2	1	5
	Peter Shilton	(Soccer)	1	1	–	5
10=	John Francome	(Racing)	1	–	1	4
11=	Frank Bruno	(Boxing)	–	1	1	3
	Dusty Hare	(Rugby Union)	1	–	–	3
	Steve Redgrave	(Rowing)	1	–	–	3
14=	Sean Kerly	(Hockey)	–	1	–	2
	Ian Rush	(Soccer)	–	–	2	2
16=	Willie Carson	(Racing)	–	–	1	1
	Henry Cecil	(Racing)	–	–	1	1
	Graham Gooch	(Cricket)	–	–	1	1
	David Gower	(Cricket)	–	–	1	1
	Barry McGuigan	(Boxing)	–	–	1	1
	Bryan Robson	(Soccer)	–	–	1	1
	Peter Scudamore	(Racing)	–	–	1	1

BRITISH SPORTSWOMAN OF THE 80s

			1st 3 pts	2nd 2 pts	3rd 1pt	
1	VIRGINIA LENG	(Equestrian)	6	5	4	32
2	Tessa Sanderson	(Athletics)	5	4	2	25
3	Jayne Torvill	(Ice Skating)	5	4	–	23
4	Lucinda Green	(Equestrian)	6	–	4	22
5	Fatima Whitbread	(Athletics)	2	5	5	21
6	Laura Davies	(Golf)	1	2	4	11
7	Princess Royal	(Equestrian/Admin)	–	2	2	6
8	Karen Briggs	(Judo)	–	1	2	4
9	Zola Budd	(Athletics)	1	–	–	3
10=	Sharron Davies	(Swimming)	–	1	–	2
	Maureen Flowers	(Darts)	–	1	–	2
	Martine Le Moignan	(Squash)	–	–	2	2
	Liz Lynch	(Athletics)	–	1	–	2
14	Carolyn Wilson	(Synchro.)	–	–	1	1

THE GUIDE TO 1990

COMMONWEALTH GAMES
The 14th Commonwealth Games take place in Auckland, New Zealand from January 24 to February 3. Package tours from Britain are being organised by Keith Prowse Sports Tours, 103 Waterloo Rd, London SE1 8UL (Tel 01 928 5511). Anyone making their own arrangements should contact 14th Commonwealth Games, PO Box 1990, Auckland, New Zealand (Tel 010 649 503550). The BBC is planning extensive coverage. The Games schedule is on page 112.

SOCCER
The FA Cup final is at Wembley on May 12. All tickets are allocated already except for the portion that goes to the two competing clubs. Details from them after the semi-finals. The World Cup takes place in Italy from June 8 to July 8. Details from World Cup Ticket Office, Football Association, 16 Lancaster Gate, London W2 3LW (Tel 01 262 4542). The soccer fixtures are on page 45.

CRICKET
England are playing three Tests and two one-day internationals in the summer of 1990 against both New Zealand and India. For the two Lord's Tests application forms are available by post (MCC, Lord's, London NW8 8QN) from January 1; credit card bookings can be made by phone (01 289 5005) after mid-April.

Enquiries and credit card bookings can be made at the other major grounds by phone: Headingley (0532 787394), Edgbaston (021 440 4292), Trent Bridge (0602 817005), Old Trafford (061 848 7021), The Oval (01 582 7764). Tickets for the two Lord's Cup finals can only be obtained from the 17 first-class counties. The full cricket fixtures start on page 143.

GOLF
The 119th Open Championship will be held on the Old Course at St Andrews from July 19-22. Admission is always available on the day. But both daily and season tickets are obtainable in advance at reduced prices. Write to Irene McKechnie, Royal and Ancient Golf Club, St Andrews, Fife KY16 9JD. The golf fixtures are on page 187.

TENNIS
The All-England Championships will take place at Wimbledon from June 25 to July 8. Tickets for Centre and No. One Courts are allocated by ballot. Application forms can be obtained (send sae) from the All-England Club, PO Box 98, Wimbledon, London SW19 5AE; they must be returned by December 31 1989. Only one application per address is allowed.

Centre Court prices range from £15 on the opening two days (£10 for restricted view) to £39 for final days (£27 restricted view). Standing room at Centre Court for the last four days is determined by a separate ballot; for this send an sae during February 1990. The tennis fixtures are on page 299.

MOTOR RACING
The British Grand Prix is at Silverstone on July 15. General admission to the track is always available on the day. However, advance booking at lower prices is recommended. And for grandstand seats very early booking – before January – is recommended. Details from Booking Office, Silverstone Circuit, Silverstone, nr Towcester, Northamptonshire NN12 8TN. Phone 0327 857273. The motor racing fixtures are on page 236.

HORSE RACING
Grand National Day is April 7. Advance booking is advisable as the best viewing areas are normally sold out. Tickets from £5 to £45 are available from Aintree Racecourse, Aintree, Liverpool L9 5AS.

Derby Day is June 6. Facilities at Epsom are limited until the new stand opens in 1992. Reserved seats are normally sold by Christmas. Grandstand and paddock admission can be purchased in advance from United Racecourses Ltd, Racecourse Paddock, Epsom, Surrey KT18 5NJ. Full racing fixtures start on page 214.

AMERICAN FOOTBALL

BEAUT MONTANA

In contrast to nearly all the previous XXII, Super Bowl XXIII in Miami provided a finish to match the trappings of the occasion. The San Francisco 49ers scored a touchdown to turn defeat into a 20-16 victory over the Cincinnati Bengals with just 34 seconds remaining: the quarterback Joe Montana engineered a 92-yard drive that culminated in a throw to John Taylor. This was the third Superbowl triumph of the 80s for both Montana and the 49ers, and a season that began with his place as starting quarterback in doubt ended with Montana completely overshadowing Boomer Esiason of the Bengals and being widely described as one of the greatest of all time.

The drama of the last quarter finally managed to distract people's attention from the other elements of the Superbowl: two broken legs (Tim Krumrie of the Bengals and Steve Wallace of the 49ers), one broken career (Stanley Wilson of the Bengals who received his fourth suspension for drug abuse hours before the start) and the Ickey Shuffle (the touchdown celebration invented by Ickey Woods of the Bengals which went unshuffled on the day) plus a major Miami race riot; the city had been trying to use the slogan "Miami Nice".

The result established Bill Walsh as one of the most successful coaches of all time and he promptly retired in favour of his chosen successor George Seifert; only Vince Lombardi had previously retired after winning a Superbowl.

The 49ers had won the NFC by beating the Chicago Bears at Soldier Field when the temperature was 10 degrees Fahrenheit with a windchill of -26. The Bengals, after winning only four games the previous year, took the AFC with a win over the Buffalo Bills. Much of their success had been built on a ploy using a no-huddle attack which was designed to prevent the opposition making substitutions; this was declared illegal by the Commissioner 75 minutes before the Buffalo game. After Cincinnati won the play-off against the Seattle Seahawks, a Seattle supporter held off police at gunpoint for two hours and threatened to kill his children before surrendering and explaining that he was devastated by his team's defeat. "We get them every year," said a police spokesman.

The regular season was the most open of all time with 15 of the 28 teams still in the running before the final weekend. The exceptions included both 1988 Superbowl teams, Washington and Denver, plus the Dallas Cowboys who had the worst season in their 29-year history. The club was bought by an Arkansas oilman, Jerry Jones, who immediately fired Tom Landry, manager throughout the 29 years. The NFL commissioner Pete Rozelle announced his retirement at the league's annual meeting, which decided to ban steroids. Notre Dame won college football's national championship, decided by a poll of sportswriters, for a record eighth time. A 12-year-old cheerleader, Angelina Perez, was reported to have given birth to a son during the third quarter of a game in Guyaco, Peru. Her jumping up and down caused premature labour.

1988-89

FINAL NFL STANDINGS

American Conference

EAST	W	L	T	Pct
Buffalo Bills	12	4	0	.750
Indianapolis Colts	9	7	0	.563
New England Patriots	9	7	0	.563
New York Jets	8	7	1	.531
Miami Dolphins	6	10	0	.375

CENTRAL	W	L	T	Pct
Cincinnati Bengals	12	4	0	.750
Cleveland Browns	10	6	0	.625
Houston Oilers	10	6	0	.625
Pittsburgh Steelers	5	11	0	.313

WEST	W	L	T	Pct
Seattle Seahawks	9	7	0	.563
Denver Broncos	8	8	0	.500
Los Angeles Raiders	7	9	0	.438
San Diego Chargers	6	10	0	.375
Kansas City	4	11	1	.281

National Conference

EAST	W	L	T	Pct
Philadelphia Eagles	10	6	0	.625
New York Giants	10	6	0	.625
Washington Redskins	7	9	0	.438
Phoenix Cardinals	7	9	0	.438
Dallas Cowboys	3	13	0	.188
CENTRAL				
Chicago Bears	12	4	0	.750
Minnesota Vikings	11	5	0	.688
Tampa Bay Rowdies	5	11	0	.313
Detroit Lions	4	12	0	.250
Green Bay Packers	4	12	0	.250
WEST				
San Francisco 49ers	10	6	0	.625
Los Angeles Rams	10	6	0	.625
New Orleans Saints	10	6	0	.625
Atlanta Falcons	5	11	0	.313

Play-offs

AFC

Wild Card Game

Houston Oilers	24-23	Cleveland Browns

Divisional Play-offs

Buffalo Bills	17-10	Houston Oilers
Cincinnati Bengals	21-13	Seattle S'Hawks

AFC Championship Game

Cincinnati Bengals	21-10	Buffalo Bills

NFC

Wild Card Game

Minnesota Vikings	27-17	LA Rams

Divisional Play-Offs

San Francisco 49ers	34-9	Minn. Vikings
Chicago Bears	20-13	Philadelphia Eagles

Championship Game

San Francisco 49ers	28-3	Chicago Bears

How the teams reached the Superbowl

CINCINNATI BENGALS

Home		Away	
21-14	Phoenix	28-24	Philadelphia
24-17	Cleveland	17-12	Pittsburgh
36-19	NY Jets	45-21	LA Raiders
44-21	Houston	21-27	New England
42-7	Pittsburgh	16-23	Cleveland
35-21	Buffalo	28-31	Kansas City
27-10	San Diego	38-24	Dallas
20-17	Washington	6-41	Houston

SAN FRANCISCO 49ERS

Home		Away	
17-34	Atlanta	34-33	New Orleans
20-13	Detroit	20-17	NY Giants
13-16	Denver	38-7	Seattle
24-21	Minnesota	24-21	LA Rams
3-9	LA Raiders	9-10	Chicago
37-21	Washington	23-24	Phoenix
30-17	New Orleans	48-10	San Diego
16-38	LA Rams	13-3	Atlanta

SUPERBOWL XXIII

January 22; John Robbie Stadium, Miami, Florida

San Francisco 49ers	0	3	10	3 - 20

Touchdowns: Rice, Taylor
Field Goals: Cofer (2)
Points After: Cofer (2)

Cincinnati Bengals	3	0	3	14 - 16

Touchdown: Jennings
Field Goals: Breech (3)
Point After: Breech
Attendance: 75,179
Most Valuable Player: Jerry Rice (San Francisco wide receiver).

■ **Superbowl: Jerry Rice (49ers) set a reception record with 215 yards. He also equalled the record for the most reception catches, 11.**

■ **Only the second Superbowl without a 1st half touchdown. The first came after 44 min 26 secs ... the longest wait in Superbowl history.**

■ **San Francisco had the worst regular season of any Superbowl winners: won 10 lost 6**

■ **San Francisco's nose tackle Michael Carter won the silver medal in the shot putt at the 1984 Los Angeles Olympics.**

AMERICAN BOWL
Wembley Stadium: Philadelphia Eagles 17 Cleveland Browns 13 (73,677)

BUDWEISER BOWL
Crystal Palace: Manchester Spartans 21 Birmingham Bulls 14 (8,000)

BOWL GAMES 1988-89
California Bowl: Fresno State 35 West Michigan 30 (31,272);
Independence Bowl: South Missouri 38 Texas, El Paso 18 (20,242);
John Hancock Sun Bowl: Alabama 29 Army 28 (48,719);
Eagle Aloha Bowl: Washington State 24 Houston 22 (35,132);
Liberty Bowl: Indiana 34 South Carolina 10 (39,210);
Mazda Gator Bowl: Georgia 34 Michigan State 27 (76,236);
Hall of Fame Bowl: Syracuse 23 Louisiana State 10 (51,112);
Florida Citrus Bowl: Clemson 13 Oklahoma 6 (53,571);
Rose Bowl: Michigan 22 So. California 14 (101,688);
USF&G Sugar Bowl: Florida State 13 Auburn 7 (61,934);
Orange Bowl: Miami 23 Nebraska 3 (79,480);
All America Bowl: Florida 14 Illinois 10 (48,218);
Freedom Bowl: Brigham Young 20 Colorado 17 (35,941):
Sea World Holiday Bowl: Oklahoma State 62 Wyoming 14 (60,718);
Peach Bowl: North Carolina State 28 Iowa 23 (44,635);
Mobil Cotton Bowl: UCLA 17 Arkansas 3 (74,304)
Sunkist Fiesta Bowl: Notre Dame 34 West Virginia 21 (74,911)

CHAMPIONS

The National Football League (NFL) has been constituted as follows:
1921-32 One League only; 1933-49 Two divisions (Eastern and Western); 1950-52 Two Divisions and National Conferences; 1953-59 Two Divisions (Eastern and Western Conferences; 1960-69 Two Leagues (American Football League (AFL) and National Football League (NFL); 1970-Two (American Football Conference (AFC) and National Football Conference (NFC)
Play-offs introduced in 1933

Champions:

1921	Chicago Staleys
1922	Canton Bulldogs (Ohio)
1923	Canton Bulldogs (Ohio)
1924	Cleveland Bulldogs
1925	Chicago Cardinals
1926	Frankford Yellowjackets
1927	New York Giants
1928	Providence Streamroller
1929	Green Bay Packers
1930	Green Bay Packers
1931	Green Bay Packers
1932	Chicago Bears

NFL Play-off

Year	Winner	Score	Loser
1933	Chicago Bears	23-21	New York Giants
1934	New York Giants	30-13	Chicago Bears
1935	Detroit Lions	26-7	New York Giants
1936	Green Bay Packers	21-6	Boston Redskins
1937	Washington Redskins	28-21	Chicago Bears
1938	New York Giants	23-17	Green Bay Packers
1939	Green Bay Packers	27-0	New York Giants
1940	Chicago Bears	73-0	Washington Reds
1941	Chicago Bears	37-9	New York Giants
1942	Washington Redskins	14-6	Chicago Bears
1943	Chicago Bears	41-21	Washington Reds
1944	Green Bay Packers	14-7	New York Giants
1945	Cleveland Rams	15-14	Washington Reds
1946	Chicago Bears	24-14	New York Giants
1947	Chicago Cardinals	28-21	Philadelphia Eagles
1948	Philadelphia Eagles	7-0	Chicago Cardinals
1949	Philadelphia Eagles	14-0	Los Angeles Rams
1950	Cleveland Browns	30-28	Los Angeles Rams
1951	Los Angeles Rams	24-17	Cleveland Browns
1952	Detroit Lions	17-7	Cleveland Browns
1953	Detroit Lions	17-16	Cleveland Browns
1954	Cleveland Browns	56-10	Detroit Lions
1955	Cleveland Browns	38-14	Los Angeles Rams
1956	New York Giants	47-7	Chicago Bears
1957	Detroit Lions	59-14	Cleveland Browns
1958	Baltimore Colts	23-17	New York Giants
1959	Baltimore Colts	31-16	New York Giants

AFL/AFC Championship

Year	Winner	Score	Loser
1960	Houston Oilers	24-16	LA Chargers
1961	Houston Oilers	10-3	S.Diego Chargers
1962	Dallas Texans	20-17	Houston Oilers
1963	San Diego Chargers	51-10	Boston Patriots
1964	Buffalo Bills	20-7	S.Diego Chargers
1965	Buffalo Bills	23-0	S.Diego Chargers
1966	Kansas City Chiefs	31-7	Buffalo Bills
1967	Oakland Raiders	40-7	Houston Oilers
1968	New York Jets	27-23	Oakland Raiders
1969	Kansas City Chiefs	17-7	Oakland Raiders
1970	Baltimore Colts	27-17	Oakland Raiders
1971	Miami Dolphins	21-0	Baltimore Colts
1972	Miami Dolphins	21-17	Pitt. Steelers
1973	Miami Dolphins	27-10	Oakland Raiders
1974	Pittsburgh Steelers	24-13	Oakland Raiders
1975	Pittsburgh Steelers	16-10	Oakland Raiders
1976	Oakland Raiders	24-7	Pitt. Steelers
1977	Denver Broncos	20-17	Oakland Raiders
1978	Pittsburgh Steelers	34-5	Houston Oilers
1979	Pittsburgh Steelers	27-13	Houston Oilers
1980	Oakland Raiders	34-27	S.Diego Chargers
1981	Cincinnati Bengals	27-7	S.Diego Chargers
1982	Miami Dolphins	14-0	New York Jets
1983	Los Angeles Raiders	30-14	Seattle Seahawks
1984	Miami Dolphins	45-28	Pitt. Steelers
1985	New England Pats	31-14	Miami Dolphins
1986	Denver Broncos	23-20	Cleveland Browns
1987	Denver Broncos	38-33	Cleveland Browns
1988	Cincinnati Bengals	21-10	Buffalo Bills

NFL/NFC Championship

Year	Winner	Score	Loser
1960	Philadelphia Eagles	17-13	Green Bay Packers
1961	Green Bay Packers	37-0	New York Giants
1962	Green Bay Packers	16-7	New York Giants
1963	Chicago Bears	14-10	New York Giants
1964	Cleveland Browns	27-0	Baltimore Colts
1965	Green Bay Packers	23-12	Cleveland Browns
1966	Green Bay Packers	34-27	Dallas Cowboys
1967	Green Bay Packers	21-17	Dallas Cowboys
1968	Baltimore Colts	34-0	Cleveland Browns
1969	Minnesota Vikings	27-7	Cleveland Browns
1970	Dallas Cowboys	17-10	San Fran 49ers
1971	Dallas Cowboys	14-3	San Fran 49ers
1972	Washington Redskins	26-3	Dallas Cowboys
1973	Minnesota Vikings	27-10	Dallas Cowboys
1974	Minnesota Vikings	14-10	Los Angeles Rams
1975	Dallas Cowboys	37-7	Los Angeles Rams
1976	Minnesota Vikings	24-13	Los Angeles Rams
1977	Dallas Cowboys	23-6	Minnesota Vikings
1978	Dallas Cowboys	28-0	Los Angeles Rams
1979	Los Angeles Rams	9-0	Tampa Bay Buccs
1980	Philadelphia Eagles	20-7	Dallas Cowboys
1981	San Francisco 49ers	28-27	Dallas Cowboys
1982	Washington Redskins	31-17	Dallas Cowboys
1983	Washington Redskins	24-21	San Fran 49ers
1984	San Francisco 49ers	23-0	Chicago Bears
1985	Chicago Bears	24-0	Los Angeles Rams
1986	New York Giants	17-0	Washington Reds
1987	Washington Redskins	17-10	Minnesota Vikings
1988	San Francisco 49ers	28-3	Chicago Bears

Superbowl

Year	Winner	Score	Loser
1967	Green Bay Packers	35-10	Kansas City Chiefs
	Memorial Coliseum, Los Angeles		
1968	Green Bay Packers	33-14	Oakland Raiders
	Orange Bowl, Miami		
1969	New York Jets	16-7	Baltimore Colts
	Orange Bowl, Miami		
1970	Kansas City Chiefs	23-7	Minnesota Vikings
	Tulane Stadium, New Orleans		
1971	Baltimore Colts	16-13	Dallas Cowboys
	Orange Bowl, Miami		
1972	Dallas Cowboys	24-3	Miami Dolphins
	Tulane Stadium, New Orleans		
1973	Miami Dolphins	14-7	Washington Redskins
	Memorial Coliseum, Los Angeles		
1974	Miami Dolphins	24-7	Minnesota Vikings
	Rice Stadium, Houston		
1975	Pittsburgh Steelers	16-6	Minnesota Vikings
	Tulane Stadium, New Orleans		
1976	Pittsburgh Steelers	21-17	Dallas Cowboys
	Orange Bowl, Miami		
1977	Oakland Raiders	32-14	Minnesota Vikings
	Rose Bowl, Pasadena		
1978	Dallas Cowboys	27-10	Denver Broncos
	Louisiana Superdrome, New Orleans		
1979	Pittsburgh Steelers	35-31	Dallas Cowboys
	Orange Bowl, Miami		
1980	Pittsburgh Steelers	31-19	Los Angeles Rams
	Rose Bowl, Pasadena		
1981	Oakland Raiders	27-10	Philadelphia Eagles
	Louisiana Superdrome, New Orleans		
1982	San Francisco 49ers	26-21	Cincinnati Bengals
	Pontiac Silverdrome, Pontiac		
1983	Washington Redskins	27-17	Miami Dolphins
	Rose Bowl, Pasadena		
1984	Los Angeles Raiders	38-9	Washington Redskins
	Tampa Stadium, Tampa		

1985	San Francisco 49ers	38-16	Miami Dolphins
	Stanford Stadium, Stanford		
1986	Chicago Bears	46-10	New England
			Patriots
	Louisiana Superdrome, New Orleans		
1987	New York Giants	39-20	Denver Broncos
	Rose Bowl, Pasadena		
1988	Washington Redskins	42-10	Denver Broncos
	Jack Murphy Stadium, San Diego		
1989	San Francisco 49ers	20-16	Cincinnati Bengals
	John Robbie Stadium, Miami		

Wins: 4 Pittsburgh Steelers; 3 Oakland/LA Raiders; 2 San Francisco 49ers, Green Bay Packers, Washington Redskins, Dallas Cowboys, Miami Dolphins; 1 Chicago Bears, New York Giants, Baltimore Colts, Kansas City Chiefs.

Appearances: 5 Dallas Cowboys, Miami Dolphins; 4 Minnesota Vikings; Oakland/LA Raiders; Pittsburgh Steelers, Washington Redskins; 3 Denver Broncos, San Francisco 49ers; 2 Baltimore Colts, Green Bay Packers, Kansas City Chiefs, Cincinnati Bengals; 1 Chicago Bears, Los Angeles Rams, New Patriots, New York Giants, New York Jets, Philadelphia Eagles.

Note: all Superbowls are played in the calendar year after the season they refer to. Thus the 1988 champions played the 1989 Superbowl.

"Joe Montana is not human. I don't want to call him a god, but he's definitely somewhere in between."
49ers' receiver Chris Collingsworth after the Superbowl

"He's the coach and I'm the player. What he says I do - unless I disagree with him."
Bengals quarterback Boomer Esiason on Bill Wyche

"If you experience tingling, numbness or change of skin colour, seek help."
Instruction to spectators at the frozen Bears-49ers game

"It's the end of an era, our era. A lot of old Cowboys are crying tonight."
Former Dallas player Bob Lilly on the sacking of Tom Landry

"I believe steroid use is rampant among the NFL and that includes my own team. It is rampant in colleges and it is rampant in high schools."
Bill Fralic of the Atlanta Falcons to US Senate investigators.

ROSEBOWL

First played in 1902, and regularly since 1916.
All games played at the Rose Bowl, Pasadena, except 1942 at Durham, N. Carolina.

Results since 1980:

1980	So. California	17-16	Ohio State
1981	Michigan	23-6	Washington
1982	Washington	28-0	Iowa
1983	UCLA	24-14	Michigan
1984	UCLA	45-9	Illinois
1985	USC	20-17	Ohio State
1986	UCLA	45-28	Iowa
1987	Arizona State	22-15	Michigan

| 1988 | Michigan | 20-17 | So. California |
| 1989 | Michigan | 22-14 | So. California |

SUMMERBOWL

All Played at Wembley Stadium

1983	Minnesota Vikings	28-10	St Louis Cardinals
1986	Chicago Bears	17-6	Dallas Cowboys
1987	Los Angeles Rams	28-27	Denver Broncos
1988	Miami Dolphins	27-21	San Francisco 49ers
1989	Philadelphia Eagles	17-3	Cleveland Browns

BUDWEISER BOWL

1986	London Ravens	20-12	Streatham Olympians
1987	London Ravens	40-23	Manchester All Stars
1988	Birmingham Bulls	30-6	London Olympians
1989	Manchester Spartans	21-14	Birmingham Bulls

EUROPEAN CHAMPIONSHIPS

1983	Italy	18-6	Finland
1985	Finland	13-2	Italy
1987	Italy	24-22	West Germany
1989	Great Britain	26-0	Finland

RECORDS

TEAM RECORDS

Record scores

Washington Redskins 0 Chicago Bears 73, 8 Dec 1940; Washington Redskins 72 New York Giants 41, 27 Nov 1966; Los Angeles Rams 70 Baltimore Colts 27, 22 Oct 1950; New York Bulldogs 20 Chicago Cardinals 65, 13 Nov 1949; Los Angeles Rams 65 Detroit Lions 24, 29 Oct 1950.

Most seasons as league champions

11 Green Bay; 9 Chicago Bears; 5 New York Giants

Most games won in regular season

15 San Francisco (1984); Chicago (1985) 14 Miami (1972, 1984); Pittsburgh (1970); Washington (1983); Chicago (1986); NY Giants (1986).

Most consecutive games won (regular season)

14 Miami (1972); 13 Chicago Bears (1934); 12 Minnesota (1969); 12 Chicago (1985).

Passing - most passes completed (career)

3686 (6467) Fran Tarkenton (Minnesota, NY Giants) 1961-71; 3297 (5604) Dan Fouts (San Diego) 1973-87; 2830 (5186) Johnny Unitas (Baltimore, San Diego) 1956-73 (figures in brackets are passes attempted)

Passing - most yards gained (career)

47,003 Fran Tarkenton (Minnesota, NY Giants) 1961-71; 43,040 Dan Fouts (San Diego) 1973-87; 40,239 Johnny Unitas (Baltimore, San Diego) 1956-73.

Most consecutive home games without defeat

30 Green Bay (1928-33); 27 Miami (1971-74); 18 Chicago Bears (1932-35, 1941-44); Oakland (1969-70); Dallas (1979-81).

Most consecutive away games without defeat

13 Chicago Bears (1941-43); 12 Green Bay (1928-30); 11 LA/San Diego Chargers (1960-61); Los Angeles Rams (1966-68).

INDIVIDUAL RECORDS

Most games played in career

340 George Blanda (Chicago Bears, Baltimore, Houston, Oakland) 1949-75; 282 Jim Marshall (Cleveland, Minnesota) 1960-79; 263 Jan Stenerud (Kansas City, Green Bay, Minnesota) 1967-85.

Most seasons as coach

40 George Halas (Chicago Bears) 1920-67; 33 Earl Lambeau (Green Bay, Chicago Cardinals, Washington) 1921-53; 29 Tom Landry (Dallas) 1960-88.

Most points (career)
2002 George Blanda (Chicago Bears, Baltimore, Houston, Oakland) 1949-75; 1699 Jan Stenerud (Kansas City, Green Bay, Minnesota) 1967-85; 1439 Jim Turner (NY Jets, Denver) 1964-79.

Most points (season)
176 Paul Hornung (Green Bay) 1960; 161 Mark Moseley (Washington) 1983; 155 Gino Cappelletti (Boston) 1964.

Most points (game)
40 Ernie Havers Chicago Cardinals v Chicago Bears 1929; 36 Dub Jones Cleveland v Chicago Bears 1951; 36 Gale Sayers Chicago v San Francisco 1965; 33 Paul Hornung Green Bay v Baltimore 1961.

Rushing - most yards gained (career)
176,726 Walter Payton (Chicago) 1975-87; 12,312 Jim Brown (Cleveland) 1957-65; 12,120 Franco Harris (Pittsburgh, Seattle) 1972-84.

1990

January 6-7: AFC and NFC Divisional play-off games; *14:* AFC and NFC Championship games; *28:* SUPERBOWL XXIV Louisiana Superdrome, New Orleans; *February 4:* AFC-NFC Pro Bowl; *August 5:* Summerbowl V (Wembley Stadium); *6:* Budweiser Bowl; *September 9-10:* NFL Regular Season starts.

ANGLING

---------- 1989 ----------

WORLD FLY FISHING CHAMPIONSHIPS
Finland, Jul 7
Individual
1 Wladyslaw Trzebuinia (Pol)
2 Slavoj Svoboda (Cze)
3 Jyrki Lamsa (Fin)
Team
1 Poland
2 France
3 Finland

WORLD FRESHWATER CHAMPIONSHIPS
Bulgaria, Sep 2-3
Individual
1 Tom Pickering (Eng)
2 Francesco Casini (Ita)
3 Richard Baynton (Wal)
Team
1 Wales
2 Italy
3 England

NATIONAL LEAGUE, FIRST DIVISION
Mallory Park, Leics, Aug 19
Individual
1 Brian Wickens (Isfield)
2 Andy Litchfield (Weybridge)
3 Geoffrey Bibby (Oundle)
Team
1 Reading and district
2 Barnsley and district
3 Bawtry and district

---------- CHAMPIONS ----------

WORLD CHAMPIONSHIPS
Fresh Water
Individual
1957	Mandeli (Ita)
1958	Garroit (Bel)
1959	Robert Tesse (Fra)
1960	Robert Tesse (Fra)
1961	Ramon Legogue (Fra)
1962	Raimondo Tedasco (Ita)
1963	William Lane (Eng)
1964	Joseph Fontanet (Fra)
1965	Robert Tesse (Fra)
1966	Henri Guiheneuf (Fra)
1967	Jacques Isenbaert (Bel)
1968	Gunter Grebenstein (FRG)
1969	Robin Harris (Eng)
1970	Marcel Van den Eynde (Bel)
1971	Dino Bassi (Ita)
1972	Hubert Levels (Hol)

1973	Pierre Michiels (Bel)
1974	Aribert Richter (FRG)
1975	Ian Heaps (Eng)
1976	Dino Bassi (Ita)
1977	Jean Mainil (Bel)
1978	Jean-Pierre Fouquet (Fra)
1979	Gerard Heulard (Fra)
1980	Wolf-Rudiger Kremkus (FRG)
1981	Dave Thomas (Eng)
1982	Kevin Ashurst (Eng)
1983	Wolf-Rudiger Kremkus (FRG)
1984	Bobby Smithers (Ire)
1985	Dave Roper (Eng)
1986	Lud Wever (Hol)
1987	Clive Branson (Wal)
1988	Jean-Pierre Fouquet (Fra)
1989	Tom Pickering (Eng)

Team
11 wins: France 1959. 1963-64, 1966, 1968, 1972, 1974-75, 1978-79, 1981
6: Belgium 1958, 1960, 1967, 1970, 1973, 1983
5: Italy 1957, 1962, 1971, 1976, 1986
3: England 1985, 1987-88
2: Holland 1969, 1982; Luxembourg 1977, 1984
1: East Germany 1961, Romania 1965, West Germany 1980, Wales 1989

Fly Fishing
Individual
1981	C Wittkamp (Hol)
1982	Viktor Diez y Diez (Spa)
1983	Segismondo Fernandez (Spa)
1984	Tony Pawson (Eng)
1985	Leslaw Frasik (Pol)
1986	Slivoj Svoboda (Cze)
1987	Brian Leadbetter (Eng)
1988	John Pawson (Eng)
1989	Wladyslaw Trzebuinia (Pol)

Team
4 wins: Italy 1982-84, 1986
2: England 1987-88, Poland 1985, 1989
1: Holland 1981

---------- 1990 ----------

Jul 21: British men's championship, Fourth Division (River Nene);

Aug 4: British Junior championships (Grand Union Canal);

Aug 11: British women's championships (Coronation Canal);

Aug 18: British men's championship, Second Division (Leeds-Liverpool Canal);

Sep 8: British men's championship, First Division (River Witham);

Sep 22: British men's championship Third Division (Royal Military Canal);

Oct 13: British men's championship, Fifth Division (River Trent).

ARCHERY

1989

WORLD CHAMPIONSHIPS
Lausanne, Switzerland, Jul 8
Men-Individual
1	Stanislav Zabrodsky (USSR)	332 pts
2	Steve Hallard (GB)	331 pts
3	Tomi Poikolainen (Fin)	331 pts

Men - Team
1	USSR	985 pts
2	United States	976 pts
3	South Korea	972 pts

Women - Individual
1	Soo Nyung-Kim (SKo)	338 pts
2	Hyung Woog-Kim (SKo)	331 pts
3	Denise Parker (US)	331 pts

Women - Team
1	South Korea	995 pts
2	Sweden	954 pts
3	USSR	953 pts

BRITISH TARGET CHAMPIONSHIPS
Lichfield, Staffs, Aug 12-13
Men
1	Stephen Hearne
2	Steve Hallard
3	Ian Pugh

Women
1	Joanne Edens (née Franks)
2	Julie Hallard
3	Linda Long

ALL BRITISH OPEN & FIELD CHAMPIONSHIPS
Glyncornel, Rhondda, May 27-28

Barebow
Men: Phillip Bowen (Falkirk Archers)
Women: K Yourstone (Sweden)

Freestyle
Men: Jonathan Shales (Raven Archers)
Women: Joanne Edens (née Franks) (Warwick Univ)

Compound Unlimited
Men: Chris Jones (GNAS)
Women: Anne Shepherd (New Century)

Traditional
Men: M Berriman (GNAS)
Women: B Berriman (GNAS)

Longbow
Men: D Cope (Hollyhall)

Home International
England

CHAMPIONS

WORLD CHAMPIONS (past 10 years)
Men
	Individual	Team
1981	Kysti Laasonen (Fin)	United States
1983	Richard McKinney (US)	United States
1985	Richard McKinney (US)	South Korea
1987	Vladimir Yesheyev (USSR)	South Korea
1989	Stanislav Zabrodsky (USSR)	USSR

Women
	Individual	Team
1981	Natalya Butuzova	USSR
1983	Kim Jin-Ho (SKo)	South Korea
1985	Irina Soldatova (USSR)	USSR
1987	Ma Xiagjun (Chn)	USSR
1989	Soo Nyung-Kim (SKo)	South Korea

OLYMPIC CHAMPIONS
Men
	Individual	Team
1972	John Williams (US)	-
1976	Darrell Pace (US)	-
1980	Tomi Poikolainen (Fin)	-
1984	Darrell Pace (US)	-
1988	Jay Barrs (US)	South Korea

Women
	Individual	Team
1972	Doreen Wilber (US)	-
1976	Luann Ryan (US)	-
1980	Keto Lossaberidze (USSR)	-
1984	Seo Hyang-Soon (SKo)	-
1988	Soo Nyung-Kim (SKo)	South Korea

1990

Apr 1: National Indoor championships;

May 26-27: All British Field championships;

Jun 9-10: UK Masters (Lilleshall);

Jul 4-6: Grand National Archery Meeting (Lilleshall);

Aug 11-12: British Target championships (Lichfield);

Aug/Sep: World Field championships and 11th Field Championships of Europe and Mediterranean (Loen, Norway);

Sep 29: National Flight championships (Burton Constable).

ASSOCIATION FOOTBALL

THE YEAR OF HILLSBOROUGH

At six minutes past three on April 15 the game and the nation were rocked by Britain's worst-ever sporting disaster. Ninety-five people were killed at Hillsborough in Sheffield at the FA Cup semi-final between Liverpool and Nottingham Forest. The disaster happened after the police opened a gate on to the terracing to avoid the possibility of people being crushed outside as latecomers clamoured to get into the already-packed Leppings Lane End, reserved for Liverpool supporters. The crowd surged forward, and people, unable to escape because of the wire fences erected to prevent pitch invasions, were asphyxiated. It was an eerie, silent tragedy which was all over before most people on the ground, including those in authority, had any idea what had occurred. There was a surreal and awful period in which many acted as though they were witnessing a routine crowd disturbance.

The vast majority of those who died came from Merseyside. Most were aged under 23 and about a third were teenagers. The dead included a father and his 14-year-old son, two sisters and two pairs of brothers. The following day, Liverpool FC opened their gates and, over the course of a week, thousands of people came in to leave flowers, or just their scarves, in memory of those who died. Lord Justice Taylor was appointed to enquire into the disaster. He said he would not be apportioning blame, but his interim report was extremely harsh on the shortcomings of the police. During the immediate recriminations, survivors accused policemen of responding to their cries for help with remarks like "Shut your fucking prattle", while *The Sun,* under a headline THE TRUTH claimed that fans had pickpocketed dead bodies and had beaten up a policeman who was trying to give the kiss of life. The Press Council received 2,500 complaints about newspaper coverage, and *The Sun* was later forced to apologise. On the following Saturday games began, at 3.06 precisely, with moving displays of mourning. And all round the country, workmen began demolishing the wire cages that hemmed in the fans amidst a temporary fashion for safety rather than control.

Hillsborough happened at a moment when many people thought football was coming through its period of trial: the season had seemed to be characterised by united opposition to the Government's Football Supporters Bill and a sense of humour...but for that one dreadful combination of circumstances on one afternoon, 1988-89 might have been remembered as the season of the inflatable banana. It was assumed by almost everyone that the Bill, forcing those who wish to attend football matches to carry identity cards, would be either postponed or forgotten as a result of the tragedy. The Prime Minister and Sports Minster did not share this assumption.

The Hillsborough disaster came less than four years after the previous occasion when Liverpool football became mixed up with death: at the Heysel Stadium in Brussels. On April 28 the Heysel trial in Brussels ended, with 14 Liverpool fans, who were found guilty of manslaughter, being sentenced to three years' imprisonment, half of it suspended; they were then allowed to go home pending appeal, having served most of the time anyway. Ten others were released because the case was not proven. Albert Roosens, former head of the Belgian Football Union and Police Captain Johan Mahieu, who was in charge of crowd control, were found guilty of criminal negligence and given suspended sentences.

BUSINESS AS USUAL

The Liverpool-Forest game was replayed at Old Trafford on May 7, although there had been many calls for the Cup to be cancelled. It was an afternoon on which everything was subdued (12,000 tickets were left unsold) except Liverpool's football; the team played brilliantly and won 3-1. Normal disservice was, however, rapidly being resumed.

Even on the Saturday immediately following the tragedy, Millwall fans at Upton Park chanted through the minute's silence and at Chelsea there were cries of "You dirty Northern bastards" at Leeds supporters. On May 13, there were 16 injuries at Selhurst Park when Birmingham fans spilled on to the pitch to escape a crush and then fighting started. 255 supporters were arrested nationwide that day, including a group from Bristol Rovers who broke up a wedding reception.

Liverpool went on to win the final in a game characterised by hyperbole. Wembley officials took the fences down and were rewarded by seven separate pitch invasions. The game itself was a strange mixture: Aldridge scored after four minutes, Liverpool tried to sit on their lead and were punished a minute from time when the Everton sub McCall equalised. There followed a hectic period when the two substitutes, McCall and Rush, traded goals before Liverpool emerged as 3-2 winners.

Liverpool then appeared to be near-certainties to win the double for the second time. They failed in a manner that in a normal season would have seemed barely credible. The post-Hillsborough rearrangements meant that Liverpool found themselves playing Arsenal in an effective championship play-off, and they only needed to avoid a two-goal home defeat to be champions yet again. However, Arsenal took the lead through Smith after 53 minutes, a goal only allowed after discussion between referee and linesman. And, in the second minute of injury time, Michael Thomas scored another. The Kop, having known such mixtures of emotion in the preceding weeks, were this time dumbfounded. Arsenal finished ahead of Liverpool, not on points or goal difference (these were identical) but because they had scored eight more goals.

Even before this, the race had twisted and turned in an unprecedented fashion. On March 1, Liverpool were 19 points behind, and, even with four games in hand, were considered to be out of the race. Norwich, who had led the League for most of the autumn, were assumed to be Arsenal's main challengers. However, Liverpool were unbeaten in 24 matches between New Year's Day and the final game.

Arsenal established their credibility as possible champions with a brilliant 3-1 win at Goodison in January, when they were applauded off the field by the Everton supporters. But as Liverpool surged, Arsenal alternated vital wins (5-0 over Norwich, 1-0 at Middlesbrough) with seemingly decisive mistakes (beaten by Derby at home and held by Wimbledon). The final twist was utterly unpredictable.

Nottingham Forest, widely-praised but inconsistent, finished third, ahead of the surprise teams of the year, Norwich and Derby, and Tottenham who recovered to finish fifth. After the season, Spurs did spectacular business by buying Lineker from Barcelona for £1.5 million and selling Waddle to Marseilles for £4.35 million. Millwall, in their debut First Division season, fell away but finished tenth. Their physio, Peter Melville, revealed that for the past two years – coincident with the club's rise – the players had been training on royal jelly. Supposedly regal Manchester United were one place behind them. Newcastle and Middlesbrough were relegated, along with West Ham, leaving the North-East without a First Division team for the first time in 25 years. West Ham went down, playing good football badly. They made a courageously useless last stand, winning five games out of six to try and avoid the drop; alas, their last game was at Anfield. They then broke tradition by sacking John Lyall after 15 years and making Lou Macari the sixth manager in their 87-year history. Macari said he would make the Academy a sterner place.

Newcastle sacked their manager, Willie McFaul, as early as October, but attempts to sack the board by dissident shareholders failed. One supporter, Eddie Knox, reported the club to the local Trading Standards Office. Jim Smith, the QPR manager, replaced McFaul and Trevor Francis took over QPR. Peter Eustace was sacked by Sheffield Wednesday and Ron Atkinson, unwanted in Spain, took over. Charlton Athletic who, unusually for them, avoided relegation before the last day of the season, announced that they would be returning home to The Valley.

APRIL 15, 3.06PM

"As you look around Hillsborough you will appreciate why it has been regarded for so long as the perfect venue for all kinds of important matches."
Bert McGee, Chairman of Sheffield Wednesday, in the match programme

"I realised it was serious when I saw one of the lasses standing near me just turn blue in the face. She went down. She was dead. That was it."
Wayne Adams, 17, Liverpool fan

"I think everyone knows there have been a few problems. It would help if you please co-operate with the police and co-operate with the first aid people."
Loudspeaker announcement by Kenny Dalglish at 3.47

POLICE: "Can we have cutting equipment for Hillsborough please, straight away?"
FIRE CONTROL: "Just a minute. Right, what's the address?"
POLICE: "Cutting equipment for Hillsborough football ground – straight away."
FIRE CONTROL: "Hillsborough football ground?"
POLICE: "Yes, Hillsborough football ground."
FIRE CONTROL: "What road is that on, do you know?"
Verbatim report given to Taylor enquiry

"We asked for a defibrillator and I was informed that there was not a defibrillator in the whole ground, which is appalling for a major event like this. We were given an oxygen tank to help with our resuscitation and it was empty. I think that is an absolute disgrace."
Dr Glyn Phillips, Liverpool fan and GP

"There was no mark on Tommy except a graze on his forehead. When I saw him, there was no look of horror on his face, no distress."
Mrs Linda Howard, on her dead 14-year-old son

"Football was the only thing we did as a family. Now we are not a family anymore."
Trevor Hicks, whose daughters died

"Kelly, you sent us to die like rats in a trap."
Enraged fan to FA Secretary Graham Kelly

"If it had not been for the fans there would probably have been more deaths. These people deserve a medal."
Gary Gillespie, Liverpool player

"I am sick of hearing how good the crowd were. Some arrived tanked up and the situation faced by officers trying to control them was simply terrifying."
PC Paul Middup, chairman of South Yorkshire Police Federation

"What sort of crowd control is it that allows numbers to build up to a dangerous level and then throws open the gates into an already packed stadium? It is the sort of control that treats fans as animals to be caged. Then, when people are dying, finds a way of getting Alsatians on the pitch but cannot clear a path for ambulances."
Liverpool Echo

"The one thing that Liverpool cannot accept is that some of its troubles might have something to do with its own people."
Charles Moore Daily Express Apr 21

"One had the impression - I am distressed to use the expression - that it was like beasts who wanted to charge into an arena. It was not far from hooliganism."
Jacques Georges, President of UEFA

"Only recently I asked what was the price of a human life. Unfortunately some clubs have not faced the question."
Sepp Blatter, Secretary - General of FIFA

"Violence, or the anticipation of violence, caused the Sheffield disaster. Nothing else."
Gazet van Antwerpen, Belgium

"It's all changed now, which is why it mattered to those young men from Liverpool that they should be there to support their team. What other group is going to troop the colours for them, present them with scarves and emblems? To what other section of society should they owe allegiance? Not to country; we're going into Europe. Not to community; we're all isolated, shut in little boxes, high-rise or low, watching another box. Not to God; science has got rid of him. Not to guilt; Freud shoved that out of the window."
Beryl Bainbridge

"The Colosseum in Rome had 80 vomitoria, exits which spewed out a full crowd of 60,000 seated spectators in three minutes. Have we learned nothing in nearly 2,000 years."
Dr Peter Ferrer, letter to The Times

"THE KOP THANKS YOU ALL. WE NEVER WALKED ALONE."
Liverpool supporters' banner

"No one has learned a bloody thing from Hillsborough."
Rogan Taylor, chairman of the Football Supporters Association

ENGLAND, OUR ENGLAND

England played ten full internationals in the 1988-89 season and remained unbeaten for the first time since 1974-75. Four of the games were World Cup ties and England won three impressively, home and away to Albania and home to Poland, which eventually gave them a place in the finals in Italy. However, the first World Cup result, a 0-0 home draw against Sweden, set the tone for a season in which the team manager, Bobby Robson, was beset by press criticism of an unprecedentedly nasty and brutish type. *The Sun* and *Daily Mirror* were so extreme in their attacks that they were counter-productive: the FA felt obliged to line up behind their manager. The press had its revenge: the *News of the World* concluded the season by printing a story linking Robson, married for 34 years, with a 37-year-old divorcee.

The purely footballing headlines included BLIND, DEAF, DUMB; DESERT PRATS (on England's draw in Saudi Arabia); IN THE NAME OF GOD, GO and ROBSON'S IN RUINS AND FA MUST ACT; this last in *The Sun* on England's 2-1 win in Athens. However, some football writers and sports editors made the mistake of allowing the BBC to film them at work during this game, and it was widely felt that they were the ones who looked like prats. A poll, commissioned by *The Sun* after the Saudi draw, Robson's worst moment, showed that even then 53% felt he should keep his job.

England then won their vital games with Albania, 2-0 away and 5-0 at home. The biggest surprise here was that the welcome in Europe's most isolated and backward country was warm and the food passable. Fortunately, the Albanians failed to understand the significance of the English spectators' Nazi salutes during the National Anthem nor the 1970s Harlow Town programmes which the poet Attila the stockbroker handed out to passers-by in Skanderbeg Square, Tirana. There was then a miserable 0-0 draw with Chile in the Rous Cup. The game was watched by only 15,628, the lowest-ever crowd at Wembley, partly due to a tube strike, partly due to the public's shrewd judgment.

However, England proceeded to win the Rous Cup with a 2-0 win over Scotland at Hampden. Steve Bull of Wolves came straight from the Third Division to score his 55th goal of the season. The England team was excellent, the fans (250 arrests) appalling. This was followed by Gary Lineker's best performance in ages, in the 3-0 World Cup win over Poland. The final game of the season, in Denmark, was largely celebratory and Peter Shilton received his 109th cap, beating Bobby Moore's record.

Scotland's passage towards the World Cup finals was much smoother. In February they enjoyed a vital victory in Cyprus when Richard Gough scored the winner after 96 minutes. The referee finally blew for time in the 97th and was immediately pelted with debris by the Cypriot supporters. The Scots followed with home wins over France and, uneasily again, Cyprus. The French game, on a soaking wet Hampden night, was dominated by Mo Johnston, then playing for Nantes, who scored in his fourth successive World Cup game and added a second besides. The Scottish edition of *The Sun* had headlined Johnston as predicting "I KO'D KRAUTS AND I'LL FLATTEN FROGS".

The Republic of Ireland, who had never reached the finals, placed themselves handily to repeat their heroics of the 1988 European Championship with home wins over Spain, Malta and much-weakened Hungary in front of capacity crowds at Lansdowne Road. Northern Ireland, heroic themselves at the 1982 World Cup, slithered towards the exit quietly, losing home and away to Spain. Wales went the same way. They staged an international at Cardiff Arms Park for the first time since 1910 and drew 0-0 against West Germany – not a bad result but not enough in a brutally tough group containing Holland as well.

Just four days before Hillsborough transformed the whole sporting landscape, UEFA had agreed to lift the ban on English clubs competing in Europe – provided the British Government agreed. The Government would only do that after the passage of what was described most memorably (by Patrick Collins of the *Mail on Sunday*) as The Bill to Abolish Professional Football by Gumming Up Turnstiles with Expired Barclaycards. The main part of the Bill, the introduction of ID cards for football supporters, was opposed by almost everyone involved, including – privately – many members of the Government. An opinion poll in *The Guardian*, however, found 52% of voters in favour (60% of women) and 33% against. There was support almost everywhere for the provisions to restrict travel for proven hooligans. The Bill was finally passed by the House of Lords on June 16.

On many League grounds, violent incidents declined and the police had some successes: 22 Bolton fans were charged after a series of dawn arrests on March 1; seven members of "The Governors", a gang attached to Manchester City, were jailed for up to 21 months in June; and seven supporters of Tamworth FC were jailed for a total of 22 years after staggering from pub to pub in Chelmsford thumping people. But there was more trouble among England followers: the 250 arrests at the England-Scotland game at Hampden reversed the traditional pattern of Tartan terror at Wembley. There were even reports of drunken chanting at an England B game in Iceland. It was becoming clearer that Britain was turning hooliganism into a successful export industry. In Holland – where the supporters' chants were mostly in English – an ID card experiment was introduced after the regular violence extended as far as explosions. It was quickly suspended as unworkable. In Italy, a Roma supporter was stabbed to death at AC Milan and the body of a fan allegedly murdered in a soccer killing seven years ago was found in a cave near Rome. Galatasaray of Turkey's win over Neuchâtel Xamax of Switzerland was set aside because of crowd trouble, and the decision was denounced by newspaper commentators as a plot to keep Turkey not only out of the European Cup but out of the European Community. But all this was nothing compared to Colombia – see below.

SEALED WITH A KISS

Footballers themselves continued to set an appalling example. The roll of dishonour included Paul Davis of Arsenal who was banned for nine games after breaking Glenn Cockerill of Southampton's jaw; Viv Anderson of Manchester United and John Fashanu of Wimbledon who had a set-to in the Plough Lane tunnel; Mark Dennis who was suspended by QPR after the 12th sending-off of his career – and in lesser surroundings the former Northern Ireland international Gerry Armstrong who head-butted an opposition committee man while playing for Brighton Reserves at Southwick. Armstrong resigned from the club and was given a conditional discharge by the magistrates. Wimbledon, and their folk-villain Vinnie Jones, attracted most of the attention until Jones was transferred in June to Leeds, a club where he was expected to feel at home. But, for the first time in seven years, Wimbledon failed to fulfil their annual summer fixture explaining their poor disciplinary record to the FA: Leeds, pre-Jones, were called in along with Southampton, Portsmouth, West Bromwich and Stockport. The most spectacular on-field violence came from Brian Clough, who chased and cuffed four youths who ran on to the City Ground pitch to celebrate a 5-2 Forest win over QPR. By way of apology, next day, he terrified two of the fans further by demanding: "Now come on, give me a kiss."

The Second Division was won by Chelsea, relegated the previous year, who went 27 games without defeat until April, and just failed to match Liverpool's divisional record of 28. Kerry Dixon broke Jimmy Greaves's club scoring record of 132, and the papers showed nostalgic pictures of Greaves circa 1961; the TV kept showing endlessly the rather bulkier 1989 version. Chelsea did their best to be efficient, rather than humorous, though Manchester City, who went up with them, enlivened the season, first when their fans began the craze for carrying inflatables and, finally, by attempting to avoid promotion when it was certain every way except mathematically. Crystal Palace also went up, after a late surge and the play-offs, thus ensuring that the supposed "team of the 80s" would be in the First Division just in time for the 90s.

Birmingham City went down to the Third Division for the first time, not so much declining as collapsing. Two other Midlands clubs accompanied them: Walsall, after one traumatic season, and Shrewsbury, after ten brave but hopeless ones. Birmingham were eventually sold to three Indian brothers from Manchester, the Kumars. A quarter of the

Division's managers were sacked: Billy Bremner of Leeds, Mark Lawrenson of Oxford (in a curious Maxwellian fashion), Tommy Coakley of Walsall (after 11 successive defeats), Alan Ball of Portsmouth, Terry Dolan of Bradford City (three weeks after they knocked Spurs out of the cup) and Eddie Gray of Hull. Sergei Baltacha became the first Soviet player to appear in the League and scored on his debut for Ipswich. Kelvin Morton of Bury St. Edmunds, refereeing the Crystal Palace-Brighton match on March 27, awarded five penalties, a League record, four of them to Palace who missed three. Palace won 2-1.

Wolves became the first club to win the Fourth and Third Division in successive seasons, which was only slightly less of an achievement than their feat in getting down that low in the first place. They went top of their division on November 5 and were never headed. Steve Bull passed 50 goals for the second successive season, and became the first man to hit a two-season century since George Camsell of Middlesbrough in 1926-8. Sheffield United also returned to the Second Division, along with Port Vale, after 32 years and, almost as interminable, the play-offs. A 39-year sequence at Vale Park ended when the defender, Phil Sproson, was forced to retire after 495 appearances; his father Roy played 832 times.

MAID IN DARTFORD

Rotherham won a much more competitive race in the Fourth Division and, at the bottom, Darlington dropped out after 68 years, though not before a fierce race against Colchester (where Jock Wallace became manager) and a writ claiming that their replacements, Maidstone, who play 20 miles away from home in Dartford, were not secure enough as tenants to be allowed in. Maidstone claimed they had prepared 28 separate schemes for a new home ground, but none had passed the Council; one was said to disturb a family of foxes. Tranmere Rovers admitted they breached the Sex Discrimination Act by refusing to let a Blackpool director, Mrs Vicki Oyston, into the boardroom. The most mixed day of the season belonged to Leyton Orient who beat Grimsby 5-0 on April 1, before armed robbers snatched the £8,000 takings.

Nottingham Forest, who again failed to fulfil Brian Clough's ambition of an FA Cup win, won two other Wembley finals. They came back from a goal down at half-time to beat Luton 3-1 in the Littlewoods Cup and Nigel Clough, who was 14 when his father last led a team out at Wembley in 1980, scored twice. Clough senior declined to show any predictable emotions, but he kissed the Luton manager Ray Harford before slipping away into the dressing room. Liverpool had gone out in the fourth round to West Ham 4-1, their heaviest defeat in a domestic cup since 1946.

TEAPOT TROPHIES

Forest also won the much-derided Simod Cup, the ersatz competition invented for clubs suffering Euro-withdrawal symptoms. The final against Everton was a thriller, settled 4-3 after extra time and 46,604 cared enough to watch it. In previous rounds, Everton had attracted only 3703 to Goodison to see Millwall, believed to be the lowest first-team gate on Merseyside this century, and 7072 to see QPR in the semi-final. On this occasion Clough received the trophy himself, but still insisted on giving the losers the recurring penalty of a kiss. If that makes them the unluckiest losers of the season, the unluckiest winner was Khotsi Moabi, who scored a last-minute goal for Brentford against Manchester United in the FA Youth Cup and had his collarbone broken when a celebrating team-mate landed on top of him.

Newport County, who dropped out of the Football League in 1988, temporarily at least dropped out of existence, sold off every asset from the players' strip to the boardroom teapot, and were expelled from the GM-Vauxhall Conference. The annulment of their record helped Maidstone overhaul Kettering in a tight race for the title. Oxford City, aged 107, also folded after being evicted from their ground and resigning from the Vauxhall-Opel League. Farnborough were top of that League when Ted Pearce passed his 1000th competitive game as club manager and they won promotion.

Gerry Allen of Whitstable Town scored after four seconds against Danson in the Kent League of March 4, possibly the quickest goal of all time. Bromley signed a striker, Simon Keith, who had had a heart transplant; and a sticker saying "Don't follow me - follow Macclesfield Town" reportedly took off with the space shuttle after being sent to NASA by a fan.

THE MIRACLE OF GANDER GREEN LANE

The most spectacular achievement by a non-league club came when Sutton United, lying 14th in the Conference, knocked Coventry City, the winners at Wembley just 20 months earlier, out of the FA Cup. Sutton's part-timers won 2-1, and the traditions of these occasions were observed: the *Sunday Express* reported that Coventry had been demolished by a 22-year-old bricklayer. An entirely untraditional element was provided by the Sutton manager Barrie Williams, a former English teacher, who quoted the Venerable Bede in his programme notes, and gave the whole enterprise an unusual degree of charm and class, which could only have come from a club with its own wine committee.

In the Fourth Round, Sutton were drawn at Norwich and Williams quoted the motto of the Benedictine order: "See everything, adjust a little, be grateful for the burden." The burden turned out to be an 8-0 defeat but Sutton were still accorded a lap of honour and were clapped off the field by their opponents. It looked like a happy enough ending but it was not a season of happy endings: on the way home Jacolyn Stephens, wife of Sutton's midfield player Micky, was critically injured in a car crash and was in a coma for four months. Williams later resigned to go into business. "Football," he said, "is a capricious taskmaster."

Scottish soccer was dominated by Rangers, who hit the front of the Premier Division race early and, without ever building a big lead, were never threatened. The only surprise came right at the end when they were beaten by Celtic 1-0 in the Cup Final. Seventy percent of Rangers was bought by 37-year-old David Murray, a steel and property tycoon and friend of the manager Graeme Souness, who bought seven percent himself, and with it a seat on the board. Souness continued to reverse a century of footballing migration patterns by buying up leading English players and, in July, reversed a much stronger and more pernicious tradition by signing a Catholic, Mo Johnston. The delight of Glasgow Catholics about the end of Rangers' sectarianism was mitigated by the fact that Celtic were convinced they had signed Johnston. This took Rangers' spending in three years to £11.5 million. Rangers also announced a £4 million sponsorship deal (with Admiral) and an £11 million overhaul of Ibrox. The manager's emotions remained touchingly human amidst all this, and he was banned from the touchline for his outbursts until 1990-91.

The most dramatic outburst of the Scottish season came from a Hearts director, Douglas Park, who protested against referee David Symes's handling of the Hearts-Rangers game by locking him in his changing-room for 18 minutes and walking off with the key. Park resigned as a Hearts director and was fined £1000 by the League. Dunfermline were promoted from the First Division and Albion Rovers (ground capacity 848) came out of the Second, after 41 years.

FIRST DIVISION RESULTS 1988-89

Home team	Arsenal	Aston V	Charlton	Coventry	Derby	Everton	Liverpool	Luton	Man Utd	M'Bro	Millwall	Newcastle	Norwich	Nottm F	QPR	Sheff W	S'ton	Tottenham	West Ham	W'don
Arsenal	-	2-3	2-2	2-0	1-2	2-0	1-1	2-0	2-1	3-0	0-0	1-0	5-0	1-3	2-1	1-1	2-2	2-0	2-1	2-2
Aston V	0-3	-	1-2	1-1	1-2	2-0	1-1	2-1	0-0	1-1	2-2	3-1	3-1	1-1	2-1	2-0	1-2	2-1	0-1	0-1
Charlton	2-3	2-2	-	0-0	3-0	1-2	0-3	3-0	1-0	2-0	0-3	2-2	1-2	0-1	1-1	2-1	2-2	2-2	0-0	1-0
Coventry	1-0	2-1	3-0	-	0-2	0-1	1-3	1-0	1-0	3-4	0-0	1-2	2-1	2-2	0-3	5-0	2-1	1-1	1-1	2-1
Derby	2-1	2-1	0-0	1-0	-	3-2	0-1	0-1	2-2	1-0	0-1	2-0	0-1	0-2	0-1	1-0	3-1	1-1	1-2	4-1
Everton	1-3	1-1	3-2	3-1	1-0	-	0-0	0-2	1-1	2-1	1-1	4-0	1-1	1-1	4-1	1-0	4-1	1-0	3-1	1-1
Liverpool	0-2	1-0	2-0	0-0	1-0	1-1	-	5-0	1-0	3-0	1-1	1-2	0-1	1-0	2-0	5-1	2-0	1-1	5-1	1-1
Luton	1-1	1-1	5-2	2-2	3-0	1-0	1-0	-	0-2	1-0	1-2	0-0	1-0	2-3	0-0	0-1	6-1	1-3	4-1	2-2
Man Utd	1-1	1-1	3-0	0-1	0-2	1-2	3-1	2-0	-	1-0	3-0	2-0	1-0	2-0	1-0	1-1	2-2	1-0	2-0	1-0
Middlesbrough	0-1	3-3	0-0	1-1	0-1	3-3	0-4	2-1	1-0	-	4-2	1-1	2-3	3-4	1-0	0-1	3-3	2-2	1-0	1-0
Millwall	1-2	2-0	1-0	1-0	1-0	2-1	1-2	3-1	0-0	2-0	-	4-0	2-3	2-2	3-2	1-0	1-1	0-5	0-1	1-0
Newcastle	0-1	1-2	0-2	0-3	0-1	2-0	2-2	0-0	0-0	3-0	1-1	-	0-2	0-1	1-2	1-3	3-3	2-2	1-2	0-1
Norwich	0-0	2-2	1-3	1-2	1-0	1-0	2-1	0-0	2-1	0-0	2-2	0-2	-	2-1	1-0	1-1	1-1	3-1	2-1	1-0
Nottm F	1-4	4-0	4-0	0-0	1-1	2-0	2-1	1-1	2-0	2-2	4-1	1-1	2-0	-	0-0	1-1	3-0	1-2	1-2	0-1
QPR	0-0	1-0	1-0	2-1	0-1	0-0	0-1	0-0	3-2	0-0	1-2	1-0	1-1	1-2	-	2-0	0-1	1-0	2-1	4-3
Sheffield W	2-1	1-0	3-1	1-2	1-1	1-1	2-2	1-0	0-2	1-0	3-0	1-2	2-2	0-3	0-2	-	1-1	0-2	0-2	1-1
Southampton	1-3	3-1	2-0	2-2	0-0	1-1	1-3	2-1	2-1	1-3	2-2	1-0	0-0	1-1	1-4	1-2	-	0-2	4-0	0-0
Tottenham H	2-3	2-0	1-1	1-1	1-3	2-1	1-2	0-0	2-2	3-2	2-0	1-0	2-1	1-2	2-2	0-0	1-2	-	3-0	3-2
West Ham	1-4	2-2	1-3	1-1	1-1	0-1	0-2	1-0	1-3	1-2	3-0	2-0	0-2	3-3	0-0	0-0	1-2	0-2	-	1-2
Wimbledon	1-5	1-0	1-1	0-1	4-0	2-1	1-2	4-0	1-1	1-1	1-0	4-0	0-2	4-1	1-0	1-0	2-1	1-2	0-1	-

Biggest wins: Luton 6 Southampton 1; Arsenal 5 Norwich 0; Coventry 5 Sheffield W 0; Liverpool 5 Luton 0; Millwall 0 Tottenham 5.

AC Milan commandingly won the European Cup, crushing Real Madrid 5-0 in the second leg of their semi-final and then, somewhat anti-climactically, rolling over Steaua Bucharest 4-0. The Italians had a club in each European final for the first time: Napoli won the UEFA Cup but Sampdoria lost the Cup-winners' final to Barcelona. However, it was Inter Milan who won the Italian League, losing only two games out of 34, which said much about the depth of the country's football as they prepared to stage the World Cup. Their capacity to get everything ready in time was in more doubt.

Real Madrid had the consolation of winning the Spanish League again – with a club record sequence of 27 undefeated games– but after losing in the European Cup semis for the third year running, Real's Dutch manager, Leo Beenhakker, went home to become technical director of Ajax. The Welshman John Toshack was appointed to replace him. Two Brits managed Atletico Madrid: Ron Atkinson for 94 days and Colin Addison for 56. Both were sacked. Manuel Lopez, goalkeeper of the Spanish Second Division side Ceuta, set a world record of 1,221 minutes without conceding a goal.

Bayern Munich won the Bundesliga in West Germany, where gates fell to their lowest for 16 years. A plan to revamp the League with teams playing two-leg ties on consecutive Saturdays was attacked by the national team manager Franz Beckenbauer as likely to cause violence.

THINGS GO BETTER WITH COKE

Brazil won the Copa America, the South American national championship, their first trophy since the 1970 World Cup. Meanwhile, Nacional of Medellin became the first Colombian team to win the Libertadores Cup, the South American club championship, beating the Paraguayan club Olimpia on penalties. However, there were worse penalties in Colombian soccer. Ten people died, mainly by shooting and stabbing, in the street celebrations that followed Nacional's qualification for the final. Colombian soccer teams were reported to be owned by rival cocaine syndicates and rigged results were said to be endemic, due to illegal betting. A leading referee was kidnapped and held for 24 hours and gangsters warned officials to call games fairly or be rubbed out; this one had allowed a game to go into 12 minutes of extra time. The season was then postponed pending inquiries into the clubs, particularly their apparent habit of buying Argentinian strikers as a means of laundering drug money. The Portuguese international Hernani Neves was not transferred to Colombia, but traces of cocaine were found in his urine after he had played for Benfica against Sporting. The match had been used to publicise the Government's anti-drug campaign and Benfica players had the message "Say No to Drugs" on their shirts.

A world cup tie between Iran and China was called off because both countries were in political crisis. Libya cancelled and forfeited their game against Algeria on safety grounds, because the pitch on which they were due to play was next to the alleged germ warfare factory at Rabta, and might be bombed by the US. The PLO XI made a European tour as part of the Palestinians' campaign for statehood, playing teams of youths, journalists and Italian dockers. In Saudi Arabia women were allowed to watch a sporting event for the first time – the World Youth Soccer Cup – apparently after pressure from the sponsors, Coca Cola. In Iraq, Emanuel Baba Daoud was sacked as national team coach for the seventh time, after the team failed to qualify for the World Cup finals.

The BBC reported – not on April 1 – that a player in Indonesia had been sent off for removing a goal-post with his trunk. Elephant soccer, using mahouts riding specially trained animals, was becoming more popular there and there was talk of organising international fixtures. Researchers at Rice University, Texas, said that the universe was largely made up of carbon molecules in the shape of truncated icosahedrons – the pattern of hexagons and pentagons on a football – thus proving that soccer is the universal as well as the world game.

THE WORLD'S WORST SOCCER TRAGEDIES

MOSCOW 1982. 340 dead (according to latest estimates in Sovietsky Sport). Moscow Spartak v Haarlem, UEFA Cup. Fans rushing for exits find all but one blocked and are crushed on icy staircase.

LIMA 1964. 318 dead. Peru v Argentina, Olympic qualifier. Uruguayan referee disallows Peruvian equaliser. The crowd get angry, the police panic and fire shots in the air; spectators fall and get trampled as they rush to get out.

HILLSBOROUGH 1989. 95 dead.

BUENOS AIRES 1968. 74 dead. River Plate v Boca Juniors. Panic and stampede after Boca fans throw burning papers on to the lower tiers.

KATMANDU 1988. 71 dead. Club game between Nepalis and Bangladeshis. Crowd stampede to avoid hailstorm.

IBROX 1971. 66 dead. Rangers v Celtic. Rangers equalise near the end of game and spectators leaving the ground turn back only

to be swept downstairs by others behind them.

BRADFORD 1985. 53 dead. Bradford City v Lincoln. Fire at Valley Parade.

CAIRO 1974. 49 dead. Zamalek v Dukla Prague. Fans crushed as they tried to get in.

KAYSERI, TURKEY 1971. 44 dead. Kayseri v Siwas. Fighting in the crowd after disputed goal leads to collapse of a platform.

BRUSSELS 1985. 39 dead. Liverpool v Juventus. Wall collapses on to Italian supporters fleeing Liverpool fans' charge.

BOLTON 1946. 33 dead. Bolton v Stoke. Wall collapses.

TRIPOLI 1988. 30 dead. Libya v Malta. Police firing shots in the air start panic.

IBROX 1902. 25 dead. Scotland v England. Part of a stand collapses.

Main source: **World Soccer**

====================== **1988-89** ======================

FOOTBALL LEAGUE
(1987-88 positions in brackets. Promoted clubs in bold. Relegated clubs in italics)

FIRST DIVISION

			P	HOME W	HOME D	HOME L	HOME F	HOME A	AWAY W	AWAY D	AWAY L	AWAY F	AWAY A	Pts	Avge Attendance H	Avge Attendance A
1	(6)	ARSENAL	38	10	6	3	35	19	12	4	3	38	17	76	35,595	24,251
2	(1)	Liverpool	38	11	5	3	33	11	11	11	5	32	17	76	38,574	27,700
3	(3)	Nottm F	38	8	7	4	31	16	9	6	4	33	27	64	20,785	21,044
4	(14)	Norwich C	38	8	7	4	23	20	9	4	6	25	25	62	16,785	19,084
5	(15)	Derby C	38	9	3	7	23	18	8	4	7	17	20	58	17,535	20,112
6	(13)	Tottenham H	38	8	6	5	31	24	7	6	6	29	22	57	24,467	24,062
7	(10)	Coventry C	38	9	4	6	28	23	5	9	5	19	19	55	16,040	18,867
8	(4)	Everton	38	10	7	2	33	18	4	5	10	17	27	54	27,765	20,538
9	(5)	QPR	38	9	5	5	23	16	5	6	8	20	21	53	12,281	19,901
10	(P)	Millwall	38	10	3	6	27	21	4	8	7	20	31	53	15,416	20,910
11	(2)	Man Utd	38	10	5	4	27	13	3	7	9	18	22	51	36,488	23,640
12	(7)	Wimbledon	38	10	3	6	30	19	4	6	9	20	27	51	7,824	18,134
13	(12)	Southampton	38	6	7	6	25	26	4	8	7	27	40	45	15,590	17,580
14	(17)	Charlton A	38	6	7	6	23	24	4	5	10	19	34	42	9,398	17,459
15	(11)	Sheffield W	38	6	6	7	21	25	4	6	9	13	26	42	20,037	18,221
16	(9)	Luton T	38	8	6	5	32	21	2	5	12	10	31	41	9,504	17,946
17	(P)	Aston V	38	7	6	6	25	22	2	7	10	20	34	40	23,310	17,936
18	(P)	*Middlesbro*	38	6	7	6	28	30	3	5	11	16	31	39	19,999	19,495
19	(16)	*West Ham U*	38	3	6	10	19	30	7	2	10	18	32	38	20,738	21,142
20	(8)	*Newcastle U*	38	3	6	10	19	28	4	4	11	13	35	31	22,921	21,264

TOP SCORERS (League and Cup)
29 John Aldridge (Liverpool)
24 Alan Smith (Arsenal)
22 Nigel Clough (Nottm F)
22 Alan McInally (Aston Villa)
20 Dean Saunders (Derby)

HOW THE LEAD CHANGED HANDS
Sep 10 Southampton; Sep 17 Norwich; Oct 1 Millwall; Oct 8 Norwich; Dec 26 Arsenal; Dec 27 Norwich; Dec 31 Arsenal; Jan 2 (2 hours) Norwich; Jan 2 Arsenal; April 8 (4 hours) Liverpool; April 8 Arsenal; April 11 Liverpool; April 15 Arsenal; May 16 Liverpool; May 17 Arsenal; May 23 Liverpool; May 26 ARSENAL.

SECOND DIVISION

			P	W	D	L	F	A	W	D	L	F	A	Pts	H	A
					HOME					AWAY					Avge	Attendance
1	(R)	CHELSEA	46	15	6	2	50	25	14	6	3	46	25	99	15,731	14,311
2	(9)	Man City	46	12	8	3	48	28	11	5	7	29	25	82	23,500	13,278
3	(6)	Crystal P	46	15	6	2	42	17	8	6	9	29	32	81	10,655	11,752
4	(R)	Watford	46	14	5	4	41	18	8	7	8	33	30	78	12,292	10,476
5	(5)	Blackburn R	46	16	4	3	50	22	6	7	10	24	37	77	8,891	10,573
6	(12)	Swindon T	46	13	8	2	35	15	7	8	8	33	38	76	8,687	10,035
7	(14)	Barnsley	46	12	8	3	37	21	8	6	9	29	37	74	7,215	9,737
8	(8)	Ipswich T	46	13	3	7	42	23	9	4	10	29	38	73	12,666	9,464
9	(20)	West Brom A	46	13	7	3	43	18	5	11	7	22	23	72	12,757	12,261
10	(7)	Leeds U	46	12	6	5	34	20	5	10	8	25	30	67	21,811	12,043
11	(P)	Sunderland	46	12	8	3	40	23	4	7	12	20	37	63	14,878	11,181
12	(17)	Bournemouth	46	13	3	7	32	20	5	5	13	21	42	62	8,087	10,744
13	(11)	Stoke C	46	10	9	4	33	25	5	5	13	24	47	59	9,817	10,953
14	(4)	Bradford C	46	8	11	4	29	22	5	6	12	23	37	56	10,524	10,568
15	(13)	Leicester C	46	11	6	6	31	20	2	10	11	25	43	55	10,694	9,794
16	(10)	Oldham A	46	9	10	4	49	32	2	11	10	26	40	54	7,204	9,589
17	(R)	Oxford U	46	11	6	6	40	34	3	6	14	22	36	54	6,352	9,264
18	(16)	Plymouth A	46	11	4	8	35	22	3	8	12	20	44	54	8,624	9,231
19	(P)	Brighton	46	11	5	7	36	24	3	4	16	21	42	51	9,048	9,528
20	(R)	Portsmouth	46	10	6	7	33	21	3	6	14	20	41	51	10,201	11,080
21	(15)	Hull C	46	7	9	7	31	25	4	5	14	21	43	47	6,666	9,326
22	(18)	*Shrewsbury*	46	4	11	8	25	31	4	7	12	15	36	42	4,706	9,310
23	(19)	*Birmingham*	46	6	4	13	21	33	2	7	14	10	43	35	6,265	10,261
24	(P)	*Walsall*	46	3	10	10	27	42	2	6	15	14	38	31	6,108	8,624

Play-offs
Blackburn R 0 1 Watford 0 1 (Blackburn won on away goals)
Swindon T 1 0 Crystal P 0 2 (Crystal P won 2-1 on agg)

Final
Blackburn R 3 0 Crystal P 1 3 (Crystal P won 4-3 on agg)

TOP SCORERS (League and Cup)
33 Ian Wright (Crystal P)
30 Keith Edwards (Hull C)
28 Kerry Dixon (Chelsea)
26 Tommy Tynan (Plymouth)
24 Mark Bright (Crystal P)

HOW THE LEAD CHANGED HANDS
Sep 10 Watford; Sep 24 Blackburn; Oct 1 Ipswich; Oct 4 Watford; Oct 15 Blackburn; Oct 25 Watford; Nov 21 Portsmouth/Watford; Nov 26 Blackburn; Dec 10 Man City; Dec 16 Chelsea; Dec 17 Blackburn; Dec 26 Chelsea; Jan 2 WBA; Jan 14 Chelsea; Feb 25 Man C; Feb 28 Chelsea; Mar 11 Man C; Mar 18 CHELSEA.

THIRD DIVISION

			P	W	D	L	F	A	W	D	L	F	A	Pts	H	A
					HOME					AWAY					Avge	Attendance
1	(P)	WOLVES	46	18	4	1	61	19	9	9	5	35	30	92	14,392	8,062
2	(R)	Sheffield U	46	16	3	4	57	21	9	6	8	36	33	84	12,222	8,182
3	(11)	Port Vale	46	15	3	5	46	21	9	9	5	32	27	84	6,944	6,331
4	(9)	Fulham	46	12	7	4	42	28	10	2	11	27	39	75	4,938	5,750
5	(8)	Bristol R	46	9	11	3	34	21	10	6	7	33	30	74	5,259	6,192
6	(16)	Preston NE	46	14	7	2	56	31	5	8	10	23	29	72	7,737	5,971
7	(12)	Brentford	46	14	5	4	36	21	4	9	10	30	40	68	5,682	5,142
8	(15)	Chester C	46	12	6	5	38	18	7	5	11	26	43	68	3,056	5,137
9	(4)	Notts C	46	11	7	5	37	22	7	6	10	27	32	67	5,675	5,045
10	(P)	Bolton W	46	12	8	3	42	23	4	8	11	16	31	64	5,705	5,714
11	(5)	Bristol C	46	10	3	10	32	25	8	6	9	21	30	63	8,121	5,410
12	(P)	Swansea C	46	11	8	4	33	22	4	8	11	18	31	61	5,088	5,529
13	(14)	Bury	46	11	7	5	27	22	5	6	12	28	45	61	3,368	5,042
14	(R)	Huddersfield	46	10	8	5	35	25	7	1	15	28	48	60	5,821	5,342
15	(19)	Mansfield T	46	10	8	5	32	22	4	9	10	16	30	59	4,006	4,849
16	(P)	Cardiff C	46	10	9	4	30	16	4	6	13	14	40	57	4,385	5,017
17	(7)	Wigan A	46	9	5	9	28	22	5	9	9	27	31	56	3,151	4,931
18	(R)	Reading	46	10	6	7	37	29	5	5	13	31	43	56	5,106	5,259
19	(10)	Blackpool	46	10	6	7	36	29	4	7	12	20	30	55	4,277	5,101
20	(6)	Northampton	46	11	2	10	41	34	5	4	14	25	42	54	3,919	5,370
21	(17)	Southend U	46	10	9	4	33	26	3	6	14	23	49	54	3,699	4,501
22	(18)	*Chesterfield*	46	9	5	9	35	35	5	2	16	16	51	49	3,717	5,129
23	(19)	*Gillingham*	46	7	3	13	25	32	5	1	17	22	49	40	3,675	4,774
24	(20)	*Aldershot*	46	7	6	10	29	29	1	7	15	19	49	37	2,609	4,881

Play-offs
Bristol R 1 4 Fulham 0 0 (Bristol R won 5-0 on agg)
Preston NE 1 1 Port Vale 1 3 (Port Vale won 4-2 on agg)

Final
Bristol R 1 0 Port Vale 1 1 (Port Vale won 2-1 on agg)

TOP SCORERS (League and Cup)
50*Steve Bull (Wolves)
33 Craig Maskell (Hudd T)
30 Tony Agana (Sheff U)
30 Brian Deane (Sheff U)
29 David Crown (Southend)
25 Jim Gilligan (Cardiff)
24 Carl Dale (Chester)
*Bull scored 55 in all games and 37 in Third Division games

HOW THE LEAD CHANGED HANDS
Sep 10 Swansea; Sep 17 Northampton; Sep 20 Sheff U; Oct 3 Port Vale;
Oct 22 Sheff U; Nov 5 WOLVES.

FOURTH DIVISION

			P	HOME W	HOME D	HOME L	HOME F	HOME A	AWAY W	AWAY D	AWAY L	AWAY F	AWAY A	Pts	Avge Attendance H	Avge Attendance A
1	(R)	ROTHERHAM U	46	13	6	4	44	18	9	10	4	32	17	82	5,064	3,964
2	(14)	**Tranmere R**	46	15	6	2	34	13	6	11	6	28	30	80	5,331	3,054
3	(17)	Crewe A	46	13	7	3	42	24	8	8	7	25	24	78	3,296	3,881
4	(4)	Scunthorpe	46	11	9	3	40	22	10	5	8	37	35	77	4,547	3,786
5	(12)	Scarborough	46	12	7	4	33	23	9	7	7	34	29	77	2,962	3,270
6	(8)	**L Orient**	46	16	2	5	61	19	5	10	8	25	31	75	3,794	3,169
7	(11)	Wrexham	46	12	7	4	44	28	7	7	9	33	35	71	2,636	3,465
8	(15)	Cambridge U	46	13	7	3	45	25	5	7	11	26	37	68	2,653	3,165
9	(R)	Grimsby T	46	11	9	3	33	18	6	6	11	32	41	66	4,302	3,434
10	(P)	Lincoln C	46	12	6	5	39	26	6	4	13	25	34	64	3,887	3,314
11	(R)	York C	46	10	8	5	43	27	7	5	11	19	36	64	2,614	3,078
12	(23)	Carlisle U	46	9	6	8	26	25	6	9	8	27	27	60	3,176	2,907
13	(22)	Exeter	46	14	4	5	46	23	4	2	17	19	45	60	2,680	3,114
14	(5)	Torquay U	46	15	2	6	32	23	2	6	15	13	37	59	2,850	2,782
15	(19)	Hereford U	46	11	8	4	40	27	3	8	12	26	45	58	2,132	2,762
16	(10)	Burnley	46	12	6	5	35	20	2	7	14	17	41	55	7,062	4,271
17	(7)	Peterborough	46	10	3	10	29	32	4	9	10	23	42	54	3,262	2,885
18	(21)	Rochdale	46	10	10	3	32	26	3	4	16	24	56	53	1,968	3,403
19	(16)	Hartlepool	46	10	6	7	33	33	4	4	15	17	45	52	2,048	3,049
20	(20)	Stockport C	46	8	10	5	31	20	2	11	10	23	32	51	2,792	3,054
21	(18)	Halifax T	46	10	7	6	42	27	3	4	16	27	48	50	1,947	3,104
22	(9)	Colchester	46	8	7	8	35	30	4	7	12	25	48	50	2,894	3,102
23	(R)	Doncaster R	46	9	6	8	32	32	4	4	15	17	46	49	2,159	2,855
24	(13)	*Darlington*	46	3	12	8	28	38	5	6	12	25	38	42	2,316	3,006

Play-offs
L Orient 2 0 Scarborough 0 1 (L Orient won 2-1 on agg)
Wrexham 3 2 Scunthorpe U 1 0 (Wrexham won 5-1 on agg)

Final
Wrexham 0 1 L Orient 0 2 (L Orient won 2-1 on agg)

TOP SCORERS (League and Cup)
32 Phil Stant (Hereford U)
28 Ian Muir (Tranmere R)
28 Bob Williamson (Rotherham U)
27 Tony Daws (Scunthorpe)
25 Terry McPhillips (Halifax T)
23 Darren Rowbotham (Exeter C)

HOW THE LEAD CHANGED HANDS
Sep 10 Burnley; Sep 17 Rotherham; Oct 4 Burnley; Oct 22 Rotherham;
Oct 29 Burnley; Nov 5 Rotherham; Nov 12 Scarborough; Nov 26 Rotherham;
Dec 26 Crewe; Dec 31 Wrexham; Jan 2 Crewe; Jan 7 Rotherham;
Jan 29 Crewe; Mar 27 Rotherham; Apr 7 Tranmere; Apr 14 Crewe;
Apr 15 Tranmere; Apr 22 ROTHERHAM

THE FIRST DIVISION IN THE 80s
(1979-80 to 1988-89)

		P	HOME					AWAY					Pts
			W	D	L	F	A	W	D	L	F	A	
1	Liverpool	414	141	44	22	447	134	92	67	48	317	205	810
2	Man Utd	414	128	54	25	370	132	66	71	70	247	248	707
3	Arsenal	414	115	59	33	331	168	75	52	80	261	272	681
4	Nottingham F	414	119	54	34	368	176	70	50	87	257	288	671
5	Everton	414	120	56	31	385	177	66	55	86	233	259	668
6	Tottenham H	414	112	45	50	386	235	64	57	86	250	298	632
7	Southampton	414	116	47	44	386	227	45	64	98	124	341	594
8	Coventry C	414	94	46	67	304	250	44	56	107	199	357	516
9	Aston V	374	98	45	44	289	191	39	53	95	211	325	509
10	West Ham U	330	75	46	44	272	194	48	34	83	176	309	449
11	Ipswich T	294	84	28	35	255	142	41	36	70	162	212	439
12	Norwich C	330	71	57	37	240	183	40	38	87	154	275	428
13	Luton T	288	71	40	33	242	158	30	37	77	140	252	380
14	West Brom A	294	65	39	43	223	167	26	43	78	129	244	355
15	QPR	246	67	29	27	195	119	29	28	66	117	193	345
16	Watford	250	62	30	33	226	147	31	28	66	160	225	337
17	Man City	252	51	40	35	174	146	22	32	72	100	213	291
18	Sheffield W	204	50	28	24	162	123	26	29	47	103	152	285
19	Stoke C	252	53	26	47	167	162	16	38	72	93	237	271
20	Newcastle U	204	45	25	32	163	137	18	35	49	93	186	249
21	Sunderland	210	38	34	33	127	111	22	21	62	93	176	235
22	Chelsea	166	40	24	19	124	94	20	27	36	99	132	231
23	Leicester C	210	44	29	32	173	137	18	16	71	105	223	231
24	Birmingham C	210	40	27	38	122	115	15	30	60	90	185	222
25	Middlesbro	164	36	27	19	117	84	13	17	52	64	134	191
26	Brighton & HA	168	34	25	25	110	92	13	23	48	72	152	189
27	Wolves	168	32	21	31	89	88	16	18	50	71	157	183
28	Wimbledon	120	29	17	14	94	61	18	16	26	71	82	174
29	Leeds U	126	26	23	14	72	56	14	13	36	52	102	156
30	Derby C	120	24	14	22	77	64	14	14	32	35	86	142
31	Notts C	126	26	16	21	100	94	12	10	41	66	118	140
32	Charlton A	120	20	21	19	74	67	10	17	33	53	98	128
33	Oxford U	124	20	22	20	88	86	7	16	39	62	143	119
34	Swansea C	84	23	7	12	66	45	8	10	24	43	75	110
35	Crystal P	84	15	13	14	58	50	3	10	29	30	83	77
36	Millwall	38	10	3	6	27	21	4	8	7	20	31	53
37	Bristol C	42	6	6	9	22	30	3	7	11	15	36	40
38	Portsmouth	40	4	8	8	21	27	3	6	11	15	39	35
39	Bolton W	42	5	11	5	19	21	0	4	17	19	52	30

Points are all based on three for a win, one for a draw. Until 1981-82 the League awarded two for a win.

THE BAD BOYS
Worst disciplinary records, Football League 1988-89

Club	Penalty Points	Fine
Portsmouth	342	£5,000
West Brom	269	£3,000
Southampton	268	£2,000
Leeds	266	£3,000
Stockport	264	£1,000

FA CUP

Winners are in capitals. Underlined teams beat a team from a higher division

FIRST ROUND
ALDERSHOT 1 Hayes 0; ALTRINCHAM 3 Lincoln C 2; BATH 2 Grays 0; BLACKPOOL 2 Scunthorpe U 1; BOGNOR REGIS 2 Exeter C 1; BRENTFORD 2 Halesowen 0; BRISTOL C 3 Southend 1; Burnley 0 CHESTER 2; CARDIFF 4 Hereford U 0; Dagenham 0 SUTTON U 4; Darlington 1 NOTTS C 2; Frickley 0 NORTHWICH V 2; Fulham 0 COLCHESTER U 1; GRIMSBY T 1 Wolves 0; Guisborough 0 BURY 1; HALIFAX T 1 York C 0; HARTLEPOOL U 2 Wigan A 0; KETTERING 2 Dartford 1; Newport C 1 MAIDSTONE 2; READING 4 Hendon 2; ROTHERHAM 4 Barrow 1; SCARBOROUGH U 2 Stockport C 1; Southport 0 PORT VALE 2; SWANSEA C 3 Northampton 1; Waterlooville 1 AYLESBURY 4; WELLING 3 Bromsgrove 0; Woking 1 CAMBRIDGE U 4; YEOVIL 3 Merthyr Tydfil 2 BRISTOL R 3 Fisher 0: Doncaster R 0 1 BRANDON 0 2; Telford U 1 1 CARLISLE U 1 4; Stafford 2 2 CREWE A 2 3; Mansfield T 1 1 SHEFFIELD U 1 2; Preston NE 1 0 TRANMERE R 1 3; RUNCORN 2 3 Wrexham 2 2; TORQUAY U 2 3 Fareham 2 2; Gillingham 3 0 PETERBOROUGH U 3 1; BOLTON W 0 3 Chesterfield 0 2; HUDDERSFIELD T 1 4 Rochdale 1 3; ENFIELD 1 2 1 Leyton Orient 1 2 0

SECOND ROUND
Altrincham 0 HALIFAX T 3; Aylesbury 0 SUTTON U 1; BLACKPOOL 3 Bury 2; Bognor 0 CAMBRIDGE U 1; Bolton W 1 PORT VALE 3; GRIMSBY T 3 Rotherham U 2; HARTLEPOOL U 1 Notts C 0; HUDDERSFIELD T 1 Chester 0; KETTERING 2 Bristol R 1; Northwich1 TRANMERE R 2; Runcorn 0 CREWE A 3; Scarborough U 0 CARLISLE U 1; Doncaster R 1 SHEFFIELD U 3; Enfield 1 CARDIFF C 4; COLCHESTER U 2 3 Swansea C 2 1; Peterborough 0 2 BRENTFORD 0 3; READING 1 2 Maidstone U 1 1; Yeovil 1 0 TORQUAY U 1 1; Bath 0 2 WELLING 0 3; Aldershot 1 0 2 0 BRISTOL C 1 0 2 1

THIRD ROUND
BARNSLEY 4 Chelsea 0; Birmingham C 0 WIMBLEDON 1; Blackpool 0 BOURNEMOUTH 1; BRADFORD C 1 Tottenham H 0; Brighton & HA 1 LEEDS 1 0; Cardiff 1 HULL C 2; Carlisle U 0 LIVERPOOL 3; CHARLTON A 2 Oldham A 1; Crewe A 2 ASTON VILLA 3; HARTLEPOOL U 1 Bristol C 0; Huddersfield T 0 SHEFFIELD U 1; MAN CITY 1 Leicester C 0; Middlesbrough 1 GRIMSBY T 2; MILLWALL 3 Luton T 2; NOTTINGHAM F 3 Ipswich T 0; PLYMOUTH A 2 Cambridge U 0; SHEFFIELD W 5 Torquay U 1; Shrewsbury T 0 COLCHESTER U 3; STOKE C 1 Crystal P 0; SUTTON U 2 Coventry C 1; Welling 0 BLACKBURN R 1; Port Vale 1 NORWICH C 3; Walsall 1 0 BRENTFORD 1 1; KETTERING 1 3 Halifax T 1 2; DERBY C 1 2 Southampton 1 1; Portsmouth 1 0 SWINDON T 1 2; WEST HAM U 2 1 Arsenal 2 0; West Bromwich A 1 0 EVERTON 1 1; Sunderland 1 0

OXFORD U 1 2; Tranmere R 1 1 READING 1 2; Newcastle U 0 2 0 0 WATFORD 0 2 0 1; MAN UTD 0 2 3 Queen's Park R 0 2 0

FOURTH ROUND
Aston Villa 0 WIMBLEDON 1; BLACKBURN R 2 Sheffield W 1; Bradford C 1 HULL C 2; BRENTFORD 3 Man City 1; CHARLTON A 2 Kettering 1; MANCHESTER U 4 Oxford U 0; NORWICH C 8 Sutton U 0; NOTTINGHAM F 2 Leeds U 0; WATFORD 2 Derby C 1; Millwall 0 LIVERPOOL 2; Stoke C 3 1 BARNSLEY 3 2; Hartlepool U 1 2 BOURNEMOUTH 1 5; SHEFFIELD U 3 2 Colchester U 3 0; Plymouth A 1 0 EVERTON 1 4; GRIMSBY T 1 2 Reading 1 1; Swindon T 0 0 WEST HAM U 0 1

FIFTH ROUND
Barnsley 0 EVERTON 1; Blackburn R 0 BRENTFORD 2; Charlton A 0 WEST HAM U 1; Hull C 2 LIVERPOOL 3; NORWICH C 3 Sheffield U 2; WIMBLEDON 3 Grimsby T 1; Watford 0 NOTTINGHAM F 3; Bournemouth 1 0 MAN UTD 1 1

SIXTH ROUND
LIVERPOOL 4 Brentford 0; Man Utd 0 NOTTINGHAM F 1; EVERTON 1 Wimbledon 0; West Ham U 0 1 NORWICH C 0 3

SEMI-FINALS
EVERTON 1 Norwich C 0 (at Villa Park); LIVERPOOL 3 Nottingham F 1 (at Old Trafford; rearranged match, 0-0 at Hillsborough abandoned after six minutes)

FINAL
LIVERPOOL (1) 3	Everton (0) 2
Aldridge, Rush 2	McCall 2

Att: 82,800

Liverpool: Grobbelaar, Nicol, Hansen, Ablett, Staunton (Venison), Houghton, Whelan, McMahon, Barnes, Beardsley, Aldridge (Rush).
Everton: Southall, McDonald, Watson, Ratcliffe, Van Den Hauwe, Nevin, Steven, Bracewell (McCall), Sheedy (Wilson), Sharp, Cottee
Ref: J Worrall, Warrington

LITTLEWOODS CUP

Winners are in capitals. Underlined teams beat a team from a higher division

FIRST ROUND
Hereford U 0 2 PLYMOUTH A 3 3; Stockport C 0 1 TRANMERE R 1 1; Wigan A 0 0 PRESTON NE 0 1; SCARBOROUGH U (#) 1 2 Halifax T 1 2; West Bromwich A 0 2 PETERBOROUGH U 3 0; Bolton W 1 1 CHESTER 0 3; BOURNEMOUTH 1 0 Bristol R 0 0; BRISTOL C 1 1 Exeter C 0 0; Cambridge U 1 1 GILLINGHAM 2 3; CARDIFF C 0 2 Swansea C 1 0; Carlisle U 1 0 BLACKPOOL 1 3; Colchester U 0 0 NORTHAMPTON T 0 5; Crewe A 1 1 LINCOLN C 1 2; Doncaster R 1 0 DARLINGTON 1 2; Fulham 2 0 BRENTFORD 2 1; Grimsby T 0 0 ROTHERHAM U 1 1; Hartlepool U 2 0 SHEFFIELD U 2 2; LEYTON 0 2 0 Aldershot 0 0; NOTTS C 5 0 Mansfield T 0 1; PORT VALE 3 1 Chesterfield 2 1; Rochdale 3 1 BURNLEY 3 2; SCUNTHORPE U 3 2 Huddersfield T 2 2; Shrewsbury T 2 0 WALSALL 2 0; SOUTHEND U 2 1 Brighton & HA 0 0; Torquay U 0 1 READING 1 3; Wolves 3 0 BIRMINGHAM C (*) 2 1; York C 0 0 SUNDERLAND 0 4; BURY 2 2 Wrexham 1 2

SECOND ROUND
Port Vale 1 0 IPSWICH T 0 3; Barnsley 0 1 WIMBLEDON 2 0; Birmingham C 0 0 ASTON VILLA 2 5; BLACKBURN R 3 3 Brentford 1 4; BLACKPOOL (*) 2 1 Sheffield W 0 3; Bournemouth 0 1 COVENTRY C 4 3;

Darlington 2 0 OLDHAM A 0 4; EVERTON 3 2 Bury 0 2; LEYTON O (#) 1 2 Stoke C 2 1; LUTON T 1 1 Burnley 1 0; MILLWALL 3 3 Gillingham 0 1; Northampton T 1 1 CHARLTON A 1 2; Notts C 1 1 TOTTENHAM H 1 2; Peterborough U 1 1 LEEDS U 2 3; Portsmouth 2 1 SCARBOROUGH U 2 3; SCUNTHORPE U 4 2 Chelsea 1 2; SHEFFIELD U 3 0 Newcastle U 0 2; Sunderland 0 1 WEST HAM U 3 2; Swindon T 1 0 CRYSTAL P 2 2; DERBY C 1 2 Southend U 0 1; Hull C 1 0 ARSENAL 2 3; LEICESTER C 4 2 Watford 1 2; Lincoln C 1 1 SOUTHAMPTON 1 3; LIVERPOOL 1 3 Walsall 0 1; MAN CITY 6 Plymouth A 0 3; Middlesbrough 0 0 TRANMERE R 0 1; NORWICH C 2 3 Preston NE 0 0; NOTTINGHAM F 6 4 Chester C 0 0; Oxford U 2 0 BRISTOL C 4 2; QUEEN'S PARK R 3 4 Cardiff C 0 1; Reading 1 1 BRADFORD C 1 2; Rotherham U 0 0 MAN UTD 1 5

THIRD ROUND
BRISTOL C 4 Crystal P 1; IPSWICH T 2 Leyton 0 0; TOTTENHAM H 0 2 Blackburn R 0 1; TRANMERE R 1 Blackpool 0; WEST HAM U 5 Derby C 0, ASTON VILLA 3 Millwall 1; BRADFORD C 1 1 Scunthorpe U 1 0; Leeds U 0 LUTON T 2; LEICESTER C 2 Norwich C 0; LIVERPOOL 1 0 2 Arsenal 1 0 1; MAN CITY 4 Sheffield U 2; NOTTINGHAM F 3 Coventry C 2; QUEEN'S PARK R 2 Charlton A 1; Scarborough 2 0 SOUTHAMPTON 2 1; WIMBLEDON 2 Man Utd 1; EVERTON 1 2 Oldham A 1 0

FOURTH ROUND
BRISTOL C 1 Tranmere R 0; LUTON T 3 Man City 1; SOUTHAMPTON 2 Tottenham H 1; ASTON VILLA 6 Ipswich T 2; Leicester C 0 1 NOTTINGHAM F 0 2; QUEEN'S PARK R 0 1 Wimbledon 0 0; WEST HAM U 4 Liverpool 1; BRADFORD C 3 Everton 1

FIFTH ROUND
Bradford C 0 BRISTOL C 1; LUTON T 1 2 Southampton 1 1; Nottingham F 5 Queen's Park R 2; WEST HAM U 2 Aston Villa 1

SEMI-FINALS
West Ham U 0 0 LUTON T 3 2; NOTTINGHAM F 1 1 Bristol C 1 0

FINAL
Wembley, Apr 9
NOTTINGHAM FOREST (0) 3   Luton Town (1) 1
Clough 2 (1 pen); Webb,   Harford
Att: 76,130
Nottingham F: Sutton, Laws, Walker, T Wilson, Pearce, Gaynor, Webb, Hodge, Parker, Clough, Chapman
Luton T: Sealey, Breacker, Foster, Beaumont, Grimes (McDonough), D Wilson, Hill, Preece, Black, Wegerle, Harford
Ref: R Milford, Bristol

Teams underlined beat a team from a higher division
(*) Won on away goals
(#) Won on penalties

FIRST DIVISION SIDES KNOCKED OUT OF THE FA CUP BY NON-LEAGUE TEAMS SINCE THE WAR

1948 Colchester U 1 Huddersfield T 0
1949 Yeovil T 2 Sunderland 1
1972 Hereford U 2 Newcastle U 1
1975 Burnley 0 Wimbledon 1
1986 Birmingham C 1 Altrincham 2
1989 Sutton U 2 Coventry C 1

THE TAYLOR REPORT

Lord Justice Taylor's interim report on Hillsborough, published on August 4, said: "the main reason for the disaster was the failure of police control". The report called the police complacent and strongly castigated Chief Superintendent David Duckinfield, who was in charge of the police operation: "Mr Duckinfield's capacity to take decisions and give orders seemed to collapse". It also criticised Sheffield Wednesday and the City Council.

MAJOR RECOMMENDATIONS

1. A safety limit should be set for each terrace or pen, and cut by 15% on existing levels (current maximum: 54 people per 10 square metres).

2. All perimeter fences must have clearly-marked gates which should be left open when spectators are inside.

3. Each section of the crowd to have its own steward or policeman to check for "overcrowding or distress".

4. Better communication and liaison - between turnstile operators; police, fire and ambulance; and the clubs, the police and the local authority.

5. Clear signposting at grounds, clearer announcements and fuller information on tickets.

6. A doctor at every game, one trained first aider per estimated 1,000 spectators and an ambulance at every game with an estimated attendance above 5,000.

Peter Wright, Chief Constable of South Yorkshire, offered his resignation after the report was published but was asked to stay on by the police authority. Chief Supt. David Duckinfield, police controller on the day, was suspended. Geoffrey Dear, Chief Constable of the West Midlands, and 90 other officers began a police investigation for the Director of Public Prosecutions with a view to possible charges.

SCOTTISH LEAGUE

Promoted teams in bold. Relegated teams in italics.

PREMIER DIVISION

		P	W	D	L	F	A	W	D	L	F	A	GD	Pts	Avge Home Att
1	(3)	**RANGERS**	36	15	1	2	39	11	11	3	4	23	15	+36	56	39,189
2	(4)	Aberdeen	36	10	7	1	26	10	8	7	3	25	15	+26	50	14,107
3	(1)	Celtic	36	13	1	4	35	18	8	3	7	31	26	+22	46	31,713
4	(5)	Dundee U	36	6	8	4	20	16	10	4	4	24	10	+18	44	12,830
5	(6)	Hibernian	36	8	4	6	20	16	5	5	8	17	20	-1	35	13,896
6	(2)	Hearts	36	7	6	5	22	17	2	7	9	13	25	-7	31	15,367
7	(9)	St Mirren	38	5	6	7	17	19	6	1	11	22	36	-16	29	8,398
8	(7)	Dundee	36	8	4	6	22	21	1	6	11	12	27	-14	28	9,352
9	(8)	Motherwell	36	5	7	6	21	21	2	6	10	14	23	-9	27	7,254
10	(P)	*Hamilton Acad*	36	5	0	13	9	42	1	2	15	10	34	-57	14	4,979

FIRST DIVISION

		P	W	D	L	F	A	W	D	L	F	A	GD	Pts	Avge Att
1	(R)	**DUNFERMLINE ATH**	39	13	5	2	37	17	9	5	5	23	19	+24	54	6,624
2	(R)	Falkirk	39	13	3	3	38	10	9	5	6	33	27	+34	52	3,782
3	(3)	Clydebank	39	12	6	2	50	29	6	6	7	30	26	+25	48	1,550
4	(6)	Airdrieonians	39	11	6	2	36	16	6	7	7	30	28	+22	47	2,355
5	(R)	Morton	39	8	5	6	20	20	8	4	8	26	26	0	41	2,091
6	(P)	St Johnstone	39	11	4	4	30	16	3	8	9	21	26	+9	40	2,946
7	(5)	Raith Rovers	39	8	6	6	29	25	7	4	8	21	27	-2	40	2,160
8	(8)	Partick Th	39	7	6	6	26	24	6	5	9	31	34	-1	37	2,686
9	(4)	Forfar Ath	39	6	9	5	24	24	4	7	8	28	32	-4	36	1,162
10	(2)	Meadowbank Th	39	8	4	7	26	26	5	6	9	19	24	-5	36	843
11	(P)	Ayr U	39	8	6	6	39	37	5	3	11	17	35	-16	35	3,541
12	(9)	Clyde	39	7	6	7	23	26	2	10	7	17	26	-12	34	1,148
13	(10)	*Kilmarnock*	39	5	7	7	19	25	5	7	8	28	35	-13	34	2,488
14	(1)	*Queen of the South**	39	1	6	13	20	47	1	2	16	18	52	-61	10	987

SECOND DIVISION

		P	W	D	L	F	A	W	D	L	F	A	GD	Pts	Avge Att
1	(12)	**ALBION R**	39	14	5	1	39	19	7	3	9	26	29	+17	50	561
2	(7)	Alloa	39	12	6	1	42	20	5	5	10	24	28	+18	45	609
3	(4)	Brechin C	39	8	5	6	27	24	7	8	5	31	25	+9	43	472
4	(5)	Stirling Albion	39	10	6	3	31	20	5	6	9	33	35	+9	42	676
5	(R)	East Fife	39	9	8	3	30	20	5	5	9	25	34	+1	41	627
6	(8)	Montrose	39	10	4	5	25	25	5	7	8	29	30	-1	41	388
7	(3)	Queen's Park	39	8	7	4	26	20	2	11	7	24	29	+1	38	641
8	(11)	Cowdenbeath*	39	6	11	2	30	27	7	3	10	18	25	-4	38	315
9	(6)	East Stirling	39	10	3	7	31	31	3	8	8	23	27	-4	37	271
10	(9)	Arbroath	39	5	6	9	29	40	6	9	4	27	23	-7	37	476
11	(14)	Stranraer	39	6	8	6	30	31	6	4	9	28	32	-5	36	733
12	(12)	Dumbarton	39	10	2	8	28	27	2	8	9	17	28	-10	34	506
13	(13)	Berwick R	39	5	7	7	18	26	5	6	9	32	33	-9	33	406
14	(10)	Stenhousemuir	39	6	8	6	27	24	3	3	13	17	35	-15	29	371

*2 points deducted for breach of rules

SCOTTISH PREMIER DIVISION IN THE 80s
(1980-81 to 1988-89)

		P	W	D	L	Pts			P	W	D	L	Pts
1	Celtic	376	235	76	65	546	11	Partick T	108	27	34	47	88
2	Aberdeen	376	214	104	58	532	12	Kilmarnock	108	19	31	58	69
3	Dundee U	376	180	108	88	468	13	Falkirk	88	18	21	49	57
4	Rangers	376	184	94	98	462	14	Airdrieonians	72	15	17	40	47
5	St. Mirren	376	131	97	148	359	15	Clydebank	80	12	20	48	44
6	Dundee	340	114	69	157	297	16	Hamilton A	80	12	11	57	35
7	Hearts	268	102	79	87	283	17	Dunfermline A	44	8	10	26	26
8	Hibernian	340	92	96	152	280	18	St. Johnstone	36	10	3	23	23
9	Motherwell	232	53	52	127	158	19	Dumbarton	36	6	7	23	19
10	Morton	224	47	48	129	142		*2 points for a win and 1 for a draw*					

——— SCOTTISH CUP ———

Winners are in capitals. Underlined teams beat a team from a higher division

FIRST ROUND

Berwick R 1 1 ALLOA A 1 2; EAST FIFE 4 Spartans 1; E STIRLING 1 Gala Fairydean 0; Inverness Thistle 0 1 DUMBARTON 0 2; MONTROSE 2 Arbroath 0; STRANRAER 2 1 Stirling A 2 0

SECOND ROUND

Cowdenbeath 1 2 STENH'SEMUIR 1 3; E STIRLING 1 MONTROSE 2; Elgin C 2 0 DUMBARTON 2 4; Inverness Caledonian 1 1 BRECHIN C 1 2; STRANRAER 2 East Fife 1; Annan 1 Queen's Park 5; Coldstream 1 0 ALBION R 1 1; Forres Mechanics 1 0 ALLOA A 1 2

THIRD ROUND

MEADOWBANK T 2 Hamilton A 0; ALLOA A 3 Albion R 1; CELTIC 2 Dumbarton 0; CLYDEBANK 2 Montrose 1; Dundee 1 DUNDEE U 2, Dunfermline A 0 1 ABERDEEN 0 3; Falkirk 1 1 MOTHERWELL 1 2; FORFAR A 1 1 Clyde 1 0; Hearts 4 Ayr U 1; HIBERNIAN 1 Brechin C 0; MORTON 0 1 Airdrie 0 0; PARTICK T 0 3 St Mirren 0 1; QUEEN OF THE SOUTH 2 1 Kilmarnock 2 0; Queen's Park 0 0 STRANRAER 0 1; Raith R 1 0 RANGERS 1 3; ST JOHNSTONE 2 Stenh'semuir 0

FOURTH ROUND

Aberdeen 1 1 0 DUNDEE U 1 1 1; CELTIC 4 Clydebank 1; HEARTS 2 Partick T 0; HIBERNIAN 2 Motherwell 1; Meadowbank T 0 MORTON 1; Queen of the South 0 2 ALLOA A 0 4; RANGERS 8 Stranraer 0; ST JOHNSTONE 2 Forfar A 1

FIFTH ROUND

CELTIC 2 Hearts 1; HIBERNIAN 1 Alloa A 0; RANGERS 2 1 Dundee U 2 0; Morton 2 2 ST JOHNSTONE 2 3

SEMI-FINALS

RANGERS 0 4 St Johnstone 0 0 (both games at Celtic Park); CELTIC 3 Hibernian 1 (at Hampden Park)

FINAL

Hampden Park
CELTIC (1) 1   Rangers (0) 0
Miller
Att: 72,069

Celtic: Bonner, Morris, McCarthy, Whyte, Rogan, Aitken, McStay, Grant, Burns, McGhee, Miller

Rangers: Woods, Stevens, Gough, Butcher, Brown, Sterland (D Cooper), I Ferguson, Munro (Souness), Drinkell, McCoist, Walters

Ref: R Valentine, Dundee

AWARDS

PFA Player of the Year

1 Mark Hughes (Man Utd)
2 Steve Nicol (Liverpool)
3 Bryan Robson (Man Utd)

PFA Young Player of the Year

1 Paul Merson (Arsenal)
2 Lee Sharpe (Man Utd)
3 Nigel Clough (Nottingham F)

PFA Merit Award

Nat Lofthouse

FWA Footballer of the Year

1 Steve Nicol (Liverpool)
2 Bryan Robson (Man Utd)
3 Peter Shilton (Derby C)

European Footballer of the Year

1 Marco Van Basten (AC Milan)
2 Ruud Gullit (AC Milan)
3 Frank Rijkaard (AC Milan)

ADIDAS European Team of the Year:

Mechelen

ADIDAS Golden Boot:

Tanju Colak (Galatasaray)

—OTHER MAJOR RESULTS IN— 1988-89

EUROPEAN CUP

QUARTER-FINALS

Gothenburg 1 1 Steaua Bucharest 0 5
PSV Eindhoven 1 1 Real Madrid 1 2
Werder Bremen 0 0 AC Milan 0 1
Monaco 0 1 Galatasaray 1 1

SEMI-FINALS

Real Madrid 1 0 AC Milan 1 5
Steaua Bucharest 4 1 Galatasaray 0 1

FINAL

Barcelona, May 24
AC Milan (3) 4   Steaua Bucharest (0) 0
Gullit 2, Van Basten 2
Attn: 97,000

EUROPEAN CUP-WINNERS' CUP

QUARTER-FINALS

Eintracht Frankfurt 0 0 Mechelen 0 1
CFKA Sredets 2 1 Roda JC 1 2
Sredets won on penalties
Dinamo Bucharest 1 0 Sampdoria 1 0
Sampdoria won on away goals
Aarhus 0 0 Barcelona 1 0

SEMI-FINALS

Barcelona 4 2 CFKA Sredets 2 1
Mechelen 2 1 Sampdoria 1 3

FINAL

Berne, May 10
Barcelona (1) 2   Sampdoria (0) 0
Salinas, Rekarce
Att: 45,000

UEFA CUP

QUARTER-FINALS

Juventus 2 0 Napoli 0 3
Hearts 1 0 Bayern Munich 0 2
Victoria Bucharest 1 0 Dynamo Dresden 1 4
VFB Stuttgart 1 0 Real Sociedad 0 1
Stuttgart won on penalties

SEMI-FINALS

Napoli 2 2 Bayern Munich 0 2
VFB Stuttgart 1 1 Dynamo Dresden 0 1

FINAL:1ST LEG

May 3
Napoli (0) 2 VFB Stuttgart (1) 1
Maradona (pen) Careca
Gaudino
Att: 83,000

FINAL: 2ND LEG

May 17
VFB Stuttgart (1) 3   Napoli (2) 3
Klinsmann, Gaudina,   Alemao, Ferrara, Careca
Schmaeler
Att: 60,800
Napoli won 5-4 on agg.

SIMOD CUP FINAL
Wembley, Apr 30
Nottingham Forest 4   Everton 3
(aet: 90 mins 2-2)
Parker (2),Chapman (2)   Cottee (2), Sharp
Att: 46,606

SHERPA VAN TROPHY
Wembley, May 28
Bolton Wanderers 4   Torquay United 1
Derby, Chandler,   Edwards
Crombie, Morgan
Att: 46,513

FA CHALLENGE TROPHY
Wembley, May 13
Telford U 1   Macclesfield 0
(aet, 90 minutes 0-0)
Crawley
Att: 18,106

FA VASE
Wembley, May 6
Sudbury 1   Tamworth 1 (aet)
Hubbick   Devaney
Att: 26,487 (record)
Replay: *Peterborough, May 10*
Tamworth 3   Sudbury 0
Stanton 2, Moores
Att: 11,500

GM VAUXHALL CONFERENCE

		P	W	D	L	F	A	Pts	Avge Home Att
1 (9)	MAIDSTONE	40	25	9	6	92	46	84	1,037
2 (3)	Kettering Town	40	23	7	10	56	39	76	2,506
3 (16)	Boston United	40	22	8	10	61	51	74	1,826
4 (18)	Wycombe Wands	40	20	11	9	68	52	71	2,248
5 (7)	Kidderminster H	40	21	6	13	68	57	69	1,504
6 (4)	Runcorn	40	19	8	13	77	53	65	785
7 (11)	Macclesfield	40	17	10	13	63	57	61	1,433
8 (2)	Barnet	40	18	7	15	64	69	61	2,431
9 (P)	Yeovil Town	40	15	11	14	68	67	56	2,395
10 (17)	Northwich Vic	40	14	11	15	64	65	53	753
11 (19)	Welling United	40	14	11	15	45	46	53	1,017
12 (8)	Sutton United	40	12	15	13	64	54	51	857
13 (12)	Enfield	40	14	8	18	62	67	50	780
14 (14)	Altrincham	40	13	10	17	51	61	49	930
15 (13)	Cheltenham Town	40	12	12	16	55	58	48	1,245
16 (5)	Telford United	40	13	9	18	37	43	48	1,235
17 (P)	Chorley	40	13	6	21	57	71	45	891
18 (15)	Fisher Athletic	40	10	11	19	55	65	41	529
19 (6)	Stafford Rangers	40	11	7	22	49	74	40	1,118
20 (P)	*Aylesbury United*	40	9	9	22	43	71	36	1,177
21 (10)	*Weymouth*	40	7	10	23	37	70	31	913

Top Scorers (League and Cup)

34 Chris Camden (Stafford)
29 Mark Gall (Maidstone)
29 Lenny Dennis (Sutton U)
27 Steve Butler (Maidstone)
26 Ken Charlery (Fisher and Maidstone)
26 Steve Burr (Macclesfield)
26 Mark West (Wycombe W)
Newport County were expelled in mid-season and their record expunged.

OTHER LEAGUES

HFS LOANS LEAGUE (Premier)   **Bottom**
   1-BARROW 87   2-Hyde United 80   3-Witton Albion 79   Worksop Town 23
HFS LOANS LEAGUE (First)
   1-COLNE DYNAMOES 98   2-Bishop Auckland 89   3- Leek Town 85   Sutton Town 23
BEAZER HOMES LEAGUE (Premier)
   1-MERTHYR TYDFIL 85   2-Dartford 82   3-VS Rugby 79   Bedworth United 19
BEAZER HOMES LEAGUE (Midland)
   1- GLOUCESTER CITY 92   2-Atherstone U. 87   3-Tamworth 87   Mile Oak Rovers 25
BEAZER HOMES LEAGUE (Southern)
   1-CHELMSFORD CITY 95   2-Gravesend 87   3-Poole Town 83   Ruislip 26
VAUXHALL OPEL LEAGUE (Premier)
   1-LEYTONSTONE ILFORD 89   2-Farnborough Town 81   3-Slough Town 78   Croydon 21
VAUXHALL OPEL LEAGUE (First)
   1-STAINES TOWN 87   2-Basingstoke 83   3-Woking 82   Basildon United 25
OVENDEN PAPERS FOOTBALL COMBINATION
   1-TOTTENHAM HOTSPUR 56   2-Arsenal 52   3-Wimbledon 51   Reading 16

CENTRAL LEAGUE (First)
1-NOTTINGHAM FOREST 66   2-Everton 64   3-Aston Villa 61   Sunderland 26
DRYBOROUGHS NORTHERN LEAGUE (First)
1-BILLINGHAM SYNTHONIA 84   2-Tow Law Town 77   3-Gretna 73   Crook Town 20
GREAT MILLS LEAGUE (Premier)
1-SALTASH UNITED 62   2-Exmouth Town 62   3-Taunton Town 56   Minehead 14
JEWSON SOUTH-WESTERN LEAGUE
1-FALMOUTH TOWN 55   2-St Blazey 53   3-Bodmin Town 53   Appledore/BAAC 15
KEY CONSULTANTS SOUTH MIDLANDS LEAGUE
1-LANGFORD 82   2-Thame United 75   3-Selby 66   Milton Keynes 21
ABACUS WELSH FOOTBALL LEAGUE
1-BARRY TOWN 88   2-Aberystwyth 76   3-Haverfordwest 63   Milford 24
HIGHLAND LEAGUE
1-PETERHEAD 73   2-Cove Rangers 69   3-Huntly 66   Fort William 13

OTHER RESULTS

EUROPEAN SUPER CUP : Mechelen (Belgium) 3 0 PSV Eindhoven (Holland) 0 1 *(Mechelen won 3-1 on agg)*
FIFA UNDER-16 WORLD CUP *Hampden*: Saudi Arabia 2 Scotland 2 *(Saudi won 4-3 on penalties)*
WORLD YOUTH TOURNAMENT *Riyadh*: Portugal 2 Nigeria 0
WORLD FIVE-A-SIDE CHAMPIONSHIP *Rotterdam:* Brazil 2 Holland 1
WELSH CUP FINAL *Swansea:* Swansea City 5 Kidderminster 0
CLUBCALL CUP *Telford:* Barnet 3 Hyde United 3 aet *(Barnet won 5-3 on penalties)*
FA COUNTY YOUTH CUP *Borehamwood*: Liverpool 2 Hertfordshire 1
FA YOUTH CUP: Manchester C 1 0 Watford 0 2 *(Watford won 2-1 on agg)*
WOMEN'S FA CUP FINAL *Old Trafford:* Leasowe Pacific 3 Friends of Fulham 2

THE JOHNSTON AFFAIR

The Scottish sporting sensation of 1989 or almost any other year came on July 10 when Mo Johnston, a Roman Catholic, signed for Rangers. It was widely and not quite correctly reported that Johnston was the first Catholic to join Rangers (historians recalled Willie Kivlichan and Pat Laverty from the distant past; modernists mentioned John Spencer, currently with Rangers Reserves). This was not quite the point. Johnston was not merely any Catholic: he was both a brilliant player and one who had been known to antagonise Rangers supporters by conspicuously crossing himself after scoring against them. He was also supposedly committed to return from Nantes to Celtic and was fined £3,000 for "unsportsmanlike behaviour" in pulling out of the deal. Johnston thus found himself in possible physical danger from both ultra-Protestant Rangers supporters and Catholics who regarded him as a traitor. Rangers hired karate experts to guard him; and his 52-year-old father Jimmy was beaten unconscious in his local. Representatives of the 97 Rangers Supporters' Clubs in Ulster voted to stage a boycott until Johnston was sold and the Daily Record reported that a mongrel in Dumbarton named Mo had also been the subject of death threats. The dog's owner Nan O'Malley said: "Some people told me I should put Mo down. Others have warned that the dog's likely to have his legs broken. What kind of mentality do people have?"

THE CARD GAME

"Does the Prime Minister want to turn every football enthusiast into a Labour Party Supporter? If not, I suggest she hesitates before introducing legislation. In the meantime, might she not be wise to instruct the ridiculous Minister of Sport, Mr Colin Moynihan to stop yapping away at us on TV like a pet Pekinese?"
John Junor, Sunday Express

"I'd like to grab him by the balls and strangle him. Have you ever seen anything like him in your bloody life?"
Brian Clough on Moynihan

"I am convinced that a marginal loss in liberty for the genuine spectator is worth the saving of a beautiful game for the future generations and worth the restoration of a decent society."
David Miller, The Times, *on Football Supporters' Bill*

"An ill-conceived, petulant and petty measure, an exercise in prejudice at the public expense and a fraud upon the citizen."
Peter Jenkins, The Independent, *on the same subject*

Mr Colin Moynihan (Sports Minister): "Why did you call me a twister?"
Mr Denis Howell (Shadow Sports Minister): "Because I couldn't call you a little shit."
Extra-parliamentary exchange reported in The Independent

ACROSS EUROPE

LEAGUE TOP THREE

ALBANIA (22)
    1-17 Nentori 32   2-Partizan 30   3- Dinamo Tirana 30
AUSTRIA (36)
    1-FCS Tyrol 39   2-Admira Wacker 33   3-Austria Vienna 31
BELGIUM (34)
    1-Mechelen 57   2-Anderlecht 53   3-FC Liège 46
BULGARIA (30)
    1-CFKA Sredets 48   2-Vitosha 39   3-Etur 34
CYPRUS (28)
    1-Omonia 43   2-Apollon 40   3-Apoel 34
CZECHOSLOVAKIA (30)
    1-Sparta Prague 45   2-Banik Ostrava 42   3-Nitra 34
DENMARK (26)
    1-Broendby 40   2-Naestved 35   3-Lyngby 35
FINLAND (22)
    1-HJK 43   2-Kuusysi 34   3-Rovaniemi 31
FRANCE (38)
    1-Marseille 73   2-Paris St Germain 70   3-Monaco 68
GERMANY, EAST (26)
    1-Dynamo Dresden 40   2-D.Berlin 32   3-Karl-Marx-Stadt 30
GERMANY, WEST (34)
    1-Bayern Munich 50   2-Cologne 45   3-Werder Bremen 44
GREECE (30)
    1-AEK Athens 44   2-Olympiakos 41   3-Panathinaikos 37
HOLLAND (34)
    1-PSV Eindhoven 53   2-Ajax 50   3-FC Twente 40
HUNGARY (30)
    1-Honved 61   2-Ferencvaros 59   3-MTK Budapest 58
ICELAND (18)
    1-Fram 49   2-Valur 41   3-IA Akranes 32
IRELAND, NORTHERN (26)
    1-Linfield 65   2-Glentoran 55   3-Coleraine 50
IRELAND, REPUBLIC OF (33)
    1-Derry City 53   2-Dundalk 51   3-Limerick 45
ITALY (34)
    1-Inter-Milan 58   2-Napoli 47   3-AC Milan 46
LUXEMBOURG (22)
    1-Spora 29   2-Jeunesse Esch 25½   3-Union 24
MALTA (16)
    1-Sliema Wanderers 26   2-Valetta 23   3-Hamrun Spartans 20
NORWAY (22)
    1-Rosenborg 45   2-Lillestrom 40   3-Molde 39
POLAND (30)
    1-Ruch Chorzow 52   2-Katowice 47   3-Gornik Zabrze 45
PORTUGAL(38)
    1-Benfica 63   2-FC Porto 56   3-Boavista 49
ROMANIA (34)
    1-Steaua Bucharest 65   2-Dinamo 62   3-Victoria 45
SPAIN (38)
    1-Real Madrid 62   2-Barcelona 49   3-Valencia 49
SOVIET UNION (30)
    1-Dnieper 46   2-Dynamo Kiev 43   3-Moscow Torpedo 42
SWEDEN (22)
    1-FC Malmo 32   2-IFK Gothenburg 31   3-Djurgaarden 27
SWITZERLAND (14)
    1-Lucerne 33   2-Grasshoppers 30   3-Young Boys 27
TURKEY (38)
    1-Fenerbahce 93   2-Besiktas 83   3-Galatasaray 69
YUGOSLAVIA (34)
    1-Vojvodina 41   2-Red Star Belgrade 38   3-Hadjuk Split 36

Figures in brackets indicate the number of league games played

CUP FINAL

Dinamo Tirana beat Partizani 1-0 (after 0-0)

FCS Tyrol beat Admira Wacker 6-4 on agg

Anderlecht beat Standard Liège 2-0

Sredets beat Chernomore 3-0

AEL Limassol beat Aris Limassol 3-2

Sparta Prague beat Slovan Breztislava 3-0

Broendby beat Ikagt 6-3

Haka Valkfakoski beat OTP Oulu 1-0 (after 2-2.)

Marseille beat Monaco 4-3

Dynamo Berlin beat Karl-Marx-Stadt 1-0

Borussia Dortmund 4 Werder Bremen 1

Panathinaikos beat Panionios 3-1

PSV Eindhoven beat FC Groningen 4-1

Honved beat Ferencvaros 1-0

Valur Reykjavik beat IB Keflavik 1-0

Ballymena United beat Larne 1-0

Derry City beat Cork City 1-0 (after 0-0)

Sampdoria beat Napoli 4-1 on agg.

Union Luxembourg beat Avenir Beggen 2-0

Hamrun Spartans beat Floriana 1-0

Rosenborg beat Brann Bergen 2-0

Legia Warsaw beat Jagiellonia 4-1

Belenenses beat Benfica 2-1

Steaua Bucharest beat Dinamo Bucharest 1-0

Real Madrid beat Valladolid 1-0

Dnieper beat Moscow Torpedo 1-0

FC Malmo beat Djurgaarden 3-0

Grasshoppers beat Aarau 2-1

Besiktas beat Fenerbahce 3-1 on agg

Partizan Belgrade beat Valez Mostar 6-1

ENGLAND'S INTERNATIONAL MATCHES 1988-89

14 Sep v. DENMARK *Wembley*, Friendly, won 1-0
Shilton (Woods) Stevens Pearce Rocastle Adams (Walker) Butcher Robson Webb[1] Harford (Cottee) Beardsley (Gascoigne) Hodge
19 Oct v. SWEDEN *Wembley*, World Cup, drew 0-0
Shilton Stevens Pearce Webb Adams (Walker) Butcher Robson Beardsley Waddle Lineker Barnes (Cottee)
16 Nov v. SAUDI ARABIA *Riyadh*, Friendly, drew 1-1
Seaman Sterland Pearce Thomas (Gascoigne) Adams[1] Pallister Robson Rocastle Beardsley (Smith) Lineker Waddle (Marwood)
8 Feb v. GREECE *Athens*, Friendly, won 2-1
Shilton Stevens Butcher Walker Pearce Rocastle Webb Robson[1] Barnes[1] Lineker Smith (Beardsley)
8 Mar v. ALBANIA *Tirana*, World Cup, Won 2-0
Shilton Stevens Butcher Walker Pearce Rocastle Webb Robson[1] Barnes[1] Lineker (Smith) Waddle (Beardsley)
26 Apr v. ALBANIA *Wembley*, World Cup, won 5-0
Shilton Stevens (Parker) Walker Butcher Pearce Rocastle (Gascoigne[1]) Webb Robson Waddle[1] Lineker[1] Beardsley[2]
23 May v. CHILE *Wembley*, Rous Cup, drew 0-0
Shilton Parker Walker Butcher Pearce Webb Robson Gascoigne Clough Fashanu (Cottee) Waddle
27 May v. SCOTLAND *Glasgow*, Rous Cup, won 2-0
Shilton Stevens Walker Butcher Pearce Steven Webb Robson Waddle[1] Fashanu (Bull[1]) Cottee (Gascoigne)
3 Jun v. POLAND *Wembley*, World Cup, won 3-0
Shilton Stevens Walker Butcher Pearce Webb[1] Robson Waddle (Smith) Lineker[1] Beardsley (Rocastle) Barnes[1]
7 Jun v. DENMARK *Copenhagen*, Friendly, drew 1-1
Shilton (Seaman) Parker Pearce Webb (McMahon) Walker Butcher Robson Rocastle Beardsley (Bull) Lineker[1] Barnes (Waddle)
(Numbers after names refer to goals scored)

ENGLAND PLAYERS 1988-89

	Appearances		Goals	
	1988-89	*Career*	*1988-89*	*Career*
Tony ADAMS	3	17	1	4
John BARNES	5	47	3	9
Peter BEARDSLEY	8	34	2	7
Steve BULL	2	2	1	1
Terry BUTCHER	9	63	-	3
Nigel CLOUGH	1	1	-	-
Tony COTTEE	4	7	-	-
John FASHANU	2	2	-	-
Paul GASCOIGNE	5	5	1	1
Mick HARFORD	1	2	-	-
Steve HODGE	1	16	-	-
Gary LINEKER	7	42	3	29
Steve McMAHON	1	5	-	-
Brian MARWOOD	1	1	-	-
Gary PALLISTER	1	2	-	-
Paul PARKER	3	3	-	-
Stuart PEARCE	10	15	-	-
Bryan ROBSON	10	79	2	24
David ROCASTLE	7	7	-	-
David SEAMAN	2	2	-	-
Peter SHILTON	9	109	-	-
Alan SMITH	4	4	-	-
Mel STERLAND	1	1	-	-
Trevor STEVEN	1	25	-	3
Gary STEVENS	7	33	-	-
Michael THOMAS	1	1	-	-
Chris WADDLE	8	44	2	6
Des WALKER	9	9	-	-
Neil WEBB	9	18	2	3
Chris WOODS	1	14	-	-

SCOTLAND 1988-89

14 Sep v Norway (a)	World Cup	won 2-1	McStay, Johnston
19 Oct v Yugoslavia (h)	World Cup	drew 1-1	Johnston
22 Dec v Italy (a)	Friendly	lost 0-2	
8 Feb v Cyprus (a)	World Cup	won 3-2	Gough (2), Johnston
8 Mar v France (h)	World Cup	won 2-0	Johnston 2
26 Apr v Cyprus (h)	World Cup	won 2-1	Johnston, McCoist
27 May v England (h)	Rous Cup	lost 0-2	
30 May v Chile (h)	Rous Cup	won 2-0	McInally, Macleod

NORTHERN IRELAND 1988-89

14 Sep v Eire (h)	World Cup	drew 0-0	
19 Oct v Hungary (a)	World Cup	lost 0-1	
21 Dec v Spain (a)	World Cup	lost 0-4	
8 Feb v Spain (h)	World Cup	lost 0-2	
26 Apr v Malta (a)	World Cup	won 2-0	Clarke, O'Neill
26 May v Chile (h)	Friendly	lost 0-1	

WALES 1988-89

14 Sep v Holland (a)	World Cup	lost 0-1	
19 Oct v Finland (h)	World Cup	drew 2-2	Saunders, own goal
8 Feb v Israel (a)	Friendly	drew 3-3	Horne, Allen, own goal
26 Apr v Sweden (h)	Friendly	lost 0-2	
31 May v W.Germany (h)	World Cup	drew 0-0	

REPUBLIC OF IRELAND 1988-89

14 Sep v N.Ireland (a)	World Cup	drew 0-0	
19 Oct v Tunisia (h)	Friendly	won 4-0	Cascarino (2), Aldridge, Sheedy
16 Nov v Spain (a)	World Cup	lost 0-2	
7 Feb v France (h)	Friendly	drew 0-0	
8 Mar v Hungary (a)	World Cup	drew 0-0	
26 Apr v Spain (h)	World Cup	won 1-0	own goal
28 May v Malta (h)	World Cup	won 2-0	Houghton, Moran
4 Jun v Hungary (h)	World Cup	won 2-0	McGrath, Cascarino

WORLD CUP

Year	Winners		Runners-up	Venue	3rd Place Play-off		
1930	Uruguay	4-2	Argentina	Montevideo	United States & Yugoslavia §		
1934	Italy	2-1†	Czechoslovakia	Rome	Germany	3-2	Austria
1938	Italy	4-2	Hungary	Paris	Brazil	4-2	Sweden
1950	Uruguay	2-1*	Brazil	Rio de Janeiro	Sweden		
1954	West Germany	3-2	Hungary	Berne	Austria	3-1	Uruguay
1958	Brazil	5-2	Sweden	Stockholm	France	6-3	West Germany
1962	Brazil	3-1	Czechoslovakia	Santiago	Chile	1-0	Yugoslavia
1966	England	4-2†	West Germany	London	Portugal	2-1	USSR
1970	Brazil	4-1	Italy	Mexico City	West Germany	1-0	Uruguay
1974	West Germany	2-1	Holland	Munich	Poland	1-0	Brazil
1978	Argentina	3-1+	Holland	Buenos Aires	Brazil	2-1	Italy
1982	Italy	3-1	West Germany	Madrid	Poland	3-2	France
1986	Argentina	3-2	West Germany	Mexico City	France	4-2	Belgium

† After extra time
* Last four teams engaged in a final pool, Uruguay played Brazil in the deciding match, Sweden finished in third place
§ No play-off match

THE LEADING NATIONS

	1st	2nd	3rd	4th	Appearances in Final Stages
Brazil	3	1	2	1	13
Italy	3	1	-	1	11
West Germany†	2	3	2	1	11
Argentina	2	1	-	-	9
Uruguay	2	-	-	2	8
England	1	-	-	-	8
Czechoslovakia	-	2	-	-	7
Hungary	-	2	-	-	9
Holland	-	2	-	-	4
Sweden	-	1	1	1	7
France	-	-	2	1	9
Poland	-	-	2	-	5
Austria	-	-	1	1	5
Chile	-	-	1	-	6
Portugal	-	-	1	-	2
United States	-	-	1	-	3
Yugoslavia	-	-	1	-	7
Belgium	-	-	-	1	7
Spain	-	-	-	1	7
USSR	-	-	-	1	6

†Germany 1930-38
Others with 5 or more appearances: 9 Mexico; 6 Scotland, Switzerland; 5 Bulgaria

WORLD CUP RECORDS

Most Appearances in Final Stages
21 Uwe Seeler (West Germany) 1958-70
21 Wladyslaw Zmuda (Poland) 1974-86

Most World Cups
5 Antonio Carbajal (Mexico) 1950, 1954, 1958, 1962, 1966

Highest Attendance
199,854 Brazil v Uruguay, 1950, Maracana Stadium, Rio de Janeiro

Highest Attendance (qualifier)
183,341 Brazil v Paraguay, 1969, Maracana Stadium, Rio de Janeiro

Lowest Attendance (qualifier)
500 United States v Bermuda, 1968, Kansas City

Most Goals One Game (Final Stages)
4 Leonidas, Brazil v Poland, 1938
4 Ernst Willimowski, Poland v Brazil, 1938
4 Gustav Wetterstorm, Sweden V Cuba, 1938
4 Juan Schiaffino, Uruguay v Bolivia, 1950
4 Ademir, Brazil v Sweden, 1950
4 Sandor Kocsis, Hungary v West Germany, 1954
4 Juste Fontaine, France v West Germany, 1958
4 Eusebio, Portugal v North Korea, 1966
4 Emilio Butragueno, Spain v Denmark, 1986

Most Goals One Tournament
13 Juste Fontaine (France) 1958

RECORDS OF BRITISH ISLES TEAMS IN THE WORLD CUP

England

1950	Group Two	Chile	won 2-0	Mortensen, Mannion
		United States	lost 0-1	
		Spain	lost 0-1	
1954	Group Four	Belgium	drew 4-4	Broadis 2, Lofthouse 2
		Switzerland	won 2-0	Wilshaw, Mullen
	Quarter-final	Uruguay	lost 2-4	Lofthouse, Finney
1958	Group Four	USSR	drew 2 2	Kevan, Finney pen
		Brazil	drew 0-0	
		Austria	drew 2-2	Kevan, Haynes
	Play-off	USSR	lost 0-1	
1962	Group Four	Hungary	lost 1-2	Flowers pen
		Argentina	won 3-1	Flowers pen, Greaves, R.Charlton
		Bulgaria	drew 0-0	
	Quarter-final	Brazil	lost 1-3	Hitchens
1966	Group One	Uruguay	drew 0-0	
		Mexico	won 2-0	R.Charlton, Hunt
		France	won 2-0	Hunt 2
	Quarter-final	Argentina	won 1-0	Hurst
	Semi-final	Portugal	won 2-1	R. Charlton 2
	Final	West Germany	won 4-2 aet	Hurst 3, Peters

1970	Group C	Romania	won 1-0	Hurst
		Brazil	lost 0-1	
		Czechoslovakia	won 1-0	Clarke pen
	Quarter-final	West Germany	lost 2-3	Mullery, Peters
1982	Group Four	France	won 3-1	Robson 2, Mariner
		Czechoslovakia	won 2-0	Mariner, T.Francis
		Kuwait	won 1-0	T.Francis
	2nd Group A	West Germany	drew 0-0	
		Spain	drew 0-0	
1986	Group F	Portugal	lost 0-1	
		Morocco	drew 0-0	
		Poland	won 3-0	Lineker 3
	Round 2	Paraguay	won 3-0	Lineker 2, Beardsley
	Quarter-final	Argentina	lost 1-2	Lineker

Scotland

1954	Group Three	Austria	lost 0-1	
		Uruguay	lost 0-7	
1958	Group Two	Yugoslavia	drew 1-1	Murray
		Paraguay	lost 2-3	Collins, Mudie
		France	lost 1-2	Baird
1974	Group Two	Zaire	won 2-0	Lorimer, Jordan
		Brazil	drew 0-0	
		Yugoslavia	drew 1-1	Jordan
1978	Group Four	Peru	lost 1-3	Jordan
		Iran	drew 1-1	own goal
		Holland	won 3-2	Gemmill 2, (1 pen) Dalglish
1982	Group Six	New Zealand	won 5-2	Wark 2, Dalglish, Archibald, Robertson
		Brazil	lost 1-4	Narey
		USSR	drew 2-2	Souness, Jordan
1986	Group E	Denmark	lost 0-1	
		West Germany	lost 1-2	Strachan
		Uruguay	drew 0-0	

Northern Ireland

1958	Group One	Czechoslovakia	won 1-0	Cush
		Argentina	lost 1-3	McParland
		West Germany	drew 2-2	McParland 2
	Play-off	Czechoslovakia	won 2-1	McParland 2
	Quarter-final	France	lost 0-4	
1982	Group Five	Yugoslavia	drew 0-0	
		Honduras	drew 1-1	Armstrong
		Spain	won 1-0	Armstrong
	2nd Group D	Austria	drew 2-2	W.Hamilton 2
		France	lost 1-4	Armstrong
1986	Group D	Algeria	drew 1-1	Whiteside
		Spain	lost 1-2	Clarke
		Brazil	lost 0-3	

Wales

1958	Group Three	Hungary	drew 1-1	J.Charles
		Mexico	drew 1-1	I.Allchurch
		Sweden	drew 0-0	
	Play-off	Hungary	won 2-1	Medwin, I.Allchurch
	Quarter-final	Brazil	lost 0-1	

British Isles teams did not enter before 1950
Republic of Ireland have never qualified for these stages

ATTENDANCES

	Nations Entered	In final Stages	Matches	Total	Average
1930	13	13	18	434,500	24,139
1934	32	16	17	395,000	23,235
1938	36	15	18	483,000	26,833
1950	34	13	22	1,337,000	60,772
1954	38	16	26	943,000	36,270
1958	51	16	35	868,000	24,800
1962	56	16	32	776,000	24,250
1966	70	16	32	1,614,677	50,458
1970	71	16	32	1,673,975	52,312
1974	95	16	38	1,774,022	46,685
1978	103	16	38	1,610,215	42,374
1982	109	24	52	1,766,277	33,967
1986	114	24	52	2,285,498	43,952
1990	112	24			

WORLD CUP 1990

Qualifying Matches

EUROPE

Group 1
Greece 1, Denmark 1; Bulgaria 1, Romania 3; Romania 3, Greece 0; Denmark 1, Bulgaria 1; Greece 0, Romania 0; Bulgaria 0, Denmark 2; Romania 1, Bulgaria 0; Denmark 7, Greece 1; Bulgaria Greece; Denmark Romania; Greece Bulgaria; Romania Denmark.

Group 2
England 0, Sweden 0; Poland 1, Albania 0; Albania 1, Sweden 2; Albania 0, England 2; England 5, Albania 0; Sweden 2, Poland 1; England 3, Poland 0; Sweden 0, England 0; Sweden 3, Albania 1; Poland 0, England 0; Poland Sweden ; Albania Poland .

Group 3
Iceland 1, USSR 1; Turkey 1, Iceland 1; USSR 2, Austria 0; E Germany 2, Iceland 0; Austria 3, Turkey 3, E Germany 1; E Germany 0, Turkey 2; USSR 3, E Germany 0; Turkey 0, USSR 1; E Germany 1, Austria 1; USSR 1, Iceland 1; Iceland 0, Austria 0; Austria 2, Iceland 1; Austria 0, USSR 0; Iceland 0, East Germany 3; Iceland 2, Turkey 1; East Germany 2, USSR 1; Turkey Austria; USSR Turkey; Austria E Germany.

Group 4
Finland 0, W Germany 4; Holland 1, Wales 0; W Germany 1, Holland 1; Wales 2, Finland 2; Holland 0, W Germany 0; Finland 0, Holland 1; Wales 0, W Germany 0; Finland 1, Wales 0; W Germany 7 Finland 1; Wales 1 Holland 2; W Germany Wales; Holland Finland.

Group 5
Norway 1, Scotland 2; France 1, Norway 0; Scotland 1, Yugoslavia 1; Cyprus 1, France 1; Cyprus 0, Norway 3; Yugoslavia 3, France 2; Yugoslavia 4, Cyprus 0; Cyprus 2, Scotland 3; Scotland 2, France 0; Scotland 2, Cyprus 1; France 0, Yugoslavia 0; Norway 3, Cyprus 1; Norway 1, Yugoslavia 2; Norway 1, France 1; Yugoslavia 3,Scotland 1; Yugoslavia Norway; France Scotland; Cyprus Yugoslavia; Scotland Norway; France Cyprus.

Group 6
N Ireland 3, Malta 0; N Ireland 0, Rep of Ireland 0; Hungary 1, N Ireland 0; Spain 2, Rep of Ireland 0; Malta 2, Hungary 2; N Ireland 0, Spain 2; Hungary 0, Rep of Ireland 0; Spain 4, Malta 0; Hungary 1, Malta 1; Rep of Ireland 1, Spain 0; Malta 0, N Ireland 2; Rep of Ireland Malta 0; Rep of Ireland 2, Hungary 0; N Ireland 1, Hungary 2; Hungary Spain; Rep of Ireland N Ireland; Spain Hungary; Malta Rep of Ireland.

Group 7
Luxembourg 1, Switzerland 4; Luxembourg 0, Czechoslovakia 2; Belgium 1, Switzerland 0; Czechoslovakia 0, Belgium 0; Portugal 1, Luxembourg 0; Portugal 1, Belgium 1; Portugal 3, Switzerland 1; Belgium 2, Czechoslovakia 1; Czechoslovakia 4, Luxembourg 0; Luxembourg 0, Belgium 5; Switzerland 0, Czechoslovakia 1; Belgium 3, Portugal 0; Switzerland 1, Portugal 2; Czechoslovakia 2, Portugal 1; Luxembourg Portugal; Switzerland Belgium; Belgium Luxembourg; Czechoslovakia Switzerland; Portugal Czechoslovakia; Switzerland Luxembourg.

Two to qualify from groups 3, 5, 6, 7; one to qualify from groups 1, 2, 4 plus best two losers from the groups = 14 European countries including Italy, the hosts.

SOUTH AMERICA

Group 1
Bolivia 2, Peru 1; Peru 0, Uruguay 2; Bolivia 2, Uruguay 1; Peru 1, Bolivia 2; Uruguay 2, Bolivia 0; Uruguay 2, Peru 0.
Uruguay qualified

Group 2
Colombia 2, Ecuador 0; Paraguay 2, Colombia 1; Ecuador 0, Colombia 0; Paraguay 2, Ecuador 1; Colombia 2, Paraguay 1; Ecuador 3, Paraguay 1.

Group 3
Venezuela 0, Brazil 4; Venezuela 1, Chile 3; Chile 1, Brazil 1; Brazil 6, Venezuela 0; Chile 5, Venezuela 0; Brazil 2, Chile 0.
Brazil qualified

Winner group 1 and 3 qualify, Winners group 2 play off against Israel = 3/4 countries, including Argentina, the hosts.

CONCACAF
(North and Central America)

FIRST ROUND
Antigua 0, Netherlands Antilles 1, Netherlands Antilles 3, Antigua 1 (agg Neth Antilles 4-1); Jamaica 1, Puerto Rico 0, Puerto Rico 1, Jamaica 2 (agg Jamaica 3-1); Guyana 0, Trinidad & Tobago 4; Trinidad & Tobago 1, Guyana 0 (agg Trinidad & Tobago 5-0); Costa Rica 1, Panama 1; Panama 0, Costa Rica 2 (agg Costa Rica 3-1); Cuba 0, Guatemala 1; Guatemala 1, Cuba 1 (agg Guatemala 2-1).

SECOND ROUND
Netherlands Antilles 0, El Salvador 1; El Salvador 5, Netherlands Antilles 0 (agg El Salvador 6-0); Trinidad & Tobago 0, Honduras 0; Honduras 1, Trinidad & Tobago 1 (agg 1-1 Trinidad & Tobago away goal); Jamaica 0, United States 0; United States 5, Jamaica 1 (agg US 5-1); Guatemala 1, Canada 0; Canada 3, Guatemala 2 (agg 3-3 Guatemala away goals); Costa Rica w/o v Mexico (banned by FIFA).

FINAL ROUND
Guatemala 1, Costa Rica 0; Costa Rica 2, Guatemala 1; Costa Rica 1, United States 0; United States 1, Costa Rica 0; United States 1, Trinidad 1; Trinidad 1, Costa Rica 1; Costa Rica 1, Trinidad 0; United States 2, Guatemala 1; El Salvador 2, Costa Rica 4; Costa Rica 1, El Salvador 0; Trinidad 2, El Salvador 0; El Salvador 0, Trinidad 0; Guatemala 0, Trinidad 1; Trinidad 2, Guatemala 1; Guatemala 0, United States 0; United States El Salvador; Trinidad United States; Guatemala El Salvador; El Salvador Guatemala; El Salvador United States.

Top two to qualify

ASIA
FIRST ROUND
Group 1
Qatar 1, Jordan 0; Iraq 1, Oman 1; Qatar 0, Oman 0; Iraq 1, Jordan 0; Jordan 2, Oman 0; Qatar 1, Iraq 0; Qatar 1, Jordan 1; Iraq 3, Oman 0; Qatar 3, Oman 0; Iraq 4 Jordan 0; Oman 0, Jordan 2; Iraq 2, Qatar 2.
Winners: Qatar.

Group 2
N Yemen 0, Syria 1; Saudi Arabia 5, Syria 4; N Yemen 1, Saudi Arabia 1; Syria 2 N Yemen 0; Syria 0, Saudi Arabia 0; Saudi Arabia 1, N Yemen 0. Bahrain withdrew.
Winners: Saudi Arabia.

Group 3
Pakistan 0, Kuwait 1; Kuwait 3, UAE 2; UAE 5, Pakistan 0; Kuwait 2; Pakistan 0; UAE 1, Kuwait 0; Pakistan 1, UAE 4.
Winners: UAE.

Group 4
Nepal 0, Malaysia 2; S Korea 3, Singapore 0; Malaysia 1, Singapore 0; S Korea 9, Nepal 0; Singapore 3, Nepal 0; S Korea 3, Malaysia 0; Singapore 2, Malaysia 2; S Korea 4, Nepal 0; S Korea 3, Malaysia 0; Singapore 7, Nepal 0; Singapore 0, S Korea 3; Malaysia 3, Nepal 0. India withdrew.
Winners: South Korea.

Group 5

Thailand 1, Bangladesh 0; China 2, Bangladesh 0;
Thailand 0, Iran 3; Bangladesh 1, Iran 2; Thailand 0, China
3; Bangladesh 0, China 2; Bangladesh 3, Thailand 1; Iran
4, Bangladesh 0; Iran 3, Thailand 0; China 2, Iran 0; China
2, Thailand 0.
Winners: China.

Group 6

Indonesia 0, N Korea 0; Hong Kong 0, Japan 0; N Korea 2,
Hong Kong 1; Indonesia 0, Japan 0; Japan 2, N Korea 1;
Hong Kong 1, Indonesia 1; Japan 5, Indonesia 0; Japan 0,
Hong Kong 0; Indonesia 3, Hong Kong 2; N Korea 2,
Japan 0; N Korea 4, Hong Kong 1, N Korea 2, Indonesia 1.
Winners: North Korea.

SECOND ROUND

Six group winners play round robin.
Two to qualify.

AFRICA

FIRST ROUND

Angola 0, Sudan 0; Sudan 1, Angola 2 (agg Angola 2-1);
Zimbabwe w/o, Lesotho; Zambia w/o, Rwanda; Uganda 1,
Malawi 0; Malawi 3, Uganda 1 (agg Malawi 3-2); Libya 3,
Burkina Faso 0; Burkina Faso 2, Libya 0 (agg Libya 3-2);
Ghana 0, Liberia 0; Liberia 2, Ghana 0 (agg Liberia 2-0);
Tunisia 5, Guinea 0; Guinea 3, Tunisia 0 (agg Tunisia 5-3);
Gabon w/o, Togo .

SECOND ROUND

Group A

Algeria 3, Zimbabwe 0; Ivory Coast 1, Libya 0 (result
expunged); Zimbabwe 0, Ivory Coast 0; Ivory Coast 0,
Algeria 0; Zimbabwe 1, Algeria 2; Ivory Coast 5,
Zimbabwe 0; Algeria 1, Ivory Coast 0
Libya withdrew after one game.
Winners: Algeria

Group B

Egypt 2, Liberia 0; Kenya 1, Malawi 1; Malawi 1, Egypt 1;
Liberia 0, Kenya 0; Liberia 1, Malawi 0; Kenya 0, Egypt 0;
Malawi 1, Kenya 0; Liberia 1, Egypt 0; Kenya 1, Liberia 0;
Egypt 1, Malawi 0; Malawi 0, Liberia 0; Egypt 2, Kenya 0.
Winners: Egypt

Group C

Nigeria 1, Gabon 0; Cameroon 1, Angola 1; Gabon 1,
Cameroon 3; Angola 2, Nigeria 2; Nigeria 2, Cameroon 0;
Angola 2, Gabon 0; Angola 1, Cameroon 2; Gabon 2,
Nigeria 1; Nigeria 1, Angola 0; Cameroon 2, Gabon 1;
Cameroon 1, Nigeria 0; Gabon 1, Angola 0.
Winners: Cameroon

Group D

Morocco 1, Zambia 0; Zaire 3, Tunisia 1; Tunisia 2,
Morocco 1; Zambia 4, Zaire 2; Zaire 0, Morocco 0;
Zambia 1, Tunisia 0; Zambia 2, Morocco 1; Tunisia 1,
Zaire 0; Morocco 0, Tunisia 0; Zaire 1 Zambia 0; Tunisia
1, Zambia 0; Morocco 1, Zaire 1.
Winners: Tunisia

THIRD ROUND

Winners A v Winners B
Winners C v Winners D
(2-leg play-offs, aggregate winners qualify for finals)
Two to qualify.

OCEANIA

FIRST ROUND

Taiwan 0, New Zealand 4; New Zealand 4, Taiwan 1 (agg
8-1); Fiji 1, Australia 0; Australia 5, Fiji 2(agg 5-3).

SECOND ROUND

Israel 1, New Zealand 0; Australia 4, New Zealand 1;
Israel 1, Australia 1; New Zealand 2, Australia 0; New
Zealand 2, Israel 2; Australia 1, Israel 1.
Israel play the winners of South America Group 2 to
qualify.

SOUTH AMERICAN CHAMPIONSHIP
1989

**Group A (Salvador and Recife): Paraguay 5,
Peru 2; Brazil 3, Venezuela 1; Colombia 4,
Venezuela 2; Brazil 0, Peru 0; Peru 1,
Venezuela 1; Paraguay 1, Colombia 0;
Paraguay 3, Venezuela 0; Brazil 0, Colombia
0; Colombia 1, Peru 1; Brazil 2, Paraguay 0.**

**Group B (Golania): Ecuador 1, Uruguay 0;
Argentina 1, Chile 0; Uruguay 3, Bolivia 0;
Ecuador 0, Argentina 0; Uruguay 3, Chile 0;
Ecuador 0, Bolivia 0; Argentina 1, Uruguay 0;
Chile 5, Bolivia 0; Argentina 0, Bolivia 0;
Chile 2, Ecuador 1.**

**Final Round (Rio de Janeiro): Brazil 2,
Argentina 0; Uruguay 3, Paraguay 0; Uruguay
2, Argentina 0; Argentina 0, Paraguay 0;
Brazil 1, Uruguay 0. Final table: Brazil 6pts;
Uruguay 4; Argentina, Paraguay 1.**

CHAMPIONS

EUROPEAN CHAMPIONSHIP

Year	Winners		Runners-up	Venue
1960	USSR	2-1†	Yugoslavia	Paris
1964	Spain	2-1	USSR	Madrid
1968	Italy	1-1	Yugoslavia	Rome
	Italy	2-0	Yugoslavia	Rome
1972	W. Germany	3-0	USSR	Brussels
1976	Czechoslovakia	2-2†	W. Germany	Belgrade
	(Czechoslovakia won 5-3 on penalties)			
1980	West Germany	2-1	Belgium	Rome
1984	France	2-0	Spain	Paris
1988	Holland	2-0	USSR	Munich

EUROPEAN CUP

Year	Winners		Runners-up
1956	Real Madrid	4-3	Rheims
1957	Real Madrid	2-0	Fiorentina
1958	Real Madrid	3-2†	AC Milan
1959	Real Madrid	2-0	Rheims
1960	Real Madrid	7-3	Eintracht
1961	Benfica	3-2	Barcelona
1962	Benfica	5-3	Real Madrid
1963	AC Milan	2-1	Benfica
1964	Inter-Milan	3-1	Real Madrid
1965	Inter-Milan	1-0	Benfica
1966	Real Madrid	2-1	Partizan Belgrade
1967	Celtic	2-1	Inter-Milan
1968	Man Utd.	4-1†	Benfica
1969	AC Milan	4-1	Ajax
1970	Feyenoord	2-1†	Celtic
1971	Ajax	2-0	Panathinaikos
1972	Ajax	2-0	Inter-Milan
1973	Ajax	1-0	Juventus
1974	Bayern Munich	1-1	Atletico Madrid
	Bayern Munich	4-0	Atletico Madrid
1975	Bayern Munich	2-0	Leeds United
1976	Bayern Munich	1-0	St. Etienne
1977	Liverpool	3-1	Borussia M/bach
1978	Liverpool	1-0	FC Bruges
1979	Nottingham F	1-0	Malmo
1980	Nottingham F	1-0	SV Hamburg

1981	Liverpool	1-0	Real Madrid
1982	Aston Villa	1-0	Bayern Munich
1983	SV Hamburg	1-0	Juventus
1984	Liverpool	1-1†	AS Roma
	(Liverpool won 4-2 on penalties)		
1985	Juventus	1-0	Liverpool
1986	Steaua Buch	0-0†	Barcelona
	(Steaua won 2-0 on penalties)		
1987	FC Porto	2-1	Bayern Munich
1988	PSV Eindhoven	0-0†	Benfica
	(Eindhoven won 6-5 on penalties)		
1989	AC Milan	4-0	Steaua Bucharest

EUROPEAN CUP-WINNERS' CUP

Year	Winners		Runners-up
1961	Rangers	0-2	Fiorentina
	Fiorentina	2-1	Rangers
	(Fiorentina won 4-1 on aggregate)		
1962	At. Madrid	1-1	Fiorentina
	At. Madrid	3-0	Fiorentina
1963	Tottenham H	5-1	Atletico Madrid
1964	Sporting Lisbon	3-3	MTK Budapest
	Sporting Lisbon	1-0	MTK Budapest
1965	West Ham U	2-0	Munich 1860
1966	B. Dortmund	2-1†	Liverpool
1967	Bayern Munich	1-0†	Rangers
1968	AC Milan	2-0	SV Hamburg
1969	Slovan Brat.	3-2	Barcelona
1970	Man City	2-1	Gornik Zabrze
1971	Chelsea	1-1	Real Madrid
	Chelsea	2-1	Real Madrid
1972	Rangers	3-2	Moscow Dynamo
1973	AC Milan	1-0	Leeds United
1974	FC Magdeburg	2-0	AC Milan
1975	Dynamo Kiev	3-0	Ferencvaros
1976	Anderlecht	4-2	West Ham United
1977	SV Hamburg	2-0	Anderlecht
1978	Anderlecht	4-0	Austria/WAC
1979	Barcelona	4-3†	Fortuna Dusseldorf
1980	Valencia	0-0†	Arsenal
	(Valencia won 5-4 on penalties)		
1981	Dynamo Tbilisi	2-1	Carl Zeiss Jena
1982	Barcelona	2-1	Standard Liège
1983	Aberdeen	2-1	Real Madrid
1984	Juventus	2-1	FC Porto
1985	Everton	3-1	R. Vienna
1986	Dynamo Kiev	3-0	Atletico Madrid
1987	Ajax	1-0	Lokomotiv Leipzig
1988	Mechelen	1-0	Ajax
1989	Barcelona	2-0	Sampdoria

† after extra time

UEFA CUP

Known as the International Industries Fairs
Inter-Cities Cup 1958-65 and European Fairs Cup 1966-70

Year	Winners			Runners-up
1958	Barcelona	6-0,	2-2†	London
1960	Barcelona	4-1,	0-0	Birmingham City
1961	AS Roma	2-0,	2-2	Birmingham City
1962	Valencia	6-2,	1-1	Barcelona
1963	Valencia	2-1,	2-0	Dynamo Zagreb
1964	Real Zaragoza	2-1		Valencia
1965	Ferencvaros	1-0		Juventus
1966	Barcelona	4-2,	0-1	Real Zaragoza
1967	Dynamo Zagreb	2-0,	0-0	Leeds United
1968	Leeds United	1-0,	0-0	Ferencvaros
1969	Newcastle Utd.	3-0,	3-2	Ujpest Dozsa
1970	Arsenal	3-0,	1-3	Anderlecht
1971	Leeds United	1-1,	2-2*	Juventus
1972	Tottenham H	2-1,	1-1	Wolverhampton W
1973	Liverpool	3-0,	0-2	Borussia M/bach
1974	Feyenoord	2-0,	2-2	Tottenham H

1975	Borussia M/bach	5-1,	0-0	Twente Enschede
1976	Liverpool	3-2,	1-1	FC Bruges
1977	Juventus	1-0,	1-2*	Ath. Bilbao
1978	PSV Eindhoven	3-0,	0-0	Bastia
1979	Borussia M/bach	1-0,	1-1	Red Star B'grade
1980	Eintracht F/furt	1-0,	2-3*	Borussia M/bach
1981	Ipswich Town	3-0,	2-4	AZ 67 Alkmaar
1982	IFK Gothenburg	1-0,	3-0	SV Hamburg
1983	Anderlecht	1-0,	1-1	Benfica
1984	Tottenham H	1-1,	1-1§	Anderlecht
1985	Real Madrid	3-0,	0-1	Videoton
1986	Real Madrid	5-1,	0-2	Cologne
1987	IFK Gothenburg	1-0,	1-1	Dundee United
1988	Bayer Leverkusen	0-3,	3-0§	Espanol
1989	Napoli	2-1,	3-3	VFB Stuttgart

* Won on away goals rule
§ Won on penalties
† Contested between cities, not clubs

EUROPE'S MOST SUCCESSFUL TEAMS

Wins	Total	EC	ECWC	UEFA
Real Madrid	8	6	-	2
Liverpool	6	4	-	2
Barcelona	6	-	3	3
AC Milan	5	3	2	-
Ajax	4	3	1	-
Bayern Munich	4	3	1	-
Juventus	3	1	1	1
Anderlecht	3	-	2	1
Tottenham Hotspur	3	-	1	2
Valencia	3	-	1	2

EUROPE'S MOST SUCCESSFUL NATIONS

Wins	Total	EC	ECWC	UEFA
England	22	8	5	9
Spain	19	6	5	8
Italy	13	6	4	3
West Germany	11	4	3	4
Holland	8	5	1	2
Portugal	4	3	1	-
Belgium	4	-	3	1
Scotland	3	1	2	-
USSR	3	-	3	-
Sweden	2	-	-	2

The following countries have each produced one winner:
Romania, Czechoslovakia, East Germany, Hungary,
Yugoslavia.

EUROPEAN SUPER CUP

Winners (aggregate scores)

1973	Ajax	6-3	Rangers
1974	Ajax	6-1	AC Milan
1975	Dynamo Kiev	3-0	Bayern Munich
1976	Anderlecht	5-3	Bayern Munich
1977	Liverpool	7-1	SV Hamburg
1978	Anderlecht	4-3	Liverpool
1979	Nottingham F	2-1	Barcelona
1980	Valencia	2-2	Nottingham F
	(Valencia won on away goals)		
1981	Not held		
1982	Aston Villa	3-1	Barcelona
1983	Aberdeen	2-0	SV Hamburg
1984	Juventus	2-0	Liverpool
	(one game; played in Turin)		
1985	Not held		
1986	Steaua Bucharest	1-0	Dynamo Kiev
	(one game; played in Monaco)		
1987	FC Porto	2-0	Ajax
1988	Mechelen	3-1	PSV Eindhoven

WORLD CLUB CHAMPIONSHIP

(1960-79 played over two games (except 1973). Not held 1975 and 1978. Scores are aggregates. Since 1980 a single game played in Tokyo for the Toyota Cup.)

Year	Winners		Runners-up
1960	Real Madrid (Spa)	5-1	Penarol (Uru)
1961	Penarol (Uru)	7-2*	Benfica (Por)
1962	Santos (Bra)	8-4	Benfica (Por)
1963	Santos (Bra)	7-6*	AC Milan (Ita)
1964	Inter Milan (Ita)	3-1*	Independiente (Arg)
1965	Inter Milan (Ita)	3-0	Independiente (Arg)
1966	Penarol (Uru)	4-0	Real Madrid (Spa)
1967	Racing Club (Arg)	3-2*	Celtic (Sco)
1968	Estudiantes (Arg)	2-1	Man Utd (Eng)
1969	AC Milan (Ita)	4-2	Estudiantes (Arg)
1970	Feyenoord (Hol)	3-2	Estudiantes (Arg)
1971	Nacional (Uru)	3-2	Panathinaikos (Gre)
1972	Ajax (Hol)	4-1	Independiente (Arg)
1973	Independiente (Arg)	1-0	Juventus (Ita)
1974	At. Madrid (Spa)	2-1	Independiente (Arg)
1976	Bayern Munich (FRG)	2-0	Cruzeiro (Bra)
1977	Boca Juniors (Arg)	5-2	B. M/gladbach (FRG)
1979	Olimpia (Par)	3-1	Malmo (Swe)
1980	Nacional (Uru)	1-0	Nottingham F (Eng)
1981	Flamengo (Bra)	3-0	Liverpool (Eng)
1982	Penarol (Uru)	2-0	Aston Villa (Eng)
1983	Gremio (Bra)	2-1	SV Hamburg (FRG)
1984	Independiente (Arg)	1-0	Liverpool (Eng)
1985	Juventus (Ita)	2-2	Argentinos Jr (Arg)
	(Juventus won 4-2 on penalties)		
1986	River Plate (Arg)	1-0	Steaua Buch. (Rom)
1987	FC Porto (Por)	2-1	Penarol (Uru)
1988	Nacional (Uru)	2-2	PSV Eindhoven (Hol)
	(Nacional won 7-6 on penalties)		

* Including a play-off match

Most Wins *Clubs:* 3 Penarol, Nacional; 2 Inter Milan, Santos, Independiente *Countries:* 6 Argentina, Uruguay; 4 Brazil, Italy *Continents:* 17 South America; 10 Europe

FOOTBALL LEAGUE

This is how membership of the Football League has changed over the years.

Year	Total Clubs	1	2	3S	3N	3	4
1888	12	-	-	-	-	-	-
1891	14	-	-	-	-	-	-
1892	28	16	12	-	-	-	-
1893	31	16	15	-	-	-	-
1894	32	16	16	-	-	-	-
1898	36	18	18	-	-	-	-
1905	40	20	20	-	-	-	-
1919	44	22	22	-	-	-	-
1920	66	22	22	-	-	22	-
1921	86	22	22	22	20	-	-
1923	88	22	22	22	22	-	-
1950	92	22	22	24	24	-	-
1958	92	22	22	-	-	24	24
1987	92	21	23	-	-	24	24
1988	92	20	24	-	-	24	24

THE FOLLOWING CLUBS HAVE JOINED AND LEFT THE FOOTBALL LEAGUE SINCE 1923

Year	Joined	Left
1923	Bournemouth	Stalybridge Celtic
	Doncaster Rovers	
	New Brighton	
1927	Torquay United	Aberdare Athletic
1928	Carlisle United	Durham City
1929	York City	Ashington
1930	Thames	Merthyr Tydfil
1931	Mansfield Town	Newport County
	Chester	Nelson
1932	Aldershot	Thames
	Newport County	Wigan Borough
1938	Ipswich Town	Gillingham
1950	Colchester United	
	Gillingham	
	Scunthorpe United	
	Shrewsbury Town	
1951	Workington	New Brighton
1960	Peterborough United	Gateshead
1962	Oxford United	Accrington
		Stanley
1970	Cambridge United	Bradford PA
1972	Hereford United	Barrow
1977	Wimbledon	Workington
1978	Wigan Athletic	Southport
1987	Scarborough	Lincoln City
1988	Lincoln City	Newport County
1989	Maidstone United	Darlington

CHAMPIONS

Double winners underlined

	FOOTBALL LEAGUE				FA CUP		
	Winners	*Pts*	*Runners-up*	*Pts*	*Winners*	*Score*	*Runners-up*
1871-72	-				Wanderers	1-0	Royal Engineers
1872-73	-				Wanderers	2-0	Oxford Univ
1873-74	-				Oxford Univ	2-0	Royal Engineers
1874-75	-				Royal Engineers	1-1 2-0	Old Etonians
1875-76	-				Wanderers	1-1 3-0	Old Etonians
1876-77	-				Wanderers	2-1	Oxford Univ
1877-78	-				Wanderers	3-1	Royal Engineers
1878-79	-				Old Etonians	1-0	Clapham R
1879-80	-				Clapham Rovers	1-0	Oxford Univ
1880-81	-				Old Carthusians	3-0	Old Etonians
1881-82	-				Old Etonians	1-0	Blackburn R
1882-83	-				Blackburn Olympic	2-1	Old Etonians
1883-84	-				Blackburn R	2-1	Queen's Park
1884-85	-				Blackburn R	2-0	Queen's Park
1885-86	-				Blackburn R	0-0 2-0	West Bromwich A
1886-87	-				Aston Villa	2-0	West Bromwich A
1887-88	-				West Bromwich A	2-1	Preston NE
1888-89	<u>Preston NE</u>	40	Aston Villa	29	<u>Preston NE</u>	3-0	Wolverhampton W
1889-90	Preston NE	33	Everton	31	Blackburn R	6-1	Sheffield W
1890-91	Everton	29	Preston NE	27	Blackburn R	3-1	Notts C
1891-92	Sunderland	42	Preston NE	37	West Bromwich A	3-0	Aston Villa
1892-93	Sunderland	48	Preston NE	37	Wolverhampton W	1-0	Everton
1893-94	Aston Villa	44	Sunderland	38	Notts C	4-1	Bolton W
1894-95	Sunderland	47	Everton	42	Aston Villa	1-0	West Bromwich A
1895-96	Aston Villa	45	Derby C	41	Sheffield W	2-1	Wolverhampton W
1896-97	<u>Aston Villa</u>	47	Sheffield U	36	<u>Aston Villa</u>	3-2	Everton
1897-98	Sheffield U	42	Sunderland	37	Nottingham F	3-1	Derby C
1898-99	Aston Villa	45	Liverpool	43	Sheffield U	4-1	Derby C
1899-00	Aston Villa	50	Sheffield U	48	Bury	4-0	Southampton
1900-01	Liverpool	45	Sunderland	43	Tottenham H	2-2 3-1	Sheffield U
1901-02	Sunderland	44	Everton	41	Sheffield U	1-1 2-1	Southampton
1902-03	Sheffield W	42	Aston Villa	41	Bury	6-0	Derby C
1903-04	Sheffield W	47	Man City	44	Man City	1-0	Bolton W
1904-05	Newcastle U	48	Everton	47	Aston Villa	2-0	Newcastle U
1905-06	Liverpool	51	Preston NE	47	Everton	1-0	Newcastle U
1906-07	Newcastle U	51	Bristol C	48	Sheffield W	2-1	Everton
1907-08	Man Utd	52	Aston Villa	43	Wolverhampton W	3-1	Newcastle U
1908-09	Newcastle U	53	Everton	46	Man Utd	1-0	Bristol C
1909-10	Aston Villa	53	Liverpool	48	Newcastle U	1-1 2-0	Barnsley
1910-11	Man Utd	52	Aston Villa	51	Bradford C	0-0 1-0	Newcastle U
1911-12	Blackburn R	49	Everton	46	Barnsley	0-0 1-0	West Bromwich A
1912-13	Sunderland	54	Aston Villa	50	Aston Villa	1-0	Sunderland
1913-14	Blackburn R	51	Aston Villa	44	Burnley	1-0	Liverpool
1914-15	Everton	46	Oldham A	45	Sheffield U	3-0	Chelsea
1919-20	West Brom. A	60	Burnley	51	Aston Villa	1-0	Huddersfield T
1920-21	Burnley	59	Man City	54	Tottenham H	1-0	Wolverhampton W
1921-22	Liverpool	57	Tottenham H	51	Huddersfield T	1-0	Preston NE
1922-23	Liverpool	60	Sunderland	54	Bolton W	2-0	West Ham U
1923-24	Huddersfield T	57	Cardiff C	57	Newcastle U	2-0	Aston Villa
1924-25	Huddersfield T	58	West Brom. A	56	Sheffield U	1-0	Cardiff C
1925-26	Huddersfield T	57	Arsenal	52	Bolton W	1-0	Man City
1926-27	Newcastle U	56	Huddersfield T	51	Cardiff C	1-0	Arsenal
1927-28	Everton	53	Huddersfield T	51	Blackburn R	3-1	Huddersfield T
1928-29	Sheffield W	52	Leicester C	51	Bolton W	2-0	Portsmouth
1929-30	Sheffield W	60	Derby C	50	Arsenal	2-0	Huddersfield T
1930-31	Arsenal	66	Aston Villa	59	West Bromwich A	2-1	Birmingham
1931-32	Everton	56	Arsenal	54	Newcastle U	2-1	Arsenal
1932-33	Arsenal	58	Aston Villa	54	Everton	3-0	Man City
1933-34	Arsenal	59	Huddersfield T	56	Man City	2-1	Portsmouth
1934-35	Arsenal	58	Sunderland	54	Sheffield W	4-2	West Bromwich A
1935-36	Sunderland	56	Derby C	48	Arsenal	1-0	Sheffield U
1936-37	Man City	57	Charlton A	54	Sunderland	3-1	Preston NE
1937-38	Arsenal	52	W'hampton W	51	Preston NE	1-0	Huddersfield T
1938-39	Everton	59	W'hampton W	55	Portsmouth	4-1	Wolverhampton W
1945-46	-				Derby C	4-1	Charlton A
1946-47	Liverpool	57	Man Utd	56	Charlton A	1-0	Burnley
1947-48	Arsenal	59	Man Utd	52	Man Utd	4-2	Blackpool
1948-49	Portsmouth	58	Man Utd	53	Wolverhampton W	3-1	Leicester C
1949-50	Portsmouth	53	W'hampton W	53	Arsenal	2-0	Liverpool
1950-51	Tottenham H	60	Man Utd	56	Newcastle U	2-0	Blackpool

FOOTBALL LEAGUE

	Winners	Pts	Runners-up	Pts
1951-52	Man Utd	57	Tottenham H	53
1952-53	Arsenal	54	Preston NE	54
1953-54	W'hampton W	57	West Brom. A	53
1954-55	Chelsea	52	W'hampton W	48
1955-56	Man Utd	60	Blackpool	49
1956-57	Man Utd	64	Tottenham H	56
1957-58	W'hampton W	64	Preston NE	59
1958-59	W'hampton W	61	Man Utd	55
1959-60	Burnley	55	W'hampton W	54
1960-61	Tottenham H	66	Sheffield W	58
1961-62	Ipswich T	56	Burnley	53
1962-63	Everton	61	Tottenham H	55
1963-64	Liverpool	57	Man Utd	53
1964-65	Man Utd	61	Leeds U	61
1965-66	Liverpool	61	Leeds U	55
1966-67	Man Utd	60	Nottingham F	56
1967-68	Man City	58	Man Utd	56
1968-69	Leeds U	67	Liverpool	61
1969-70	Everton	66	Leeds U	57
1970-71	Arsenal	65	Leeds U	64
1971-72	Derby C	58	Leeds U	57
1972-73	Liverpool	60	Arsenal	57
1973-74	Leeds U	62	Liverpool	57
1974-75	Derby C	53	Liverpool	51
1975-76	Liverpool	60	QPR	59
1976-77	Liverpool	57	Man City	56
1977-78	Nott'ham F	64	Liverpool	57
1978-79	Liverpool	68	Nott'ham F	60
1979-80	Liverpool	60	Man Utd	58
1980-81	Aston Villa	60	Ipswich T	56
1981-82	Liverpool	87	Ipswich T	83
1982-83	Liverpool	82	Watford	71
1983-84	Liverpool	80	Southampton	77
1984-85	Everton	90	Liverpool	77
1985-86	Liverpool	88	Everton	86
1986-87	Everton	86	Liverpool	77
1987-88	Liverpool	90	Man Utd	81
1988-89	Arsenal	76	Liverpool	76

FA CUP

Winners	Score	Runners-up
Newcastle U	1-0	Arsenal
Blackpool	4-3	Bolton W
West Bromwich A	3-2	Preston NE
Newcastle U	3-1	Man City
Man City	3-1	Birmingham C
Aston Villa	2-1	Man Utd
Bolton W	2-0	Man Utd
Nottingham F	2-1	Luton T
Wolverhampton W	3-0	Blackburn R
Tottenham H	2-0	Leicester C
Tottenham H	3-1	Burnley
Man Utd	3-1	Leicester C
West Ham U	3-2	Preston NE
Liverpool	2-1	Leeds U
Everton	3-2	Sheffield W
Tottenham H	2-1	Chelsea
West Bromwich A	1-0	Everton
Man City	1-0	Leicester C
Chelsea	2-2 2-1	Leeds U
Arsenal	2-1	Liverpool
Leeds U	1-0	Arsenal
Sunderland	1-0	Leeds U
Liverpool	3-0	Newcastle U
West Ham U	2-0	Fulham
Southampton	1-0	Man Utd
Man Utd	2-1	Liverpool
Ipswich T	1-0	Arsenal
Arsenal	3-2	Man Utd
West Ham U	1-0	Arsenal
Tottenham H	1-1 3-2	Man City
Tottenham H	1-1 1-0	Queens Park R
Man Utd	2-2 4-0	Brighton & Hove A
Everton	2-0	Watford
Man Utd	1-0	Everton
Liverpool	3-1	Everton
Coventry C	3-2	Tottenham H
Wimbledon	1-0	Liverpool
Liverpool	3-2	Everton

FOOTBALL LEAGUE

Most titles

Div 1: 17 Liverpool; 9 Arsenal, Everton; 7 Manchester U, Aston Villa; 6 Sunderland

Div 2: 6 Leicester C, Man City; 5 Sheffield W; 4 Derby C, Liverpool, Birmingham C; 3 Notts C, Preston NE, Middlesbrough

Div 3: 2 Portsmouth, Oxford U

Div 4: 2 Chesterfield, Doncaster R, Peterborough U

Div 3(S): 3 Bristol C; 2 Charlton A, Ipswich T, Millwall, Notts C, Plymouth A, Swansea T

Div 3(N): 3 Barnsley, Doncaster R, Lincoln C; 2 Chesterfield, Grimsby T, Hull C, Port Vale, Stockport C

FA CUP

Venues (Excluding replays)
61 times Wembley 1923-39, 1946-89; 20 Kennington Oval 1872, 1874-92, Crystal Palace 1895-1914; 3 Stamford Bridge 1920-22; 1 Lillie Bridge 1873, Fallowfield 1893, Goodison Park 1894, Old Trafford 1915

Replay Venues
Kennington Oval 1875, 1876;
Derby 1886;
Burnden Park 1901;
Crystal Palace 1902;
Goodison Park 1910;
Old Trafford 1911, 1970;
Bramall Lane 1912;
Wembley 1981, 1982, 1983.

THE TOP TEAMS: FA CUP

	Wins	Finals	SF
Aston Villa	7	9	17
Tottenham Hotspur	7	8	12
Newcastle United	6	11	13
Manchester United	6	10	17
Blackburn Rovers	6	8	16
Arsenal	5	11	16
West Bromwich Albion	5	10	19
The Wanderers	5	5	5
Everton	4	11	22
Liverpool	4	9	17
Wolverhampton Wanderers	4	8	13
Manchester City	4	8	10
Bolton Wanderers	4	7	12
Sheffield United	4	6	10
Sheffield Wednesday	3	5	15
West Ham United	3	4	5
Preston North End	2	7	10
Old Etonians	2	6	6
Sunderland	2	3	10
Nottingham Forest	2	2	10
Bury	2	2	2

Most wins at Wembley
5 Arsenal, Newcastle U, Tottenham H; 4 Bolton W, Liverpool; 3 Everton, Manchester C, Man Utd, West Bromwich A, West Ham U

Most appearances at Wembley
11 Arsenal; 9 Man Utd; 8 Liverpool; 7 Everton, Manchester C

THOSE LOVABLE WOMBLES

"Stop yer squealing. You deserve it."
Attributed to Vinny Jones after tackling Gary Stevens and putting him in hospital.

"Wimbledon are killing the dreams that have made football the world's greatest game."
Terry Venables

"I want Vinny to manage the team in years to come. He possesses just the right character and epitomises the true spirit of Wimbledon."
Sam Hammam, Wimbledon chairman

"Vinny Jones once said he would like to tear off the head of Kenny Dalglish and spit down the hole. He was widely pictured squeezing the testicles of Paul Gascoigne, a real footballer . . . Sam Hammam is proud of Jones? He too should be kicked out of the game. What charge? Bringing the game into disrepute on a daily basis."
James Lawton, Daily Express

"Without contact with Europe English football's dominant characteristics are liable to turn monstrous. A few years and who knows what mutants it will produce. I see Vinniana Jones and the Temple of Doom. I see Creatures the World Forgot."
Robert Pryce, The Guardian

"I know for a fact that anyone who has played Sunday morning park football will wonder what all the fuss is about. Those who want to watch two million-pound players wrapped up in cotton wool playing with a balloon on the front carpet have not got any right to comment on real football anyway."
Geoff Martin, Wimbledon Labour Councillor

"One day they'll try and stick the sinking of the Titanic on me."
Dave Bassett, former Wimbledon Manager

"I have a saying: the only people who like you are the ones nicking your dough or bonking your woman."
Sam Hammam

"Just when you thought it was safe to go to Elland Road, along came Vinny Jones."
T-shirt seen in Leeds after Jones's transfer

FOOTBALL LEAGUE CUP

Known as the Milk Cup 1982-85 and the Littlewoods Cup since 1986. All finals 1961-66 were over two legs; since then they have been single games at Wembley.

Finals

1961	Aston Villa	3-0† 0-2	Rotherham U
1962	Norwich C	3-0 1-0	Rochdale
1963	Birmingham C	3-1 0-0	Aston Villa
1964	Leicester C	1-1 3-2	Stoke C
1965	Chelsea	3-2 0-0	Leicester C
1966	West Bromwich A	1-2 4-1	West Ham U
1967	Queen's Park R	3-2	West Brom. A
1968	Leeds U	1-0	Arsenal
1969	Swindon T	3-1	Arsenal
1970	Man City	2-1	West Brom. A
1971	Tottenham H	2-0	Aston V
1972	Stoke C	2-1	Chelsea
1973	Tottenham H	1-0	Norwich C
1974	Wolverhampton W	2-1	Man City
1975	Aston Villa	1-0	Norwich C
1976	Man City	2-1	Newcastle U
1977	Aston Villa	0-0. 1-1† 3-2	Everton
1978	Nottingham F	0-0† 1-0	Liverpool
1979	Nottingham F	3-2	Southampton
1980	Wolverhampton W	1-0	Nottingham F
1981	Liverpool	1-1† 2-1	West Ham U
1982	Liverpool	3-1†	Tottenham H
1983	Liverpool	2-1†	Man Utd
1984	Liverpool	0-0† 1-0	Everton
1985	Norwich C	1-0	Sunderland
1986	Oxford U	3-0	Queen's Park R
1987	Arsenal	2-1	Liverpool
1988	Luton T	3-2	Arsenal
1989	Nottingham F	3-1	Luton T

† after extra time

Most wins:
4 Liverpool; 3 Aston Villa, Nottingham F

Most finals:
6 Liverpool; 5 Aston Villa; 4 Arsenal, Norwich C, Nottingham F; 3 Manchester C, Tottenham H

MOST SUCCESSFUL ENGLISH CLUBS (All Major Tournaments)

Total		FL	FAC	FLC	Eur.
31	Liverpool	17	4	4	6
18	Aston Villa	7	7	3	1
16	Arsenal	9	5	1	1
14	Everton	9	4	-	1
14	Manchester United	7	6	-	1
13	Tottenham Hotspur	2	7	2	2
11	Newcastle United	4	6	-	1
9	Wolverhampton W.	3	4	2	-
9	Manchester City	2	4	2	1
8	Sunderland	6	2	-	-
8	Blackburn Rovers	2	6	-	-
8	Nottingham Forest	1	2	3	2
7	Sheffield Wednesday	4	3	-	-
7	West Bromwich Albion	1	5	1	-
6	Leeds United	2	1	1	2

SCOTLAND

	LEAGUE Winners	Pts	Runners-up	Pts	CUP Winners	Score	Runners-up
1873-74	-				Queen's Park	2-0	Clydesdale
1874-75	-				Queen's Park	3-0	Renton
1875-76	-				Queen's Park	1-1 2-0	Third Lanark
1876-77	-				Vale of Leven	1-1 1-1 3-2	Rangers
1877-78	-				Vale of Leven	1-0	Third Lanark
1878-79	-				(a)		
1879-80	-				Queen's Park	3-0	Thornlibank
1880-81	-				Queen's Park	3-1	Dumbarton
1881-82	-				Queen's Park	2-2 4-1	Dumbarton
1882-83	-				Dumbarton	2-2 2-1	Vale of Leven
1883-84	-				(b)		
1884-85	-				Renton	0-0 3-1	Vale of Leven
1885-86	-				Queen's Park	3-1	Renton
1886-87	-				Hibernian	2-1	Dumbarton
1887-88	-				Renton	6-1	Cambuslang
1888-89	-				Third Lanark	2-1	Celtic
1889-90	-				Queen's Park	1-1 2-1	Vale of Leven
1890-91	Dumbarton/ Rangers	29			Hearts	1-0	Dumbarton
1891-92	Dumbarton	37	Celtic	35	Celtic	5-1	Queen's Park
1892-93	Celtic	29	Rangers	28	Queen's Park	2-1	Celtic
	Division I						
1893-94	Celtic	29	Hearts	26	Rangers	3-1	Celtic
1894-95	Hearts	31	Celtic	26	St. Bernard's	2-1	Renton
1895-96	Celtic	30	Rangers	26	Hearts	3-1	Hibernian
1896-97	Hearts	28	Hibernian	26	Rangers	5-1	Dumbarton
1897-98	Celtic	33	Rangers	29	Rangers	2-0	Kilmarnock
1898-99	Rangers	36	Hearts	26	Celtic	2-0	Rangers
1899-00	Rangers	32	Celtic	25	Celtic	4-3	Queen's Park
1900-01	Rangers	35	Celtic	29	Hearts	4-3	Celtic
1901-02	Rangers	28	Celtic	26	Hibernian	1-0	Celtic
1902-03	Hibernian	37	Dundee	31	Rangers	1-1 0-0 2-0	Hearts
1903-04	Third Lanark	43	Hearts	39	Celtic	3-2	Rangers
1904-05	Celtic	41	Rangers	41	Third Lanark	0-0 3-1	Rangers
1905-06	Celtic	49	Hearts	43	Hearts	1-0	Third Lanark
1906-07	Celtic	55	Dundee	48	Celtic	3-0	Hearts
1907-08	Celtic	55	Falkirk	51	Celtic	5-1	St. Mirren
1908-09	Celtic	51	Dundee	50	(c)		
1909-10	Celtic	54	Falkirk	52	Dundee	2-2 0-0 2-1	Clyde
1910-11	Rangers	52	Aberdeen	48	Celtic	0-0 2-0	Hamilton A
1911-12	Rangers	51	Celtic	45	Celtic	2-0	Clyde
1912-13	Rangers	53	Celtic	49	Falkirk	2-0	Raith R
1913-14	Celtic	65	Rangers	59	Celtic	0-0 4-1	Hibernian
1914-15	Celtic	65	Hearts	61	-		
1915-16	Celtic	67	Rangers	56	-		
1916-17	Celtic	64	Morton	54	-		
1917-18	Rangers	56	Celtic	55	-		
1918-19	Celtic	58	Rangers	57	-		
1919-20	Rangers	71	Celtic	68	Kilmarnock	3-2	Albion R
1920-21	Rangers	76	Celtic	66	Partick T	1-0	Rangers
1921-22	Celtic	67	Rangers	66	Morton	1-0	Rangers
1922-23	Rangers	55	Airdrieonians	50	Celtic	1-0	Hibernian
1923-24	Rangers	59	Airdrieonians	50	Airdrieonians	2-0	Hibernian
1924-25	Rangers	60	Airdrieonians	57	Celtic	2-1	Dundee
1925-26	Celtic	58	Airdrieonians	50	St. Mirren	2-0	Celtic
1926-27	Rangers	56	Motherwell	51	Celtic	3-1	East Fife
1927-28	Rangers	60	Celtic	55	Rangers	4-0	Celtic
1928-29	Rangers	67	Celtic	51	Kilmarnock	2-0	Rangers
1929-30	Rangers	60	Motherwell	55	Rangers	0-0 2-1	Partick T
1930-31	Rangers	60	Celtic	58	Celtic	2-2 4-2	Motherwell
1931-32	Motherwell	66	Rangers	61	Rangers	1-1 3-0	Kilmarnock
1932-33	Rangers	62	Motherwell	59	Celtic	1-0	Motherwell
1933-34	Rangers	66	Motherwell	62	Rangers	5-0	St. Mirren
1934-35	Rangers	55	Celtic	52	Rangers	2-1	Hamilton A
1935-36	Celtic	66	Rangers	61	Rangers	1-0	Third Lanark
1936-37	Rangers	61	Aberdeen	54	Celtic	2-1	Aberdeen
1937-38	Celtic	61	Hearts	58	East Fife	1-1 4-2	Kilmarnock
1938-39	Rangers	59	Celtic	48	Clyde	4-0	Motherwell
1946-47	Rangers	46	Hibernian	44	Aberdeen	2-1	Hibernian
1947-48	Hibernian	48	Rangers	46	Rangers	1-1 1-0	Morton
1948-49	Rangers	46	Dundee	45	Rangers	4-1	Clyde
1949-50	Rangers	50	Hibernian	49	Rangers	3-0	East Fife
1950-51	Hibernian	48	Rangers	38	Celtic	1-0	Motherwell

	LEAGUE				CUP		
	Winners	Pts	Runners-up	Pts	Winners	Score	Runners-up
1951-52	Hibernian	45	Rangers	41	Motherwell	4-0	Dundee
1952-53	Rangers	43	Hibernian	43	Rangers	1-1 1-0	Aberdeen
1953-54	Celtic	43	Hearts	38	Celtic	2-1	Aberdeen
1954-55	Aberdeen	49	Celtic	46	Clyde	1-1 1-0	Celtic
1955-56	Rangers	52	Aberdeen	46	Hearts	3-1	Celtic
1956-57	Rangers	55	Hearts	53	Falkirk	1-1 2-1	Kilmarnock
1957-58	Hearts	62	Rangers	49	Clyde	1-0	Hibernian
1958-59	Rangers	50	Hearts	48	St. Mirren	3-1	Aberdeen
1959-60	Hearts	54	Kilmarnock	50	Rangers	2-0	Kilmarnock
1960-61	Rangers	51	Kilmarnock	50	Dunfermline A	0-0 2-0	Celtic
1961-62	Dundee	54	Rangers	51	Rangers	2-0	St. Mirren
1962-63	Rangers	57	Kilmarnock	48	Rangers	1-1 3-0	Celtic
1963-64	Rangers	55	Kilmarnock	49	Rangers	3-1	Dundee
1964-65	Kilmarnock	50	Hearts	50	Celtic	3-2	Dunfermline A
1965-66	Celtic	57	Rangers	55	Rangers	0-0 1-0	Celtic
1966-67	Celtic	58	Rangers	55	Celtic	2-0	Aberdeen
1967-68	Celtic	63	Rangers	61	Dunfermline A	3-1	Hearts
1968-69	Celtic	54	Rangers	49	Celtic	4-0	Rangers
1969-70	Celtic	57	Rangers	45	Aberdeen	3-1	Celtic
1970-71	Celtic	56	Aberdeen	54	Celtic	1-1 2-1	Rangers
1971-72	Celtic	60	Aberdeen	50	Celtic	6-1	Hibernian
1972-73	Celtic	57	Rangers	56	Rangers	3-2	Celtic
1973-74	Celtic	53	Hibernian	49	Celtic	3-0	Dundee U
1974-75	Rangers	56	Hibernian	49	Celtic	3-1	Airdrieonians
	Premier Division						
1975-76	Rangers	54	Celtic	48	Rangers	3-1	Hearts
1976-77	Celtic	55	Rangers	46	Celtic	1-0	Rangers
1977-78	Rangers	55	Aberdeen	53	Rangers	2-1	Aberdeen
1978-79	Celtic	48	Rangers	45	Rangers	0-0 0-0 3-2	Hibernian
1979-80	Aberdeen	48	Celtic	47	Celtic	1-0	Rangers
1980-81	Celtic	56	Aberdeen	49	Rangers	0-0 4-1	Dundee U
1981-82	Celtic	55	Aberdeen	53	Aberdeen	4-1	Rangers
1982-83	Dundee U	56	Celtic	55	Aberdeen	1-0	Rangers
1983-84	Aberdeen	57	Celtic	50	Aberdeen	2-1	Celtic
1984-85	Aberdeen	59	Celtic	52	Celtic	2-1	Dundee U
1985-86	Celtic	50	Hearts	50	Aberdeen	3-0	Hearts
1986-87	Rangers	69	Celtic	63	St. Mirren	1-0	Dundee U
1987-88	Celtic	72	Hearts	62	Celtic	2-1	Dundee U
1988-89	Rangers	56	Aberdeen	50	Celtic	1-0	Rangers

(a) Cup awarded to Vale of Leven, Rangers failed to appear for replay after 1-1 draw
(b) Cup awarded to Queen's Park, Vale of Leven failed to appear for the final
(c) After two drawn games (2-2 and 1-1) between Celtic and Rangers, the Cup was withdrawn following a riot

LEAGUE

Most titles:

Premier/1st Division:
39 Rangers; **35** Celtic; **4** Aberdeen, Hearts, Hibernian;
1st/2nd Division:
6 Ayr United, Morton; **5** Clyde; **4** Hibernian, Motherwell,
Partick Thistle, Raith Rovers, St. Johnstone, Stirling
Albion
(New) 2nd Division: **2** Clyde

CUP

Most wins:
29 Celtic; **24** Rangers; **10** Queen's Park; **6** Aberdeen; **5**
Hearts; **3** Clyde, St. Mirren, Vale of Leven

Most finals:
45 Celtic; **40** Rangers; **12** Aberdeen, Queen's Park; **10**
Hearts, Hibernian; **7** Kilmarnock, Vale of Leven; **6** Clyde,
Dumbarton, St. Mirren, Third Lanark

Venues (excl. replays)
Matches played at various Glasgow venues until 1924,
except Logie Green, Edinburgh 1896. Current Hampden
Park first used 1904 and every year since 1925. All replays
have been in Glasgow and at Hampden Park regularly
since 1930

SCOTTISH LEAGUE CUP

Skol Cup since 1984-85

1946-47	Rangers	4-0	Aberdeen
1947-48	East Fife	1-1† 4-1	Falkirk
1948-49	Rangers	2-0	Raith R
1949-50	East Fife	3-0	Dunfermline A
1950-51	Motherwell	3-0	Hibernian
1951-52	Dundee	3-2	Rangers
1952-53	Dundee	2-0	Kilmarnock
1953-54	East Fife	3-2	Partick T
1954-55	Hearts	4-2	Motherwell
1955-56	Aberdeen	2-1	St. Mirren
1956-57	Celtic	0-0† 3-0	Partick T
1957-58	Celtic	7-1	Rangers
1958-59	Hearts	5-1	Partick T
1959-60	Hearts	2-1	Third Lanark
1960-61	Rangers	2-0	Kilmarnock
1961-62	Rangers	1-1† 3-1	Hearts
1962-63	Hearts	1-0	Kilmarnock
1963-64	Rangers	5-0	Morton
1964-65	Rangers	2-1	Celtic
1965-66	Celtic	2-1	Rangers
1966-67	Celtic	1-0	Rangers
1967-68	Celtic	5-3	Dundee
1968-69	Celtic	6-2	Hibernian

1969-70	Celtic	1-0	St. Johnstone	1984-85	Rangers	1-0	Dundee U
1970-71	Rangers	1-0	Celtic	1985-86	Aberdeen	3-0	Hibernian
1971-72	Partick T	4-1	Celtic	1986-87	Rangers	2-1	Celtic
1972-73	Hibernian	2-1	Celtic	1987-88	Rangers	3-3†	Aberdeen
1973-74	Dundee	1-0	Celtic		*(Rangers won 5-3 on penalties)*		
1974-75	Celtic	6-3	Hibernian	1988-89	Rangers	3-2	Aberdeen

1975-76 Celtic 1-0 Celtic — **Venues:**

All finals and replays at Hampden Park except 1980 replay and 1981 final, which were played at Dens Park, Dundee

Most wins:

16 Rangers; 9 Celtic; 4 Hearts; 3 Aberdeen, Dundee, East Fife

Most finals:

21 Rangers; 19 Celtic; 8 Aberdeen; 5 Dundee, Hearts, Hibernian; 4 Dundee U, Partick T

1975-76	Rangers	1-0	Celtic
1976-77	Aberdeen	2-1	Celtic
1977-78	Rangers	2-1	Celtic
1978-79	Rangers	2-1	Aberdeen
1979-80	Dundee U	0-0 3-0	Aberdeen
1980-81	Dundee U	3-0	Dundee
1981-82	Rangers	2-1	Dundee U
1982-83	Celtic	2-1	Rangers
1983-84	Rangers	3-2†	Celtic

NON-LEAGUE
(since 1970)

	Northern Premier	Southern League	FA Challenge Trophy		
1969-70	Macclesfield Town	Cambridge United	Macclesfield Town	2-0	Telford United
1970-71	Wigan Athletic	Yeovil Town	Telford United	3-2	Hillingdon B
1971-72	Stafford Rangers	Chelmsford City	Stafford Rangers	3-0	Barnet
1972-73	Boston United	Kettering Town	Scarborough	2-1†	Wigan Athletic
1973-74	Boston United	Dartford	Morecambe	2-1	Dartford
1974-75	Wigan Athletic	Wimbledon	Matlock Town	4-0	Scarborough
1975-76	Runcorn	Wimbledon	Scarborough	3-2†	Stafford Rangers
1976-77	Boston United	Wimbledon	Scarborough	2-1	Dagenham
1977-78	Boston United	Bath City	Altrincham	3-1	Leatherhead
1978-79	Mossley	Worcester City	Stafford Rangers	2-0	Kettering Town

	Alliance Premier League			FA Challenge Trophy			
1979-80	Altrincham	56	Weymouth	54	Dagenham	2-1	Mossley
1980-81	Altrincham	54	Kettering Town	51	Bishop's Stortford	1-0	Sutton United
1981-82	Runcorn	93	Enfield	86	Enfield	1-0†	Altrincham
1982-83	Enfield	84	Maidstone United	83	Telford United	2-1	Northwich Vic
1983-84	Maidstone Utd	70	Nuneaton Borough	69	Northwich Vic	1-1† 2-1	Bangor City
1984-85	Wealdstone	62	Nuneaton Borough	58	Wealdstone	2-1	Boston United
1985-86	Enfield	76	Frickley Athletic	69	Altrincham	1-0	Runcorn
1986-87	Scarborough	91	Barnet	85	Kidderminster H	0-0† 2-1	Burton Albion
1987-88	Lincoln City	82	Barnet	80	Enfield	0-0† 3-2	Telford U
1988-89	Maidstone Utd	84	Kettering Town	76	Telford U	1-0†	Macclesfield

† after extra time
Alliance Premier League 1979-83, Gola League 1984-85, GM Vauxhall Conference 1986-

---

"Even the most brilliant football manager could not deal with Manchester United as long as the club is run from the chairman's office in the way that it is."
Michael Crick and David Smith, authors of Manchester United: The Betrayal of a Legend

"When the television people asked me if I'd like to play a football manager I asked how long it would take. They told me about 10 days and I said 'That's about par for the course'." *Tommy Docherty on acting*

"You'd think taking a club from 18th to third in three months was good enough."
Ron Atkinson, sacked by Atletico Madrid

"There are some coaches who sign a contract and then act as though they've won the lottery."
Jesus Gil, president of Atletico

"Here I am. Tear me limb from limb."
Gordon McKeag, chairman of Newcastle, to the Press after relegation

"If I go, Barnet goes. I am the club. If supporters get silly, they are in for a shock."
Stan Flashman, chairman of Barnet

"I don't know if we can help the Hammers or not, but we are going to pray for them."
Billy Graham, addressing a rally at Upton Park

"We have worked very hard to win an international reputation for Birmingham, and yet the club with our name is a place of flaking paint, rust and filth."
Bryan Bird, City Councillor

"No one in British soccer gives a damn about technique any more. It's all about up-and-unders."
Keith Burkinshaw

"I don't believe in these high transfer fees."
Chris Waddle

— ENGLISH HONOURS BOARD - QUICK REFERENCE GUIDE —

	Football League	*FA Cup*	*Football League Cup*
Arsenal	1931, 1933, 1934, 1935, 1938, 1948, 1953, 1971, 1989	1930, 1936, 1950, 1971, 1979	1987
Aston Villa	1894, 1896, 1897, 1899,1900, 1910, 1981	1887, 1895, 1897, 1905, 1913, 1920,1957	1961, 1975, 1977
Barnsley		1912	
Birmingham City			1963
Blackburn Olympic		1883	
Blackburn Rovers	1912, 1914	1884, 1885, 1886, 1890, 1891, 1928	
Blackpool		1953	
Bolton Wanderers		1923, 1926,1929, 1958	
Bradford City		1911	
Burnley	1921, 1960	1914	
Bury		1900, 1903	
Cardiff City		1927	
Charlton Athletic		1947	
Chelsea	1955	1970	1965
Clapham Rovers		1880	
Coventry City		1987	
Derby County	1972, 1975	1946	
Everton	1891, 1915, 1928, 1932, 1939, 1963, 1970, 1985, 1987	1906, 1933,1966, 1984	
Huddersfield Town	1924, 1925, 1926	1922	
Ipswich Town	1962	1978	
Leeds United	1969, 1974	1972	1968
Leicester City			1964
Liverpool	1901, 1906, 1922, 1923, 1947, 1964, 1966, 1973, 1976, 1977, 1979, 1980, 1982, 1983, 1984, 1986, 1988	1965, 1974, 1986, 1989	1981, 1982, 1983, 1984
Luton Town			1988
Manchester City	1937, 1968	1904, 1934,1956, 1969	1970, 1976
Manchester United	1908, 1911, 1952, 1956, 1957, 1965, 1967	1909, 1948, 1963, 1977, 1983, 1985	
Newcastle United	1905, 1907, 1909, 1927	1910, 1924, 1932, 1951, 1952, 1955	
Norwich City			1962, 1985
Nottingham Forest	1978	1898, 1959	1978, 1979, 1989
Notts County		1894	
Old Carthusians		1881	
Old Etonians		1879, 1882	
Oxford United			1986
Oxford University		1874	
Portsmouth	1949, 1950	1939	
Preston North End	1889, 1890	1889, 1938	
Queen's Park R			1967
Royal Engineers		1875	
Sheffield United	1898	1899, 1902, 1915, 1925	
Sheffield Wed	1903, 1904, 1929, 1930	1896, 1907, 1935	
Southampton		1976	
Stoke City			1972
Sunderland	1892, 1893, 1895, 1902, 1913, 1936	1937, 1973	
Swindon Town			1969
Tottenham Hotspur	1951, 1961	1901, 1921, 1961, 1962, 1967, 1981, 1982	1971, 1973
Wanderers		1872, 1873, 1876, 1877, 1878	
West Bromwich A	1920	1888, 1892, 1931, 1954, 1968	1966
West Ham United		1964, 1975, 1980	
Wimbledon		1988	
Wolverhampton W	1954, 1958, 1959	1893, 1908, 1949, 1960	1974, 1980

RECORDS

(to end of 1988-89 season)

APPEARANCES
Football League
PLAYERS WITH 750 OR MORE APPEARANCES:
864 Peter Shilton (Leicester C, Stoke C, Nottingham F, Southampton, Derby C) 1966-
824 Terry Paine (Southampton and Hereford U) 1957-77
777 Alan Oakes (Manchester C, Chester, Port Vale) 1959-84
770 John Trollope (Swindon T) 1960-80
764 Jimmy Dickinson (Portsmouth) 1946-65
762 Roy Sproson (Port Vale) 1950-72
Trollope's 770 games for Swindon T are a record for one club.

The most appearances in the Scottish League:
626 by Bob Ferrier (Motherwell) 1918-37

International Matches
BRITISH ISLES PLAYERS WITH OVER 100 CAPS:
119 Pat Jennings (Northern Ireland) 1964-86
109 Peter Shilton (England) 1970-89
108 Bobby Moore (England) 1962-73
106 Bobby Charlton (England) 1958-70
105 Billy Wright (England) 1946-59
102 Kenny Dalglish (Scotland) 1971-86
The most caps won by the other two nations:
Most for Wales: 72 Joey Jones 1972-86
Most for Republic of Ireland: 70 Liam Brady 1974-89

OTHER LEADING CAPPED PLAYERS:
150 Hector Chumpitaz (Peru) 1963-82
120 Rivelino (Brazil) 1968-79
115 Bjorn Nordqvist (Sweden) 1963-78
112 Dino Zoff (Italy) 1968-83
111 Pele (Brazil) 1957-71

ENGLAND'S CENTURIONS

109 Peter Shilton
First match: 25 Nov 1970 v E Germany

108 Bobby Moore
First match: 20 May 1962 v Peru
Last match: 14 Nov 1973 v Italy

106 Bobby Charlton
First match: 19 Apr 1958 v Scotland
Last match: 14 Jun 1970 v W Germany

105 Billy Wright
First match: 28 Sep 1946 v N Ireland
Last match: 28 May 1959 v United States

ATTENDANCES
Record Attendances
European Championship: 103,000 USSR v Hungary 1968, Moscow
International (Britain): 149,547 Scotland v England, 1937 Hampden Park
Club match (World): 177,656 Flamengo v Fluminese, 1963 (Brazilian League) Maracaña Stadium, Rio de Janeiro
Club match (Europe): 146,433 Celtic v Aberdeen 1937, (Scottish Cup Final), Hampden Park
European Cup: 136,505 Celtic v Leeds U, 1970, Hampden Park
FA Cup Final: 126,047 Bolton W v West Ham U, 1923, Wembley Stadium

FA Cup (other than final): 84,569 Manchester C v Stoke C, 1934 (6th Round), Maine Road
Football League Cup (other than final): 63,418 Manchester U v Manchester C, 1969 (Semi-final), Old Trafford
Football League:
Div 1: 83,260 Man Utd v Arsenal, 1948, Maine Road
Div 2: 68,029 Aston Villa v Coventry C, 1937, Villa Park
Div 3: 49,309 Sheffield W v Sheffield U, 1979, Hillsborough
Div 4: 37,774 Crystal P v Millwall, 1961, Selhurst Park
Div 3 (S): 51,621 Cardiff C v Bristol C, 1947, Ninian Park
Div 3 (N): 49,655 Hull C v Rotherham U, 1948, Boothferry Park
Highest Post-War Average: 57,552 Manchester U 1967-68
Scottish League
Div 1/Premier: 118,567 Rangers v Celtic, 1939, Ibrox Stadium
Lower Divisions: 27,205 Queen's Park v Kilmarnock, 1961, Hampden Park
Scottish FA Cup: 146,433 Celtic v Aberdeen (as above)
Scottish League Cup: 107,647 Celtic v Rangers, 1965, Hampden Park
GM Vauxhall Conference: 7,522 Lincoln C v Boston U, 1988, Sincil Bank

Lowest attendances
(Excluding matches played behind closed doors)
Football League: 13 Stockport C v Leicester C (Div 2), 1921, Old Trafford (*); 450 Rochdale v Cambridge U (Div 3), 1974, Spotland
Football League Div 1: 4,026 Wimbledon v Norwich C, 1987, Plough Lane
Scottish League: 80 Meadowbank T v Stenhousemuir (Div 2), 1979 Meadowbank Stadium
Major European Cup match: 483 Rapid Vienna v Juventus, (UEFA Cup), 1971
Home International: 2,315 Wales v Northern Ireland, 1982, Wrexham
England International at Wembley: 15,628 v Chile, 1989
(*)Disputed. Up to 2,000 believed present despite official figure

WINS
Most in a season
33(42) Doncaster R, Div 3(N), 1946-47
Div 1 record: 31(42) Tottenham H, 1960-61
Scottish record: 35(42) Rangers, 1920-21

Fewest in a season
1(34) Loughborough T, Div 2, 1899-1900
Div 1 record: 3(38) Woolwich Arsenal, 1912-13; 3(42) Stoke City, 1984-85
Scottish record: 0(22) Vale of Leven, 1891-92; post-war 1(34) Ayr U, Div 1, 1966-67.

DEFEATS
Most in a season
33(40) Rochdale, Div 3(N), 1931-32
33(46) Cambridge U, Div 3, 1984-85
33(46) Newport C, Div 4, 1987-88
Div 1 record: 31(42) Stoke C, 1984-85
Scottish record: 31(42) St Mirren, Div 1, 1920-21

Fewest in a season
0(22) Preston NE, Football League, 1888-89
0(28) Liverpool, Div 2, 1893-94

0(18) Celtic, Scottish Div 1, 1897-98
0(18) Rangers, Scottish Div 1, 1898-99
0(18) Kilmarnock, Scottish Div 2 1898-99
Post-war record: 2(42) Leeds U, Div 1, 1968-69; 2(40)
Liverpool, Div 1, 1987-88; 2(39) St Mirren, Scottish Div 1,
1976-77; 2(38) Morton, Scottish Div 2, 1966-67
Figures in brackets indicate matches played

DRAWS
Most in a season
Football League
23(42) Norwich C, Div 1, 1978-79
23(46) Exeter C, Div 4, 1986-87
Scottish record: 21(44) East Fife, Div 1, 1986-87
Figures in bracket indicate matches played

**Following John Lyall's removal as West Ham
manager in June 1989 the longest serving
Football league managers were:**

		Date Apptd.
Brian Clough	Nottingham F	Jan 1975
Joe Royle	Oldham A	Jul 1982
Lennie Lawrence	Charlton A	Nov 1982
Frank Clark	Leyton O	May 1983
Dario Gradi	Crewe A	Jun 1983
Harry Redknapp	Bournemouth	Oct 1983
John Rudge	Port Vale	Dec 1983

POINTS
Most points in a season
(Points available in brackets)
Football League (2pts for a win): 74(92) Lincoln C,
Div 4, 1975-76
Div 1: 68(84) Liverpool, 1978-79
Football League (3 pts for a win): 102(138) Swindon
T, Div 4, 1985-86
Div 1: 90(120) Liverpool, 1987-88; 90(126) Everton,
1984-85
Scottish League (2pts for a win): 76(84) Rangers,
Div 1, 1920-21
Premier Division: 72(88) Celtic, 1987-88
Fewest points in a season
(Since expansion in 1898)
Football League: 8(68) Loughborough T, Div 2, 1899-
1900; Doncaster R, Div 2, 1904-05
Div 1: 17(126) Stoke C, 1984-85 (since expansion in 1905)
Scottish League: 6(60) Stirling A, Div 1, 1954-55
Premier Division: 11(72) St Johnstone, 1975-76
In 1896-97 Abercorn collected just 3 points in the Scottish
1st Division from their 18 games, an all-time low for a
British League side.

GOALSCORING
Fast Scoring
Fastest Football League Goals:
(From kick-off): all 6 secs: Albert Mundy, Aldershot v
Hartlepool U, 1958, Div 4; Barrie Jones, Notts C v
Torquay U, 1962, Div 3; Keith Smith, Crystal P v Derby C,
1964, Div 2; Tommy Langley, Queen's Park R v Bolton W,
1980, Div 2
Fastest FA Cup Goal:
8 secs; Vic Lambden, Bristol R v Aldershot, 1951, 3rd
Round
Fastest Goal for England:
27 secs; Bryan Robson, v France, 1982 World Cup

Fastest hat-trick:
2¹/₂ mins: Jimmy Scarth, Gillingham v Leyton O, 1952,
Div 3(S)
Fastest International hat-trick:
3¹/₂ mins: Willie Hall, England v Ireland, 1938
Fastest own goal:
6 secs: Pat Kruse, Torquay U v Cambridge U, 1977, Div 4

Individual Scoring Records
Most Goals in a Single Game:
First Class Match: 16 Stephan Stanis, Racing Club Lens
v Aubry-Asturies, (French Cup) 1942
Internationals: 10 Sofus Nielsen, Denmark v France,
1908 Olympics; 10 Gottfried Fuchs, Germany v Russia,
1912 Olympics
British International Football: 6 Joe Bambrick, N.
Ireland v Wales, 1930
The record for England is: 5 Oliver Vaughton, v Ireland,
1882, 5 Steve Bloomer, v Wales, 1896; 5 Gilbert Smith, v
Ireland, 1899; 5 Willie Hall, v Ireland, 1938; 5 Malcolm
Macdonald, v Cyprus, 1975
European Club Competition: 6 Lothar Emmerich,
Borussia Dortmund v Floriana, Cup-winners' Cup, 1965
British Record in Europe: 5 Ray Crawford, Ipswich T v
Floriana (European Cup), 1962; 5 Peter Osgood, Chelsea v
Jeunesse Hautcharage (Cup-winners' Cup), 1971
Football League: 10 Joe Payne, Luton T v Bristol R,
Div 3(S), 1936
Div 1 record: 7 Jimmy Ross, Preston NE v Stoke, 1888; 7
Ted Drake, Arsenal v Aston Villa, 1935
FA Cup: *Preliminary competition:* 10 Chris Marron,
South Shields v Radcliffe Borough, 1947
Competition proper: 9 Ted MacDougall, Bournemouth v
Margate, 1st round, 1971
Scottish League: 8 Owen McNally, Arthurlie v
Armadale, Div 2, 1927; 8 Jimmy McGrory, Celtic v
Dumfermline A, Div 1, 1928; 8 Jim Dyet, King's Park v
Forfar A, Div 2, 1930; 8 John Calder, Morton v Raith R,
Div 2, 1936; 8 Norman Haywood, Raith R v Brechin C,
Div 2, 20 Aug 1937
Scottish Cup: 13 John Petrie, Arbroath v Bon Accord,
1885
Most Goals in a season
World Record: 127 Pele (Santos, Brazil) 1959
European Cup: 14 Jose Altafini (AC Milan) 1962-63
European Cup-winners' Cup:
14 Lothar Emmerich (Borussia Dortmund) 1965-66
Football League:
60 Dixie Dean (Everton), Div 1, 1927-28
The leading scorers in the other divisions have been:
Div 2: 59 George Camsell (Middlesbrough), 1927-28; Div
3: 39 Derek Reeves (Southampton), 1959-60; Div 4: 52
Terry Bly (Peterborough U), 1960-61; Div 3(S): 55 Joe
Payne (Luton T), 1936-37; Div 3(N): 55 Ted Harston
(Mansfield R), 1936-37
Scottish League: 66 Jim Smith (Ayr U), Div 2, 1927-28
FA Cup: 15 Albert Brown (Tottenham H), 1900-01
Football League Cup: 12 Clive Allen (Tottenham H),
1986-87
Most Goals in a Career
World Record: 1329 Artur Friedenreich (Germanio, CA
Ipiranga, Americano, CA Paulistano, Sao Paulo,
Flamengo, Brazil) 1909-35
*Two other players have scored more than 1000 first class
goals:* 1280 Pele 1956-77; 1006 Franz Binder 1930-50
Internationals: 97 Pele (Brazil), 1957-70
British Internationals: 49 Bobby Charlton (England);
44 Jimmy Greaves (England); 30 Tom Finney (England);

30 Nat Lofthouse (England); 30 Denis Law (Scotland); 30 Kenny Dalglish (Scotland); 29 Vivian Woodward (England); 29 Gary Lineker (England); 26 Steve Bloomer (England)
The records for the other countries are:
Northern Ireland: 12 Joe Bambrick, Billy Gillespie, Gerry Armstrong; *Wales:* 23 Ivor Allchurch, Trevor Ford; *Republic of Ireland:* 19 Don Givens
European Cup: 49 Alfredo de Stefano (Real Madrid) 1955-64
British Record: 30 Peter Lorimer (Leeds U), 1965-77
Football League: 434 Arthur Rowley (West Bromwich A, Fulham, Leicester C, Shrewsbury T), 1946-65
Scottish League: 410 Jimmy McGrory (Celtic, Clydebank), 1922-38
FA Cup: 41 Denis Law (Huddersfield T, Man City, Man Utd)

WEST HAM MANAGERS

Syd King	**1902-32**
Charlie Paynter	**1932-50**
Ted Fenton	**1950-61**
Ron Greenwood	**1961-74**
John Lyall	**1974-89**
Lou Macari	**1989-**

Hat Tricks

Football League

Most in a career: 37 Dixie Dean (Tranmere R, Everton, Notts C), 1923-37

Most in one season: 9 George Camsell (Middlesbrough), Div 2, 1926-27

Hat tricks in FA Cup finals: William Townley, Blackburn R v Sheffield W, 1890; Jimmy Logan, Notts C v Bolton W, 1894; Stanley Mortensen, Blackpool v Bolton W, 1953

Team Records
Most goals scored in a season

Football League: 134 Peterborough U, Div 4, 1960-61
Div 1 record: 128 Aston Villa, 1930-31

Scottish League: 142 Raith R, Div 2, 1937-38
Div 1/Premier Division record: 132 Hearts, Div 1, 1957-58

Fewest goals scored in a season

Football League *(since expansion in 1905):*
24 Watford, Div 2, 1971-72; 24 Stoke C, Div 1, 1984-85

Scottish League: 18 Stirling A, Div 1, 1980-81

Most goals conceded in a season

Football League: 141 Darwen, Div 2, 1898-99
Div 1 record: 125 Blackpool, 1930-31

Scottish League: 146 Edinburgh C, Div 2 1931-32
Div 1/Premier Division record: 137 Leith A, Div 1, 1931-32

Fewest goals conceded in a season
(since expansion in 1905)

Football League: 16 Liverpool, Div 1, 1978-79

Scottish League: 14 Celtic, Div 1, 1913-14

Record Scores

Football League:
13-0 Stockport C v Halifax T, Div 3(N), 1933-34; 13-0 Newcastle U v Newport C 1946-47; 13-4 Tranmere R v Oldham A, Div 3(N), 1935-36;
Div 1 record: 12-0 West Bromwich v Darwen, 1891-92; 12-0 Nottingham F v Leicester F, 1908-09
Record Away Win: 10-0 Sheffield U at Burslem Port Vale, Div 2, 1892-93

Scottish League:
15-1 Airdrieonians v Dundee W, Div 2, 1894-95
Div 1/Premier Division: 11-0 Celtic v Dundee, 1895-95

THE WORLD'S MOST EXPENSIVE PLAYERS

£ million	Player	From	To	Date
6.0	Ruud Gullitt	PSV Eindhoven	AC Milan	Jun 1987
5.0	Diego Maradona	Barcelona	Napoli	Jun 1984
4.8	Diego Maradona	Boca Juniors	Barcelona	Jun 1982
4.3	Chris Waddle	Tottenham H	Marseille	Jul 1989
4.0	Rui Barros	FC Porto	Juventus	Jul 1989
4.0	Ronald Koeman	PSV Eindhoven	Barcelona	Jul 1989
3.5	Ruggi Rizzitelli	Cesena	Roma	May 1988
3.4	Karl-H Rummenigge	Bayern Munich	Inter Milan	Jul 1984
3.2	Ian Rush	Liverpool	Juventus	Jun 1987
2.8	Careca	Sao Paulo	Napoli	May 1987
2.8	Ian Rush	Juventus	Liverpool	Aug 1988

The top fees involving British players have been:
£ million
4.3 Chris Waddle, Tottenham to Marseille, 1989
3.2 Ian Rush, Liverpool to Juventus, 1987
2.8 Ian Rush, Juventus to Liverpool, 1988
2.75 Gary Lineker, Everton to Barcelona, 1986
2.5 Tony Cottee, West Ham U to Everton, 1988
2.3 Mark Hughes, Man Utd to Barcelona, 1986

━━━ 1990 ━━━

GENERAL FIXTURES

JANUARY 6 FA Cup Third Round: 17 Littlewoods Cup Fifth Round; 20 Scottish Cup Third Round; 27 FA Cup Fourth Round.

FEBRUARY 14 Littlewoods Cup semi-final first leg; 17 FA Cup Fifth Round; 24 Scottish Cup Fourth Round; 28 Littlewoods Cup semi-final second leg.

MARCH 7 European Cups quarter-finals first leg; 10 FA Cup Sixth Round; 17 Scottish Cup Fifth Round; 21 European Cups quarter-finals second leg; 28 Internationals, to be arranged.

APRIL 4 European Cups semi-finals first leg; 7 FA Cup semi-finals; 14 Scottish Cup semi-finals; 18 European Cups semi-finals second leg; 25 England v Czechoslovakia (Wembley); 29 Littlewoods Cup final (Wembley).

MAY 2 UEFA Cup final first leg; 5 FA Vase final (Wembley); 9 European Cup-winners' Cup final; 12 FA Cup final (Wembley); Scottish Cup final (Hampden); 15 England v ? , Rous Cup (Wembley); 16 UEFA Cup final second leg; 19 FA Trophy final (Wembley); 22 England v Scotland, Rous Cup (Wembley); 23 European Cup final.

JUNE 8 - JULY 8 World Cup finals: see below

THIRD DIVISION PLAYERS TO HAVE PLAYED FOR ENGLAND

Tommy Lawton, Notts County, 1947

Reg Matthews, Coventry City, 1956

Johnny Byrne, Crystal Palace, 1961

Peter Taylor, Crystal Palace, 1976

Steve Bull, Wolverhampton W, 1989

━━━ WORLD CUP FINALS 1990 ━━━

FIRST PHASE

Day	Date	City	Match	Teams	Kickoff	Group
Friday	June 8	Milan	1	5 v 6	5pm	B
Saturday	June 9	Bari	2	7 v 8	4pm	B
		Rome	3	1 v 2	8pm	A
		Bologna	4	15 v 16	8pm	D
Sunday	June 10	Florence	5	3 v 4	4pm	A
		Turin	6	9 v 10	8pm	C
		Milan	7	13 v 14	8pm	D
Monday	June 11	Genoa	8	11 v 12	4pm	C
		Cagliari	9	21 v 22	8pm	F
Tuesday	June 12	Verona	10	17 v 18	4pm	E
		Palermo	11	23 v 24	8pm	F
Wednesday	June 13	Udine	12	19 v 20	4pm	E
		Naples	13	5 v 7	8pm	B
Thursday	June 14	Bologna	14	14 v 16	4pm	D
		Rome	15	1 v 3	8pm	A
		Bari	16	6 v 8	8pm	B
Friday	June 15	Florence	17	2 v 4	4pm	A
		Milan	18	13 v 15	8pm	D
Saturday	June 16	Turin	19	9 v 11	4pm	C
		Genoa	20	10 v 12	8pm	C
		Cagliari	21	21 v 23	8pm	F
Sunday	June 17	Palermo	22	22 v 24	4pm	F
		Verona	23	17 v 19	8pm	E
		Udine	24	18 v 20	8pm	E
Monday	June 18	Naples	25	5 v 8	8pm	B
		Bari	26	6 v 7	8pm	B
Tuesday	June 19	Milan	27	13 v 16	4pm	D
		Bologna	28	14 v 15	4pm	D
		Rome	29	1 v 4	8pm	A
		Florence	30	2 v 3	8pm	A
Wednesday	June 20	Turin	31	9 v 12	8pm	C
		Genoa	32	10 v 11	8pm	C
Thursday	June 21	Verona	33	17 v 20	4pm	E
		Udine	34	18 v 19	4pm	E
		Cagliari	35	21 v 24	8pm	F
		Palermo	36	22 v 23	8pm	F

SECOND PHASE (LAST 16)

Saturday	June 23	Naples	37	Winner Group B v Third in A/C/D	4pm
		Bari	38	Second Group A v Second Group C	8pm
Sunday	June 24	Turin	39	Winner Group C v Third in A/B/F	4pm
		Milan	40	Winner Group D v Third in B/E/F	8pm
Monday	June 25	Rome	41	Winner Group A v Third in C/D/E	4pm
		Genoa	42	Second Group F v Second Group B	8pm
Tuesday	June 26	Verona	43	Winner Group E v Second Group D	4pm
		Bologna	44	Winner Group F v Second Group E	8pm

QUARTER-FINALS

Saturday	June 30	Florence	45	Winner Game 39 v Winner Game 43	4pm
		Rome	46	Winner Game 41 v Winner Game 42	8pm
Sunday	July 1	Milan	47	Winner Game 38 v Winner Game 40	4pm
		Naples	48	Winner Game 37 v Winner Game 44	8pm

SEMI-FINALS

Tuesday	July 3	Naples	49	Winner Game 45 v Winner Game 46	7pm
Wednesday	July 4	Turin	50	Winner Game 47 v Winner Game 48	7pm

THIRD PLACE MATCH

Saturday	July 7	Bari	51	Loser Game 49 v Loser Game 50	7pm

FINAL

Sunday	July 8	Rome	52	Winner Game 49 v Winner Game 50	7pm

All times BST. Italian times one hour later.

FIRST DIVISION FIXTURES 1989-90

Home Team \ Away Team	Arsenal	Aston V	Charlton	Chelsea	Coventry	C.Palace	Derby	Everton	Liverpool	Luton	Man City	Man Utd	Millwall	Norwich	Nottm F	QPR	Sheff W	S'ton	Tottenham	Wimbledon
Arsenal	-	Apr 7	Sep 23	Mar 17	Aug 22	Jan 1	Oct 28	Mar 31	Feb 24	Dec 16	Oct 11	Feb 12	Apr 28	Nov 4	Feb 10	Nov 18	Sep 9	Aug 16	Jan 20	Aug 26
Aston V	Dec 12	-	Aug 8	Apr 14	Nov 11	Oct 28	Sep 30	Nov 4	Aug 23	Mar 10	Mar 31	Dec 26	Apr 21	Apr 28	Dec 2	Sep 23	Feb 10	Jan 20	Sep 9	Feb 24
Charlton	Feb 3	Jan 13	-	Aug 29	Oct 28	Dec 16	Aug 19	Sep 16	Apr 7	Feb 17	Nov 25	Nov 4	Dec 9	Mar 3	Mar 17	Mar 31	Apr 28	Jan 1	Oct 14	Apr 16
Chelsea	Sep 30	Jan 1	Jan 20	-	Sep 23	Apr 16	Oct 21	Apr 28	Dec 16	Apr 7	Oct 28	Feb 24	Nov 4	Mar 10	Sep 9	Aug 22	Nov 18	Nov 11	Feb 10	Dec 2
Coventry	Dec 9	Mar 3	Mar 24	Feb 3	-	Jan 13	Apr 7	Aug 19	May 5	Sep 16	Aug 30	Oct 21	Feb 17	Nov 25	Oct 14	Apr 16	Mar 17	Nov 11	Feb 10	Dec 16
Crystal Palace	Apr 14	Mar 24	Apr 21	Dec 26	Aug 26	-	Mar 10	Sep 30	Jan 20	Nov 11	May 5	Aug 22	Oct 21	Dec 30	Sep 23	Dec 2	Feb 24	Feb 10	Nov 18	Sep 9
Derby	Mar 24	Mar 17	Dec 2	Oct 21	Dec 30	Oct 14	-	Dec 26	Sep 9	May 5	Nov 11	Aug 26	Apr 14	Apr 21	Jan 20	Feb 10	Nov 18	Sep 23	Feb 24	Aug 23
Everton	Oct 21	Oct 14	Feb 10	Apr 21	Dec 26	Apr 16	Feb 3	-	Sep 23	Dec 16	Sep 9	Dec 23	Mar 24	Sep 16	Nov 18	Apr 7	Aug 26	Aug 30	Mar 31	Jan 13
Liverpool	Nov 25	Dec 9	Dec 30	Nov 11	Sep 9	Feb 17	Sep 9	Sep 23	-	Jan 13	Dec 16	Sep 23	Mar 3	Apr 21	Dec 26	Apr 28	Aug 22	Apr 14	Oct 28	Aug 26
Luton	Apr 21	Oct 14	Sep 9	Nov 11	Aug 19	Nov 4	May 5	Apr 14	Aug 26	-	Sep 30	Feb 3	Jan 13	Dec 9		Apr 16	Mar 3	Mar 17	Dec 2	Feb 3
Man City	Mar 10	Oct 21	Feb 24	Jan 20	Aug 30	May 5	Nov 11	Sep 9	Dec 16	Aug 19	-	Mar 17	Sep 16	Apr 7	Aug 23	Sep 9	Dec 26	Nov 4	Jan 13	Sep 16
Man Utd	Aug 19	Apr 17	Feb 24	Mar 24	Oct 21	Aug 22	Aug 26	Apr 21	Feb 3	Nov 18	Mar 17	-	Dec 30	Aug 30	Nov 11	Jan 1	Feb 24	Dec 16	Aug 26	Oct 21
Millwall	Nov 11	Dec 16	Nov 18	May 5	Feb 17	Oct 21	Apr 14	Mar 24	Mar 3	Jan 13	Feb 3	Dec 30	-	Sep 16	Nov 11	Feb 24	Sep 23	Dec 2	Dec 16	Apr 7
Norwich	May 5	Nov 11	Oct 21	Nov 18	Nov 25	Dec 30	Apr 21	Sep 16	Apr 21	Dec 9	Apr 7	Aug 30	Sep 16	-	Aug 26	Sep 30	Sep 9	Apr 21	Mar 24	Apr 14
Nottm F	Sep 16	Aug 19	Sep 30	Feb 24	Oct 14	Apr 7	Jan 20	Nov 18	Dec 26		Apr 16	Nov 11	Mar 17	Jan 13	-	Oct 28	Dec 2	Sep 9	Apr 16	Mar 31
QPR	Mar 3	Feb 3	Oct 21	Dec 9	Apr 16	Mar 3	Feb 10	Apr 7	Apr 28	Jan 20	Sep 9	Jan 1	Feb 24	Aug 26		-	Dec 16	Mar 10	Sep 30	Nov 4
Sheffield W	Feb 17	Sep 16	Nov 11	Jan 13	Sep 30	Nov 25	Apr 14	Mar 3	Aug 22	Apr 21	Oct 14	Aug 19	Feb 3	Aug 19	Feb 10	Dec 16	-	Apr 7	Mar 31	May 5
Southampton	Dec 26	Aug 29	Apr 14	Apr 28	Sep 30	Nov 25	Feb 3	Jan 13	Oct 21	Nov 25	Dec 9	Mar 24	Aug 19	Feb 17	Apr 21	Mar 10	Dec 30	-	Nov 4	Sep 30
Tottenham	Oct 18	Feb 17	Mar 10	Sep 16	Dec 9	Mar 3	Nov 25	Mar 3	Mar 24	Aug 19	Jan 13	Apr 21	Dec 26	Apr 14	Dec 30	Oct 21	Oct 21	May 5	-	Nov 11
Wimbledon	Jan 13	Nov 25	Dec 26	Aug 19	Apr 14	Feb 17	Feb 3	Mar 3	Oct 14	Feb 3	Sep 16	Oct 21	Apr 7	Apr 14	Oct 21	Nov 4	Mar 24	Mar 17	Apr 28	-

ATHLETICS

CONFESSION IS GOOD FOR THE SPORT

The athletics event of the year took place nowhere near a track or stadium but inside an anonymous office block in downtown Toronto. On a cool June morning, the fallen Olympian Ben Johnson arrived and finally admitted to the Canadian government inquiry into drugs in sport that his coach Charlie Francis had started giving him little blue and pink pills in 1981, and that he had knowingly been taking anabolic steroids ever since.

The revelation surprised no one. But as athletics attempts to recover from the sport's disgrace, it may be the cathartic moment. All over the world, the veil surrounding the hidden truth of athletics – and other sports – was lifting just a fraction. Prince Alexandre de Merode, chairman of the Olympic medical commission, said that more sophisticated tests carried out since the Seoul Games had shown 50 males had used steroids there even though their tests at the time had proved negative. The East German sports doctor and defector Hans-Georg Aschenbach said that all East German sportsmen since the 1960s had been using drugs from childhood, stopping 10 days before their events. Some had electric shock treatment to inflate their muscles.

CHEMICAL CORNER

Robert Armstrong QC: "Why did you not tell the truth?"

Ben Johnson: "Cos I lied and I was ashamed for my family and other Canadian athletes and the kids who looked up to me. I was just in a mess."

Armstrong: "Do you want to run again?"

Johnson: "I'll be back."

Armstrong: "Do you believe you can be the fastest man in the world without taking drugs?"

Johnson: "I know I can be."
Exchange at the Dubin Inquiry, Toronto

"How blind we were. We saw our kids become muscle-bound overnight and we gave the credit to a healthy California diet."
Editorial in the Toronto Star

"If there was any athlete not on them (steroids) they were probably from Sri Lanka or Timbuktoo or some other God-forsaken place."
Johnson's doctor Jamie Astaphan's account of the 1988 Olympics

"Let me blow the lid on this affair and the prevalent double standards. After I'm through, the IOC will have to resign."
Jamie Astaphan

"Charlie Francis said that anabolic steroids were worth one metre in a 100 metre race. Well I set that record and I won my Olympic races by a lot more than one metre. How does he account for the other four?"
Florence Griffith-Joyner

"I'm sorry. I don't think a woman can run 10.49. Not yet at least. Not legal."
Angella Issajenko, Canadian sprinter

"In my mind, he's Satan with a stopwatch."
Skip Stolley on fellow US coach Chuck DeBus, alleged advocate of steroids

"I wish I'd never heard of steroids"
David Jenkins on his release from jail

American athletics officials began investigating Chuck DeBus, alleged steroid-peddler to top athletes. A Moscow newspaper said that 290 Soviet sportsmen had been punished for using drugs in the past three years. The Bulgarian team coach Stoyan Slavkov was dismissed after a positive test on a heptathlete, Svetia Dimitrova. The British athlete David Jenkins, jailed in California for seven years on charges of supplying steroids in December 1988, was released in June but only because a federal judge said his assistance had led to 20 other people being caught. And, day after day in

Toronto, the inquiry chaired by Judge Charles Dubin heard damning evidence about the prevalence of drug use in Canada. Canadian athletics was not uniquely wicked; it was merely uniquely determined to bring the truth into the open. None of this meant that the days of athletics as an extension of the pharmaceutical industry were actually over. But the drug-users were under pressure and there were signs that a more hopeful and wholesome era might be on the way.

BATTLING BRITS

The actual sport, in the thinnest year of the Olympic cycle, was less dramatic. But there were still two excuses for big outpourings of British patriotism. First, Britain's male athletes had what was widely described as their greatest triumph in history when they won the European Cup in Gateshead. That put them into the World Cup in Barcelona. There the men came third, behind the United States and the combined European team.

Even optimists had thought that Britain would do no more than nick second at the European Cup. Only dreary realists mentioned the mitigating factors – home advantage in the European Cup, the absence from the World Cup of stars like Carl Lewis, the retirement of 50 East Germans since the Seoul Olympics, the low-key approach of many athletes in the post-Olympic year. Nonetheless, as Britain's great generation of middle-distance runners began to fade into the background (not quietly though, see below), a set of new stars began to emerge – the hurdler Colin Jackson, Steve Backley in the javelin, Dalton Grant in the high jump – to suggest that Britain's apparent status as a world athletic power might be ratified in the years ahead.

The absence of so many East Germans was in itself a possible indication of a new caution concerning drugs. It was the most delicious of ironies that the East German men qualified for the World Cup final only because a dope test on the Soviet shot-putter Alexander Bagach found high levels of testosterone. Bagach had finished third in his event. His disqualification knocked his country out of second place and enabled the East Germans to qualify instead.

The World Cup involved athletes from four individual countries – the two European qualifiers, the US and the hosts Spain – plus five continents. The weather was terrible and a thunderstorm almost forced the whole event to be abandoned. But there was evidence that the track surface, Mondo, was fast and will see some spectacular times when the Olympics are held in the same stadium in 1992. The most dramatic race came in the 100 metres hurdles when the American Roger Kingdom ran the fastest time in history, 12.87, just edging out Colin Jackson, his rival in many exciting races all summer, by 0.08 of a second. The following wind prevented Kingdom's time being a world record; but no one took the wet track into account either.

Seb Coe was beaten – amid mild jostling – by Abdi Bile in the World Cup 1500 metres and, despite speculation that he would immediately retire and concentrate on Tory politics, aimed himself at the Commonwealth Games. What was almost certainly Coe's last race against his old rival Steve Ovett had astonishing results. They were facing each other at the AAA in Birmingham, their first meeting in Britain for 17 years, their first anywhere since the LA Olympics. The race was remarkable enough. Steve Crabb fell, Coe was almost brought down but then fought back to win. But that was only a fraction of the drama: Steve Ovett claimed that he had been offered money to compete and threatened to withdraw on principle when he learned that Coe had not.

Ovett trailed in ninth in the race and afterwards burst into tears when being interviewed on TV. He claimed the money had been offered by Andy Norman, the AAA's promotions officer, long ago his best man and best friend; Norman denied it vigorously. Most viewers were baffled; it would have been more understandable if Ovett had been the one not offered money. It was later revealed that Norman had had 39,000 dollars in cash stolen from his hotel room at Crystal Palace a month earlier. Briefly, another corner of athletics' murky undergrowth came into view. A committee was set up to discover which of the two was lying.

Among the AAA's other achievements was to bar, briefly, the runner Brian Whittle from competing for Haringey in the British League because he lived in Scotland. "It almost seems racist," said Whittle. "And this from a body which bent over backwards to allow Zola Budd to run for England."

RECORD BREAKERS

There was a burst of world record breaking on the late summer circuit. The Cuban Javier Sotomayor passed one of athletics' great improbable landmarks by becoming the first man to jump eight feet (2.44 metres, or a soccer crossbar). And on a boiling hot afternoon in Cologne Said Aouita finally expunged Henry Rono's 11-year-old time in the 3,000 metres, the oldest athletics record apart from Bob Beamon's long jump. Aouita also made two attempts in a week on the world mile record. He failed, though his 3:52.93 at Gateshead beat the Emsley Carr mile best which had stood for 23 years. Roger Kingdom broke the eight-year-old world 110m hurdles record in Zurich. And Arturo Barrios of Mexico sliced 5.68 secs off the five-year-old world 10,000m record in Berlin; Barrios's Polish coach Tadaus Koppka jogged the curve on some laps shouting encouragement, which pushed the rules about receiving assistance. Among other world records to change was the 100 metres: Ben Johnson's famous time of 9.83 at the 1987 World Championships was expunged because of his drug use. At the New York Games, the first major summer invitational in the US for more than 20 years, Carl Lewis won his 61st successive long jump.

Florence Griffith-Joyner announced her retirement in February after signing a million dollars' worth of deals since the Olympics; she was considering an offer to play a female James Bond. The Afrikaaner waif Zola Budd announced in June that she would not return to England. She made certain she would not return to international athletics (unless world politics changed) by entering – and winning – a road race near her home in Bloemfontein. The Romanian Maricica Puica, winner of the Olympic 3,000 metres in which Budd tangled with Mary Decker-Slaney, also retired.

Douglas Wakiihuri, the Japan-based Kenyan, won the London marathon, beating 29,999 other entries. Véronique Marot, the British-based French émigrée, won the women's section. Ian Thompson, starting from the back of the field, overtook 19,489 runners, a record. One C. Lee finished 22,655th and last in 8 hours 21.41. A hundred and thirty-five people were caught cheating. Princess Diana came second in the mother's race at Prince William's school sports day and received more publicity in the British press than any of the above.

THE OVETT AFFAIR: Who said what to whom?

"They got me here under false pretences, and lied to a lot of other people . . . . . There are some people in this sport who are trying to use it and they should be stopped."
Steve Ovett

"I think he knew he was going to be beaten and was looking for a cop-out."
Andy Norman

"Andy Norman is a powerful man. He controls the sport in this country. He has friends abroad too and a lot of athletes are afraid to say anything otherwise the door will be shut on them."
Steve Ovett

"Steve is one of life's caring people."
Sebastian Coe

"I said 'Look me in the eyes, Andy. Tell me you didn't make that phone call to Steve.' And in front of everybody he looked straight at me and said 'I didn't make that phone call.' It was an awful moment. I just cried." *Rachel Ovett, Steve's wife*

"If something positive does not come out in a short space of time, it will be necessary for an independent body to find out what is happening in this sport. To witness this humiliation, off the track, of one of the world's great athletes is extremely serious, for whatever sport."
Peter Yarranton, chairman of the Sports Council

━━━ 1989 ━━━

EUROPEAN CUP
Gateshead, Aug 6-7
Men
100 Metres
1 Linford Christie (GB) 10.33s
2 Daniel Sangouma (Fra) 10.39s
3 Vladimir Krylov (USSR) 10.43s
200 Metres
1 John Regis (GB) 20.62s
2 Stefano Tilli (Ita) 20.66s
3 Daniel Sangouma (Fra) 20.83s
400 Metres
1 Edgar Itt (FRG) 45.43s
2 Jens Carlowitz (GDR) 45.44s
3 Cayetano Cornet (Spa) 45.82s
800 Metres
1 Tom McKean (GB) 1m 46.94s
2 Peter Braun (FRG) 1m 47.53s
3 Hauke Fuhlbruegge (GDR) 1m 48.20s
1500 Metres
1 Pascal Thiebaut (Fra) 3m 48.05s
2 Sergei Afanasayev (USSR) 3m 48.35s
3 Gennaro di Napoli (Ita) 3m 48.61s
5000 Metres
1 Salvatore Antibo (Ita) 13m 43.84s
2 Jack Buckner (GB) 13m 44.77s
3 Mikhail Dasko (USSR) 13m 47.56s
10,000 Metres
1 Francesco Panetta (Ita) 28m 27.02s
2 Tim Hutchings (GB) 28m 27.21s
3 Jose Manuel Albentosa (Spa) 28m 29.78s
110 Metres Hurdles
1 Colin Jackson (GB) 13.56s
2 Vladimir Shishkin (USSR) 13.76s
3 Florian Schwarthoff (FRG) 13.88s
400 Metres Hurdles
1 Kriss Akabusi (GB) 48.95s
2 Harald Schmid (FRG) 49.26s
3 Vladimir Budko (USSR) 49.60s
3000 Metres Steeplechase
1 Alessandro Lambruschini (Ita) 8m 34.06s
2 Hagen Melzer (GDR) 8m 34.90s
3 Raymond Pannier (Fra) 8m 35.33s
4 x 100 Metres Relay
1 Great Britain 38.39s
2 France 38.46s
3 Italy 38.98s
4 x 400 Metres Relay
1 Great Britain 3m 03.16s
2 West Germany 3m 03.33s
3 East Germany 3m 04.21s
High Jump
1 Dalton Grant (GB) 2.32m
2 Rudolph Povarnitsyn (USSR) 2.32m
3 Robert Ruffini (Cze) 2.29m
Long Jump
1 Vladimir Ratushkov (USSR) 8.09m
2 Christia Thomas (FRG) 8.05m
3 Stewart Faulkner (GB) 7.97m
Triple Jump
1 Oleg Sakirkin (USSR) 17.18m
2 Wolfgang Zinser (FRG) 16.71m
3 Dario Badinelli (Ita) 16.50m
Pole Vault
1 Rodion Gataulin (USSR) 5.70m
2 Bernhard Zintl (FRG) 5.50m
3 Uwe Langhammer (GDR) 5.40m

Discus
1 Jürgen Schult (GDR) 66.54m
2 Romas Ubartas (USSR) 63.98m
3 Rolf Danneberg (FRG) 63.12m
Hammer
1 Heinz Weis (FRG) 79.86m
2 Igor Astapkovitch (USSR) 79.68m
3 Ralf Haber (GDR) 77.76m
Javelin
1 Steve Backley (GB) 82.92m
2 Jan Zelezny (Cze) 79.44m
3 Volke Hadwich (GDR) 79.38
Shot
1 Ulf Timmermann (GDR) 21.72m
2 Karsten Stolz (FRG) 20.45m
3 Alessandro Andrei (Ita) 20.03m
Alexandr Bagach (USSR) disqualified from 3rd place following positive drugs test. This cost USSR a place in the World Cup final.
Final Placings
1 Great Britain 115 pts
2 East Germany 103 pts
3 USSR 101 pts
4 Italy 95 pts
5 France 95 pts
6 West Germany 91 pts
7 Czechoslovakia 63 pts
8 Spain 54 pts
Women
100 Metres
1 Kathrin Krabbe (GDR) 11.14s
2 Paula Dunn (GB) 11.24s
3 Irina Sergeyeva (USSR) 11.26s
200 Metres
1 Silke Moeller (GDR) 23.00s
2 Paula Dunn (GB) 23.45s
3 Ewa Kasprzyk (Pol) 23.72s
400 Metres
1 Grit Breuer (GDR) 50.52s
2 Linda Keough (GB) 51.66s
3 Helga Arendt (FRG) 51.80s
800 Metres
1 Doina Melinte (Rom) 1m 58.04s
2 Sigrun Wodars (GDR) 1m 58.55s
3 Dalia Matsaviciene (USSR) 1m 59.74s
1500 Metres
1 Doina Melinte (Rom) 4m 05.83s
2 Yvonne Mai (GDR) 4m 06.50s
3 Svetlana Kitova (USSR) 4m 07.62s
3000 Metres
1 Paula Ivan (Rom) 8m 38.48s
2 Yvonne Murray (GB) 8m 44.34s
3 Natalya Artyomova (USSR) 9m 03.39s
10,000 Metres
1 Kathrin Ullrich (GDR) 32m 17.88s
2 Viorica Ghican (Rom) 32m 41.34s
3 Angela Pain (GB) 32m 42.84s
100 Metres Hurdles
1 Cornelia Oschkenat (GDR) 12.74s
2 Claudia Zaczkiewicz (FRG) 12.82s
3 Yelena Charnyshova (USSR) 12.85s
400 Metres Hurdles
1 Petra Krug (GDR) 54.72s
2 Sally Gunnell (GB) 54.98s
3 Tatayana Ledovskaya (USSR) 55.35s
4 x 100 Metres Relay
1 East Germany 41.87s

2 USSR 42.84s
3 West Germany 43.64s

4 x 400 Metres Relay
1 East Germany 3m 24.02s
2 USSR 3m 24.75s
3 Great Britain 3m 26.54s

High Jump
1 Galina Astafei (Rom) 2.00m
2 Tamara Bykova (USSR) 1.97m
3 Heike Balck (GDR) 1.94m

Long Jump
1 Galina Chistiakova (USSR) 7.10m
2 Helga Radtke (GDR) 6.89m
3 Fiona May (GB) 6.88m

Discus
1 Ilke Wyludda (GDR) 73.04m
2 Tsvetanka Khristova (Bul) 62.62m
3 Dagmar Galler (FRG) 60.46m

Javelin
1 Petra Felke (GDR) 66.92m
2 Brigita Graune (FRG) 62.04m
3 Tessa Sanderson (GB) 59.72m

Shot
1 Heike Hartwig (GDR) 20.59m
2 Claudia Losch (FRG) 20.17m
3 Lyudmila Peleshenko (USSR) 19.32m

Final Placings
1 East Germany 120pts
2 USSR 95pts
3 Great Britain 84pts
4 West Germany 79pts
5 Romania 72pts
6 Poland 56pts
7 Bulgaria 43pts
8 Czechoslovakia 26pts

"I wouldn't be surprised if one day his halo slipped and choked him."
Allan Wells on Carl Lewis

"You know what I wish? I would like to see them have races for men and women together. If I could race against Carl Lewis and Ben Johnson I'd run 10.2."
Florence Griffith-Joyner

"Not only will I be there next time, I'll probably win."
Daley Thompson on the 1992 Olympics

"This is the dawning of a new golden era."
British coach Frank Dick after the European Cup

"When I quit this sport, I should have made a million dollars."
Roger Kingdom

"I hope to pursue a career which is altogether quieter, less controversial, more reflective and more physical – in politics."
Sebastian Coe, aspirant Tory MP

"To judge by the tone of many of Coe's remarks and values over the years .... our Seb is not so much a natural Thatcherite as a natural Democrat."
The Guardian

WORLD CUP
Barcelona, Sep 8-10
Men
100 Metres
1 Linford Christie (GB) 10.10s
2 Leroy Burrell (US) 10.15s
3 Daniel Sangouma (Europe) 10.17s

200 Metres
1 Robson da Silva (Americas) 20.00s
2 Floyd Heard (US) 20.36s
3 Oladape Adeniken (Africa) 20.38s

400 Metres
1 Roberto Hernandez (Americas) 44.58s
2 Jens Carlowitz (GDR) 44.86s
3 Gabriel Tiacoh (Africa) 44.97s

800 Metres
1 Tom McKean (GB) 1m 44.95s
2 Jens-Peter Herold (GDR) 1m 45.04s
3 Nixon Kiprotich (Africa) 1m 45.08s

1500 Metres
1 Abdi Bile (Africa) 3m 35.56s
2 Sebastian Coe (GB) 3m 35.79s
3 Jens-Peter Herold (GDR) 3m 35.87s

5000 Metres
1 Said Aouita (Africa) 13m 23.14s
2 John Doherty (Europe) 13m 25.39s
3 Jose-Luis Carreira (Spa) 13m 25.94s

10,000 Metres
1 Salvatore Antibo (Europe) 28m 05.26s
2 Abdi Abebe (Africa) 28m 06.43s
3 Antonio Prieto (Spa) 28m 07.42s

3000 Metres Steeplechase
1 Julius Kariuki (Africa) 8m 20.84s
2 Alessandro Lambruschini (Europe) 8m 21.75s
3 Hagen Melzer (GDR) 8m 23.21s

110 Metres Hurdles
1 Roger Kingdom (US) 12.87s
2 Colin Jackson (GB) 12.95s
3 Emilio Valle (Americas) 13.21s

400 Metres Hurdles
1 Dave Patrick (US) 48.74s
2 Henry Amike (Africa) 49.24s
3 Kriss Akabusi (GB) 49.24s

4 x 100 Metres Relay
1 United States 38.29s
2 Great Britain 38.34s
3 Europe 38.47s

4 x 400 Metres Relay
1 Americas 3m 00.65s
2 United States 3m 00.99s
3 Africa 3m 01.88s

High Jump
1 Patrik Sjoberg (Swe) 2.34m
2 Dalton Grant (GB) 2.31m
3 Javier Sotomayor (Americas) 2.25m

Pole Vault
1 Philippe Collet (Fra) 5.75m
2 Tim Bright (US) 5.70m
3 Uwe Langhammer (GDR) 5.55m

Long Jump
1 Larry Myricks (US) 8.29m
2 Yasuf Ali (Africa) 8.00m
3 Stewart Faulkner (GB) 7.84s

Triple Jump
1 Mike Conley (US) 17.49m
2 Vladimir Inozemtsev (Europe) 17.31m
3 Jon Edwards (GB) 17.28m

Shot
1 Ulf Timmermann (GDR) 21.68m

2 Werner Günthoer (Europe) 21.40m
3 Randy Barnes (US) 21.10m

Discus
1 Jürgen Schult (GDR) 67.12m
2 Luis-Mariano Delis (Americas) 66.72m
3 Rolf Danneberg (Europe) 65.30m

Hammer
1 Heinz Weis (Europe) 77.68m
2 Lance Deal (US) 76.38m
3 Ralf Haber (GDR) 76.28m

Javelin
1 Steve Backley (GB) 85.90m
2 Kazuhiro Mizoguchi (Asia) 82.30m
3 Volker Hadwich (GDR) 80.30m

Final Standings
1 United States 133pts
2 Europe 127pts
3 Great Britain 119pts
4 East Germany 116.5pts
5 Africa 107pts
6 Americas 97pts
7 Asia 68.5pts
8 Spain 64.5pts
9 Oceania 64.5pts

Women
100 Metres
1 Sheila Echols (US) 11.18s
2 Mary Onyali (Africa) 11.23s
3 Silke Moeller (GDR) 11.24s

200 Metres
1 Silke Moeller (GDR) 22.46s
2 Mary Onyali (Africa) 22.82s
3 Grace Jackson (Americas) 22.87s

400 Metres
1 Ana Quirot (Americas) 50.60s
2 Grit Breuer (GDR) 50.67s
3 Falilat Ogunkoya (Africa) 51.67s
*Marie Perec (Europe) disqualified from first place (50.30s)
for stepping out of lane.*

800 Metres
1 Ana Quirot (Americas) 1m 54.44s
2 Sigrun Wodars (GDR) 1m 55.70s
3 Doina Melinte (Europe) 1m 56.55s

1500 Metres
1 Paula Ivan (Europe) 4m 18.60s
2 Yelena Podkopeyeva (USSR) 4m 19.44s
3 Yvonne Mai (GDR) 4m 20.30s

3000 Metres
1 Yvonne Murray (Europe) 8m 44.32s
2 Tatyana Pozdynyakova (USSR) 8m 49.42s
3 Patti Sue Plumer (US) 8m 54.33s

10,000 Metres
1 Kathrin Ullrich (GDR) 31m 33.92s
2 Ingrid Kristiansen (Europe) 31m 42.01s
3 Natalya Sorokivskaya (USSR) 32m 15.53s

100 Metres Hurdles
1 Cornelia Oschkenat (GDR) 12.60s
2 Lyudmila Narojilenko (USSR) 12.80s
3 Lynda Tolbert (US) 12.86s

400 Metres Hurdles
1 Sandra Farmer-Patrick (US) 53.84s
2 Tatanya Ledovskaya (USSR) 54.68s
3 Sally Gunnell (Europe) 55.25s

4 x 100 Metres Relay
1 East Germany 42.21s
2 USSR 42.76s
3 United States 42.83s

4 x 400 Metres Relay
1 Americas 3m 23.09s
2 East Germany 3m 23.97s
3 USSR 3m 26.15s

High Jump
1 Sylvia Costa (Americas) 2.04m
2 Tamara Bykova (USSR) 1.97m
3 Galina Astafei (Europe) 1.94m

Long Jump
1 Galina Chistiakova (USSR) 7.10m
2 Marieta Ilcu (Europe) 6.71m
3 Nicole Boegman (Oceania) 6.64m

Shot
1 Zhihong Huang (Asia) 20.73m
2 Heike Hartwig (GDR) 20.62m
3 Claudia Losch (Europe) 20.10m

Discus
1 Ilke Wyludda (GDR) 71.54m
2 Xuemei Hou (Asia) 66.04m
3 Maritza Marten (Americas) 65.40m

Javelin
1 Petra Felke (GDR) 70.32m
2 Zhang Li (Asia) 61.50m
3 Laverne Eve (Americas) 60.32m

Final Standing
1 East Germany 124pts
2 USSR 106pts
3 Americas 94pts
4 Europe 89pts
5 United States 84.5pts
6 Asia 67.5pts
7 Africa 58pts
8 Spain 48pts
9 Oceania 40pts

MOBIL GRAND PRIX
Final Standings
N.B. Some events not held

Men
200 Metres
1 Robson Da Silva (Bra) 59pts
2 Henry Thomas (US) 47pts
3 Calvin Smith (US) 41pts

400 Metres
1 Danny Everett (US) 51pts
2 Harry Reynolds (US) 50pts
3 Mohammed Al Malky (Oma) 45pts

1500 Metres
1 Abdi Bile (Som) 61pts
2 Wilfred Kirochi (Ken) 50pts
3 Kip Cheruiyot (Ken) 47pts

5000 Metres
1 Arturo Barrios (Mex) 60pts
2 Said Aouita (Mor) 51pts
3 Sidney Maree (US) 43pts

110 Metres Hurdles
1 Roger Kingdom (US) 63pts
2 Tonie Campbell (US) 57pts
3 Colin Jackson (GB) 53pts

Pole Vault
1 Radion Gataulin (USSR) 61pts
2 Sergey Bubka (USSR) 55 pts
3 Earl Bell (US) 40pts

Long Jump
1 Larry Myricks (US) 61pts
2 Mike Powell (US) 53pts
3 Mike Conley (US) 41pts

Discus
1 Wolfgang Schmidt (FRG) 52pts
2 Luis-Mariano Delis (Cub) 50pts
3 Erik De Bruin (Hol) 37pts

Javelin
1 Steve Backley (GB) 63pts
2 Kazuhiro Mizoguchi (Jap) 54pts
3 Sigurdur Einarsson (Ice) 45pts

Overall
1 Said Aouita (Mor) 69pts
2 Roger Kingdom (US) 63pts
3 Steve Backley (GB) 63pts
4 Rodion Gataulin (USSR) 61pts
5 Abdi Bile (Som) 61pts
6 Larry Myricks (US) 61pts

Women
100 Metres
1 Merlene Ottey (Jam) 63pts
2 Sheila Echols (US) 49pts
3 Pauline Davis (Bah) 47pts

800 Metres
1 Ana Quirot (Cub) 63pts
2 Caby Lesch (FRG) 39pts
3 Christine Wachtel (GDR) 37pts

Mile
1 Paula Ivan (Rom) 51pts
2 Doina Melinte (Rom) 51pts
3 Svetlana Kitova (USSR) 49pts

3000 Metres
1 Patti Sue Plumer (US) 55pts
2 Elly van Hulst (Hol) 39pts
3 Yvonne Murray (GB) 34pts

400 Metres Hurdles
1 Sandra Farmer-Patrick (US) 63pts
2 Sally Gunnell (GB) 45pts
3 Schowonda Williams (US) 41pts

High Jump
1 Jan Wohlschlag (US) 59pts
2 Silvia Costa (Cub) 48pts
3 Tamara Bykova (USSR) 38pts

Long Jump
1 Galina Chistiakova (USSR) 63pts
2 Marieta Ilcu (Rom) 44pts
3 Vali Ionescu (Rom) 38pts

Shot
1 Natalya Lisovskaya (USSR) 61pts
2 Grit Hammer-Haupt (GDR) 44pts
3 Stephani Storp (FRG) 43pts

Overall
1 Paula Ivan (Rom) 67pts
2 Galina Chistiakova (USSR) 63pts
3 Sandra Farmer-Patrick (US) 63pts
4 Merlene Ottey (Jam) 63pts
5 Ana Quirot (Cub) 63pts
6 Natalya Lisovskaya (USSR) 61pts

IAAF WORLD CROSS COUNTRY CHAMPIONSHIPS
Stavanger, Norway, Mar 19
Senior Men
Individual
1 John Ngugi (Ken) 39m 42s
2 Tim Hutchings (GB) 40m 10s
3 Wilfred Kirochi (Ken) 40m 21s

Team
1 Kenya 44pts
2 Great Britain 147pts
3 Ethiopia 162pts

Senior Women
Individual
1 Annette Sergent (Fra) 22m 27s
2 Nadezhda Stepanova (USSR) 22m 34s
3 Lynn Williams (Can) 22m 41s

Team
1 Soviet Union 58pts
2 France 60pts
3 United States 68pts

EUROPEAN CUP FOR CLUBS
Belgrade, Jun 3-4
1 Red Star (Yug)	118pts
2 Larios (Spa)	110½
3 Racing Club (Fra)	109½
4 Fiamme Oro (Ita)	107½
5 Haringey (GB)	97
6 Bayer Leverkusen (FRG)	81½
7 Benfica (Por)	63
8 Tjalve (Nor)	49

GRE BRITISH LEAGUE
Division 1
1 Birchfield H 31pts
2 Haringey 22pts
3 Shaftesbury-Barnet 19pts
Relegated: Sale/Wolverhampton

Division 2
1 Thames Valley H 24pts
2 Old Gaytonians 17½pts
3 Edinburgh AC 12pts
Relegated: Cardiff/Windsor

Division 3
1 Woodford Green 23pts
2 Leeds 18pts
3 Enfield 14pts
Relegated: Hillingdon/Southampton

Division 4
1 Sheffield 21pts
2 Cambridge H 19pts
3 Hercules Wimbledon 18pts
Relegated: Luton/North London

Division 5
1 Stretford 21pts
2 Swansea 19pts
3 Liverpool 17pts

GUARDIAN ROYAL EXCHANGE GOLD CUP *(Men)*
1 Haringey	127pts
2 Birchfield	106pts
3 Wolverhampton	101pts
4 Enfield	86pts
5 Thames Valley	84pts
6 Blackheath	81pts
7 Belgrave	71pts
8 Sale	71pts

JUBILEE CUP *(Women)*
1 Birchfield	97pts
2 Essex Ladies	96½pts
3 Stretford	85pts
4 Sale	76pts
5 Bromley	61pts
6 Cardiff	51pts
7 Hounslow	44pts
8 Derby Ladies	42½pts

MARATHON WORLD CUP
Milan, Apr 16
Individual Men
1 Keleke Metafeira (Eth) 2h 10m 28s
2 Dereje Nedi (Eth) 2h 10m 36s
3 Gianni Poli (Ita) 2h 10m 49s
Team Men
1 Ethiopia 6h 37m 20s
2 Italy 6h 37m 51s
3 France 6h 38m 51s
Individual Women
1 Sue Marchiano (US) 2h 30m 48s
2 Misako Miyahara (Jap) 2h 35m 16s
3 Uta Pippig (GDR) 2h 35m 17s
Team Women
1 USSR 7h 51m 29s

2 United States 7h 56m 17s
3 China 7h 57m 07s

LONDON MARATHON
Apr 23
Men
1 Douglas Wakiihuri (Ken) 2h 09m 03s

2 Steve Moneghetti (Aus) 2h 09m 06s
3 Ahmed Salah (Dji) 2h 09m 09s

Women
1 Véronique Marot (GB) 2h 25m 56s
2 Wanda Panfill (Pol) 2h 27m 05s
3 Aurora Cunha (Por) 2h 28m 11s

	EUROPEAN INDOOR CHAMPIONSHIPS The Hague, Feb 19-20	WORLD INDOOR CHAMPIONSHIP Budapest, Mar 3-5
Men		
60 metres:	Andreas Berger (Aut) 6.65s	Andreas Gomez (Cub) 6.52s
200 metres:	Ade Mafe (GB) 20.92s	John Regis (GB) 20.54s
400 metres:	Cayetano Cornet (Spa) 46.21s	Antonio McKay (US) 45.59s
800 metres:	Steve Heard (GB) 1m 48.84s	Paul Ereng (Ken) 1m 44.84s
1500 metres:	Herve Philippeau (Fra) 3m 47.42s	Marcus O'Sullivan (Ire) 3m 36.64s
3000 metres:	Dieter Baumann (FRG) 7m 50.43s	Said Aouita (Mor) 7m 47.94s
60 metres hurdles:	Colin Jackson (GB) 7.59s	Roger Kingdom (US) 7.43s
5km walk:	Mikhail Schennikov (USSR) 18m 35.60s	Mikhail Schennikov (USSR) 18m 27.10s
High jump:	Dietmar Moegenburg (FRG) 2.33m	Javier Sotomayor (Cub) 2.43m
Pole vault:	Grigory Yegorov (USSR) 5.75m	Rodion Gataullin (USSR) 5.85m
Triple jump:	Nikolai Musienko (USSR) 17.29m	Mike Conley (US) 17.65m
Long jump:	Emmiel Mellaard (Hol) 8.14m	Larry Myricks (US) 8.37m
Shot	Ulf Timmermann (GDR) 21.68m	Ulf Timmermann (GDR) 21.75m
Women		
60 metres:	Nellie Fiere-Cooman (Hol) 7.15s	Nellie Fiere-Cooman (Hol) 7.05s
200 metres:	Marie Josee Perec (Fra) 23.21s	Merlene Ottey (Jam) 22.34s
400 metres:	Sally Gunnell (GB) 52.04s	Helga Arendt (FRG) 51.52s
800 metres:	Doina Melinte (Rom) 1m 59.89s	Christine Wachtel (GDR) 1m 59.24s
1500 metres:	Paula Ivan (Rom) 4m 07.16s	Doina Melinte (Rom) 4m 04.79s
3000 metres:	Elly van Hulst (Hol) 9m 10.01s	Elly van Hulst (Hol) 8m 33.82s
60 metres hurdles:	Yordanka Donkova (Bul) 7.87s	Elizaveta Chernishova (USSR) 7.82s
3km walk:	Beate Anders (GDR) 12m 21.91s	Kerry Saxby (Aus) 12m 01.65s
High jump:	Galina Astafei (Rom) 1.96m	Stefka Kostadinova (Bul) 2.02m
Long jump:	Galina Chistiakova (USSR) 6.98m	Galina Chistiakova (USSR) 6.98m
Shot	Stephanie Storp (FRG) 20.30m	Claudia Losch (FRG) 20.45m

CHAMPIONS

OLYMPIC GAMES
Men
100 Metres
1896	Thomas Burke (US) 12.0s
1900	Francis Jarvis (US) 11.0s
1904	Archie Hahn (US) 11.0s
1908	Reginald Walker (SA) 10.8s
1912	Ralph Craig (US) 10.8s
1920	Charles Paddock (US) 10.8s
1924	Harold Abrahams (GB) 10.6s
1928	Percy Williams (Can) 10.8s
1932	Eddie Tolan (US) 10.38s
1936	Jesse Owens (US) 10.3s
1948	Harrison Dillard (US) 10.3s
1952	Lindy Remigino (US) 10.79s
1956	Bobby Morrow (US) 10.62s
1960	Armin Hary (FRG) 10.32s
1964	Robert Hayes (US) 10.06s
1968	James Hines (US) 9.95s
1972	Valeriy Borzov (USSR) 10.14s
1976	Hasely Crawford (Tri) 10.06s
1980	Allan Wells (GB) 10.25s
1984	Carl Lewis (US) 9.99s
1988	Carl Lewis (US) 9.92s

200 Metres
1900	Walter Tewksbury (US) 22.2s
1904	Archie Hahn (US) 21.6s
1908	Robert Kerr (Can) 22.6s
1912	Ralph Craig (US) 21.7s
1920	Allen Woodring (US) 22.0s
1924	Jackson Scholz (US) 21.6s
1928	Percy Williams (Can) 21.8s
1932	Eddie Tolan (US) 21.12s

1936	Jesse Owens (US) 20.7s
1948	Melvin Patton (US) 21.1s
1952	Andrew Stanfield (US) 20.81s
1956	Bobby Morrow (US) 20.75s
1960	Livio Berrutti (Ita) 20.62s
1964	Henry Carr (US) 20.36s
1968	Tommie Smith (US) 19.83s
1972	Valeriy Borzov (USSR) 20.00s
1976	Donald Quarrie (Jam) 20.22s
1980	Pietro Mennea (Ita) 20.19s
1984	Carl Lewis (US) 19.80s
1988	Joe DeLoach (US) 19.75s

400 Metres
1896	Thomas Burke (US) 54.2s
1900	Maxie Long (US) 49.4s
1904	Harry Hillman (US) 49.2s
1908	Wyndham Halswelle (GB) 50.0s
1912	Charles Reidpath (US) 48.2s
1920	Bevil Rudd (SA) 49.6s
1924	Eric Liddell (GB) 47.6s
1928	Ray Barbuti (US) 47.8s
1932	Bill Carr (US) 46.28s
1936	Archie Williams (US) 46.66s
1948	Arthur Wint (Jam) 46.2s
1952	George Rhoden (Jam) 46.09s
1956	Charles Jenkins (US) 46.86s
1960	Otis Davis (US) 45.07s
1964	Michael Larrabee (US) 45.15s
1968	Lee Evans (US) 43.86s
1972	Vincent Matthews (US) 44.66s
1976	Alberto Juantorena (Cub) 44.26s
1980	Viktor Markin (USSR) 44.60s
1984	Alonzo Babers (US) 44.27s
1988	Steve Lewis (US) 43.87s

800 Metres
1896	Edwin Flack (Aus)	2m 11.0s
1900	Alfred Tysoe (GB)	2m 01.2s
1904	James Lightbody (US)	1m 56.0s
1908	Mel Sheppard (US)	1m 52.8s
1912	James Meredith (US)	1m 51.9s
1920	Albert Hill (GB)	1m 53,4s
1924	Douglas Lowe (GB)	1m 52.4s
1928	Douglas Lowe (GB)	1m 51.8s
1932	Tom Hampson (GB)	1m 49.70s
1936	John Woodruff (US)	1m 52.9s
1948	Malvin Whitfield (US)	1m 49.2s
1952	Malvin Whitfield (US)	1m 49.34s
1956	Thomas Courtney (US)	1m 47.75s
1960	Peter Snell (NZ)	1m 46.48s
1964	Peter Snell (NZ)	1m 45.1s
1968	Ralph Doubell (Aus)	1m 44.40s
1972	David Wottle (US)	1m 45.86s
1976	Alberto Juantorena (Cub)	1m 43.50s
1980	Steve Ovett (GB)	1m 45.40s
1984	Joaquim Cruz (Bra)	1m 43.00s
1988	Paul Ereng (Ken)	1m 44.06s

1500 Metres
1896	Edwin Flack (Aus)	4m 33.2s
1900	Charles Bennett (GB)	4m 06.2s
1904	James Lightbody (US)	4m 05.4s
1908	Mel Sheppard (US)	4m 03.4s
1912	Arnold Jackson (GB)	3m 56.8s
1920	Albert Hill (GB)	4m 01.8s
1924	Paavo Nurmi (Fin)	3m 53.6s
1928	Harri Larva (Fin)	3m 53.2s
1932	Luigi Beccali (Ita)	3m 51.20s
1936	Jack Lovelock (NZ)	3m 47.8s
1948	Henry Eriksson (Swe)	3m 49.8s
1952	Josef Barthel (Lux)	3m 45.28s
1956	Ron Delany (Ire)	3m 41.49s
1960	Herbert Elliott (Aus)	3m 35.6s
1964	Peter Snell (NZ)	3m 38.1s
1968	Kipchoge Keino (Ken)	3m 34.91s
1972	Pekka Vasala (Fin)	3m 36.33s
1976	John Walker (NZ)	3m 39.17s
1980	Sebastian Coe (GB)	3m 38.40s
1984	Sebastian Coe (GB)	3m 32.53s
1988	Peter Rono (Ken)	3m 36.21s

5000 Metres
1912	Hannes Kolehmainen (Fin)	14m 36.6s
1920	Joseph Guillemot (Fra)	14m 55.6s
1924	Paavo Nurmi (Fin)	14m 31.2s
1928	Ville Ritola (Fin)	14m 38.0s
1932	Lauri Lehtinen (Fin)	14m 30.0s
1936	Gunnar Hockert (Fin)	14m 22.2s
1948	Gaston Reiff (Bel)	14m 17.6s
1952	Emil Zatopek (Cze)	14m 06.72s
1956	Vladimir Kuts (USSR)	13m 39.86s
1960	Murray Halberg (NZ)	13m 43.4s
1964	Robert Schul (US)	13m 48.8s
1968	Mohamed Gammoudi (Tun)	14m 05.0s
1972	Lasse Viren (Fin)	13m 26.42s
1976	Lasse Viren (Fin)	13m 24.76s
1980	Miruts Yifter (Eth)	13m 20.91s
1984	Said Aouita (Mor)	13m 05.59s
1988	John Ngugi (Ken)	13m 11.70s

10,000 Metres
1912	Hannes Kolehmainen (Fin)	31m 20.8s
1920	Paavo Nurmi (Fin)	31m 45.8s
1924	Ville Ritola (Fin)	30m 23.2s
1928	Paavo Nurmi (Fin)	30m 18.8s
1932	Janusz Kushocinski (Pol)	30m 11.4s
1936	Ilmari Salminen (Fin)	30m 15.4s
1948	Emil Zatopek (Cze)	29m 59.6s
1952	Emil Zatopek (Cze)	29m 17.0s
1956	Vladimir Kuts (USSR)	28m 45.60s
1960	Pyotr Bolotnikov (USSR)	28m 32.18s

1964	William Mills (US)	28m 24.4s
1968	Naftali Temu (Ken)	29m 27.4s
1972	Lasse Viren (Fin)	27m 38.35s
1976	Lasse Viren (Fin)	27m 40.38s
1980	Miruts Yifter (Eth)	27m 42.69s
1984	Alberto Cova (Ita)	27m 47.54s
1988	Moulay Brahim Boutaib (Mor)	27m 21.46s

Marathon
1896	Spyridon Louis (Gre)	2h 58m 50.0s
1900	Michel Theato (Fra)	2h 59m 45.0s
1904	Thomas Hicks (US)	3h 28m 35.0s
1908	John Hayes (US)	2h 55m 18.4s
1912	Kenneth McArthur (SA)	2h 36m 54.8s
1920	Hannes Kolehmainen (Fin)	2h 32m 35.8s
1924	Albin Stenroos (Fin)	2h 41m 22.6s
1928	Mohamed El Ouafi (Fra)	2h 32m 57.0s
1932	Juan Zabala (Arg)	2h 31m 36.0s
1936	Kitei Son (Jap)	2h 29m 19.2s
1948	Delfo Cabrera (Arg)	2h 34m 51.6s
1952	Emil Zatopek (Cze)	2h 23m 03.2s
1956	Alain Mimoun (Fra)	2h 25m 00.0s
1960	Abebe Bikila (Eth)	2h 15m 16.2s
1964	Abebe Bikila (Eth)	2h 12m 11.2s
1968	Mamo Wolde (Eth)	2h 20m 26.4s
1972	Frank Shorter (US)	2h 12m 19.8s
1976	Waldemar Cierpinski (GDR)	2h 09m 55s
1980	Waldemar Cierpinski (GDR)	2h 11m 03s
1984	Carlos Lopes (Por)	2h 09m 21s
1988	Gelindo Bordin (Ita)	2h 10m 32s

110 Metres Hurdles
1896	Thomas Curtis (US)	17.6s
1900	Alvin Kraenzlein (US)	15.4s
1904	Fred Schule (US)	16.0s
1908	Forrest Smithson (US)	15.0s
1912	Fred Kelly (US)	15.1s
1920	Earl Thomson (Can)	14.8s
1924	Daniel Kinsey (US)	15.0s
1928	Sydney Atkinson (SA)	14.8s
1932	George Saling (US)	14.56s
1936	Forrest Towns (US)	14.2s
1948	William Porter (US)	13.9s
1952	Harrison Dillard (US)	13.91s
1956	Lee Calhoun (US)	13.70s
1960	Lee Calhoun (US)	13.98s
1964	Hayes Jones (US)	13.67s
1968	Willie Davenport (US)	13.33s
1972	Rodney Milburn (US)	13.24s
1976	Guy Drut (US)	13.30s
1980	Thomas Munkelt (GDR)	13.39s
1984	Roger Kingdom (US)	13.20s
1988	Roger Kingdom (US)	12.98s

400 Metres Hurdles
1900	Walter Tewksbury (US)	57.6s
1904	Harry Hillman (US)	53.0s
1908	Charles Bacon (US)	55.0s
1920	Frank Loomis (US)	54.0s
1924	Morgan Taylor (US)	52.6s
1928	Lord Burghley (GB)	53.4s
1932	Robert Tisdall (Ire)	51.67s
1936	Glenn Hardin (US)	52.4s
1948	Roy Cochran (US)	51.1s
1952	Charles Moore (US)	51.06s
1956	Glenn Davis (US)	50.29s
1960	Glenn Davis (US)	49.51s
1964	Rex Cawley (US)	49.69s
1968	David Hemery (GB)	48.12s
1972	John Akii-Bua (Uga)	47.82s
1976	Edwin Moses (US)	47.63s
1980	Volker Beck (GDR)	48.70s
1984	Edwin Moses (US)	47.75s
1988	Andre Phillips (US)	47.19s

3000 Metres Steeplechase
1920	Percy Hodge (GB)	10m 00.4s

1924	Ville Ritola (Fin) 9m 33.6s
1928	Toivo Loukola (Fin) 9m 21.8s
1932	Volmari Iso-Hollo (Fin) 10m 33.4s*
1936	Volmari Iso-Hollo (Fin) 9m 03.8s
1948	Tore Sjöstrand (Swe) 9m 04.6s
1952	Horace Ashenfelter (US) 8m 45.68s
1956	Christopher Brasher (GB) 8m 41.35s
1960	Zdzislaw Kryszkowiak (Pol) 8m 34.31s
1964	Gaston Roelants (Bel) 8m 30.8s
1968	Amos Biwott (Ken) 8m 51.0s
1972	Kipchoge Keino (Ken) 8m 23.64s
1976	Anders Gärderud (Swe) 8m 08.02s
1980	Bronislaw Malinowski (Pol) 8m 09.70s
1984	Julius Korir (Ken) 8m 11.80s
1988	Julius Kariuki (Ken) 8m 05.51s

Competitors ran an extra lap in error.

20,000 Metres Walk

1956	Leonid Spirin (USSR) 1h 31m 27.4s
1960	Vladimir Golubnichiy (USSR) 1h 34m 07.2s
1964	Kenneth Matthews (GB) 1h 29m 34.0s
1968	Vladimir Golubnichiy (USSR) 1h 33m 58.4s
1972	Peter Frenkel (GDR) 1h 26m 42.4s
1976	Daniel Bautista (Mex) 1h 24m 40.6s
1980	Maurizio Damilano (Ita) 1h 23m 35.5s
1984	Ernesto Canto (Mex) 1h 23m 13s
1988	Jozef Pribilinec (Cze) 1h 19m 57s

50,000 Metres Walk

1932	Thomas Green (GB) 4h 50m 10.0s
1936	Harold Whitlock (GB) 4h 30m 41.1s
1948	John Ljunggren (Swe) 4h 41m 52.0s
1952	Giuseppe Dordoni (Ita) 4h 28m 07.8s
1956	Norman Read (NZ) 4h 30m 42.8s
1960	Don Thompson (GB) 4h 25m 30.0s
1964	Abdon Pamich (Ita) 4h 11m 12.4s
1968	Christophe Höhne (GDR) 4h 20m 13.6s
1972	Bernd Kannenberg (GDR) 3h 56m 11.6s
1980	Hartwig Gauder (GDR) 3h 49m 24s
1984	Raul Gonzales (Mex) 3h 47m 26s
1988	Viacheslav Ivanenko (USSR) 3h 38m 29s

4 x 100 Metres Relay

1912	Great Britain 42.4s
1920	United States 42.2s
1924	United States 41.0s
1928	United States 41.0s
1932	United States 40.0s
1936	United States 39.8s
1948	United States 40.6s
1952	United States 40.26s
1956	United States 39.59s
1960	West Germany 39.66s
1964	United States 39.06s
1968	United States 38.23s
1972	United States 38.19s
1976	United States 38.83s
1980	USSR 38.26s
1984	United States 37.83s
1988	USSR 38.19s

4 x 400 Metres Relay

1912	United States 3m 16.6s
1920	Great Britain 3m 22.2s
1924	United States 3m 16.0s
1928	United States 3m 14.2s
1932	United States 3m 08.2s
1936	Great Britain 3m 09.0s
1948	United States 3m 10.4s
1952	Jamaica 3m 04.04s
1956	United States 3m 04.80s
1960	United States 3m 02.37s
1964	United States 3m 00.71s
1968	United States 2m 56.16s
1972	Kenya 2m 59.83s
1976	United States 2m 58.66s
1980	USSR 3m 01.08s

1984	United States 2m 57.91s
1988	United States 2m 56.16s

High Jump

1896	Ellery Clark (US) 1.81m
1900	Irving Baxter (US) 1.90m
1904	Samuel Jones (US) 1.80m
1908	Harry Porter (US) 1.90m
1912	Alma Richards (US) 1.93m
1920	Richard Landon (US) 1.94m
1924	Harold Osborn (US) 1.98m
1928	Robert King (US) 1.94m
1932	Duncan McNaughton (Can) 1.97m
1936	Cornelius Johnson (US) 2.03m
1948	John Winter (Aus) 1.98m
1952	Walter Davis (US) 2.04m
1956	Charles Dumas (US) 2.12m
1960	Robert Shavlakadze (USSR) 2.16m
1964	Valeriy Brumel (USSR) 2.18m
1968	Dick Fosbury (US) 2.24m
1972	Yuriy Tarmak (USSR) 2.23m
1976	Jacek Wszola (Pol) 2.25m
1980	Gerd Wessig (GDR) 2.36m
1984	Dietmar Mögenburg (FRG) 2.35m
1988	Gennady Avdeyenko (USSR) 2.38m

Pole Vault

1896	William Hoyt (US) 3.30m
1900	Irving Baxter (US) 3.30m
1904	Charles Dvorak (US) 3.50m
1908	Edward Cooke & Alfred Gilbert (US) 3.71m
1912	Harry Babcock (US) 3.95m
1920	Frank Foss (US) 4.09m
1924	Lee Barnes (US) 3.95m
1928	Sabin Carr (US) 4.20m
1932	Bill Miller (US) 4.31m
1936	Earle Meadows (US) 4.35m
1948	Guinn Smith (US) 4.30m
1952	Robert Richards (US) 4.55m
1956	Robert Richards (US) 4.56m
1960	Dinald Bragg (US) 4.70m
1964	Frederick Hansen (US) 5.10m
1968	Bob Seagren (US) 5.40m
1972	Wolfgang Nordwig (GDR) 5.50m
1976	Tadeusz Slusarski (Pol) 5.50m
1980	Wladyslaw Kozakiewicz (Pol) 5.78m
1984	Pierre Quinon (Fra) 5.75m
1988	Sergey Bubka (USSR) 5.90m

Long Jump

1896	Ellery Clark (US) 6.35m
1900	Alvin Kraenzlein (US) 7.18m
1904	Myer Prinstein (US) 7.34m
1908	Francis Irons (US) 7.48m
1912	Albert Gutterson (US) 7.60m
1920	William Pettersson (Swe) 7.15m
1924	William De Hart Hubbard (US) 7.44m
1928	Edward Hamm (US) 7.73m
1932	Edward Gordon (US) 7.64m
1936	Jesse Owens (US) 8.06m
1948	William Steele (US) 7.82m
1952	Jerome Biffle (US) 7.57m
1956	Gregory Bell (US) 7.83m
1960	Ralph Boston (US) 8.12m
1964	Lynn Davies (GB) 8.07m
1968	Bob Beamon (US) 8.90m
1972	Randy Williams (US) 8.24m
1976	Arnie Robinson (US) 8.35m
1980	Lutz Dombrowski (GDR) 8.54m
1984	Carl Lewis (US) 8.54m
1988	Carl Lewis (US) 8.72m

Triple Jump

1896	James Connolly (US) 13.71m
1900	Myer Prinstein (US) 14.47m
1904	Myer Prinstein (US) 14.35m
1908	Tim Ahearne (GB) 14.91m

1912	Gustaf Lindblom (Swe) 14.76m
1920	Vilho Tuulos (Fin) 14.50m
1924	Anthony Winter (Aus) 15.52m
1928	Mikio Oda (Jap) 15.21m
1932	Chuhei Nambu (Jap) 15.72m
1936	Naoto Tajima (Jap) 16.00m
1948	Arne Ahman (Swe) 15.40m
1952	Adhemar Ferreira da Silva (Bra) 16.22m
1956	Adhemar Ferreira da Silva (Bra) 16.35m
1960	Jozef Schmidt (Pol) 16.81m
1964	Jozef Schmidt (Pol) 16.85m
1968	Viktor Saneyev (USSR) 17.39m
1972	Viktor Saneyev (USSR) 17.35m
1976	Viktor Saneyev (USSR) 17.29m
1980	Jaak Uudmae (USSR) 17.35m
1984	Al Joyner (US) 17.26m
1988	Hristo Markov (Bul) 17.61m

Shot

1896	Robert Garrett (US) 11.22m
1900	Richard Sheldon (US) 14.10m
1904	Ralph Rose (US) 14.80m
1908	Ralph Rose (US) 14.21m
1912	Patrick McDonald (US) 15.34m
1920	Ville Porhola (Fin) 14.81m
1924	Clarence Houser (US) 14.99m
1928	John Kuck (US) 15.87m
1932	Leo Sexton (US) 16.00m
1936	Hans Woellke (Ger) 16.20m
1948	Wilbur Thompson (US) 17.12m
1952	Parry O'Brien (US) 17.41m
1956	Parry O'Brien (US) 18.57m
1960	William Nieder (US) 19.68m
1964	Dallas Long (US) 20.33m
1968	Randy Matson (US) 20.54m
1972	Wladyslaw Komar (Pol) 21.18m
1976	Udo Beyer (GDR) 21.05m
1980	Vladimir Kiselyov (USSR) 21.35m
1984	Alessandro Andrei (Ita) 21.26m
1988	Ulf Timmermann (GDR) 22.47m

Discus

1896	Robert Garrett (US) 29.15m
1900	Rudolf Bauer (Hun) 36.04m
1904	Martin Sheridan (US) 39.28m
1908	Martin Sheridan (US) 40.89m
1912	Armas Taipale (Fin) 45.21m
1920	Elmer Niklander (Fin) 44.68m
1924	Clarence Houser (US) 46.15m
1928	Clarence Houser (US) 47.32m
1932	John Anderson (US) 49.49m
1936	Ken Carpenter (US) 50.48m
1948	Adolfo Consolini (Ita) 52.78m
1952	Sim Iness (US) 55.03m
1956	Al Oerter (US) 56.36m
1960	Al Oerter (US) 59.18m
1964	Al Oerter (US) 61.00m
1968	Al Oerter (US) 64.78m
1972	Ludvik Danek (Cze) 64.40m
1976	Mac Wilkins (US) 67.50m
1980	Viktor Rashchupkin (USSR) 66.64m
1984	Rolf Danneberg (FRG) 66.60m
1988	Jürgen Schult (GDR) 68.82m

Javelin

1908	Erik Lemming (Swe) 54.82m
1912	Erik Lemming (Swe) 60.64m
1920	Jonni Myyrä (Fin) 65.78m
1924	Jonni Myyrä (Fin) 62.96m
1928	Erik Lundkvist (Swe) 66.60m
1932	Matti Järvinen (Fin) 72.71m
1936	Gerhard Stöck (Ger) 71.84m
1948	Tapio Rautavaara (Fin) 69.77m
1952	Cyrus Young (US) 73.78m
1956	Egil Danielsen (Nor) 85.71
1960	Viktor Tsibulenko (USSR) 84.64m

1964	Pauli Nevala (Fin) 82.66m
1968	Janis Lusis (USSR) 90.10m
1972	Klaus Wolfermann (FRG) 90.48m
1976	Miklos Nemeth (Hun) 94.58m
1980	Dainis Kula (USSR) 91.20m
1984	Arto Harkönen (Fin) 86.76m
1988	Tapio Korjus (Fin) 84.28m

Hammer

1900	John Flanagan (US) 49.73m
1904	John Flanagan (US) 51.23m
1908	John Flanagan (US) 51.92m
1912	Matt McGrath (US) 54.74m
1920	Patrick Ryan (US) 52.87m
1924	Fred Tootell (US) 53.29m
1928	Patrick O'Callaghan (Ire) 51.39m
1932	Patrick O'Callaghan (Ire) 53.92m
1936	Karl Hein (Ger) 56.49m
1948	Imre Nemeth (Hun) 56.07m
1952	Jozsef Csermak (Hun) 60.34m
1956	Harold Connolly (US) 63.19m
1960	Vasiliy Rudenkov (USSR) 67.10m
1964	Romuald Klim (USSR) 69.74m
1968	Gyula Zsivotzky (Hun) 73.36m
1972	Anatoliy Bondarchuk (USSR) 75.50m
1976	Yuriy Sedykh (USSR) 77.52m
1980	Yuriy Sedykh (USSR) 81.80m
1984	Juha Tiainen (Fin) 78.08m
1988	Sergey Litvinov (USSR) 84.80m

Decathlon

Points converted to 1984 tables.

1904	Thomas Kiely (Ire) 6036pts
1912	Jim Thorpe (US) 6564pts†
1920	Helge Løvland (Nor) 5804pts
1924	Harold Osborn (US) 6476pts
1928	Paavo Yrjola (Fin) 6607pts
1932	James Bausch (US) 6735pts
1936	Glenn Morris (US) 7254pts
1948	Robert Mathias (US) 6628pts
1952	Robert Mathias (US) 7580pts
1956	Milton Campbell (US) 7565 pts
1960	Rafer Johnson (US) 7901pts
1964	Willi Holdorf (FRG) 7726pts est
1968	Bill Toomey (US) 8158pts
1972	Nikolai Avilov (USSR) 8466pts
1976	Bruce Jenner (US) 8634pts
1980	Daley Thompson (GB) 8522pts
1984	Daley Thompson (GB) 8847pts
1988	Christian Schenk (GDR) 8488pts

† *Thorpe disqualified for professionalism, and gold medal awarded to Hugo Weislander (Swe) 5965. Thorpe was posthumously re-instated in 1982.*

Women

100 Metres

1928	Elizabeth Robinson (US) 12.2s
1932	Stanislawa Walasiewicz (Pol) 11.9s
1936	Helen Stephens (US) 11.5s
1948	Fanny Blankers-Koen (Hol) 11.9s
1952	Marjorie Jackson (Aus) 11.65s
1956	Betty Cuthbert (Aus) 11.82s
1960	Wilma Rudolph (US) 11.08s
1964	Wyomia Tyus (US) 11.49s
1968	Wyomia Tyus (US) 11.08s
1972	Renate Stecher (GDR) 11.07s
1976	Annegret Richter (FRG) 11.08s
1980	Lyudmila Kondratyeva (USSR) 11.06s
1984	Evelyn Ashford (US) 10.97s
1988	Florence Griffith-Joyner (US) 10.54s

200 Metres

1948	Fanny Blankers-Koen (Hol) 24.4s
1952	Marjorie Jackson (Aus) 23.89s
1956	Betty Cuthbert (Aus) 23.55s
1960	Wilma Rudoph (US) 24.03s
1964	Edith Maguire (US) 23.05s

1968 Irena Szewinska (Pol) 22.58s
1972 Renate Stecher (GDR) 22.40s
1976 Barbel Eckert (GDR) 22.37s
1980 Barbel Wockel (née Eckert) (GDR) 22.03s
1984 Valerie Brisco-Hooks (US) 21.81s
1988 Florence Griffith-Joyner (US) 21.34s

400 Metres
1964 Betty Cuthbert (Aus) 52.01s
1968 Colette Besson (Fra) 52.03s
1972 Monika Zehrt (GDR) 51.08s
1976 Irena Szewinska (Pol) 49.29s
1980 Marita Koch (GDR) 48.88s
1984 Valerie Brisco-Hooks (US) 48.83s
1988 Olga Bryzgina (USSR) 48.65s

800 Metres
1928 Lina Radke (Ger) 2m 16.8s
1960 Lyudmila Shevtsova (USSR) 2m 04.50s
1964 Ann Packer (GB) 2m 01.1s
1968 Madeline Manning (US) 2m 00.92s
1972 Hildegard Falck (FRG) 1m 58.55s
1976 Tatyana Kazankina (USSR) 1m 54.94s
1980 Nadezhda Olizarenko (USSR) 1m 53.43s
1984 Doina Melinte (Rom) 1m 57.60s
1988 Sigrun Wodars (GDR) 1m 56.10s

1500 Metres
1972 Lyudmila Bragina (USSR) 4m 01.38s
1976 Tatyana Kazankina (USSR) 4m 05.48s
1980 Tatyana Kazankina (USSR) 3m 56.56s
1984 Gabriella Doria (Ita) 4m 03.25s
1988 Paula Ivan (Rom) 3m 53.96s

3000 Metres
1984 Maricica Puica (Rom) 8m 35.96s
1988 Tatyana Samolenko (USSR) 8m 26.53s

10,000 Metres
1988 Olga Bondarenko (USSR) 31m 05.21s

Marathon
1984 Joan Benoit (US) 2h 24m 52s
1988 Rosa Mota (Por) 2h 25m 40s

100 Metres Hurdles
(80 metres 1936-68)
1932 Mildred Didrikson (US) 11.7s
1936 Trebisonda Valla (Ita) 11.74s
1948 Fanny Blankers-Koen (Hol) 11.2s
1952 Shirley Strickland (Aus) 11.03s
1956 Shirley Strickland (Aus) 10.96s
1960 Irina Press (USSR) 10.94s
1964 Karin Balzar (GDR) 10.54s
1968 Maureen Caird (Aus) 10.39s
1972 Annelie Ehrhardt (GDR) 12.59s
1976 Johanna Schaller (GDR) 12.77s
1980 Vera Komisova (USSR) 12.56s
1984 Benita Fitzgerald-Brown (US) 12.84s
1988 Jordanka Donkova (Bul) 12.38s

400 Metres Hurdles
1984 Nawal el Moutawakil (Mor) 54.61s
1988 Debbie Flintoff-King (Aus) 53.17s

4 x 100 Metres Relay
1928 Canada 48.4s
1932 United States 47.0s
1936 United States 46.9s
1948 Netherlands 47.5s
1952 United States 46.14s
1956 Australia 44.65s
1960 United States 44.72s
1964 Poland 43.69s
1968 United States 42.87s
1972 West Germany 42.81s
1976 East Germany 42.55s
1980 East Germany 41.60s
1984 United States 41.65s
1988 United States 41.98s

4 x 400 Metres Relay
1972 East Germany 3m 22.95s
1976 East Germany 3m 19.23s
1980 USSR 3m 20.12s
1984 United States 3m 18.29s
1988 USSR 3m 15.18s

High Jump
1928 Ethel Catherwood (Can) 1.59m
1932 Jean Shiley (US) 1.65m
1936 Ibolya Csak (Hun) 1.60m
1948 Alice Coachman (US) 1.68m
1952 Esther Brand (SA) 1.67m
1956 Mildred McDaniel (US) 1.76m
1960 Iolanda Balas (Rom) 1.85m
1964 Iolanda Balas (Rom) 1.90m
1968 Miloslava Rezkova (Cze) 1.82m
1972 Ulrike Meyfarth (FRG) 1.92m
1976 Rosi Ackermann (GDR) 1.93m
1980 Sara Simeoni (Ita) 1.97m
1984 Ulrike Meyfarth (FRG) 2.02m
1988 Louise Ritter (US) 2.03m

Long Jump
1948 Olga Gyarmati (Hun) 5.69m
1952 Yvette Williams (NZ) 6.24m
1956 Elzbieta Krzesinska (Pol) 6.35m
1960 Vyera Krepkina (USSR) 6.37m
1964 Mary Rand (GB) 6.76m
1968 Viorica Viscopoleanu (Rom) 6.82m
1972 Heide Rosendahl (FRG) 6.78m
1976 Angela Voigt (GDR) 6.72m
1980 Tatyana Kolpakova (USSR) 7.06m
1984 Anisora Stanciu (Rom) 6.96m
1988 Jackie Joyner-Kersee (US) 7.40m

Shot
1948 Micheline Ostermeyer (Fra) 13.75m
1952 Galina Zybina (USSR) 15.28m
1956 Tamara Tishkyevich (USSR) 16.59m
1960 Tamara Press (USSR) 17.32m
1964 Tamara Press (USSR) 18.14m
1968 Margitta Gummel (GDR) 19.61m
1972 Nadezhda Chizhova (USSR) 21.03m
1976 Ivanka Khristova (Bul) 21.16m
1980 Ilona Slupianek (GDR) 22.41m
1984 Claudia Losch (FRG) 20.48m
1988 Natalya Lisovskaya (USSR) 22.24m

Discus
1928 Helena Konopacka (Pol) 39.62m
1932 Lillian Copeland (US) 40.58m
1936 Gisela Mauermayer (Ger) 47.63m
1948 Micheline Ostermeyer (Fra) 41.92m
1952 Nina Ponomaryeva (USSR) 51.42m
1956 Olga Fikotova (Cze) 53.69m
1960 Nina Ponomaryeva (USSR) 55.10m
1964 Tamara Press (USSR) 57.27m
1968 Lia Manoliu (Rom) 58.28m
1972 Faina Melnik (USSR) 66.62m
1976 Evelin Schlaak (GDR) 69.00m
1980 Evelin Jahl (née Schlaak) (GDR) 69.96m
1984 Ria Stalmach (Hol) 65.36m
1988 Martina Hellman (GDR) 72.30m

Javelin
1932 Mildred Didrikson (US) 43.68m
1936 Tilly Fleischer (Ger) 45.18m
1948 Herma Bauma (Aut) 45.57m
1952 Dana Zatopkova (Cze) 50.47m
1956 Inese Jaunzeme (USSR) 53.86m
1960 Elvira Ozolina (USSR) 55.98m
1964 Mihaela Penes (Rom) 60.54m
1968 Angela Nemeth (Hun) 60.36m
1972 Ruth Fuchs (GDR) 63.88m
1976 Ruth Fuchs (GDR) 65.94m
1980 Maria Colon (Cub) 68.40m

| 1984 | Tessa Sanderson (GB) 69.56m |
| 1988 | Petra Felke (GDR) 74.68m |

Pentathlon
1964	Irina Press (USSR) 5246pts
1968	Ingrid Becker (FRG) 5098pts
1972	Mary Peters (GB) 4801pts
1976	Sigrun Siegl (GDR) 4745pts
1980	Nadezhda Tkachenko (USSR) 5083pts

Heptathlon
| 1984 | Glynis Nunn (Aus) 6390pts |
| 1988 | Jackie Joyner-Kersee (US) 7291pts |

SAID AOUITA'S WORLD RECORDS

23 Aug 1985: 1500 metres 3m 29.46s; Berlin
28 May 1987: 2 miles 8m 13.45s; Turin
16 Jul 1987: 2000 metres 4m 50.81s; Paris
22 Jul 1987: 5000 metres 12m 58.39s; Rome
20 Aug 1989: 3000 metres 7m 29.45s; Cologne.

WORLD CHAMPIONSHIPS
Inaugurated 1983

Men	1983, Helsinki	1987, Rome
100m:	Carl Lewis (US) 10.07s	Ben Johnson (Can) 9.83s
200m:	Calvin Smith (US) 20.14s	Calvin Smith (US) 20.16s
400m:	Bert Cameron (Jam) 45.05s	Thomas Schoenlebe (GDR) 44.33s
800m:	Willi Wullbeck (FRG) 1m 43.65s	Billy Konchellah (Ken) 1m 43.06s
1500m:	Steve Cram (GB) 3m 41.59s	Abdi Bile (Som) 3m 36.80s
5000m:	Eamonn Coghlan (Ire) 13m 28.53s	Said Aouita (Mor) 13m 26.44s
10,000m:	Alberto Cova (Ita) 28m 01.04s	Paul Kipkoech (Ken) 27m 38.63s
Marathon:	Rob de Castella (Aus) 2h 10m 03s	Douglas Wakiihuri (Ken) 2h 11m 48s
3000m S/chase:	Patriz Ilg (FRG) 8m 15.06s	Francesco Panetta (Ita) 8m 08.57s
110m Hurdles:	Greg Foster (US) 13.42s	Greg Foster (US) 13.21s
400m Hurdles:	Edwin Moses (US) 47.50s	Edwin Moses (US) 47.46s
20km Walk:	Ernesto Canto (Mex) 1h 20m 49s	Maurizio Damilano (Ita) 1h 20m 45s
50km Walk:	Ronald Weigel (GDR) 3h 43m 08s	Hartwig Gauder (GDR) 3h 40m 53m
4 x 100m Relay:	United States 37.86s	United States 37.90s
4 x 400m Relay:	USSR 3m 00.79s	United States 2m 57.29s
High Jump:	Gennadiy Avdeyenko (USSR) 2.32m	Patrik Sjoberg (Swe) 2.38m
Long Jump:	Carl Lewis (US) 8.55m	Carl Lewis (US) 8.67m
Triple Jump:	Zdzislaw Hoffmann (Pol) 17.42m	Hristo Markov (Bul) 17.92m
Pole Vault:	Sergey Bubka (USSR) 5.70m	Sergey Bubka (USSR) 5.85m
Shot:	Edward Sarul (Pol) 21.29m	Werner Guenthoer (Swi) 22.23m
Javelin:	Detlef Michel (GDR) 89.48m	Seppo Raty (Fin) 83.54m
Discus:	Imrich Bugar (Cze) 67.72m	Jurgen Schult (GDR) 68.74m
Hammer:	Sergey Litvinov (USSR) 82.68m	Sergey Litvinov (USSR) 83.06m
Decathlon:	Daley Thompson (GB) 8714pts	Torsten Voss (GDR) 8680pts

Women	1983, Helsinki	1987, Rome
100m:	Marlies Gohr (GDR) 10.97s	Silke Gladisch (GDR) 10.90s
200m:	Marita Koch (GDR) 22.13s	Silke Gladisch (GDR) 21.74s
400m:	Jarmila Kratochvilova (Cze) 47.99s	Olga Bryzgina (USSR) 49.38s
800m:	Jarmila Kratochvilova (Cze) 1m 54.68s	Sigrun Wodars (GDR) 1m 55.26s
1500m:	Mary Decker (US) 4m 00.90s	Tatyana Samolenko (USSR) 3m 58.56s
3000m:	Mary Decker (US) 8m 34.62s	Tatyana Samolenko (USSR) 8m 38.73s
Marathon:	Greta Waitz (Nor) 2h 28m 09s	Rosa Mota (Por) 2h 25m 17s
100m Hurdles:	Bettina Jahn (GDR) 12.35s	Ginka Zagorcheva (Bul) 12.34s
400m Hurdles:	Ekaterina Fesenko (USSR) 54.14s	Sabine Busche (GDR) 53.62s
4 x 100m Relay:	East Germany 41.76s	United States 41.58s
4 x 400m Relay:	East Germany 3m 19.73s	East Germany 3m 18.63s
High Jump:	Tamara Bykova (USSR) 2.01m	Stefka Kostadinova (Bul) 2.09m
Long Jump:	Heike Daute (GDR) 7.27m	Jackie Joyner-Kersee (US) 7.36m
Shot:	Helena Fibingerova (Cze) 21.05m	Natalya Lisovskaya (USSR) 21.24m
Discus:	Martina Opitz (GDR) 68.94m	Martina Hellman (GDR) 71.62m
Javelin:	Tiina Lillak (Fin) 70.82m	Fatima Whitbread (GB) 76.64m
Heptathlon:	Ramona Neubert (GDR) 6770pts	Jackie Joyner-Kersee (US) 7128pts

WORLD CUP

1977 Düsseldorf

Men		Women	
1 East Germany	127pts	Europe	107pts
2 United States	120pts	East Germany	102pts
3 West Germany	112pts	USSR	89pts
4 Europe	111pts	United States	59pts
5 Americas	92pts	Americas	55pts
6 Oceania	48pts	Oceania	45pts
7 Africa	46pts	Africa	31pts
8 Asia	44pts	Asia	29pts

1979 Montreal

Men		Women	
1 United States	119pts	East Germany	106pts
2 Europe	112pts	USSR	98pts
3 East Germany	108pts	Europe	88pts
4 USSR	102pts	United States	76pts
5 Americas	98pts	Americas	68pts
6 Africa	84pts	Oceania	47pts
7 Oceania	58pts	Africa	30pts
8 Asia	36pts	Asia	26pts

1981 Rome

Men		Women	
1 Europe	147pts	East Germany	120.5pts
2 East Germany	130pts	Europe	110pts
3 United States	127pts	USSR	98pts
4 USSR	118pts	United States	89pts
5 Americas	95pts	Americas	72pts
6 Italy	93pts	Italy	68.5pts
7 Africa	66pts	Oceania	58pts
8 Oceania	62pts	Asia	32pts
9 Asia	59pts	Africa	26pts

1985 Canberra

1 United States	123pts	East Germany	121pts
2 USSR	115pts	USSR	105.5pts
3 East Germany	114pts	Europe	86pts
4 Europe	97.5pts	Americas	62.5pts
5 Africa	81pts	United States	61pts
6 Americas	80pts	Oceania	52pts
7 Oceania	65pts	Asia	42pts
8 Asia	39.5pts	Africa	41pts

1989 Barcelona

1 United States	133pts	East Germany	124pts
2 Europe	127pts	USSR	106pts
3 Great Britain	119pts	Americas	94pts
4 East Germany	116.5pts	Europe	89pts
5 Africa	107pts	United States	84.5pts
6 Americas	97pts	Asia	67.5pts
7 Asia	68.5pts	Africa	58pts
8 Spain	64.5pts	Spain	48pts
9 Oceania	64.5pts	Oceania	40pts

BRITISH WINNERS AT THE WORLD CUP

Representing Britain
Men:

Linford Christie,	100 metres,	1989
Tom McKean,	800 metres,	1989
Steve Backley,	javelin,	1989

Representing Europe
Men:

Steve Ovett,	1500 metres,	1977 1981
Alian Wells,	100 metres,	1981
Sebastian Coe,	800 metres,	1981
Women:		
Yvonne Murray,	3000 metres,	1989
Sonia Lannaman,		
Andrea Lynch,	4 x 100 metre relay,	1977
Heather Hunte,	4 x 400 metres relay,	1979

EUROPEAN CUP
Winners

	Men	Women
1965	USSR	USSR
1967	USSR	USSR
1970	East Germany	East Germany
1973	USSR	East Germany
1975	East Germany	East Germany
1977	East Germany	East Germany
1979	East Germany	East Germany
1981	East Germany	East Germany
1983	East Germany	East Germany
1985	USSR	USSR
1987	USSR	East Germany
1989	Great Britain	East Germany

IAAF/MOBIL GRAND PRIX

	Men	Women
1985	Doug Padilla (US)	Mary Slaney (US)
1986	Said Aouita (Mor)	Yordanka Donkova (Bul)
1987	Tonie Campbell (US)	Merlene Ottey (Jam)
1988	Said Aouita (Mor)	Paula Ivan (Rom)
1989	Said Aouita (Mor)	Paula Ivan (Rom)

MARATHON WORLD CUP
Inaugurated 1985
Men

	Individual	Team
1985	Ahmed Saleh (Dji)	Djibouti
1987	Ahmed Saleh (Dji)	Italy
1989	Keleke Metafeira (Eth)	Ethiopia

Women

	Individual	Team
1985	Katrine Dorre (GDR)	Italy
1987	Zoya Ivanova (USSR)	USSR
1989	Sue Marchiano (US)	USSR

LONDON MARATHON
Men

1981	Dick Beardsley (US) & Inge Simonsen (Nor)	2h 11m 48s
1982	Hugh Jones (GB)	2h 09m 24s
1983	Mike Gratton (GB)	2h 09m 43s
1984	Charlie Spedding (GB)	2h 09m 57s
1985	Steve Jones (GB)	2h 08m 16s
1986	Toshihiko Seko (Jap)	2h 10m 02s
1987	Hiromi Taniguchi (Jap)	2h 09m 50s
1988	Henryk Jorgensen (Den)	2h 10m 20s
1989	Douglas Wakiihuri (Ken)	2h 09m 03s

Women

1981	Joyce Smith (GB)	2h 29m 57s
1982	Joyce Smith (GB)	2h 29m 43s
1983	Grete Waitz (Nor)	2h 25m 29s
1984	Ingrid Kristiansen (Nor)	2h 24m 26s
1985	Ingrid Kristiansen (Nor)	2h 21m 06s
1986	Grete Waitz (Nor)	2h 24m 54s
1987	Ingrid Kristiansen (Nor)	2h 22m 48s
1988	Ingrid Kristiansen (Nor)	2h 25m 41s
1989	Veronique Marot (GB)	2h 25m 56s

WORLD CROSS COUNTRY CHAMPIONS
Winners since 1980
Men

	Individual	Team
1980	Craig Virgin (US)	England
1981	Craig Virgin (US)	Ethiopia
1982	Mohamed Kedir (Eth)	Ethiopia
1983	Bekele Debele (Eth)	Ethiopia
1984	Carlos Lopes (Por)	Ethiopia
1985	Carlos Lopes (Por)	Ethiopia
1986	John Ngugi (Ken)	Kenya
1987	John Ngugi (Ken)	Kenya
1988	John Ngugi (Ken)	Kenya
1989	John Ngugi (Ken)	Kenya

Women

	Individual	Team
1980	Grete Waitz (Nor)	USSR
1981	Grete Waitz (Nor)	USSR
1982	Maricica Puica (Rom)	USSR
1983	Grete Waitz (Nor)	United States
1984	Maricica Puica (Rom)	United States
1985	Zola Budd (Eng)	United States
1986	Zola Budd (Eng)	England
1987	Annette Sergent (Fra)	United States
1988	Ingrid Kristiansen (Nor)	USSR
1989	Annette Sergent (Fra)	USSR

RECORDS

WORLD OUTDOOR RECORDS
(September 1989)

Men

100m:	9.92s Carl Lewis (US); Seoul, Sep 24 1988*
200m:	19.72s Pietro Mennea (Ita); Mexico City, Sep 12, 1979
400m:	43.29s Harry Reynolds (US); Zürich, Aug 17, 1988
800m:	1m 41.73s Sebastian Coe (GB); Florence, Jun 10, 1981
1000m:	2m 12.18s Sebastian Coe (GB); Oslo, Jul 11, 1981
1500m:	3m 29.46s Said Aouita (Mor); Berlin, Aug 23, 1985
Mile:	3m 46.32s Steve Cram (GB); Oslo, Jul 27, 1985
2000m:	4m 50.81s Said Aouita (Mor); Paris, Jul 16, 1987
3000m:	7m 29.45s Said Aouita (Mor); Cologne, Aug 20, 1989
5000m:	12m 58.39s Said Aouita (Mor); Rome, Jul 27, 1987
10,000m:	27m 08.23s Arturo Barrios (Mex); Berlin, Aug 18, 1989
20,000m:	57m 24.2s Jos Hermens (Hol); Papendal, Holland, May 1, 1976
1 Hour:	20,994 metres Jos Hermens (Hol); Papendal, Holland, May 1, 1976
25,000m:	1h 13m 55.8s Toshihiko Seko (Jap); Christchurch, NZ, Mar 22, 1981
30,000m:	1h 29m 18.8s Toshihiko Seko (Jap); Christchurch, NZ, Mar 22, 1981
110m Hdles:	12.92s Roger Kingdom (US); Zürich, Aug 16, 1989
400m Hdles:	47.02s Edwin Moses (US); Koblenz, Aug 31, 1983
3000m S/chase:	8m 05.35s Peter Koech (Ken); Stockholm, Jul 3, 1989
4 x 100m Relay:	37.83s United States; Los Angeles, Aug 11, 1984
4 x 200m Relay:	1m 20.26s Univ. of S. California; Tempe, Arizona, May 27, 1978
4 x 400m Relay:	2m 56.16s United States; Mexico City, Oct 20, 1968
	2m 56.16s United States; Seoul, Oct 1 1988
4 x 800m Relay:	7m 03.89s Great Britain; London, Aug 30, 1982
4 x 1500m Relay:	West Germany; Cologne, Aug 17, 1977
High Jump:	2.44m Javier Sotomayor (Cub); San Juan, Puerto Rico, Jul 30 1989
Pole Vault:	6.06m Sergey Bubka (USSR); Nice, Jul 10, 1988
Long Jump:	8.90m Bob Beamon (US); Mexico City, Oct 18, 1968
Triple Jump:	17.97m Willie Banks (US); Indianapolis, Jun 16, 1985
Shot:	23.06m Ulf Timmermann (GDR); Hania, May 22, 1988
Discus:	74.08m Jürgen Schult (GDR); Neubrandenburg, GDR, Jun 6, 1986
Hammer:	86.74m Yuriy Sedykh (USSR); Stuttgart, Aug 30, 1986
Javelin:	87.66m Jan Zelezny (Cze); Nitra, Czechoslovakia, May 31, 1987
Decathlon:	8847pts Daley Thompson (GB); Los Angeles, Aug 8/9, 1984
Marathon (†):	2h 06m 50s Belayneh Dinsamo (Eth); Rotterdam, Apr 17, 1988

NEW WORLD RECORDS IN 1989

Men

3000m Steeplechase
New Record: 8m 05.35s Peter Koech (Ken); Stockholm, Jul 3, 1989
Old Record: 8m 05.40s Henry Rono (Ken); Seattle, May 13, 1978

High Jump
New Record: 2.44m Javier Sotomayor (Cub); San Juan, Puerto Rico, Jul 30, 1989
Old Record: 2.43m Javier Sotomayor (Cub); Salamanca, Cuba, Sep 8, 1988

110 Metres Hurdles
New Record: 12.92s Roger Kingdom (US); Zurich, Aug 16, 1989
Old Record: 12.93s Renaldo Nehemiah (US); Zurich, Aug 19, 1981

10,000 Metres
New Record: 27m 08.23s Arturo Barrios (Mex); Berlin, Aug 18, 1989
Old Record: 27m 13.81s Fernando Mamede (Por); Stockholm, Jul 2, 1984

3000 Metres
New Record: 7m 29.45s Said Aouita (Mor); Cologne, Aug 20, 1989
Old Record: 7m 32.10s Henry Rono (Ken); Oslo, Jun 27, 1978

Women

Mile
New Record: 4m 15.61s Paula Ivan (Rom); Nice, Jul 10, 1989
Old Record: 4m 16.71s Mary Decker-Slaney (US); Zurich, Aug 21, 1985

Women

100m:	10.49s Florence Griffith-Joyner (US); Indianapolis, Jul 16, 1988
200m:	21.34s Florence Griffith-Joyner (US); Seoul, Sep 29, 1988
400m:	47.60s Marita Koch (GDR); Canberra, Oct 6, 1985
800m:	1m 53.28s Jarmila Kratochvilova (Cze); Munich, Jul 26, 1983
1500m:	3m 52.47s Tatyana Kazankina (USSR); Zürich, Aug 13, 1980
Mile:	4m 15.61s Paula Ivan (Rom); Nice, Jul 10, 1989
2000m:	5m 28.69s Maricica Puica (Rom); London, Jul 11, 1986
3000m:	8m 22.62s Tatyana Kazankini (USSR); Leningrad, Aug 26, 1984
5000m:	14m 37.33s Ingrid Kristiansen (Nor); Stockholm, Aug 5, 1986
10,000m:	30m 13.74s Ingrid Kristiansen (Nor); Oslo, Jul 5, 1986
20,000m:	1h 29m 29.2s Karolina Szabo (Hun); Budapest, Apr 22, 1988
30,000m:	1h 49m 05.6s Karolina Szabo (Hun); Budapest, Apr 22, 1988
100m Hurdles:	12.21s Yordanka Donkova (Bul); Stara Zagora, Bul, Aug 20, 1988
400m Hurdles:	52.94s Marina Stepanova (USSR); Tashkent, Sep 17, 1986
4 x 100m Relay:	41.37s East Germany; Canberra, Oct 6, 1985
4 x 200m Relay:	1m 28.15s East Germany; Jena, GDR, Aug 9, 1980
4 x 400m Relay:	3m 15.17s USSR; Seoul, Oct 1, 1988
4 x 800m Relay:	7m 50. 17s USSR; Moscow, Aug 5, 1984
High Jump:	2.09m Stefka Kostadinova (Bul); Rome, Aug 30, 1987
Long Jump:	7.52m Galina Chistyakova (USSR); Leningrad, Jun 11, 1988
Shot:	22.63m Natalya Lisovskaya (USSR); Moscow, Jun 7, 1987
Discus:	76.80m Gabriele Reinsch (GDR); Neubrandenburg, GDR, Jul 9, 1988
Javelin:	80.00m Petra Felke (GDR); Potsdam, GDR, Sep 9, 1988
Heptathlon:	7,291pts Jackie Joyner-Kersee (US); Seoul, Sep 23/24, 1988
Marathon (†):	2h 21m 06s Ingrid Kristiansen (Nor); London, Apr 21, 1985

† *World records not recognised for the Marathon, only best time*
* *Unofficial record pending formal removal of Ben Johnson's 9.83s*

UP TO EIGHT FEET: WORLD HIGH JUMP ALTIMETER

MILESTONES

First 6 ft
1.83m Hon. Marshall Brooks (GB) Mar 17, 1876

First 7 ft
2.15m Charles Dumas (US) Jun 29, 1956

7 ft 3 in
2.22m John Thomas (US) Jul 1, 1960

First 7 ft 6 in
2.29m Patrick Matzdorf (US) Jul 3, 1971

First 7 ft 9 in
2.38m Jianhua Zhu (Chn) Sep 22, 1983

First 8 ft
2.44m Javier Sotomayor (Cub) Jul 30, 1989

TOWARDS SEVEN FEET: WOMEN'S HIGH JUMP MARKS

First 6 ft
1.83m Iolanda Balas (Rom) Oct 18, 1958

First 6 ft 3 in
1.91m Iolanda Balas (Rom) Jul 16, 1961

First 6 ft 6 in
2.00m Rosie Ackermann (GDR) Aug 26, 1977

First 6 ft 9 in
2.07m Ludmilla Andonova (Bul) Jul 20, 1984

Current Record
2.09m Stefka Kostadinova (Bul) Aug 30, 1987

1990

FIXTURES

Mar 3-4: European Indoor Championships (Kelvin Hall, Glasgow); Mar 25: World Cross-country championships (Aix Les-Bains, France); Apr 22: London Marathon; May 7: Belfast Marathon; Jul 6: Grand Prix meeting (Edinburgh); Jul 20: Grand Prix meeting (Crystal Palace); Aug 8-12 World Junior championships (Plovdiv, Bulgaria); Aug 27-Sep 1: 15th EUROPEAN CHAMPIONSHIPS (Split, Yugoslavia).

AUSTRALIAN RULES FOOTBALL

1989

VICTORIA FOOTBALL LEAGUE (VFL) CHAMPIONSHIP
Final League Positions

		P	W	L	Pts
1	Hawthorn	22	19	3	76
2	Essendon	22	17	5	68
3	Geelong	22	16	6	64
4	Melbourne	22	14	8	56
5	Collingwood	22	13	9	52
6	Fitzroy	22	12	10	48
7	Sydney	22	11	11	44
8	Carlton	22	9	12	38
9	Nth Melbourne	22	9	13	36
10	Brisbane	22	8	14	32
11	West Coast	22	7	15	28
12	St Kilda	22	7	15	28
13	Footscray	22	6	15	26
14	Richmond	22	5	17	20

Play-offs
Elimination Final
Melbourne beat Collingwood 133-88
Qualifying Final
Essendon beat Geelong 157-77
Semi-finals
Geelong beat Melbourne 153-99
Hawthorn beat Essendon 112-76
Preliminary Final
Geelong beat Essendon 164-70
Grand Final
Melbourne Cricket Ground, September 30
Hawthorn beat Geelong 144-138

CHAMPIONS

VICTORIA FOOTBALL LEAGUE GRAND FINAL
Winners

1897	Essendon
1898	Fitzroy
1899	Fitzroy
1900	Melbourne
1901	Essendon
1902	Collingwood
1903	Collingwood
1904	Fitzroy
1905	Fitzroy
1906	Carlton
1907	Carlton
1908	Carlton
1909	South Melbourne
1910	Collingwood
1911	Essendon
1912	Essendon
1913	Fitzroy
1914	Carlton
1915	Carlton
1916	Fitzroy
1917	Collingwood
1918	South Melbourne
1919	Collingwood
1920	Richmond
1921	Richmond
1922	Fitzroy
1923	Essendon
1924	Essendon
1925	Geelong
1926	Melbourne
1927	Collingwood
1928	Collingwood
1929	Collingwood
1930	Collingwood
1931	Geelong
1932	Richmond
1933	South Melbourne
1934	Richmond
1935	Collingwood
1936	Collingwood
1937	Geelong
1938	Carlton
1939	Melbourne
1940	Melbourne
1941	Melbourne
1942	Essendon
1943	Richmond
1944	Fitzroy
1945	Carlton
1946	Essendon
1947	Carlton
1948	Melbourne
1949	Essendon
1950	Essendon
1951	Geelong
1952	Geelong
1953	Collingwood
1954	Footscray
1955	Melbourne
1956	Melbourne
1957	Melbourne
1958	Collingwood
1959	Melbourne
1960	Melbourne
1961	Hawthorn
1962	Essendon
1963	Geelong
1964	Melbourne
1965	Essendon
1966	St Kilda
1967	Richmond
1968	Carlton
1969	Richmond
1970	Carlton
1971	Hawthorn
1972	Carlton
1973	Richmond
1974	Richmond
1975	North Melbourne
1976	Hawthorn
1977	North Melbourne
1978	Hawthorn
1979	Carlton
1980	Richmond
1981	Carlton
1982	Carlton
1983	Hawthorn
1984	Essendon
1985	Essendon
1986	Hawthorn
1987	Carlton
1988	Hawthorn
1989	Hawthorn

Wins
15 Carlton; **14** Essendon; **13** Collingwood; **12** Melbourne; **10** Richmond; **8** Fitzroy, Hawthorn; **6** Geelong; **3** South Melbourne; **2** North Melbourne; **1** Footscray, St Kilda

BADMINTON

1989

WORLD CHAMPIONSHIPS
Jakarta, May 28-Jun 4

Men's singles

QUARTER-FINALS
Yang Yang (Chn) beat Paul-Erik Hoyer Larsen (Den) 15-11 17-15; I Sugiarto (Ina) beat Zhao Jianhua (Chn) 15-8 1-15 17-15; Eddie Kurniawan (Ina) beat Xiong Guobao (Chn) 15-10 15-13; Ardi Wiranata (Ina) beat Hermawan Susanto (Ina) 15-8 15-10

SEMI-FINALS
Yang Yang beat Sugiarto 13-15 15-7 15-9; Wiranata beat Kurniawan 14-18 15-10 15-13

FINAL
Yang Yang beat Wiranata 15-10 2-15 15-5

Women's singles

QUARTER-FINALS
Li Lingwei (Chn) beat C Magnusson (Swe) 10-12 11-2 11-6; Tang Juihong (Chn) beat E Rybkina (USSR) 11-2 11-5; Huang Hua (Chn) beat Susi Susanti (Ina) 11-5 11-6; Sarwendah Kusumawardhani (Ina) beat Eline Coene (Hol) 11-6 6-11 11-7

SEMI-FINALS
Li Lingwei beat Tang Juihong 6-11 11-8 11-2; Huang Hua beat Kusumawardhani 8-11 11-7 11-2

FINAL
Li Lingwei beat Huang Hua 11-6 12-9

Men's doubles

FINAL
Tian Bingyi/Lin Yongbo beat Kang/Hongyong 15-3 15-12

Women's doubles

FINAL
Guan Weizhan/Lin Ying beat Chung Myung Hee/Hwang Hye Young 15-1 15-7

Mixed doubles

FINAL
Park Joo Bong/Chung Myung Hee beat Hartono/Farjin 15-9 15-9

YONEX ALL-ENGLAND CHAMPIONSHIPS
Wembley, Mar15-19

Men's singles

QUARTER-FINALS
Yang Yang (Chn) beat A Kusuma (Ina) 15-9 15-5 Poul-Erik Hoyer Larsen (Den) beat Darren Hall (GB) 15-2 17-18 17-14; Ardi Wiranata (Ina) beat Steve Baddeley (GB) 15-5 10-15 15-11; Morten Frost (Den) beat Eddie Kurniawan (Ina) 15-8 15-8

SEMI-FINALS
Frost beat Wiranata 15-5 15-7; Yang Yang beat Hoyer Larsen 15-4 18-13

FINAL
Yang Yang beat Frost 15-6 15-7

Women's singles

QUARTER-FINALS
Li Lingwei (Chn) beat K Larsen (Den) 11-3 11-0; Lee Yung Suk (SKo) beat C Hattens (Den) 11-2 11-2; Susi Susanti (Ina) beat P Nedergaard (Den) 12-9 11-9; Hwang Hye Young (SKo) beat A Van Der Knaap (Hol) 9-12 11-6 12-9

SEMI-FINALS
Li-Lingwei beat Lee Yung Suk 10-12 11-7 11-2; Susi Susanti beat Hwang Hye Young 3-11 11-6 11-8

FINAL
Li Lingwei beat Susanti 11-8 11-4

Men's doubles

QUARTER-FINALS
R Gunawan/E Hartono (Ina) beat Cheah Soon Kit/Ong Beng Leong (Mal) 17-15 15-7; Lee Sang Bok/Park Joo Bong (SKo) beat J-E Antonsson/P-G Johnsson (Swe) 15-2 15-6; J & R Sidek (Mal) beat J Paulsen/H Svarrer (Den) 15-9 15-6; Li Yongho/Tian Bingyi (Chn) beat M Christiansen/M Kjeldsen (Den) 15-8 15-5

SEMI-FINALS
Gunawan/Hartono beat Li Yongho/Tian Bingyi 5-15 17-15 17-14; Lee Sang Bok/Park Joo Bong beat J & R Sidek 15-11 15-11

FINAL
Lee Sang Bok/Park Joo Bong beat Gunawan/Hartono 15-8 15-7

Women's doubles

QUARTER-FINALS
V Fajrin/Y Kusmaitie (Ina) beat M & C Bengtsson (Swe) 15-3 15-11; Chung Myung Hee/Chung So Young (SKo) beat Li Lingwei/Shang Fume (Chn) 15-9 15-4; Sun Xiaoging/Zhou Lei (Chn) beat E Sulistianingsifi/R Tendean (Ina) 15-10 15-11; Eline Coene/Erica Van Dijck (Hol) beat G Clark/S Sankey (GB) 15-11 15-9

SEMI-FINALS
Chung Myung Hee/Chung So Young beat Fajrin/Kusmiatie 15-6 15-17 15-5; Sun Xiaoging/Zhou Lei beat Coene/Van Dijck 15-11 15-3

FINAL
Chung Myung Hee/Chung So Young beat Sun Xiaoging/Zhou Lei 15-7 15-4

Mixed Doubles

QUARTER-FINALS
J Paulsen (Den)/G Gowers (GB) beat D Wright/O Palmer (GB) 15-10 15-6; E Hartong/V Fajrin (Ina) beat Wang Pengren/Shi Fangjing (Chn) 12-15 15-11 15-9; J-E Antonsson/M Bengtsson (Swe) beat Kee Sang Bok/Chung So Young (SKo) 15-9 18-15; Park Joo Bong/Chung Myung Hee (SKo) beat H Svarrer/D Kjaer (Den) 15-4 15-7

SEMI-FINALS
Park Joo Bong/Chung Myung Hee beat Paulsen/Gowers 15-11 15-4; Antonsson/Bengtsson beat Hartono/Fajrin 15-6 12-15 17-14

FINAL
Park Joo Bong/Chung Hee beat Antonsson/Bengtsson 15-1 15-9

CHAMPIONS

MEN'S WORLD TEAM CHAMPIONSHIP
(For the Thomas Cup)

1949	Malaya
1952	Malaya
1955	Malaya
1958	Indonesia
1961	Indonesia
1964	Indonesia
1967	Malaysia
1970	Indonesia
1973	Indonesia
1976	Indonesia
1979	Indonesia
1982	China
1984	Indonesia
1986	China
1988	China

Most wins: 8 Indonesia

WOMEN'S WORLD TEAM CHAMPIONSHIP
(For the Uber Cup)

1957	United States
1960	United States
1963	United States
1966	Japan
1969	Japan
1972	Japan
1975	Indonesia
1978	Japan
1981	Japan
1984	China
1986	China
1988	China

Most wins: 5 Japan

WORLD CHAMPIONSHIPS
Men's singles

1977	Flemming Delfs (Den)
1980	Rudy Hartono (Ina)
1983	Icuk Sugiarto (Ina)
1985	Han Jian (Chn)
1987	Yang Yang (Chn)
1989	Yang Yang (Chn)

Women's singles

1977	Lene Koppen (Den)
1980	Wiharjo Verawaty (Ina)
1983	Li Lingwei (Chn)
1985	Han Aiping (Chn)
1987	Han Aiping (Chn)
1989	Li Lingwei (Chn)

Men's doubles

1977	Tjun Tjun & Johan Wahjudi (Ina)
1980	Ade Chandra & Hadinata Christian (Ina)
1983	Steen Fladberg & Jesper Helledie (Den)
1985	Park Joo Bong & Kim Moon Soo (SKo)
1987	Tian Bingyi & Li Yongbo (Chn)
1989	Tian Bingyi & Li Yongbo (Chn)

Women's doubles

1977	Etsuko Tuganoo & Emiko Vero (Jap)
1980	Nora Perry & Jane Webster (GB)
1983	Wu Dixi & Liu Ying (Chn)
1985	Han Aiping & Li Lingwei (Chn)
1987	Guan Weizhan & Lin Ying (Chn)
1989	Guan Weizhan & Lin Ying (Chn)

Mixed doubles

1987	Steen Stovgaard & Lene Koppen (Den)
1980	Hadinata Christian & Imelda Wigoeno (Ina)
1983	Thomas Kihlstrom (Swe) & Nora Perry (GB)
1985	Park Joo Bong & Yoo Sang Hee (SKo)
1987	Wang Pengrin & Shi Fangjing (Chn)
1989	Park Joo Bong & Chung Myung Hee (SKo)

Most titles: 3 Han Aiping, Li Limgwei, Lin Ying, Park Joo Bong

ALL-ENGLAND CHAMPIONSHIPS
Inaugurated 1899 for doubles only. Singles first held 1900.

Post-war winners
Men's Singles

1947	Conny Jepsen (Swe)
1948	Jörn Skaarup (Den)
1949	Dave Freeman (US)
1950	Wong Peng Soon (Mal)
1951	Wong Peng Soon (Mal)
1952	Wong Peng Soon (Mal)
1953	Eddie Choong (Mal)
1954	Eddie Choong (Mal)
1955	Wong Peng Soon (Mal)
1956	Eddie Choong (Mal)
1957	Eddie Choong (Mal)
1958	Erland Kops (Den)
1959	Tan Joe Hok (Ina)
1960	Erland Kops (Den)
1961	Erland Kops (Den)
1962	Erland Kops (Den)
1963	Erland Kops (Den)
1964	Knud Nielsen (Den)
1965	Erland Kops (Den)
1966	Tan Aik Huang (Mal)
1967	Erland Kops (Den)
1968	Rudy Hartono (Ina)
1969	Rudy Hartono (Ina)
1970	Rudy Hartono (Ina)
1971	Rudy Hartono (Ina)
1972	Rudy Hartono (Ina)
1973	Rudy Hartono (Ina)
1974	Rudy Hartono (Ina)
1975	Sven Pri (Den)
1976	Rudy Hartono (Ina)
1977	Flemming Delfs (Den)
1978	Liem Swie King (Ina)
1979	Liem Swie King (Ina)
1980	Prakash Padukone (Ind)
1981	Liem Swie King (Ina)
1982	Morten Frost (Den)
1983	Luan Jin (Chn)
1984	Morten Frost (Den)
1985	Zhao Jianhua (Chn)
1986	Morten Frost (Den)
1987	Morten Frost (Den)
1988	Ib Frederiksen (Den)
1989	Yang Yang (Chn)

Most wins:
8 Rudy Hartono; 6 Frank Devlin (Ire) 1925-29 1931, Erland Kops; 5 Ralph Nicholls (Eng) 1932, 1934, 1936-38; 4 George Thomas (Eng) 1920-23 Wong Peng Soon, Eddie Choong, Morten Frost

Women's singles

1947	Marie Ussing (Den)
1948	Kirsten Thorndahl (Den)
1949	Aase Jacobsen (Den)
1950	Tonny Olsen-Ahm (Den)
1951	Aase Jacoben (Den)
1952	Tonny Olsen-Ahm (Den)
1953	Marie Ussing (Den)
1954	Judy Devlin (US)
1955	Margaret Varner (US)
1956	Margaret Varner (US)
1957	Judy Devlin (US)
1958	Judy Devlin (US)

1959	Heather Ward (Eng)
1960	Judy Devlin (US)
1961	Judy Hashman (née Devlin) (US)
1962	Judy Hashman (US)
1963	Judy Hashman (US)
1964	Judy Hashman (US)
1965	Ursula Smith (Eng)
1966	Judy Hashman (US)
1967	Judy Hashman (US)
1968	Eva Twedberg (Swe)
1969	Hiroe Yuki (Jap)
1970	Etsuko Takenaka (Jap)
1971	Eva Twedberg (Swe)
1972	Noriko Nakayama (Jap)
1973	Margaret Beck (Eng)
1974	Hiroe Yuki (Jap)
1975	Hiroe Yuki (Jap)
1976	Gillian Gilks (Eng)
1977	Hiroe Yuki (Jap)
1978	Gillian Gilks (Eng)
1979	Lene Köppen (Den)
1980	Lene Köppen (Den)
1981	Sun Ai Hwang (SKo)
1982	Zang Ailing (Chn)
1983	Zang Ailing (Chn)
1984	Li Lingwei (Chn)
1985	Han Aiping (Chn)
1986	Kim Yun-Ja (SKo)
1987	Kirsten Larsen (Den)
1988	Gu Jiaming (Chn)
1989	Li Lingwei (Chn)

Most wins:

10 Judy Hashman (née Devlin); 6 Meriel Lucas (Eng) 1902, 1905, 1907-10; 5 Ethel Thomson (Eng) 1900-01, 1903-04, 1906, Marjorie Barrett (Eng) 1926-27, 1929-31; 4 Kitty McKane (Eng) 1920-22, 1924.

Winners since 1980
Men's Doubles

1980	Tjun Tjun & Johan Wahjudi (Ina)
1981	Hariamanto Kartono & Rudy Heryanto (Ina)
1982	Razif Sidek & Jalaini Sidek (Mal)
1983	Stefan Karisson & Thomas Kihlstrom (Swe)

1984	Hariamanto Kartono & Rudy Heryanto (Ina)
1985	Kim Moon-Soo & Park Joo-Bong (SKo)
1986	Kim Moon-Soo & Park Joo-Bong (SKo)
1987	Li Yongbo & Tian Bingyi (Chn)
1988	Li Yongbo & Tian Bingyi (Chn)
1989	Lee Sang Bok & Park Joo Bong (SKo)

Women's Doubles

1980	Gillian Gilks & Nora Perry (Eng)
1981	Nora Perry & Jane Webster (Eng)
1982	Lin Ying & Wu Dixi (Chn)
1983	Xu Rong & Wu Jiangiu (Chn)
1984	Lin Ying & Wu Dixi (Chn)
1985	Li Lingwei & Han Aiping (Chn)
1986	Chung Myung-Hee & Hwang Hye-Young (SKo)
1987	Chung Myung-Hee & Hwang Hye-Young (SKo)
1988	Chung So-Young & Kim Yun-Ja (SKo)
1989	Chung Myung-Hee & Chung So-Young (SKo)

Mixed Doubles

1980	Mike Tredgett & Nora Perry (Eng)
1981	Mike Tredgett & Nora Perry (Eng)
1982	Martin Dew & Gillian Gilks (Eng)
1983	Thomas Kihlstrom (Swe) & Nora Perry (Eng)
1984	Martin Dew & Gillian Gilks (Eng)
1985	Billy Gilliland & Nora Perry (Eng)
1986	Park Joo-Bong & Chung Myung-Hee (SKo)
1987	Lee Deuk-Choon & Chung Myung-Hee (SKo)
1988	Wang Pengren & Shi Fangjiing (Chn)
1989	Park Joo-Bong & Chung Myung-Hee (SKo)

Most Overall All-England titles:

21 George Thomas 1903-28; 18 Frank Devlin 1922-31; 17 Meriel Lucas 1899-1910, Judy Hashman (née Devlin) 1954-67

————— **1990** —————

Feb 23-25: Thomas and Uber Cups qualifying rounds (Villach, Austria and Kuala Lumpur); *Mar 12-13:* All-England Championships, qualifying rounds (Watford); *Mar 14-17:* All-England Championships (Wembley Arena); *May 25-27:* Thomas and Uber Cup finals (Tokyo); *Dec 14-16:* World Grand Prix finals (Singapore)

BASEBALL

ROSE AND FALL

The traditional autumn thrill of tight pennant races was overshadowed in 1989 by one of baseball's most sensational scandals. Pete Rose, manager of the Cincinnati Reds and the man with more major league hits than anyone else, was banned from the game for life for betting on his team's games.

This was the culmination of months of whispers and rumours and investigations and denials, with evidence constantly being produced and Rose constantly denying it. Although there was no suggestion that he had thrown games, Rose had broken a baseball rule posted in every clubhouse and a taboo dating back to the Black Sox scandal of 1919. He was the first person banned for life in 46 years. There was a hint of plea bargaining before the final decision and Rose was convinced he would be reinstated in 1990 when he can appeal. Others were less sure.

The man who pursued and punished Rose was A. Bartlett Giamatti, the former president of Yale University who became commissioner of baseball early in the year. Eight days after he announced the Rose decision and five months after taking office, Giamatti died of a heart attack. He was succeeded, without dissent, by his friend and deputy Francis R. "Fay" Vincent, the former chief executive of Columbia Pictures.

Even leaving Rose out of it, the season was notable for a succession of titillating scandalettes involving leading players in matters that did not come under the Commissioner's remit. This followed the revelations about Wade Boggs of the Red Sox's love life in 1988. These refused to go away. Margo Adams, Boggs's girlfriend, who sued him for 12 million dollars' palimony, revealed the ultimate baseball statistic: Boggs's batting average when he went on away trips with his wife was .221; with Margo it rose to .341.

Meanwhile, Pedro Guerrero of the St Louis Cardinals was allegedly drugged and robbed by a girl in a hotel. Debra Brice, a former girlfriend of Kevin Mitchell of the San Francisco Giants, claimed he beat her and threatened her with a gun. José Canseco of the Oakland A's revealed that he carried a gun to signing sessions; he was later charged with carrying one unlawfully.

There were also some major achievements on the ball park. The San Francisco Giants and the Oakland Athletics reached the World Series, making it the first local series since 1956. The Baltimore Orioles, who lost their first 21 games in 1988 and finished hopelessly last in the American League East, made a sensational recovery and led the division for 98 consecutive days until September 2 when they were overhauled by the Toronto Blue Jays. Ken Griffey snr of Cincinnati and Ken Griffey jr of the Seattle Mariners became the first father and son ever to play simultaneaously in the major leagues. Ken jr, 19, had a chocolate bar named after him. Nolan Ryan, 42, now with the Texas Rangers, became the first pitcher to pass 5,000 strikeouts. No 5,000 – against Rickey Henderson of Oakland – was timed at 96mph. Cal Ripken jr, the Baltimore Orioles' short-stop played his 1,208th consecutive game on August 17, passing Steve Garvey and moving into third place in the all-time list behind Everett Scott (1,307) and Lou Gehrig (2,130). Jim Abbott, who has only one hand, established himself in the California Angels pitching rotation. Dave Dravecky of the San Francisco Giants made a heart-warming comeback after having a cancerous growth removed from his pitching arm; he broke the same arm the following week.

"I'd be willing to bet you, if I was a betting man, that I have never bet on baseball."
    Pete Rose, April 4

"I've been in baseball three decades and to think I'm going to be out of baseball for a very short period of time hurts. My life is baseball. I hope to get back in as soon as I possibly can. I'm never looking forward to a birthday like I'm looking forward to my new daughter's birthday. Because two days after that I can apply for reinstatement."
    Pete Rose, Aug 25

"In keeping with the central theme of his tragedy, Pete Rose has been banned from baseball for life and is the only one who doesn't know it yet. His almost infinite capacity for self-delusion completed a full and sad circle as a watching nation saw the horrible power of psychological denial . . . He always liked to say 'I was raised, but I never did grow up.' For his

sake, let's hope he starts soon. Because, at the moment, Pete Rose seems to have regressed past childhood, all the way to a world of fantasy."
    Thomas Boswell, Washington Post

"Sitting in front of my locker every day was like watching The Untouchables."
    Former Cincinnati Reds player on Pete Rose's unsavoury friends

"Babe Ruth retired, Ted Williams retired, Willie Mays retired, I retired and baseball is still as popular as ever. Baseball was here before Pete, myself or anyone else. No one person is bigger than the show."
    Hank Aaron

"There's nothing wrong with his shoulder except some pain – and pain don't hurt you."
    Detroit manager Sparky Anderson discussing injuries

The Toronto Blue Jays moved to the Skydome, the first stadium in North America with a retractable roof. At the opening ceremony people were drenched by a sudden shower; no one had brought umbrellas and it took 34 minutes to put the roof up. Three deaths in two weeks among elderly spectators were put down to the 1/2 mile walk to the station and the unreliable lifts. It was, however, a very handsome arena, and Toronto attendances soared above three million, breaking the American League record. Dallas Green, the manager of the New York Yankees, feuded with the owner George Steinbrenner, calling him "manager George". Eight days later, this had the usual effect: Green was sacked in Steinbrenner's 17th managerial change in 17 years. Bucky Dent was the new incumbent.

Mike Schmidt of the Philadelphia Phillies, 7th on the all-time home run list and one of the all-time great third base men, retired in May. Donnie Moore, a former Angels pitcher, shot and wounded his wife and then killed himself. It was said that Moore had become mentally ill after blaming himself for a bad pitch which gave away a decisive home-run in the 1986 play-offs against the Red Sox. Before he died, Commissioner Giamatti refused a request to reinstate "Shoeless" Joe Jackson, one of the eight Chicago White Sox players banned after 1919. Giamatti said he did not "wish to play God with history". Michael Bush of Phelps, New York, was arrested for trespass after carrying a sign to school games protesting that his 17-year-old son was being left out of the Midlakes High team. The Soviet baseball team lost all nine games on their first US tour, by scores of up to 21-1. The first baseball instruction book was published in Russian.

1989

MAJOR LEAGUE BASEBALL (US)
Final Standings
(Last season's position in brackets)

American League – East

	Won	Lost	Pct	GB
1 (4) Toronto Blue Jays	89	73	.549	-
2 (7) Baltimore Orioles	87	75	.537	2
3 (1) Boston Red Sox	83	79	.512	6
4 (3) Milwaukee Brewers	81	81	.500	8
5 (5) New York Yankees	74	87	.460	14 1/2
6 (6) Cleveland Indians	73	89	.451	16
7 (2) Detroit Tigers	59	103	.364	30

American League – West

	Won	Lost	Pct	GB
1 (1) Oakland Athletics	99	63	.611	-
2 (3) Kansas City Royals	92	70	.568	7
3 (4) California Angels	91	71	.562	8
4 (6) Texas Rangers	83	79	.512	16
5 (2) Minnesota Twins	80	82	.494	19
6 (7) Seattle Mariners	73	89	.451	26
7 (5) Chicago White Sox	69	92	.429	29 1/2

National League – East

	Won	Lost	Pct	GB
1 (4) Chicago Cubs	93	69	.571	-
2 (1) New York Mets	87	75	.537	6
3 (5) St Louis Cardinals	86	76	.531	7
4 (3) Montreal Expos	81	81	.500	12
5 (2) Pittsburgh Pirates	74	88	.457	19
6 (6) Philadelphia Phillies	67	95	.414	26

National League – West

	Won	Lost	Pct	GB
1 (4) San Francisco Giants	92	70	.568	-
2 (3) San Diego Padres	89	73	.549	3
3 (5) Houston Astros	86	76	.531	6
4 (1) Los Angeles Dodgers	77	83	.481	14
5 (2) Cincinnati Reds	75	87	.463	17
6 (6) Atlanta Braves	63	97	.394	28

60th ALL-STAR GAME
Anaheim, California, Jul 12
NATIONAL LEAGUE 2 0 0 0 0 0 0 1 0 – 3
AMERICAN LEAGUE 2 1 2 0 0 0 0 0 x – 5
MVP: Bo Jackson (AL)
Attendance: 64,036
American League lead series 37-22 (one tie).

OTHER RESULTS
Scottish Amicable European Championship
Reading, Jun 18
Final
University of Paris beat Sokol Prague 9-8
3rd Place Play-off
German Tornadoes beat Enfield Spartans 19-9
Scottish Amicable National League Play-offs
Semi-finals
Southern Tigers beat Lancashire Red Sox 33-16
Humberside Bears beat London Warriors 18-5
Final
Richmond, Aug 12
Southern Tigers beat Humberside Bears 8-7

——— CHAMPIONS ———

WORLD SERIES

Year	Team	
1903	Boston Red Sox (AL)	5
	Pittsburgh Pirates (NL)	3
1904	Not held	
1905	New York Giants (NL)	4
	Philadelphia Athletics (AL)	1
1906	Chicago White Sox (AL)	4
	Chicago Cubs (NL)	2
1907	Chicago Cubs (NL)	4(*)
	Detroit Tigers (AL)	0
1908	Chicago Cubs (NL)	4
	Detroit Tigers (AL)	1
1909	Pittsburgh Pirates (NL)	4
	Detroit Tigers (AL)	3
1910	Philadelphia Athletics (AL)	4
	Chicago Cubs (NL)	1
1911	Philadelphia Athletics (AL)	4
	New York Giants (NL)	2
1912	Boston Red Sox (AL)	4
	New York Giants (NL)	3(*)
1913	Philadelphia Athletics (AL)	4
	New York Giants (NL)	1
1914	Boston Braves (NL)	4
	Philadelphia Athletics (AL)	0
1915	Boston Red Sox (AL)	4
	Philadelphia Phillies (NL)	1
1916	Boston Red Sox (AL)	4
	Brooklyn Dodgers (NL)	1
1917	Chicago White Sox (AL)	4
	New York Giants (NL)	2
1918	Boston Red Sox (AL)	4
	Chicago Cubs (NL)	2
1919	Cincinnati Reds (NL)	5
	Chicago White Sox (AL)	3
1920	Cleveland Indians (AL)	5
	Brooklyn Dodgers (NL)	2
1921	New York Giants (NL)	4
	New York Yankees (AL)	3
1922	New York Giants (NL)	4
	New York Yankees (AL)	0(*)
1923	New York Yankees (AL)	4
	New York Giants (NL)	2
1924	Washington Senators (AL)	4
	New York Giants (NL)	3
1925	Pittsburgh Pirates (NL)	4
	Washington Senators (AL)	3
1926	St Louis Cardinals (NL)	4
	New York Yankees (AL)	3
1927	New York Yankees (AL)	4
	Pittsburgh Pirates (NL)	0
1928	New York Yankees (AL)	4
	St Louis Cardinals (NL)	0
1929	Philadelphia Athletics (AL)	4
	Chicago Cubs (NL)	1
1930	Philadelphia Athletics (AL)	4
	St Louis Cardinals (NL)	2
1931	St Louis Cardinals (NL)	4
	Philadelphia Athletics (AL)	3
1932	New York Yankees (AL)	4
	Chicago Cubs (NL)	0
1933	New York Giants (NL)	4
	Washington Senators (AL)	1
1934	St Louis Cardinals (NL)	4
	Detroit Tigers (AL)	3
1935	Detroit Tigers (AL)	4
	Chicago Cubs (NL)	2
1936	New York Yankees (AL)	4
	New York Giants (NL)	2
1937	New York Yankees (AL)	4
	New York Giants (NL)	1
1938	New York Yankees (AL)	4
	Chicago Cubs (NL)	0
1939	New York Yankees (AL)	4
	Cincinnati Reds (NL)	0
1940	Cincinnati Reds (NL)	4
	Detroit Tigers (AL)	3
1941	New York Yankees (AL)	4
	Brooklyn Dodgers (NL)	1
1942	St Louis Cardinals (NL)	4
	New York Yankees (AL)	1
1943	New York Yankees (AL)	4
	St Louis Cardinals (NL)	1
1944	St Louis Cardinals (NL)	4
	St Louis Browns (AL)	2
1945	Detroit Tigers (AL)	4
	Chicago Cubs (NL)	3
1946	St Louis Cardinals (NL)	4
	Boston Red Sox (AL)	3
1947	New York Yankees (AL)	4
	Brooklyn Dodgers (NL)	3
1948	Cleveland Indians (AL)	4
	Boston Braves (NL)	2
1949	New York Yankees (AL)	4
	Brooklyn Dodgers (NL)	1
1950	New York Yankees (AL)	4
	Philadelphia Phillies (NL)	0
1951	New York Yankees (AL)	4
	New York Giants (NL)	2
1952	New York Yankees (AL)	4
	Brooklyn Dodgers (NL)	3
1953	New York Yankees (AL)	4
	Brooklyn Dodgers (NL)	2

1954	New York Giants (NL)	4
	Cleveland Indians (AL)	0
1955	Brooklyn Dodgers (NL)	4
	New York Yankees (AL)	3
1956	New York Yankees (AL)	4
	Brooklyn Dodgers (NL)	3
1957	Milwaukee Braves (NL)	4
	New York Yankees (AL)	3
1958	New York Yankees (AL)	4
	Milwaukee Braves (NL)	3
1959	Los Angeles Dodgers (NL)	4
	Chicago White Sox (AL)	2
1960	Pittsburgh Pirates (NL)	4
	New York Yankees (AL)	3
1961	New York Yankees (AL)	4
	Cincinnati Reds (NL)	1
1962	New York Yankees (AL)	4
	San Francisco Giants (NL)	3
1963	Los Angeles Dodgers (NL)	4
	New York Yankees (AL)	0
1964	St Louis Cardinals (NL)	4
	New York Yankees (AL)	3
1965	Los Angeles Dodgers (NL)	4
	Minnesota Twins (AL)	3
1966	Baltimore Orioles (AL)	4
	Los Angeles Dodgers (NL)	0
1967	St Louis Cardinals (NL)	4
	Boston Red Sox (AL)	3
1968	Detroit Tigers (AL)	4
	St Louis Cardinals (NL)	3
1969	New York Mets (NL)	4
	Baltimore Orioles (AL)	1
1970	Baltimore Orioles (AL)	4
	Cincinnati Reds (NL)	1
1971	Pittsburgh Pirates (NL)	4
	Baltimore Orioles (AL)	3
1972	Oakland A's (AL)	4
	Cincinnati Reds (NL)	3
1973	Oakland A's (AL)	4
	New York Mets (NL)	3
1974	Oakland A's (AL)	4
	Los Angeles Dodgers (NL)	1
1975	Cincinnati Reds (NL)	4
	Boston Red Sox (AL)	3
1976	Cincinnati Reds (NL)	4
	New York Yankees (AL)	0
1977	New York Yankees (AL)	4
	Los Angeles Dodgers (NL)	3
1978	New York Yankees (AL)	4
	Los Angeles Dodgers (NL)	2
1979	Pittsburgh Pirates (NL)	4
	Baltimore Orioles (AL)	3
1980	Philadelphia Phillies (NL)	4
	Kansas City Royals (AL)	2
1981	Los Angeles Dodgers (NL)	4
	New York Yankees (AL)	2
1982	St Louis Cardinals (NL)	4
	Milwaukee Brewers (AL)	3
1983	Baltimore Orioles (AL)	4
	Philadelphia Phillies (NL)	1
1984	Detroit Tigers (AL)	4
	San Diego Padres (NL)	1
1985	Kansas City Royals (AL)	4
	St Louis Cardinals (NL)	3
1986	New York Mets (NL)	4
	Boston Red Sox (AL)	3
1987	Minnesota Twins (AL)	4
	St Louis Cardinals (NL)	3
1988	Los Angeles Dodgers (NL)	4
	Oakland Athletics (AL)	1

(*) Included one tied game
(AL) American League (NL) National League

Most Wins
22 New York Yankees; 9 St Louis Cardinals; 5 Boston Red Sox, Pittsburgh Pirates, Philadelphia Athletics, Los Angeles Dodgers, New York Giants; 4 Cincinnati Reds, Detroit Tigers

PLAY-OFFS IN THE 1980s
(Between winners of East division and West division)
American League
1980	Kansas City (W) beat New York (E)	3-0
1981	New York (E) beat Oakland (W)	3-0
1982	Milwaukee (E) beat California (W)	3-2
1983	Baltimore (E) beat Chicago (W)	3-1
1984	Detroit (E) beat Kansas City (W)	3-0
1985	Kansas City (W) beat Toronto (E)	4-3
1986	Boston (E) beat California (W)	4-3
1987	Minnesota (W) beat Detroit (E)	4-1
1988	Oakland (W) beat Boston (E)	4-0
1989	Oakland (W) beat Toronto (E)	4-1

National League
1980	Philadelphia (E) beat Houston (W)	3-2
1981	Los Angeles (W) beat Montreal (E)	3-2
1982	St Louis (E) beat Atlanta (W)	3-0
1983	Philadelphia (E) beat Los Angeles (W)	3-1
1984	San Diego (W) beat Chicago (E)	3-2
1985	St Louis (E) beat Los Angeles (W)	4-2
1986	New York (E) beat Houston (W)	4-2
1987	St Louis (E) beat San Francisco (W)	4-3
1988	Los Angeles (W) beat New York (E)	4-3
1989	San Francisco (W) beat Chicago (E)	4-1

RECORDS

MOST HITS
4256 Pete Rose
4191 Ty Cobb
3771 Hank Aaron
3630 Stan Musial
3515 Tris Speaker

MOST HOME RUNS
755 Hank Aaron
714 Babe Ruth
660 Willie Mays
586 Frank Robinson
573 Harmon Killibrew
563 Reggie Jackson
Leading Current Player
414 Darrell Evans (Atlanta)
(as at Sep 14, 1989)

MOST STRIKEOUTS
5052 Nolan Ryan
(as at Sep 14, 1989)
4131 Steve Carlton
3640 Tom Seaver
3534 Gaylord Perry
3530 Don Sutton
3508 Walter Johnson

BASKETBALL

The Detroit Pistons won the US National Basketball Association (NBA) Championship, basketball's World Series, for the first time in the 41-year history of the franchise with a dramatic 4-0 sweep of the Los Angeles Lakers. The Lakers, Champions in 1987 and 1988, were badly hit by injuries, notably to Magic Johnson, and the Pistons, known not without reason as Bad Boys, overpowered and outplayed them.

The Lakers were also diverted by the nostalgia surrounding the retirement of their 7ft 2in 42-year-old icon, Kareem-Abdul Jabbar (née Lew Alcindor). Jabbar finished his extraordinary career with 38, 387 points in the NBA, 44,149 in all, far ahead of anyone else. At the end of his 20-year career he received presents from every NBA club, including a Rolls-Royce (from his own team-mates), an 1886 Winchester rifle, a scholarship in his name and the key to the city of Indianapolis. "He always looked like he was playing to music," said his team-mate Magic Johnson.

In Britain, Glasgow Rangers won the League and beat Murray Livingston in the Championship play-off. However, Rangers were immediately closed down and Livingston converted into an amateur club by David Murray, who found himself owning both finalists as a by-product of his football dealings and became fed up with spending money on importing Americans.

The international ruling body, FIBA, decided to open world championships and Olympics to all professionals, making it a near-certainty that the US will regain the Olympics title in 1992. Fifty-eight percent of American pros said they would be willing to play.

In Esperanza, Philippines, 26 people, many of them children, were reported killed at a local tournament when unidentified men threw grenades during the presentations. In New York, drug dealers were said to be running neighborhood teams and staking huge bets on tournaments in local playgrounds. One referee was murdered, allegedly after his decision in a close game cost a dealer a $50,000 bet.

━━━━━ 1989 ━━━━━

NBA FINAL STANDINGS
Eastern Conference

CENTRAL

	W	L	Pct
Detroit Pistons	63	19	.768
Cleveland Cavaliers	57	25	.695
Atlanta Hawks	52	30	.634
Milwaukee Bucks	49	33	.598
Chicago Bulls	47	35	.573
Indiana Pacers	28	54	.341

ATLANTIC

	W	L	Pct
New York Knicks	52	30	.634
Philadelphia 76ers	46	36	.561
Boston Celtics	42	40	.512
Washington Bullets	40	42	.488
New Jersey Nets	26	56	.317
Charlotte Hornets	20	62	.244

Western Conference

MID WEST

	W	L	Pct
Utah Jazz	51	31	.622
Houston Rockets	45	37	.549
Denver Nuggets	44	38	.537
Dallas Mavericks	38	44	.463
San Antonio Spurs	21	61	.256
Miami Heat	15	67	.183

PACIFIC

	W	L	Pct
Los Angeles Lakers	57	25	.695
Phoenix Suns	55	27	.671
Seattle Sonics	47	35	.573
Golden State Warriors	43	39	.524
Portland Trail Blazers	39	43	.476
Sacramento Kings	27	55	.329
Los Angeles Clippers	21	61	.256

KAREEM ABDUL-JABBER retired at the end of the 1989 season. Born Lew Alcindor, he converted to Islam in 1969 and turned professional with Milwaukee in 1970. Among his all-time records are:

Leading NBA Scorer: 38,987 points

Leading scorer in all games: 4,708 points

Most seasons played in NBA: 20

Most games played in NBA: 1,560

He had a cameo role in the 1980 film *Airplane*.

NATIONAL BASKETBALL ASSOCIATION (NBA)

Conference Play-Offs

Eastern Conference

First Round

Detroit Pistons beat Boston Celtics 3-0
Milwaukee Bucks beat Atlanta Hawks 3-2
New York Knicks beat Philadelphia 76ers 3-0
Chicago Bulls beat Cleveland Cavaliers 3-2

Semi-finals

Detroit Pistons beat Milwaukee Bucks 4-0
Chicago Bulls beat New York Knicks 4-2

Conference Final

Detroit Pistons beat Chicago Bulls 4-2

Western Conference

First Round

L.Angeles Lakers beat Portland Trail Blazers 3-0
Seattle Sonics beat Houston Rockets 3-1
Golden State Warriors beat Utah Jazz 3-0
Phoenix Suns beat Denver Nuggets 3-0

Semi-finals

Los Angeles Lakers beat Seattle Sonics 4-0
Phoenix Suns beat Golden State Warriors 4-1

Final

Los Angeles Lakers beat Phoenix Suns 4-0

NBA Championship

Game 1: Detroit Pistons beat Los Angeles Lakers 109-97
Game 2: Detroit Pistons beat Los Angeles Lakers 108-105
Game 3: Detroit Pistons beat Los Angeles Lakers 114-110
Game 4: Detroit Pistons beat Los Angeles Lakers 106-97
Detroit won the best-of-seven series 4-0
Series MVP: Joe Dumars (Detroit Pistons)

NBA PLAYERS WITH 10,000 POINTS

When Michael Jordan (Chicago Bulls) scored against Philadelphia 76ers on 25 January 1989 he became the sixth NBA player to score 10,000 points. The other 10,000 point men, and number of games taken to get there are:

Games	Player
236	Wilt Chamberlain
303	Michael Jordan
318	Kareem Abdul-Jabbar
334	Oscar Robertson
336	Elgin Baylor
358	Bob McAdoo

ENGLISH BASKETBALL ASSOCIATION

Carlsberg League

		P	W	L	For	Agst	Pts
1	Glasgow	20	18	2	1965	1634	36
2	Livingston	20	16	4	1901	1640	32
3	Bracknell	20	15	5	1928	1627	30
4	Leicester	20	14	6	1764	1604	28
5	Manchester	20	13	7	1608	1563	26
6	Sunderland	20	12	8	1754	1724	24
7	Hemel Hempstead	20	9	11	1771	1803	18
8	Olympic City	20	4	16	1644	1837	8
9	Solent	20	4	16	1803	1977	8
10	Derby	20	3	17	1502	1840	6
11	Crystal Palace	20	2	18	1493	1824	4

National League

Men: Division One

		P	W	L	For	Agst	Pts
1	Oldham	20	17	3	2053	1564	34
2	Brixton	20	17	3	1857	1625	34
3	Birmingham	20	16	4	1962	1645	32
4	Worthing	20	15	5	2068	1777	30
5	Gateshead	20	14	6	1872	1655	28
6	Plymouth	20	10	10	1935	1887	20
7	Oxford	20	8	12	1715	1903	16
8	Cheshire	20	6	14	1488	1637	12
9	Corby	20	4	16	1717	2088	8
10	Stockport	20	3	17	1453	1886	6
11	Tower Hamlets	20	0	20	1527	1990	0

Women: Division One

		P	W	L	For	Agst	Pts
1	Northampton	22	21	1	1826	1113	42
2	London YMCA	22	19	3	1734	1301	38
3	Stockport	22	17	5	1642	1417	34
4	Tyneside	22	15	7	1530	1263	30
5	Nottingham	22	13	9	1372	1265	26
6	Crystal Palace	22	13	9	1434	1363	26
7	Sheffield	22	12	10	1248	1184	24
8	Ipswich	22	8	14	1268	1440	16
9	Brixton	22	5	17	1152	1472	10
10	Cardiff	22	4	18	1114	1516	8
11	Kingston	22	3	19	1200	1626	6
12	London Jets	22	2	20	1078	1638	4

Championship Play-offs

NEC Birmingham: Att. 5,000

Men

Glasgow Rangers beat Murray Livingston 89-86

Women

Avon Northampton beat Stockport Louvolite 66-65

Coca-Cola National Cup Finals

London Arena, Isle of Dogs; Att. 5,000

Men

Bracknell Tigers beat Manchester Eagles 87-75

Women

Avon Northampton beat London Bobcats 94-61

Coach of the Year: Kevin Cadle (Glasgow Rangers)
Most Valuable Player of the Year: Alan Cunningham (Glasgow Rangers)

EUROPEAN CHAMPIONSHIPS

Men:	1st/2nd Yugoslavia beat Greece 98-77
	3rd/4th USSR beat Italy 104-76
	5th/6th Spain beat France 95-87
	7th/8th Bulgaria beat Netherlands 91-86
Women:	1st/2nd USSR beat Czechoslovakia 64-61
	3rd/4th Bulgaria beat Yugoslavia 79-67
	5th/6th Hungary beat France 84-66
	7th/8th Italy beat Netherlands 51-42

EUROPEAN CUP FINALS

Men:	1st: KK Jugoplastika (Yug)
	2nd: Maccabi Elite (Isr)
Women:	Jedinstvo Aida beat AS Primigi 74-70

EUROPEAN CUP

Korac Cup: KK Partizan (Yug) beat Wiwa Vismara (Ita) 177-171 (agg)
Ronchetti Cup: CSKA Moscow (USSR) beat Basket Femminile (Ita) 92-86

———— CHAMPIONS ————

OLYMPIC GAMES
Men
1936	United States
1948	United States
1952	United States
1956	United States
1960	United States
1964	United States
1968	United States
1972	USSR
1976	United States
1980	Yugoslavia
1984	United States
1988	USSR

Women
1976	USSR
1980	USSR
1984	United States
1988	United States

WORLD CHAMPIONSHIPS
Men
1950	Argentina
1954	United States
1959	Brazil
1963	Brazil
1967	USSR
1970	Yugoslavia
1974	USSR
1978	Yugoslavia
1982	USSR
1986	United States

Women
1953	United States
1957	United States
1959	USSR
1964	USSR
1967	USSR
1971	USSR
1975	USSR
1979	United States
1983	USSR
1987	United States

EUROPEAN CHAMPIONSHIPS
Men
1935	Latvia
1937	Lithuania
1939	Lithuania
1946	Czechoslovakia
1947	USSR
1949	Egypt
1951	USSR
1953	USSR
1955	Hungary
1957	USSR
1959	USSR
1961	USSR
1963	USSR
1965	USSR
1967	USSR
1969	USSR
1971	USSR
1973	Yugoslavia
1975	Yugoslavia
1977	Yugoslavia
1979	USSR
1981	USSR
1983	Italy
1985	USSR
1987	Greece
1989	Yugoslavia

Women
1938	Italy
1950	USSR
1952	USSR
1954	USSR
1956	USSR
1958	Bulgaria
1960	USSR
1962	USSR
1964	USSR
1966	USSR
1968	USSR
1970	USSR
1972	USSR
1974	USSR
1976	USSR
1978	USSR
1980	USSR
1981	USSR
1983	USSR
1985	USSR
1987	USSR
1989	USSR

NBA
1947	Philadelphia Warriors
1948	Baltimore Bullets
1949	Minneapolis Lakers
1950	Minneapolis Lakers
1951	Rochester Royals
1952	Minneapolis Lakers
1953	Minneapolis Lakers
1954	Minneapolis Lakers
1955	Syracuse Nationals
1956	Philadelphia Warriors
1957	Boston Celtics
1958	St Louis Hawks
1959	Boston Celtics
1960	Boston Celtics
1961	Boston Celtics
1962	Boston Celtics
1963	Boston Celtics
1964	Boston Celtics
1965	Boston Celtics
1966	Boston Celtics
1967	Philadelphia 76ers
1968	Boston Celtics
1969	Boston Celtics
1970	New York Knicks
1971	Milwaukee Bucks
1972	Los Angeles Lakers
1973	New York Knicks
1974	Boston Celtics
1975	Golden State Warriors
1976	Boston Celtics
1977	Portland Trail Blazers
1978	Washington Bullets
1979	Seattle Supersonics
1980	Los Angeles Lakers
1981	Boston Celtics
1982	Los Angeles Lakers
1983	Philadelphia 76ers
1984	Boston Celtics
1985	Los Angeles Lakers
1986	Boston Celtics
1987	Los Angeles Lakers
1988	Los Angeles Lakers
1989	Detroit Pistons

ENGLISH BASKETBALL ASSOCIATION
National Champions
Men

1936	Hoylake YMCA
1937	Hoylake YMCA
1938	Catford Saints
1939	Catford Saints
1940	Birmingham Athletic Inst.
1947	Carpathians
1948	Latter Day Saints
1949	Latter Day Saints
1950	Latter Day Saints
1951	Birmingham Dolobran
1952	London Polytechnic
1953	London Polytechnic
1954	London Polytechnic
1955	London Polytechnic
1956	-
1957	Central YMCA
1958	Central YMCA
1959	Aspley O.B.
1960	Central YMCA
1961	London University
1962	Central YMCA
1963	Central YMCA
1964	Central YMCA
1965	Aldershot Warriors
1966	Oxford University
1967	Central YMCA
1968	Oxford University
1969	Central YMCA
1970	Liverpool Police
1971	Mancester University
1972	Avenue (Leyton)
1973	London Latvian SK
1974	Sutton & C,Palace
1975	Embassy All Stars
1976	Crystal Palace
1977	Crystal Palace
1978	Crystal Palace
1979	Crystal Palace
1980	Crystal Palace
1981	Sunderland
1982	Crystal Palace
1983	Sunderland
1984	Solent
1985	Manchester Untied
1986	Kingston
1987	BCP London
1988	Murray Livingston
1989	Glasgow Rangers

Women

1981	Southgate
1982	Southgate
1983	Southgate
1984	A.C. Northampton
1985	A.C. Northampton
1986	Crystal Palace
1987	A.C. Northampton
1988	Stockport
1989	Northampton

National Cup Winners (since 1980)
Men

1980	Crystal Palace
1981	Crystal Palace
1982	Solent
1983	Solent
1984	Solent
1985	Kingston
1986	Kingston
1987	Kingston
1988	Kingston
1989	Bracknell

Women

1980	Tigers
1981	Southgate
1984	Manchester
1985	Northampton
1986	Crystal Palace
1987	BCP London
1988	Northampton
1989	Northampton

Carlsberg League
(Inaugurated 1987-88 and comprising leading clubs from National League)

1988	Portsmouth
1989	Glasgow Rangers

National League
Men

	Division 1	Division 2
1973	Avenue (Leyton)	-
1974	Crystal Palace	-
1975	E.A.S. Islington	-
1976	Crystal Palace	V.M. Bedford
1977	Crystal Palace	Stockport B
1978	Crystal Palace	Sunderland
1979	Doncaster	S.P. Guildford
1980	Crystal Palace	Nottingham
1981	T.F.Birmingham	Solent
1982	Crystal Palace	Leicester
1983	Crystal Palace	Bolton
1984	Solent	Sandwell
1985	Kingston	Tyneside
1986	Manchester Untied	Calderdale
1987	Portsmouth	Walsall
1988	Portsmouth	Worthing
1989	Oldham	Teeside

Women

	Division 1	Division 2
1976	Tigers (Herts)	-
1977	Tigers (Herts)	Waltham Abbey
1978	Cleveland E	S.H. Solent
1979	Cleveland E	Crystal Palace
1980	Tigers (Herts)	Brinnington
1981	Southgate	Brinnington
1982	Southgate	T.C.B. Brighton
1983	Southgate	Newcastle
1984	Northampton	Bath
1985	Northampton	Rugby
1986	Crystal Palace	Hemel & Watford
1987	Northampton	Ipswich
1988	Northampton	Cardiff

	Division 1	Division 2(N)	Division 2(S)
1989	Northampton	Wirral	Birmingham

BILLIARDS

1989

CHAMPIONS

WORLD PROFESSIONAL CHAMPIONSHIP
Leura, Australia

FIRST ROUND
EDDIE CHARLTON(Aus) beat Stephen Naisby (Eng) 889 – 844; RAY EDMONDS (Eng) beat Jack Karnehm (Eng) 1209 – 973; NORMAN DAGLEY (Eng) beat Hugh Nimmo (Sco) 1422 – 866; MIKE RUSSELL (Eng) beat Howard Griffiths (Wal) 2106 – 826; IAN WILLIAMSON (Eng) beat Michael Ferreira (Ind) 999 – 998; BOB CLOSE (Eng) beat Geet Sethi (Ind) 1477 – 984; EUGENE HUGHES (Ire) beat Robbie Foldvari (Aus) 990 – 932; PETER GILCHRIST (Eng) beat Mark Wildman (Eng) 1493 – 851

QUARTER-FINALS
NORMAN DAGLEY beat Bob Close 1547 – 983; MIKE RUSSELL beat Ian Williamson 1155 – 857; PETER GILCHRIST beat Eugene Hughes 1577 – 874; EDDIE CHARLTON beat Ray Edmonds 1143 – 766

SEMI-FINALS
MIKE RUSSELL beat Norman Dagley 1685 – 1001; PETER GILCHRIST beat Eddie Charlton 1336 – 743

FINAL
MIKE RUSSELL beat Peter Gilchrist 2242 – 1347

STRACHAN UK CHAMPIONSHIP
Middlesbrough
QUARTER-FINALS
Bob Close (Eng) beat Ian Williamson (Eng) 4 – 0; Michael Ferreira (Ind) beat Clive Everton (Wal) 4 – 1; Mike Russell (Eng) beat Robbie Foldvari (Aus) 4 – 1; Norman Dagley (Eng) beat Peter Gilchrist (Eng) 4 – 3

SEMI-FINALS
Close beat Ferreira 4 – 1; Russell beat Dagley 4 – 0

FINAL
Russell beat Close 7 – 0

BRITISH OPEN
Middlesbrough
QUARTER-FINALS
Mike Russell (Eng) beat Ian Williamson (Eng) 709 – 549; Hugh Nimmo (Sco) beat Clive Everton (Wal) 449 – 416; Peter Gilchrist beat Michael Ferreira (Ind) 782 – 632; Bob Close (Eng) beat Norman Dagley (Eng) 622 – 561

SEMI-FINALS
Gilchrist beat Nimmo 846 – 518; Russell beat Close 1054 – 576

FINAL
Gilchrist beat Russell 1489 – 974

ROTHMANS WORLD MATCH-PLAY CHAMPIONSHIP
Manchester

QUARTER-FINALS
Norman Dagley (Eng) beat Jack Karnehm (Eng) 4 – 0; Mike Russell (Eng) beat Mark Wildman (Eng) 4 – 1; Ian Williamson (Eng) beat Bob Close (Eng) 4-1; Michael Ferreira (Ind) beat Robbie Foldvari (Aus) 4 – 1

SEMI-FINALS
Russell beat Dagley 4 – 3; Williamson beat Ferreira 4 – 2

FINAL
Russell beat Williamson 6 – 1

WORLD PROFESSIONAL CHAMPIONSHIP
1870–1909 operated on a challenge system and again 1951-71. Since 1980 it has been held on a knockout basis
All winners British unless otherwise stated

1870	William Cook
1870	John Roberts, Jnr
1870	Joseph Bennett
1871	John Roberts, Jnr
1871	William Cook
1875	John Roberts, Jnr
1880	Joseph Bennett
1885	John Roberts, Jnr
1889	Charles Dawson
1901	H. W. Stevenson
1901	Charles Dawson
1901	H. W. Stevenson
1903	Charles Dawson
1908	Melbourne Inman
1909	H. W. Stevenson
1910	H. W. Stevenson
1911	H. W. Stevenson
1912	Melbourne Inman
1913	Melbourne Inman
1914	Melbourne Inman
1919	Melbourne Inman
1920	Willie Smith
1921	Tom Newman
1922	Tom Newman
1923	Willie Smith
1924	Tom Newman
1925	Tom Newman
1926	Tom Newman
1927	Tom Newman
1928	Joe Davis
1929	Joe Davis
1930	Joe Davis
1931	Not held
1932	Joe Davis
1933	Walter Lindrum (Aus)
1934	Walter Lindrum (Aus)
1951	Clark McConachy (NZ)
1968	Rex Williams
1971	Leslie Driffield
1971	Rex Williams
1980	Fred Davis
1982	Rex Williams
1983	Rex Williams
1984	Mark Wildman
1985	Ray Edmonds
1986	Robbie Foldvari (Aus)
1987	Norman Dagley
1988	Norman Dagley
1989	Mike Russell

WORLD AMATEUR CHAMPIONSHIP

1926	Joe Earlham (Eng)
1927	Allan Prior (SA)
1929	Les Hayes (Aus)
1931	Laurie Steeples (Eng)
1933	Sydney Lee (Eng)
1935	Horace Coles (Wal)
1936	Robert Marshall (Aus)
1938	Robert Marshall (Aus)
1951	Robert Marshall (Aus)
1952	Leslie Driffield (Eng)

1954	Tom Cleary (Aus)
1958	Wilson Jones (Ind)
1960	Herbert Beetham (Eng)
1962	Robert Marshall (Aus)
1964	Wilson Jones (Ind)
1967	Leslie Driffield (Eng)
1969	Jack Karnehm (Eng)
1971	Norman Dagley (Eng)
1973	Mohammed Lafir (Sri)
1975	Norman Dagley (Eng)
1977	Michael Ferreira (Ind)
1979	Paul Mifsud (Malta)
1981	Michael Ferreira (Ind)
1983	Michael Ferreira (Ind)
1985	Geet Sethi (Ind)
1987	Geet Sethi (Ind)

UNITED KINGDOM PROFESSIONAL CHAMPIONSHIP
(Not held 1952-1978)

1934	Joe Davis
1935	Joe Davis
1936	Joe Davis
1937	Joe Davis
1938	Joe Davis
1939	Joe Davis
1946	John Barrie
1947	Joe Davis
1948	Sidney Smith
1950	John Barrie
1951	Fred Davis

1979	Rex Williams
1980	Jack Karnehm
1981	Rex Williams
1983	Mark Wildman
1987	Norman Dagley
1988	Ian Williamson
1989	Mike Russell

EUROPEAN CHAMPIONSHIP
(First held 1988)

| 1988 | Mike Russell (Eng) |

BRITISH OPEN
(First held 1989)

| 1989 | Peter Gilchrist |

WORLD MATCH-PLAY
(First held 1989)

| 1989 | Mike Russell (Eng) |

─── RECORDS ───

Highest break: 499,135 Tom Reece 3 Jun – 6 Jul 1907 (this incorporated the cradle cannon which is no longer allowed)

Highest break since introduction of 25-hazard rule (1926): 4,137 Walter Lindrum 1932

Highest break under current 'two pot' rule: 962 (unfinished) Michael Ferreira 29 Apr 1986

BOWLS

Two 15-year-olds played in the EBA Championships at Worthing. Nicky Jones of Bournemouth became the Hampshire champion and the youngest-ever competitor in the singles; he beat the England international Bill Hobart in the first round before going out. Neil Karge of the Carlisle Subscription club, five months younger than Jones, was the youngest-ever competitor in the pairs. Playing with Ronnie Little (55) he beat two former singles champions, Ron Keating and David Cutler, in the second round before going out on the last end in the third. Two teams from one club, Blackheath and Greenwich, reached the semi-finals of the Fours Championship; one of the rinks lost by one shot and the first one-club final in 84 years just failed to materialise. The smallest bowls county in England reached the finals of the Middleton Cup: Lancashire has only a handful of clubs because of the prevalence of crown green. The former world champion Peter Belliss was excluded from the New Zealand Commonwealth Games team because he had played in South Africa.

1989

MEN'S OUTDOOR

WOOLWICH EBA NATIONAL CHAMPIONSHIPS
Worthing, Aug 14-25
Semi-finals
John Ottaway (Norfolk) beat Tony Allcock (Gloucestershire) 25-21; Barry Croad (Isle of Wight) beat Norman Burns (Leicestershire) 25-21.
Final
John Ottaway beat Barry Croad 26-13

Pairs
Semi-finals
Paul Maynard and David McCathie (Essex County) beat David Rhys-Jones and David Byrant (Clevedon) 24-15; Charles Tattersall and Mick Leach (Newton Hall, Blackpool) beat Tony Baily and Rick Collins (Mail Cart, Spalding) 19-13
Final
Maynard and McCathie beat Leach and Tattersall 25-16

Triples
Semi-finals
Swindon (Wilts) beat Blackheath & Greenwich (Kent) 15-14; Southbourne (Sussex) beat Poole Park (Dorset) 16-15
Final
Southbourne beat Swindon 20-18

Fours
Semi-finals
Blackheath & Greenwich (Skip: Martin Sejker) beat Rodbourne Cheney (Wilts) 16-12: Brush (Leics) beat Blackheath & Greenwich (Skip: Andy Thomson) 16-15
Final
Blackheath & Greenwich beat Brush 17-16

NATWEST MIDDLETON CUP
Worthing, Aug 26
Semi-finals
Kent beat Devon 120-104; Lancashire beat Nottinghamshire 115-106
Final
Kent beat Lancashire 117-107

NATWEST BRITISH ISLES CHAMPIONSHIP
Worthing, Jul 7
1 England 2 Scotland 3 Wales 4 Ireland

WOOLWICH MASTERS
Worthing, Jun 11
Play-offs
1st-2nd:	David Bryant (Eng) beat Willie Wood (Sco) 25-8
3rd-4th:	Ken Williams (Aus) beat John Ottaway (Eng) 25-24
5th-6th:	Tony Allcock (Eng) beat George Souza (HK) 25-16

MEN'S INDOOR

EMBASSY WORLD CHAMPIONSHIPS
Guildhall, Preston, Mar 12
Singles
Quarter-finals
Gary Smith (Eng) beat John Price (Wal) 7-1 7-2 7-5; Hugh Duff (Sco) beat Stephen Rees (Wal) 7-6 7-1 2-7 7-2; Willie Wood (Sco) beat Wynne Richards (Eng) 7-6 7-6 7-5; Richard Coursie (Sco) beat Mark McMahon (HK) 7-1 6-7 7-6 7-0
Semi-finals
Willie Wood beat Hugh Duff 6-7 7-5 7-1 4-7 7-1 Richard Coursie beat Gary Smith 7-1 7-5 7-5
Final
Richard Coursie beat Willie Wood 7-2 7-5 7-6 7-3 7-2

Pairs
Semi-finals
David Bryant and Tony Allcock (Eng) beat Gary Smith and Andy Thomson (Eng) 6-1 9-2 6-5; Rowan Brassey and Peter Belliss (NZ) beat Gerry Smyth and Steve Halmai (Eng) 8-3 5-6 6-1 5-3
Final
David Bryant and Tony Allcock beat Rowan Brassey and Peter Belliss 9-5 8-2 9-3

ENGLISH NATIONAL CHAMPIONSHIP
Melton Mowbray, Mar 18
Singles
Andy Thomson (Cyphers, Beckenham) beat Tony Allcock (Cotswold) 21-17
Pairs
Boston beat Paddington 28-9
Triples
Mote Park (Maidstone) beat Ipswich 20-12

Fours
Cyphers, Beckenham beat Paddington 29-16

CIS BRITISH CHAMPIONSHIPS
Swansea, Apr 4
Singles
Bryan Kingdom (Wal) beat Jim Baker (Ire) 21-12
Pairs
Ireland beat England 21-12
Triples
England beat Ireland 17-16
Fours
England beat Wales 25-8
Junior Singles
Richard Coursie (Sco) beat Mark Hopson (Wal) 21-11
Home International Championship
Hilton Trophy
1 England 2 Scotland 3 Wales 4 Ireland

SUN LIFE ENGLISH BOWLS PLAYERS ASSOCIATION CHAMPIONSHIP
Wellingborough, Jan 22
Mike Marsden (Northavon) beat John Evans (Torbay) 7-6 7-6

WOMEN'S OUTDOOR

LIVERPOOL VICTORIA NATIONAL CHAMPIONSHIPS
Leamington Spa, Aug 13
Singles
Jean Baker (Alfreton) beat Wendy Line (Southampton) 21-13
Two-wood Singles
Catherine Anton (Peterborough) beat Edna Bessell (Yeovil) 14-9
Pairs
Ropner Park, Stockton beat Springhead Park, Hull 19-18
Triples
North Walsham beat Sherwood 27-7
Fours
Kingsway beat West Cornwall 20-13

WOMEN'S INDOOR

WORLD CHAMPIONSHIP
Edinburgh, April 23
Semi-finals
Margaret Johnston (Ire) beat Marion Mungall (Sco) 7-5 7-0 1-7 7-5; Mavis Steele (Eng) beat Joyce Lindores (Sco) 7-1 7-4 7-5
Third Place Play-off
Joyce Lindores beat Marion Mungall 4-7 7-4 7-6
Final
Margaret Johnston beat Mavis Steele 2-7 3-7 7-1 7-4 4-7 7-2 7-6

CIS BRITISH CHAMPIONSHIPS
Glasgow, March 13
Singles
Marion Mungall (Sco) beat Sylvia Froud (Wal) 21-18
Pairs
Ireland beat England 19-7
Triples
Wales beat Ireland 22-12
Fours
Wales beat Scotland 23-14

CROWN GREEN BOWLS

WATERLOO CUP
Waterloo Hotel, Blackpool, completed Sep 13
Quarter-finals
ROBERT EATON (Holmes Chapel) beat Ken Humphries (Kirkham) 21-16; BRIAN DUNCAN (Preston) beat Darryl Pryce (Sychdyn, Mold) 21-8; KEVIN WAINWRIGHT (Warrington) beat Ian Rigby (Tarleton) 21-13; DAVID SLATER (Blackburn) beat Peter Fielding (Rochdale) 21-13
Semi-finals
DUNCAN beat Eaton 21-10; WAINWRIGHT beat Slater 21-10
Final
DUNCAN beat Wainwright 21-12
Ladies Final
DIANE HUNT (Swinton) beat Pat Holt (Blackburn) 21-20

━━━━ CHAMPIONS ━━━━

WORLD CHAMPIONSHIPS
Men-Outdoors
Singles
1966	David Bryant (Eng)
1972	Malwyn Evans (Wal)
1976	Doug Watson (SA)
1980	David Bryant (Eng)
1984	Peter Belliss (NZ)
1988	David Bryant (Eng)

Pairs
1966	Geoff Kelly & Bert Palm (Aus)
1972	Clementi Delgado & Eric Liddell (HK)
1976	Doug Watson & William Moseley (SA)
1980	Alf Sandercock & Peter Rheuben (Aus)
1984	George Adrain & Skippy Arculli (US)
1988	Rowan Brassey & Peter Belliss (NZ)

Triples
1966	Australia
1972	United States
1976	South Africa
1980	England
1984	Ireland
1988	New Zealand

Fours
1966	New Zealand
1972	England
1976	South Africa
1980	Hong Kong
1984	England
1988	Ireland

Men-Indoors
Singles

		Team	
1979	David Bryant (Eng)	(Leonard Trophy)	
1980	David Bryant (Eng)	1966	Australia
1981	David Bryant (Eng)	1972	Scotland
1982	John Watson (Sco)	1976	South Africa
1983	Bob Sutherland (Sco)	1980	England
1984	Jim Baker (Ire)	1984	Scotland
1985	Terry Sullivan (Wal)	1988	England
1986	Tony Allcock (Eng)		
1987	Tony Allcock (Eng)		
1988	Hugh Duff (Sco)		
1989	Richard Coursie (Sco)		

Women-Outdoors
Singles
1969	Gladys Doyle (PNG)
1973	Elsie Wilke (NZ)
1977	Elsie Wilke (NZ)
1981	Norma Shaw (Eng)
1985	Merle Richardson (Aus)
1988	Janet Ackland (Wal)

Pairs
1969	E McDonald & M Cridlan (SA)
1973	Lorna Lucas & Dot Jenkinson (Aus)
1977	Helen Wong & Elvie Chok (HK)
1981	Eileen Bell & Nan Allely (Ire)
1985	Merle Richardson & Fay Craig (Aus)
1988	Margaret Johnston & Phyllis Nolan (Ire)

Triples
1969	South Africa
1973	New Zealand
1977	Wales
1981	Hong Kong
1985	Australia
1988	Australia

Fours
1969	South Africa
1973	New Zealand
1977	Australia
1981	England
1985	Scotland
1988	Australia

Team
1969	South Africa
1973	New Zealand
1977	Australia
1981	England
1985	Australia
1988	England

Women-Indoors
Singles
1988	Margaret Johnston (Ire)
1989	Margaret Johnston (Ire)

EBA CHAMPIONSHIPS
Inaugurated 1903. Winners since 1980:
Singles
1980	T Buller, Durham
1981	Andy Thomson, Kent
1982	Chris Ward, Norfolk
1983	John Bell, Cumbria
1984	Wynne Richards, Surrey
1985	Roy Keating, Devon
1986	Wynne Richards, Surrey
1987	David Holt, Lancs
1988	Richard Bray, Cornwall
1989	John Ottaway, Norfolk

Pairs
1980	Framlingham House, Suffolk
1981	Burton House, Lincs
1982	Bedford Borough, Buckinghamshire
1983	Eldon Grove, Durham
1984	Lenham, Kent
1985	Haxby Road, Yorks
1986	Owton Lodge, Durham
1987	Bolton, Lancs
1988	Leicester
1989	Essex County

Triples
1980	Heaton Hall, Lancashire
1981	St Peter's Hampshire
1982	Lenham, Kent
1983	Marlborough, Suffolk
1984	Clevedon, Somerset
1985	Clevedon, Somerset
1986	Poole Park, Dorset
1987	Worcester County
1988	Belgrave, Leicester
1989	Southbourne, Sussex

Fours
1980	Cromer & District, Norfolk
1981	Owton Lodge, Durham
1982	Castle, Nottinghamshire
1983	Bolton, Lancs
1984	Boscombe Cliff, Hampshire
1985	Aldershot, Essex
1986	Stony Stratford, Bucks
1987	Aylesbury Town, Bucks
1988	Summertown, Oxon
1989	Blackheath & Greenwich, Kent

WOOLWICH MASTERS
Inaugurated 1978
Kodak Masters 1978-83, Gateway Masters 1984-87, Woolwich since 1988
1978	David Bryant (Eng)
1979	David Bryant (Eng)
1980	William Moseley (SA)
1981	William Moseley (SA)
1982	David Bryant (Eng)
1983	George Souza (HK)
1984	David Bryant (Eng)
1985	David Bryant (Eng)
1986	David Bryant (Eng)
1987	David Bryant (Eng)
1988	David Bryant (Eng)
1989	David Bryant (Eng)

MIDDLETON CUP
Inaugurated 1911. Winners since 1980:
1980	Northamptonshire
1981	Somerset
1982	Berkshire
1983	Surrey
1984	Somerset
1985	Northumberland
1986	Wiltshire
1987	Kent
1988	Northumberland
1989	Kent

CROWN GREEN BOWLS
Waterloo Cup
Inaugurated 1907. Played at Waterloo Hotel, Blackpool. Winners since 1980:
Men
1980	Vernon Lee
1981	Roy Nicholson
1982	Dennis Mercer
1983	Stan Frith
1984	Steve Ellis
1985	Tommy Johnstone
1986	Brian Duncan
1987	Brian Duncan
1988	Ingham Gregory
1989	Brian Duncan

Most wins: Brian Duncan 4

Women
(Inaugurated 1988)
1988	Barbara Rawcliffe
1989	Diane Hunt

--- **1990** ---

Jul 6 British Isles championships, men (Edinburgh); Aug 13-24 Woolwich English National championships, men (Worthing); Aug 25 Middleton Cup finals (Worthing); Sep 1-2 Champion of Champions, men (Bath).

BOXING

HYPE, HYPE, HOORAY

The world heavyweight champion Mike Tyson successfully defended his title twice in the period under review. The second contest, against Carl "The Truth" Williams, lasted 93 seconds. The first, against Frank Bruno, lasted months.

The actual fighting lasted until the fifth round and Tyson's title and Bruno's pride and brain were all left intact. It was the least undistinguished British challenge since Henry Cooper and perhaps since Don Cockell. But the actual contest was nothing compared to the prolonged build-up which produced five postponements and endless newspaper copy as Tyson's contractual, physical, mental and marital problems multiplied.

Eleven days before the bout Tyson took Valentine's Day off training to divorce Robin Givens in the Dominican Republic due to "irreconcilable differences". Three days after that a $10 million writ arrived from his ex-trainer Kevin Rooney. The champ was also involved in a street brawl with one of his former opponents, Mitch Green, and several arguments involving cars. Bruno trained steadily under a hypnotist, amongst others, as this went on. British punters were sufficiently fooled to put £1 million on him; closer observers, seeing Tyson finally knuckle down in the weeks before the fight, thought Bruno would not last a round. It turned into a raw, no-prisoners, fight with Tyson looking murderous even if he was short of his lethal best; Bruno went down briefly after only 8 seconds but he got up and clung on extremely well (often literally), rocking the champ more than once with rights and doing something to erase the tradition of horizontal British heavyweights.

In Leeds, Keith Raby, 28, died after a pre-fight argument in a Chinese takeaway about who would win. Bruno came home to replace Derek Jameson as host of the BBC programme People, which wanted to move up-market, and to be cast as Wishee-Washee's minder in a London production of Aladdin. Tyson went on to be made an honorary doctor of humane letters by Central State University, Ohio, get a writ from Mitch Green demanding $30 million and a rematch in the ring and endure a great many revelations from his ex-wife, who said Tyson hit her too.

His contest with Williams was short and bitter. It ended after 93 seconds with an axe-like left hook to the jaw. Williams claimed the fight should never have been stopped, which was not a widespread view. Tyson's popularity as a box-office draw appeared to be waning because there was no one in sight who could even make a contest interesting, though Tyson v Givens could have filled any hall.

The most hyped contest of the year involved the two ageing troupers, Sugar Ray Leonard and Thomas Hearns, whose meeting in Las Vegas ended in a draw even though Hearns knocked Leonard down twice and most people thought he had won. More important, Leonard (33) made $13m and Hearns (30) $11m. There was talk of yet another rematch; up-and-coming fighters complained that they could never get a look in because TV was only interested in nostalgic names. Hearns' brother Henry was arrested 24 hours before the fight and charged with first-degree murder after the shooting of his girlfriend in the boxer's house in Southfield, Michigan.

Five British boxers held world titles at different times with varying degrees of conviction. By the autumn, Britons held only two crowns, both trivial. Dave McAuley, the Larne chef, won the IBF flyweight title from another Briton, Duke McKenzie, at Wembley Arena on June 7. Glenn McCrory became IBF cruiserweight champion when he outpointed Patrick Lumumba of Kenya in the un-Vegas-like setting of Stanley, Co. Durham, which had the twin advantages of being 300 yards from his own house and had a local council willing to stage the fight on the rates. McCrory had lost four of his five bouts in 1986 and almost retired. "It seemed a pity to spoil the fun." wrote John Rodda in *The Guardian*, "but outside in the cool night air one could not recall such an appalling world title fight."

BITTER HONEY

Lloyd Honeyghan, after much pre-fight cockiness, lost his WBC welterweight title to Marlon Starling when he was stopped in the ninth. Honeyghan suffered a pinched nerve and was taken from Caesars Palace to Valley Hospital, a route taken before by several other British fighters including McGuigan, Hope, Boza-Edwards and Minter. It was only Honeyghan's second defeat in 34 fights. He then became the first boxer to test positive in a drugs test after a WBC title fight when traces of the dentists' pain-killer Lidocaine were found. It had not helped his performance much; Honeyghan was fined $1500.

BEFORE

"This time it's war."
Advertisement for Tyson-Bruno fight

"Bored, bored, bored man, is what I am of this place. Stuck in here all the time drives me crazy and I've got another five weeks of it."
Mike Tyson at training camp

"Yeah, I do get scared. I get scared at night when I get chased by monsters. Happens all the time. I dream a lot and I'm always getting chased by monsters."
Mike Tyson

"The problem is that Michael and I are very similar. We're both fighters."
Robin Givens, Tyson's ex-wife

"Tyson's troubles are mounting so inexorably he may have agreed to fight Frank Bruno for an interlude of comparative affection and calm in his life."
Jonathan Foster, The Independent

"It only takes him a minute to put me to sleep and when I wake up I feel as if I could fight King Kong, let alone Mike Tyson."
Frank Bruno on his hypnotist, David Silverman

"The fact that Bruno is going into the ring with me is taken by some people to mean that he has a chance. In fact, it really means he has no chance. I'm not normally a hostile person but I have to say he's in trouble, real trouble."
Mike Tyson

"Bruno figures to be the biggest British disaster since the Titanic... Las Vegas will bet you even money Bruno doesn't last the first round. He's 7¹/₂ to 1 to lose, 6 to 1 to get knocked out, he's probably 7 to 5 to get killed. If Bruno lasts much past the introductions, if he is still upright as the strains of God Save The Queen die on the night air – and are not quickly followed by him – Tyson may have to leave town in disgrace and incognito."
Jim Murray, Los Angeles Times

"There is going to be a war and I want to put a disclaimer out that whatever happens is no indication of anything that would be offensive to the Honourable Margaret Thatcher, Prime Minister of England. By no stretch of the imagination do we mean to be offensive when we send back Bruno in an incapacitated state."
Don King, promoter

"Don King has made Mike Tyson out to be Superman. But I've got the Kryptonite to beat him."
Frank Bruno

...AND AFTER

"I'm sorry and that's cricket, you know."
Frank Bruno

"Frank is one of the Lord's chosen. Whatever happens he always comes sunny side up."
Terry Lawless, Bruno's manager

"I was thinking when he got up he meant business after all, man. He was throwing a great deal of hard punches but I refuse to go down."
Mike Tyson

"Bruno was Bruno. Tyson was terrible."
Bert Randolph Sugar, Boxing Illustrated

"How dare these people challenge me with their primitive boxing skills? They are all as good as dead. I've said it all along. I'm the best in the world."
Mike Tyson

"Carl, I'm sorry man. This is bullshit."
Mike Tyson, after the Williams fight was stopped in 93 seconds

"I was just a little stunned. I wasn't on Queer Street. I wasn't wandering round the ring, disbobulating."
Carl Williams, ditto

"The fact is Carl fights better after he gets stunned and gets up."
Williams' manager Carmen Graziano, ditto

"In my mind they're nothing more than legalised extortion."
Joseph Spinelli, New York state inspector-general, on Don King's contracts

"I will not allow Tyson to be added to the scores of boxers who claim to have been raped and pillaged by King. I will do everything in my power to keep him from committing economic suicide."
Bill Cayton, Tyson's estranged manager

"Mr Cayton is an inveterate liar. He's a tyrant, a despot, a power zealot. He's an egotistical maniac. Nobody likes Bill Cayton. He's never been liked by anybody."
Don King

LEONARD: Are you talking rematch, Tommy?
HEARNS: If you want to, I do.

"I don't think they should fight again. I don't think they should be allowed to fight again. But I don't know who can stop them."
Ferdie Pacheco, NBC TV

"I'm afraid Herol Graham just doesn't figure in our plans now or in the future. I find him utterly boring."
Bob Arum, US promoter

"My opinion is that the brain should not be a target in any sport and no amount of juggling with the regulations can take away the risk."
J.A.N. Corsallis, professor of neuropathology, British Medical Journal

"There could be a clash of heads. You might have a cut, he might have a cut, you get into some fighting inside, heads are rubbing together, blood is mingling."
Barry McGuigan on refusing to fight homosexuals

"After the sixth round I decided to give the boy a chance, let him have the title. He's a nice boy but I could have beaten him if I had tried."
Patrick Lumumba, after being beaten by Glenn McCrory

"Francesco Damiani ... is the perfect champion for the WBO, a new organisation that is even less needed than the WBA, the WBC and the IBF. At least Damiani's appearance will calm the notion that boxing is a brutal sport. He punches with all the violence and bad intentions of Mahatma Gandhi."
Jerry Izenberg, Newark Star-Ledger

Two weeks after that, Dennis Andries, the persevering light-heavyweight from Hackney (age: thirtysomething), won back the WBC title he had lost to Thomas Hearns in 1987 to become the third Briton to regain a world title – after Honeyghan and Ted "Kid" Lewis. Much credit was given to Andries for going to the Kronk gym in Detroit and restoring his career. His next scheduled opponent Donny Lalonde promptly retired and Andries was expected to have an easy ride against Jeff Harding, the Australian stand-in. Harding stopped him in the 12th.

Herol Graham almost became the WBA middleweight champion when he went down to Mike McCallum on a split points decision. In effect Graham missed out by the single point the referee deducted when he was warned for wrestling in the eighth. Sammy Reeson was much further away when he fought Carlos de Leon for the vacant WBC cruiserweight title: he was stopped in the ninth. Two former British world champions tried to come back: Barry McGuigan gave up after being stopped by Jim McDonnell; Terry Marsh never got into the ring. He claimed that the apparent epilepsy which had forced him to retire in the first place was in fact a condition brought on by eating too many Mars bars. The British Boxing Board were unconvinced.

The most potent all-British fight for years took place in Finsbury Park on May 21 when Nigel Benn (after 22 fights, 22 wins and just 41 rounds) lost both his Commonwealth title and his unbeaten record to the much less publicised Michael Watson. Benn was reported to have insured his hands for £10 million at an annual premium of £35,000. He forgot to insure his chin and was knocked out in the sixth. His second most difficult contest came when the police mistakenly issued his picture as a wanted gunman. Two people tried to effect citizen's arrests, one grabbing hold and jumping on top of him. Later, Benn opted to go to the US to train under Kevin Rooney. "I'm going to lead a monk's life," he said. The unluckiest ex-champion of all was René Jacquot of France, who lost his WBC super-welterweight title to John Mugabi of Uganda when he twisted his ankle in the first. The most troubled reigning champion was the IBF super-middleweight Graciano Rocchigniani who was arrested in Berlin on charges of white slavery, procuring and extortion.

THE HARDER THEY FALL

Former champions also continued to have the difficulties traditional in their calling. Carlos Monzon, former world middleweight champion, was sentenced to 11 years in jail (probably under five years in practice) in Mar del Plata, Argentina, for the murder of his third ex-wife who died after falling from a second-floor balcony after a row over alimony. A court in Knoxville, Tennessee ordered an auction of the possessions of John Tate, the former heavyweight champion. It secured $45 for his shorts, $200 for his robe and $300 for his gloves. The former British heavyweight challenger Richard Dunn was found working happily on a North Sea oil rig and living in Scarborough. The former world light-heavyweight champion John Conteh was briefly declared bankrupt on a tax claim of £48,000. Marvin Hagler and his family were ordered to get their troublesome cocker spaniel Cuddles out of Hanover, Massachusetts by the local council.

Pro boxing was staged in the Soviet Union in May. In China, where all boxing was illegal from 1959 to 1986, the sport was reported to be booming with thousands of people pouring in to watch fighters contest £10 purses. In the west, boxing faced tougher times. Roy Hodgson, a 21-year-old soldier with the Royal Irish Rangers, died from brain damage after a bout at the barracks. A study showed that an average of 67 American soldiers were taken to hospital each year between 1980 and 1985 because of boxing injuries. An 18-year-old amateur from Tennessee, Guydell Williams, died of a stroke after fighting twice in one day in an amateur championship. The International Amateur Boxing Association decided that amateurs would in future be allowed to receive prize money, thus presumably creating a new sport to be known as professional boxing.

THE WORLD TITLE FIGHTS OF MIKE TYSON

Date	Opponent	Venue	Titles	Won
Nov 22, 1986	Trevor Berbick	Las Vegas	WBC	ko 2nd
Jul 3, 1987	James Smith	Las Vegas	WBC/WBA	pts 12
May 30, 1987	Pinklon Thomas	Las Vegas	WBC/WBA	ko 6th
Aug 1, 1987	Tony Tucker	Las Vegas	WBC/WBA/IBF	pts 12
Oct 16, 1987	Tyrell Biggs	Atlantic City	WBC/WBA/IBF	ko 7th
Jan 22, 1988	Larry Holmes	Atlantic City	WBC/WBA/IBF	ko 4th
Mar 21, 1988	Tony Tubbs	Tokyo	IBF	ko 2nd
Jun 27, 1988	Michael Spinks	Atlantic City	WBC/WBA/IBF	ko 1st
Feb 25, 1989	Frank Bruno	Las Vegas	WBC/WBA/IBF	rsf 5th
Jul 21, 1989	Carl Williams	Atlantic City	WBC/WBA/IBF	rsf 1st

— WORLD TITLE FIGHTS 1989 —

(new champions underlined)

Heavyweight

Champions on Jan 1; WBC/WBA/IBF Mike Tyson, (US); WBO Vacant

WBC/WBA/IBF: 25, Las Vegas: Mike Tyson beat Frank Bruno (GB), rsf 5th

WBO: May 6, Syracuse, Italy: <u>Francesco Damiani (Ita)</u> beat Johnny Du Ploy (SA), ko 3rd

WBC/WBA/IBF: Jul 21, Atlantic City: Mike Tyson beat Carl 'The Truth' Williams (US), rsf 1st

Cruiserweight

Champions on Jan 1: all titles vacant

WBA: Mar 25, Casablanca: <u>Taoufik Belbouli (Fra)</u> beat Michael Greer (US), rsf 8th

WBC: May 17, Dockland Arena, London: <u>Carlos De Leon (PR)</u> beat Sammy Reeson (GB), rsf 9th

IBF: Jun 3, Stanley, Co. Durham: <u>Glenn McCrory (GB)</u> beat Patrick Lumumba (Ken), pts

Light-heavyweight

Champions on Jan 1: WBC vacant; WBA Virgil Hill (US); IBF Prince Charles Williams (US); WBO: Michael Moorer (US)

WBO: Feb 19, Monessen, Pennsylvania: Michael Moorer beat Frankie Swindell (US), rsf 6th.

WBC: Feb 22, Tucson, Arizona: <u>Dennis Andries (GB)</u> beat Tony Willis (US), rsf 5th.

WBA: Mar 4, Bismarck, North Dakota, Virgil Hill beat Bobby Czyz (US), pts.

WBO: Apr 22, Auburn Hills, Michigan: Michael Moorer beat Freddie Delgado (PR), rsf 1st

WBA: May 27, Bismarck, North Dakota; Virgil Hill beat Joe Lasisi (Nig), rsf 7th.

WBC: Jun 24, Atlantic City: <u>Jeff Harding (Aus)</u> beat Dennis Andries, rsf 12th.

IBF: Jun 25, Atlantic City; Prince Charles Williams beat Bobby Czyz, (US) TKO 10th.

WBO: Jun 25, Atlantic City; Michael Moorer beat Leslie Stewart (Tri), rsf 8th.

Super-middleweight

Champions on Jan 1: WBC: Sugar Ray Leonard (US); WBA: Fulgencio Obelmejias (Ven); IBF: Graciano Rocchigniani (FRG); WBO: Thomas Hearns (US).

IBF Jan 27, Berlin: Graciano Rocchigniani beat Tulane 'Sugar Boy' Malinga, (SA) pts.

WBA: May 27, Seoul: <u>In-Chul Baek (SKo)</u> beat Fulgencio Obelmejias, rsf 11th.

WBC: Jun 12, Las Vegas: Sugar Ray Leonard and Thomas Hearns (US), drew.

Middleweight

Champions on Jan 1: WBC Iran Barkley (US); WBA: Sambu Kalambay (Ita); IBF: Michael Nunn (US); WBO Vacant

WBC: Feb 24, Atlantic City: <u>Roberto Duran (Pan)</u> beat Iran Barkley, pts.

IBF: Mar 25, Las Vegas: Michael Nunn beat Sumbu Kalambay (Ita), ko 1st.

WBO: Apr 18, Atlantic City: Doug DeWitt (US) beat Robbie Simms (US), pts

WBA: May 10, Albert Hall, London: <u>Mike McCallum</u> (US) beat Herol Graham (GB), pts.

IBF: Aug 19, Reno, Nevada: Michael Nunn beat Iran Barkley (US), pts.

Junior-middleweight

Champions on Jan 1; WBC: Don Curry (US); WBA: Julian Jackson (VI); IBF: Robert Hines (US); WBO: John David Jackson (US)

IBF: Feb 4, Atlantic City: <u>Darrin Van Horn (US)</u> beat Robert Hines, pts.

WBC: Feb 11, Grenoble: <u>René Jacquot (Fra)</u> beat Don Curry, pts.

WBA: Feb 24, Las Vegas: Julian Jackson beat Francisco De Jesus (Bra), ko 8th.

WBO: Apr 22, Auburn Hills, Michigan: John David Jackson beat Steve Little (US), rsf 8th.

WBC: Jul 8, Paris: <u>John Mugabi (Uga)</u> beat René Jacquot, ko 1st.

IBF: Jul 16, Atlantic City: <u>Gianfranco Rossi (Ita)</u> beat Darrin van Horn, pts.

WBA: Jul 30, Atlantic City: Julian Jackson beat Terry Norris (US), rsf 2nd.

Welterweight

Champions on Jan 1: WBC Lloyd Honeyghan (GB); WBA Vacant; IBF Simon Brown (Jan); WBO: Vacant

WBA: Feb 4, Las Vegas: <u>Mark Breland (US)</u> beat Seung-Soon Lee (SKo), rsf 1st.

WBC: Feb 4, Las Vegas: <u>Marlon Starling (US)</u> beat Lloyd Honeyghan, rsf 9th.

IBF: Feb 18, Budapest: Simon Brown beat Jorge Maysonet (PR), rsf 3rd.

WBA: Apr 22, Atlantic City: Mark Breland beat Rafael Pineda (Col), ret 5th.

IBF: Apr 25, Washington: Simon Brown beat Al Long (US), rsf 7th.

WBO: May 6: Santa Ana, California: <u>Genaro Leon (Mex)</u> beat Danny Garcia (PR), rsf 1st.

Junior-welterweight

Champions on Jan 1: WBC Roger Mayweather (US); WBA Juan Martin Coggi (Arg); IBF Meldrick Taylor (US); WBO: Vacant.

IBF: Jan 21, Atlantic City: Meldrick Taylor beat John Meekins (US), rsf 7th

WBA: Jan 21, Vasto, Italy: Juan Martin Coggi beat Harold Brazier (USA), pts

WBO: Mar 6, Reno, Nevada: <u>Hector Camacho (PR)</u> beat Ray Mancini (US), pts.

WBA: Apr 29, Vasto, Italy: Juan Martin Coggi beat Akinobu Hiranaka (Jap), pts.

WBC: May 13, Los Angeles: <u>Julio Cesar Chavez (Mex)</u> beat Roger Mayweather, rsf 10th.

Lightweight

Champions on Jan 1; WBC/WBA: Julio Cesar Chavez (Mex); IBF: Greg Haugen (US); WBO: Vacant

WBO: Jan 21, Monteria, Colombia: <u>Amancio Castro (Col)</u> and Mauricio Aceves (Mex), drew.

IBF: Feb 20, Hampton, Virginia, <u>Pernell Whitaker (US)</u> beat Greg Haugen, pts.

IBF: May 1, Norfolk, Virginia; Pernell Whitaker beat Louie Lomeli (Ita), rsf 3rd.

WBO: May 6, Santa Ana, California: <u>Mauricio Aceves (Mex)</u> beat Amancio Castro (Col), pts.

WBA: Jul 9, Atlantic City: <u>Edwin Rosario (US)</u> beat Anthony 'Baby' Jones (US), rsf 6th.

WBC/IBF: Aug 20, Norfolk, Virginia: Pernell Whitaker beat Jose Luis Ramirez (Mex), pts.

Super-featherweight

Champions on Jan 1: WBC: Azumah Nelson (Gha); WBA: Brian Mitchell (SA); IBF: Tony Lopez (US); WBO: Vacant

WBA: Feb 10, Capo D'Orlando, Italy: Brian Mitchell beat Salvatore Bottiglieri (Ita), ko 8th.

WBC: Feb 25, Las Vegas: Azumah Nelson beat Mario Martinez (Mex), rsf 12th.

IBF: Mar 5, Sacramento: Tony Lopez beat Rocky Lockridge (US), pts.

WBO: Apr 29, San Juan, Puerto Rico: <u>Juan 'John-John' Molina (PR)</u> beat Juan Laporte (PR), pts.

IBF: Jun 21, Nevada: Tony Lopez beat Tyrone Jackson (US), rsf 8th.

WBA: Jul 1, Crotone, Italy: Brian Mitchell beat Jackie Beard (US), tko 9th.

Featherweight

Champions on Jan 1: WBC: Jeff Fenech (Aus); WBA: Antonio Esparragoza (Ven); IBF: Jorge Paez (Mex); WBO: Vacant.

WBO: Jan 28, Milan, Italy: Maurizio Stecca (Ita) beat Pedro Nolasco (Dom), rsf 6th.

WBA: Mar 25, Kawasaki, Japan: Antonio Esparragoza beat Mitsuru Sugiya (Jap), ko 10th.

IBF: Mar 30, Mexicali, Mexico: Jorge Paez beat Calvin Grove (US), ko 11th.

WBC: Apr 8, Melbourne: Jeff Fenech beat Marcos Villasana (Mex), pts.

IBF: May 22, Phoenix: Jorge Paez and Louie Espinoza (US), drew

WBA: Jun 3, Manur, Belgium: Antonio Esparragoza beat Jean-Marc Renard (Bel), ko 6th.

WBO: Jun 16, Milan: Maurizio Stecca beat Angel Levi Mayor (Ven), rsf 9th.

IBF: Aug 6, El Paso, Texas: Jorge Paez beat Steve Cruz (US), pts.

Super-bantamweight/Junior-featherweight

Champions on Jan 1: WBC: Daniel Zaragoza (Mex); WBA: Juan Jose Estrada (Mex); IBF: Jose Sanabria (Ven); WBO: Vacant.

IBF: Mar 10, Limoges: Fabrice Benichou (Fra) beat Jose Sanabria, pts.

WBA: Apr 5, Los Angeles: Juan Jose Estrada beat Jesus Poll (Ven), rsf 10th.

WBO: Apr 29, San Juan, Puerto Rico: Kenny Mitchell (US) beat Julio Gervacio (Dom), pts.

IBF: Jun 11, Frosinone, Italy: Fabrice Benichou beat Frans Cornelius Badenhorst (SA), ko 5th.

WBC: Jun 24, Los Angeles: Daniel Zaragoza beat Paul Banke (US), pts.

WBA: Jul 12, Tijuana, Mexico: Juan Jose Estrada beat Luis Mendoza (Col), pts.

Bantamweight

Champions on Jan 1: WBC: Raul Perez (Mex); WBA: Sung-Kil Moon (SKo); IBF: Orlando Canizales (US); WBO Vacant.

WBO: Feb 4, Caracas: Israel Contreras (Ven) beat Maurizio Lupino (Ita), ko 1st.

WBA: Feb 18, Seoul: Sung-Kil Moon beat Giaki Kobayashi (Jap), ko 5th.

WBC: Mar 10, Los Angeles: Raul Perez beat Lucio Lopez (Arg), pts.

IBF: Jun 24, Atlantic City: Orlando Canizales beat Kelvin Seabrooks (US), rsf 11th.

WBA: Jul 7, Bangkok: Khaokor Galaxy (Tha) beat Sung-Kil Moon, pts.

WBC: Aug 26, Talcahuano, Chile: Raul Perez beat Cerdenio Ulloa (Chi), tko 8th.

Super-flyweight/Junior-bantamweight

Champions on Jan 1: WBC Gilberto Roman (Mex); WBA Khaosai Galaxy (Tha); IBF Ellyas Pical (Ina) WBO: Vacant.

WBA: Jan 15, Bangkok, Thailand: Khaosai Galaxy beat Tae-Il Chang (SKo), ko 2nd.

IBF: Feb 25, Singapore: Ellyas Pical beat Mike Phelps (US), pts.

WBA: Apr 8, Yokohama, Japan: Khaosai Galaxy beat Kenji Matsumura (Jap), pts.

WBO: Apr 29, San Juan, Puerto Rico: Jose Ruiz (PR) beat Sugar Baby Rojas (Col), pts.

WBC: Jun 5, Los Angeles; Gilberto Roman beat Juan Carazo (PR), pts.

WBA: Jul 29, Surin, Thailand: Khaosai Galaxy beat Alberto Castro (Col), ret 10th.

Flyweight

Champions on Jan 1: WBC: Yung Kang-Kim (SKo); WBA: Fidel Bassa (Col); IBF: Duke McKenzie (GB); WBO: Vacant.

WBO: Mar 3, Medellin, Colombia: Elvis Alvarez (Col) beat Miguel Mercedes (Dom), pts.

WBC: Mar 5, Aomori, Japan; Yung Kang-Kim beat Yukhito Tamakuma (Jap), pts.

IBF: Mar 9, Royal Albert Hall, London: Duke McKenzie beat Tony DeLuca (US), rsf 4th.

WBA: Apr 15, Barranquilla, Colombia: Fidel Bassa beat Julio Gudino (Pan), rsf 6th.

WBC: Jun 3, Trang, Thailand: Sot Chitlada (Tha) beat Yung Kang-Kim, pts.

IBF: Jun 7, Wembley Arena: Dave McAuley (GB) beat Duke McKenzie (GB), pts.

Light-flyweight

Champions on Jan 1: WBC: German Torres (Mex); WBA: Myung-Woo Yuh (SKo); IBF: Tacy Macalos (Phi); WBO: Vacant.

WBC: Mar 19, Seoul: Yol-Woo Lee (SKo) beat German Torres, rsf 9th.

IBF: May 2, Bangkok: Muangchai Kittikasem (Tha) beat Tacy Macalos (Phi), pts.

WBO: May 19, San Juan, Puerto Rico: Jose de Jesus (PR) beat Fernando Martinez (Mex), rsf 9th.

WBA: Jun 11, Inchon, Korea: Myung-Woo Yuh beat Mario DeMarco (Arg), pts.

WBC: Jun 25, Chongju, Korea: Humberto Gonzalez (Mex) beat Yol-Woo Lee, pts.

Straw-weight

Champions on Jan 1: WBC: Napa Kiatwanchai (Tha); WBA: Leo Gomez (Dom): IBF: Samuth Sithnaruepol (Tha); WBO: Vacant.

WBC: Feb 11, Korat: Napa Kiatwanchai beat John Arief (Ina), pts.

IBF: Mar 23, Jakarta, Samuth Sithanaruepol and Nico Thomas (Ina), drew.

WBA: Apr 16, Pohang, S. Korea: Kim Bong-Jun (SKo) beat Agustin Garcia (Col), rsf 7th.

WBC: Jun 10, Osaka, Japan: Napa Kiatwanchai beat Hiroki Ioka (Jap), rsf 11th.

IBF: Jun 17, Jakarta, Nico Thomas (Ina) beat Samuth Sithanaruepol, pts.

WBA: Aug 6, Seoul:Kim Bong-Jun beat Lee Sam-Jung (SKo), pts.

BRITISH TITLE FIGHTS 1989
Heavyweight

Champions as at Jan 1: Vacant

Jan 18, Kensington: Gary Mason (Chatham) beat Trevor Hughroy Currie (Catford), ko 4th.

Jun 28, Brentwood: Gary Mason beat Jess Harding (Potters Bar), rsf 2nd.

Cruiserweight

Champion as at Jan 1: Andy Straughn (Hitchin)

May 21, Finsbury Park: Johnny Nelson (Sheffield) beat Andy Straughn, ko 8th.

Light-heavyweight

Champion as at Jan 1: Tony Wilson (Wolverhampton)

Jan 25, Bethnal Green: Tony Wilson beat Brian Schumacher (Liverpool), rsf 3rd.

Mar 22, Reading: Tom Collins (Leeds) beat Tony Wilson, rsf 2nd.

Super middleweight

(title inaugurated 1989)

Sep 19, Belfast: Sam Storey (Belfast) beat Tony Burke (Croydon), pts

Middleweight
Champion as at Jan 1: Herol Graham (Sheffield)
No fights

Light-middleweight
Champion as at Jan 1: Gary Stretch (St Helens)
No fights

Welterwight
Champion as at Jan 1: Kirkland Laing (Nottingham)
No fights

Light-welterweight
Champion as at Jan 1: Lloyd Christie (Coventry)
Jan 24, King's Heath, Birmingham: <u>Clinton McKenzie</u> (Croydon) beat Lloyd Christie ko 2nd. McKenzie relinquished title.

May 9, St. Albans: <u>Pat Barrett</u> (Manchester) beat Tony Willis (Liverpool) ko 9th.

Lightweight
Champion as at Jan 1: Steve Boyle (Glasgow)
No fights

Super-featherweight
Champion as at Jan 1: Floyd Havard (Merthyr)
Sep 7, Port Talbot: <u>John Doherty</u> (Bradford) beat Floyd Havard, ret 11th.

Featherweight
Champion as at Jan 1: Paul Hodkinson (Kirkby)
Sep 7, Port Talbot: Paul Hodkinson beat Peter Harris (Swansea), rsf 9th.

Bantamweight
Champion as at Jan 1: Billy Hardy (Sunderland)
Feb 14, Sunderland: Billy Hardy beat Ronnie Carroll (Glasgow) pts.

Flyweight
Champion as at Jan 1: Pat Clinton (Glasgow) No fights

BRITISH BOXERS IN WORLD HEAVYWEIGHT TITLE FIGHTS

Jan 25, 1894   James J. Corbett beat CHARLIE MITCHELL, Jacksonville, Florida, ko 3rd.

Mar 17, 1897   BOB FITZSIMMONS beat James J. Corbett, Carson City, Nevada, ko 14th.

Jun 9, 1899   James J. Jeffries beat BOB FITZSIMMONS, Coney Island, New York, ko 11th.

Jul 25, 1902   James J. Jeffries beat BOB FITZSIMMONS, San Francisco, ko 8th.

Dec 2, 1907   Tommy Burns beat GUNNER MOIR, London, ko 10th.

Feb 10, 1908   Tommy Burns beat JACK PALMER, London, ko 4th.

Apr 18, 1908   Tommy Burns beat JEWEY SMITH, Paris, ko 5th.

Aug 30, 1937   Joe Louis beat TOMMY FARR, New York, pts 15.

May 16, 1955   Rocky Marciano beat DON COCKELL, San Francisco, rsf 9th.

May 1, 1959   Floyd Patterson beat BRIAN LONDON, Indianapolis, ko 11th.

May 21, 1966   Muhammad Ali beat HENRY COOPER, London, rsf 6th.

Aug 6, 1966   Muhammad Ali beat BRIAN LONDON, London, ko 3rd.

Jul 1, 1975   Muhammad Ali beat JOE BUGNER, Kuala Lumpur, pts 15.

May 25, 1976   Muhammad Ali beat RICHARD DUNN, Munich, rsf 5th.

Jul 20, 1986   Tim Witherspoon beat FRANK BRUNO, London, ko 11th.

Feb 25, 1989   Mike Tyson beat FRANK BRUNO, Las Vegas, rsf 5th.

COMMONWEALTH CHAMPIONS 1989

Weight	Champion on Jan 1	New Champion(s) during 1989
HEAVYWEIGHT	Derek Williams (Eng)	None
CRUISERWEIGHT	Glenn McCrory (Eng)	Apollo Sweet (Aus)
LIGHT-HEAVYWEIGHT	Willie Featherstone (Can)	Guy Waters (Aus)
MIDDLEWEIGHT	Nigel Benn (Eng)	Michael Watson (Eng)
LIGHT-MIDDLEWEIGHT	Troy Waters (Aus)	None
WELTERWEIGHT	Gary Jacobs (Sco)	None
LIGHT-WELTERWEIGHT	Lester Ellis (Aus)	Steve Larramore (Bah)
LIGHTWEIGHT	Mo Hussein (Eng)	Pat Doherty (Eng), Najib Daho (Eng)
SUPER-FEATHERWEIGHT	John Sichula (Zam)	None
FEATHERWEIGHT	Thunder Ayeh (Ghana)	Oblitei Commey (Gha)
BANTAMWEIGHT	Ray Minus Jr (Bah)	None
FLYWEIGHT	Nana Yaw Konandu (Gha)	None

EUROPEAN CHAMPIONS 1989

Weight	Champion as at Jan 1	New Champion(s) 1989
HEAVYWEIGHT	Francesco Damiani (Ita)	None
CRUISERWEIGHT	Vacant	Angelo Rottoli (Ita)
LIGHT-HEAVYWEIGHT	Jan Lefeber (Hol)	None
MIDDLEWEIGHT	Christophe Tiozzo (Fra)	Francesco dell'Aquila (Ita)
LIGHT-MIDDLEWEIGHT	René Jacquot (Fra)	Edip Secovic (Aut), Giuseppe Leto (Ita)
WELTERWEIGHT	Vacant	Nino La Rocca (Ita)
LIGHT-WELTERWEIGHT	Tex N'Kalankete (Fra)	Efrem Calmati (Ita)
LIGHTWEIGHT	Policarpo Diaz (Spa)	None
SUPER-FEATHERWEIGHT	Racheed Lawal (Den)	Daniel Londas (Fra)
FEATHERWEIGHT	Jean-Marc Renard (Bel)	Paul Hodkinson (GB)
BANTAMWEIGHT	Vincenzo Balcastro (Ita)	None
FLYWEIGHT	Vacant	Eyup Can (Den)

AMATEUR BOXING

ABA FINALS 1989

SUPER-HEAVYWEIGHT	Patrick Passley (Lynn) beat Walter Harewood (Horseley Hill), pts.
HEAVYWEIGHT	Henry Akinwande (Lynn) beat Herbie Hide (Norwich Lads), pts.
LIGHT-HEAVYWEIGHT	Nick Piper (Penarth) beat Les Hudson (Royal Navy), pts.
MIDDLEWEIGHT	Seymour Johnson (Gloucester) beat Henry Wharton (Bass St Patrick's), disq.
LIGHT-MIDDLEWEIGHT	Neville Brown (Burton Boys) beat Carlo Colarusso (Trostre), rsf 1st.
WELTERWEIGHT	Mark Elliot (Bennetts Banks) beat John Jones (Sefton), pts.
LIGHT-WELTERWEIGHT	Alan Hall (Shildon) beat Robert McCracken (Birmingham City), pts.
LIGHTWEIGHT	Mark Ramsey (Small Heath) beat Jason Matthews (Aberbargoed), pts.
FEATHERWEIGHT	Peter Richardson (Phil Thomas) beat John Williams (Pontypool & Panteg), pts.
BANTAMWEIGHT	Keith Howlett (Army) beat Marlon Jones (Newco Repton), pts.
FLYWEIGHT	John Lyon (Greenalls St Helens) beat John McLean (Army), pts.
LIGHT-FLYWEIGHT	Mickey Cantwell (Eltham & District) beat Ian Lang (Everton Red Triangle), pts.

WORLD CHAMPIONS

Heavyweight
1882	John L. Sullivan (US)	
1892	James J. Corbett (US)	
1897	Bob Fitzsimmons (GB)	
1899	James J. Jefferies (US)	
1905	Marvin Hart (US)	
1906	Tommy Burns (Can)	
1908	Jack Johnson (US)	
1915	Jess Willard (US)	
1919	Jack Dempsey (US)	
1926	Gene Tunney (US)	
1930	Max Schmeling (Ger)	
1932	Jack Sharkey (US)	
1933	Primo Carnera (Ita)	
1934	Max Baer (US)	
1935	James J. Braddock (US)	
1937	Joe Louis (US)	
1949	Ezzard Charles (US)	
1951	Jersey Joe Walcott (US)	
1952	Rocky Marciano (US)	
1956	Floyd Patterson (US)	
1959	Ingemar Johansson (Swe)	
1960	Floyd Patterson (US)	
1962	Sonny Liston (US)	
1964	Cassius Clay (US)	
1965	Ernie Terrell (US)	(WBA)
1968	Jimmy Ellis (US)	(WBA)
1970	Joe Frazier (US)	
1973	George Foreman (US)	
1974	Muhammad Ali (US)	
1978	Leon Spinks (US)	
1978	Ken Norton (US)	(WBC)
1978	Muhammad Ali (US)	(WBA)
1978	Larry Holmes (US)	(WBC)
1979	John Tate (US)	(WBA)
1980	Mike Weaver (US)	(WBA)
1982	Mike Dokes (US)	(WBA)
1983	Gerrie Coetzee (SA)	(WBA)
1984	Larry Holmes (US)	(IBF)
1984	Tim Witherspoon (US)	(WBC)
1984	Pinklon Thomas (US)	(WBC)
1984	Greg Page (US)	(WBA)
1985	Michael Spinks (US)	(IBF)
1985	Tony Tubbs (US)	(WBA)
1986	Tim Witherspoon (US)	(WBA)
1986	Trevor Berbick (Jam)	(WBC)
1986	James Smith (US)	(WBA)
1987	Mike Tyson (US)	(WBA/WBC)
1987	Tony Tucker (US)	(IBF)
1987	Mike Tyson (US)	
1989	Francesco Damiani (Ita)	(WBO)
1989	Mike Tyson (US)	(WBA/WBC/IBF)

Cruiserweight
1979	Marvin Camel (US)	(WBC)
1980	Carlos de Leon (PR)	(WBC)
1982	Ossie Ocasio (PR)	(WBA)
1982	S.T. Gordon (US)	(WBC)
1983	Carlos de Leon (PR)	(WBC)
1983	Marvin Camel (US)	(IBF)
1984	Lee Roy Murphy (US)	(IBF)
1984	Piet Crous (SA)	(WBA)
1985	Alfonso Ratliff (US)	(WBC)
1985	Dwight Muhammad Qawi (US)	(WBA)
1985	Bernard Benton (US)	(WBC)
1986	Carlos de Leon (PR)	(WBC)
1986	Evander Holyfield (US)	(WBA)
1986	Rickey Parkey (US)	(IBF)
1987	Francesco Damiani (Ita)	(WBA)
1987	Evander Holyfield (US)	(IBF)
1988	Evander Holyfield (US)	
1989	Taoufik Belbouli (Fra)	(WBA)
1989	Carlos de Leon (PR)	(WBC)
1989	Glenn McCrory (GB)	(IBF)

Light-heavyweight
1903	Jack Root (Aut)	
1903	George Gardner (Ire)	
1903	Bob Fitzsimmons (GB)	
1905	Jack O'Brien (US)	
1912	Jack Dillon (US)	
1916	Battling Levinsky (US)	

1920	Georges Carpentier (Fra)	
1922	Battling Siki (Sen)	
1923	Mike McTigue (Ire)	
1925	Paul Berlenbach (US)	
1926	Jack Delaney (Can)	
1927	Jim Slattery (US)	
1927	Tommy Loughran (US)	
1930	Jim Slattery (US)	
1930	Maxie Rosenbloom (US)	
1934	Bob Olin (US)	
1935	John Henry Lewis (US)	
1939	Melio Bettina (US)	
1939	Billy Conn (US)	
1941	Anton Christoforidis (Gre)	
1941	Gus Lesnevich (US)	
1948	Freddie Mills (GB)	
1950	Joey Maxim (US)	
1952	Archie Moore (US)	
1962	Harold Johnson (US)	
1963	Willie Pastrano (US)	
1965	Jose Torres (PR)	
1966	Dick Tiger (Nig)	
1968	Bob Foster (US)	
1971	Vicente Rondon (Ven)	(WBA)
1974	John Conteh (GB)	(WBC)
1974	Victor Galindez (Arg)	(WBA)
1977	Miguel Cuello (Arg)	(WBC)
1978	Mate Parlov (Yug)	(WBC)
1978	Mike Rossman (US)	(WBA)
1978	Marvin Johnson (US)	(WBC)
1979	Victor Galindez (Arg)	(WBA)
1979	Matthew Saad Muhammad (US)	(WBC)
1979	Marvin Johnson (US)	(WBA)
1980	Eddie Mustafa Muhammad (US)	(WBA)
1981	Michael Spinks (US)	(WBA)
1981	Dwight Muhammah Qawi (US)	(WBC)
1983	Michael Spinks (US)	
1985	J.B. Williamson (US)	(WBC)
1985	Slobodan Kacar (Yug)	(IBF)
1986	Marvin Johnson (US)	(WBA)
1986	Dennis Andries (GB)	(WBC)
1986	Bobby Czyz (US)	(IBF)
1987	Thomas Hearns (US)	(WBC)
1987	Leslie Stewart (Jam)	(WBA)
1987	Virgil Hill (US)	(WBA)
1987	Prince Charles Williams (US)	(IBF)
1988	Donny Lalonde (Can)	(WBC)
1988	Sugar Ray Leonard (US)	(WBC)
1988	Michael Moorer (US)	(WBO)
1989	Dennis Andries (GB)	(WBC)
1989	Jeff Harding (Aus)	(WBC)

ALL-BRITISH WORLD TITLE FIGHTS (Since 1946)

1946 Jackie Peterson beat Joe Curran, Flyweight

1948 Rinty Monaghan beat Jackie Paterson, Flyweight

1949 Rinty Monaghan beat Terry Allen, Flyweight

1980 Jim Watt beat Charlie Nash, Lightweight

1986 Dennis Andries beat Tony Sibson, Light-heavyweight

1989 Dave McAuley beat Duke McKenzie, Flyweight

Super-middleweight

1984	Murray Sutherland (Can)	(IBF)
1984	Chong-Pal Park (SKo)	(WBA)
1988	Graciano Rocchigniani (FRG)	(IBF)
1988	Fulgencio Obelmejias (Ven)	(WBA)
1988	Sugar Ray Leonard (US)	(WBC)
1988	Thomas Hearns (US)	(WBO)
1989	In-Chul Baek (SKo)	(WBA)

Middleweight

1891	Nonpareil Jack Dempsey (Ire)	
1891	Bob Fitzsimmons (GB)	
1897	Kid McCoy (US)	
1898	Tommy Ryan (US)	
1908	Stanley Ketchel (US)	
1908	Billy Papke (US)	
1908	Stanley Ketchel (US)	
1910	Billy Papke (US)	
1911	Cyclone Thompson (US)	
1911	Billy Papke (US)	
1912	Frank Mantell (US)	
1912	Billy Papke (US)	
1913	Frank Klaus (US)	
1913	George Chip (US)	
1914	Al McCoy (US)	
1917	Mike O'Dowd (US)	
1920	Johnny Wilson (US)	
1923	Harry Greb (US)	
1926	Tiger Flowers (US)	
1926	Mickey Walker (US)	
1931	Gorilla Jones (US)	
1932	Marcel Thil (Fra)	
1937	Fred Apostoli (US)	
1939	Ceferino Garcia (Phi)	
1940	Ken Overlin (US)	
1941	Billy Soose (US)	
1941	Tony Zale (US)	
1947	Rocky Graziano (US)	
1948	Tony Zale (US)	
1948	Marcel Cerdan (Alg)	
1949	Jake la Motta (US)	
1951	Sugar Ray Robinson (US)	
1951	Randolph Turpin (GB)	
1951	Sugar Ray Robinson (US)	
1953	Carl Bobo Olsen (Haw)	
1955	Sugar Ray Robinson (US)	
1957	Gene Fullmer (US)	
1957	Sugar Ray Robinson (US)	
1957	Carmen Basilio (US)	
1958	Sugar Ray Robinson (US)	
1960	Paul Pender (US)	
1961	Terry Downes (GB)	
1962	Paul Pender (US)	
1962	Dick Tiger (Nig)	
1963	Joey Giardello (US)	
1965	Dick Tiger (Nig)	
1966	Emile Griffith (VI)	
1968	Nino Benvenuti (Ita)	
1970	Carlos Monzon (Arg)	
1974	Rodrigo Valdez (Col)	(WBC)
1976	Carlos Monzon (Arg)	
1977	Rodrigo Valdez (Col)	
1978	Hugo Corro (Arg)	
1979	Vito Antuofermo (Ita)	
1980	Alan Minter (GB)	
1980	Marvin Hagler (US)	
1987	Sugar Ray Leonard (US)	(WBC)
1987	Frank Tate (US)	(IBF)
1987	Sambu Kalambay (Zai)	(WBA)
1987	Thomas Hearns (US)	(WBC)
1988	Iran Barkley (US)	(WBC)
1988	Michael Nunn (US)	(IBF)
1989	Roberto Duran (Pan)	(WBC)
1989	Mike McCallum (US)	(WBA)

Junior-middleweight

1962	Denny Moyer (US)	
1963	Ralph Dupas (US)	
1963	Sandro Mazzinghi (Ita)	
1965	Nino Benvenuti (Ita)	
1966	Ki-Soo Kim (SKo)	
1968	Sandro Mazzinghi (Ita)	
1969	Freddie Little (US)	
1970	Carmelo Bossi (Ita)	
1971	Koichi Wajima (Jap)	
1974	Oscar Albarado (US)	
1975	Koichi Wajima (Jap)	
1975	Miguel de Oliviera (Bra)	(WBC)
1975	Jae-Do Yuh (SKo)	(WBA)
1975	Elisha Obed (Bah)	(WBC)
1976	Koichi Wajima (Jap)	(WBA)
1976	Jose Duran (Spa)	(WBA)
1976	Eckhard Dagge (FRG)	(WBC)
1976	Angel Castellini (Arg)	(WBA)
1977	Eddie Gazo (Nic)	(WBA)
1977	Rocky Mattioli (Ita)	(WBC)
1978	Masashi Kudo (Jap)	(WBA)
1979	Maurice Hope (GB)	(WBC)
1979	Ayube Kalule (Uga)	(WBA)
1981	Wilfred Benitez (US)	(WBC)
1981	Sugar Ray Leonard (US)	(WBA)
1981	Tadashi Mihara (Jap)	(WBA)
1982	Davey Moore (US)	(WBA)
1982	Thomas Hearns (US)	(WBC)
1983	Roberto Duran (Pan)	(WBA)
1984	Mark Medal (US)	(IBF)
1984	Mike McCallum (Jam)	(WBA)
1984	Carlos Santos (PR)	(IBF)
1986	Buster Drayton (US)	(IBF)
1986	Duane Thomas (US)	(WBC)
1987	Matthew Hilton (Can)	(IBF)
1987	Lupe Aquino (Mex)	(WBC)
1988	Gianfranco Rossi (Ita)	(WBC)
1988	Don Curry (US)	(WBC)
1988	Julian Jackson (VI)	(WBA)
1988	Robert Hines (US)	(IBF)
1988	John David Jackson (US)	(WBO)
1989	Darrin Van Horn (US)	(IBF)
1989	René Jacquot (Fra)	(WBC)
1989	John Mugabi (Uga)	(WBC)
1989	Gianfranco Rossi (Ita)	(IBF)

Welterweight

1892	Billy Smith (US)	
1894	Tommy Ryan (US)	
1898	Billy Smith (US)	
1900	Rube Ferns (US)	
1900	Matty Matthews (US)	
1901	Rube Ferns (US)	
1901	Joe Walcott (Bar)	
1904	Dixie Kid (US)	
1905	Joe Walcott (Bar)	
1906	Honey Mellody (US)	
1907	Mike Sullivan (US)	
1908	Harry Lewis (US)	
1914	Waldemar Holberg (Den)	
1914	Tom McCormick (Ire)	
1914	Matt Wells (GB)	
1915	Mike Glover (US)	
1915	Jack Britton (US)	
1915	Ted Kid Lewis (GB)	
1916	Jack Britton (US)	
1917	Ted Kid Lewis (GB)	
1919	Jack Britton (US)	
1922	Mickey Walker (US)	
1926	Pete Latzo (US)	
1927	Joe Dundee (Ita)	
1928	Jack Thompson (US)	
1929	Jackie Fields (US)	
1930	Jack Thompson (US)	

1930	Tommy Freeman (US)	
1931	Jack Thompson (US)	
1931	Lou Brouillard (Can)	
1932	Jackie Fields (US)	
1933	Young Corbett III (Ita)	
1933	Jimmy McLarnin (Ire)	
1934	Barney Ross (US)	
1934	Jimmy McLarnin (Ire)	
1935	Barney Ross (US)	
1938	Henry Armstrong (US)	
1940	Fritzie Zivic (US)	
1941	Red Cochrane (US)	
1946	Marty Servo (US)	
1946	Sugar Ray Robinson (US)	
1951	Johnny Bratton (US)	
1951	Kid Gavilan (Cub)	
1954	Johnny Saxton (US)	
1955	Tony de Marco (US)	
1955	Carmen Basilio (US)	
1956	Johnny Saxton (US)	
1956	Carmen Basilio (US)	
1958	Virgil Atkins (US)	
1958	Don Jordon (Dom)	
1960	Benny Kid Paret (Cub)	
1961	Emile Griffith (VI)	
1961	Benny Kid Paret (Cub)	
1962	Emile Griffith (VI)	
1963	Louis Rodriguez (Cub)	
1963	Emile Griffith (VI)	
1966	Curtis Cokes (US)	
1969	Jose Napoles (Cub)	
1970	Billy Backus (US)	
1971	Jose Napoles (Cub)	
1975	Angel Espada (PR)	(WBA)
1975	John H. Stracey (GB)	(WBC)
1976	Carlos Palomino (Mex)	(WBC)
1976	Pipino Cuevas (Mex)	(WBA)
1979	Wilfred Benitez (US)	(WBC)
1979	Sugar Ray Leonard (US)	(WBC)
1980	Roberto Duran (Pan)	(WBC)
1980	Thomas Hearns (US)	(WBA)
1980	Sugar Ray Leonard (US)	(WBC)
1981	Sugar Ray Leonard (US)	
1983	Don Curry (US)	(WBA)
1983	Milton McCrory (US)	(WBC)
1984	Don Curry (US)	(IBF)
1985	Don Curry (US)	
1986	Lloyd Honeyghan (GB)	
1987	Mark Breland (US)	(WBA)
1987	Lloyd Honeyghan (GB)	(WBC/IBF)
1987	Marlon Starling (US)	(WBA)
1987	Jorge Vaca (Mex)	(WBC)
1988	Simon Brown (Jam)	(IBF)
1988	Tomas Molinares (Col)	(WBA)
1988	Lloyd Honeyghan (GB)	(WBC)
1989	Mark Breland (US)	(WBA)
1989	Marlon Starling (US)	(WBC)
1989	Genaro Leon (Mex)	(WBO)

Junior-welterweight

1922	Pinky Mitchell (US)	
1926	Mushy Callahan (US)	
1930	Jackie Kid Berg (GB)	
1931	Tony Canzoneri (US)	
1932	Johnny Jaddick (US)	
1933	Battling Shaw (Mex)	
1933	Tony Canzoneri (US)	
1933	Barney Ross (US)	
1946	Tippy Larkin (US)	
1959	Carlos Ortiz (PR)	
1969	Duilio Loi (Ita)	
1962	Eddie Perkins (US)	
1962	Duilio Loi (Ita)	
1963	Roberto Cruz (Phi)	
1963	Eddie Perkins (US)	

1965	Carlos Hernandez (Ven)	
1966	Sandro Lopoplo (Ita)	
1967	Paul Fujii (Haw)	
1968	Nicolino Loche (Arg)	(WBA)
1968	Pedro Adigue (Phi)	(WBC)
1970	Bruno Acari (Ita)	(WBC)
1972	Alfonso Frazer (Pan)	(WBA)
1972	Antonio Cervantes (Col)	(WBA)
1974	Perico Fernandez (Spa)	(WBC)
1975	Saensak Muangsurin (Tha)	(WBC)
1976	Wilfred Benitez (US)	(WBA)
1976	Miguel Velasquez (Spa)	(WBC)
1976	Saensak Muangsurin (Tha)	(WBC)
1977	Antonio Cervantes (Col)	(WBA)
1978	Sang-Hyun Kim (SKo)	(WBC)
1980	Saoul Mamby (US)	(WBC)
1980	Aaron Pryor (US)	(WBA)
1982	Leroy Haley (US)	(WBC)
1983	Aaron Pryor (US)	(IBF)
1983	Bruce Curry (US)	(WBC)
1984	Johnny Bumphus (US)	(WBA)
1984	Billy Costello (US)	(WBC)
1984	Gene Hatcher (US)	(WBA)
1985	Ubaldo Sacco (Arg)	(WBA)
1985	Lonnie Smith (US)	(WBC)
1986	Patrizio Oliva (Ita)	(WBA)
1986	Gary Hinton (US)	(IBF)
1986	René Arredondo (Mex)	(WBC)
1986	Tsuyoshi Hamada (Jap)	(WBC)
1986	Joe Louis Manley (US)	(IBF)
1987	Terry Marsh (GB)	(IBF)
1987	Juan Martin Coggi (Arg)	(WBA)
1987	René Arredondo (Mex)	(WBC)
1988	James Buddy McGirt (US)	(IBF)
1988	Roger Mayweather (US)	(WBC)
1988	Meldrick Taylor (US)	(IBF)
1989	Hector Camacho (PR)	(WBO)
1989	Julio Cesar Chavez (Mex)	(WBC)

Lightweight

1896	George Lavigne (US)	
1899	Frank Erne (Swi)	
1902	Joe Gans (US)	
1908	Battling Nelson (Den)	
1910	Ad Wolgast (US)	
1912	Willie Ritchie (US)	
1914	Freddie Welsh (GB)	
1917	Benny Leonard (US)	
1925	Jimmy Goodrich (US)	
1925	Rocky Kansas (US)	
1926	Sammy Mandell (US)	
1930	Al Singer (US)	
1930	Tony Canzeroni (US)	
1933	Barney Ross (US)	
1935	Tony Canzeroni (US)	
1936	Lou Ambers (US)	
1938	Henry Armstrong (US)	
1939	Lou Ambers (US)	
1940	Lew Jenkins (US)	
1941	Sammy Angott (US)	
1942	Beau Jack (US)	
1943	Bob Montgomery (US)	
1943	Sammy Angott (US)	
1944	Juan Zurita (Mex)	
1945	Ike Williams (US)	
1951	Jimmy Carter (US)	
1952	Lauro Salas (Mex)	
1952	Jimmy Carter (US)	
1954	Paddy de Marco (US)	
1954	Jimmy Carter (US)	
1955	Wallace Bud Smith (US)	
1956	Joe Brown (US)	
1962	Carlos Ortiz (PR)	
1965	Ismael Laguna (Pan)	
1965	Carlos Ortiz (PR)	

1968	Carlos Teo Cruz (Dom)	
1969	Mando Ramos (US)	
1970	Ismael Laguna (Pan)	
1970	Ken Buchanan (GB)	(WBA)
1971	Pedro Carrasco (Spa)	(WBC)
1972	Mando Ramos (US)	(WBC)
1972	Roberto Duran (Pan)	(WBA)
1972	Chango Carmona (Mex)	(WBC)
1972	Rodolfo Gonzalez (Mex)	(WBC)
1974	Guts Ishimatsu (Jap)	(WBC)
1976	Esteban de Jesus (PR)	(WBC)
1978	Roberto Duran (Pan)	
1979	Jim Watt (GB)	(WBC)
1979	Ernesto Espana (Ven)	(WBA)
1980	Hilmer Kenty (US)	(WBA)
1981	Sean O'Grady (US)	(WBA)
1981	Alexis Arguello (Nic)	(WBC)
1981	Claude Noel (Tri)	(WBA)
1981	Arturo Frias (US)	(WBA)
1982	Ray Mancini (US)	(WBA)
1983	Edwin Rosario (PR)	(WBC)
1984	Charlie Brown (US)	(IBF)
1984	Livingstone Bramble (US)	(WBA)
1984	Harry Arroyo (US)	(IBF)
1984	Jose Luis Ramirez (Mex)	(WBC)
1985	Jimmy Paul (US)	(IBF)
1985	Hector Camacho (PR)	(WBC)
1986	Edwin Rosario (PR)	(WBA)
1986	Greg Haugen (US)	(IBF)
1987	Vinny Pazienza (US)	(IBF)
1987	Jose Luis Ramirez (Mex)	(WBC)
1987	Julio Cesar Chavez (Mex)	(WBA)
1988	Greg Haugen (US)	(IBF)
1988	Julio Cesar Chavez (Mex)	(WBC/WBA)
1989	Amancio Castro (Col)	(WBO)
1989	Pernell Whitaker (US)	(IBF)
1989	Mauricio Aceves (Mex)	(WBO)
1989	Edwin Rosario (PR)	(WBA)

Super-featherweight

1921	Johnny Dundee (Ita)	
1923	Jack Bernstein (US)	
1923	Johnny Dundee (Ita)	
1924	Kid Sullivan (US)	
1925	Mike Ballerino (US)	
1925	Tod Morgan (US)	
1929	Benny Bass (US)	
1931	Kid Chocolate (Cub)	
1933	Frankie Klick (US)	
1959	Harold Gomes (US)	
1960	Flash Elorde (Phi)	
1967	Yoshiaki Numata (Jap)	
1967	Hiroshi Kobayashi (Jap)	
1969	Rene Barrientos (Phi)	(WBC)
1970	Yoshiaki Numata (Jap)	(WBC)
1971	Alfredo Marcano (Ven)	(WBA)
1971	Ricardo Aredondo (Mex)	(WBC)
1972	Ben Villaflor (Phi)	(WBA)
1973	Kuniaki Shibata (Jap)	(WBA)
1973	Ben Villaflor (Phi)	(WBA)
1974	Kuniaki Shibata (Jap)	(WBC)
1975	Alfredo Escalera (PR)	(WBC)
1976	Sam Serrano (PR)	(WBA)
1978	Alexis Arguello (Nic)	(WBC)
1980	Yasutsune Vehare (Jap)	(WBA)
1980	Rafael Limon (Mex)	(WBC)
1981	Cornelius Boza Edwards (Uga)	(WBC)
1981	Sam Serrano (PR)	(WBA)
1981	Rolando Navarette (Phi)	(WBC)
1982	Rafael Limon (Mex)	(WBC)
1982	Bobby Chacon (US)	(WBC)
1983	Roger Mayweather (US)	(WBA)
1983	Hector Camacho (PR)	(WBC)
1984	Rocky Lockridge (US)	(WBA)
1984	Hwan-Kil Yuh (SKo)	(IBF)

1984	Julio Cesar Chavez (Mex)	(WBC)
1985	Lester Ellis (Aus)	(IBF)
1985	Wilfredo Gomez (PR)	(WBA)
1985	Barry Michael (Aus)	(IBF)
1986	Alfredo Layne (Pan)	(WBA)
1986	Brian Mitchell (SA)	(WBA)
1987	Julio Cesar Chavez (Mex)	(WBC)
1987	Rocky Lockridge (US)	(IBF)
1988	Azumah Nelson (Gha)	(WBC)
1988	Tony Lopez (US)	(IBF)
1989	Juan Molina (PR)	(WBO)

Featherweight

1891	Young Griffo (Aus)	
1892	George Dixon (Can)	
1897	Solly Smith (US)	
1898	Dave Sullivan (Ire)	
1898	George Dixon (Can)	
1900	Terry McGovern (US)	
1901	Young Corbett II (US)	
1904	Jimmy Britt (US)	
1904	Tommy Sullivan (US)	
1906	Abe Attell (US)	
1912	Johnny Kilbane (US)	
1923	Eugene Criqui (Fra)	
1923	Johnny Dundee (Ita)	
1925	Kid Kaplan (US)	
1927	Benny Bass (US)	
1928	Tony Canzoneri (US)	
1928	André Routis (Fra)	
1929	Battling Battalino (US)	
1932	Kid Chocolate (Cub)	
1933	Freddie Miller (US)	
1936	Petey Sarron (US)	
1937	Henry Armstrong (US)	
1938	Joey Archibald (US)	
1940	Harry Jeffra (US)	
1941	Joey Archibald (US)	
1941	Chalky Wright (Mex)	
1942	Willie Pep (US)	
1948	Sandy Saddler (US)	
1949	Willie Pep (US)	
1950	Sandy Saddler (US)	
1957	Hogan Kid Bassey (Nig)	
1959	Davey Moore (US)	
1963	Sugar Ramos (Cub)	
1964	Vicente Saldivar (Mex)	
1968	Howard Winstone (GB)	(WBC)
1968	Raul Rojas (US)	(WBA)
1968	Jose Legra (Cub)	(WBC)
1968	Shozo Saijyo (Jap)	(WBA)
1969	Johnny Famechon (Fra)	(WBC)
1970	Vicente Saldivar (Mex)	(WBC)
1970	Kuniaki Shibata (Jap)	(WBC)
1971	Antonio Gomez (Ven)	(WBA)
1972	Clemente Sanchez (Mex)	(WBC)
1972	Ernesto Marcel (Pan)	(WBA)
1972	Jose Legra (Cub)	(WBC)
1973	Eder Jofre (Bra)	(WBC)
1974	Ruben Olivares (Mex)	(WBA)
1974	Bobby Chacon (US)	(WBC)
1974	Alexis Arguello (Nic)	(WBA)
1975	Ruben Olivares (Mex)	(WBC)
1975	David Kotey (Gha)	(WBC)
1976	Danny Lopez (US)	(WBC)
1977	Rafael Ortega (Pan)	(WBA)
1977	Cecilio Lastra (Spa)	(WBA)
1978	Eusebio Pedroza (Pan)	(WBA)
1980	Salvador Sanchez (Mex)	(WBC)
1982	Juan Laporte (PR)	(WBC)
1984	Min-Keum Oh (SKo)	(IBF)
1984	Wilfredo Gomez (PR)	(WBC)
1984	Azumah Nelson (Gha)	(WBC)
1985	Barry McGuigan (Ire)	(WBA)
1985	Ki-Young Chung (SKo)	(IBF)

1986	Steve Cruz (US)	(WBA)
1986	Antonio Rivera (PR)	(IBF)
1987	Antonio Esparragoza (Ven)	(WBA)
1988	Calvin Grove (US)	(IBF)
1988	Jeff Fenech (Aus)	(WBC)
1988	Jorge Paez (Mex)	(IBF)
1989	Maurizio Stecca (Ita)	(WBO)

Junior-featherweight

1922	Jack Kid Wolfe (US)	
1923	Carl Duane (US)	
1976	Rigoberto Riasca (Pan)	(WBC)
1976	Royal Kobayashi (Jap)	(WBC)
1976	Dong-Kyun Yum (SKo)	(WBC)
1977	Wilfredo Gomez (PR)	(WBC)
1977	Soo-Hwan Hong (SKo)	(WBA)
1978	Ricardo Cardona (Col)	(WBA)
1980	Leo Randolph (US)	(WBA)
1980	Sergio Palma (Arg)	(WBA)
1982	Leo Cruz (Dom)	(WBA)
1983	Jaime Garza (US)	(WBC)
1983	Bobby Berna (Phi)	(IBF)
1984	Loris Stecca (Ita)	(WBA)
1984	Seung-Il Suh (SKo)	(IBF)
1984	Victor Callejas (PR)	(WBA)
1984	Juan Meza (Mex)	(WBC)
1985	Ji-Won Kim (SKo)	(IBF)
1985	Lupe Pintot (Mex)	(WBC)
1986	Samart Payakarun (Tha)	(WBC)
1987	Louis Espinoza (US)	(WBA)
1987	Seung-Hoon Lee (SKo)	(IBF)
1987	Jeff Fenech (Aus)	(WBC)
1987	Julio Gervacio (Dom)	(WBA)
1988	Bernardo Pinango (Ven)	(WBA)
1988	Daniel Zaragoza (Mex)	(WBC)
1988	Jose Sanabria (Ven)	(IBF)
1988	Juan Jose Estrada (Mex)	(WBA)
1989	Fabrice Benichou (Fra)	(IBF)
1989	Kenny Mitchell (US)	(WBO)

Bantamweight

1891	George Dixon (Can)	
1892	Billy Plimmer (GB)	
1895	Pedlar Palmer (GB)	
1899	Terry McGovern (US)	
1901	Harry Forbes (US)	
1903	Frankie Neil (US)	
1904	Joe Bowker (GB)	
1905	Jimmy Walsh (US)	
1907	Owen Moran (GB)	
1908	Johnny Coulon (Can)	
1914	Kid Williams (Den)	
1917	Pete Herman (US)	
1920	Joe Lynch (US)	
1921	Pete Herman (US)	
1921	Johnny Buff (US)	
1922	Joe Lynch (US)	
1924	Abe Goldstein (US)	
1924	Eddie Martin (US)	
1925	Charlie Rosenberg (US)	
1927	Bud Taylor (US)	
1928	Bushy Graham (Ita)	
1929	Al Brown (Pan)	
1935	Baltazar Sangchilli (Spa)	
1936	Tony Marino (US)	
1936	Sixto Escobar (Spa)	
1937	Harry Jeffra (US)	
1938	Sixto Escobar (Spa)	
1940	Lou Salica (US)	
1942	Manuel Ortiz (US)	
1947	Harold Dade (US)	
1947	Manuel Ortiz (US)	
1950	Vic Toweel (SA)	
1952	Jimmy Carruthers (Aus)	
1954	Robert Cohen (Alg)	
1956	Mario D'Agata (Ita)	

1957	Alphonse Halimi (Alg)	
1959	Joe Becerra (Mex)	
1960	Eder Jofre (Bra)	
1965	Fighting Harada (Jap)	
1968	Lionel Rose (Aus)	
1969	Ruben Olivares (Mex)	
1970	Chucho Castillo (Mex)	
1971	Ruben Olivares (Mex)	
1972	Rafael Herrera (Mex)	
1972	Enrique Pinder (Pan)	
1973	Romeo Anaya (Mex)	(WBA)
1973	Rafael Herrera (Mex)	(WBC)
1973	Arnold Taylor (SA)	(WBA)
1974	Soo-Hwan Hong (SKo)	(WBA)
1974	Rudolfo Martinez (Mex)	(WBC)
1975	Alfonso Zamora (Mex)	(WBA)
1976	Carlos Zarate (Mex)	(WBC)
1977	Jorge Lujan (Pan)	(WBA)
1979	Lupe Pintor (Mex)	(WBC)
1980	Julian Solis (PR)	(WBA)
1980	Jeff Changler (US)	(WBA)
1983	Alberto Davila (US)	(WBC)
1984	Richard Sandoval (US)	(WBA)
1984	Satoshi Shingaki (Jap)	(IBF)
1985	Jeff Fenech (Aus)	(IBF)
1985	Daniel Zaragoza (Mex)	(WBC)
1985	Miguel Lora (Col)	(WBC)
1986	Gaby Canizales (US)	(WBA)
1986	Bernardo Pinanago (Ven)	(WBA)
1987	Takuya Muguruma (Jap)	(WBA)
1987	Kelvin Seabrooks (US)	(IBF)
1987	Chang-Young Park (SKo)	(WBA)
1987	Wilfredo Vasquez (PR)	(WBA)
1988	Kaokor Galaxy (Tha)	(WBA)
1988	Orlando Canizales (US)	(IBF)
1988	Sung-Kil Moon (SKo)	(WBA)
1988	Raul Perez (Mex)	(WBC)
1989	Israel Contreras (Ven)	(WBO)
1989	Khaokor Galaxy (Tha)	(WBA)

Super-flyweight

1980	Rafael Orono (Ven)	(WBC)
1981	Chul-Ho Kim (SKo)	(WBC)
1981	Gustavo Ballas (Arg)	(WBA)
1981	Rafael Pedroza (Pan)	(WBA)
1982	Jiro Watanabe (Jap)	(WBA)
1982	Rafael Orono (Ven)	(WBC)
1983	Payao Poontarat (Tha)	(WBC)
1983	Joo-Do Chun (SKo)	(IBF)
1984	Jiro Watanabe (Jap)	(WBC)
1984	Kaosai Galaxy (Tha)	(WBA)
1985	Ellyas Pical (Ina)	(IBF)
1986	Cesar Polanco (Dom)	(IBF)
1986	Gilberto Roman (Mex)	(WBC)
1986	Tae-Il Chang (SKo)	(IBF)
1986	Ellyas Pical (Ina)	(IBF)
1987	Santos Laciar (Arg)	(WBC)
1987	Jesus Rojas (Col)	(WBC)
1988	Gilberto Roman (Mex)	(WBC)
1989	Jose Ruiz (PR)	(WBO)

Flyweight

1913	Sid Smith (GB)	
1913	Bill Ladbury (GB)	
1914	Percy Jones (GB)	
1915	Joe Symonds (GB)	
1916	Jimmy Wilde (GB)	
1923	Pancho Villa (Phi)	
1925	Fidel la Barba (US)	
1928	Frankie Genaro (US)	
1929	Emile Pladner (Fra)	
1929	Frankie Genaro (US)	
1931	Young Perez (Tun)	
1932	Jackie Brown (Eng)	
1935	Benny Lynch (GB)	
1938	Peter Kane (GB)	

1943	Jackie Paterson (GB)	
1948	Rinty Monaghan (GB)	
1950	Terry Allen (GB)	
1950	Dado Marino (Haw)	
1952	Yoshio Shirai (Jap)	
1954	Pascual Perez (Arg)	
1960	Pone Kingpetch (Tha)	
1960	Fighting Harada (Jap)	
1963	Pone Kingpetch (Tha)	
1963	Hiroyuki Ebihara (Jap)	
1964	Pone Kingpetch (Tha)	
1965	Salvatore Burruni (Ita)	
1966	Horacio Accavallo (Arg)	(WBA)
1966	Walter McGowan (GB)	(WBC)
1966	Chartchai Chionoi (Tha)	(WBC)
1969	Efren Torres (Mex)	(WBC)
1969	Hiroyuki Ebihara (Jap)	(WBA)
1969	Bernabe Villacampo (Phi)	(WBA)
1970	Chartchai Chionoi (Tha)	(WBC)
1970	Berkrerk Chartvanchai (Tha)	(WBA)
1970	Masao Ohba (Jap)	(WBA)
1970	Erbito Salavarria (Phi)	(WBC)
1972	Venice Borkorsor (Tha)	(WBC)
1973	Chartchai Chionoi (Tha)	(WBA)
1973	Betulio Gonzalez (Ven)	(WBC)
1974	Shoji Oguma (Jap)	(WBC)
1974	Susumu Hanagata (Jap)	(WBA)
1975	Miguel Canto (Mex)	(WBC)
1975	Erbito Salavarria (Phi)	(WBA)
1976	Alfonso Lopez (Pan)	(WBA)
1976	Guty Espadas (Mex)	(WBA)
1978	Betulio Gonzalez (Ven)	(WBA)
1979	Chan-Hee Park (SKo)	(WBC)
1979	Luis Ibarra (Pan)	(WBA)
1980	Tae-Shik Kim (SKo)	(WBA)
1980	Shoji Oguma (Jap)	(WBA)
1980	Peter Mathebula (SA)	(WBA)
1981	Santos Laciar (Arg)	(WBA)
1981	Antonio Avelar (Mex)	(WBC)
1981	Luis Ibarra (Pan)	(WBA)
1981	Juan Herrera (Mex)	(WBA)
1982	Prudencio Cardona (Col)	(WBC)
1982	Santos Laciar (Arg)	(WBA)
1982	Freddie Castillo (Mex)	(WBC)
1982	Eleoncio Mercedes (Dom)	(WBC)
1983	Charlie Magri (GB)	(WBC)
1983	Frank Cedeno (Phi)	(WBC)
1983	Soon-Chun Kwon (SKo)	(IBF)
1984	Koji Kobayashi (Jap)	(WBC)
1984	Gabriel Bernal (Mex)	(WBC)
1984	Sot Chitalada (Tha)	(WBC)
1985	Hilario Zapata (Pan)	(WBA)
1985	Chong-Kwan Chung (SKo)	(IBF)
1986	Bi-Won Chung (SKo)	(IBF)
1986	Hi-Sup Shin (SKo)	(IBF)
1987	Fidel Bassa (Col)	(WBA)
1987	Dodie Penalosa (Phi)	(IBF)
1987	Chang-Ho Choi (SKo)	(IBF)
1988	Rolando Bohol (Phi)	(IBF)
1988	Yung-Kang Kim (SKo)	(WBC)
1988	Duke McKenzie (GB)	(IBF)
1989	Elvis Alvarez (Col)	(WBO)
1989	Sot Chitalda (Tha)	(WBC)
1989	Dave McAuley (GB)	(IBF)

Light-flyweight

1975	Franco Udella (Ita)	(WBC)
1975	Jaime Rios (Pan)	(WBA)
1975	Luis Estaba (Ven)	(WBC)
1976	Juan Jose Guzman (Dom)	(WBA)
1976	Yoko Gushiken (Jap)	(WBA)
1978	Freddie Castillo (Mex)	(WBC)
1978	Netrnoi Vorasingh (Tha)	(WBC)
1978	Sung-Jun Kim (SKo)	(WBC)
1980	Shigeo Nakajima (Jap)	(WBC)

1980	Hilario Zapata (Pan)	(WBC)
1981	Pedro Flores (Mex)	(WBA)
1981	Hwan-Jin Kim (SKo)	(WBA)
1981	Katsuo Takashiki (Jap)	(WBA)
1982	Amado Ursua (Mex)	(WBC)
1982	Tadashi Tomori (Jap)	(WBC)
1982	Hilario Zapata (Pan)	(WBC)
1983	Jung-Koo Chang (Kor)	(WBC)
1983	Lupe Madera (Mex)	(WBA)
1983	Dodie Penalosa (Phi)	(IBF)
1984	Francisco Quiroz (Dom)	(WBA)
1985	Joey Olivo (US)	(WBA)
1985	Myung-Woo Yuh (SKo)	(WBA)
1986	Chong-Hwan Choi (SKo)	(IBF)

1988	Tacy Macalos (Phi)	(IBF)
1988	German Torres (Mex)	(WBC)
1989	Yol-Woo Lee (SKo)	(WBC)
1989	Muancgchai Kittikasem (Tha)	(IBF)
1989	Jose de Jesus (PR)	(WBO)
1989	Humberto Gonzalez (Mex)	(WBC)

Straw-weight

1987	Kyung-Yung Lee (SKo)	(WBC)
1988	Leo Gomez (Dom)	(WBA)
1988	Hiroki Ioka (Jap)	(WBC)
1988	Samuth Sithnaruepol (Tha)	(IBF)
1988	Napa Kiatwanchai (Tha)	(WBC)
1989	Kim Bong-Jun (SKo)	(WBA)
1989	Nico Thomas (Ina)	(IBF)

HEAVYWEIGHT CHAMPIONS

British

1891	Ted Pritchard
1895	Jem Smith
1897	George Crisp
1903	Jack Palmer
1906	Gunner Jim Moir
1909	William 'Iron' Hague
1911	Bombardier Billy Wells
1919	Joe Beckett
1919	Frank Goddard
1919	Joe Beckett
1923	Frank Goddard
1926	Phil Scott
1931	Reggie Meen
1932	Jack Petersen
1933	Len Harvey
1934	Jack Petersen
1936	Ben Foord
1937	Tommy Farr
1938	Len Harvey
1944	Jack London
1945	Bruce Woodcock
1950	Jack Gardner
1952	Johnny Williams
1953	Don Cockell
1956	Jack Erskine
1958	Brian London
1959	Henry Cooper
1969	Jack Bodell
1970	Henry Cooper
1971	Joe Bugner
1971	Jack Bodell
1972	Danny McAlinden
1975	Bunny Johnson
1975	Richard Dunn
1976	Joe Bugner
1978	John L Gardner
1981	Gordon Ferris
1981	Neville Meade
1983	David Pearce
1985	Hughroy Currie
1986	Horace Notice
1989	Gary Mason

European

1906	Gunner Moir (GB)
1909	Iron Hague (GB)
1911	Bombardier Billy Wells (GB)
1913	Georges Carpentier (Fra)
1922	Battling Siki (Sen)
1923	Erminio Spalla (Ita)
1926	Paolino Uzcudin (Spa)
1929	Pierre Charles (Bel)
1931	Heinz Muller (Ger)
1932	Pierre Charles (Bel)
1933	Paolino Uzcudin (Spa)
1933	Primo Carnera (Ita)
1935	Pierre Charles (Bel)
1937	Arno Kollin (Ger)
1938	Heinz Lazek (Aut)
1939	Adolph Heuser (Ger)
1939	Max Schmeling (Ger)
1943	Olle Tandberg (Swe)
1943	Karel Sys (Bel)
1946	Bruce Woodcock (GB)
1950	Jo Weidin (Aus)
1951	Jack Gardner (GB)
1951	Hein Ten Hoff (Ger)
1952	Karel Sys (Bel)
1952	Heinz Neuhaus (Ger)
1955	Franco Cavicchi (Ita)
1956	Ingemar Johansson (Swe)
1960	Dick Richardson (GB)
1962	Ingemar Johansson (Swe)
1964	Henry Cooper (GB)
1964	Karl Mildenberger (Ger)
1968	Henry Cooper (GB)
1969	Peter Weiland (Ger)
1970	Jose Urtain (Spa)
1970	Henry Cooper (GB)
1971	Joe Bugner (GB)
1971	Jack Bodell (GB)
1971	Jose Urtain (Spa)
1972	Jurgen Blin (Ger)
1972	Joe Bugner (GB)
1976	Richard Dunn (GB)
1976	Joe Bugner (GB)
1977	Jean-Pierre Coopman (Bel)
1977	Lucien Rodriguez (Fra)
1977	Alfredo Evangelista (Spa)
1979	Lorenzo Zanon (Ita)
1980	John L Gardner (GB)
1981	Lucien Rodriguez (Fra)
1984	Steffen Tangstad (Nor)
1985	Anders Eklund (Swe)
1985	Frank Bruno (GB)
1986	Steffen Tangstad (Nor)
1987	Alfredo Evangelista (Spa)
1987	Anders Eklund (Swe)
1988	Francesco Damiani (Ita)

Commonwealth

1910	Tommy Burns (Can)
1911	Matthew Curran (Eng)
1911	Bombardier Billy Wells (Eng)
1919	Joe Beckett (Eng)
1926	Phil Scott (Eng)
1931	Larry Gains (Can)
1934	Len Harvey (Eng)
1934	Jack Petersen (Wal)
1936	Ben Foord (SA)
1937	Tommy Farr (Wal)
1939	Len Harvey (Eng)
1944	Jack London (Eng)
1945	Bruce Woodcock (Eng)
1950	Jack Gardner (Eng)
1952	Johnny Williams (Wal)
1953	Don Cockell (Eng)
1956	Joe Bygraves (Jam)
1957	Joe Erskine (Wal)
1958	Brian London (Eng)
1959	Henry Cooper (Eng)
1971	Joe Bugner (Eng)
1971	Jack Bodell (Eng)
1972	Danny McAlinden (NI)
1975	Bunny Johnson (Eng)
1975	Richard Dunn (Eng)
1976	Joe Bugner (Eng)
1978	John L Gardner (Eng)
1981	Trevor Berbick (Can)
1986	Horace Notice (Eng)
1988	Derek Williams (Eng)

OLYMPIC CHAMPIONS

Super-heavyweight
1984	Tyrell Biggs (US)
1988	Lennox Lewis (Can)

Heavyweight
1904	Samuel Berger (US)
1908	A.L. Oldham (GB)
1912	Not held
1920	Ronald Rawson (GB)
1924	Otto von Porat (Nor)
1928	Arturo Rodriguez Jurado (Arg)
1932	Santiago Lovell (Arg)
1936	Herbert Runge (Ger)
1948	Rafael Iglesias (Arg)
1952	Edward Sanders (US)
1956	Peter Rademacher (US)
1960	Franco de Piccoli (Ita)
1964	Joe Frazier (US)
1968	George Foreman (US)
1972	Teofilio Stevenson (Cub)
1976	Teofilio Stevenson (Cub)
1980	Teofilio Stevenson (Cub)
1984	Henry Tillman (US)
1988	Ray Mercer (US)

Light-heavyweight
1920	Eddie Eagan (US)
1924	Harry Mitchell (GB)
1928	Victor Avendano (Arg)
1932	David Carstens (SA)
1936	Roger Michelot (Fra)
1948	George Hunter (SA)
1952	Norvel Lee (US)
1956	James Boyd (US)
1960	Cassius Clay (US)
1964	Cosimo Pinto (Ita)
1968	Dan Poznyak (USSR)
1972	Mate Parlov (Yug)
1976	Leon Spinks (US)
1980	Slobodan Kacar (Yug)
1984	Anton Jospovic (Yug)
1988	Andrew Maynard (US)

Middleweight
1904	Charles Mayer (US)
1908	John Douglas (GB)
1920	Harry Mallin (GB)
1924	Harry Mallin (GB)
1928	Piero Toscani (Ita)
1932	Carmen Barth (US)
1936	Jean Despeaux (Fra)
1948	Laszlo Papp (Hun)
1952	Floyd Patterson (US)
1956	Genaddy Schatkov (USSR)
1960	Edward Crook (US)
1964	Valery Popenchenko (USSR)
1968	Chris Finnegan (GB)
1972	Vyacheslav Lewechev (USSR)
1976	Michael Spinks (US)
1980	Jose Gomez (Cub)
1984	Sin-Joon Sup (SKo)
1988	Henry Maske (GDR)

Light-middleweight
1952	Laszlo Papp (Hun)
1956	Laszlo Papp (Hun)
1960	Wilbert McClure (US)
1964	Boris Lagutin (USSR)
1968	Boris Lagutin (USSR)
1972	Dieter Kottysch (FRG)
1976	Jerzy Rybicki (Pol)
1980	Armando Martinez (Cub)
1984	Frank Tate (US)
1988	Park Si-Hun (Kor)

Welterweight
1904	Albert Young (US)
1908	not held
1920	Albert Schneider (Can)
1924	Jean Delarge (Bel)
1928	Edward Morgan (NZ)
1932	Edward Flynn (US)
1936	Sten Suvio (Fin)
1948	Julius Torma (Cze)
1952	Zygmunt Chychia (Pol)
1956	Nicolae Linca (Rom)
1960	Giovanni Benvenuti (Ita)
1964	Marian Kasprzyk (Pol)
1968	Manfred Wolke (GDR)
1972	Emilio Correa (Cub)
1976	Jochen Bachfeld (GDR)
1980	Andres Aldama (Cub)
1984	Mark Breland (US)
1988	Robert Wangila (Ken)

Light-welterweight
1952	Charles Adkins (US)
1956	Vladimir Yengibaryan (USSR)
1960	Bohumil Nemecek (Cze)
1964	Jerzy Kulej (Pol)
1968	Jerzy Kulej (Pol)
1972	Ray Seales (US)
1976	Ray Leonard (US)
1980	Patrizio Oliva (Ita)
1984	Jerry Page (US)
1988	Viatcheslav Janovski (USSR)

Lightweight
1904	Harry Spanger (US)
1908	Frederick Grace (GB)
1920	Samuel Mosberg (US)
1924	Hans Neilsen (Den)
1928	Carlo Orlando (Ita)
1932	Lawrence Stevens (SA)
1936	Imre Harangi (Hun)
1948	Gerald Dreyer (SA)
1952	Aureliano Bolognesi (Ita)
1956	Dick McTaggart (GB)
1960	Kazimierz Pazdzior (Pol)
1964	Jozef Grudzien (Pol)
1968	Ron Harris (US)
1972	Jan Szczepanski (Pol)
1976	Howard Davis (US)
1980	Angel Herrera (Cub)
1984	Pernell Whitaker (US)
1988	Andreas Zuelow (GDR)

Featherweight
1904	Oliver Kirk (US)
1908	Richard Gunn (GB)
1920	Paul Fritsch (Fra)
1924	John Fields (US)
1928	Lambertus van Klavaren (Hol)
1932	Carmelo Robledo (Arg)
1936	Oscar Casanovas (Arg)
1948	Ernesto Formenti (Ita)
1952	Jan Zachara (Cze)
1956	Vladimir Safronov (USSR)
1960	Francesco Musso (Ita)
1964	Stanislav Stepashkin (USSR)
1968	Antonio Roldan (Mex)
1972	Boris Kousnetsov (USSR)
1976	Angel Herrera (Cub)
1980	Rudi Fink (GDR)
1984	Meldrick Taylor (US)
1988	Giovanni Parisi (Ita)

Bantamweight
1904	Oliver Kirk (US)
1908	Henry Thomas (GB)
1920	Clarence Walker (SA)

1924	William Smith (SA)
1928	Vittorio Tamagnini (Ita)
1932	Horace Gwynne (Can)
1936	Ulderico Sergo (Ita)
1948	Tibor Csik (Hun)
1952	Pentti Hamalainen (Fin)
1956	Wolfgang Behrendt (FRG)
1960	Oleg Grigoryev (USSR)
1964	Takao Sakurai (Jap)
1968	Valery Sokolov (USSR)
1972	Orlando Martinez (Cub)
1976	Yung-Jo Gu (NKo)
1980	Juan Hernandez (Cub)
1984	Maurizio Stecca (Ita)
1988	Kennedy McKinney (US)

Flyweight

1904	George Finnegan (US)
1908	not held
1920	Frank Di Gennara (US)
1924	Fidel La Barba (US)
1928	Antal Kocsis (Hun)
1932	Istvan Enekes (Hun)
1936	Willi Kaiser (Ger)
1948	Pascual Perez (Arg)
1952	Nathan Brooks (US)
1956	Terry Spinks (GB)
1960	Gyula Torok (Hun)
1964	Fernando Atzori (Ita)
1968	Ricardo Delgado (Mex)
1972	Georgi Kostadinov (Bul)
1976	Leo Randolph (US)
1980	Peter Lessov (Bul)
1984	Steve McCrory (US)
1988	Kim Kwang-Sun (Kor)

Light-flyweight

1968	Francisco Rodriguez (Ven)
1972	Gyorgy Gedo (Hun)
1976	Jorge Hernandez (Cub)
1980	Shamil Sabyrov (USSR)
1984	Paul Gonzales (US)
1988	Ivalio Hristov (Bul)

RECORDS

MOST WORLD TITLES
(at different weights)
5 Thomas Hearns; Sugar Ray Leonard.
4 Roberto Duran.
3 Terry McGovern; Bob Fitzsimmons; Stanley Ketchel; Tony Canzoneri; Barney Ross; Henry Armstrong; Emile Griffiths; Wilfred Benitez; Alexis Arguello; Wilfredo Gomez; Hector Camacho.

UNDEFEATED WORLD CHAMPIONS
Jimmy Barry (70 bouts); Jack McAuliffe (53 bouts); Rocky Marciano (49 bouts).

LONGEST REIGNING WORLD CHAMPION
11 years 252 days Joe Louis (heavyweight) 22 June 1937 to 1 March 1949.

MOST SUCCESSFUL WORLD TITLE DEFENCES
25 Joe Louis (heavyweight) 1937-48

MOST WORLD TITLE FIGHTS
27 Joe Louis (heavyweight) 1937-50

SHORTEST WORLD TITLE FIGHTS
45 seconds Al McCoy (US) v George Chip (US), middleweight 1914
45 seconds Lloyd Honeyghan (GB) v Gene Hatcher (US) welterweight 1987.

MOST KNOCKDOWNS IN WORLD TITLE FIGHT
14 – Vic Toweel (SA) knocked down Danny O'Sullivan (GB) 14 times during their bantamweight contest in 1950.

OLDEST WORLD CHAMPION
48 yr 59 dy Archie Moore (light-heavyweight). Moore may have been only 45. Either way, he is still the oldest world champion.

HEAVIEST WORLD CHAMPION
270 lb Primo Carnera (heavyweight)

1990

AMATEUR FIXTURES
Jan 22: Young England v Young Scotland (Royal Lancaster Hotel, London); *Feb 26:* Young England v Opponents to be arranged (Hilton Hotel, London); *Apr 24 -May 2:* Multi-Nations InterCup Tournament (Karlsruhe, West Germany); *May 2:* George Wimpey ABA finals (Royal Albert Hall); *May 26:* Daily Star Junior ABA finals (York Hall, London); *Jun 14-15:* Daily Star Golden Gloves Tournament (York Hall, London); *Jul 14-22:* European junior championships (Usti, Czechoslovakia); *Aug 30-Sep 8:* World Cup competition (Dublin); *Sept 14-23:* World junior championships (Lima, Peru); *Oct 2-7:* Multi-Nations Tournament (Berlin, East Germany).

CANOEING

1989

WORLD CANOE RACING CHAMPIONSHIPS
Savage River, Montana, Jun 15-26

Men

500 Metres Kayak Singles
1 Martin Hunter (Aus) 1m 41.65s
2 Kay Bluhm (GDR) 1m 41.76s
3 Mike Herbert (US) 1m 42.96s

1000 Metres Kayak Singles
1 Zsolt Gyulay (Hun) 3m 38.87s
2 Torsten Krentz (GDR) 3m 40.17s
3 Kalle Sundqvist (Swe) 3m 41.30s

10,000 Metres Kayak Singles
1 Attila Szabo (Cze) 42m 48.94s
2 Stanislav Boreyko (USSR) 42m 49.78s
3 José Garcia (Por) 42m 49.84s

500 Metres Kayak Pairs
1 Kay Bluhm & Torsten Gutsche (GDR) 1m 31.58s
2 Sergey Kalesnik & Anatoliy Tishtenko (USSR) 1m 31.73s
3 Maciej Freimut & Wotjek Kurpiewski (Pol) 1m 32.53s

1000 Metres Kayak Pairs
1 Kay Bluhm & Torsten Gutsche (GDR) 3m 11.62s
2 Vladimir Bobreshov & Arturas Veta (USSR) 3m 14.67s
3 Attila Adrivcz & Zoltan Berkes (Hun) 3m 16.49s

10,000 Metres Kayak Pairs
1 Attila Abraham & Sandor Hodosi (Hun) 39m 24.99s
2 Grayson Bourne & Ivan Lawler (GB) 39m 26.30s
3 Vladimir Gordiley & Genadiy Vasilenko (USSR) 39m 27.05s

500 Metres Kayak Fours
1 USSR 1m 22.50s
2 West Germany 1m 22.84s
3 Bulgaria 1m 22.90s

1000 Metres Kayak Fours
1 Hungary 2m 55.30s
2 Poland 2m 56.18s
3 East Germany 2m 56.34s

10,000 Metres Kayak Fours
1 USSR 35m 58.54s
2 Hungary 35m 59.69s
3 Poland 36m 00.37s

500 Metres Canadian Singles
1 Mikhail Slivinsky (USSR) 1m 53.17s
2 Olaf Heukrodt (GDR) 1m 54.03s
3 Martin Marinov (Bul) 1m 54.92s

1000 Metres Canadian Singles
1 Ivan Klementiev (USSR) 4m 00.04s
2 Larry Cain (Can) 4m 02.96s
3 Gaspar Boldiszar (Hun) 4m 03.70s

10,000 Metres Canadian Singles
1 Ivan Klementiev (USSR) 46m 49.96s
2 Zsolt Bohacs (Hun) 46m 50.10s
3 Jan Bartunek (Cze) 47m 44.38s

500 Metres Canadian Pairs
1 Nikolay Juravsky & Viktor Reneysky (USSR) 1m 40.90s
2 Tomasz Goliasz & Marek Lbik (Pol) 1m 42.32s
3 Joel Bettin & Philippe Renaud (Fra) 1m 42.45s

1000 Metres Canadian Pairs
1 C. Frederiksen & Arne Nielsson (Den) 3m 37.08s
2 Olivier Boivin & Didier Hoyer (Fra) 3m 37.60s
3 Yuri Gurin & Valeriy Veshko (USSR) 3m 39.46s

10,000 Metres Canadian Pairs
1 C. Frederiksen & Arne Nielsson (Den) 42m 42.59s
2 Olivier Boivin & Didier Hoyer (Fra) 43m 21.12s
3 Andrei Balabonov & Viktor Dobrotvorsky (USSR) 43m 39.85s

500 Metres Canadian Fours
1 USSR 1m 31.10s
2 Hungary 1m 33.12s
3 France 1m 33.69s

1000 Metres Canadian Fours
1 USSR 3m 19.94s
2 Hungary 3m 22.30s
3 Bulgaria 3m 22.54s

Women

500 Metres Kayak Singles
1 Katrin Borchert (GDR) 1m 53.38s
2 Isabella Dylewska (Pol) 1m 53.99s
3 Josefa Idem (FRG) 1m 54.39s

5000 Metres Kayak Singles
1 Katrin Borchert (GDR) 22m 15.80s
2 Isabella Dylewska (Pol) 22m 24.45s
3 Josefa Idem (FRG) 22m 24.88s

500 Metres Kayak Pairs
1 Anke Nothnagel & Heike Singer (GDR) 1m 43.17s
2 Eva Donusz & Erika Meszaros (Hun) 1m 44.63s
3 Irina Salomikova & Galina Savenko (USSR) 1m 44.83s

5000 Metres Kayak Pairs
1 Monika Bunke & Ramona Portwich (GDR) 20m 27.05s
2 Marina Bituleanu & Luminita Hertea (Rom) 20m 34.83s
3 Alexandra Apanovich & Nadejda Kovalekevich (USSR) 20m 35.70s

500 Metres Kayak Fours
1 East Germany 1m 32.90s
2 Hungary 1m 34.10s
3 USSR 1m 35.50s

CHAMPIONS

OLYMPIC GAMES

Men

500 Metres Kayak Singles
1976	Vasile Diba (Rom)
1980	Vladimir Parfenovich (USSR)
1984	Ian Ferguson (NZ)
1988	Zsolt Gyulay (Hun)

1000 Metres Kayak Singles
1936	Gregor Hradetzky (Aut)
1948	Gert Fredriksson (Swe)
1952	Gert Fredriksson (Swe)
1956	Gert Fredriksson (Swe)
1960	Erik Hansen (Den)
1964	Rolf Peterson (Swe)
1968	Mihaly Hesz (Hun)
1972	Alexandr Shaparenko (USSR)
1976	Rudiger Helm (GDR)
1980	Rudiger Helm (GDR)
1984	Alan Thompson (NZ)
1988	Greg Barton (US)

500 Metres Kayak Pairs
1976	East Germany
1980	USSR

1984 New Zealand
1988 New Zealand

1000 Metres Kayak Pairs
1936 Austria
1948 Sweden
1952 Finland
1956 West Germany
1960 Sweden
1964 Sweden
1968 USSR
1972 USSR
1976 USSR
1980 USSR
1984 Canada
1988 United States

1000 Metres Kayak Fours
1964 USSR
1968 Norway
1972 USSR
1976 USSR
1980 East Germany
1984 New Zealand
1988 Hungary

500 Metres Canadian Singles
1976 Alexandr Rogov (USSR)
1980 Sergey Postrekhin (USSR)
1984 Larry Cain (Can)
1988 Olaf Heukrodt (GDR)

1000 Metres Canadian Singles
1936 Francis Amyot (Can)
1948 Josef Holecek (Cze)
1952 Josef Holecek (Cze)
1956 Leon Rotman (Rom)
1960 Josef Parti (Hun)
1964 Jürgen Eschert (FRG)
1968 Tibor Tatai (Hun)
1972 Ivan Patzaichin (Rom)
1976 Matija Ljubek (Yug)
1980 Lubomir Lubenov (Bul)
1984 Ulrich Eicke (FRG)
1988 Ivan Klementiev (USSR)

500 Metres Canadian Pairs
1976 USSR
1980 Hungary
1984 Yugoslavia
1988 USSR

1000 Metres Canadian Pairs
1936 Czechoslovakia
1948 Czechoslovakia
1952 Denmark
1956 Romania
1960 USSR
1964 USSR
1968 Romania
1972 USSR
1976 USSR
1980 Romania
1984 Romania
1988 USSR

Women
500 Metres Kayak Singles
1948 Karen Hoff (Den)
1952 Sylvi Saimo (Fin)
1956 Elisaveta Dementyeva (USSR)
1960 Anatonina Seredina (USSR)
1964 Lyudmila Khvedosyuk (USSR)
1968 Lyudmila Pinayeva (USSR)
1972 Yulia Ryabchinskaya (USSR)
1976 Carola Zirzow (GDR)
1980 Birgit Fischer (GDR)
1984 Agneta Anderson (Swe)
1988 Vania Guecheva (USSR)

500 Metres Kayak Pairs
1960 USSR
1964 West Germany
1968 West Germany
1972 USSR
1976 USSR
1980 East Germany
1984 Sweden
1988 East Germany

500 Metres Kayak Fours
1984 Romania
1988 East Germany

WORLD CHAMPIONS
Inaugurated 1938. Not held in Olympic years
Winners since 1981

Men
500 Metres Kayak Singles
1981 Vladimir Perfenovich (USSR)
1982 Vladimir Perfenovich (USSR)
1983 Vladimir Perfenovich (USSR)
1985 Andreas Stahle (GDR)
1986 Jeremy West (GB)
1987 Peter MacDonald (NZ)
1989 Martin Hunter (Aus)

1000 Metres Kayak Singles
1981 Rudiger Helm (GDR)
1982 Rudiger Helm (GDR)
1983 Rudiger Helm (GDR)
1985 Ferenc Csipes (Hun)
1986 Jeremy West (GB)
1987 Greg Barton (US)
1989 Zsolt Gyulay (Hun)

10,000 Metres Kayak Singles
1981 Einar Rasmussen (Nor)
1982 Milan Janic (USSR)
1983 Einar Rasmussen (Nor)
1985 Greg Barton (US)
1986 Ferenc Csipes (Hun)
1987 Greg Barton (US)
1989 Attila Szabo (Cze)

500 Metres Kayak Pairs
1981 USSR
1982 USSR
1983 East Germany
1985 New Zealand
1986 West Germany
1987 Hungary
1989 East Germany

1000 Metres Kayak Pairs
1981 USSR
1982 USSR
1983 East Germany
1985 France
1986 Romania
1987 New Zealand
1989 East Germany

10,000 Metres Kayak Pairs
1981 USSR
1982 France
1983 Great Britain
1985 Sweden
1986 Hungary
1987 France
1989 Hungary

500 Metres Kayak Fours
1981 USSR
1982 USSR
1983 East Germany
1985 Hungary
1986 East Germany

| 1987 | USSR |
| 1989 | USSR |

1000 Metres Kayak Fours
1981	East Germany
1982	Sweden
1983	Romania
1985	Sweden
1986	Hungary
1987	Hungary
1989	Hungary

10,000 Metres Kayak Fours
1981	East Germany
1982	USSR
1983	USSR
1985	Hungary
1986	USSR
1987	Norway
1989	USSR

500 Metres Canadian Singles
1981	Olaf Heokrodt (GDR)
1982	Olaf Heokrodt (GDR)
1983	Costica Alaru (Rom)
1985	Olaf Heokrodt (GDR)
1986	Olaf Heokrodt (GDR)
1987	Olaf Heokrodt (GDR)
1989	Mikhail Slivinsky (USSR)

1000 Metres Canadian Singles
1981	Ulrick Papke (GDR)
1982	Schmidt (GDR)
1983	Vladimir Beresa (USSR)
1985	Ivan Klementiev (USSR)
1986	Aurel Macarencu (Rom)
1987	Olaf Heokrodt (GDR)
1989	Ivan Klementiev (USSR)

10,000 Metres Canadian Singles
1981	Tamas Wichmann (Hun)
1982	Tamas Wichmann (Hun)
1983	Jiri Vrdlovec (Cze)
1985	Jiri Vrdlovec (Cze)
1986	Aurel Macarencu (Rom)
1987	Ivan Sabjan (Yug)
1989	Ivan Klementiev (USSR)

500 Metres Canadian Pairs
1981	Hungary
1982	Yugoslavia
1983	Yugoslavia
1985	Hungary
1986	Hungary
1987	Poland
1989	USSR

1000 Metres Canadian Pairs
| 1981 | Romania |
| 1982 | East Germany |

1983	Romania
1985	East Germany
1986	Hungary
1987	USSR
1989	Denmark

10,000 Metres Canadian Pairs
1981	Hungary
1982	Romania
1983	Hungary
1985	Yugoslavia
1986	Poland
1987	Denmark
1989	Denmark

500 Metres Canadian Fours
First held 1989
| 1989 | USSR |

1000 Metres Canadian Fours
First held 1989
| 1989 | USSR |

Women
500 Metres Kayak Singles
1981	Birgit Fischer (GDR)
1982	Birgit Fischer (GDR)
1983	Birgit Fischer (GDR)
1985	Birgit Fischer (GDR)
1986	Vania Gesheva (Bul)
1987	Birgit Schmidt (GDR)
1989	Katrin Borchert (GDR)

5000 Metres Kayak Singles
First held 1989
| 1989 | Katrin Borchert (GDR) |

500 Metres Kayak Pairs
1981	East Germany
1982	East Germany
1983	East Germany
1985	East Germany
1986	Hungary
1987	East Germany
1989	East Germany

5000 Metres Kayak Pairs
First held 1989
| 1989 | East Germany |

500 Metres Kayak Fours
1981	East Germany
1982	East Germany
1983	East Germany
1985	East Germany
1986	Hungary
1987	East Germany
1989	East Germany

COMMONWEALTH GAMES

VENUES

Year	Venue	Competing Nations
1930	Hamilton, Canada	11
1934	London, England	16
1938	Sydney, Australia	15
1950	Auckland, New Zealand	13
1954	Vancouver, Canada	24
1958	Cardiff, Wales	35
1962	Perth, Australia	35
1966	Kingston, Jamaica	34
1970	Edinburgh, Scotland	42
1974	Christchurch, New Zealand	38
1978	Edmonton, Canada	46
1982	Brisbane, Australia	46
1986	Edinburgh, Scotland	27
1990	Auckland, New Zealand	

Leading Gold Medal Winners

24	England	20	Canada	6	South Africa
29	England	17	Canada	8	Australia
24	Australia	15	England	13	Canada
34	Australia	19	England	10	New Zealand
23	England	20	Australia	16	South Africa
29	England	27	Australia	13	South Africa
38	Australia	29	England	10	New Zealand
34	England	23	Australia	14	Canada
36	Australia	27	England	18	Canada
32	Australia	28	England	23	Canada
44	Canada	27	England	25	Australia
39	Australia	38	England	26	Canada
52	England	51	Canada	40	Australia

THE GOLD MEDAL WINNING NATIONS

Golds	
373	England
345	Australia
252	Canada
77	New Zealand
60	South Africa
51	Scotland
29	Kenya
24	India
22	Wales
20	Pakistan
18	Jamaica
14	Nigeria
14	Northern Ireland
12	Ghana
8	Malaysia
7	Trinidad
6	Uganda
4	Hong Kong
4	Singapore
3	Bahamas
3	Tanzania
3	Zimbabwe (formerly S. Rhodesia)
2	Fiji
2	Guyana (formerly British Guiana)
2	Isle of Man
2	Sri Lanka (formerly Ceylon)
2	Zambia
1	Barbados
1	St Vincent

ARCHERY

Men
1982	Mark Blenkarne (Eng)	

Women
1982	Neroli Fairhall (NZ)	

ATHLETICS
w - Wind Assisted

Men

100 Metres (100 yards 1930-66)

Year		time
1930	Percy Williams (Can)	9.9
1934	Arthur Sweeney (Eng)	10.0
1938	Cyril Holmes (Eng)	9.7
1950	John Treloar (Aus)	9.7
1954	Mike Agostini (Tri)	9.6
1958	Keith Gardner (Jam)	9.66
1962	Seraphino Antao (Ken)	9.50
1966	Harry Jerome (Can)	9.41
1970	Don Quarrie (Jam)	10.24
1974	Don Quarrie (Jam)	10.38
1978	Don Quarrie (Jam)	10.03
1982	Allan Wells (Sco)	10.05
1986	Ben Johnson (Can)	10.07

200 Metres (220 yards 1930-66)

1930	Stanley Engelhart (Eng)	21.8
1934	Arthur Sweeney (Eng)	21.9
1938	Cyril Holmes (Eng)	21.2
1950	John Treloar (Aus)	21.5
1954	Donald Jowett (NZ)	21.5
1958	Tom Robinson (Bah)	21.08
1962	Seraphino Antao (Ken)	21.28
1966	Stanley Allotey (Gha)	20.65
1970	Don Quarrie (Jam)	20.56
1974	Don Quarrie (Jam)	20.73
1978	Allan Wells (Sco)	20.12
1982	Allan Wells (Sco) & Mike Mc Farlane (Eng)	20.43
1986	Atlee Mahorn (Can)	20.31

400 Metres (440 yards 1930-66)

1930	Alex Wilson (Can)	48.8
1934	Godfrey Rampling (Eng)	48.0
1938	Bill Roberts (Eng)	47.9
1950	Edwin Carr (Aus)	47.9
1954	Kevin Gosper (Aus)	47.2
1958	Mikha Singh (Ind)	46.71
1962	George Kerr (Jam)	46.74
1966	Wendell Mottley (Tri)	45.08
1970	Charles Assati (Ken)	45.01
1974	Charles Assati (Ken)	46.04
1978	Rick Mitchell (Aus)	46.43
1982	Bert Cameron (Jam)	45.89
1986	Roger Black (Eng)	45.57

800 Metres (880 yards 1930-66)

1930	Thomas Hampson (Eng)	1:52.4
1934	Phil Edwards (Guy)	1:54.2
1938	Vernon Boot (NZ)	1:51.2
1950	John Parlett (Eng)	1:53.1
1954	Derek Johnson (Eng)	1:50.7
1958	Herb Elliott (Aus)	1:49.32
1962	Peter Snell (NZ)	1:47.64
1966	Noel Clough (Aus)	1:46.9
1970	Robert Ouko (Ken)	1:46.89
1974	John Kipkurgat (Ken)	1:43.85
1978	Mike Boit (Ken)	1:46.39
1982	Peter Bourke (Aus)	1:45.18
1986	Steve Cram (Eng)	1:43.22

1,500 Metres (1 mile 1930-66)

1930	Reg Thomas (Eng)	4:14.0
1934	Jack Lovelock (NZ)	4:12.8
1938	Jim Alford (Wal)	4:11.6
1950	William Parnall (Can)	4:11.0
1954	Roger Bannister (Eng)	3:58.8
1958	Herb Elliott (Aus)	3:59.03
1962	Peter Snell (NZ)	4:04.58
1966	Kipchoge Keino (Ken)	3:55.34
1970	Kipchoge Keino (Ken)	3:36.60
1974	Filbert Bayi (Tan)	3:12.16
1978	David Moorcroft (Eng)	3:35.48
1982	Steve Cram (Eng)	3:42.37
1986	Steve Cram (Eng)	3:50.87

5,000 Metres (3 miles 1930-66)

1930	Stan Tomlin (Eng)	14:27.4
1934	Walter Beavers (Eng)	14:32.6
1938	Cecil Matthews (NZ)	13:59.6
1950	Len Eyre (Eng)	14:23.6
1954	Chris Chataway (Eng)	13:35.2
1958	Murray Halberg (NZ)	13:14.96
1962	Murray Halberg (NZ)	13:34.15
1966	Kipchoge Keino (Ken)	12:57.4
1970	Ian Stewart (Sco)	13:22.8
1974	Ben Jipcho (Ken)	13:14.4
1978	Henry Rono (Ken)	13:23.04
1982	David Moorcroft (Eng)	13:33.00
1986	Steve Ovett (Eng)	13:24.11

10,000 Metres (6 miles 1930-66)

1930	John Savidan (NZ)	30:49.6
1934	Arthur Penny (Eng)	31:00.6
1938	Cecil Matthews (NZ)	30:14.5
1950	Harold Nelson (NZ)	30:29.6
1954	Peter Driver (Eng)	29:09.4
1958	David Power (Aus)	28:48.16
1962	Bruce Kidd (Can)	28:26.13
1966	Naftali Temu (Ken)	27:14.21
1970	Lachie Stewart (Sco)	28:11.71
1974	Richard Taylor (NZ)	27:46.4
1978	Brendan Foster (Eng)	28:13.65
1982	Gidamis Shahanga (Tan)	28:10.15
1986	Jonathan Solly (Eng)	27:57.42

Marathon

1930	Duncan McL.Wright (Sco)	2:43:43
1934	Harold Webster (Can)	2:40:36
1938	Johannes Coleman (SA)	2:30:49.8
1950	Jack Holden (Eng)	2:32:57
1954	Joseph Mc Gee (Sco)	2:39:36
1958	David Power (Aus)	2:22:45.6
1962	Brian Kilby (Eng)	2:21:17
1966	Jim Alder (Sco)	2:22:07.8
1970	Ron Hill (Eng)	2:09:28
1974	Ian Thompson (Eng)	2:09:12
1978	Gidamis Shahanga (Tan)	2:15:39.8
1982	Rob de Castella (Aus)	2:09:18
1986	Rob de Castella (Aus)	2:10:15

3,000 Metres Steeplechase
(8 laps in 1930; 2 miles in 1934)

1930	George Bailey (Eng)	9:52.0
1934	Stanley Scarsbrook (Eng)	10:23.4
1962	Trevor Vincent (Aus)	8:43.4
1966	Peter Welsh (NZ)	8:29.44
1970	Tony Manning (Aus)	8:26.2
1974	Ben Jipcho (Ken)	8:20.8
1978	Henry Rono (Ken)	8:26.54
1982	Julius Korir (Ken)	8:23.94
1986	Graeme Fell (Can)	8:24.49

110 Metres Hurdles
(120 yards 1930-66)

1930	Lord Burghley (Eng)	14.6
1934	Don Finlay (Eng)	15.2

1938	Tom Lavery (SA)	14.0w
1950	Peter Gardner (Aus)	14.3
1954	Keith Gardner (Jam)	14.2
1958	Keith Gardner (Jam)	14.20
1962	Ghulam Raziq (Pak)	14.34
1966	David Hemery (Eng)	14.1
1970	David Hemery (Eng)	13.66
1974	Fatwel Kimaiyo (Ken)	13.69
1978	Berwyn Price (Wal)	13.70
1982	Mark McKoy (Can)	13.37
1986	Mark McKoy (Can)	13.31

400 Metres Hurdles
(440 yards 1930-66)

1930	Lord Burghley (Eng)	54.4
1934	Alan Hunter (Sco)	55.2
1938	John Loaring (Can)	52.9
1950	Duncan White (Sri)	52.5
1954	David Lean (Aus)	52.4
1958	Gerhardus Potgeiter (SA)	49.73
1962	Ken Roche (Aus)	51.5
1966	Ken Roche (Aus)	50.95
1970	John Sherwood (Eng)	50.03
1974	Alan Pascoe (Eng)	48.83
1978	Daniel Kimaiyo (Ken)	49.48
1982	Garry Brown (Aus)	49.37
1986	Phil Beattie (NI)	49.60

4 x 100 Metres Relay
(4 x 110 yards 1930-66)

1930	Canada	42.2
1934	England	42.2
1938	Canada	41.6
1950	Australia	42.2
1954	Canada	41.3
1958	England	40.72
1962	England	40.62
1966	Ghana	39.8
1970	Jamaica	39.46
1974	Australia	39.31
1978	Scotland	39.24
1982	Nigeria	39.15
1986	Canada	39.15

4 x 400 Metres Relay
(4 x 440 yards 1930-66)

1930	England	3:19.4
1934	England	3:16.8
1938	Canada	3:16.9
1950	Australia	3:17.8
1954	England	3:11.2
1958	South Africa	3:08.21
1962	Jamaica	3:10.2
1966	Trinidad & Tobago	3:02.8
1970	Kenya	3:03.63
1974	Kenya	3:04.4
1978	Kenya	3:03.54
1982	England	3:05.45
1986	England	3:07.19

High Jump

		metres
1930	Johannes Viljoen (SA)	1.90
1934	Edwin Thacker (SA)	1.90
1938	Edwin Thacker (SA)	1.96
1950	John Winter (Aus)	1.98
1954	Emmanuel Ifeajuna (Nig)	2.03
1958	Ernest Haisley (Jam)	2.06
1962	Percy Hobson (Aus)	2.11
1966	Lawrie Peckham (Aus)	2.08
1970	Lawrie Peckham (Aus)	2.14
1974	Gordon Windeyer (Aus)	2.16
1978	Claude Ferragne (Can)	2.20
1982	Milt Ottey (Can)	2.31
1986	Milt Ottey (Can)	2.30

Long Jump

1930	Leonard Hutton (Can)	7.20
1934	Sam Richardson (Can)	7.17
1938	Harold Brown (Can)	7.43
1950	Neville Price (SA)	7.31
1954	Ken Wilmshurst (Eng)	7.54
1958	Paul Foreman (Jam)	7.47
1962	Michael Ahey (Gha)	8.05w
1966	Lynn Davies (Wales)	7.99
1970	Lynn Davies (Wales)	8.06w
1974	Alan Lerwill (Eng)	7.94
1978	Roy Mitchell (Eng)	8.06
1982	Gary Honey (Aus)	8.13
1986	Gary Honey (Aus)	8.08

Triple Jump

1930	Gordon Smallacombe (Can)	14.76
1934	Jack Metcalfe (Aus)	15.63
1938	Jack Metcalfe (Aus)	15.49
1950	Brian Oliver (Aus)	15.61
1954	Ken Wilmshurst (Eng)	15.28
1958	Ian Tomlinson (Aus)	15.74
1962	Ian Tomlinson (Aus)	16.20
1966	Samuel Igun (Nig)	16.40
1970	Phil May (Aus)	16.72
1974	Joshua Owusu (Gha)	16.50
1978	Keith Connor (Eng)	17.21
1982	Keith Connor (Eng)	17.81w
1986	John Herbert (Eng)	17.27

Pole Vault

1930	Victor Pickard (Can)	3.73
1934	Sylvanus Apps (Can)	3.88
1938	Andries Du Plessis (SA)	4.11
1950	Tim Anderson (Eng)	3.97
1954	Geoff Elliott (Eng)	4.26
1958	Geoff Elliott (Eng)	4.16
1962	Trevor Bickle (Aus)	4.49
1966	Trevor Bickle (Aus)	4.80
1970	Mike Bull (NI)	5.10
1974	Don Baird (Aus)	5.05
1978	Bruce Simpson (Can)	5.10
1982	Ray Boyd (Aus)	5.20
1986	Andrew Ashurst (Eng)	5.20

Shot

1930	Henrick Hart (SA)	14.58
1934	Henrick Hart (SA)	14.67
1938	Louis Fouche (SA)	14.48
1950	Maitaika Tuicakau (Fij)	14.64
1954	John Savidge (Eng)	16.77
1958	Arthur Rowe (Eng)	17.57
1962	Martyn Lucking (Eng)	18.08
1966	David Steen (Can)	18.79
1970	David Steen (Can)	19.21
1974	Geoff Capes (Eng)	20.74
1978	Geoff Capes (Eng)	19.77
1982	Bruno Pauletto (Can)	19.55
1986	Billy Cole (Eng)	18.16

Javelin

1930	Stanley Lay (NZ)	63.12
1934	Robert Dixon (Can)	60.02
1938	James Courtwright (Can)	62.80
1950	Leo Roininen (Can)	57.10
1954	James Achurch (Eng)	68.52
1958	Colin Smith (Eng)	71.28
1962	Alfred Mitchell (Aus)	78.10
1966	John FitzSimons (Eng)	79.78
1970	David Travis (Eng)	79.50
1974	Charles Clover (Eng)	84.92
1978	Phil Olsen (Can)	84.00
1982	Michael O'Rourke (NZ)	89.48
1986	David Ottley (Eng)	80.62

Discus

1930	Hendrick Hart (SA)	41.44
1934	Hendrick Hart (SA)	41.54
1938	Eric Coy (Can)	44.76
1950	Ian Reed (Aus)	47.72
1954	Stephanus du Plessis (SA)	51.70
1958	Stephanus du Plessis (SA)	55.94
1962	Warwick Selvey (Aus)	56.48
1966	Les Mills (NZ)	56.18
1970	George Puce (Can)	59.02
1974	Robin Tait (NZ)	63.08
1978	Borys Chambul (Can)	59.70
1982	Brad Cooper (Bah)	64.04
1986	Raymond Lazdins (Can)	58.86

Hammer

1930	Malcolm Nokes (Eng)	47.12
1934	Malcolm Nokes (Eng)	48.24
1938	George Sutherland (Can)	48.70
1950	Duncan Clark (Sco)	49.94
1954	Muhammad Iqbal (Pak)	55.38
1958	Mike Ellis (Eng)	62.90
1962	Howard Payne (Eng)	61.64
1966	Howard Payne (Eng)	61.98
1970	Howard Payne (Eng)	67.80
1974	Ian Chipchase (Eng)	69.56
1978	Peter Farmer (Aus)	71.10
1982	Robert Weir (Eng)	75.08
1986	David Smith (Eng)	74.06

Decathlon (Adjusted to 1984 tables)

		pts
1966	Roy Williams (NZ)	7133
1970	Geoff Smith (Aus)	7420
1974	Mike Bull (NI)	7363
1978	Daley Thompson (Eng)	8470
1982	Daley Thompson (Eng)	8424
1986	Daley Thompson (Eng)	8663

30 km Walk
(20 miles/32.18 km 1966-74)

		time
1966	Ron Wallwork (Eng)	2:44:42.8
1970	Noel Freeman (Aus)	2:33:33
1974	John Warhurst (Eng)	2:35:23.0
1978	Ollie Flynn (Eng)	2:22:03.7
1982	Steve Barry (Wales)	2:10:16
1986	Simon Baker (Aus)	2:07:47

Women

100 Metres (100 yards 1934-66)

1934	Eileen Hiscock (Eng)	11.3
1938	Decima Norman (Aus)	11.1
1950	Marjorie Jackson (Aus)	10.8
1954	Marjorie Nelson (née Jackson) (Aus)	10.7
1958	Marlene Willard (Aus)	10.70
1962	Dorothy Hyman (Eng)	11.2
1966	Dianne Burge (Aus)	10.6
1970	Raelene Boyle (Aus)	11.26
1974	Raelene Boyle (Aus)	11.27
1978	Sonia Lannaman (Eng)	11.27
1982	Angella Taylor (Can)	11.00
1986	Heather Oakes (Eng)	11.20

200 Metres (220 yards 1934-66)

1934	Eileen Hiscock (Eng)	25.0
1938	Decima Norman (Aus)	24.7
1950	Marjorie Jackson (Aus)	24.3
1954	Marjorie Nelson (née Jackson)(Aus)	24.0
1958	Marlene Willard (Aus)	23.65
1962	Dorothy Hyman (Eng)	24.00
1966	Dianne Burge (Aus)	23.73
1970	Raelene Boyle (Aus)	22.75
1974	Raelene Boyle (Aus)	22.50
1978	Denise Boyd (Aus)	22.82
1982	Merlene Ottey (Jam)	22.19
1986	Angella Issajenko (née Taylor) (Can)	22.91

400 Metres (440 yards 1934-66)

1966	Judy Pollock (Aus)	53.0
1970	Marilyn Neufville (Jam)	51.02
1974	Yvonne Saunders (Can)	51.67
1978	Donna Hartley (Eng)	51.69
1982	Raelene Boyle (Aus)	51.26
1986	Debbie Flintoff (Aus)	51.29

800 Metres (880 yards 1934-66)

1934	Gladys Lunn (Eng)	2:19.4
1962	Dixie Willis (Aus)	2:03.85
1966	Abigail Hoffman (Can)	2:04.3
1970	Rosemary Stirling (Sco)	2:06.24
1974	Charlene Redina (Aus)	2:01.1
1978	Judy Peckham (Aus)	2:02.82
1982	Kirsty McDermott (Wales)	2:01.31
1986	Kirsty Wade (née McDermott) (Wales)	2:00.94

1,500 Metres

1970	Rita Ridley (Eng)	4:18.8
1974	Glenda Reiser (Can)	4:07.8
1978	Mary Stewart (Eng)	4:06.34
1982	Christina Boxer (Eng)	4:08.28
1986	Kirsty Wade (Wales)	4:10.91

3,000 Metres

1978	Paula Fudge (Eng)	9:13.0
1982	Anne Audain (NZ)	8:45.53
1986	Lynn Williams (Can)	8:54.29

Marathon

1986	Lisa Martin (Aus)	2:27:07

80 Metres Hurdles

1934	Marjorie Clark (SA)	11.8
1938	Barbara Burke (SA)	11.7
1950	Shirley Strickland (Aus)	11.6
1954	Edna Maskell (Zam)	10.9
1958	Norma Thrower (Aus)	10.72
1962	Pam Kilborn (Aus)	11.07
1966	Pam Kilborn (Aus)	10.9

100 Metres Hurdles

1970	Pam Kilborn (Aus)	13.27
1974	Judy Vernon (Eng)	13.45
1978	Lorna Boothe (Eng)	12.98
1982	Shirley Strong (Eng)	12.78
1986	Sally Gunnell (Eng)	13.29

400 Metres Hurdles

1982	Debbie Flintoff (Aus)	55.89
1986	Debbie Flintoff (Aus)	54.94

4 x 100 Metres Relay
(4 x 110 yards 1934-66)

1954	Australia	46.8
1958	England	45.37
1962	Australia	46.71
1966	Australia	45.3
1970	Australia	44.14
1974	Australia	43.51
1978	England	43.70
1982	England	43.15
1986	England	43.39

4 x 400 Metres Relay

1974	England	3:29.2
1978	England	3:27.19
1982	Canada	3:27.70
1986	Canada	3:28.92

Discontinued Sprint Relays
(2 x 110 yards 1 x 220 yards)

1934	England	49.4
1938	Australia	49.1
1950	Australia	47.9

(2 x 220 yards 2 x 110 yards)

1934	Canada	1:14.4
1938	Australia	1:15.2
1950	Australia	1:13.4

High Jump

metres

1934	Marjorie Clark (SA)	1.60
1938	Dorothy Odam (Eng)	1.60
1950	Dorothy Tyler (née Odam) (Eng)	1.60
1954	Thelma Hopkins (NI)	1.67
1958	Michele Mason (Aus)	1.70
1962	Robyn Woodhouse (Aus)	1.78
1966	Michele Brown (née Mason) (Aus)	1.73
1970	Debbie Brill (Can)	1.78
1974	Barbara Lawton (Eng)	1.84
1978	Katrina Gibbs (Aus)	1.93
1982	Debbie Brill (Can)	1.88
1986	Christine Stanton (Aus)	1.92

Long Jump

1934	Phyllis Bartholomew (Eng)	5.47
1938	Decima Norman (Aus)	5.80
1950	Yvette Williams (NZ)	5.90
1954	Yvette Williams (NZ)	6.08
1958	Sheila Hoskin (Eng)	6.02
1962	Pam Kilborn (Aus)	6.27
1966	Mary Rand (Eng)	6.36
1970	Sheila Sherwood (Eng)	6.73
1974	Modupe Oshikoya (Nig)	6.46
1978	Sue Reeve (Eng)	6.59
1982	Shonel Ferguson (Bah)	6.91w
1986	Joyce Oladapo (Eng)	6.43

Shot

1954	Yvette Williams (NZ)	13.96
1958	Valerie Sloper (NZ)	15.54
1962	Valerie Young (née Sloper) (NZ)	15.23
1966	Valerie Young (NZ)	16.50
1970	Mary Peters (NI)	15.93
1974	Jane Haist (Can)	16.12
1978	Gael Mulhall (Aus)	17.31
1982	Judy Oakes (Eng)	17.92
1986	Gael Martin (née Mulhall) (Aus)	19.00

Javelin

1934	Gladys Lunn (Eng)	32.18
1938	Robina Higgins (Can)	38.28
1950	Charlotte MacGibbon-Weeks (Aus)	38.84
1954	Magdelena Swanepoel (SA)	43.82
1958	Anna Pazera (Aus)	57.40
1962	Susan Platt (Eng)	50.24
1966	Margaret Parker (Aus)	51.38
1970	Petra Rivers (Aus)	52.00
1974	Petra Rivers (Aus)	55.48
1978	Tessa Sanderson (Eng)	61.34
1982	Suzanne Howland (Aus)	64.46
1986	Tessa Sanderson (Eng)	69.80

Discus

1954	Yvette Williams (NZ)	45.02
1958	Suzanne Allday (Eng)	45.91
1962	Valerie Young (NZ)	50.20
1966	Valerie Young (NZ)	49.78
1970	Rosemary Payne (Sco)	54.46
1974	Jane Haist (Can)	55.52
1978	Carmen Ionescu (Can)	62.16
1982	Margaret Ritchie (Sco)	62.98
1986	Gael Martin (Aus)	56.42

Pentathlon

(Adjusted to 1971 tables)   *pts*

1970	Mary Peters (NI)	4515
1974	Mary Peters (NI)	4455
1978	Diane Konihowski (Can)	4768

Heptathlon

1982	Glynis Nunn (Aus)	6254
1986	Judy Simpson (Eng)	6282

Leading Gold Medal Countries in athletics:
Men - England 86, Australia 48, Canada 21, Kenya 21, New Zealand 18, South Africa 16, Jamaica 14, Scotland 11. *Women* - Australia 55, England 39, Canada 17, New Zealand 10.

BADMINTON
Men
Singles
1966 Tan Aik Huang (Mal)
1970 Jamie Paulson (Can)
1974 Punch Gunalan (Mal)
1978 Padukone Prakash (Ind)
1982 Syed Modi (Ind)
1986 Steve Baddeley (Eng)
Doubles
1966 Huang & Hoe (Mal)
1970 Bee & Gunalam (Mal)
1974 Talbot & Stuart (Eng)
1978 Stevens & Tredgett (Eng)
1982 Sidek & Ong (Mal)
1986 Gilliland & Travers (Sco)
Women
Singles
1966 Angela Bairstoe (Eng)
1970 Margaret Beck (Eng)
1974 Gillian Gilks (Eng)
1978 Sylvia Ng (Mal)
1982 Helen Troke (Eng)
1986 Helen Troke (Eng)
Doubles
1966 Horton & Smith (Eng)
1970 Boxall & Whetnall (Eng)
1974 Beck & Gilks (Eng)
1978 Perry & Statt (Eng)
1982 Backhouse & Falardeau (Can)
1986 Clark & Gowers (Eng)
Mixed Doubles
1966 Mills & Bairstow (Eng)
1970 Talbot & Boxall (Eng)
1974 Talbot & Gilks (Eng)
1978 Tredgett & Perry (Eng)
1982 Dew & Chapman (Eng)
1986 Scandolera & Tucket (Aus)
Team
1978 England
1982 England
1986 England

BOWLS
Men
Singles
1930 Robert Colquhoun (Eng)
1934 Robert Sprot (Sco)
1938 Horace Harvey (SA)
1950 James Pirret (NZ)
1954 Ralph Hodges (Zim)
1958 Phineas Danilowitz (SA)
1962 David Bryant (Eng)
1970 David Bryant (Eng)
1974 David Bryant (Eng)
1978 David Bryant (Eng)
1982 William Wood (Sco)
1986 Ian Dickison (NZ)
Pairs
1930 Hills & Wright (Eng)
1934 Hills & Wright (Eng)
1938 Macey & Denison (NZ)
1950 Henry & Exelby (NZ)
1954 Rosbotham & Watson (NZ)
1958 Morris & Pilkington (NZ)
1962 McDonald & Robson (NZ)
1970 King & Line (Eng)
1974 Christie & McIntosh (Sco)
1978 Liddell & Delgado (HK)
1982 Watson & Gourlay (Sco)
1986 Adrain & Knox (Sco)

Fours
1930 England
1934 England
1938 New Zealand
1950 South Africa
1954 South Africa
1958 England
1962 England
1970 Hong Kong
1974 New Zealand
1978 Hong Kong
1982 Australia
1986 Wales
Women
Singles
1986 Wendy Line (Eng)
Pairs
1986 Freda Elliott & Margaret Johnstone (NI)
Triples
1986 Zimbabwe
Fours
1986 Wales

BOXING
Super-heavyweight
1986 Lennox Lewis (Can)
Heavyweight
1930 Victor Stuart (Eng)
1934 Pat Floyd (Eng)
1938 Thomas Osborne (Can)
1950 Frank Creagh (NZ)
1954 Brian Harper (Eng)
1958 Daniel Bekker (SA)
1962 George Oywello (Uga)
1966 William Kini (NZ)
1970 Benson Masanda (Uga)
1974 Neville Meade (Eng)
1978 Julius Awome (Eng)
1982 Willie DeWit (Can)
1986 James Peau (NZ)
Light-heavyweight
1930 Joe Goyder (Eng)
1934 George Brennan (Eng)
1938 Nicholas Wolmarans (SA)
1950 Donald Scott (Eng)
1954 Piet Van Vuuren (SA)
1958 Tony Madigan (Aus)
1962 Tony Madigan (Aus)
1966 Roger Tighe (Eng)
1970 Fatai Ayinla (Nig)
1974 William Knight (Eng)
1978 Roger Fortin (Can)
1982 Fine Sani (Fiji)
1986 James Moran (Eng)
Middleweight
1930 Frederick Mallin (Eng)
1934 Alf Shawyer (Eng)
1938 Denis Reardon (Wales)
1950 Theunis va Schalkwyk (SA)
1954 Johnannes van der Kolff (SA)
1958 Terry Milligan (NI)
1962 Cephas Coquhoun (Jam)
1966 Joe Darkey (Gha)
1970 John Conteh (Eng)
1974 Frankie Lucas (SVI)
1978 Philip McElwaine (Aus)
1982 Jimmy Price (Eng)
1986 Rod Douglas (Eng)
Light-middleweight
1954 Wilfred Greaves (Can)
1958 Grant Webster (SA)

1962	Harold Mann (Can)
1966	Mark Rowe (Eng)
1970	Tom Imrie (Sco)
1974	Lotti Mwale (Zam)
1978	Kelly Perlette (Can)
1982	Shawn O'Sullivan (Can)
1986	Dan Sherry (Can)

Welterweight
1930	Leonard Hall (SA)
1934	David McCleave (Eng)
1938	Bill Smith (Aus)
1950	Terence Ratcliffe (Eng)
1954	Nicholas Gargano (Eng)
1958	Joseph Grayling (SA)
1962	Wallace Coe (NZ)
1966	Eddie Blay (Gha)
1970	Emma Ankudey (Gha)
1974	Muhamad Muruli (Uga)
1978	Michael McCallum (Jam)
1982	Christopher Pyatt (Eng)
1986	Darren Dyer (Eng)

Light-welterweight
1954	Mickey Bergin (Can)
1958	Henry Loubscher (SA)
1962	Clement Quartey (Gha)
1966	James McCourt (NI)
1970	Muhamad Muruli (Uga)
1974	Obisia Nwakpa (Nig)
1978	Winfield Braithwaite (Guy)
1982	Christopher Ossai (Nig)
1986	Howard Grant (Can)

Lightweight
1930	James Rolland (Sco)
1934	Leslie Cook (Aus)
1938	Harry Groves (Eng)
1950	Ronald Latham (Eng)
1954	Piet van Staden (Zim)
1958	Dick McTaggart (Sco)
1962	Eddie Blay (Gha)
1966	Anthony Andeh (Nig)
1970	Abayomi Adeyemi (Nig)
1974	Ayub Kalule (Uga)
1978	Gerard Hamil (NI)
1982	Hussein Khalili (Ken)
1986	Asif Dar (Can)

Featherweight
1930	F.R. Meacham (Eng)
1934	Charles Catterall (SA)
1938	Anadale Henricus (Sri)
1950	Henry Gilliland (Sco)
1954	Leonard Leisching (SA)
1958	Wally Taylor (Aus)
1962	John McDermott (Sco)
1966	Philip Waruinge (Ken)
1970	Philip Waruinge (Ken)
1974	Edward Ndukwa (Nig)
1978	Nelson Azumah (Gha)
1982	Peter Knoyegwachie (Nig)
1986	Bill Downey (Can)

Bantamweight
1930	Hyman Mizler (Eng)
1934	Freddy Ryan (Eng)
1938	William Butler (Eng)
1950	Johannes van Rensburg (SA)
1954	John Smillie (Sco)
1958	Howard Winstone (Wales)
1962	Jeffery Dynevor (Aus)
1966	Edward Ndukwu (Nig)
1970	Sulley Shittu (Gha)
1974	Pat Cowdell (Eng)
1978	Barry McGuigan (NI)
1982	Joe Orewa (Nig)
1986	Sean Murphy (Eng)

Flyweight
1930	Jacob Smith (SA)
1934	Patrick Palmer (Eng)
1938	Johannes Joubert (SA)
1950	Hugh Riley (Sco)
1954	Richard Currie (Sco)
1958	Jackie Brown (Sco)
1962	Robert Mallon (Sco)
1966	Sulley Shittu (Gha)
1970	David Needham (Eng)
1974	David Lamour (NI)
1978	Michael Irungu (Ken)
1982	Michael Mutua (Ken)
1986	John Lyon (Eng)

Light-flyweight
1970	James Odwori (Uga)
1974	Stephen Muchoki (Ken)
1978	Stephen Muchoki (Ken)
1982	Abraham Wachire (Ken)
1986	Scott Olson (Can)

CYCLING
Sprint
1934	Ernest Higgins (Eng)
1938	Edgar Gray (Aus)
1950	Russell Mockridge (Aus)
1954	Cyril Peacock (Eng)
1958	Dick Ploog (Aus)
1962	Thomas Harrison (Aus)
1966	Roger Gibbon (Tri)
1970	John Nicholson (Aus)
1974	John Nicholson (Aus)
1978	Kenrick Tucker (Aus)
1982	Kenrick Tucker (Aus)
1986	Gary Neiwand (Aus)

1,000 Metres Time Trial
1934	Edgar Gray (Aus)
1938	Robert Porter (Aus)
1950	Russell Mockridge (Aus)
1954	Dick Ploog (Aus) & Alfred Swift (SA)
1958	Neville Tong (Eng)
1962	Peter Bartels (Aus)
1966	Roger Gibbon (Tri)
1970	Harry Kent (NZ)
1974	Dick Paris (Aus)
1978	Jocelyn Lovell (Can)
1982	Craig Adair (NZ)
1986	Martin Vinnicombe (Aus)

4,000 Metres Individual Pursuit
1950	Cyril Cartwright (Eng)
1954	Norman Sheil (Eng)
1958	Norman Sheil (Eng)
1962	Maxwell Langshaw (Aus)
1966	Hugh Porter (Eng)
1970	Ian Hallam (Eng)
1974	Ian Hallam (Eng)
1978	Michael Richards (NZ)
1982	Michael Turtur (Aus)
1986	Dean Woods (Aus)

4,000 Metres Team Pursuit
1974	England
1978	Australia
1982	Australia
1986	Australia

100 km Team Time Trial
1982	England
1986	England

Tandem Sprint
1970	Johnson & Jonker (Aus)
1974	Cook & Crutchlow (Eng)
1978	Lovell & Singleton (Can)

10 Mile Track Race
1934	Robert McLeod (Can)
1938	William Maxfield (Eng)
1950	William Heseltine (Aus)
1954	Lindsay Cocks (Aus)
1958	Ian Browne (Aus)
1962	Douglas Adams (Aus)
1966	Ian Alsop (Eng)
1970	Jocelyn Lovell (Can)
1974	Stephen Heffernan (Eng)
1978	Jocelyn Lovell (Can)
1982	Kevin Nichols (Aus)
1986	Wayne McCarney (Aus)

Road Race
1938	Hendrick Binneman (SA)
1950	Hector Sutherland (Aus)
1954	Eric Thompson (Eng)
1958	Ray Booty (Eng)
1962	Wesley Mason (Eng)
1966	Peter Buckley (IOM)
1970	Bruce Biddle (NZ)
1974	Clyde Sefton (Aus)
1978	Philip Anderson (Aus)
1982	Malcolm Elliott (Eng)
1986	Paul Curran (Eng)

FENCING
(Discontinued 1970)
Men
Foil
	Individual	Team
1950	Rene Paul (Eng)	England
1954	Rene Paul (Eng)	England
1958	Raymond Paul (Eng)	England
1962	Alex Leckie (Sco)	England
1966	Allan Jay (Eng)	England
1970	Mike Breckin (Eng)	England

Epee
	Individual	Team
1950	Chas-L. de Beaumont (Eng)	Australia
1954	Ivan Lund (Aus)	England
1958	William Hoskyns (Eng)	England
1962	Ivan Lund (Aus)	England
1966	William Hoskyns (Eng)	England
1970	William Hoskyns (Eng)	England

Sabre
	Individual	Team
1950	Arthur Pilbrow (Eng)	England
1954	Michael Amberg (Eng)	Canada
1958	William Hoskyns (Eng)	England
1962	Ralph Cooperman (Eng)	England
1966	Ralph Cooperman (Eng)	England
1970	Alex Leckie (Sco)	England

Women
Foil
	Individual	Team
1950	Mary Glen-Haig (Eng)	-
1954	Mary Glen-Haig (Eng)	-
1958	Gillian Sheen (Eng)	-
1962	Melody Coleman (NZ)	-
1966	Janet Wardell-Yerburgh (Eng)	England
1970	Janet Wardell-Yerburgh (Eng)	England

GYMNASTICS
(Only held 1978)
Men
	Individual	Team
1978	Philip Delesalle (Can)	Canada

Women
	Individual	Team
1978	Elfi Schlegel (Can)	Canada

ROWING
Men
Single Sculls
1930	Bobby Pearce (Aus)
1938	Herbert Turner (Aus)
1950	Mervyn Wood (Aus)
1954	Donald Rowlands (NZ)
1958	Stuart Mackenzie (Aus)
1962	James Hill (NZ)
1986	Steven Redgrave (Eng)

Double Sculls
1930	Bole & Richards (Can)
1950	Wood & Riley (Aus)
1954	Wood & Riley (Aus)
1958	Spracklen & Baker (Eng)
1962	Justice & Birkmyre (Eng)
1986	Walter & Ford (Can)

Coxless Pairs
1950	Lambert & Webster (Aus)
1954	Parker & Douglas (NZ)
1958	Parker & Douglas (NZ)
1962	Farquharson & Lee-Nicholson (Eng)
1986	Redgrave & Holmes (Eng)

Coxless Fours
1930	England
1958	England
1962	England
1986	Canada

Coxed Fours
1930	New Zealand
1938	Australia
1950	New Zealand
1954	Australia
1958	England
1962	New Zealand
1986	England

Eights
1930	England
1938	England
1950	Australia
1954	Canada
1958	Canada
1962	Australia
1986	Australia

Lightweight Single Sculls
1986	Peter Antonie (Aus)

Lightweight Coxless Fours
1986	England

Women
(First held 1986)
Single Sculls
1986	Stephanie Foster (NZ)

Double Sculls
1986	Foster & Clark (NZ)

Coxless Pairs
1986	Barr & Schreiner (Can)

Coxed Fours
1986	Canada

Eights
1986	Australia

Lightweight Single Sculls
1986	Adair Ferguson (Aus)

Lightweight Coxless Fours
1986	England

SHOOTING
Small Bore Rifle
1966   Gilmour Boa (Can)
1974   Yvonne Gowland (Aus)
1978   Alister Allan (Sco)
Small Bore Rifle - Prone
Individual
1982   Alan Smith (Aus)
1986   Alan Smith (Aus)
Pairs
1982   Cooper & Sullivan (Eng)
1986   Ashcroft & Stewart (Can)
Small Bore Rifle - Three Positions
Individual
1982   Alister Allan (Sco)
1986   Malcolm Cooper (Eng)
Pairs
1982   Cooper & Dagger (Eng)
1986   Cooper & Cooper (Eng)
Full Bore Rifle
Individual
1966   Lord John Swansea (Wales)
1974   Maurice Gordon (NZ)
1978   Desmond Vamplew (Can)
1982   Arthur Clarke (Sco)
1986   Stan Golinski (Aus)
Pairs
1982   Affleck & Ayling (Aus)
1986   Marion & Baldwin (Can)
Free Pistol
Individual
1966   Charles Sexton (Eng)
1974   Jules Sobrian (Can)
1978   Yvon Trempe (Can)
1982   Tom Guinn (Can)
1986   Greg Yelavich (NZ)
Pairs
1982   Adams & Tremelling (Aus)
1986   Guinn & Beaulieu (Can)
Centre Fire Pistol
Individual
1966   James Lee (Can)
1982   John Cooke (Eng)
1986   Robert Northover (Eng)
Pairs
1982   Ryan & Taransky (Aus)
1986   Adams & Hack (Aus)
Rapid Fire Pistol
Individual
1966   Anthony Clark (Eng)
1974   William Hare (Can)
1978   Jules Sobrian (Can)
1982   Solomon Lee (HK)
1986   Pat Murray (Aus)
Pairs
1982   Heuke & Taransky (Aus)
1986   Girling & Turner (Eng)
Olympic Trap
Individual
1974   John Primrose (Can)
1978   John Primrose (Can)
1982   Peter Boden (Eng)
1986   Ian Peel (Eng)
Pairs
1982   Ellis & Rumbel (Aus)
1986   Peel & Boden (Eng)
Skeet
Individual
1974   Harry Willsie (Can)
1978   John Woolley (NZ)
1982   John Woolley (NZ)
1986   Nigel Kelly (IOM)

Pairs
1982   Gabriel & Altmann (Can)
1986   Neville & Harman (Eng)
Air Pistol
Individual
1982   George Darling (Eng)
1986   Greg Yelavich (NZ)
Pairs
1982   Adams & Colbert (Aus)
1986   Leatherdale & Reid (Eng)
Air Rifle
Individual
1982   Jean-Francois Senecal (Can)
1986   Guy Lorion (Can)
Pairs
1982   Allan & McNeil (Sco)
1986   Lorion & Bowes (Can)

SWIMMING
Men

100 Metres Freestyle (100 yards 1930-34; 110 yards 1938-66)

		time
1930	Munroe Bourne (Can)	56.0
1934	George Burleigh (Can)	55.0
1938	Bob Pirie (Can)	59.6
1950	Peter Salmon (Can)	1:00.4
1954	Jon Henricks (Aus)	56.5
1958	John Devitt (Aus)	56.6
1962	Richard Pound (Can)	55.8
1966	Mike Wenden (Aus)	54.0
1970	Mike Wenden (Aus)	53.06
1974	Mike Wenden (Aus)	52.73
1978	Mark Morgan (Aus)	52.70
1982	Neil Brooks (Aus)	51.14
1986	Greg Fasala (Aus)	50.95

200 Metres Freestyle (400 yards 1930; 440 yards 1934-66)

1970	Mike Wenden (Aus)	1:56.69
1974	Stephen Badger (Aus)	1:56.72
1978	Ron McKeon (Aus)	1:52.06
1982	Andrew Astbury (Eng)	1:51.52
1986	Robert Gleria (Aus)	1:50.57

400 Metres Freestyle (400 yards 1930; 440 yards 1934-66)

1930	Noel Ryan (Aus)	4:39.38
1934	Noel Ryan (Aus)	5:03.0
1938	Bob Pirie (Can)	4:54.6
1950	Garrick Agnew (Aus)	4:49.4
1954	Gary Chapman (Aus)	4:39.8
1958	John Konrads (Aus)	4:25.9
1962	Murray Rose (Aus)	4:20.0
1966	Robert Windle (Aus)	4:15.0
1970	Graham White (Aus)	4:08.48
1974	John Kulasalu (Aus)	4:01.44
1978	Ron McKeon (Aus)	3:54.43
1982	Andrew Astbury (Eng)	3:53.29
1986	Duncan Armstrong (Aus)	3:52.25

1,500 Metres Freestyle (1,500 yards 1930-34; 1,650 yards 1938-66)

1930	Noel Ryan (Aus)	18:55.4
1934	Noel Ryan (Aus)	18:25.4
1938	Robert Leivers (Eng)	19:46.4
1950	Graham Johnston (SA)	19:55.7
1954	Graham Johnston (SA)	19:01.4
1958	John Konrads (Aus)	17:45.4
1962	Murray Rose (Aus)	17:18.1
1966	Ron Jackson (Aus)	17:25.9
1970	Graham Windeatt (Aus)	16:23.82
1974	Steve Holland (Aus)	15:34.73
1978	Max Metzker (Aus)	15:31.92

1982	Max Metzker (Aus)	15:23.94
1986	Jason Plummer (Aus)	15:12.62

100 Metres Backstroke
(100 yards 1930-34; 110 yards 1938-66)

1930	John Trippett (Eng)	1:05.4
1934	Willie Francis (Sco)	1:05.2
1938	Percy Oliver (Aus)	1:07.9
1950	Jacobus Wiid (SA)	1:07.7
1954	John Brockway (Wales)	1:06.5
1958	John Monckton (Aus)	1:01.7
1962	Graham Sykes (Eng)	1:04.5
1966	Peter Reynolds (Aus)	1:02.4
1970	Bill Kennedy (Can)	1:01.65
1974	Mark Tonelli (Aus)	59.65
1978	Glenn Patching (Aus)	57.90
1982	Michael West (Aus)	57.12
1986	Mark Tewksbury (Can)	56.45

200 Metres Backstroke
(200 yards 1962-66)

1962	Julian Carroll (Aus)	2:20.9
1966	Peter Reynolds (Aus)	2:12.0
1970	Mike Richards (Wales)	2:14.53
1974	Brad Cooper (Aus)	2:06.31
1978	Gary Hurring (NZ)	2:04.37
1982	Cameron Henning (Can)	2:02.58
1986	Sandy Goss (Can)	2:02.55

100 Metres Breaststroke
(110 yards 1962-66)

1962	Ian O'Brien (Aus)	1:11.4
1966	Ian O'Brien (Aus)	1:08.2
1970	Bill Mahoney (Can)	1:09.0
1974	David Leigh (Eng)	1:06.52
1978	Graham Smith (Can)	1:03.81
1982	Adrian Moorhouse (Eng)	1:02.93
1986	Victor Davis (Can)	1:03.01

200 Metres Breaststroke
(200 yards 1930-34)

1930	Jack Aubin (Can)	2:38.4
1934	Norman Hamilton (Sco)	2:41.4
1938	John Davies (Eng)	2:51.9
1950	David Hawkins (Aus)	2:54.1
1954	John Doms (NZ)	2:52.6
1958	Terry Gathercole (Aus)	2:41.6
1962	Ian O'Brien (Aus)	2:38.2
1966	Ian O'Brien (Aus)	2:29.3
1970	Bill Mahoney (Can)	2:30.29
1974	David Wilkie (Sco)	2:24.42
1978	Graham Smith (Can)	2:20.86
1982	Victor Davis (Can)	2:16.25
1986	Adrian Moorhouse (Eng)	2:16.35

100 Metres Butterfly (110 yards 1962-66)

1962	Kevin Berry (Aus)	59.5
1966	Ron Jacks (Can)	1:00.3
1970	Byron MacDonald (Can)	58.44
1974	Neil Rogers (Aus)	56.58
1978	Dan Thompson (Can)	55.04
1982	Dan Thompson (Can)	54.71
1986	Andrew Jameson (Eng)	54.07

200 Metres Butterfly (220 yards 1958-66)

1958	Ian Black (Sco)	2:22.6
1962	Kevin Berry (Aus)	2:10.8
1966	David Gerrard (NZ)	2:12.7
1970	Tom Arusoo (Can)	2:08.97
1974	Brian Brinkley (Eng)	2:04.51
1978	George Nagy (Can)	2:01.99
1982	Phil Hubble (Eng)	2:00.98
1986	Anthony Mosse (NZ)	1:57.27

200 Metres Individual Medley

1970	George Smith (Can)	2:13.72
1974	David Wilkie (Sco)	2:10.11
1978	Graham Smith (Can)	2:05.25

1982	Alex Baumann (Can)	2:02.25
1986	Alex Baumann (Can)	2:01.80

400 Metres Individual Medley
(440 yards 1962-66)

1962	Alex Alexander (Aus)	5:15.3
1966	Peter Reynolds (Aus)	4:50.8
1970	George Smith (Can)	4:48.87
1974	Mark Treffers (NZ)	4:35.90
1978	Graham Smith (Can)	4:27.34
1982	Alex Baumann (Can)	4:23.53
1986	Alex Baumann (Can)	4:18.29

4 x 100 Metres Freestyle Relay
(4 x 110 yards 1962-66)

1962	Australia	3:43.9
1966	Australia	3:35.6
1970	Australia	3:36.02
1974	Canada	3:33.79
1978	Canada	3:27.94
1982	Australia	3:24.17
1986	Australia	3:21.58

4 x 200 Metres Freestyle Relay
(4 x 200 yards 1930-34; 4 x 220 yards 1938-66)

1930	Canada	8:42.4
1934	Canada	8:40.6
1938	England	9:19.0
1950	New Zealand	9:27.7
1954	Australia	8:47.6
1958	Australia	8:33.4
1962	Australia	8:13.4
1966	Australia	7:59.5
1970	Australia	7:50.77
1974	Australia	7:50.13
1978	Australia	7:34.83
1982	Australia	7:28.81
1986	Australia	7:23.49

4 x 100 Metres Medley Relay
(3 x 100 yards 1934; 3 x 110 yards 1938-54; 4 x 110 yards 1958-66.
Butterfly included from 1958)

1934	Canada	3:11.2
1938	England	3:28.2
1950	England	3:26.6
1954	Australia	3:22.0
1958	Australia	4:14.2
1962	Australia	4:12.4
1966	Canada	4:10.5
1970	Canada	4:01.10
1974	Canada	3:52.93
1978	Canada	3:49.76
1982	Australia	3:47.34
1986	Canada	3:44.00

Springboard Diving

1930	Alfred Phillips (Can)
1934	J. Briscoe Ray (Eng)
1938	Ron Masters (Aus)
1950	George Athans (Can)
1954	Peter Heatly (Sco)
1958	Keith Collin (Eng)
1962	Brian Phelps (Eng)
1966	Brian Phelps (Eng)
1970	Donald Wagstaff (Aus)
1974	Donald Wagstaff (Aus)
1978	Chris Snode (Eng)
1982	Chris Snode (Eng)
1986	Shaun Panayi (Aus)

Highboard Diving

1930	Alfred Phillips (Can)
1934	Tommy Mather (Eng)
1938	Doug Tomalin (Eng)

1950	Peter Heatly (Sco)
1954	William Patrick (Can)
1958	Peter Heatly (Sco)
1962	Brian Phelps (Eng)
1966	Brian Phelps (Eng)
1970	Donald Wagstaff (Aus)
1974	Donald Wagstaff (Aus)
1978	Chris Snode (Eng)
1982	Chris Snode (Eng)
1986	Craig Rogerson (Aus)

Water Polo
1950	Australia

Women
100 Metres Freestyle
(100 yards 1930-34; 110 yards 1938-66)
1930	Joyce Cooper (Eng)	1:07.0
1934	Phyllis Dewar (Can)	1:03.5
1938	Evelyn de Lacy (Aus)	1:10.1
1950	Marjorie McQuade (Aus)	1:09.0
1954	Lorraine Crapp (Aus)	1:05.8
1958	Dawn Fraser (Aus)	1:01.4
1962	Dawn Fraser (Aus)	59.5
1966	Marion Lay (Aus)	1:02.3
1970	Angela Coughlan (Can)	1:01.22
1974	Sonya Gray (Aus)	59.13
1978	Carol Klimpel (Can)	57.78
1982	June Croft (Eng)	56.97
1986	Jane Kerr (Can)	57.62

200 Metres Freestyle
1970	Karen Moras (Aus)	2:09.78
1974	Sonya Gray (Aus)	2:04.27
1978	Rebecca Perrott (NZ)	2:00.63
1982	June Croft (Eng)	1:59.74
1986	Susie Baumer (Aus)	2:00.61

400 Metres Freestyle
(400 yards 1930; 440 yards 1934-66)
1930	Joyce Cooper (Eng)	5:25.4
1934	Phyllis Dewar (Can)	5:45.6
1938	Dorothy Green (Aus)	5:39.7
1950	Joan Harrison (SA)	5:26.4
1954	Lorraine Crapp (Aus)	5:11.4
1958	Ilsa Konrads (Aus)	4:49.4
1962	Dawn Fraser (Aus)	4:51.4
1966	Kathy Wainwright (Aus)	4:38.8
1970	Karen Moras (Aus)	4:27.38
1974	Jenny Turrall (Aus)	4:22.09
1978	Tracey Wickham (Aus)	4:08.45
1982	Tracey Wickham (Aus)	4:08.82
1986	Sarah Hardcastle (Eng)	4:07.68

800 Metres Freestyle
1970	Karen Moras (Aus)	9:02.45
1974	Jaynie Parkhouse (NZ)	8:58.49
1978	Tracey Wickham (Aus)	8:24.62
1982	Tracey Wickham (Aus)	8:29.05
1986	Sarah Hardcastle (Eng)	8:24.77

100 Metres Backstroke
(100 yards 1930-34; 110 yards 1938-66)
1930	Joyce Cooper (Eng)	1:15.0
1934	Phyllis Harding (Eng)	1:13.8
1938	Pat Norton (Aus)	1:19.5
1950	Judy-Joy Davies (Aus)	1:18.6
1954	Joan Harrison (SA)	1:15.2
1958	Judy Grinham (Eng)	1:11.9
1962	Linda Ludgrove (Eng)	1:11.1
1966	Linda Ludgrove (Eng)	1:09.2
1970	Lynne Watson (Aus)	1:07.10
1974	Wendy Cook (Can)	1:06.37
1978	Debra Forster (Aus)	1:03.97
1982	Lisa Forrest (Aus)	1:03.48
1986	Sylvia Hume (NZ)	1:04.00

200 Metres Backstroke
(220 yards 1962-66)
1962	Linda Ludgrove (Eng)	2:35.2
1966	Linda Ludgrove (Eng)	2:28.5
1970	Lynne Watson (Aus)	2:22.86
1974	Wendy Cook (Can)	2:20.37
1978	Cheryl Gibson (Can)	2:16.57
1982	Lisa Forrest (Aus)	2:13.36
1986	Georgina Parkes (Aus)	2:14.88

100 Metres Breaststroke
(110 yards 1962-66)
1962	Anita Lonsbrough (Eng)	1:21.3
1966	Diana Harris (Eng)	1:19.7
1970	Beverley Whitfield (Aus)	1:17.40
1974	Catherine Gaskell (Eng)	1:16.42
1978	Robin Corsiglia (Can)	1:13.56
1982	Kathy Bald (Can)	1:11.89
1986	Alison Higson (Can)	1:10.84

200 Metres Breaststroke
(200 yards 1930-34; 220 yards 1938-66)
1930	Celia Wolstenholme (Eng)	2:54.8
1934	Claire Dennis (Aus)	2:50.2
1938	Doris Storey (Eng)	3:06.3
1950	Elenor Gordon (Sco)	3:01.7
1954	Elenor Gordon (Sco)	2:59.2
1958	Anita Lonsbrough (Eng)	2:53.5
1962	Anita Lonsbrough (Eng)	2:51.7
1966	Jill Slattery (Eng)	2:50.3
1970	Beverley Whitfield (Aus)	2:44.12
1974	Pat Beaan (Wales)	2:43.11
1978	Lisa Borsholt (Can)	2:37.70
1982	Anne Ottenbrite (Can)	2:32.07
1986	Allison Higson (Can)	2:31.20

100 Metres Butterfly
(110 yards 1958-66)
1958	Beverley Bainbridge (Aus)	1:13.5
1962	Mary Stewart (Can)	1:10.1
1966	Elaine Tanner (Can)	1:06.8
1970	Diane Lansley (Eng)	1:07.90
1974	Patti Stenhouse (Can)	1:05.38
1978	Wendy Quirk (Can)	1:01.92
1982	Lisa Curry (Aus)	1:01.22
1986	Caroline Cooper (Eng)	1:02.12

200 Metres Butterfly
(220 yards 1966)
1966	Elaine Tanner (Can)	2:29.9
1970	Maree Robinson (Aus)	2:24.67
1974	Sandra Yost (Aus)	2:20.57
1978	Michele Ford (Aus)	2:11.29
1982	Michele Ford (Aus)	2:11.89
1986	Donna McGinnis (Can)	2:11.97

200 Metres Individual Medley
1970	Denise Langford (Aus)	2:28.89
1974	Leslie Cliff (Can)	2:24.13
1978	Sharron-Davies (Eng)	2:18.37
1982	Lisa Curry (Aus)	2:16.94
1986	Suzanne Landells (Aus)	2:17.02

400 Metres Individual Medley
(440 yards 1962-66)
1962	Anita Lonsbrough (Eng)	5:38.6
1966	Elaine Tanner (Can)	5:26.3
1970	Denise Langford (Aus)	5:10.74
1974	Leslie Cliff (Can)	5:01.35
1978	Sharron Davies (Eng)	4:52.44
1982	Lisa Curry (Aus)	4:51.95
1986	Suzanne Landells (Aus)	4:45.82

4 x 100 Metres Freestyle Relay
(4 x 100 yards 1930-34; 4 x 110 yards
1938-66)

1930	England	4:32.8
1934	Canada	4:21.8
1938	Canada	4:48.3
1950	Australia	4:44.9
1954	South Africa	4:33.9
1958	Australia	4:17.4
1962	Australia	4:11.0
1966	Canada	4:10.8
1970	Australia	4:06.41
1974	Canada	3:57.14
1978	Canada	3:50.28
1982	England	3:50.28
1986	Canada	3:48.45

4 x 200 Metres Freestyle Relay

1986	Australia	8:12.09

4 x 100 Metres Medley Relay
(3 x 100 yards 1934; 3 x 110 yards
1938-54; 4 x 110 yards 1958.
Butterfly included from 1958)

1934	Canada	3:42.0
1938	England	3:57.7
1950	Australia	3:53.8
1954	Scotland	3:51.0
1958	England	4:54.0
1962	Australia	4:45.9
1966	England	4:40.6
1970	Australia	4:30.66
1974	Canada	4:24.77
1978	Canada	4:15.26
1982	Canada	4:14.33
1986	England	4:13.48

Springboard Diving

1930	Oonagh Whitsett (SA)
1934	Judy Moss (Can)
1938	Irene Donnett (Aus)
1950	Edna Child (Eng)
1954	Ann Long (Eng)
1958	Charmain Welsh (Eng)
1962	Susan Knight (Aus)
1966	Kathy Rowlatt (Eng)
1970	Beverley Boys (Can)
1974	Cindy Shatto (Can)
1978	Janet Nutter (Can)
1982	Jenny Donnett (Aus)
1986	Debbie Fuller (Can)

Highboard Diving

1930	Pearl Stoneham (Can)
1934	Elizabeth Macready (Eng)
1938	Lurline Hook (Aus)
1950	Edna Child (Eng)
1954	Barbara McAulay (Aus)
1958	Charmain Welsh (Eng)
1962	Susan Knight (Aus)
1966	Joy Newman (Eng)
1970	Beverley Boys (Can)
1974	Beverley Boys (Can)
1978	Linda Cuthbert (Can)
1982	Valerie Beddoe (Aus)
1986	Debbie Fuller (Can)

Synchronised Swimming
Solo

1986	Sylvie Frechette (Can)

Duet

1986	Waldo & Cameron (Can)

Leading Gold Medal countries in swimming.
Men Australia 78, Canada 46, England 27, Scotland 8, New Zealand 6. *Women* Australia 59, Canada 44, England 40, South Africa 4, Scotland and New Zealand 3.

WEIGHTLIFTING
Flyweight

1970	George Vasiliades (Aus)
1974	Precious McKenzie (Eng)
1978	Ekambaram Karunakaran (Ind)
1982	Nick Voukelatos (Aus)
1986	Greg Hayman (Aus)

Bantamweight

1950	Tho Fook Hung (Mal)
1954	Maurice Magennis (Eng)
1958	Reginald Gaffley (SA)
1962	Chua Phung Kim (Sin)
1966	Precious McKenzie (Eng)
1970	Precious McKenzie (Eng)
1974	Michael Adams (Aus)
1978	Precious McKenzie (NZ)
1982	Geoffrey Laws (Eng)
1986	Nick Voukelatos (Aus)

Featherweight

1950	Koh Eng Tong (Mal)
1954	Rodney Wilkes (Tri)
1958	Tan Ser Cher (Sin)
1962	George Newton (Eng)
1966	Kum Weng Chung (Wales)
1970	George Perrin (Eng)
1974	George Vasiliades (Aus)
1978	Michel Mercier (Can)
1982	Dean Willey (Eng)
1986	Raymond Williams (Wales)

Lightweight

1950	James Halliday (Eng)
1954	Verdi Barberis (Aus)
1958	Tan Howe Liang (Sin)
1962	Carlton Goring (Eng)
1966	Hugo Gittens (Tri)
1970	George Newton (Eng)
1974	George Newton (Eng)
1978	Bill Stellios (Aus)
1982	David Morgan (Wales)
1986	Dean Willey (Eng)

Middleweight

1950	Gerard Gratton (Can)
1954	James Halliday (Eng)
1958	Blair Blenman (Bar)
1962	Tan Howe Laing (Sin)
1966	Pierre St Jean (Can)
1970	Russell Perry (Aus)
1974	Tony Ebert (NZ)
1978	Sam Castiglione (Aus)
1982	Stephen Pinsent (Eng)
1986	Bill Stellios (Aus)

Light-heavyweight

1950	James Varaleau (Can)
1954	Gerry Gratton (Can)
1958	Phil Caira (Sco)
1962	Phil Caira (Sco)
1966	George Vakakis (Aus)
1970	Nicolo Ciancio (Aus)
1974	Tony Ford (Eng)
1978	Robert Kabbas (Aus)
1982	Newton Burrowes (Eng)
1986	David Morgan (Wales)

Middle-heavyweight

1954	Keevil Daly (Can)
1958	Manoel Santos (Aus)
1962	Louis Martin (Eng)
1966	Louis Martin (Eng)
1970	Louis Martin (Eng)
1974	Nicolo Ciancio (Aus)
1978	Gary Langford (Eng)
1982	Robert Kabbas (Aus)
1986	Keith Boxell (Eng)

Sub-heavyweight
1978   John Burns (Wales)
1982   Oliver Orok (Nig)
1986   Denis Garon (Can)

Heavyweight
1950   Harold Cleghorn (NZ)
1954   Doug Hepburn (Can)
1958   Ken McDonald (Eng)
1962   Arthur Shannos (Aus)
1966   Donald Oliver (NZ)
1970   Russell Prior (Can)
1974   Russell Prior (Can)
1978   Russell Prior (Can)
1982   John Burns (Wales)
1986   Kevin Roy (Can)

Super-heavyweight
1970   Ray Rigby (Aus)
1974   Graham May (NZ)
1978   Jean-Marc Cardinal (Can)
1982   Dean Lukin (Aus)
1986   Dean Lukin (Aus)

WRESTLING (Freestyle)
Light-flyweight
1970   Ved Prakash (Ind)
1974   Mitchell Kawasaki (Can)
1978   Ashok Kumar (Ind)
1982   Ram Cahnder Sarang (Ind)
1986   Ron Moncur (Can)

Flyweight
1950   Bert Harris (Aus)
1954   Louis Base (SA)
1958   Ian Epton (SA)
1962   Muhammad Niaz (Pak)
1966   Mohammad Nazir (Pak)
1970   Sudesh Kumar (Ind)
1974   Sudesh Kumar (Ind)
1978   Ray Takahashi (Can)
1982   Mahabir Singh (Ind)
1986   Chris Woodcroft (Can)

Bantamweight
1930   James Trifunov (Can)
1934   Edward Melrose (Sco)
1938   Ted Purcell (Aus)
1950   Douglas Mudgeway (NZ)
1954   Geoffrey Jameson (Aus)
1958   Mohammad Akhtar (Pak)
1962   Siraj-ud-Din (Pak)
1966   Bishambar Singh (Ind)
1970   Sadar Mohd (Pak)
1974   Premnath (Ind)
1978   Satbir Singh (Ind)
1982   Brian Aspen (Eng)
1986   Mitch Ostberg (Can)

Featherweight
1930   Clifford Chilcott (Can)
1934   Robert McNab (Can)
1938   Roy Purchase (Aus)
1950   John Armitt (NZ)
1954   Abraham Geldenhuys (SA)
1958   Abraham Geldenhuys (SA)
1962   Ala-ud-Din (Pak)
1966   Mohammad Akhtar (Pak)
1970   Mohammad Saeed (Pak)
1974   Egon Beiler (Can)
1978   Egon Beiler (Can
1982   Bob Robinson (Can)
1986   Paul Hughes (Can)

Lightweight
1930   Howard Thomas (Can)
1934   Richard Garrard (Aus)
1938   Richard Garrard (Aus)
1950   Richard Garrard (Aus)

1954   Godfrey Pienaar (SA)
1958   Muhammad Ashraf (Pak)
1962   Muhammad Akhtar (Pak)
1966   Mukhtiar Singh (Ind)
1970   Udey Chand (Ind)
1974   Jagrup Singh (Ind)
1978   Zsigmund Kelevitz (Aus)
1982   Jagminder Singh (Ind)
1986   David McKay (Can)

Welterweight
1930   Reg Priestley (Can)
1934   Joseph Schleimer (Can)
1938   Thomas Trevaskis (Aus)
1950   Henry Hudson (Can)
1954   Nicholas Laubscher (SA)
1958   Muhammad Bashir (Pak)
1962   Muhammad Bashir (Pak)
1966   Muhammad Bashir (Pak)
1970   Mukhtiar Singh (Ind)
1974   Raghunath Pawar (Ind)
1978   Rajinder Singh (Ind)
1982   Rajinder Singh (Ind)
1986   Gary Holmes (Can)

Middleweight
1930   Mike Chepwick (Can)
1934   Terry Evans (Can)
1938   Terry Evans (Can)
1950   Maurice Vachon (Can)
1954   Hermanus van Zyl (SA)
1958   Hermanus van Zyl (SA)
1962   Muhammad Faiz (Pak)
1966   Muhammad Faiz (Pak)
1970   Harish Rajindra (Ind)
1974   David Aspin (NZ)
1978   Richard Deschatelets (Can)
1982   Chris Rinke (Can)
1986   Chris Rinke (Can)

Light-heavyweight
1930   Bill McIntyre (Can)
1934   Mick Cubbin (SA)
1938   Edward Scarf (Aus)
1950   Patrick Morton (SA)
1954   Jacob Theron (SA)
1958   Jacob Theron (SA)
1962   Anthony Buck (Eng)
1966   Robert Chamberot (Can)
1970   Muhammad Faiz (Pak)
1974   Terry Paice (Can)
1978   Stephen Danier (Can)
1982   Clark Davis (Can)
1986   Noel Loban (Eng)

Heavyweight
1930   Earl McCready (Can)
1934   Jack Knight (Aus)
1938   Jack Knight (Aus)
1950   James Armstrong (Aus)
1954   Kenneth Richmond (Eng)
1958   Lila Ram (Ind)
1962   Muhammad Niaz (Pak)
1966   Bhim Singh (Ind)
1970   Edward Millard (Can)
1974   Claude Pilon (Can)
1978   Wyatt Wishart (Can)
1982   Richard Deschatelets (Can)
1986   Clark Davis (Can)

Super-heavyweight
1970   Ikram Ilahi (Pak)
1974   Bill Benko (Can)
1978   Robert Gibbons (Can)
1982   Wyatt Wishart (Can)
1986   Wayne Brightwell (Can)

═══ SCHEDULE ═══

COMMONWEALTH GAMES
Auckland, New Zealand (Jan 24-Feb 3, 1990)

Events and venues
Athletics	Mt Smart Stadium
Badminton	Badminton Hall
Bowls	Pakuranga Combined Bowls Centre
Boxing	Logan Campbell Centre
Cycling	Manukau Veladrome
Gymnastics	Chase Stadium
Judo	Carter Holt Pavilion
Shooting	Waitemata Gun Club (shotgun),
	Mangatawhiri Range (full bore),
	Ardmore Range (small bore, pistols, airweapons and running boar)
Swimming	West Auckland Swimming Centre
Weightlifting	East Pavilion, Expo Centre, Epsom

Programme of events at a glance

	Day 1	Day 2	Day 3	Day 4	Day 5	Day 6	Day 7	Day 8	Day 9	Day 10	Day 11
	Wed Jan 24	Thu Jan 25	Fri Jan 26	Sat Jan 27	Sun Jan 28	Mon Jan 29	Tue Jan 30	Wed Jan 31	Thu Feb 1	Fri Feb 2	Sat Feb 3
Opening Ceremony	E										
Athletics				A	A	A	M	M	A	MA	A
Badminton		MAE	MAE	MAE		ME	ME	A	E	ME	
Bowls		MA	MA	MA	MA	MA	MA	MA	MA	A	
Boxing		E	AE	AE	AE	AE	E	E	E	E	
Cycling		M		ME	ME	ME		ME	ME		M
Gymnastics		A	A	MA	MA		E	E	E		
Judo								AE	E	E	AE	MA
Shooting		MA	MA	MA	MA	MA	M	MA	MA	MA	
Swimming		MA	MA	MA	MA	MA	M				
Weightlifting		AE	AE	AE	AE	AE					
Closing Ceremony											E
Netball*										A	
Triathlon*				M							

M = Morning A = Afternoon E = Evening *Demonstration Sports

Day-by-day timetable guide to events
M = men, W = women, Q = qualifying, P = Preliminaries, H = heats, R = rounds, F = final
Athletics – D = Decathlon, Hp = Heptathlon, Cycling – R = reselection, TT = Team Trials, ITT = Individual team trial, IP = Individual pursuit, TP = Team pursuit, RR = Road Race.
Note: All times local. GMT is 13 hours behind New Zealand – eg 0900 Thursday is 2000 Wednesday in London.

Day 1 – Wednesday, Jan 24
Opening Ceremony (Mt Smart)

Day 2 – Thursday, Jan 25

Badminton:	0900 hrs – Team event
	1400 hrs – Team event
	1900 hrs – Team event
Bowls:	0900 hrs – W Singles
	M Pairs
	M Fours
	1330 hrs – W Singles
	M Pairs
	M Fours
	1600 hrs – W Singles

Boxing:	1930 hrs – Preliminaries	
Cycling:	1100 hrs – 100km Road TT	
Gymnastics:	1400 hrs – M Artistic team	
	1900 hrs – M Artistic team	
Shooting:	0900 hrs – Fullbore rifle pairs	
	Air rifle	
	Rapid Fire Pistol	
	1300 hrs – Free Pistol	
Swimming:	0900 hrs – W 100m free	(H)
	M 100m breast	(H)
	W 400m medley	(H)
	M 200m free	(H)
	W 4 x 200m free	(H)
	Synchro solo routine	
	(or figure)	(P)
	1630 hrs – W 100m free	(F)
	M 100m breast	(F)
	W 400m medley	(F)
	M 200m free	(F)
	W 4 x 200m free	(F)
	Diving:	
	W 1m springbd	(P)
	M 1m springbd	(P)

Weightlifting:	1400 hrs – 52 kg class	
	1900 hrs – 56 kg class	

Day 3 – Friday, Jan 26

Badminton:	0900 hrs – Team event	
	1400 hrs – Team event	
	1900 hrs – Team event	
Bowls:	0900 hrs – W Singles	
	M Pairs	
	M Fours	
	1300 hrs – W Singles	
	M Pairs	
	M Fours	
	1600 hrs – W Singles	
Boxing:	1400 hrs – Preliminaries	
	1930 hrs – Preliminaries	
Gymnastics:	1400 hrs – W Artistic team	
	1900 hrs – W Artistic team	
Shooting:	0900 hrs – Trench pairs	
	Rapid Fire Pistol pairs	
	1300 hrs – Air Pistol pairs	
Swimming:	0900 hrs – M 100m B/fly	(H)
	W 200m free	(H)
	M 400m medley	(H)
	W 200m breast	(H)
	M 4 x 200m free	(H)
	Diving:	
	W 1m springbd	(F)
	M 1m springbd	(F)
	1630 hrs – M 100m B/fly	(F)
	W 200m free	(F)
	M 400m medley	(F)
	W 200m breast	(F)
	M 4 x 200m free	(F)
	Synchro figures	
	(or solo routine)	(P)
Weightlifting:	1400 hrs – 60 kg class	
	1900 hrs – 67.5 kg class	

Day 4 – Saturday, Jan 27

Athletics:	1200 hrs – M Hammer	(Q)
	1230 hrs – W 100m hurdles	(Hp)
	1330 hrs – M 100m	(R1)
	1330 hrs – W High jump	(Hp)
	1345 hrs – W Discus	(Q)
	1400 hrs – W 400m	(R1)
	1425 hrs – M 400m	(R1)
	1455 hrs – M 110m hurdles	(H)
	1525 hrs – W 100m	(H)
	1530 hrs – W Shot	(Hp)
	1555 hrs – M 3000m st'ch	(H)
	1630 hrs – M Hammer	(F)
	1630 hrs – M 100m	(R2)
	1700 hrs – M 110m hurdles	(SF)
	1725 hrs – W 200m	(Hp)
	1745 hrs – W 400m	(SF)
	1805 hrs – M 400m	(R2)
	1830 hrs – W 3000m	(H1)
	1850 hrs – W 3000m	(H2)
	1910 hrs – M 10000m	(F)
Badminton:	0900 hrs – Team event	
	1400 hrs – Team event	
	1900 hrs – Team event	
Bowls:	0900 hrs – W Singles	
	M Pairs	
	M Fours	
	1330 hrs – W Singles	
	M Pairs	
	M Fours	
Boxing:	1400 hrs – Preliminaries	
	1930 hrs – Preliminaries	
Cycling:	1100 hrs – M Sprint	(Q)
	W Sprint	(Q)
	1900 hrs – M 1000m ITT	(F)
	W Sprint (R1 and Res)	

Gymnastics:	1000 hrs – M Artistic all round	
	1500 hrs – W Artistic all round	
Shooting:	0900 hrs – Fullbore rifle Stage 1 & 2	
	Air Rifle individual	
	Skeet pairs	
	1300 hrs – Free pistol individual	
Swimming:	0900 hrs – W 400m free	(H)
	M 100m free	(H)
	W 100m back	(H)
	M 200m back	(H)
	W 4 x 100m free (H)	
	Synchro solo routine	(F)
	1630 hrs – W 400m free	(F)
	M 100m free	(F)
	W 100m back	(F)
	M 200m back	(F)
	W 4 x 100m free	(F)
	Diving:	
	W highboard	(P)
	M 3m springbd	(P)
Weightlifting:	1400 hrs – 75 kg class	
	1900 hrs – 82.5 kg class	

Day 5 – Sunday, Jan 28

Athletics:	1200 hrs – M 100m	(D)
	1300 hrs – M Long jump	(D)
	1345 hrs – W Shot	(Q)
	1445 hrs – W Longjump	(Hp)
	1500 hrs – W 400m hurdles	(H)
	1500 hrs – M Shot	(D)
	1525 hrs – M 400m hurdles	(H)
	1545 hrs – M 400m	(SF)
	1615 hrs – M 110m hurdles	(F)
	1615 hrs – W Javelin	(Hp)
	1635 hrs – W 100m	(SF)
	1645 hrs – M High jump	(D)
	1655 hrs – M 100m	(SF)
	1715 hrs – M 3000m st'ch	(F)
	1745 hrs – W 400m	(F)
	1745 hrs – W Discus	(F)
	1800 hrs – M 400m	(F)
	1820 hrs – W 800m	(Hp)
	1850 hrs – W 100m	(F)
	1910 hrs – M 100m	(F)
	1930 hrs – W 3000m	(F)
	1945 hrs – M 400m	(D)
Bowls:	0900 hrs – W Singles	(SF)
	M Singles	
	W Pairs	
	M Fours	
	1300 hrs – W Singles	(F)
	M Singles	
	M Pairs	
	M Fours	
	1600 hrs – M Singles	
Boxing:	1400 hrs – Preliminaries	
	1930 hrs – Preliminaries	
Cycling:	1100 hrs – M Sprint (R1 and Res)	
	M 4000m IP	(Q)
	1900 hrs – M Sprint (R2 and Res)	
	W Sprint	(QF)
	M 4000 IP	(QF)
Gymnastics:	1000 hrs – M Apparatus	(F)
	1500 hrs – W Apparatus	(F)
Shooting:	0900 hrs – Smallbore rifle 3 position pairs	
	Running Boar Pairs	
	1300 hrs – Centre Fire Pairs	
Swimming:	0900 hrs – M 400m free	(H)
	W 100m B/fly	(H)
	M 200m breast	(H)
	W 100m breast	(H)
	M 4 x 100m free	(H)
	W 800m free	(H)

Diving:
W highboard (F)
M 3m springbd (F)
1630 hrs – M 400m free (F)
W 100m B/fly (F)
M 200m breast (F)
W 100m breast (F)
M 4 x 100m free (F)
Synchro – Duet
routine (P)
Weightlifting: 1400 hrs – 90 kg class
1900 hrs – 100 kg class

Day 6 – Monday, Jan 29
Athletics: 1330 hrs – M 110m hurdles (D)
1350 hrs – M 800m (H)
1410 hrs – M High jump (Q)
1420 hrs – W 400m hurdles (SF)
1430 hrs – M Discus (D)
1440 hrs – M 400m hurdles (SF)
1500 hrs – W 200m (H)
1530 hrs – M 200m (R1)
1600 hrs – W Javelin (Q)
1600 hrs – M Pole Vault (D)
1620 hrs – W 800m (H)
1640 hrs – M 800m (SF)
1700 hrs – W 200m (SF)
1710 hrs – W Shot (F)
1720 hrs – M 200m (R2)
1750 hrs – W 400m hurdles (F)
1800 hrs – M Javelin (D)
1810 hrs – M 400m hurdles (F)
1830 hrs – M 5000m (H1)
1900 hrs – M 5000m (H2)
1930 hrs – M 1500m (D)
Badminton: 1000 hrs – M Singles (R1 and 2)
1700 hrs – W Singles (R1 and 2)
M Doubles (R1)
W Doubles (R1)
Bowls: 0900 hrs – M Singles
M Pairs (SF)
W Pairs
M Fours
W Fours
1300 hrs – M Singles
M Pairs (F)
W Pairs
Boxing: 1400 hrs – Quarter-finals
1930 hrs – Quarter-finals
Cycling: 1100 hrs – M Sprint (QF)
M Sprint (SF)
M 4000m IP (SF)
1900 hrs – W Sprint (F)
M Sprint (SF)
M 4000m IP (F)
W 3000m IP (Q)
Shooting: 0900 hrs – Fullbore rifle (F)
Trench 1st 100 individual
Running Boar Pairs
1300 hrs – Centre Fire Pairs
Swimming: 0900 hrs – W 200m medley (H)
M 200m B/fly (H)
M 100m back (H)
M 4 x 100m medley (H)
M 50m free (H)
M 1500m free (H)
Synchro-duet
routine (F)
1630 hrs – W 200m medley (F)
M 200m B/fly (F)
M 50m free (F)
W 800m free (F)
M 100m back (F)
W 4 x 100m medley (F)

Diving:
W 3m springbd (P)
M highboard (P)
Weightlifting: 1400 hrs – 110 kg class
1900 hrs – 110+ kg class

Day 7 – Tuesday, Jan 30
Athletics: 0700 hrs – M Marathon
Badminton: 1000 hrs – M Singles (R3)
W Singles (R3)
M Doubles (R2)
W Doubles (R2)
1700 hrs – Mixed Doubles (R1, 2, 3)
Bowls: 0900 hrs – M Singles
W Pairs
M Fours (SF)
1330 hrs – M Singles
W Pairs
M Fours (F)
W Fours
Boxing: 1930 hrs – Semi-finals
Gymnastics: 1900 hrs – Rhythmic Individual
2 Apparatus
Judo: 1400 hrs – M Heavyweight
W Heavyweight
1900 hrs – M Half heavyweight
W Half heavyweight
Shooting: 0900 hrs – Smallbore rifle Prone Pairs
Air Pistol Individual
Trench 2nd 100 Individual
Running Boar Individual
Swimming: 0900 hrs – M 200m medley (H)
W 200m B/fly (H)
W 200m back (H)
M 4 x 100m medley (H)
W 50m free (H)
Diving:
W 3m springbd (F)
M highboard (F)
1630 hrs – M 200m medley (F)
W 200m B/fly (F)
W 50m free (F)
M 1500m free (F)
W 200m back (F)
M 4 x 100m medley (F)

Day 8 – Wednesday, Jan 31
Athletics: 0700 hrs – W Marathon
Badminton: 1300 hrs – All events (QF)
Bowls: 0900 hrs – M Singles (SF)
W Pairs
W Fours
1330 hrs – M Singles (F)
W Pairs
W Fours
Boxing: 1930 hrs – Semi-finals
Cycling: 1100 hrs – W 3000m IP (QF)
M 4000m TP (Q)
1900 hrs – M Sprint (F)
W 3000m IP (SF)
M 50 km points (F)
Gymnastics: 1900 hrs – Rhythmic Individual
2 Apparatus
Judo: 1900 hrs – M Middleweight
W Middleweight
Shooting: 0900 hrs – Smallbore rifle 3 position
Individual
Rapid Fire Pistol Individual

Day 9 – Thursday, Feb 1
Athletics: 1300 hrs – M Long jump (Q)
1300 hrs – W High jump (Q)
1300 hrs – M Pole Vault (Q)
1300 hrs – M Discus (Q)
1500 hrs – W Long jump (Q)
1500 hrs – M High jump (F)

	1600 hrs – W 100m hurdles	(H)
	1630 hrs – M 200m	(SF)
	1700 hrs – W 800m	(F)
	1700 hrs – M Long jump	(F)
	1730 hrs – W Javelin	(F)
	1730 hrs – M 800m	(F)
	1750 hrs – W 200m	(F)
	1810 hrs – M 200m	(F)
	1840 hrs – W 100m hurdles	(SF)
	1910 hrs – M 5000m	(F)
Badminton:	1800 hrs – All events	(SF)
Bowls:	0900 hrs – W Pairs	(SF)
	W Fours	
	1330 hrs – W Pairs	(F)
Boxing:	1930 hrs – Finals	
Cycling:	1100 hrs – M 4000m TP	(SF)
	1900 hrs – M 4000m TP	(F)
	W 3000m IP	(F)
	M 10m Scratch	(F)
Gymnastics:	1900 hrs – Rhythmic Individual	(F)
Judo:	1900 hrs – M Half middleweight	
	W Half middleweight	
Shooting:	0900 hrs – Skeet 1st 100 Individual	
	Running Boar Slow Individual	
	1300 hrs – Centre fire individual	

Day 10 – Friday, Feb 2

Athletics:	0700 hrs – M Road walk	(30km)
	1045 hrs – W Road walk	(10km)
	1400 hrs – M Javelin	(Q)
	1400 hrs – M Triple Jump	(Q)
	1400 hrs – M Shot	(Q)
	1430 hrs – M Pole Vault	(F)
	1510 hrs – W 4 x 100m relay	(H)
	1530 hrs – M 4 x 100m relay	(H)
	1555 hrs – W 1500m	(H)
	1600 hrs – W Long jump	(F)
	1615 hrs – W High jump	(F)
	1640 hrs – M 1500m	(H)

	1750 hrs – M Discus	(F)
	1735 hrs – W 100m hurdles	(F)
	1805 hrs – W 4 x 400m relay	(H)
	1840 hrs – M 4 x 400m relay	(H)
	1910 hrs – W 10000m	(F)
Badminton:	1200 hrs – All events play off for Bronze	
	1800 hrs – All events play off for	
	Gold/Silver	
Bowls:	0900 hrs – W Fours	(SF)
	1330 hrs – W Fours	(F)
Boxing:	1930 hrs – Finals	
Cycling:	0800 hrs – W 72 km RR	
	1030 hrs – M 173 km RR	
Judo:	1400 hrs – M Lightweight	
	W Lightweight	
	1900 hrs – M Half lightweight	
	W Half lightweight	
Shooting:	0900 hrs – Smallbore rifle Prone	
	Individual	
	Skeet 2nd 100 Individual	
	Running Boar Fast Individual	
	1300 hrs – Centre Fire Individual	

Day 11 – Saturday, Feb 3

Athletics:	1600 hrs – M Javelin	(F)
	1615 hrs – W 1500m	(F)
	1630 hrs – M Triple jump	(F)
	1640 hrs – W 4 x 100m relay	(F)
	1700 hrs – M 4 x 100m relay	(F)
	1715 hrs – M Shot	(F)
	1725 hrs – M 1500m	(F)
	1755 hrs – W 4 x 400m relay	(F)
	1815 hrs – M 4 x 400m relay	(F)
Judo:	0930 hrs – M Extra lightweight	
	W Extra lightweight	
	1330 hrs – M Open	
	W Open	

Closing Ceremony: 1900 hrs – 2030 hrs (Mt Smart)

CRICKET

THE YEAR IT ALL WENT WRONG

One of the most beautiful English summers of the century produced probably the most traumatic season of Test cricket the nation has ever endured. The England team, starting the summer in a mood of jaunty confidence under new management, finished it in unprecedented tatters. Australia regained the Ashes four-nil, with England lucky to get the nil. On August 1, the day Australia's victory was secured, South Africa announced a 16-man English team who would be touring there in early 1990 and would thus be barred from Test cricket for the foreseeable future.

David Gower, made captain for the entire Ashes series, was not merely sacked afterwards but excluded from the touring party to the West Indies. That squad of remnants faced a task so apparently hopeless that gloomier souls began to wonder, not whether they might win a match, but whether they might score a run or take a wicket. Given this prognosis, the tour could only come as a pleasant surprise.

The Ashes summer began in a mood of English optimism that soon became bizarre to recall. Ted Dexter, who had replaced Peter May as chairman of selectors, revamped the selection process and immediately began dashing everywhere on his motor bike, creating an impression of vigour and enthusiasm which lasted until the cricket actually started.

When he was appointed, Gower said he was "supremely confident" of beating the Australians. The mood was widely shared, remembering other Australian teams of the recent past. It turned out that this one was different – with mature, composed batting led first by Steve Waugh (who scored 393 runs before getting out) and latterly by Mark Taylor (who scored 839 in the series), effective bowling led by Terry Alderman (41 wickets) and carefully-laid plans that contrasted vividly with Gower's come-day, go-day approach. Any luck that was going went with Australia: England were beset by injuries and ill-fortune as well as incompetence. The headlines from these matches are culled from *The Sun*; their use does not necessarily imply endorsement of the sentiments.

1. GOWER'S GOONS: Border later said he believed the series was won and lost on the first day of the First Test when England, remembering past explosive Headingley wickets, chose to bowl first, did so terribly and watched Australia compile 601, to the satisfaction of one Englishman anyway: the Headingley groundsman Keith Boyce. England avoided the follow-on, chairman Dexter went home and with the game apparently safe England collapsed to Alderman. 0-1.

2. CAP'N CALAMITY: At Lord's England chose to bat but did so profligately. Australia's early batsmen also struggled but the tailenders doubled the score on a bleak Saturday which concluded with Gower walking out of his press conference so he could attend a West End show: "Anything Goes". Gower redeemed some of his own reputation, but not the team's, with a century on Monday. It was too late. 0-2.

3. THE PITS: After 11 failures in a row, Border won a toss against Gower, Australia batted on a plumb Edgbaston pitch but scored a mere 424. On Thursday evening, perhaps the most furious storm ever seen on an English cricket ground broke and it was impossible to see the far side. On Friday and Saturday, only three hours' play were possible and Gower said the game was drawn unless "something beyond belief" happened. England promptly collapsed, all too believably, to 75 for 5 but recovered to let the last pair Dilley and Jarvis nervously avoid the follow-on. Still 0-2.

4. KICK THE TWITS OUT! England were bowled out for 260 on a slow pitch at Old Trafford, an innings relieved only by a marvellous century by Robin Smith. Australia then piled up a big lead. Gower was reprimanded by Dexter for giving a surreptitious V-sign to barrackers. Luckily, he did not appear at a press conference on either Saturday or Monday. Had he done so, he would probably have resigned there and

then. As it was, England were saved from defeat until the Tuesday by Manchester rain, and by then attention had been diverted by the announcement of the South Africans' captures, who included three of the team on the field. Jack Russell became the first Englishman since Billy Griffith in 1947-48 to score his maiden century in a Test and came close to saving the game. Everyone was too preoccupied to give him due credit. 0-3.

5. GIVE US A BREAK, BORDER: The selectors had to revamp the team but not as dramatically as many of their critics wanted. The makeshift side had a horrendous first day when the Australian openers Taylor and Geoff Marsh became the first pair ever to bat through the opening day of a Test in England (the ninth in any Test), eventually constructing a stand of 329, a record for either side in the Ashes and the highest for any wicket in a Trent Bridge Test. Australia batted on until the third morning but won in four days by an innings and 180, the heaviest defeat in an Ashes Test since Brisbane, 1946-7. 0-4. England were brought back on Tuesday for "naughty-boy" nets. A man in his 30s was reported to have been admitted to a local hospital having taken an overdose of pills "because of the situation at the Test match". Two days later an England XI under Peter Roebuck, comprising precisely those young players advocated by the selectors' critics, lost by three runs in a 40-over match – to Holland. (In September, an MCC team lost to France; in 1989, nothing was impossible.)

6. OUR OVAL 'ORRORS: With the fortune that always attends failing sides, England struggled to find 11 fit men, never mind 11 good ones. Derek Pringle and Alan Igglesden, brought in as late replacements, were reckoned by manager Stewart to be approximately the 16th and 17th choice seam bowlers. Igglesden had to borrow his neighbour's spanner to fix his washing machine and wash his kit. England used 29 players in the series, Australia 12. Dean Jones scored a brilliant hundred. Australia totalled 468, fewer than expected on a belting pitch. England avoided the follow-on and secured a draw with a spirited innings by Gladstone Small but no one was on the team balcony to applaud him. The Vicar of Scarborough offered special prayers for cricket lovers. After the match, Gower went on holiday to Portugal and his team even lost a game against the Port Wine XI in Oporto. He was once again dismissed by an Australian. Andrew Peacock, leader of the Australian opposition, said Border should be knighted.

Gower told reporters who tracked him down in Portugal that he had been sacked as England captain. Lord's denied this. Gower was sacked, but they did not tell him until after the news that Graham Gooch had been re-appointed was officially announced. England then selected a team for the West Indies including no reserve opener, no left-hand specialist batsmen, no recognised blocker and no one with any substantial Test experience other than Gooch and his vice-captain Allan Lamb. Botham, having changed his mind and made himself available, was excluded to his own astonishment; Gower was excluded, to everyone's astonishment; Roebuck, widely regarded as a possible England captain, did not make either the main party or the A tour to Zimbabwe.

THE BOYS IN THE RAND

The alternative England team, put together by Ali Bacher of the South African Cricket Union, also seemed in better shape than the original side. The year had started with a deal at the International Cricket Conference at which the black countries agreed to forgive players (like Gooch) associated with South Africa in the past provided anyone who went there in future was banned from Test cricket – four years for coaching there, five years for going on an organised tour. The ban was agreed despite the misgivings of the Cricketers' Association, the English players' trade union, and an improbable attempt to summons Lt-Col John Stephenson, secretary of the MCC and the ICC, under Section 21 of the Theft Act 1968, which covers blackmail.

SUMMER OF LOVE

"I would like England to be the most likeable and watchable team in the world."
Ted Dexter, Feb 1

"The mood of optimism is building up and I'd like to see it transmitted to the players."
David Gower, Apr 5

"A Test match without Ian Botham is like a horror film without Boris Karloff."
Fred Trueman on the First Test

"Things have not gone exactly according to plan."
Ted Dexter, after the first day of the series

"They have outplayed us in all departments. But we have five more chances of winning a match this summer and, as far as the home side is concerned, whatever the disappointments we have had at Leeds, they will not stop us coming back with a vengeance at Lord's."
David Gower, after the First Test

"It's never right to panic yourself."
David Gower, after the Second Test.

"These tactics were incomprehensible."
Mike Brearley, Sunday Times, on David Gower's handling of the Second Test

"Micky Stewart said the England players do not think about defeat. Some of them do not seem to think very much at all."
Mike Selvey, The Guardian, on the Third Test

"Fight? Resist? Our lot fought and resisted with the guts and spunk of a butterfly. With blokes like these in the trenches, Hitler would have had as easy a campaign as Allan Border."
John Sadler, The Sun, on the Fourth Test

"I have the support of my England committee colleagues, from my colleagues in the England team and, I think, from the majority of the English public."
David Gower, after the Fourth Test

"And don't forget Malcolm Devon."
Ted Dexter

"I suppose he might just get in the Windward Islands side – but not the Leewards, who must have dozens as good."
John Woodcock, The Times, on Devon Malcolm

"If what the selection committee came up with for Trent Bridge is rebuilding, I don't want them doing my renovations."
Ian Chappell, Adelaide Advertiser, on the Fifth Test

"Mr Gower is the most disastrous leader since Ethelred the Unready. Beyond question he should now stand down in favour of Ken Dodd."
Sun leader, after the Fifth Test

"All your press and media just batter on rubbishing the England boys – thinking their boys set out to play like idiots and not giving it their best shot. That's not been the story at all. Why not a mention in the media that the better side won?"
Allan Border

"The cricketers available this season have not been markedly inferior, man for man, to Australia's. What has been lacking is leadership, thought and application."
Mike Brearley, Sunday Times

"Unobtrusive, persevering, much respected and as tough as a pebble, what would England not give for Border's like!"
John Woodcock, The Times

"All I am trying to do is to retain some sort of confidence in, first, what I can do as a captain and a player and secondly, what the eleven can do as a team. And keep plugging on."
David Gower, after the Fifth Test

"I wish the critics would stop knocking David Gower. It really appals me the way he is kicked in the teeth every time his back is turned."
Letter in Daily Star from A. Daniels, Manchester

"Let's face it, David does not give the appearance on the field that he has got the job by the balls. He doesn't appear to be on top of the job and he's not the greatest communicator on the field – though he's great on A Question of Sport."
Don Tebbutt, Leicestershire chairman

"The cast of England's summer tragi-comedy might have changed as often as the Mousetrap but the script has never been rewritten."
Peter Johnson, Daily Mail, on the Sixth Test

"Grim as England's record was before the series, I met nobody in May who wasn't confident it would improve against the Aussies. Instead, total disarray. Love-four down, skipper in a daze, half the side we thought was going to win the Ashes knee-deep in krugerrands, all the quickies crippled and the dressing room festooned in nappies to make pramfuls of new players feel at home. I mean, I ask you."
John Thicknesse, Evening Standard, on the Sixth Test

"I am not aware of any errors I have made."
Ted Dexter, after the Sixth Test

"No errors? Give me strength. Dexter promised such a lot. He had style, flair, energy and zest. But the Aussies scratched off the veneer. And there was little underneath."
John Thicknesse, Evening Standard

> "Bungling Ted Dexter has shown himself up as the Pontius Pilate of cricket – the man who keeps washing his hands of any blame."
> Geoffrey Boycott, Daily Mirror

> "Ted Dexter and I both speak English, although obviously not the same version."
> David Gower, September 4, after Dexter denied sacking him

> "To be honest I'll be delighted if someone else can cop the flak. Some of the stuff that has been written or spoken this year has been diabolical – of that there is no doubt."
> David Gower, September 7, after Dexter did sack him

> "This is different and certainly a clarification of matters. I hadn't anticipated it and it's come as a bit of a shock. I was sad yesterday and even sadder now, but I'm not bitter and still on speaking terms with everyone."
> David Gower, September 8, after being left out of the winter tour

> "I am shattered by this decision. It is macabre."
> Ian Botham, September 8, on being left out of the winter tour

The South African 16, announced on the day Australia won the Ashes, included Mike Gatting as captain, leading two other sacked England captains, John Emburey and Chris Cowdrey, and 12 other Test players plus David Graveney, the player-manager. Bacher had no trouble putting the party together owing to erratic England selection policy which had created a large number of capped but disillusioned cricketers; the money on offer – thought to be £200,000 for Gatting, about £80,000 for others – contrasted vividly with county cricket's feeble pay. Phil DeFreitas and Roland Butcher, the only two black players in the squad, withdrew because of adverse reaction (threats, said Gatting) within the black community. Blacks in South Africa also condemned the tour; a delegation visited Britain and met Gatting and Emburey in an attempt to talk them out of it.

Gatting said, amidst other clichés, that he knew nothing about apartheid. His team-mate Simon Hughes reported that Gatting received 230 letters; 160 supported him, 59 were against, 10 were abusive and one contained only a picture of a gorilla. Anti-apartheid demonstrations began at English grounds and Gatting was prevented taking strike for five minutes in a Sunday League match at Lord's. 300 people demonstrated at the NatWest Trophy final. An *Observer* reader spotted Gatting going in to a record shop to buy a cassette by Ladysmith Black Mambazo, a black South African rock band.

With English cricket in turmoil, the Australians, meanwhile, conducted a triumphal procession round the country. They lost only one match – on a ridiculous wicket at Worcester – and won 12, prompting comparisons with Bradman's unbeaten 1948 side. Dean Jones scored 248 v Warwickshire, believed to be the highest-ever by a player on his first-class debut in England. The Waugh twins scored centuries for opposing sides when the Australians played Essex. Even the players who spent most of the Test series watching their team-mates grab the glory had their moments. Tom Moody reportedly broke the Scottish haggis-throwing record (230 feet) and Greg Campbell's girlfriend Kimbra Wittison said yes after he stuck a notice saying Will U Marry Me on the team balcony during the Lord's Test. A letter-writer to *Private Eye* noted the resemblance between Merv Hughes and Lech Walesa. A correspondent of *The Independent* said the same of Derek Pringle and Princess Anne. An Australian police team, about to tour England, approached the former Test bowler Michael Whitney for technical advice. "Don't drink the Pommy beer," said Whitney. "It makes you fat."

A DUBIOUS TITLE

Through it all, county cricket continued on its ancient way and Worcestershire became champions for the second consecutive year and the fifth time in all. However, this title will always be regarded with a smidgin of doubt: Essex actually won 19 points more than Worcestershire but the TCCB deducted 25 of them for a substandard pitch under a new rule. It happened after Essex beat Yorkshire at Southchurch Park, Southend where the ground is under the control of the local council, not the club. The TCCB said there was no suggestion of malpractice, reminiscent of Peter May's acceptance that there was no impropriety before he sacked Mike Gatting as captain. When Essex officials whinged the secretary, Peter Edwards, was summoned to Lord's and warned. The decision certainly cost Essex the Championship both arithmetically and because the team lost their momentum completely after the deduction. The effect was particularly unjust: it was widely felt that, overall, the Worcester pitch, once the best in the country, had degenerated to become the worst. It is now to be dug up.

However, helped by the Board, Worcestershire were able to overturn a 52-point deficit in eight days. They took the lead on August 1 by beating Kent. Hardly anyone noticed because that was the day all hell broke loose at Old Trafford (see above). Hardly anyone noticed either that on the same day Essex lost at Trent Bridge on a pitch producing what their acting captain Derek Pringle called "chin-high leg-breaks" and on which Franklyn Stephenson took 15 wickets for 106, the best Championship analysis since 1967. Nottinghamshire were later docked 25 points themselves after a two-day win against Derbyshire. The match was suspended because the original pitch was considered dangerous and then – unprecedentedly – the game was switched to an adjoining strip, the one on which Australia scored 602. Derbyshire scored 64 between them; Michael Holding was so disgusted by it all that he went on strike and refused to bat.

Having taken the lead, Worcestershire played like worthy champions. They won nine of their last 13 games and became mathematically uncatchable (barring further deductions) on August 29, the earliest date for 10 years. Their attack was seriously depleted by injuries but two local youngsters, Steve McEwan and Stuart Lampitt, deputised superbly. Worcestershire even coped with a mildly indifferent season by Graeme Hick; he was merely the second leading run-getter in the country.

Middlesex came third ahead of Lancashire and Northamptonshire, both of whom under-achieved. The Northants batting collapsed with alarming regularity; four of their batsmen were then selected in the England touring party to the West Indies. Hampshire had an outside chance of the Championship and then lost five successive late-season games leaving them equal sixth with Derbyshire, who surged having been last on July 21, and just ahead of Warwickshire, who did not win a game until August.

Glamorgan finished bottom for the third year out of four. They were unbeaten and in mid-table until July but then fell apart. The young captain Hugh Morris resigned to try and recapture his batting form; he was replaced by Alan Butcher. When they lost their fourth successive Championship match, the clock at Sophia Gardens responded by ticking backwards. However, they were only just behind Yorkshire and Kent, who fell from second to 15th, the steepest decline since Gloucestershire (from second to 17th) in 1970.

In January, Viv Richards had asked to join Yorkshire. The committee rejected the idea of signing Richards or any other non-Yorkshire-born player after a five-minute discussion. Instead, Yorkshire set up a cricket academy on the old Park Avenue ground at Bradford and Richards joined Glamorgan, though he never played because of his piles. In September, the Yorkshire captain Phil Carrick wrote to the committee asking for the club's rule to be relaxed and suggesting a maximum of three outsiders to help the team compete. The club promised a discussion; its length was not specified. Yorkshire were four points off bottom place; Lancashire did the Roses match double over them for the first time since 1960.

The leading batsman was Jimmy Cook of Somerset, the 36-year-old South African who in his first year of county cricket made up for lost time. He impressed everyone with his attitude and technique, became the first to 1000 runs (on June 21) and raced to 2000 by August 5, the earliest date since John Edrich on July 17 1965. Against Nottinghamshire at Trent Bridge, he became the second man ever to carry his bat and score a century in both innings of a match. He later lost form, presumed knackered. This was a problem in 1989. Bowlers, in particular, resented the loss of the normal time off provided by rain and found their work tiring on hard grounds under a hot sun. No one took 100 wickets, which last happened in the comparably hot summer of 1976.

JIMMY COOK'S SUMMER 1989

APRIL	v Hampshire	85 and 44*	JUL	v Derbys	44 and 85
	v Glam	42 and 79		v Surrey	105
				v Notts	120* and 131*
MAY	v Sussex	91 and 36		v Leics	148
	v Austs	11 and 57		v Sussex	6 and 130
	v Lancs	156 and 17			
	v Essex	147* and 10	AUG	v Middlesex	25 and 50
				v Worcs	9 and 44
JUN	v Glam	61		v Warwicks	4 and 16
	v Yorks	34		v Hants	25 and 3
	v Kent	49 and 72		v Worcs	10 and 3
	v Gloucs	12 and 147	SEP	v Gloucs	18 and 35
	v Northants	25 and 46		v Warwicks	9

BAD LUCK, YOUNG LEVER

There were surprise results in both Lord's Cup finals. Nottinghamshire beat Essex in the Benson and Hedges Cup in extraordinary circumstances. John Lever (age 40 years 141 days) bowled to Eddie Hemmings (age 40 years 145 days) with Hemmings needing to hit four for victory. Obviously, experience told. Hemmings made contact and the ball beat the fielder to the cover point boundary by inches. The result reversed two other close Essex-Notts finishes: the 1984 Championship and the 1985 NatWest. The early part of the competition was enlivened by the Combined Universities, the traditional fall-guys. A team mainly comprising Durham and other non-Oxbridge men beat Surrey and Worcestershire to reach the quarter-finals. There they lost to Somerset only in the last over. Nasser Hussain scored a century. The previous day he had been taking his finals; three months later he was on the edge of the Test team.

In the NatWest final Neil (NMK) Smith, son of Mike (MJK) and possessor of what looked like a hand-me-down pair of his gold-rimmed specs, gave Warwickshire an unexpected win over Middlesex. Warwickshire needed 10 off the last over. Smith hit the second ball from Simon Hughes over long-off for six and won the game with a comparatively comfortable two balls to spare. Dermot Reeve, man of the match for Sussex in 1986, won the award for Warwickshire this time. Mike Gatting, the Middlesex captain, had a wretched day. He bucked history by choosing to bat first (12 of the last 15 winners have now batted second), was heckled by anti-apartheid demonstrators and bowled for one. In seven Lord's finals, Gatting has scored 124.

Essex were again unlucky in the Sunday League. They looked like winning a vital game at Old Trafford before rain intervened. It should be a while before Lancashire supporters complain on this subject again. Their team were then able to clinch the title on the final Sunday when Paul Allott hit a six off Martin Bicknell of Surrey at the start of the last over – just before Essex began what would have been an enthralling last over at Northampton. Lancashire, Sunday League champions in the first two years, 1969 and 70, had not won it since. Essex had to be content with the piffling Refuge Assurance Cup on the last day of the season. This involved yet another last-over finish between them and Nottinghamshire. But by then the public had lost interest. Richard Blakey of Yorkshire scored five successive Sunday League 50s, a feat surpassed only by Barry Richards.

Tim Robinson and Paul Pollard of Nottinghamshire became the first batsmen in England to share two double-century opening stands in the same game: 222 and 282 against Kent on the Trent Bridge terror-track. Kent won by four wickets. On that same day, June 13, Robinson, Ravi Shastri of Glamorgan and David Capel of Northants all completed two centuries in a match. At Worksop, Graham Lloyd scored his maiden century for Lancashire; David Constant was umpiring, just as he was when Graham's father David scored his maiden century in 1969. Mike Gatting broke the benefit record, collecting £205,000 before accepting a similar amount from the South Africans. Bill Athey resigned as Gloucestershire captain after only one season. Vic Marks, after his first season as Somerset captain, decided to retire and become cricket correspondent of *The Observer*. Jack Simmons, Lancashire's best-loved character, retired at 48, along with John Lever at 40, Michael Holding at 35, Rodney Ontong (knee injury) at 33, Steve O'Shaughnessy at 28 and John Carr at 26. Geoff Miller, capped 34 times by England, was released by Essex and returned to Derbyshire. Surrey sacked Sylvester Clarke, the fourth Test player in a year they had dismissed (after David Smith, Jack Richards and Tony Gray) for stroppiness rather than cricketing failure.

The normally mild Derek Pringle made two angry gestures in a week and was fined £150 by the TCCB. The less mild Somerset fast bowler Adrian Jones was also fined £150 for "an audible obscenity". His arguments with umpire Ray Julian in a cup-tie at Taunton were described by Julian as "an insult to cricket". At Hove, the microphone in the telephone commentary box had to be turned down to prevent Jones's language contravening the Telecommunications Act.

THE SHEILAS

Warren Hegg of Lancashire and Alec Stewart of Surrey both equalled the world wicket-keeping record of 11 catches in a match. County players began to wear baseball caps. Cricket ceased at Priory Meadow, Hastings after 125 years; the ground is being turned into a shopping precinct. Fred Trueman organised a dinner in London which raised £70,000 for his former new-ball partner Brian Statham, who has the bone disease osteoporosis. David Gower revealed that he had been rejected as a playing member of MCC because he could not play the requisite number of qualifying matches and was on the ordinary waiting list, which can take 30 years. Stuart Welch, 18, a member of the MCC ground staff, won the search-for-a-spinner competition at Lord's. First prize: a place on the MCC ground staff. MCC appointed a female PR adviser, Karen Earl; 70% of MCC members who answered a club questionnaire were against admitting women to the club. Sheila Nicholls, 19, did a naked cartwheel in front of the Warner Stand during a one-day international. Sheila Ford, 31, was fined £500 by Leeds magistrates for running half-naked across the Headingley pitch with "No Tax" printed across the back of her panties.

Oxfordshire became Minor Counties champions, beating Hertfordshire in the final. Hertfordshire had won the East division title when Andy Needham bowled six successive deliberate and gentle no-balls at Northumberland batsman Peter Graham. The aim was to keep the batsmen interested in victory and stop them playing for a draw. It worked. Two slow-left-armers, Paul Meehan, 51, and Matt Holland, 17, bowled together for Wiltshire against Wales. Wiltshire scored 506 for 7 against Devon at Torquay, the highest in the Minor Counties for 42 years. Durham launched a campaign to become a first-class county in 1991. Stockport and Littleborough both thought they had won the Central Lancashire League owing to a mix-up over Stockport's points; Littleborough were unlucky. Hambledon, the best club in England in the 18th century, reached the final of the national village competition only to lose to a less evocative team from Cheshire called Toft, who promptly had the trophy stolen.

THE SILLY SEASON

The following stories must all be true; most were in Simon Barnes's column in *The Times*. A fund-raising match at Twyford, Bristol brought in £44; unfortunately the club had to pay £45 to repair a window broken by a six. In Surrey, a bowler called Malik of Limpsfield Chart took all 11 Chaldon wickets – the teams each had an extra man and agreed to play 12-a-side. In Gloucestershire, Dave Debidin of Old Emanuel bowled an over to Ian Payne of Wingate in which the ball did not touch the playing surface – six full tosses were all hit for six. A ball hit into an adjoining field at Kentisbeare, Devon was eaten by a cow. John Overy, umpiring Wimbledon v Stanmore, walked off the pitch with 10 overs to go, claiming that several Wimbledon players were drunk. Two Pembrokeshire XIs, Burton and Lawrenny, playing each other in the 22-over Alex Colley Cup, tied three successive matches before Burton won the fourth game by nine wickets. The second tie was caused by the non-striker thinking the ball had gone for four and omitting to run. George Smith, 44, of Coventry lay down on the wicket for 15 minutes at the Coventry and North Warwickshire ground (site of a first-class game in 1990) to protest against the ball being hit through his sitting-room window. A game between Burridge in Hampshire and a touring team from Yorkshire was reportedly interrupted continually by the Burridge players' portable telephones; several misfields were attributed to fielders taking calls. Prajapati All-Indian Club in the West Riding Sunday Cricket Council registered 43 players for the season, 39 of them called Mistry, thus outdoing by some way the Indian Panthers who had 16 Singhs.

Christopher Thomason, 16, made 265 with 20 sixes in a 32-over match for Richard Taunton College in Southampton against Hill College, then took four for six. Ian Harris, 18, returned to the village team at Veryan, Cornwall, two years after his leg was amputated. Liam Botham, 11, (born Doncaster Royal Infirmary, son of someone or other) took 2 for 12 and hit 20* for Yorkshire Schools under-13 v Lancashire. Zac Morris, 10, took five wickets in his first over for Barnsley under-11s against Derby and was then barred from bowling by teachers in the interests of fairness. Derby won.

"This House calls on the BBC to show due respect for our cultural heritage by reversing its decision to fundamentally alter the British summer by pulling the plug on continuous ball-by-ball Test match commentaries and thus help preserve a traditional, if somewhat eccentric, part of the British way of life."
Commons motion tabled by David Wilshire, Conservative MP for Spelthorne

"A programme that was once a jewel in radio's crown has descended to self-parody, lurching between chocolate-cake chortles and the bovine pomposities of the golf club bar."
Patrick Collins, Mail on Sunday

"The thing I wanted to do was to play my sport again. I was going to do everything possible not to let anything take that away."
Simon O'Donnell on returning to the Australian team

"I've stood in over 30 international games. Cricket has been my life. Now I am an outcast. I am sure even Mr Gatting would not wish me to finish up like this."
Pakistani umpire Shakoor Rana on being sacked

"With a full squad we can just about cope. Any injuries to key players under the 'Yorkshire-born' system means we do not compete on level terms and are always having our backs to the wall."
Phil Carrick, Yorkshire captain, in a letter to the committee

"If Yorkshire sign an overseas player, a foreign player, the first membership card they'll receive will be mine. I never want to see overseas players in the side. The quicker that overseas players are kicked out of the other 16 first-class county sides and replaced with 11 all qualified for England, the quicker we'll be on the road to recovery."
Fred Trueman

"Tactics are, in fact, my only weapon, confusing the batsman my only threat . . . If, perchance, he is an impressionable youngster I try to look wily and sage, as if I have something up my sleeve. Actually, this is not difficult. My life has been ruined by the fact that people think I'm plotting something even on the rare occasions when I'm not."
Peter Roebuck on his bowling

"We have been advised to go to the European Court of human rights to protest about the points deduction, so the destiny of the championship may not be settled until 1995."
Peter Edwards, Essex secretary

Hubert Doggart, treasurer of MCC: "Have you seen our new Mound Stand, sir?"

Duke of Edinburgh: "Seen it? I only bloody opened it."
Exchange reported in Private Eye

"If you want a straight answer, it's maybe yes, maybe no."
A C Smith, TCCB Chief Executive

In New Zealand, Graeme Hick became the second batsman (after Martin Crowe) to score 1,000 runs in a Shell Trophy season. Hick scored his 10,000th run aged 22 years 237 days, 10 days older than Javed Miandad in 1980, but in 185 innings against 252. In India, six leading players, including captain Dilip Vengsarkar, were banned from all cricket for a year for going on an unauthorised tour of North America. The ban was rescinded after six weeks, longer than usual. The Indian Test player Navjot Singh Sidhu toured the West Indies while on bail charged with "culpable homicide short of murder" after a man died in a dispute after a car crash. The charge was later dropped. Sachin Tendulkar, aged 15 years 7 months, scored 100 on debut in the Ranji Trophy for Bombay against Gujarat. Two former Indian Test players, Jasu Patel and R H Shodhan, went on hunger strike until the deputy Mayor of Ahmedabad agreed to consider their plea that important matches should be staged at the city's renovated Sardar Patel stadium.

In Pakistan, Haroon Rashid resigned from the selection panel after escaping injury in a gunshot attack on him in Karachi. It is believed the attackers were supporters of players overlooked for the under-19 squad. Mike Gatting's least favourite umpire, Shakoor Rana, was dropped from the Test panel for refusing to undergo a refresher course on umpiring. Farook Mohammed, 37, who beat an umpire unconscious with a bat in Winnipeg, Canada, was acquitted of attempted murder but found guilty of aggravated assault and possession of a dangerous weapon.

Simon O'Donnell returned to the Australian one-day team, 13 months after he was found to have cancer; he was cheered all the way to the wicket. The Victorian Health Promotion Foundation offered the Australian Cricket Board £5.7m to buy out the rest of Benson and Hedges' contract to sponsor Australian cricket. VicHealth is funded by a levy on each packet of cigarettes and has already bought into soccer sponsorship and stuck "Quit Smoking" messages next to B and H's at big games. It was claimed, in a letter to *The Times*, that a competitive cricket league was operating among the native women of the French Pacific Island of New Caledonia, with men traditionally only doing the scoring. It was suggested that they would be worthy opponents for England.

1989

ENGLAND v AUSTRALIA

CORNHILL TESTS

First Test *Headingley, Jun 8-13*

Gatting (broken thumb) and Botham (fractured cheekbone) withdrew from original England 12; Barnett and Smith replaced them; Emburey England 12th man. Debut: Campbell (Australia). England won toss.

AUSTRALIA

1st innings		2nd innings	
G.R. Marsh lbw b DeFreitas	16	c Russell b Foster	6
M.R. Taylor lbw b Foster	136	c Broad b Pringle	60
D.C. Boon c Russell b Foster	9	lbw b DeFreitas	43
*A.R. Border c Foster b DeFreitas	66	not out	60
D.M. Jones c Russell b Newport	79	not out	40
S.R. Waugh not out	177		
†I.A. Healy c & b Newport	16		
M.G. Hughes c Russell b Foster	71		
G.F. Lawson not out	10		
Extras (1b13, w1, nb7)	21	Extras (b2, lb5, w9, nb5)	21
Total (7 wkts dec)	601	Total (3 wkts dec)	230

Fall: 1-44, 2-57, 3-174, 4-273, 5-411, 6-441, 7-588   Fall: 1-14, 2-97, 2-129

Did not bat:
1st innings G.D. Campbell, T.M. Alderman
2nd innings S.R. Waugh, † I.A. Healy, G.F. Lawson, G.D. Campbell, M.G. Hughes, T.M. Alderman

Bowling:
1st innings DeFreitas 45. 3-8-140-2; Foster 46-14-109-3; Newport 39-5-153-2; Pringle 33-5-123-0; Gooch 9-1-31-0; Barnett 6-0-32-0
2nd innings Foster 19-4-65-1; DeFreitas 18-2-76-1; Pringle 12.5-1-60-1; Newport 5-2-22-0

ENGLAND

1st innings		*2nd innings*	
G.A. Gooch lbw b Alderman	13	lbw b Hughes	68
B.C. Broad b Hughes	37	lbw b Alderman	7
K.J. Barnett lbw b Alderman	80	c Taylor b Alderman	34
A.J. Lamb c Boon b Alderman	125	c Boon b Alderman	4
*D.I. Gower c Healy b Lawson	26	c Healy b Lawson	34
R.A. Smith lbw b Alderman	66	c Border b Lawson	0
D.R. Pringle lbw b Campbell	6	c Border b Alderman	0
P.J. Newport c Boon b Lawson	36	c Marsh b Alderman	8
†R.C. Russell c Marsh b Lawson	15	c Healy b Hughes	2
P.A.J. De Freitas lbw b Alderman	1	b Hughes	21
N.A. Foster not out	2	not out	1
Extras (b5, lb7, w1, nb10)	23	Extras (b4, lb3, nb5)	12
Total	430	Total	191

Fall: 1-35, 2-81, 3-195, 4-243, 5-323,
6-338, 7-392, 8-421, 9-424

Fall: 1-17, 2-67, 3-77, 4-134 5-134
6-153, 7-153, 8-166, 9-170

Bowling:
1st innings Alderman 37-7-107-5; Lawson 34. 5-6-105-3; Campbell 14-0-82-1; Hughes 28-7-92-1; Waugh 6-2-27-0; Border 2-1-5-0
2nd innings Alderman 20-7-44-5; Lawson 11-2-58-2; Campbell 10-0-42-0; Hughes 9.2-2-36-3; Border 5-3-4-0.
Australia's 601-7 was their highest score at Headingley
Man of the match: Alderman
Australia won by 210 runs

Second Test *Lord's, Jun 22-27*
Lamb (injured finger) withdrew. Fraser England 12th man.
England won toss.

ENGLAND

1st innings		*2nd innings*	
G.A. Gooch c Healy b Waugh	60	b Alderman	0
B.C. Broad lbw b Alderman	18	b Lawson	20
K.J. Barnett c Boon b Hughes	14	c Jones b Alderman	3
M.W. Gatting c Boon b Hughes	0	lbw b Alderman	22
*D.I. Gower b Lawson	57	c Border b Hughes	106
R.A. Smith c Hohns b Lawson	32	b Alderman	96
J.E. Emburey b Alderman	0	not out	36
†R.C. Russell not out	64	c Boon b Lawson	29
N.A. Foster c Jones b Hughes	16	lbw b Alderman	4
P.W. Jarvis c Marsh b Hughes	6	lbw b Alderman	5
G.R. Dilley c Border b Alderman	7	c Boon b Hughes	24
Extras (lb9, nb3)	12	Extras (b6, lb6, nb2)	14
Total	286	Total	359

Fall: 1-31, 2-52, 3-58, 4-131, 5-180,
6-185, 7-191, 8-237, 9-253

Fall: 1-0, 2-18, 3-28, 4-84,
5-223, 6-274, 7-300, 8-304, 9-314

Bowling:
1st innings Alderman 20.5-4-60-3; Lawson 27-8-88-2; Hughes 26-3-71-4; Waugh 9-3-49-1; Hohns 7-3-9-0
2nd innings Alderman 38-6-128-6; Lawson 39-10-99-2; Hughes 24-8-44-2; Border 9-3-23-0; Hohns 13-6-33-0; Waugh 7-2-20-0

AUSTRALIA

1st innings		*2nd innings*	
G.R. Marsh c Russell b Dilley	3	b Dilley	1
M.A. Taylor lbw b Foster	62	c Gooch b Foster	27
D.C. Boon c Gooch b Dilley	94	not out	58
*A.R. Border c Smith b Emburey	35	c sub b Foster	1
D.M. Jones lbw b Foster	27	c Russell b Foster	0
S.R. Waugh not out	152	not out	21
†I.A. Healy c Russell b Jarvis	3		
M.G. Hughes c Gooch b Foster	30		
T.V. Hohns b Emburey	21		
G.F. Lawson c Broad b Emburey	74		
T.M. Alderman lbw b Emburey	8		
Extras (lb11, nb8)	19	Extras (b3, lb4, nb4)	11
Total	528	Total (for 4 wkts)	119

Fall: 1-6, 2-151, 3-192, 4-221, 5-235,
6-265, 7-331, 8-381, 9-511

Fall: 1-9, 2-51, 3-61, 4-67

Did not bat:
2nd innings †I.A. Healy, M.G. Hughes, G.F. Lawson, T.V. Hohns, T. M. Aiderman

Bowling:
1st innings Dilley 34-3-141-2; Foster 45-7-129-3; Jarvis 31-3-150-1; Emburey 42-12-88-4;
Gooch 6-2-9-0
2nd innings Dilley 10-2-27-1; Foster 18-3-39-3; Emburey 3-0-8-0; Jarvis 9.2-0-38-0
*Gower's eighth successive defeat as captain, a record in all tests. England have not beaten
Australia at Lord's since 1934. Receipts: £1.1 million, an English record.*
Man of the match: Waugh.
Australia won by six wickets

Third Test *Edgbaston, Jul 6-11*
Lamb (shoulder), Smith (hamstring), Foster (hand), Gatting (death of mother-in-law) withdrew.
Curtis, Jarvis and Tavaré replacements.
Debut: Fraser (England)
Australia won toss

AUSTRALIA

1st innings		*2nd innings*	
G.R. Marsh lbw Botham	42	b Jarvis	42
M.A. Taylor st Russell b Emburey	43	c Botham b Gooch	51
D.C. Boon run out	38	not out	22
*A.R. Border b Emburey	8		
D.M. Jones c sub b Fraser	157		
S.R. Waugh b Fraser	43		
†I.A. Healy b Fraser	2	not out	33
M.G. Hughes c Botham b Dilley	2		
T.V. Hohns c Gooch b Dilley	40		
G.F. Lawson b Fraser	12		
T.M. Alderman not out	0		
Extras (lb20, nb17)	37	**Extras** (b4, lb4, nb2)	10
Total	424	**Total** (2 wkts)	158

Fall: 1-8, 2-94, 3-105, 4-201, 5-272,
6-289, 7-299, 8-391, 9-421

Fall: 1-81, 2-109

Did not bat:
2nd innings A.R. Border, D.M. Jones, S.R. Waugh, M.G. Hughes, T.V. Hohns, G.F. Lawson,
T.M. Alderman
Bowling:
1st innings Dilley 31-3-123-2; Jarvis 23-4-82-0; Fraser 33-8-63-4; Botham 25-5-75-1;
Emburey 29-5-61-2
2nd innings Dilley 10-4-27-0; Fraser 12-0-29-0; Emburey 20-8-37-0; Jarvis 6-1-20-1;
Gooch 14-5-30-1; Curtis 3-0-7-0

ENGLAND

1st innings	
G.A. Gooch lbw b Lawson	8
T.S. Curtis lbw b Hughes	41
*D.I. Gower lbw b Alderman	8
C.J. Tavaré c Taylor b Alderman	2
K.J. Barnett c Healy b Waugh	10
I.T. Botham b Hughes	46
†R.C. Russell c Taylor b Hohns	42
J.E. Emburey c Boon b Lawson	26
A.R.C. Fraser run out	12
G.R. Dilley not out	11
P.W. Jarvis lbw b Alderman	22
Extras (b1, lb2, nb11)	14
Total	242

Fall: 1-17, 2-42, 3-47, 4-75, 5-75, 6-171,
7-171, 8-185, 9-215
Bowling:
Alderman 26.3-6-61-3; Lawson 21-4-54-2; Hughes 22-4-68-2; Waugh 11-3-38-1; Hohns 16-8-18-1

Border became the fourth man to pass 8,000 test runs.
Man of the match: Jones
Match drawn.

Fourth Test *Old Trafford, Jul 27-Aug 1*
Dilley withdrew (knee); Jarvis called in but 12th man.
England won toss

ENGLAND

1st innings

G.A. Gooch b Lawson	11
T.S. Curtis b Lawson	22
R.T. Robinson lbw b Lawson	0
R.A. Smith c Hohns b Hughes	143
*D.I. Gower lbw b Hohns	35
I.T. Botham b Hohns	0
†R.C. Russell lbw b Lawson	1
J.E. Emburey lbw b Hohns	5
N.A. Foster c Border b Lawson	39
A.R.C. Fraser lbw b Lawson	2
N.G.B. Cook not out	0
Extras (lb2)	2
Total	260

2nd innings

c Alderman b Lawson	13
c Boon b Alderman	0
lbw b Lawson	12
c Healy b Alderman	1
c Marsh b Lawson	15
lbw b Alderman	4
not out	128
b Alderman	64
b Alderman	6
lbw b Hohns	3
c Healy b Hughes	5
Extras (lb6, w2, nb5)	13
Total	264

Fall: 1-23, 2-23, 3-57, 4-132, 5-140,
6-147, 7-158, 8-232, 9-252

Fall: 1-10, 2-25, 3-27, 4-28,
5-38, 6-59, 7-201, 8-223, 9-255

Bowling:
1st innings Alderman 26-13-49-0; Lawson 33-11-77-6; Hughes 17-6-55-1; Hohns 27-7-59-3; Waugh 6-1-23-0
2nd innings Lawson 31-8-81-3; Alderman 27-7-66-5; Hohns 26-15-37-1; Hughes 14.4-2-45-1; Border 8-2-12-0; Waugh 4-0-17-0

AUSTRALIA

1st innings

M.A. Taylor st Russell b Emburey	85
G.R. Marsh c Russell b Botham	47
D.C. Boon b Fraser	12
*A.R. Border c Russell b Foster	80
D.M. Jones b Botham	69
S.R. Waugh c Curtis b Fraser	92
†I.A. Healy lbw b Foster	0
T.V. Hohns c Gower b Cook	17
M.G. Hughes b Cook	3
G.F. Lawson b Fraser	17
T.M. Alderman not out	6
Extras (b5, lb7, w1, nb6)	19
Total	447

2nd innings

not out	37
c Robinson b Emburey	31
not out	10
Extras (nb3)	3
Total (1 wkt)	81

Fall: 1-135, 2-143, 3-154, 4-274, 5-362, 6-362
7-413, 8-423, 9-423

Fall: 1-62

Did not bat:
2nd innings *A.R. Border, D.M. Jones, S.R. Waugh, †I.A. Healy, T.V. Hohns, M.G. Hughes, G.F. Lawson, T. M. Alderman

Bowling:
1st innings Foster 34-12-74-2; Fraser 36.5-4-95-3; Emburey 45-9-118-1; Cook 28-6-85-2; Botham 24-6-63-2
2nd innings Foster 5-2-5-0; Fraser 10-0-28-0; Emburey 13-3-30-1; Cook 4.5-0-18-0

Australia's 100th test win over England. They regained the Ashes in England for the first time since 1934. Russell became the fourth Englishman to score his maiden century in tests (H. Wood, 1891-2; A.J.L. Hill, 1895-6; S.C. Griffith, 1947-8).
Man of the match: Lawson
Australia won by 9 wickets.

Fifth Test *Trent Bridge, Aug 10-14*
Players contracted to South Africa not considered for selection. Gooch also asked to be left out. Small (strained side) withdrew. Thomas, his replacement, 12th man.
Debuts: Atherton, Malcolm (England)
Australia won toss.

AUSTRALIA

1st innings

G.R. Marsh c Botham b Cook	138
M.A. Taylor st Russell b Cook	219
D.C. Boon st Russell b Cook	73
*A.R. Border not out	65
D.M. Jones c Gower b Fraser	22
S.R. Waugh c Gower b Malcolm	0
†I.A. Healy b Fraser	5
T.V. Hohns not out	19
Extras (b6, lb23, w3, nb29)	61
Total (6 wkts dec)	602

Fall: 1-329, 2-430, 3-502, 4-543, 5-553, 6-560
Did not bat: M.G. Hughes, G.F. Lawson, T.M. Alderman
Bowling:
Fraser 52.3-18-108-2; Malcolm 44-2-166-1; Botham 30-4-103-0; Hemmings 33-8-81-0;
Cook 40-10-91-3; Atherton 7-0-24-0

ENGLAND

1st innings			*2nd innings*	
T.S. Curtis lbw b Alderman	2		(2) lbw b Alderman	6
M.D. Moxon c Waugh b Alderman	0		(5) b Alderman	18
M.A. Atherton lbw b Alderman	0		c & b Hohns	47
R.A. Smith c Healy b Alderman	101		b Hughes	26
*D.I. Gower c Healy b Lawson	11		(1) b Lawson	5
†R.C. Russell c Healy b Lawson	20		b Lawson	1
E.E. Hemmings b Alderman	38		lbw b Hughes	35
A.R.C. Fraser b Hohns	29		b Hohns	1
I.T. Botham c Waugh b Hohns	12		absent hurt	
N.G.B. Cook not out	2		not out	7
D.E. Malcolm c Healy b Hughes	9		b Hughes	5
Extras (lb18, nb13)	31		Extras (b3, lb6, w1, nb6)	16
Total	255		Total	167

Fall: 1-1, 2-1, 3-14, 4-37, 5-119, 6-172, 7-214, 8-243, 9-244

Fall: 1-5, 2-13, 3-67, 4-106, 5-114, 6-120, 7-134, 8-160, 9-167

Bowling
1st innings Alderman 19-2-69-5; Lawson 21-5-57-2; Hohns 18-8-48-2; Hughes 7.5-0-40-1; Waugh 11-4-23-0
2nd innings Alderman 16-6-32-2; Lawson 15-3-51-2; Hughes 12.3-1-46-3; Hohns 12-3-29-2

Australia batted throughout the first day without losing a wicket. 329 was the highest opening stand in Ashes history. England's worst Ashes defeat since 1946-7.
Man of the match: Taylor
Australia won by an innings and 180 runs.

Sixth Test *The Oval, Aug 24-29*

Malcolm (back) and Fraser (knee) withdrew. DeFreitas, Malcolm's replacement, withdrew (hamstring). Thomas, expected replacement for Fraser, withdrew (South Africa). Pringle and Igglesden came in. Hussain and Hemmings left out of squad.
Debuts: Stephenson, Igglesden (England)
Australia won toss.

AUSTRALIA

1st innings			*2nd innings*	
G.R. Marsh c Igglesden b Small	17		lbw b Igglesden	4
M.A. Taylor c Russell b Igglesden	71		c Russell b Small	48
D.C. Boon c Atherton b Small	46		run out	37
*A.R. Border c Russell b Capel	76		not out	51
D.M. Jones c Gower b Small	122		b Capel	50
S.R. Waugh b Igglesden	14		not out	7
†I.A. Healy c Russell b Pringle	44			
T.V. Hohns c Russell b Pringle	30			
M.G. Hughes lbw b Pringle	21			
G.F. Lawson b Pringle	2			
T.M. Alderman not out	6			
Extras (b1, lb9, nb9)	19		Extras (b2, lb7, nb13)	22
Total (132.3 overs)	468		Total (for 4 wkts dec)	219

Fall: 1-48, 2-130, 3-149, 4-345, 5-347, 6-386, 7-409, 8-447, 9-453

Fall: 1-7, 2-100, 3-101, 4-189

Bowling:
1st innings Small 40-8-141-3; Igglesden 24-2-91-2; Pringle 24.3-6-70-4; Capel 16-2-66-1; Cook 25-5-78-0; Atherton 1-0-10-0; Gooch 2-1-2-0
2nd innings Small 20-4-57-1; Igglesden 13-1-55-1; Capel 8-0-35-1; Pringle 16-0-53-0; Cook 6-2-10-0

ENGLAND

1st innings			*2nd innings*	
G.A. Gooch lbw b Alderman	0		c & b Alderman	10
J.P. Stephenson c Waugh b Alderman	25		lbw b Alderman	11
M.A. Atherton c Healy b Hughes	12		b Lawson	14
R.A. Smith b Lawson	11		not out	77
*D.I. Gower c Healy b Alderman	79		c Waugh b Lawson	7
D.J. Capel lbw b Alderman	4		c Taylor b Hohns	17
†R.C. Russell c Healy b Alderman	12		not out	0
D.R. Pringle c Taylor b Hohns	27			
G.C. Small c Jones b Lawson	59			
N.G.B. Cook c Jones b Lawson	31			
A.P. Igglesden not out	2			
Extras (b2, lb7, w1, nb13)	23		Extras (lb1, w1, nb5)	7
Total (92.1 overs)	285		Total (for 5 wkts)	143

Fall: 1-0, 2-28, 3-47, 4-80, 5-84, 6-98, 7-169, 8-201, 9-274

Fall: 1-20, 2-27, 3-51, 4-67, 5-138

Bowling:

1st innings Alderman 27-7-66-5; Lawson 29.1-9-85-3; Hughes 23-3-84-1; Hohns 10-1-30-1; Waugh 3-0-11-0
2nd innings Alderman 13-3-30-2; Lawson 15.1-2-41-2; Hughes 8-3-34-0; Hohns 10-2-37-1
Australia passed 400 in the first innings for the 8th successive Test, a record.
Man of the match: Jones
Man of the series (Australia) Alderman; (England) Russell
Match Drawn

Test Averages: England v Australia, 1989
England – Batting

	M	I	NO	RUNS	BEST	AVGE	M	I	NO	RUNS	BEST	AVGE

	M	I	NO	RUNS	BEST	AVGE	M	I	NO	RUNS	BEST	AVGE
A.J. Lamb (Northants)	1	2	0	129	125	64.50	57	100	9	3098	137*	34.04
R.A. Smith (Hants)	5	10	1	553	143	61.44	8	16	2	698	143	49.85
G.C. Small (Warwicks)	1	1	0	59	59	59.00	6	8	3	120	59	24.00
R.C. Russell (Glos)	6	11	3	314	128*	39.25	7	12	3	408	128*	45.33
E.E. Hemmings (Notts)	1	2	0	73	38	36.50	9	14	3	280	95	24.45
D.I. Gower (Leics)	6	11	0	383	106	34.81	106	183	13	7383	215	43.43
J.E. Emburey (Middx)	3	5	1	131	64	32.75	60	89	18	1540	75	21.69
K.J. Barnett (Derbys)	3	5	0	141	80	28.20	4	7	0	207	80	29.57
N.G.B. Cook (Northants)	3	5	3	45	31	22.50	15	25	4	179	31	8.52
P.J. Newport (Worcs)	1	2	0	44	36	22.00	2	3	0	70	36	23.33
G.R. Dilley (Worcs)	2	3	1	42	24	21.00	41	58	19	521	56	13.36
B.C. Broad (Notts)	2	4	0	82	37	20.50	25	44	2	1661	162	39.55
G.A. Gooch (Essex)	5	9	0	183	68	20.33	73	132	4	4724	196	36.90
M.A. Atherton (Lancs)	2	4	0	73	47	18.25	2	4	0	73	47	18.25
J.P. Stephenson (Essex)	1	2	0	36	25	18.00	1	2	0	36	25	18.00
N.A. Foster (Essex)	3	6	2	68	39	17.00	28	47	7	410	39	10.25
I.T. Botham (Worcs)	3	4	0	62	46	15.50	97	155	5	5119	208	34.13
T.S. Curtis (Worcs)	3	5	0	71	41	14.20	5	9	0	140	41	15.56
P.A.J. DeFreitas (Lancs)	1	2	0	22	21	11.00	13	19	1	204	40	11.33
M.W. Gatting (Middx)	1	2	0	22	22	11.00	68	117	14	3870	207	37.57
P.W. Jarvis (Yorks)	2	3	0	33	22	11.00	6	9	2	109	29*	15.57
D.R. Pringle (Essex)	2	3	0	33	27	11.00	21	36	3	512	63	15.51
D.J. Capel (Northants)	1	2	0	21	17	10.50	11	18	0	293	98	16.27
A.R.C. Fraser (Middx)	3	5	0	47	29	9.40	3	5	0	47	29	9.40
M.D. Moxon (Yorks)	1	2	0	18	18	9.00	10	17	1	455	99	28.44
D.E. Malcolm (Derbys)	1	2	0	14	9	7.00	1	2	0	14	9	7.00
R.T. Robinson (Notts)	1	2	0	12	12	6.00	29	49	5	1601	175	36.39
C.J. Tavaré (Somerset)	1	1	0	2	2	2.00	31	56	2	1755	149	32.50
A.P. Igglesden (Kent)	1	1	1	2	2*	–	1	1	1	2	2*	–

Updated career figures

Career records of members of the 1989-90 touring party to West Indies who did not play against the Australians

	M	I	NO	RUNS	BEST	AVGE
R.J. Bailey (Northants)	1	2	0	46	43	23.00
W. Larkins (Northans)	6	11	0	176	34	16.00

England – Bowling

	BALLS	RUNS	WKTS	5wI	10wM	BEST	AVGE	BALLS	RUNS	WKTS	5wI	10wM	BEST	AVGE
Foster	1002	421	12	0	0	3-39	35.08	6081	2797	88	5	1	8-107	31.78
Fraser	866	323	9	0	0	4-63	35.88	866	323	9	0	0	4-63	35.88
Emburey	912	342	8	0	0	4-88	42.75	14227	5105	138	6	0	7-78	36.99
Igglesden	222	146	3	0	0	2-91	48.66	222	146	3	0	0	2-91	48.66
Small	360	198	4	0	0	3-141	49.50	1443	652	24	2	0	5-48	27.16
Capel	144	101	2	0	0	1-35	50.50	1256	628	12	0	0	2-13	52.33
Cook	623	282	5	0	0	3-91	56.40	4174	1689	52	4	1	6-65	32.48
Pringle	518	306	5	0	0	4-70	61.20	3750	1807	48	2	0	5-95	37.64
Dilley	510	318	5	0	0	2-123	63.60	8192	4107	138	6	0	6-38	29.76
Gooch	186	72	1	0	0	1-30	72.00	1617	622	14	0	0	2-12	44.42
DeFreitas	381	216	3	0	0	2-140	72.00	2719	1296	29	1	0	5-86	49.84
Botham	480	241	3	0	0	2-63	80.33	21281	10633	376	27	4	8-34	28.28
Newport	264	175	2	0	0	2-153	87.50	549	339	9	0	0	4-87	37.67
Jarvis	416	290	2	0	0	1-20	145.00	1345	708	14	0	0	4-107	50.57
Malcolm	264	166	1	0	0	1-166	166.00	166	1	0	0	0	1-166	166.00

Updated career records

Australia – Batting

	M	I	NO	RUNS	BEST	AVGE		Updated career figures				
							M	I	NO	RUNS	BEST	AVGE
S.R. Waugh	6	8	4	506	177*	126.50	32	49	9	1605	177*	40.13
M.A. Taylor	6	11	1	839	219	83.90	8	15	1	906	219	64.71
A.R. Border	6	9	3	442	80	73.66	108	188	33	8273	205	53.37
D.M. Jones	6	9	1	566	157	70.75	27	48	6	2102	216	50.05
D.C. Boon	6	11	3	442	94	55.25	42	77	7	2852	184*	40.74
T.V. Hohns	5	5	1	127	40	31.75	7	7	1	136	49	22.67
G.R. Marsh	6	11	0	347	138	31.54	33	61	6	2017	138	36.67
G.F. Lawson	6	5	1	115	74	28.75	44	66	12	871	74	16.13
M.G. Hughes	6	5	0	127	71	25.40	17	19	3	280	72*	17.50
T.M. Alderman	6	4	3	20	8	20.00	30	40	18	145	25	6.59
I.A. Healy	6	7	1	103	44	17.16	14	19	1	315	52	17.50

G.D. Campbell played one match but did not bat.

Australia – Bowling

	BALLS	RUNS	WKTS	5wI	10wM	BEST	AVGE	Updated career records						
								BALLS	RUNS	WKTS	5wI	10wM	BEST	AVGE
Alderman	1622	712	41	6	1	6-128	17.36	7476	2478	127	11	1	6-128	27.39
Hohns	834	300	11	0	0	3-59	27.27	1558	580	17	0	0	3-59	34.12
Lawson	1663	791	29	1	0	6-72	27.27	10560	5308	177	11	2	8-112	29.99
Hughes	1136	615	19	0	0	4-71	32.36	3606	1910	54	3	1	8-87	35.37
Waugh	342	208	2	0	0	1-38	104.00	3584	1781	42	2	0	5-69	42.40
Campbell	144	124	1	0	0	1-82	124.00	144	124	1	0	0	1-82	124.00

Texaco Trophy: One-Day Internationals

Old Trafford, May 25
England won by 95 runs
ENGLAND 231-9 (55 overs) (G.A. Gooch 52)
AUSTRALIA 136 (47.1 overs).

Trent Bridge, May 27
Match Tied
ENGLAND 226-5 (55 overs) (A.J. Lamb 100no)
AUSTRALIA 226-8 (55 overs)

Lord's, May 29
Australia won by 6 wickets
ENGLAND 278-7 (55 overs) G.A. Gooch 136, D.I. Gower 61)
AUSTRALIA 279-4 (54.3 overs) (G.R. Marsh 111no, A.R. Border 53).

England won series because of fewer wickets lost in tied match

OTHER AUSTRALIAN FIXTURES

First-class games

WINS: Middlesex, 3 wickets (Lord's); Derbyshire 11 runs (Derby); Lancashire 9 wickets (Old Trafford); Northants 272 runs (Northampton); Gloucestershire innings and 146 (Bristol); Notts 196 runs (Trent Bridge); Leics 9 wkts (Leicester); Essex 150 runs (Chelmsford).

DRAWS: Somerset (Taunton); Warwickshire (Edgbaston); Glamorgan (Neath); Hampshire (Southampton); Kent (Canterbury).

DEFEAT: Worcestershire 3 wickets (Worcester).

One-day games

WINS: League Cricket Conference 165 runs (West Bromwich); Lavinia, Duchess of Norfolk's XI 120 runs (Arundel); MCC 101 runs (Lord's); Yorkshire 109 runs (Headingley); Combined Universities 99 runs (The Parks); Scotland 97 runs (Glasgow); Minor Counties 27 runs (Trowbridge).

DEFEAT: Sussex 4 wickets (Hove).

AUSTRALIAN TOURING SIDES IN ENGLAND

(First-class games only)

	P	W	D	L
1948	31	23	8	0
1953	33	16	16	1
1956	31	9	19	3
1961	32	13	18	1
1964	30	11	16	3
1968	25	8	14	3
1972	26	11	10	5
1975	15	8	5	2
1977	22	5	13	4
1980	5	1	2	2
1981	17	3	11	3
1985	20	4	13	3
1989	20	12	7	1

AUSTRALIA v WEST INDIES
First Test

Brisbane, Nov 18-21 1988
West Indies won by 9 wickets
AUSTRALIA 167 & 289; WEST INDIES 394 & 63-1
Richards' 100th Test. Walsh took the first Test hat-trick in 12 years without realising it: he dismissed Dodemaide at the end of Australia's first innings then Veletta and Wood when he came on in the second.

Second Test

Perth, Dec 2-6 1988
West Indies won by 169 runs
WEST INDIES 449 (I.V.A. Richards 146; M.G. Hughes 5-130) & 349-9 dec (D.L. Haynes 100; M.G. Hughes 8-87)
AUSTRALIA 395 - 8 dec (G.M. Wood 111; C.E.L. Ambrose 5-72) & 234
Hughes emulated Walsh, with three wickets not only in two innings but spanning three separate overs. Hughes went on to become the first Australian to take 12 wickets in a Test v West Indies. Ambrose broke Lawson's jaw with a bouncer.

Third Test
Melbourne, Dec 24-29 1988
West Indies won by 285 runs
WEST INDIES 280 & 361-9 dec (R.B. Richardson 122;
S.R. Waugh 5-92)
AUSTRALIA 242 & 114 (B.P. Patterson 5-39)
Border's 100th Test: he scored his first nought since his
43rd. Marshall becomes 9th bowler to take 300 Test
wickets with lowest average of any (20.88). Four
Australian players were hit and hurt in the fourth innings.

Fourth Test
Sydney, Jan 26-30
Australia won by 7 wickets
WEST INDIES 224 (A.R. Border 7-46) and 256 (D.L.
Haynes 143)
AUSTRALIA 401 (D.C. Boon 149; M.D. Marshall 5-29)
and 82-3.
Australia's second successive win over West Indies at
Sydney. Border's best bowling performance in any form of
cricket.

Fifth Test
Adelaide, Feb 3-7
Match Drawn
AUSTRALIA 515 (D.M. Jones 216) and 224-4 dec
WEST INDIES 369 (R.B. Richardson 106; M.R. Whitney
7-89) and 233-4 (C.G. Greenidge 104).
Merv Hughes supports Jones with improbable 72. Ambrose
voted player of the series; Haynes international cricketer of
the year.

West Indies won series 3-1

NEW ZEALAND v PAKISTAN
First Test
Dunedin, Feb 3-7
Match abandoned without a ball being bowled
The fourth washed-out test in history.

Second Test
Wellington, Feb 10-14
Match Drawn
NEW ZEALAND 447 (M.D. Crowe 174) and 186-8
(Salim Jaffer 5-40)
PAKISTAN 438-7 dec (Shoaib Mohammed 163, Javed
Miandad 118).
Shoaib scores slowest 150 in Tests: 10 hours 24 minutes

Third Test
Auckland, Feb 24-28
Match Drawn
PAKISTAN 616-5 dec (Javed Miandad 271, Shoaib
Mohammed 112)
NEW ZEALAND 403 (Abdul Qadir 6-160) and 99-3
Javed's sixth Test double century.

Series Drawn 0-0

WEST INDIES v INDIA
First Test
Georgetown, Mar 25-30
Match Drawn
WEST INDIES 437 (R.B. Richardson 194; Arshad Ayub
5-104)
INDIA 86-1
Only two days' play due to rain

Second Test
Bridgetown, Apr 7-12
West Indies won by 8 wickets
INDIA 321 (S.V. Manjrekar 108; I.R. Bishop 6-76) & 251
(R.J. Shastri 107; M.D. Marshall 5-60)
WEST INDIES 377 (C.G. Greenidge 117) & 196-2 (D.L.
Haynes 112no)
Marshall overtook Gibbs as West Indies' leading wicket-
taker.

Third Test
Port of Spain, Apr 15-20
West Indies won by 217 runs
WEST INDIES 314 (Arshad Ayub 5-117) & 266 (Kapil
Dev 5-58)
INDIA 150 (M.D. Marshall 5-34) & 213 (M.D. Marshall
6-55)
Marshall took 10 wickets in a Test for the fourth time.

Fourth Test
Kingston, Apr 28-May 3
West Indies won by 7 wickets
INDIA 289 (N.S. Sidhu 116; C.A. Walsh 6-62) & 152
WEST INDIES 384 (R.B. Richardson 156; I.V.A. Richards
110; Kapil Dev 6-84) & 60-3
Game interrupted by bottle-throwing. Home captain
Richards accused of inciting it, and given a suspended
£150 fine. Indian captain Vengsarkar accused un-named
teammates of cowardice and faking injuries.

West Indies won series 3-0

HAPPY DAYS: Australia v West Indies

"You'll get yours."
  *Patrick Patterson to Steve Waugh after Waugh
  bowled bouncers at him.*

**"Intimidation has got so out of hand, when
conditions encourage it, that it is a job to
know who is going to stop it, and how."**
  *John Woodcock, The Times, from the Perth
  Test*

**"They scarred the evening with a foul-
mouthed blend of rampant alcoholism,
blatant exhibitionism, overt racism and
downright violence."**
  *Sydney Daily Mirror on the crowd at the WSC
  final*

**"They (the police) stand with their backs to
the cricket on the Hill at Sydney or in the
Southern Stand at Melbourne, watching
the hooting, seething, retching mass.
Asked if he ever got scared, a Melbourne
police officer said, 'Yes, you get scared
and you learn to hate them.'"**
  John Woodcock, The Times

**"It's been bloody unpleasant out there all
summer. Quite honestly, if it goes on like
this for much longer, it can do so without
my help."**
  *Australian umpire Tony Crafter on the West
  Indies series*

**"My personal belief is that in 10 years Test
matches will be attracting crowds no
bigger than the ones we get now at
Sheffield Shield matches."**
  *Bob Radford, executive director of the New
  South Wales Cricket Association*

**"It's all right for a bit of a laugh, I suppose,
but it's crap really, and the players know
it."**
  Jeff Thomson on one-day cricket

**"I can't ever remember getting seven
wickets, not even in my glory days in the
under-12s."**
  *Allan Border, after bowling out the West Indies
  at Sydney*

DELOITTE RATINGS
September 1989

Computerised rankings of Test players
(September 1988 in brackets)

BATTING

1	(5)	**Javed Miandad** (Pak)	**903**
2	(14)	**Richie Richardson** (WI)	**891**
3	(1)	**Dilip Vengsarkar** (Ind)	**769**
4	(3)	**Viv Richards** (WI)	**758**
5	(4)	**Martin Crowe** (NZ)	**757**
6	(2)	**Allan Border** (Aus)	**757**
7	(–)	**Mark Taylor** (Aus)	**757**
8	(38)	**Robin Smith** (Eng)	**746**
9	(12)	**Desmond Haynes** (WI)	**745**
10	(33)	**Steve Waugh** (Aus)	**695**

BOWLING

1	(2)	**Richard Hadlee** (NZ)	**900**
2	(1)	**Malcolm Marshall** (WI)	**883**
3	(3)	**Imran Khan** (Pak)	**815**
4	(–)	**Terry Alderman** (Aus)	**694**
5	(12)	**Kapil Dev** (Ind)	**656**
6	(–)	**Geoff Lawson** (Aus)	**647**
7	(13)	**Courtney Walsh** (WI)	**636**
8	(–)	**Arshad Ayub** (Ind)	**625**
9	(21)	**Curtly Ambrose** (WI)	**619**
10	(10)	**Bruce Reid** (Aus)	**603**

THE ENGLISH SEASON 1989
First-Class Averages
Batting

			Runs	Avge
1	(–)	Dean Jones	1510	88.82
2	(3)	Steve Waugh	1030	64.37
3	(–)	Jimmy Cook	2241	60.56
4	(31)	Robin Smith	1577	58.40
5	(110)	Keith Brown	522	58.00
6	(–)	Mark Taylor	1669	57.55
7	(2)	Graeme Hick	1824	57.00
8	(–)	David Boon	1306	56.78
9	(19)	Mike Gatting	1503	55.66
10	(35)	Monte Lynch	383	54.71
11	(8)	Allan Border	979	54.38
12	(64)	Mark Benson	1299	54.12
13	(47)	Roy Pienaar	1321	52.84
14	(61)	Alan Wells	1629	52.54
15	(11)	Allan Lamb	733	52.35
Others with 1500 runs				
18	(68)	Alan Butcher	1632	46.62
24	(62)	Alec Stewart	1637	44.24
26	(–)	Mark Waugh	1537	43.91
28	(45)	John Morris	1638	43.10
31	(126)	Wayne Larkins	1787	42.54
34	(42)	Tim Robinson	1516	42.11
43	(132)	Chris Broad	1512	38.76

Bowling

			Wkts	Avge
1	(33)	Terry Alderman	70	15.64
2	(14)	Allan Donald	86	16.25
3	(1)	Malcolm Marshall	64	16.67
4	(–)	Stuart Lampitt	31	16.96
5	(20)	Wasim Akram	63	17.73
6	(3)	Winston Benjamin	69	17.94
7	(58)	Derek Pringle	94	18.64
8	(8)	Franklyn Stephenson	92	18.77
9	(–)	Ricardo Ellcock	32	19.21

10	(–)	Steve McEwan	52	19.21
11	(50)	Patrick Patterson	32	19.31
12	(85)	Graeme Hick	26	19.96
13	(11)	Angus Fraser	92	20.22
14	(2)	Ole Mortensen	43	20.41
15	(111)	Courtney Walsh	81	20.67
Others with 75 wickets				
20	(32)	Neil Foster	85	21.60
27	(29)	Paul-Jan Bakker	77	22.49
30	(48)	Neal Radford	75	23.00
40	(87)	Steve Watkin	94	25.09
43	(6)	Paul Jarvis	76	25.31

(1988 positions in brackets)

WICKET-KEEPERS: 1 Warren Hegg 79 (77 ct 2 st); 2 Bobby Parks 71 (67 ct 4 st); 3 Paul Downton 69 (63 ct 6 st).

FIELDERS: 1 Graeme Hick 43; 2 Paul Terry 39; 3 Bill Athey 31.

Highest Totals

602-6d	Australia v England	(Trent Bridge)
601-7d	Australia v England	(Headingley)
528	Australia v England	(Lord's)
526-7d	Kent v Somerset	(Bath)
522-3d	Essex v Derbys	(Chelmsford)
505	Northants v Glos	(Bristol)
498	Leics v Kent	(Folkestone)
477-6d	Surrey v Kent	(The Oval)
475-4d	Lancs v Hants	(Portsmouth)
475-8d	Notts v Surrey	(Guildford)

Lowest Totals

43	Middlesex v Lancs	(Lord's)
48	Glos v Hants	(Portsmouth)
51	Northants v Warwicks	(Northampton)
57	Derbys v Leics	(Chesterfield)
60	Northants v Glam	(Swansea)
64	Derbys v Notts	(Trent Bridge)
65	Glamorgan v Essex	(Swansea)
67	Cambridge U v Sussex	(Hove)
73	Somerset v Gloucs	(Bath)
78	Derbys v Leics	(Leicester)

Highest Individual Scores
248 Dean Jones
Australians v Warwicks (Edgbaston)
228 David Gower
Leicestershire v Glam (Leicester)
219 Mark Taylor
Australia v England (Trent Bridge)
206* Desmond Haynes
Middlesex v Kent (Uxbridge)
206 Alec Stewart
Surrey v Essex (The Oval)
201* Ian Hutchinson
Middlesex v Oxford U (Oxford)
199* Alec Stewart
Surrey v Sussex (The Oval)
199 Alan Fordham
Northants v Yorkshire (Northampton)
191* Matthew Maynard
Glamorgan v Gloucs (Cardiff)
182 Robin Smith
Hampshire v Kent (Southampton)

Best Bowling
8-41 Rajesh Maru
Hampshire v Kent (Southampton)
8-47 Franklyn Stephenson
Notts v Essex (Trent Bridge)
7-18 Derek Pringle
Essex v Glamorgan (Swansea)
7-19 Courtney Walsh
Glos v Somerset (Bath)
7-21 Phil DeFreitas
Lancashire v Middlesex (Lord's)

7-27 John Emburey
Middlesex v Glos (Cheltenham)
7-31 Cardigan Connor
Hampshire v Glos (Portsmouth)
7-35 John Childs
Essex v Cambridge U (Cambridge)
7-38 John Childs
Essex v Hampshire (Ilford)
7-38 Franklyn Stephenson
Notts v Yorkshire (Headingley)

Most Centuries
8 Jimmy Cook (Somerset)
6 Graeme Hick (Worcs)
  Robin Smith (Hampshire)
5 Mark Benson (Kent)
  Dean Jones (Australians)

Mark Nicholas (Hampshire)
Peter Roebuck (Somerset)

Fastest Century
69 balls Darren Bicknell, Surrey v Essex (The Oval)

One-Day Centuries
4 Chris Tavaré (Somerset)
3 Jimmy Cook (Somerset)
  Graham Gooch (Essex)
  Robin Smith (Hampshire)

Man of the Match Awards
(all recognised one-day games combined)
3 Phil DeFreitas (Lancs)
  Robin Smith (Hampshire)
  Chris Tavaré (Somerset)
  Paul Prichard (Essex)

Britannic Assurance Championship 1989

(Championship games only)

		P	W	L	D	BAT	BONUS BOWL	POINT	Leading run-getter		Leading wicket-taker	
1 (1)	WORCS	22	12	3	7	44	83	319	Graeme Hick	1595	Neal Radford	67
2 (3)	Essex	22	13	2	7	59	71	313	Mark Waugh	1288	Derek Pringle	89
3 (8)	Middx	22	9	2	11	50	72	266	Mike Gatting	1337	Angus Fraser	78
4 (9)	Lancs	22	8	5	9	57	65	250	Neil Fairbrother	1336	Phil DeFreitas	65
5 (12)	Northants	22	7	8	7	47	63	222	Wayne Larkins	1419	Greg Thomas	66
6½ (14)	Derbys	22	6	6	10	45	75	216	John Morris	1555	Simon Base	51
6½ (15)	Hants	22	6	8	8	55	65	216	Paul Terry	1198	Paul-Jan Bakker	77
8 (6)	Warwicks	22	5	4	13	44	75	207	Andy Lloyd	1116	Allan Donald	86
9 (10)	Glos	22	6	11	5	38	70	204	Kevin Curran	1186	Courtney Walsh	81
10 (16)	Sussex	22	4	4	14	60	68	192	Alan Wells	1629	Tony Dodemaide	65
11 (5)	Notts	22	6	6	10	54	65	190	Tim Robinson	1454	Franklyn Stephenson	89
12 (4)	Surrey	22	4	7	11	50	69	183	Alec Stewart	1633	Martin Bicknell/	
											Tony Murphy	65
13 (7)	Leics	22	4	8	10	43	74	181	James Whitaker	1252	Jonathan Agnew	66
14 (11)	Somerset	22	4	6	12	50	54	168	Jimmy Cook	2173	Adrian Jones	69
15 (2)	Kent	22	3	8	11	53	53	154	Neil Taylor	1495	Alan Igglesden	53
16 (13)	Yorks	22	3	9	10	41	60	149	Ashley Metcalfe	1279	Paul Jarvis	74
17 (17)	Glam	22	3	6	13	38	59	145	Alan Butcher	1527	Steve Watkin	89

Warwickshire + 8 pts: still batting in draw with scores level; Essex and Notts -25 pts for sub-standard pitches.
Top of the table: Apr 24 Worcs; May 1 Northants; May 8 Essex; May 19 Northants; May 23 Lancs; June 23 Essex; Aug 1 Worcs; Aug 31 Worcs become champions.
Bottom of the table: May 1 Yorks; May 8 Derbys; May 19 Glos; May 23 Yorks; May 26 Glos; Jun 20 Warwicks; Jun 23 Derbys; Jul 25 Kent; Aug 15 Glam.
(1988 positions in brackets)

COUNTY CHAMPIONSHIP IN THE 80s

		P	W	L	D	T	BONUS BAT	BOWL	PTS
1	Essex	230	82	39	109	–	558	728	2589
2	Middlesex	230	80	44	106	–	543	704	2527
3	Nottinghamshire	230	73	48	109	–	526	709	2374
4	Surrey	230	67	52	111	–	574	706	2352
5	Leicestershire	230	62	41	127	–	518	688	2206
6	Hampshire	230	59	61	110	–	514	682	2136
7	Worcestershire	230	57	58	115	–	530	661	2103
8	Northamptonshire	230	54	52	123	1	522	614	2004
9	Kent	230	49	58	121	2	511	652	1963
10	Sussex	230	49	60	120	1	507	649	1944
11	Somerset	230	43	56	131	–	559	640	1903
12	Derbyshire	230	47	52	130	1	498	652	1902
13	Gloucestershire	230	47	67	115	1	501	628	1889
14	Lancashire	230	47	54	129	–	464	626	1846
15	Warwickshire	230	40	65	125	–	540	619	1807
16	Yorkshire	230	41	49	140	–	505	601	1770
17	Glamorgan	230	27	68	135	–	446	600	1486

80s seasonal records: WINS: Most – 13 Essex 1984 and 89; fewest – 0 Warwickshire 1982. DEFEATS: Most – 13 Hampshire 1984; fewest – 1 Yorkshire 1982, Sussex 1985 and Nottinghamshire 1987. DRAWS: Most – 19 Leicestershire 1985, Somerset 1987; fewest – 5 Gloucestershire 1989. BATTING POINTS: Most – 71 Warwickshire 1984; fewest – 26 Lancashire 1980. BOWLING POINTS: Most – 85 Middlesex 1985; fewest – 45 Somerset 1985. POINTS: Most – 355 Essex 1984; fewest – 102 Hampshire 1980.

Notes: Since 1981 16 points have been awarded for a win and 8 for a tie. In this table 1980 figures (12 and 6) have been brought into line. Figures do not add precisely because (a) counties are awarded only 12 for a win when play restricted to one innings match (b) some counties have gained eight points for batting in drawn game with scores level and (c) Essex and Nottinghamshire were docked 25 points for bad pitches under 1989 rules.

CHAMPIONSHIP RESULTS CHART

Away Team →

Home team	Derbys	Essex	Glam	Glos	Hants	Kent	Lancs	Leics	Middx	Northants	Notts	Somerset	Surrey	Sussex	Warwicks	Worcs	Yorks	Headquarters
Derbys	–	D	H 9W	X	D	X	D[1]	A[1] 9W	X	D	H 1W	D	H 9W	D	X	X	H[1] 3W	Derby
Essex	H 1&212	–	X	X	H[2] 102R	H[3] 1&6	X	D	H 9W	H[4] 120R	X	D	H 2W	X	H[2] 5W	D[4]	H[3]† 3W	Chelmsford
Glam	X	A[5] 188R	–	D	D	X	X	A 9W	D[6]	H[5] 244R	D	D	X	D[5]	A[5] 8W	D[7]	X	Cardiff
Glos	D[9]	A 116R	H 1&123	–	D	X	H[9] 1&23	X	A[9] 188R	A 9W	A[8] 1&4	H 141R	X	D[8]	X	A 79R	X	Bristol
Hants	X	X	A 30R	H[12] 1&118	–	H 123R	H[12] 3W	H[10] 119R	X	X	X	D	H[11] 8W	D	A[10] 60R	A[10] 1&91	A 3W	Southampton
Kent	A 8W	D	A 101R	A[14] 47R	D[13]	–	X	D[15]	D	D[14]	X	X	A 7W	A[13] 3W	A 10W	X	X	Canterbury
Lancs	D	A[18] 7W	A 9R	X	X	D	–	X	X	D[17]	D	X	H 97R	D[16]	H 62R	A 36R	H 181R	Old Trafford
Leics	H 10W	A 10W	D	A 9W	H 4W	D	D	–	X	D	H 1&101	X	A 4W	X	D[19]	X	A 49R	Leicester
Middx	H 70R	D[20]	X	A 8W	H 4W	D[20]	A 218R	D	–	H 7W	D	X	H 125R	X	X	X	D	Lord's
Northants	A 8W	H 4W	X	H 9W	A 9W	A 4W	A 6W	H 1W	X	–	H 60R	A[21] 12R	D	X	A 1&31	A 1&19	H 6W	Northampton
Notts	H† 70R	H 115R	X	A 8W	D	D	A[22] 6W	H 1&47	D	X	–	H 1&67	X	X	D	A 9W	D	Trent Bridge
Somerset	X	X	D	H 8W	D	D	D	X	D[24]	X	X	–	X	H 5W	D	A[24] 9W	D	Taunton
Surrey	X	A 8W	D	H 3W	D	D	D	D	D	X	D[25]	D[25]	–	D	D	X	D	The Oval
Sussex	X	D[26]	D	H 3W	H 9W	D	X	D[27]	A[28] 9W	D	A[27] 3W	D	D	–	X	H 4W	X	Hove
Warwicks	D[29]	X	D	H	X	X	D	H 10W	A 8W	D	X	D	A 4R	D	–	D*	D	Edgbaston
Worcs	H 145R	X	X	H	X	H 10W	A 66R	H[30] 10W	X	X	D	H 5W	H 103R	D	D	–	X	Worcester
Yorks	D	X	X	D[31]	X	A[34] 5W	A[34] 184R	X	A 3W	A[32] 42R	A 10W	X	X	H[33] 8R	D	D[32]	–	Headingley

H = Home win A = Away win D = Draw X = No fixture

Championship matches are played at county headquarters where no number is given.

Matches played on out-grounds as follows: 1. Chesterfield; 2. Ilford; 3. Southend; 4. Colchester; 5. Swansea; 6. Abergavenny; 7. Pontypridd; 8. Gloucester; 9. Cheltenham; 10. Bournemouth; 11. Basingstoke; 12. Portsmouth; 13. Tunbridge Wells; 14. Maidstone; 15. Folkestone; 16. Liverpool; 17. Southport; 18. Lytham; 19. Hinckley; 20. Uxbridge; 21. Luton; 22. Worksop; 23. Bath; 24. Weston-super-Mare; 25. Guildford; 26. Horsham; 27. Eastbourne; 28. Hastings; 29. Nuneaton; 30. Kidderminster; 31. Harrogate; 32. Sheffield; 33. Middlesbrough; 34. Scarborough.

*Warwickshire awarded eight points – still batting with scores level

† Essex and Nottinghamshire deducted 25 points for sub-standard pitches

Biggest wins: Essex beat Derbyshire by innings and 212; Gloucestershire beat Glamorgan by innings and 123.

Narrowest wins: Glamorgan beat Lancashire by 9 runs; Yorkshire beat Sussex by 8 runs; Surrey beat Sussex by 8 runs; Northamptonshire beat Leicestershire by 1 wicket; Derbyshire beat Nottinghamshire by 1 wicket.

Earliest wins: Warwickshire beat Northamptonshire 12.45pm, second day; Nottinghamshire beat Yorkshire 2.24pm, second day (four-day match).

ONE-DAY CRICKET
NatWest Bank Trophy
First Round

March: WORCESTERSHIRE beat Cambridgeshire by 9 wkts; Telford: LEICESTERSHIRE beat Shropshire by 6 wkts; Hitchin: NOTTINGHAMSHIRE beat Hertfordshire by 5 wkts; Canterbury: KENT beat Dorset by 198 runs; Oxford: GLOUCESTERSHIRE beat Oxfordshire by 43 runs; Darlington: MIDDLESEX beat Durham by 54 runs; Kendal: LANCASHIRE beat Cumberland by 4 wkts; Derby: DERBYSHIRE beat Ireland by 63 runs; Bury St Edmunds: NORTHAMPTONSHIRE beat Suffolk by 32 runs; Edgbaston: WARWICKSHIRE beat Wiltshire by 186 runs; Headingley: YORKSHIRE beat Scotland by 3 wkts; Chester: HAMPSHIRE beat Cheshire by 147 runs; Jesmond: SURREY beat Northumberland by 4 wkts; Taunton: SOMERSET beat Essex by 55 runs; Cardiff: GLAMORGAN beat Staffordshire by 167 runs; Hove: SUSSEX beat Berkshire by 35 runs.

Second Round

Cardiff: HAMPSHIRE beat Glamorgan by 7 wkts; Gloucester: LANCASHIRE beat Gloucester by 1 wkt; Canterbury: WARWICKSHIRE beat Kent by 49 runs; Uxbridge: MIDDLESEX beat Nottinghamshire by 36 runs; Taunton: NORTHAMPTONSHIRE beat Somerset by 5 wkts; SUSSEX beat Leicestershire by 68 runs; Worcester: WORCESTERSHIRE beat Derbyshire by 38 runs

Quarter-finals

Lord's: MIDDLESEX beat Sussex by 78 runs; Worcester: WORCESTERSHIRE beat Lancashire by 7 wkts; The Oval: HAMPSHIRE beat Surrey by 5 wkts; Northampton: WARWICKSHIRE beat Northamptonshire by 3 wkts

Semi-finals

Edgbaston: WARWICKSHIRE beat Worcestershire by 100 runs; Southampton: MIDDLESEX beat Hampshire by 3 runs.

Final
Lord's, Sep 2

MIDDLESEX	
J.D. Carr c Humpage b Reeve	17
D.L. Haynes b N.M.K. Smith	50
*M.W. Gatting b Munton	1
M.R. Ramprakash b Donald	24
M.A. Roseberry c Asif Din b Small	26
†P.R. Downton not out	43
J.E. Emburey not out	21
Extras (lb16, w9, nb3)	28
Total (5 wkts, innings closed)	210

Fall: 1-40, 2-41, 3-98, 4-111, 5-148
Did not bat:
Middlesex: S.P. Hughes, A.R.C. Fraser, N.G. Cowans, R.M. Ellcock
Warwickshire: G.C. Small, A.A. Donald, T.A. Munton
Bowling:
Warwickshire: Donald 12-1-41-1; Small 12-3-35-1; Reeve 12-4-27-1; Munton 11-3-37-1; P.A. Smith 4-0-21-0; N.M.K. Smith 9-0-33-1
Middlesex: Ellcock 10-1-45-0; Cowans 12-4-23-1; Fraser 12-3-30-2; Hughes 10.4-2-45-0; Emburey 12-2-46-1; Carr 3-0-11-1
Man of the match: D.A. Reeve
Warwickshire won by four wickets

WARWICKSHIRE	
A.J. Moles b Fraser	10
*T.A. Lloyd b Emburey	34
A.I. Kallicharran c Downton b Fraser	0
†G.W. Humpage c Gatting b Cowans	36
P.A. Smith b Carr	24
D.A. Reeve run out	42
Asif Din not out	34
N.M.K. Smith not out	15
Extras (b4, lb7, w5)	16
Total (6wkts, 59.4 overs)	211

Fall: 1-16, 2-26, 3-66, 4-99, 5-122, 6-191

Benson & Hedges Cup

Group A

Cardiff: KENT beat Glamorgan by 6 wkts; Hove: ESSEX beat Sussex by 63runs; Chelmsford: ESSEX beat Hampshire by 7 wkts; Canterbury: SUSSEX beat Kent by 5 wkts; Southampton: GLAMORGAN beat Hampshire by 8 wkts; Canterbury: ESSEX beat Kent by 4 wkts; Chelmsford: ESSEX beat Glamorgan by 10 wkts; Hove: HAMPSHIRE beat Sussex by 65 runs; Swansea: SUSSEX beat Glamorgan by 47 runs; Southampton: KENT beat Hampshire by 4 wkts

ESSEX and KENT qualified

Group B

Fenners: COMBINED UNIVS beat Surrey by 9 runs; Lord's: WORCESTERSHIRE beat Middlesex by one run; Bristol: GLOUCESTERSHIRE beat Middlesex by 6 wkts; The Oval: SURREY beat Worcestershire by 1 wkt; Worcester: GLOUCESTERSHIRE beat Worcestershire by 48 runs; The Parks: MIDDLESEX beat Combined Univs by 8 wkts; The Oval: GLOUCESTERSHIRE beat Surrey by 144 runs; Worcester: COMBINED UNIVS beat Worcestershire by 5 wkts; Lord's: MIDDLESEX beat Surrey by 76 runs; Bristol: GLOUCESTERSHIRE beat Combined Univs by 3 wkts.

GLOUCESTERSHIRE & COMBINED UNIVERSITIES qualified

CUP FINALS DECIDED OFF THE LAST BALL

1981 NatWest DERBYSHIRE beat Northants. Griffiths bowling to Tunnicliffe. Single wanted: Miller, the non-striker, just beat Lamb's throw.

1984 NatWest MIDDLESEX beat Kent. Ellison to Emburey . One wanted: Emburey hit overpitched ball for four.

1985 NatWest ESSEX beat Notts. Pringle to Randall. Two wanted: Randall caught at short mid-wicket.

1986 B and H MIDDLESEX beat Kent. Hughes to Dilley. Six wanted: three scored.

1987 B and H YORKSHIRE beat Northants. Davis to Love, who blocked last ball knowing that was enough for victory on fewer wickets lost.

1989 B and H NOTTS beat Essex. Lever to Hemmings. Four wanted: Hemmings hits four to square-leg.

Group C
Derby: SOMERSET beat Derbyshire by 7 wkts; Jesmond: YORKSHIRE beat Minor Counties by 5 wkts; Trent Bridge: NOTTINGHAMSHIRE beat Derbyshire by 5 wkts; Taunton: SOMERSET beat Minor Counties by 35 runs; Headingley: SOMERSET beat Yorkshire by 62 runs; Oxton: NOTTINGHAMSHIRE beat Minor Counties by 5 wkts; Derby: DERBYSHIRE beat Minor Counties by 7 wkts; Trent Bridge: NOTTINGHAMSHIRE beat Yorkshire by 33 runs; Headingley: YORKSHIRE beat Derbyshire by 7 wkts; Taunton: SOMERSET beat Nottinghamshire by 7 wkts

SOMERSET & NOTTINGHAMSHIRE qualified

Group D
Old Trafford: LANCASHIRE beat Leicestershire by 7 wkts; Edgbaston: NORTHAMPTONSHIRE beat Warwickshire by 4 wkts; Leicester: LEICESTERSHIRE

beat Warwickshire by 31 runs: Perth: LANCASHIRE beat Scotland by 7 wkts Northampton; NORTHAMPTONSHIRE beat Lancashire by 38 runs; Leicester: LEICESTERSHIRE beat Scotland by 111 runs; Edgbaston: WARWICKSHIRE beat Scotland by 6 wkts; Northampton: Northamptonshire v Leicestershire match abandoned; Old Trafford: LANCASHIRE beat Warwickshire by 5 wkts; Glasgow: NORTHAMPTONSHIRE beat Scotland by 9 wkts

NORTHAMPTONSHIRE & LANCASHIRE qualified

Quarter-finals
Northampton: KENT beat Northamptonshire by 21 runs; Taunton: SOMERSET beat Combined Univs by 3 runs; Bristol: NOTTINGHAMSHIRE beat Gloucestershire by 5 runs; Chelmsford: ESSEX beat Lancashire by 3 wkts.

Semi-finals
Trent Bridge: NOTTINGHAMSHIRE beat Kent by 69 runs; Taunton: ESSEX beat Somerset by 4 runs

Final
Lord's, Jul 15

ESSEX

*G.A. Gooch b Afford	48
B.R. Hardie b Stephenson	0
A.W. Lilley not out	95
M.E. Waugh c Robinson b Evans	41
P.J. Pritchard lbw b Cooper	1
J.P. Stephenson run out	9
D.P. Pringle run out	15
†M.A. Garnham c Johnson b Evans	0
N.A. Foster not out	2
Extras (b1, lb26, w4, nb1)	32
Total (7 wkts, 55 overs)	243

Fall: 1-4, 2-74, 3-156, 4-162, 5-185, 6-220, 7-235
Did not bat:
Essex G. Miller, J.K. Lever

NOTTINGHAMSHIRE

B.C. Broad c Garnham b Lever	6
P. Pollard lbw b Lever	2
*R.T. Robinson run out	86
P. Johnson b Foster	54
D.W. Randall c Waugh b Pringle	49
F.D. Stephenson c Gooch b Miller	0
K.P. Evans run out	26
†B.N. French not out	8
E.E. Hemmings not out	6
Extras (b1, lb3, w2, nb1)	7
Total (7 wkts, 55 overs)	244

Fall: 1-5, 2-17, 3-149, 4-162, 5-162 6-221, 7-234
Nottinghamshire K.E. Cooper, J.A. Afford

Bowling:
Nottinghamshire Stephenson 11-0-61-1; Cooper 11-3-30-1; Evans 11-0-28-2; Afford 11-0-50-1; Hemmings 11-0-47-0
Essex Lever 11-2-43-2; Foster 11-1-40-1; Gooch 11-0-57-0; Pringle 11-1-38-1; Miller 9-0-50-0; Stephenson 2-0-12-0
Man of the match: R.T. Robinson
Nottinghamshire won by 3 wickets

Refuge Assurance (Sunday) League

		P	W	L	T	A	PTS
1	Lancashire (3)	16	12	2	0	2	52
2	Worcestershire (1)	16	11	4	0	1	46
	Essex (10)	16	11	4	0	1	46
4	Nottinghamshire (17)	16	9	6	0	1	38
	Derbyshire (12)	16	9	6	0	1	38
6	Surrey (5)	16	9	7	0	0	36
	Hampshire (9)	16	8	6	1	1	36
	Northamptonshire (14)	16	8	6	0	2	36
9	Middlesex (4)	16	8	7	1	0	34
10	Somerset (12)	16	7	8	1	0	30
11	Kent (7)	16	7	9	0	0	28
	Yorkshire (8)	16	7	9	0	0	28
	Sussex (14)	16	6	8	1	1	28
14	Warwickshire (10)	16	5	10	0	1	22
	Leicestershire (14)	16	5	10	0	1	22
16	Gloucestershire (2)	16	3	13	0	0	12
	Glamorgan (5)	16	2	12	0	2	12

1988 positions in brackets

Refuge Assurance Cup

Semi-finals
ESSEX beat Worcestershire by 101 runs
NOTTINGHAMSHIRE beat Lancashire by 5 wickets
Final
ESSEX beat Nottinghamshire by 5 runs
ESSEX 160-5 (40 overs) (P.J. Prichard 56)
NOTTINGHAMSHIRE 155 (39.4 overs) (D.R. Pringle 4-20)

Refuge Assurance League Results Chart

Team	Derbys	Ess	Gla	Glo	Han	Ke	Lan	Lei	Mx	Nor	Not	Som	Sur	Sus	War	Wor	Yor
Derbys	–	L	W	W	L	W	L	W	L	A	L	W	W	W	W	L	W
Essex	W	–	W	W	W	W	A	W	W	L	L	W	L	W	W	L	W
Glam	L	L	–	L	W	L	L	A	W	L	L	L	L	A	L	L	L
Glos	L	L	W	–	W	L	W	L	W	L	L	L	L	L	L	L	L
Hants	W	L	L	L	–	W	L	W	T	A	W	W	L	W	W	W	W
Kent	L	L	W	W	L	–	L	W	W	L	L	L	W	W	W	L	L
Lancs	W	A	W	W	W	W	–	L	W	W	W	W	W	W	A	W	L
Leics	L	L	A	L	L	L	W	–	L	W	L	L	W	L	W	L	W
Middx	W	L	L	W	T	L	L	W	–	W	L	L	W	W	L	W	W
Northants	A	W	W	W	A	W	L	L	L	–	W	L	W	L	W	L	W
Notts	W	W	W	W	L	W	L	W	W	L	–	L	W	L	W	A	L
Somerset	L	L	W	W	L	W	L	W	W	W	W	–	L	T	L	L	L
Surrey	L	W	W	W	W	L	L	L	L	L	L	W	–	W	W	W	W
Sussex	L	L	A	W	L	L	L	W	L	W	W	T	L	–	L	W	W
Warwicks	L	L	W	W	L	L	A	L	W	L	L	W	L	W	–	L	L
Worcs	W	W	W	W	W	W	L	W	L	W	A	W	L	L	W	–	W
Yorks	L	L	W	W	L	W	W	L	L	L	W	W	L	L	W	L	–

W = won L = lost T = tied A = abandoned

Sunday League in the 80s

	W	L	Tied	A	Pts
Essex	87	55	3	15	384
Sussex	80	57	3	20	366
Hampshire	79	63	5	13	352
Somerset	79	63	1	17	352
Middlesex	73	61	3	23	344
Worcestershire	77	69	3	11	336
Lancashire	69	62	5	24	334
Kent	71	65	3	21	332
Derbyshire	72	69	2	17	326
Nottinghamshire	71	71	2	16	320
Surrey	64	71	3	22	306
Northamptonshire	63	74	3	20	298
Yorkshire	63	75	2	20	296
Warwickshire	61	75	6	18	292
Leicestershire	53	76	1	30	274
Gloucestershire	57	83	3	17	268
Glamorgan	53	83	2	22	260

80s seasonal records: Most points: Sussex 58, 1982. Fewest points: Glamorgan, Gloucestershire 12, 1989. Most wins: Sussex 14, 1982. Fewest wins: Glamorgan 2, 1989. Fewest defeats: Sussex 1, 1982. Most defeats: Gloucestershire 13, 1989. Most ties: Worcestershire 3, 1983. Most wash-outs: Leicestershire 7, 1987.

ENGLISH LEAGUE CRICKET 1989
Top three clubs in leading leagues
Bassetlaw: 1 Farnsfield; 2 Blidworth Colliery; 3 Bridon.
Birmingham: 1 Stourbridge; 2 Walsall; 3 Old Hill.
Bradford: 1 Hanging Heaton; 2 Bradford & Bingley; 3 Yorkshire Bank.
Central Lancashire: 1 Stockport; 2 Littleborough; 3 Middleton.
Durham Senior: 1 Eppleton; 2 Burnmoor; 3 Gateshead Fell.
Lancashire: 1 Haslingden; 2 Accrington; 3 East Lancashire.
Middlesex County: 1 Richmond; 2 Teddington; 3 Southgate.
Northern: 1 Blackpool; 2 Netherfield; 3 Leyland Motors.
Western: 1 Cheltenham; 2 Weston-super-Mare; 3 Newport.
Yorkshire: 1 Harrogate; 2 York; 3 Barnsley.

OTHER CRICKET 1989
Youth Tests: (three match series) Scarborough, Canterbury and Old Trafford – NEW ZEALAND under-19 beat England under-19 1-0.
Minor Counties Championship: Final (55 overs) – Worcester: OXFORDSHIRE beat Hertfordshire by 7 wickets.
Rapid Cricketline Championship, Second XIs: 1 MIDDLESEX; 2 Warwickshire: 3 Kent.
Bain Clarkson Trophy (55 overs, county 2nd XIs) – Canterbury: MIDDLESEX beat Kent by 6 wickets.
Cockspur Cup (45 overs, clubs) – Edgbaston: TEDDINGTON beat Old Hill by 11 runs.
Hydro Village Championship – Beckenham: TOFT (Cheshire) beat Hambledon (Hants) by 6 wickets.

OVERSEAS CRICKET
Sheffield Shield Final
Perth, Mar 25-29
Match Drawn. Western Australia retained Shield
WESTERN AUSTRALIA 535 (T.M. Moody 162, C.R. Miller 7-112) and 289-2 (T.M. Moody 155, G.R. Marsh 105no)
SOUTH AUSTRALIA 494 (P.R. Sleep 146no)

CHAMPIONS

WORLD CUP
1975	West Indies beat Australia by 17 runs
1979	West Indies beat England by 92 runs
1983	India beat West Indies by 43 runs
1987	Australia beat England by 7 runs

COUNTY CHAMPIONS

1864	Surrey	1904	Lancashire	1953	Surrey
1865	Nottinghamshire	1905	Yorkshire	1954	Surrey
1866	Middlesex	1906	Kent	1955	Surrey
1867	Yorkshire	1907	Nottinghamshire	1956	Surrey
1868	Nottinghamshire	1908	Yorkshire	1957	Surrey
1869	Notts & Yorks (shared)	1909	Kent	1958	Surrey
1870	Yorkshire	1910	Kent	1959	Yorkshire
1871	Notts	1911	Warwickshire	1960	Yorkshire
1872	Notts	1912	Yorkshire	1961	Hampshire
1873	Gloucs & Notts (shared)	1913	Kent	1962	Yorkshire
1874	Gloucestershire	1914	Surrey	1963	Yorkshire
1875	Nottinghamshire	1915-18	Not held	1964	Worcestershire
1876	Gloucestershire	1919	Yorkshire	1965	Worcestershire
1877	Gloucestershire	1920	Middlesex	1966	Yorkshire
1878	Undecided	1921	Middlesex	1967	Yorkshire
1879	Lancs & Notts (shared)	1922	Yorkshire	1968	Yorkshire
1880	Nottinghamshire	1923	Yorkshire	1969	Glamorgan
1881	Lancashire	1924	Yorkshire	1970	Kent
1882	Lancs & Notts (shared)	1925	Yorkshire	1971	Surrey
1883	Nottinghamshire	1926	Lancashire	1972	Warwickshire
1884	Nottinghamshire	1927	Lancashire	1973	Hampshire
1885	Nottinghamshire	1928	Lancashire	1974	Worcestershire
1886	Nottinghamshire	1929	Nottinghamshire	1975	Leicestershire
1887	Surrey	1930	Lancashire	1976	Middlesex
1888	Surrey	1931	Yorkshire	1977	Kent & Middx (shared)
1889	Lancs, Notts & Surrey (shared)	1932	Yorkshire	1978	Kent
		1933	Yorkshire	1979	Essex
1890	Surrey	1934	Lancashire	1980	Middlesex
1891	Surrey	1935	Yorkshire	1981	Nottinghamshire
1892	Surrey	1936	Derbyshire	1982	Middlesex
1893	Yorkshire	1937	Yorkshire	1983	Essex
1894	Surrey	1938	Yorkshire	1984	Essex
1895	Surrey	1939	Yorkshire	1985	Middlesex
1896	Yorkshire	1940-45	Not held	1986	Essex
1897	Lancashire	1946	Yorkshire	1987	Nottinghamshire
1898	Yorkshire	1947	Middlesex	1988	Worcestershire
1899	Surrey	1948	Glamorgan	1989	Worcestershire
1900	Yorkshire	1949	Middx & Yorks (shared)	**Most outright wins**	
1901	Yorkshire	1950	Lancs & Surrey (shared)	31 Yorkshire; 18 Surrey; 14	
1902	Yorkshire	1951	Warwickshire	Nottinghamshire; 9 Middlesex; 8	
1903	Middlesex	1952	Surrey	Lancashire; 6 Kent; 5 Worcestershire.	

NATWEST BANK TROPHY
(Gillette Cup 1963-80)

1963	Sussex beat Worcestershire by 14 runs
1964	Sussex beat Warwickshire by 8 wickets
1965	Yorkshire beat Surrey by 175 runs
1966	Warwickshire beat Worcs by 5 wickets
1967	Kent beat Somerset by 32 runs
1968	Warwickshire beat Sussex by 4 wickets
1969	Yorkshire beat Derbyshire by 69 runs
1970	Lancashire beat Sussex by 6 wickets
1971	Lancashire beat Kent by 24 runs
1972	Lancashire beat Warwickshire by 4 wickets
1973	Gloucestershire beat Sussex by 40 runs
1974	Kent beat Lancashire by 4 wickets
1975	Lancashire beat Middlesex by 7 wickets
1976	Northants beat Lancashire by 4 wickets
1977	Middlesex beat Glamorgan by 5 wickets
1978	Sussex beat Somerset by 5 wickets
1979	Somerset beat Northants by 45 runs
1980	Middlesex beat Surrey by 7 wickets
1981	Derbyshire beat Northants fewer wickets lost (scores level)
1982	Surrey beat Warwickshire by 9 wickets
1983	Somerset beat Kent by 24 runs
1984	Middlesex beat Kent by 4 wickets
1985	Essex beat Nottinghamshire by 1 run
1986	Sussex beat Lancashire by 7 wickets
1987	Nottinghamshire beat Northants by 3 wickets

1988   Middlesex beat Worcestershire by 3 wickets
1989   Warwickshire beat Middlesex by 4 wickets
Most wins
4 Lancashire, Sussex, Middlesex

REFUGE ASSURANCE LEAGUE
(John Player League 1969-86)

		Pts
1969	Lancashire	49
1970	Lancashire	53
1971	Worcestershire	44
1972	Kent	45
1973	Kent	50
1974	Leicestershire	54
1975	Hampshire	52
1976	Kent	40
1977	Leicestershire	52
1978	Hampshire	48
1979	Somerset	50
1980	Warwickshire	46
1981	Essex	50
1982	Sussex	58
1983	Yorkshire	46
1984	Essex	50
1985	Essex	44
1986	Hampshire	50
1987	Worcestershire	46
1988	Worcestershire	50
1989	Lancashire	52

Most wins
3 Essex, Kent, Hampshire, Worcestershire, Lancashire

BENSON & HEDGES CUP
1972   Leicestershire beat Yorkshire by 5 wickets
1973   Kent beat Worcestershire by 39 runs
1974   Surrey beat Leicestershire by 27 runs
1975   Leicestershire beat Middlesex by 5 wickets
1976   Kent beat Worcestershire by 43 runs
1977   Gloucestershire beat Kent by 64 runs
1978   Kent beat Derbyshire by 6 wickets
1979   Essex beat Surrey by 35 runs
1980   Northants beat Essex by 6 runs
1981   Somerset beat Surrey by 7 wickets
1982   Somerset beat Nottinghamshire by 9 wickets
1983   Middlesex beat Essex by 4 runs
1984   Lancashire beat Warwickshire by 6 wickets
1985   Leicestershire beat Essex by 5 wickets
1986   Middlesex beat Kent by 2 runs
1987   Yorkshire beat Northants fewer wickets lost (scores level)
1988   Hampshire beat Derbyshire by 7 wickets
1989   Nottinghamshire beat Essex by 3 wickets
Most wins
3 Leicestershire, Kent

CARRYING BAT IN BOTH INNINGS OF A MATCH

H. Jupp
43/95 and 109/193 Surrey v Yorkshire, The Oval 1874
S. Kinneir
70/239 and 69/166 Warwicks v Leics, Leicester 1907
C.J.B. Wood
107/309 and 117/296 Leics v Yorkshire, Bradford 1911
V.M. Merchant
135/271 and 77/161 Indians v Lancs, Liverpool 1936
S.J. Cook
120/186 and 131/218 Somerset v Notts, Nottingham 1989

RECORDS

BATTING RECORDS
Most Runs in a Career
61,237 J.B. Hobbs; 58,969 F.E. Woolley; 57,611 E.H. Hendren; 55,061 C.P. Mead; 54,896 W.G. Grace; 50,551 W.R. Hammond; 50,138 H. Sutcliffe

Highest Individual Scores
499 Hanif Mohammad, Karachi v Bahawalpur (Karachi) 1958-59; 452* D.G. Bradman NSW v Queensland (Sydney) 1929-30; 443* B.B. Nimbalkar, Maharashtra v Kathiawar (Poona) 1948-49

Most Runs in an Over
36: G.S. Sobers off M.A. Nash, Nottinghamshire v Glamorgan (Swansea) 1968; R.J. Shastri off Tilak Raj, Bombay v Baroda (Bombay) 1984-85

Most Sixes
In an innings: 15 J.R. Reid, Wellington v Northern Districts (Wellington) 1962-63
In a match: 17 W.J. Stewart, Warwickshire v Lancashire (Blackpool) 1959
In a season: 80 I.T. Botham, Somerset 1985

Separate Hundreds in a Match
Eight times: Zaheer Abbas; seven times: W.R. Hammond; six times: J.B. Hobbs, G.M. Turner

Most Consecutive Hundreds
Six: C.B. Fry 1901; D.G. Bradman 1938-39; M.J. Procter 1970-71. Five E.D. Weekes 1955-56

Most Hundreds in a Season
18 D.C.S. Compton 1947. 16 J.B. Hobbs 1925. 15 W.R. Hammond 1938. 14 H. Sutcliffe 1932

Most Runs in a Season
3816 D.C.S. Compton 1947; 3539 W.J. Edrich 1947; 3518 T.W. Hayward 1906

Most Hundreds in a Career
197 J.B.Hobbs; 170 E.H. Hendren; 167 W.R. Hammond; 153 C.P. Mead; 151 G. Boycott

Highest Average in an English Season
115.66 D.G. Bradman 1938; 102.53 G. Boycott 1979; 102.00 W.A. Johnston 1953; 100.12 G. Boycott 1971

Fastest Fifty
Eight minutes: C.C. Inman (57), Leicestershire v Nottinghamshire (Nottingham) 1965

Fastest Hundred
35 minutes: P.G.H. Fender (113*), Surrey v Northamptonshire (Northampton) 1920; 35 minutes: S.J. O'Shaughnessy (105), Lancashire v Leicestershire (Manchester) 1983

Fastest Double Hundred
113 minutes: R.J. Shastri (200*), Bombay v Baroda (Bombay) 1984-85

Fastest Triple Hundred
181 minutes: D.C.S. Compton (300), MCC v N E Transvaal (Benoni) 1948-49

Highest Partnerships
577: V.S. Hazare (288) and Gul Mahomed (319), fourth wicket, Baroda v Holkar (Baroda) 1946-47; 574*: F.M. Worrell (255*) and C.L. Walcott (314*), fourth wicket, Barbados v Trinidad (Port of Spain) 1945-46; 561: Waheed Mirza (324) and Mansoor Akhtar (224*), first wicket, Karachi Whites v Quetta (Karachi) 1976-77

1,000 Runs before June
1,000 in May: W.G. Grace 1895; W.R. Hammond 1927; C. Hallows 1928
1,000 before June: T.W. Hayward 1900; D.G. Bradman 1930, 1938; W.J. Edrich 1938; G.M. Turner 1973; G.A. Hick 1988

BOWLING RECORDS

Most Wickets in a Career
4,187 W. Rhodes, 1898-1930; 3,776 A.P. Freeman, 1914-36; 3,278 C.W.L. Parker, 1903-35; 3,061 J.T. Hearne, 1888-1923

Most Wickets in a Match
19-90 J.C. Laker, England v Australia (Manchester) 1956

Most Wickets in a Day
17-48 C. Blythe, Kent v Northamptonshire (Northampton) 1907; 17-91 H. Verity, Yorkshire v Essex (Leyton) 1933; 17-106 T.W. Goddard, Gloucestershire v Kent (Bristol) 1939

Most Hat-Tricks in a Career
Seven: D.V.P. Wright; six: T.W. Goddard, C.W.L. Parker; five: S. Haigh, V.W.C. Jupp, A.E.G. Rhodes, F.A. Tarrant

Most Wickets in a Season
304 A.P. Freeman 1928; 298 A.P. Freeman 1933; 290 T. Richardson 1895

100 Wickets in a Season Most Times
23 W. Rhodes; 20 D. Shackleton (in successive seasons 1949-68); 17 A.P. Freeman

The Double: 1,000 Runs and 100 Wickets in a Season
16 W. Rhodes; 14 G.H. Hirst; 10 V.W.C. Jupp

WICKETKEEPING RECORDS

Most Dismissals in an Innings
Eight (all ct): A.T.W. Grout, Queensland v Western Australia (Brisbane) 1959-60; D.E. East, Essex v Somerset (Taunton) 1985

Most Dismissals in a Match
12: (8ct 4st) E. Pooley, Surrey v Sussex (The Oval) 1868; (9ct 3st) D. Tallon, Queensland v New South Wales (Sydney) 1938-39; (9ct 3st) H.B. Taber, New South Wales v South Australia (Adelaide) 1968-69

Most Dismissals in a Season
128 (79ct 49st) L.E.G. Ames 1929; 122 (70ct 52st) L.E.G. Ames 1928; 110 (63ct 47st) H. Yarnold 1949

Most Dismissals in a Career
1,648 R.W. Taylor 1960-86; 1,527 J.T. Murray 1952-75; 1,497 H. Strudwick 1902-27; 1,344 A.P.E. Knott 1964-85; 1,310 F.H. Huish 1895-1914

FIELDING RECORDS

Most Catches in an Innings
Seven: M.J. Stewart, Surrey v Northamptonshire (Northampton) 1957; A.S. Brown, Gloucestershire v Nottinghamshire (Nottingham) 1966

Most Catches in a Match
Ten: W.R. Hammond, Gloucestershire v Surrey (Cheltenham) 1928

Most Catches in a Season
78 W.R. Hammond 1928; 77 M.J. Stewart 1957; 73 P.M. Walker 1961; 71 P.J. Sharpe 1962

Most Catches in a Career
1,018 F.E. Woolley 1906-38; 887 W.G. Grace 1865-1908; 831 G.A.R. Lock 1946-70; 819 W.R. Hammond 1920-51; 813 D.B. Close 1949-86

TEAM RECORDS

Highest Totals
1,107: Victoria v New South Wales (Melbourne) 1926-27; 1,059: Victoria v Tasmania (Melbourne) 1922-23 County Championship 887: Yorkshire v Warwickshire (Birmingham) 1896

Lowest Totals
12: Oxford University v MCC and Ground (Oxford) 1877, Northamptonshire v Gloucestershire (Gloucester) 1907

Largest Victories
Inns and 851 runs: Railways (910-6 dec) v Dera Ismail Khan (Lahore) 1964-65; Inns and 666 runs: Victoria (1,059) v Tasmania (Melbourne) 1922-23; Inns and 656 runs: Victoria (1,107) v New South Wales (Melbourne) 1926-27

TEST MATCH RECORDS

BATTING

Most Runs in a Career
10,122 S.M. Gavaskar 1971-87; 8273 A.R. Border 1974-89; 8114 G. Boycott 1964-82; 8032 G.S. Sobers 1954-74; 7849 I.V.A. Richards 1978-89; 7624 M.C. Cowdrey 1954-75; 7515 C.H. Lloyd 1966-85

Highest Individual Innings
365* G.S. Sobers, West Indies v Pakistan (Kingston) 1957-58; 364 L. Hutton, England v Australia (The Oval) 1938; 337 Hanif Mohammad, Pakistan v West Indies (Bridgetown) 1957-58; 336* W.R. Hammond, England v New Zealand (Auckland) 1932-33; 334 D.G. Bradman, Australia v England (Leeds) 1930

Most Runs in a Series
974 D.G. Bradman 1930; 905 W.R. Hammond 1928-29; 839 M.A. Taylor 1989

Highest Career Averages
99.94 D.G. Bradman; 60.97 R.G. Pollock; 60.83 G.A. Headley; 60.73 H. Sutcliffe

Most Hundreds
34 S.M. Gavaskar; 29 D.G. Bradman; 26 G.S. Sobers; 24 G.S. Chappell, I.V.A. Richards; 23 A.R. Border

LONGEST TEST INNINGS

16h 10m: Hanif Mohammed (337), Pakistan v West Indies, Bridgetown, 1957-58

13h 20m: Len Hutton (364) England v Australia, The Oval, 1938

12h 56m: Brendan Kuruppu (201*), Sri Lanka v New Zealand, Colombo, 1986-87

12 hr: Shoaib Mohammed (163), Pakistan v New Zealand, Wellington, 1988-89

†*Hanif and Shoaib are father and son*

BOWLING

Most Wickets in a Career
396 R.J. Hadlee 1973-89; 376 I.T. Botham 1977-89; 355 D.K. Lillee 1971-84; 347 Kapil Dev 1978-89; 341 Imran Khan 1971-89; 326 M.D. Marshall 1978-89; 325 R.G.D. Willis 1971-84; 309 L.R. Gibbs 1958-76; 307 F.S. Trueman 1952-65

Most Wickets in an Innings
10-53 J.C. Laker, England v Australia (Manchester) 1956

Most Wickets in a Match
19-90 J.C. Laker, England v Australia (Manchester) 1956; 17-159 S.F. Barnes, England v South Africa (Johannesburg) 1913-14

Most Wickets in a Series
49 S.F. Barnes 1913-14; 46 J.C. Laker 1956; 44 C.V. Grimmett 1935-36; 42 T.M. Alderman 1981

800 RUNS IN A TEST SERIES

RUNS				TESTS	AVGE
974	Don Bradman	Australia v England	1930	5	139.14
905	Walter Hammond	England v Australia	1928-9	5	113.12
839	Mark Taylor	Australia v England	1989	6	83.90
834	Neil Harvey	Australia v S. Africa	1952-3	5	92.66
829	Viv Richards	W. Indies v England	1976	4	118.42
827	Clyde Walcott	W. Indies v Australia	1954-5	5	82.70
824	Garfield Sobers	W. Indies v Pakistan	1957-8	5	137.33
810	Don Bradman	Australia v England	1936-7	5	90.00
806	Don Bradman	Australia v S. Africa	1931-2	5	201.50

40 WICKETS IN A TEST SERIES

WICKETS				TESTS	AVGE
49	Sydney Barnes	England v S. Africa	1913-14	4	10.93
46	Jim Laker	England v Australia	1956	5	9.60
44	Clarrie Grimmett	Australia v S. Africa	1935-6	5	14.59
42	Terry Alderman	Australia v England	1981	6	21.26
41	Rodney Hogg	Australia v England	1978-9	6	12.85
41	Terry Alderman	Australia v England	1989	6	17.36
40	Imran Khan	Pakistan v India	1982-3	6	13.95

WICKETKEEPING

Most Dismissals in a Career
355 R.W. Marsh; 269 A.P.E. Knott; 228 Wasim Bari; 219 T.G. Evans

Most Dismissals in One Test
10 R.W. Taylor, England v India (Bombay) 1979-80

Most Dismissals in an Innings
7: Wasim Bari, Pakistan v New Zealand (Auckland) 1978-79, R.W. Taylor, England v India (Bombay) 1979-80

FIELDING

Most Catches in an Innings
5: V.Y. Richardson, Australia v South Africa (Durban) 1935-36; Yajurvindra Singh, India v England (Bangalore) 1976-77

Most Catches in a Career
122 G.S. Chappell; 120 M.C. Cowdrey; 118 A.R. Border; 112 I.V.A. Richards, I.T. Botham; 110 R.B. Simpson; 110 W.R. Hammond

TEAM RECORDS

Highest Team Totals
903-7 dec England v Australia (The Oval) 1938; 849 England v West Indies (Kingston) 1929-30; 790-3 dec West Indies v Pakistan (Kingston) 1957-58; 758-8 dec Australia v West Indies (Kingston) 1954-55

Lowest Team Totals
26: New Zealand v England (Auckland) 1954-55; 30: South Africa v England (Port Elizabeth) 1895-96; South Africa v England (Birmingham) 1924; 35: South Africa v England (Cape Town) 1898-99

ENGLAND AGAINST THE OTHER COUNTRIES
v. Australia

	W	L	D		W	L	D		W	L	D
1876-77	1	1	0	1905	2	0	3	1961	1	2	2
1878-79	0	1	0	1907-08	1	4	0	1962-63	1	1	3
1880	1	0	0	1909	1	2	2	1964	0	1	4
1881-82	0	2	2	1911-12	4	1	0	1965-66	1	1	3
1882	0	1	0	1912	1	0	2	1968	1	1	2
1882-83	2	2	0	1920-21	0	5	0	1970-71	2	0	4
1884	1	0	2	1921	0	3	2	1972	2	2	1
1884-85	3	2	0	1924-25	1	4	0	1974-75	1	4	1
1886	3	0	0	1926	1	0	4	1975	0	1	3
1886-87	2	0	0	1928-29	4	1	0	1976-77	0	1	0
1887-88	1	0	0	1930	1	2	2	1977	3	0	2
1888	2	1	0	1932-33	4	1	0	1978-79	5	1	0
1890	2	0	0	1934	1	2	2	1979-80	0	3	0
1891-92	1	2	0	1936-37	2	3	0	1980	0	0	1
1893	1	0	2	1938	1	1	2	1981	3	1	2
1894-95	3	2	0	1946-47	0	3	2	1982-83	1	2	2
1896	2	1	0	1948	0	4	1	1985	3	1	2
1897-98	1	4	0	1950-51	1	4	0	1986-87	2	1	2
1899	0	1	4	1953	1	0	4	1987-88	0	0	1
1901-02	1	4	0	1954-55	3	1	1	1989	0	4	2
1902	1	2	2	1956	2	1	2				
1903-04	3	2	0	1958-59	0	4	1	Totals	88	101	80

TEST MATCHES IN THE 80s

	P	W	L	D	T	Win %
West Indies	82	44	8	30	-	53
Pakistan	77	23	13	41	-	29
New Zealand	59	17	15	27	-	28
Australia	94	26	32	35	1	27
England	104	20	39	45	-	19
India	77	11	21	44	1	14
Sri Lanka	27	2	15	10	-	7

Includes all Tests with play Jan 1980-Aug 1989

v South Africa

	E	SA	D
1888-89	2	0	0
1891-92	1	0	0
1895-96	3	0	0
1898-99	2	0	0
1905-06	1	4	0
1907	1	0	2
1909-10	2	3	0
1912	3	0	0
1913-14	4	0	1
1922-23	2	1	2
1924	3	0	2
1927-28	2	2	1
1929	2	0	3
1930-31	0	1	4
1935	0	1	4
1938-39	1	0	4
1947	3	0	2
1948-49	2	0	3
1951	3	1	1
1955	3	2	0
1956-57	2	2	1
1960	3	0	2
1964-65	1	0	4
1965	0	1	2
Total	46	18	38

v West Indies

	E	WI	D
1928	3	0	0
1929-30	1	1	2
1933	2	0	1
1934-35	1	2	1
1939	1	0	2
1947-48	0	2	2
1950	1	3	0
1953-54	2	2	1
1957	3	0	2
1959-60	1	0	4
1963	1	3	1
1966	1	3	1
1967-68	1	0	4
1969	2	0	1
1973	0	2	1
1973-74	1	1	3
1976	0	3	2
1980	0	1	4
1980-81	0	2	2
1984	0	5	0
1985-86	0	5	0
1988	0	4	1
Total	21	39	35

v New Zealand

	E	NZ	D
1929-30	1	0	3
1931	1	0	2
1932-33	0	0	2
1937	1	0	2
1946-47	0	0	1
1949	0	0	4
1950-51	1	0	1
1954-55	2	0	0
1958	4	0	1
1958-59	1	0	1
1962-63	3	0	0
1965	3	0	0
1965-66	0	0	3
1969	2	0	1
1970-71	1	0	1
1973	2	0	1
1974-75	1	0	1
1977-78	1	1	1
1978	3	0	0
1983	3	1	0
1983-84	0	1	2
1986	0	1	2
1987-88	0	0	3
Totals	30	4	32

v India

	E	I	D
1932	1	0	0
1933-34	2	0	1
1936	2	0	1
1946	1	0	2
1951-52	1	1	3
1952	3	0	1
1959	5	0	0
1961-62	0	2	3
1963-64	0	0	5
1967	3	0	0
1971	0	1	2
1972-73	1	2	2
1974	3	0	0
1976-77	3	1	1
1979	1	0	3
1979-80	1	0	0
1981-82	0	1	5
1982	1	0	2
1984-85	2	1	2
1986	0	2	1
Total	30	11	34

v Pakistan

	E	P	D
1954	1	1	2
1961-62	1	0	2
1962	4	0	1
1967	2	0	1
1968-69	0	0	3
1971	1	0	2
1972-73	0	0	3
1974	0	0	3
1977-78	0	0	3
1978	2	0	1
1982	2	1	0
1983-84	0	1	2
1987	0	1	4
1987-88	0	1	2
Totals	13	5	29

v Sri Lanka

	E	SL	D
1981-82	1	0	0
1984	0	0	1
1988	1	0	0
Totals	2	0	1

ENGLAND CAPTAINS IN THE 80s

(Test matches since January 1, 1980)

	P	W	D	L	% of wins
Mike Brearley	7	4	1	2	57
Graham Gooch	2	1	0	1	50
Bob Willis	18	7	6	5	38
David Gower	32	5	9	18	15
Keith Fletcher	7	1	5	1	14
Mike Gatting	23	2	16	5	8
Ian Botham	12	0	8	4	0
Chris Cowdrey	1	0	0	1	0
John Emburey	2	0	0	2	0

1990

ENGLAND TEAMS OVERSEAS 1989-90
England Test Team in the West Indies
Graham Gooch (Essex, capt), Allan Lamb (Northants, vice-capt), Robert Bailey (Northants), David Capel (Northants), Phillip DeFreitas (Lancs), Ricardo Ellcock (Middlesex), Angus Fraser (Middlesex), Eddie Hemmings (Notts), Nasser Hussain (Essex), Wayne Larkins (Northants), Devon Malcolm (Derbyshire), Keith Medlycott (Surrey), Jack Russell (Glos), Gladstone Small (Warwicks), Robin Smith (Hampshire), Alec Stewart (Surrey)

England A Team in Zimbabwe
Mark Nicholas (Hampshire, capt), Michael Atherton (Lancs, vice-capt), Andy Afford (Notts), Darren Bicknell (Surrey), Martin Bicknell (Surrey), Alan Igglesden (Kent), Richard Illingworth (Worcs), Chris Lewis (Leics), Derek Pringle (Essex), Steve Rhodes (Worcs), John Stephenson (Essex), Graham Thorpe (Surrey), Steve Watkin (Glamorgan), James Whitaker (Leics)

England Under-19 in Australia
Alex Barnett (Middlesex), Jeremy Batty (Yorkshire), Kim Butler (Essex), Dominic Cork (Derbyshire), John Crawley (Lancashire), Darren Gough (Yorkshire), Paul Grayson (Yorkshire), Aftab Habib (Middlesex), Jeremy Hallett (Somerset), Piran Holloway (Warwickshire), Ronnie Irani (Lancashire), Matthew Keech (Middlesex), Wayne Noon (Northants), Toby Radford (Middlesex), Andrew Robson (Surrey)

Very Unofficial England in South Africa
Mike Gatting (Middlesex, capt), Bill Athey (Glos), Kim Barnett (Derbyshire), Chris Broad (Notts), Chris Cowdrey (Kent), Graham Dilley (Worcs), Richard Ellison (Kent), John Emburey (Middlesex), Neil Foster (Essex), Bruce French (Notts), David Graveney (Glos, player/manager), Paul Jarvis (Yorkshire), Matthew Maynard (Glamorgan), Tim Robinson (Notts), Greg Thomas (Northants), Alan Wells (Sussex)

TRAITORS!
Headline in the Sun *and* Daily Mirror

". . .Both headline writers got it wrong. Facile, avaricious, blithe in their pursuit of self-interest and quite unable to conceive of an ethical realm beyond that of their own insular little world, the so-called rebel tourists in fact represent their nation only too well."
Dave Hill, New Statesman

"I am a sportsman and should be allowed to play anywhere in the world."
Mike Gatting

"No one pays anything for loyalty."
Paul Jarvis

"I know nothing about apartheid."
Mike Gatting

"We all know that nobody will believe us when we say that we are not just going for the fat cheque, but it is the truth that I and others feel we will be helping to break down the system."
David Graveney

"Blessed are the truly naïve, for they shall go to Johannesburg."
Patrick Collins, Mail on Sunday

"The African National Congress should now admit that it had its tactics wrong all along. Nelson Mandela, instead of pointlessly getting himself locked up for life merely because he wanted his people to be free, should have concentrated on his batting skills."
Phillip Cole, letter in The Guardian

"They disgust me. They shouldn't be allowed to show their faces in sports arenas in Britain again. They have betrayed black sportsmen and black people in Britain."
John Regis, athlete, on Phillip DeFreitas and Roland Butcher

"When I decided to go it was purely a cricketing decision. When I decided not to go it was a family decision."
Roland Butcher

"I would rather be with England. But I have been forced into a corner. Call me a victim of war."
Mike Gatting

"This is a gang of mercenaries who will be gambolling on the cricket fields while our people are in detention. It is an obscenity for them to come to South Africa at this stage of our crisis."
Archbishop Tutu

"Why the hell don't we stand up straight just for once and tell the whole goddamned lot to get lost?"
John Junor, Sunday Express

"They are brave young men. Good luck to them."
John Carlisle, Tory MP

FIXTURES

England Tour to West Indies

Jan 24 arrive; Jan 30-31 Two-day practice match (Barbados); Feb 3-6 Windward Islands (tba); Feb 9-12 Leeward Islands (St Kitts, prov); Feb 14 First one-day international (Port of Spain); Feb 17 Second one-day international (Port of Spain); Feb 19-21 Jamaica (Kingston); Feb 24-Mar 1 (rest day Feb 27) FIRST TEST (Kingston); Mar 3 Third one-day international (Kingston); Mar 6 Fourth one-day international (Georgetown); Mar 9-14 (rest day Mar 12) SECOND TEST (Georgetown); Mar 17-20 President's XI (Guaracara Park, Trinidad); Mar 23-28 (rest day Mar 26) THIRD TEST (Port of Spain); Mar 30-Apr 1 Barbados (Bridgetown); Apr 3 Fifth one-day international (Bridgetown); Apr 5-10 (rest day Apr 9) FOURTH TEST (Bridgetown); Apr 12-17 (rest day Apr 13) FIFTH TEST (Antigua)

England A Tour to Zimbabwe

Feb 15 arrive; Feb 18 Zimbabwe Districts (Harare South); Feb 20-22 Young Zimbabwe (tba); Feb 24 Zimbabwe (Harare); Feb 25 Zimbabwe (Harare); Feb 27-Mar 2 Zimbabwe B (Harare); Mar 4 Zimbabwe (Bulawayo); Mar 6-8 Young Zimbabwe (Bulawayo); Mar 10-15 (rest day Mar 13) Zimbabwe (Harare); Mar 18-21 Zimbabwe B (Harare); Mar 24-28 Zimbabwe (Harare)

Other Winter Tests

AUSTRALIA V PAKISTAN: Jan 12-16 First Test (Melbourne); Jan 19-23 Second Test (Adelaide); Feb 3-7 Third Test (Sydney)

NEW ZEALAND V INDIA: Feb 2-6 First Test (Christchurch); Feb 9-13 Second Test (Napier); Feb 22-26 Third Test (Auckland)

ENGLISH SEASON 1990

The season will be on the pattern of the past two summers but there are three Tests against New Zealand followed by three against India, with two one-day internationals against each. There is no Test match at Headingley for the first time in 30 years. In the Britannic Assurance Championship counties play 22 matches, 16 over three days and six over four days. Warwickshire play their first-ever match at the Coventry and North Warwickshire ground against Lancashire on July 18. On July 25 Sussex stage their first Championship match at Arundel Castle. There are non-Test tours by Sri Lanka and Zimbabwe, and extra games involving them are being arranged.

Duration of Matches

Cornhill Insurance Test Series	5 days
Britannic Assurance Championship	3 days unless stated
Tourist Matches	3 days unless stated
Universities v Counties	3 days
Texaco Trophy One Day Internationals	1 day
Benson & Hedges Cup	1 day
NatWest Bank Trophy	1 day
Refuge Assurance League/ Refuge Assurance Cup	1 day

Date	Venue	Match
APRIL		
Sat 14	Fenner's	Cambridge Univ v Northamptonshire
	The Parks	Oxford Univ v Gloucestershire
Tues 17	Lord's	MCC v Champion County (four days)
Wed 18	Fenner's	Cambridge Univ v Derbyshire
	The Parks	Oxford Univ v Somerset
Sun 22		**Refuge Assurance League**
	Chelmsford	Essex v Kent
	Bristol	Gloucestershire v Glamorgan
	Old Trafford	Lancashire v Middlesex
	Leicester	Leicestershire v Northamptonshire
	Trent Bridge	Nottinghamshire v Yorkshire
	Taunton	Somerset v Worcestershire
	Hove	Sussex v Derbyshire
Tues 24		**Benson & Hedges Cup**
	Bristol	Gloucestershire v Worcestershire
	Edgbaston	Warwickshire v Glamorgan
	Derby	Derbyshire v Sussex
	Lord's	Middlesex v Minor Counties
	Southampton	Hampshire v Yorkshire
	Old Trafford	Lancashire v Surrey
	Chelmsford	Essex v Nottinghamshire
	Leicester	Leicestershire v Northamptonshire
Thu 26		**Britannic Assurance Championship (four days)**
	Cardiff	Glamorgan v Leicestershire
	Canterbury	Kent v Hampshire
	Old Trafford	Lancashire v Worcestershire
	Lord's	Middlesex v Essex
	Trent Bridge	Nottinghamshire v Derbyshire
	Taunton	*Somerset v Gloucestershire
	Hove	Sussex v Surrey
	Headingley	Yorkshire v Northamptonshire
		Other Match
	Fenner's	Cambridge Univ v Warwickshire
Sun 29		**Refuge Assurance League**
	Derby	Derbyshire v Worcestershire
	Cardiff	Glamorgan v Leicestershire
	Canterbury	Kent v Hampshire
	Lord's	Middlesex v Essex
	Trent Bridge	Nottinghamshire v Lancashire
	Hove	Sussex v Surrey
	Edgbaston	Warwickshire v Northamptonshire

*Includes Sunday play

MAY

Tues 1		**Benson & Hedges Cup**
	Worcester	Worcestershire v Kent
	Cardiff	Glamorgan v Gloucestershire
	Marlow	Minor Counties v Sussex
	Taunton	Somerset v Derbyshire
	Fenner's/The Parks	Combined Universities v Lancashire
	The Oval	Surrey v Hampshire
	Glasgow	Scotland v Essex
	Trent Bridge	Nottinghamshire v Leicestershire
Thu 3		**Britannic Assurance Championship** (four days)
	Chelmsford	Essex v Leicestershire
	Cardiff	*Glamorgan v Somerset
	Folkestone	Kent v Sussex
	Northampton	Northamptonshire v Derbyshire
	The Oval	Surrey v Lancashire
	Edgbaston	Warwickshire v Yorkshire
	Worcester	Worcestershire v Nottinghamshire
		Other Matches
	Fenner's	Cambridge Univ v Middlesex
	The Parks	Oxford Univ v Hampshire
Sun 6		**Refuge Assurance League**
	Southampton	Hampshire v Gloucestershire
	Folkestone	Kent v Middlesex
	Leicester	Leicestershire v Essex
	Northampton	Northamptonshire v Derbyshire
	The Oval	Surrey v Lancashire
	Edgbaston	Warwickshire v Yorkshire
	Worcester	Worcestershire v Nottinghamshire
		Tourist Match
Mon 7	Lord's	MCC v New Zealand
	Arundel	Lavinia, Duchess of Norfolk's XI v New Zealand (one-day)
Tues 8		**Benson & Hedges Cup**
	Worcester	Worcestershire v Glamorgan
	Canterbury	Kent v Warwickshire
	Hove	Sussex v Middlesex
	Taunton	Somerset v Minor Counties
	Headingley	Yorkshire v Combined Universities
	Old Trafford	Lancashire v Hampshire
	Titwood, Glasgow	Scotland v Nottinghamshire
	Northampton	Northamptonshire v Essex
		Tourist Match
Wed 9		**Tourist Match**
	Downpatrick	Ireland v New Zealand (one-day)
Thu 10		**Benson & Hedges Cup**
	Canterbury	Kent v Gloucestershire
	Edgbaston	Warwickshire v Worcestershire
	Lord's	Middlesex v Somerset
	Wellington (Salop)	Minor Counties v Derbyshire
	Headingley	Yorkshire v Lancashire
	Fenner's/The Parks	Combined Universities v Surrey
	Northampton	Northamptonshire v Scotland
	Chelmsford	Essex v Leicestershire
		Tourist Match
	Ormeau, Belfast	Ireland v New Zealand (one day)
Sat 12		**Benson & Hedges Cup**
	Bristol	Gloucestershire v Warwickshire
	Swansea	Glamorgan v Kent
	Derby	Derbyshire v Middlesex
	Hove	Sussex v Somerset
	Southampton	Hampshire v Combined Universities
	The Oval	Surrey v Yorkshire
	Leicester	*Leicestershire v Scotland
	Trent Bridge	Nottinghamshire v Northamptonshire
Sat 12		**Tourist Match**
	Worcester	§Worcestershire v New Zealand
Sun 13		**Refuge Assurance League**
	Chelmsford	Essex v Gloucestershire
	Llanelli	Glamorgan v Kent
	Lord's	Middlesex v Nottinghamshire
	Taunton	Somerset v Hampshire
	Headingley	Yorkshire v Derbyshire

§Reserve day Sunday
*Includes Sunday play

Tues 15		**Britannic Assurance Championship** (four days)
	Derby	Derbyshire v Lancashire
	Bristol	Gloucestershire v Glamorgan
	Southampton	Hampshire v Sussex
	Leicester	Leicestershire v Nottinghamshire
	Lord's	Middlesex v Kent
	Northampton	Northamptonshire v Warwickshire
Wed 16		**Tourist Match**
	Taunton	Somerset v New Zealand
		Other Matches
	Fenner's	Cambridge Univ v Essex
	The Parks	Oxford Univ v Surrey
Sat 19		**Britannic Assurance Championship**
	Old Trafford	Lancashire v Leicestershire
	Taunton	Somerset v Derbyshire
	The Oval	Surrey v Hampshire
	Hove	Sussex v Glamorgan
	Edgbaston	Warwickshire v Nottinghamshire
	Worcester	Worcestershire v Essex
		Tourist Match
	Lord's	*Middlesex v New Zealand
Sun 20		**Refuge Assurance League**
	Moreton-in-Marsh	Gloucestershire v Warwickshire
	Canterbury	Kent v Yorkshire
	Old Trafford	Lancashire v Leicestershire
	Trent Bridge	Nottinghamshire v Surrey
	Taunton	Somerset v Derbyshire
	Hove	Sussex v Glamorgan
	Worcester	Worcestershire v Essex
Wed 23		**Texaco Trophy**
	Headingley	ENGLAND v NEW ZEALAND
		(First One-day International)
		Britannic Assurance Championship
	Chesterfield	Derbyshire v Yorkshire
	Swansea	Glamorgan v Kent
	Southampton	Hampshire v Essex
	Lord's	Middlesex v Surrey
	Trent Bridge	Nottinghamshire v Northamptonshire
	Taunton	Somerset v Sussex
		Other Matches
	Fenner's	Cambridge Univ v Gloucestershire
	The Parks	Oxford Univ v Leicestershire
Fri 25		**Texaco Trophy**
	The Oval	ENGLAND v NEW ZEALAND
		(Second One-day International)
Sat 26		**Britannic Assurance Championship**
	Derby	*Derbyshire v Nottinghamshire
	Colwyn Bay	Glamorgan v Lancashire
	Leicester	Leicestershire v Somerset
	Lord's	Middlesex v Gloucestershire
	Edgbaston	Warwickshire v Worcestershire
	Headingley	Yorkshire v Hampshire
		Tourist Match
	Hove	*Sussex v New Zealand
Sun 27		**Refuge Assurance League**
	Aberystwyth	Glamorgan v Lancashire
	Leicester	Leicestershire v Lancashire
	Lord's	Middlesex v Gloucestershire
	Northampton	Northamptonshire v Kent
	Worcester	Worcestershire v Warwickshire
	Headingley	Yorkshire v Hampshire
Wed 30		**Benson & Hedges Cup**
		Quarter-finals
		Tourist Match
	Edgbaston or	
	Old Trafford	Warwickshire or Lancashire v New Zealand

*Includes Sunday play

JUNE

Sat 2		**Britannic Assurance Championship**
	Ilford	Essex v Middlesex
	Bristol	Gloucestershire v Somerset
	Tunbridge Wells	Kent v Nottinghamshire
	Leicester	Leicestershire v Hampshire
	Horsham	Sussex v Lancashire
	Edgbaston	Warwickshire v Northamptonshire
	Worcester	Worcestershire v Yorkshire
		Tourist Match
	Derby	*Derbyshire v New Zealand
		Other Match
	The Parks	Oxford Univ v Glamorgan
Sun 3		**Refuge Assurance League**
	Ilford	Essex v Glamorgan
	Bristol	Gloucestershire v Somerset
	Leicester	Leicestershire v Hampshire
	Lord's	Middlesex v Warwickshire
	The Oval	Surrey v Northamptonshire
	Horsham	Sussex v Lancashire
	Worcester	Worcestershire v Yorkshire
Wed 6		**Britannic Assurance Championship**
	Ilford	Essex v Gloucestershire
	Basingstoke	Hampshire v Somerset
	Tunbridge Wells	Kent v Yorkshire
	Lord's	Middlesex v Warwickshire
	Northampton	Northamptonshire v Leicestershire
	The Oval	Surrey v Derbyshire
		Other Match
	The Parks	Oxford Univ v Nottinghamshire
Thu 7		**CORNHILL INSURANCE TEST MATCH**
	Trent Bridge	ENGLAND v NEW ZEALAND
		(First Test Match)
Sat 9		**Britannic Assurance Championship**
	Canterbury	Kent v Somerset
	Old Trafford	Lancashire v Gloucestershire
	Northampton	Northamptonshire v Glamorgan
	Edgbaston	Warwickshire v Essex
	Harrogate	Yorkshire v Surrey
Sun 10		**Refuge Assurance League**
	Heanor	Derbyshire v Nottinghamshire
	Basingstoke	Hampshire v Middlesex
	Canterbury	Kent v Somerset
	Old Trafford	Lancashire v Gloucestershire
	Leicester	Leicestershire v Sussex
	Hitchin	Northamptonshire v Glamorgan
	Edgbaston	Warwickshire v Essex
	Hull	Yorkshire v Surrey
Wed 13		**Benson & Hedges Cup**
		Semi-finals
		Tourist Match
	Old Trafford	
	or Edgbaston	Lancashire or Warwickshire v New Zealand
Sat 16		**Britannic Assurance League**
	Derby	Derbyshire v Warwickshire
	Southampton	Hampshire v Glamorgan
	Leicester	Leicestershire v Middlesex
	Bath	Somerset v Essex
	The Oval	Surrey v Worcestershire
	Hove	Sussex v Gloucestershire
		Tourist Match
	Northampton	*Northamptonshire v New Zealand
		Other Matches
	Fenner's	Cambridge Univ v Nottinghamshire
	The Parks	Oxford Univ v Lancashire
Sun 17		**Refuge Assurance League**
	Derby	Derbyshire v Warwickshire
	Bournemouth	Hampshire v Glamorgan
	Canterbury	Kent v Nottinghamshire
	Leicester	Leicestershire v Middlesex
	Bath	Somerset v Essex
	The Oval	Surrey v Worcestershire
	Hove	Sussex v Yorkshire

*Includes Sunday play

Wed 20		**Britannic Assurance Championship**
	Gloucester	Gloucestershire v Hampshire
	Old Trafford	Lancashire v Middlesex
	Leicester	Leicestershire v Derbyshire
	Trent Bridge	Nottinghamshire v Surrey
	Bath	Somerset v Glamorgan
	Worcester	Worcestershire v Sussex
	Sheffield	Yorkshire v Warwickshire
		Other Match
	Fenner's	Cambridge Univ v Kent
Thu 21		**CORNHILL INSURANCE TEST MATCH**
	Lord's	**ENGLAND v NEW ZEALAND**
		(Second Test Match)
Sat 23		**Britannic Assurance Championship**
	Cardiff	Glamorgan v Yorkshire
	Gloucester	Gloucestershire v Leicestershire
	Old Trafford	Lancashire v Hampshire
	Luton	Northamptonshire v Middlesex
	Edgbaston	Warwickshire v Kent
Sun 24		**Refuge Assurance League**
		Glamorgan v Yorkshire
	Gloucester	Gloucestershire v Leicestershire
	Old Trafford	Lancashire v Hampshire
	Luton	Northamptonshire v Middlesex
	Bath	Somerset v Nottinghamshire
	The Oval	Surrey v Derbyshire
	Edgbaston	Warwickshire v Kent
	Worcester	Worcestershire v Sussex
Wed 27		**NatWest Bank Trophy**
		First Round
	Swansea	Glamorgan v Dorset
	Downpatrick	Ireland v Sussex
	Northampton	Northants v Staffordshire
	Amersham	Buckinghamshire v Nottinghamshire
	Headingley	Yorkshire v Norfolk
	St Albans	Hertfordshire v Warwickshire
	Chesterfield	Derbyshire v Shropshire
	Old Trafford	Lancashire v Durham
	Gloucester	Gloucestershire v Lincolnshire
	Oxford	
	(Christ Church)	Oxfordshire v Kent
	Lord's	Middlesex v Berkshire
	Swindon/Trowbridge	Wiltshire v Surrey
	Chelmsford	Essex v Scotland
	Leicester	Leicestershire v Hampshire
	Torquay	Devon v Somerset
	Bury St Edmunds	Suffolk v Worcestershire
		Tourist Match
	Fenner's	Oxbridge v New Zealand
Thu 28		**Tourist Match**
		League Cricket Conference v India (one-day)
Sat 30		**Britannic Assurance Championship**
	Derby	Derbyshire v Gloucestershire
	Cardiff	Glamorgan v Surrey
	Maidstone	Kent v Lancashire
	Lord's	Middlesex v Worcestershire
	Trent Bridge	Nottinghamshire v Leicestershire
	Taunton	Somerset v Nothamptonshire
		Tourist Matches
	Chelmsford	*Essex v New Zealand
	Headingley	*Yorkshire v India
		Other Match
	Hove	Sussex v Cambridge Univ
JULY		
Sun 1		**Refuge Assurance League**
	Derby	Derbyshire v Gloucestershire
	Cardiff	Glamorgan v Surrey
	Maidstone	Kent v Lancashire
	Lord's	Middlesex v Worcestershire
	Trent Bridge	Nottinghamshire v Leicestershire
	Taunton	Somerset v Northamptonshire
	Hove	Sussex v Hampshire

*Includes Sunday play

Wed 4		**Britannic Assurance Championship**
	Swansea	Glamorgan v Gloucestershire
	Maidstone	Kent v Essex
	Taunton	Somerset v Warwickshire
	The Oval	Surrey v Northamptonshire
	Hove	Sussex v Derbyshire
	Sheffield	Yorkshire v Nottinghamshire
		Tourist Match
	Southampton	Hampshire v India
		Other Match
	Lord's	Oxford Univ v Cambridge Univ
Thu 5		**CORNHILL INSURANCE TEST MATCH**
	Edgbaston	ENGLAND v NEW ZEALAND
		(Third Test Match)
Sat 7		**Britannic Assurance Championship**
	Liverpool	Lancashire v Derbyshire
	Leicester	*Leicestershire v Glamorgan
	Northampton	Northamptonshire v Yorkshire
	Trent Bridge	Nottinghamshire v Sussex
	The Oval	Surrey v Warwickshire
	Worcester	Worcestershire v Gloucestershire
		Tourist Match
	Canterbury	*Kent v India
Sun 8		**Refuge Assurance League**
	Southampton	Hampshire v Essex
	Old Trafford	Lancashire v Derbyshire
	Lord's	Middlesex v Somerset
	Tring	Northamptonshire v Yorkshire
	Trent Bridge	Nottinghamshire v Sussex
	The Oval	Surrey v Warwickshire
	Worcester	Worcestershire v Gloucestershire
Wed 11		**NatWest Bank Trophy**
		Second Round
(Possible fixtures subject to first round results)		
	Cardiff	Glamorgan v Sussex
	Northampton	Northants v Nottinghamshire
	Headingley	Yorkshire v Warwickshire
	Derby	Derbyshire v Lancashire
	Bristol	Gloucestershire v Kent
	Uxbridge	Middlesex v Surrey
	Chelmsford	Essex v Leics/Hampshire
	Taunton	Somerset v Worcestershire
		Tourist Match
		Minor Counties v India
Sat 14	Lord's	**BENSON & HEDGES CUP FINAL**
		Tourist Match
	Titwood, Glasgow	Scotland v India (one-day)
Sun 15		**Refuge Assurance League**
	Cheadle, Staffs	Derbyshire v Leicestershire
	Chelmsford	Essex v Northamptonshire
	Swindon or	
	Trowbridge	Gloucestershire v Sussex
	Southampton	Hampshire v Nottinghamshire
	Old Trafford	Lancashire v Worcestershire
	The Oval	Surrey v Middlesex
	Edgbaston	Warwickshire v Glamorgan
	Scarborough	Yorkshire v Somerset
Mon 16		**Tourist Match**
	Chesterfield	†Derbyshire v India (one-day)
Wed 18		**Texaco Trophy**
	Headingley	ENGLAND v INDIA
		(First One-day International)
		Britannic Assurance Championship
	Colchester	Essex v Derbyshire
	Portsmouth	Hampshire v Nottinghamshire
	Uxbridge	Middlesex v Yorkshire
	Northampton	Northamptonshire v Kent
	Guildford	Surrey v Sussex
	Coventry	Warwickshire v Lancashire
	Worcester	Worcestershire v Somerset

*Includes Sunday play

†Or another county if Derbyshire in B & H Cup Final

Fri 20		**Texaco Trophy**
	Trent Bridge	ENGLAND v INDIA
		(Second one-day International)
Sat 21		**Britannic Assurance Championship**
	Colchester	Essex v Lancashire
	Abergavenny	Glamorgan v Worcestershire
	Cheltenham	Gloucestershire v Yorkshire
	Portsmouth	Hampshire v Derbyshire
	Uxbridge	Middlesex v Somerset
	Northampton	Northamptonshire v Sussex
	Guildford	Surrey v Kent
		Tourist Match
	Leicester	*Leicestershire v India
Sun 22		**Refuge Assurance League**
	Colchester	Essex v Lancashire
	Newport	Glamorgan v Somerset
	Cheltenham	Gloucestershire v Yorkshire
	Portsmouth	Hampshire v Derbyshire
	Wellingborough	Northamptonshire v Sussex
	The Oval	Surrey v Kent
	Edgbaston	Warwickshire v Nottinghamshire
Wed 25		**Britannic Assurance Championship**
	Derby	Derbyshire v Worcestershire
	Swansea	Glamorgan v Warwickshire
	Cheltenham	Gloucestershire v Northamptonshire
	Canterbury	Kent v Middlesex
	Southport	Lancashire v Nottinghamshire
	Hinckley	Leicestershire v Essex
	Arundel	Sussex v Hampshire
	Scarborough	Yorkshire v Somerset
Thu 26		**CORNHILL INSURANCE TEST MATCH**
	Lord's	ENGLAND v INDIA
		(First Test Match)
Sat 28		**Britannic Assurance Championship**
	Chelmsford	Essex v Sussex
	Cheltenham	Gloucestershire v Surrey
	Canterbury	Kent v Worcestershire
	Old Trafford	Lancashire v Somerset
	Trent Bridge	Nottinghamshire v Middlesex
	Edgbaston	Warwickshire v Hampshire
	Sheffield	Yorkshire v Leicestershire
Sun 29		**Refuge Assurance League**
	Chelmsford	Essex v Sussex
	Neath	Glamorgan v Derbyshire
	Cheltenham	Gloucestershire v Surrey
	Canterbury	Kent v Worcestershire
	Old Trafford	Lancashire v Somerset
	Trent Bridge	Nottinghamshire v Northamptonshire
	Edgbaston	Warwickshire v Hampshire
	Sheffield	Yorkshire v Leicestershire
AUGUST		
Wed 1		**NatWest Bank Trophy**
		Quarter-finals
		Tourist Match
	The Oval or	
	Trent Bridge	Surrey or Nottinghamshire v India
Thu 2	Jesmond	England XI v Rest of the World XI (one-day)
Fri 3	Jesmond	England XI v Rest of the World XI (one-day)
Sat 4		**Britannic Assurance Championship**
	Chesterfield	Derbyshire v Kent
	Southend	Essex v Nottinghamshire
	Bournemouth	Hampshire v Northamptonshire
	Leicester	Leicestershire v Worcestershire
	Lord's	Middlesex v Glamorgan
	Weston-super-Mare	Somerset v Surrey
	Eastbourne	Sussex v Warwickshire
	Headingley	Yorkshire v Lancashire
		Tourist Match
	Bristol ·	*Gloucestershire v India
Sun 5		**Refuge Assurance League**
	Chesterfield	Derbyshire v Kent
	Southend	Essex v Nottinghamshire
	Bournemouth	Hampshire v Northamptonshire

*Includes Sunday play

	Leicester	Leicestershire v Worcestershire
	Lord's	Middlesex v Glamorgan
	Weston-super-Mare	Somerset v Surrey
	Eastbourne	Sussex v Warwickshire
	Scarborough	Yorkshire v Lancashire
Wed 8		**Britannic Assurance Championship**
	Chesterfield	Derbyshire v Northamptonshire
	Southend	Essex v Glamorgan
	Bristol	Gloucestershire v Warwickshire
	Bournemouth	Hampshire v Middlesex
	Dartford	Kent v Leicestershire
	Weston-super-Mare	Somerset v Nottinghamshire
	Eastbourne	Sussex v Yorkshire
	Kidderminster	Worcestershire v Lancashire
Thu 9		**CORNHILL INSURANCE TEST MATCH**
	Old Trafford	ENGLAND v INDIA
		(Second Test Match)
Sat 11		**Britannic Assurance Championship**
	Bristol	Gloucestershire v Kent
	Lord's	Middlesex v Sussex
	Northampton	Northamptonshire v Lancashire
	Worksop	Nottinghamshire v Glamorgan
	The Oval	Surrey v Leicestershire
	Worcester	Worcestershire v Hampshire
	Middlesbrough	Yorkshire v Essex
Sun 12		**Refuge Assurance League**
	Bristol	Gloucestershire v Kent
	Lord's	Middlesex v Sussex
	Northampton	Northamptonshire v Lancashire]
	Trent Bridge	Nottinghamshire v Glamorgan
	Weston-super-Mare	Somerset v Warwickshire
	The Oval	Surrey v Leicestershire
	Worcester	Worcestershire v Hampshire
	Middlesbrough	Yorkshire v Essex
Mon 13 or		
Tues 14		Bain Clarkson Trophy semi-finals (one-day)
Wed 15		**NatWest Bank Trophy**
		Semi-finals
		Tourist Match
	Edgbaston	TCCB Under 25 XI v India
Sat 18		**Britannic Assurance Championship**
	Derby	Derbyshire v Middlesex
	Chelmsford	Essex v Surrey
	Old Trafford	*Lancashire v Yorkshire (4 days)
	Trent Bridge	Nottinghamshire v Gloucestershire
	Taunton	*Somerset v Hampshire (4 days)
	Hove	Sussex v Kent
	Edgbaston	Warwickshire v Leicestershire
	Worcester	Worcestershire v Northamptonshire
		Tourist Match
	Swansea	*Glamorgan v India
Sun 19		**Refuge Assurance League**
	Derby	Derbyshire v Middlesex
	Chelmsford	Essex v Surrey
	Canterbury	Kent v Sussex
	Trent Bridge	Nottinghamshire v Gloucestershire
	Edgbaston	Warwickshire v Leicestershire
	Worcester	Worcestershire v Northamptonshire
Thu 23		**CORNHILL INSURANCE TEST MATCH**
	The Oval	ENGLAND v INDIA
		(Third Test Match)
		Britannic Assurance Championships (four days)
	Derby	Derbyshire v Essex
	Southampton	Hampshire v Surrey
	Leicester	Leicestershire v Kent
	Northampton	Northamptonshire v Gloucestershire

*Includes Sunday play

	Hove	Sussex v Somerset
	Worcester	Worcestershire v Warwickshire
	Headingley	Yorkshire v Middlesex
Sun 26		**Refuge Assurance League**
	Derby	Derbyshire v Essex
	Swansea	Glamorgan v Worcestershire
	Southampton	Hampshire v Surrey
	Old Trafford	Lancashire v Warwickshire
	Leicester	Leicestershire v Kent
	Northampton	Northamptonshire v Gloucestershire
	Hove	Sussex v Somerset
	Scarborough	Yorkshire v Middlesex
Wed 29		**Britannic Assurance Championship**
	Cardiff	Glamorgan v Derbyshire
	Bournemouth	Hampshire v Kent
	Blackpool	Lancashire v Surrey
	Leicester	Leicestershire v Sussex
	Northampton	Northamptonshire v Essex
	Trent Bridge	Nottinghamshire v Worcestershire

SEPTEMBER

Sat 1	Lord's	**NATWEST BANK TROPHY FINAL**
Mon 3		Bain Clarkson Trophy Final (one-day)
	Taunton	Somerset v Sri Lanka
Wed 5		**Refuge Assurance Cup**
		Semi-finals
Fri 7		**Britannic Assurance Championship** (four days)
	Chelmsford	*Essex v Northamptonshire
	Pontypridd	*Glamorgan v Hampshire
	Bristol	*Gloucestershire v Worcestershire
	Canterbury	*Kent v Surrey
	Lord's	*Middlesex v Nottinghamshire
	Edgbaston	*Warwickshire v Somerset
	Scarborough	*Yorkshire v Derbyshire
Wed 12		**Britannic Assurance Championship** (four days)
	Chelmsford	Essex v Kent
	Bristol	Gloucestershire v Sussex
	Leicester	Leicestershire v Northamptonshire
	Trent Bridge	Nottinghamshire v Lancashire
	Taunton	Somerset v Worcestershire
	The Oval	Surrey v Middlesex
	Edgbaston	Warwickshire v Glamorgan
Sun 16		**REFUGE ASSURANCE CUP FINAL**
Tues 18		**Britannic Assurance Championship** (four days)
	Derby	Derbyshire v Leicestershire
	Southampton	Hampshire v Gloucestershire
	Old Trafford	Lancashire v Warwickshire
	Trent Bridge	Nottinghamshire v Yorkshire
	The Oval	Surrey v Essex
	Hove	Sussex v Middlesex
	Worcester	Worcestershire v Glamorgan

*Includes Sunday play

CROQUET

1989

CONTINENTAL AIRLINES WORLD SINGLES CHAMPIONSHIPS
Hurlingham, Jul 16-23
Semi-finals
JOE HOGAN (NZ) beat David Openshaw (Eng) 2-0 (+26TP, +6); MARK AVERY (Eng) beat Colin Irwin (Ire) 2-1 (+26,-12,+14)
Final
HOGAN beat Avery 2-0 (+3; +3)

BRITISH OPEN
Hurlingham, Jul 16-23
Singles Final
Joe Hogan (NZ) beat Mark Avery (Eng) 2-0 (+3,+3)
Doubles Final
Joe Hogan & Bob Jackson (NZ) beat Robert Fulford & Chris Clarke (Eng) 2-1 (+26; -26;+26)

NATIONAL CHAMPIONSHIPS
Cheltenham, Jun 22
Men
Keith Aiton beat Dayal Gunasekera 2-1 (+26,-9,+2)
Women
Bo Harris beat Dab Wheeler 2-0 (+13,+14)
Mixed Doubles
Ian Maugham & Bo Harris beat Ian Bond & Veronica Carlisle 1-0 (+10)

HOME INTERNATIONAL CHAMPIONSHIP
Budleigh Salterton, Jun 5
1 England 2 Ireland 3 Wales 4 Scotland

BRITISH RANKINGS
Issued Aug 24
1 Steve Mulliner
2 Nigel Aspinall
3 Mark Avery
4 David Openshaw
5 William Prichard
6 Martin Murray

CHAMPIONS

WORLD CHAMPIONSHIP
Inaugurated 1989
1989 Joe Hogan (NZ)

OPEN SINGLES
Inaugurated 1867
Winners since 1980 (British unless stated)
1980 William Prichard
1981 David Openshaw
1982 Nigel Aspinall
1983 Nigel Aspinall
1984 Nigel Aspinall
1985 David Openshaw
1986 Joe Hogan (NZ)
1987 Mark Avery
1988 Steve Mulliner
1989 Joe Hogan (NZ)
Most wins
10 John Solomon 1953, 1956, 1959, 1961, 1963-68; 8 Nigel Aspinall 1969, 1974-76, 1978, 1982-84; 7 Humphrey

Hicks 1932, 1939, 1947-50, 1952; 5 Cyril Corbally 1902-03, 1906, 1908, 1913

OPEN DOUBLES
Inaugurated 1924
Winners since 1980
1980 William Prichard & Steve Mulliner
1981 Steve Mulliner & M Ormerod
1982 Martin Murray & A B Hope
1983 John McCullough & Phil Cordingley
1984 Nigel Aspinall & Steve Mulliner
1985 David Openshaw & Mark Avery
1986 Nigel Aspinall & Steve Mulliner
1987 David Openshaw & Mark Avery
1988 Nigel Aspinall & Steve Mulliner
1989 Joe Hogan & Bob Jackson (NZ)

NATIONAL CHAMPIONSHIPS
Men
Inaugurated 1925
Winners since 1980
1980 Martin Murray
1981 David Openshaw
1982 Martin Murray
1983 Nigel Aspinall
1984 Steve Mulliner
1985 Steve Mulliner
1986 David Foulser
1987 Keith Aiton
1988 Mark Saurin
1989 Keith Aiton

Most wins
10 John Solomon 1951, 1953, 1958-60, 1962, 1964-65, 1971-72; 9 Humphrey Hicks 1930, 1932, 1948-50, 1955-56, 1961, 1966

Women
Inaugurated 1869
Winners since 1980
1980 Mrs B Meachem
1981 Mrs H B H Carlisle
1982 Mrs W R D Wiggins (NZ)
1983 Mrs W R D Wiggins (NZ)
1984 Mrs H B H Carlisle
1985 Mary Collin
1986 Mrs W R D Wiggins (NZ)
1987 Mary Collin
1988 Debbie Cornelius
1989 Bo Harris

Most wins
15 Dorothy Steel 1919, 1922, 1925-27, 1929-30, 1932-39; 6 Mrs E Rotherham 1952-53, 1955, 1959, 1963-64; Miss E Warwick 1960, 1962, 1965-66, 1968-69

Mixed Doubles
Inaugurated 1899
Winners since 1980
1980 B C Sykes & Mrs B C Sykes
1981 Martin Murray & Mrs B Meachem
1982 Nigel Aspinall & Mrs C Knox
1983 Martin Murray & Mrs K G Yeoman
1984 Ian Bond & Mrs H B H Carlisle
1985 Keith Aiton & Mary Collin
1986 T Griffith & Jan Macleod
1987 Nigel Aspinall & Debbie Cornelius
1988 P J Smith & Lady Bazley
1989 Ian Maugham & Bo Harris

CYCLING

TWO, LEMOND

The American Greg LeMond won what was probably the most exciting Tour de France in its 86-year history, recapturing the lead from Laurent Fignon on the final time trial in Paris to take the Tour by eight seconds, having been 50 seconds down and apparently out the previous day.

There was huge excitement on the Champs Elysées as news came through of LeMond's exceptionally fast ride in the time trial. And when Fignon arrived everyone knew exactly what he had to do as the clock ticked away. When he just failed (and he still came third in the time trial) there was an enormous cheer; Fignon remains less than universally loved in his own country.

It was the closest-ever winning margin and only the second Tour when the lead had changed hands on the final day: in 1968 Jan Janssen of Holland caught Herman van Springel of Belgium. That, however, had been largely expected. Fignon had snatched the lead on L'Alpe d'Huez, the mountain where he took the yellow jersey in his winning years of 1983 and 84, and had boasted the night before entering Paris that he could not be caught. LeMond, the 1986 winner, had had a succession of problems ever since, including an emergency appendix operation, an ankle operation and being wounded by his brother in a shooting accident.

Pedro Delgado, the 1988 winner, came third. Delgado's efforts to catch up had provided a marvellous undercurrent to the Tour after he had lost almost three minutes at the start in Luxembourg because he was signing autographs. For a time he was *lanterne rouge* rather than *maillot jaune* but he moved up the field steadily until his efforts in the Pyrenees left him with little extra for the Alps.

Sean Kelly won the points prize for a record fourth time and his PDM team won every jersey except the yellow. For the second year running a Dutchman – Gert-Jan Theunisse – improbably became King of the Mountains. Fignon won the Prix Citron, awarded by press photographers to the least courteous rider, winning 35 votes out of 37. All 87 dope tests during the tour were negative.

LeMond then completed a rare double by winning the world road race championships in an equalling thrilling finish. After 6³/₄ hours round Chambery, six men dashed for the line and LeMond won by a wheel. He is the fourth man to complete the double after Louison Bobet, Eddy Merckx and Stephen Roche. None of them had been shot.

LeMond later signed a three-year, 5.5 million dollar contract with the French 'Z' Peugeot team. On the track at Lyons, the world championships were dominated by the East Europeans and the Italians but then 20-year-old Colin Sturgess of Britain beat the Australian Dean Woods in the 5 km professional individual pursuit. Sturgess, the youngest-ever winner, emulated two other Brits: Hugh Porter (winner four times) and Tony Doyle (twice). It was hardly an accident: "I've thought about being world champion since I was eight," he said.

It was a good year all round for British riders. Malcolm Elliott was the points winner of the Tour of Spain to become the first Briton ever to win a major award on a leading tour. Meanwhile, Sean Yates was the first British winner of the 81-year-old Tour of Belgium – by one second. Jeannie Longo of France won the World Championship pursuit, the points race and then the women's road race at Chambery to become the first female rider to win three golds at the same championships. She said she planned to retire.

1989

WORLD CHAMPIONSHIPS
Lyon/Chambery, France, Aug 14-27

Men-Professional
Sprint
1 Claudio Golinelli (Ita) 11.09s 11.05s
2 Yuichiro Kamiyami (Jap) –
3 Hideyami Matsui (Jap) –

Individual Pursuit
1 Colin Sturgess (GB) 5m 52.40s
2 Dean Woods (Aus) 5m 54.06s
3 Regis Clere (Fra) –

Kierin
1. Claudio Golinelli (Ita) 10.88s
2 Patrick Da Rocha (Fra) –
3 Masatoshi Sako (Jap) –

Motor Paced
1 Giovanni Renosto (Ita) 1h 00m 13.40s
2 Walter Brugna (Ita) at 2s
3 Torsten Rellensmann (FRG) at 4s

Points Race
1 Urs Freuler (Swi) 45pts
2 Gary Sutton (Aus) 39pts
3 Martin Penc (Cze) 33pts

Road Race
1 Greg LeMond (US) 6h 45m 59s
2 Dimitry Konychev (USSR) same time
3 Sean Kelly (Ire) same time

Men – Amateur
1 km Individual Time Trial
1 Jens Glücklich (GDR) 1m 04.032s
2 Martin Vinnicombe (Aus) 1m 04.950s
3 Alexandre Kiritchenko (USSR) 1m 05.060s

Individual Pursuit
1 Viatcheslav Ekimov (USSR) 4m 35.58s
2 Jens Lehmann (GDR) 4m 42.17s
3 Steffen Blochwitz (GDR) –

Team Pursuit
1 East Germany 4m 16.59s
2 USSR 4m 18.54s
3 Italy –

Sprint
1 Bill Huck (GDR) 11.71s 10.94s
2 Michael Hubner (GDR) –
3 Nikolai Kovsch (USSR) –

Points Race
1 Marat Satybaldiev (USSR) 52 pts
2 Fabio Baldato (Ita) 44 pts
3 Leo Peelen (Hol) 32 pts

Tandem
1 Fabrice Colas/Frédéric Magne (Fra) 20.52s 10.68s
2 Jiri Illek/Lubomir Hargas (Cze)
3 Andrea Faccini/Federico Paris (Ita)

Motor Paced
1 Roland Konigshoffer (Aut) 42m 32.19s
2 Tonino Vittigli (Ita) at 1 lap
3 Thomas Konigshoffer (Aut) at 1 lap, 2s

Road Team Time Trial
1 East Germany 2h 02m 36s
2 Poland 2h 03m 19s
3 USSR 2h 03m 37s

Road Race
1 Joachim Halupczok (Pol) 4 h 52m 54s
2 Eric Pichon (Fra) at 2m 54s
3 Christophe Manin (Fra) at 2m 58s

Women
Sprint
1 Erika Salumiae (USSR) 12.90s 11.95s
2 Galina Enuhina (USSR) –
3 Isabelle Gautheron (Fra) –

Pursuit
1 Jeannie Longo (Fra) 3m 54.45s
2 Petra Rossner (GDR) 3m 55.31s
3 Barbara Ganz (Swi) –

Points Race
1 Jeannie Longo (Fra) 35 pts
2 Barbara Ganz (Swi) 29 pts
3 Jayne Eickhoff (US) 28 pts

Road Team Time Trial
1 USSR 1h 08m 05s
2 Italy 1h 08m 05s
3 France 1h 08m 35s

Road Race
1 Jeannie Longo (Fra) 1h 56m 41s
2 Catherine Marsal (Fra) at 4m 05s
3 Maria Canins (Ita) at 4m 05s

Medal Table

	G	S	B	Total
France	4	3	4	11
USSR	4	3	3	10
East Germany	4	2	2	8
Italy	3	4	3	10
Switzerland	1	1	1	3
Austria	1	1	0	2
Poland	1	1	0	2
United States	1	0	1	2
Great Britain	1	0	0	1
Australia	0	3	0	3
Japan	0	1	2	3
Czechoslovakia	0	1	1	2
Holland	0	0	1	1
West Germany	0	0	1	1
Ireland	0	0	1	1

TOUR DE FRANCE
Started Luxembourg, July 1: Finished Paris July 23

Individual
1 Greg LeMond (US/ADR) 87h 38m 5s
2 Laurent Fignon (Fra/Super-U) at 8s
3 Pedro Delgado (Spa/Reynolds) at 3m 34s
4 Gert-Jan Theunisse (Hol/PDM) at 7m 30s
5 Marino Lejaretta (Spa/Paternina at 9m 39s
6 Charly Mottet (Fra/RMO) at 10m 6s
7 Steven Rooks (Hol/PDM) at 11m 10s
8 Raul Alcala (Mex/PDM) at 14m 21s
9 Sean Kelly (Ire/PDM) at 18m 25s
10 Robert Millar (GB/Z-Peugeot) at 18m 46s
11 Gianni Bugno (Ita/Château d'Ax) at 24m 21s
12 Eric Cartioux (Fra/RMO) at 28m 14s
13 Pascal Simon (Fra/Super-U) at 28m 28s
14 Bruno Cornillet (Fra/Z-Peugeot) at 28m 31s
15 Steve Bauer (Can/Helvetia) at 31m 16s

Team
1 PDM 263h 19m 48s; 2 Reynolds 263h 21m 7s; 3 Z-Peugeot 264h 4m 10s; 4 Super-U 264h 11m 14s; 5 RMO 264h 32m 07s; 6 Helvetia 264h 35m 14s.

Points:
1 Sean Kelly (Ire/PDM) 277 pts; 2 Etienne De Wilde (Bel/Histor); 3 Steven Rooks (Hol/PDM).

King of the Mountains:
1 Gert-Jan Theunisse (Hol/PDM) 441 pts; 2 Pedro Delgado (Spa/Reynolds); 3 Steve Rooks (Hol/PDM).

Stage Winners

	Stage Winner	Yellow Jersey
Prologue:	Eric Breukink (Hol/Panasonic)	Eric Breukink
Stage 1:	Acacio da Silva (Por/Carrera)	Acacio da Silva
Stage 2:	Super U (team time trial)	Acacio da Silva
Stage 3:	Raul Alcala (Mex/PDM)	Acacio da Silva
Stage 4:	Jelle Nijdam (Hol/Superconfex)	Acacio da Silva
Stage 5:	Greg LeMond (US/ADR)	Greg LeMond
Stage 6:	Joel Pelier (Fra/BH)	Greg LeMond
Stage 7:	Etienne de Wilde (Bel/Histor)	Greg LeMond
Stage 8:	Martin Earley (Ire/PDM)	Greg LeMond
Stage 9:	Miguel Indurain (Spa/Reynolds)	Greg LeMond
Stage 10:	Robert Millar (GB/Z-Peugeot)	Laurent Fignon
Stage 11:	Mathieu Hermans (Hol/Paternia)	Laurent Fignon
Stage 12:	Valérie Tebaldi (Ita/Château d'Ax)	Laurent Fignon
Stage 13:	Vincent Barteau (Fra/Super-U)	Laurent Fignon
Stage 14:	Jelle Nijdam (Hol/Superconfex)	Laurent Fignon
Stage 15:	Steven Rooks (Hol/PDM)	Greg LeMond
Stage 16:	Pascal Richard (Swi/Helvetia)	Greg LeMond
Stage 17:	Gert-Jan Theunisse (Hol/PDM)	Laurent Fignon
Stage 18:	Laurent Fignon (Fra/Super-U)	Laurent Fignon
Stage 19:	Greg LeMond (US/ADR)	Laurent Fignon
Stage 20:	Giovanni Fidanza (Ita/Château d'Ax)	Laurent Fignon
Stage 21:	Greg LeMond (US/ADR)	Greg LeMond

WOMEN'S TOUR DE FRANCE (Tour Féminin)
1 Jeannie Longo (Fra) 21h 59m 38s
2 Maria Canins (Ita) at 8m 44s
3 Inga Thompson (US) at 12m 24s

TOUR OF SPAIN
Apr 24 to May 15
1 Pedro Delgado (Spa) 93h 01m 17s
2 Fabbio Parra (Col) at 35s
3 Oscar Vargas (Col) at 3m 09s
4 Federico Echave (Spa) at 3m 24s
5 Alvaro Pino (Spa) at 4m 28s
6 Ivan Ivanov (USSR) at 5m 00s

TOUR OF ITALY
May 21 to Jun 11
1 Laurent Fignon (Fra) 93h 30m 16s
2 Flavio Giupponi (Ita) at 1m 15s
3 Andy Hampsten (US) at 2m 46s
4 Erik Breukink (Hol) at 5m 02s
5 Franco Chioccioli (Ita) at 5m 43s
6 Urs Zimmermann (Swi) at 6m 28s

KELLOGG'S TOUR OF BRITAIN
Aug 29 to Sep 3
Individual
1 Robert Millar (GB, Z-Peugeot) 20h 45m 10s
2 Mauro Gianetti (Swi, Helvetia) at 8s
3 Remig Stumpf (FRG, Toshiba) at 4m 22s
4 Martin Earley (Ire, PDM) at 4m 34s

5 Malcolm Elliott (GB, Teka) at 4m 45s
6 Paul Curren (GB, Percy Bilton) at 4m 57s
Team
1 Helvetia (Swi) 62h 30m 11s; 2 PDM (Hol) 62h 35m 15s; 3 Teka (Spa) 62h 35m 23s.

MILK RACE
May 28 to Jun 10
Individual
1 Brian Walton (Can) 43h 34m 41s
2 Keith Reynolds (GB) at 25s
3 Olaf Lurvik (Nor) at 48s
4 Kim Andersen (Den) at 59s
5 M Karlowicz (Pol) at 1m 05s
6 Nigel Bishop (GB) at 1m 16s
Team
1 Z-Peugeot 131h 56m 32s; 2 Great Britain at 1m 36s; 3 France at 3m 06s.

WORLD CYCLO CROSS CHAMPIONSHIPS
Pontchâteau, France, January 28/29,
Professional
1 Danny De Bie (Bel) 1h 00m 58s
2 Adri Van Der Poel (Hol) at 24sec
3 Christophe Lavainne (Fra) at 27 sec
Amateur
1 Ondrej Glajza (Cze) 54m 28 sec
2 R Simunek (Cze)
3 R Honegger (Swi)

═══ CHAMPIONS ═══

TOUR DE FRANCE

1903	Maurice Garin (Fra)	1914	Philippe Thys (Bel)	1929	Maurice de Waele (Bel)
1904	Henri Cornet (Fra)	1919	Firmin Lambot (Bel)	1930	André Leducq (Fra)
1905	Louis Trousselier (Fra)	1920	Philippe Thys (Bel)	1931	Antonin Magne (Fra)
1906	René Pottier (Fra)	1921	Leon Scieur (Bel)	1932	Andre Leducq (Fra)
1907	Lucien Petit-Breton (Fra)	1922	Firmin Lambot (Bel)	1933	Georges Speicher (Fra)
1908	Lucien Petit-Breton (Fra)	1923	Henri Pelissier (Fra)	1934	Antonin Magne (Fra)
1909	François Faber (Lux)	1924	Ottavio Bottecchia (Ita)	1935	Romain Maes (Bel)
1910	Octave Lapize (Fra)	1925	Ottavio Bottecchia (Ita)	1936	Sylvère Maes (Bel)
1911	Gustave Garrigou (Fra)	1926	Lucien Buysse (Bel)	1937	Roger Lapebie (Fra)
1912	Odile Defraye (Bel)	1927	Nicholas Frantz (Lux)	1938	Gino Bartali (Ita)
1913	Philippe Thys (Bel)	1928	Nicholas Frantz (Lux)	1939	Sylvère Maes (Bal)

POST-WAR WINNERS OF THE THREE MAJOR TOURS

	Tour de France	Tour of Italy	Tour of Spain
1947	Jean Robic (Fra)	Fausto Coppi (Ita)	E Van Dyck (Bel)
1948	Gino Bartali (Ita)	Fiorenzo Magni (Ita)	B Ruiz (Spa)
1949	Fausto Coppi (Ita)	Fausto Coppi (Ita)	–
1950	Ferdinand Kebler (Swi)	Hugo Koblet (Swi)	E Rodriquez (Spa)
1951	Hugo Koblet (Swi)	Fiorenzo Magni (Ita)	–
1952	Fausto Coppi (Ita)	Fausto Coppi (Ita)	–
1953	Louison Bobet (Fra)	Fausto Coppi (Ita)	–
1954	Louison Bobet (Fra)	Carlo Clerici (Swi)	–
1955	Louison Bobet (Fra)	Fiorenzo Magni (Ita)	J Dotto (Spa)
1956	Roger Walkowiak (Fra)	Charly Gaul (Lux)	A Contero (Ita)
1957	Jacques Anquetil (Fra)	Gastone Nencini (Ita)	J Lorono (Spa)
1958	Charly Gaul (Lux)	Ercole Baldani (Ita)	Jean Stablinski (Fra)
1959	Federico Bahamontès (Spa)	Charly Gaul (Lux)	A Suarez (Spa)
1960	Gastone Nencini (Ita)	Jacques Anquetil (Fra)	F de Mulder (Bel)
1961	Jacques Anquetil (Fra)	Arn Pambianco (Ita)	A Soler (Spa)
1962	Jacques Anquetil (Fra)	Franco Balmamion (Ita)	Rudi Altig (FRG)
1963	Jacques Anquetil (Fra)	Franco Balmamion (Ita)	Jacques Anquetil (Fra)
1964	Jacques Anquetil (Fra)	Jacques Anquetil (Fra)	Raymond Poulidor (Fra)
1965	Felice Gimondi (Ita)	Vittorio Ardoni (Ita)	R Wolfshohl (FRG)
1966	Lucien Aimar (Fra)	Gianni Motta (Ita)	F Gabicagogeascoa (Spa)
1967	Roger Pingeon (Fra)	Felice Gimondi (Ita)	Jan Janssen (Hol)
1968	Jan Janssen (Hol)	Eddy Merckx (Bel)	Felice Gimondi (Ita)
1969	Eddy Merckx (Bel)	Felice Gimondi (Ita)	Roger Pingeon (Fra)
1970	Eddy Merckx (Bel)	Eddy Merckx (Bel)	Luis Ocana (Spa)
1971	Eddy Merckx (Bel)	Gosta Petterson (Swe)	F Bracke (Bel)
1972	Eddy Merckx (Bel)	Eddy Merckx (Bel)	José-Manuel Fuente (Spa)
1973	Luis Ocana (Spa)	Eddy Merckx (Bel)	Eddy Merckx (Bel)
1974	Eddy Merckx (Bel)	Eddy Merckx (Bel)	José-Manuel Fuente (Spa)
1975	Bernard Thevenet (Fra)	F Bertoglio (Ita)	G Tamames (Spa)
1976	Lucien van Impe (Bel)	Felice Gimondi (Ita)	J Pesarrodona (Spa)
1977	Bernard Thevenet (Fra)	Michel Pollentier (Bel)	Freddie Maertens (Bel)
1978	Bernard Hinault (Fra)	Johan De Muynck (Bel)	Bernard Hinault (Fra)
1979	Bernard Hinault (Fra)	Giuseppe Saronni (Ita)	Joop Zoetemelk (Hol)
1980	Joop Zoetemelk (Hol)	Bernard Hinault (Fra)	Faustino Ruperez (Spa)
1981	Bernard Hinault (Fra)	Giovanni Bartaglin (Ita)	Giovanni Bartaglin (Ita)
1982	Bernard Hinault (Fra)	Bernard Hinault (Fra)	Marino Lejaretta (Spa)
1983	Laurent Fignon (Fra)	Giuseppe Saronni (Ita)	Bernard Hinault (Fra)
1984	Laurent Fignon (Fra)	Francesco Moser (Ita)	Eric Caritoux (Fra)
1985	Bernard Hinault (Fra)	Bernard Hinault (Fra)	Pedro Delgado (Spa)
1986	Greg LeMond (US)	Roberto Visentini (Ita)	Alvaro Pino (Spa)
1987	Stephen Roche (Ire)	Stephen Roche (Ire)	Luis Herrera (Col)
1988	Pedro Delgado (Spa)	Andy Hampsten (US)	Sean Kelly (Ire)
1989	Greg LeMond (US)	Laurent Fignon (Fra)	Pedro Delgado (Spa)

Most Wins

Tour de France: 5 Jacques Anquetil, Eddy Merckx, Bernard Hinault

Tour of Italy: 5 Alfredo Binda (Ita) 1925, 1927-29, 1933;
Fausto Coppi 1940, 1947, 1949, 1952-53; Eddy Merckx

Tour of Spain: 2 Gustave Deloor (Bel) 1935-36; Julio Barrendero (Spa) 1941-42; José-Manuel Fuente; Bernard Hinault; Pedro Delgado.

LEMOND'S CAREER HIGHLIGHTS

1979 World junior road race champion.

1980 Won Circuit de la Sarthe.

1981 Turned pro. Won Coors Classic.

1982 Won Tour de l'Avenir; second in world pro road race championship.

1983 Won world pro road race championship at Altenrhein.

1984 Third in Tour de France.

1985 Won Tour of Americas; second in Tour de France.

1986 Won Tour de France.

1989 Won Tour de France; won world pro road race championship at Chambery.

WOMEN'S TOUR DE FRANCE

(Inaugurated 1984)

1984	M Martin (US)
1985	Maria Canins (Ita)
1986	Maria Canins (Ita)
1987	Jeannie Longo (Fra)
1988	Jeannie Longo (Fra)
1989	Jeannie Longo (Fra)

WORLD PROFESSIONAL ROAD RACE CHAMPIONSHIP

(Post-war winners)

1946	Hans Knecht (Swi)
1947	Theo Middlekamp (Hol)
1948	Alberic Scotte (Bel)
1949	Rik van Steenbergen (Bel)
1950	Alberic Schotts (Bel)
1951	Ferdi Kubler (Swi)
1952	Heinz Muller (Ger)
1953	Fausto Coppi (Ita)
1954	Louison Bobet (Fra)
1955	Stan Ockers (Bel)

1956	Rik van Steenbergen (Bel)
1957	Rik van Steenbergen (Bel)
1958	Ercole Baldini (Ita)
1959	André Darrigade (Fra)
1960	Rik van Looy (Bel)
1961	Rik van Looy (Bel)
1962	Jean Stablinski (Fra)
1963	Renoni Beheyt (Bel)
1964	Jan Janssen (Hol)
1965	Tom Simpson (GB)
1966	Rudi Altig (FRG)
1967	Eddy Merckx (Bel)
1968	Vittorio Adorni (Ita)
1969	Harm Ottenbros (Hol)
1970	Jean-Pierre Monsère (Bel)
1971	Eddy Merckx (Bel)
1972	Marino Basso (Ita)
1973	Felice Gimondi (Ita)
1974	Eddy Merckx (Bel)
1975	Hennie Kuiper (Hol)
1976	Freddy Maertens (Bel)
1977	Francesco Moser (Ita)
1978	Gerrie Knetemann (Hol)
1979	Jan Raas (Hol)
1980	Bernard Hinault (Fra)
1981	Freddy Maertens (Bel)
1982	Giuseppe Saronni (Ita)
1983	Greg LeMond (US)
1984	Claude Criquielon (Bel)
1985	Joop Zoetemelk (Hol)
1986	Moreno Argentin (Ita)
1987	Stephen Roche (Ire)
1988	Maurizio Fondriest (Ita)
1989	Greg LeMond (US)

Most Wins
3 Alfredo Binda (Ita) 1927, 1930, 1932;
Rik van Steenbergen, Eddy Merckx

TOUR OF BRITAIN (Milk Race)

1951	Ian Steel (GB)
1952	Ken Russell (GB)
1953	Gordon Thomas (GB)
1954	Eugène Tamburlini (Fra)
1955	Anthony Hewson (GB)
1958	Richard Durlacher (Aut)
1959	Bill Bradley (GB)
1960	Bill Bradley (GB)
1961	Billy Holmes (GB)
1962	Eugen Pokorny (Pol)
1963	Peter Chisman (GB)
1964	Arthur Metcalfe (GB)
1965	Les West (GB)
1966	Josef Gawliczek (Pol)
1967	Les West (GB)
1968	Gosta Pettersson (Swe)
1969	Fedor Den Hertog (Hol)
1970	Jiri Mainus (Cs)
1971	Fedor Den Hertog (Hol)
1972	Hennie Kuiper (Hol)
1973	Piet van Katwijk (Hol)
1974	Roy Schuiten (Hol)
1975	Bernt Johansson (Swe)
1976	Bill Nickson (GB)
1977	Said Gusseinov (USSR)
1978	Jan Brzezny (Pol)
1979	Yuriy Kashirin (USSR)
1980	Ivan Mitchtenko (USSR)
1981	Sergey Krivocheyev (USSR)
1982	Yuriy Kashirin (USSR)
1983	Matt Eaton (USA)
1984	Oleg Czougeda (USSR)
1985	Eric van Lancker (Bel)
1986	Joey McLoughlin (GB)
1987	Malcolm Elliott (GB)
1988	Vasiliy Zhdanov (USSR)
1989	Brian Walton (Can)

KELLOGG'S TOUR OF BRITAIN
(Inaugurated 1987)

1987	Joey McLoughlin (GB)
1988	Malcolm Elliott (GB)
1989	Robert Millar (GB)

OLYMPIC GAMES
Men
1000 Metres Sprint

1896	Paul Masson (Fra)
1900	Georges Taillandier (Fra)
1908	No gold medal awarded
1920	Maurice Peeters (Hol)
1924	Lucien Michard (Fra)
1928	René Beaufrand (Fra)
1932	Jacobus van Egmond (Hol)
1936	Toni Merkens (Ger)
1948	Mario Ghella (Ita)
1952	Enzo Sacchi (Ita)
1956	Michel Rousseau (Fra)
1960	Sante Gaiardoni (Ita)
1964	Giovanni Pettenella (Ita)
1968	Daniel Morelon (Fra)
1972	Daniel Morelon (Fra)
1976	Anton Tkac (Cze)
1980	Lutz Hesslich (GDR)
1984	Mark Gorski (US)
1988	Lutz Hesslich (GDR)

1000 Metres Time Trial

1896	Paul Masson (Fra)
1928	Willy Falck-Hansen (Den)
1932	Edgar Gray (Aus)
1936	Arie van Vliet (Hol)
1948	Jacques Dupont (Fra)
1952	Russell Mockridge (Aus)
1956	Leandro Faggin (Ita)
1960	Sante Gaiardoni (Ita)
1964	Patrick Sercu (Bel)
1968	Pierre Trentin (Fra)
1972	Niels-Christian Fredborg (Den)
1976	Klaus-Jürgen Grunke (GDR)
1980	Lothar Thoms (GDR)
1984	Freddy Schmidtke (FRG)
1988	Alexander Kirchenko (USSR)

100 km Team Time Trial

1912	Sweden
1920	France
1924	France
1928	Denmark
1932	Italy
1936	France
1948	Belgium
1952	Belgium
1956	France
1960	Italy
1964	Holland
1968	Holland
1972	USSR
1976	USSR
1980	USSR
1984	Italy
1988	East Germany

4000 Metres Individual Pursuit

1964	Jiri Daler (Cze)
1968	Daniel Rebillard (Fra)
1972	Knut Knudsen (Nor)
1976	Gregor Braun (GDR)
1980	Robert Dill-Bundi (Swi)
1984	Steve Hegg (US)
1988	Giantautus Umarus (USSR)

4000 Metre Team Pursuit

1908	Great Britain
1920	Italy
1924	Italy

1928	Italy
1932	Italy
1936	France
1948	France
1952	Italy
1956	Italy
1960	Italy
1964	West Germany
1968	Denmark
1972	West Germany
1976	West Germany
1980	USSR
1984	Australia
1988	USSR

Points Races
| 1984 | Roger Ilegems (Bel) |
| 1988 | Dan Frost (Den) |

Road Race
1896	Aristidis Konstantinidis (Gre)
1912	Rudolph Lewis (SAf)
1920	Harry Stenqvist (Swe)
1924	Armand Blanchonnet (Fra)
1928	Henry Hansen (Den)
1932	Attilio Pavesi (Ita)
1936	Robert Charpentier (Fra)
1948	José Beyaert (Fra)
1952	André Noyelle (Bel)
1956	Ercole Baldini (Ita)
1960	Viktor Kapitonov (USSR)
1964	Mario Zanin (Ita)
1968	Pierfranco Vianelli (Ita)
1972	Hennie Kuiper (Hol)
1976	Bernt Johansson (Swe)
1980	Sergey Sukhoruchenkov (USSR)
1984	Alexi Grewal (US)
1988	Olaf Ludwig (GDR)

Women
1000 Metres Sprint
| 1988 | Erika Saloumiae (USSR) |

Road Race
| 1984 | Connie Carpenter-Phinney (US) |
| 1988 | Monique Knol (Hol) |

WORLD CHAMPIONS
(Since 1980)
(In Olympic years, if an event is included at the Games then it is not contested at the World Championships that year)

Men – Professional
Sprint
1980	Koichi Nakano (Jap)
1981	Koichi Nakano (Jap)
1982	Koichi Nakano (Jap)
1983	Koichi Nakano (Jap)
1984	Koichi Nakano (Jap)
1985	Koichi Nakano (Jap)
1986	Koichi Nakano (Jap)
1987	Nabuyuki Tawara (Jap)
1988	Stephen Pate (Aus)
1989	Claudio Golinelli (Ita)

Individual Pursuit
1980	Tony Doyle (GB)
1981	Alain Bondue (Fra)
1982	Alain Bondue (Fra)
1983	Steele Bishop (Aus)
1984	Hans-Henrik Oersted (Den)
1985	Hans-Henrik Oersted (Den)
1986	Tony Doyle (GB)
1987	Hans-Henrik Oersted (Den)
1988	Lech Piasecki (Pol)
1989	Colin Sturgess (GB)

Kierin
1980	Danny Clark (Aus)
1981	Danny Clark (Aus)
1982	Gordon Singleton (Can)
1983	Urs Freuler (Swi)
1984	Robert Dill-Bundi (Swi)
1985	Urs Freuler (Swi)
1986	Michel Vaarten (Bel)
1987	Hazuni Honda (Jap)
1988	Claudio Golinelli (Ita)
1989	Claudio Golinelli (Ita)

Motor Paced
1980	Wilfried Peffgen (FRG)
1981	Rene Kos (Hol)
1982	Martin Venix (Hol)
1983	Bruno Vicini (Ita)
1984	Horst Schutz (FRG)
1985	Bruno Vicini (Ita)
1986	Bruno Vicini (Ita)
1987	Max Hurzeler (Swi)
1988	Danny Clark (Aus)
1989	Giovanni Renosto (Ita)

Points Race
1980	Stan Tourne (Bel)
1981	Urs Freuler (Swi)
1982	Urs Freuler (Swi)
1983	Urs Freuler (Swi)
1984	Urs Freuler (Swi)
1985	Urs Freuler (Swi)
1986	Urs Freuler (Swi)
1987	Urs Freuler (Swi)
1988	Daniel Wyder (Swi)
1989	Urs Freuler (Swi)

Men – Amateur
1 km Individual Time Trial
1981	Lothar Thoms (GDR)
1982	Fredy Schmidteke (FRG)
1983	Sergey Kopylov (USSR)
1985	Jens Glücklich (GDR)
1986	Maik Malchow (GDR)
1987	Martin Vinnicombe (Aus)
1989	Jens Glücklich (GDR)

Individual Pursuit
1981	Detlef Macha (GDR)
1982	Detlef Macha (GDR)
1983	Viktor Kupovets (USSR)
1985	Vyacheslav Yekimov (USSR)
1986	Vyacheslav Yekimov (USSR)
1987	Guintautas Umaros (USSR)
1989	Vyacheslav Yekimov (USSR)

Team Pursuit
1981	East Germany
1982	USSR
1983	West Germany
1985	Italy
1986	Czechoslovakia
1987	USSR
1989	East Germany

Sprint
1981	Sergey Kopylov (USSR)
1982	Sergey Kopylov (USSR)
1983	Lutz Hesslich (GDR)
1985	Lutz Hesslich (GDR)
1986	Michael Hubner (GDR)
1987	Lutz Hesslich (GDR)
1989	Bill Huck (GDR)

Points Race
1981	Lutz Haueisen (GDR)
1982	Hans-Jaochim Pohl (GDR)
1983	Michael Marcussen (Den)

1985 Martin Penc (Cze)
1986 Dan Frost (Den)
1987 Marat Ganeev (USSR)
1989 Marat Satybaliev (USSR)

Tandem
1980 Ivan Kucirek & Pavel Martinek (Cze)
1981 Ivan Kucirek & Pavel Martinek (Cze)
1982 Ivan Kucirek & Pavel Martinek (Cze)
1983 Philippe Vernet & Frank Depine (Fra)
1984 Jürgen Greil & Frank Weber (FRG)
1985 Vitezlav Voboril & Roman Rekhousek (Cze)
1986 Vitezlav Voboril & Roman Rekhousek (Cze)
1987 Fabrice Colas & Frédéric Magne (Fra)
1988 Fabrice Colas & Frédéric Magne (Fra)
1989 Fabrice Colas & Frédéric Magne (Fra)

Motor Paced
1980 Gaby Minneboo (Hol)
1981 Matthe Pronk (Hol)
1982 Gaby Minneboo (Hol)
1983 Rainer Podlesch (GDR)
1984 Jan de Nijs (Hol)
1985 Roberto Dotti (Ita)
1986 Mario Gentilo (Ita)
1987 Mario Gentilo (Ita)
1988 Vincenzo Colamartino (Ita)
1989 Roland Konigshoffer (Aut)

Road Team Time Trial
1981 East Germany
1982 Netherlands
1983 USSR
1985 USSR
1986 Netherlands
1987 Italy
1989 East Germany

Road Race
1981 Andrey Vedernikov (USSR)
1982 Bernd Drogan (GDR)
1983 Uwe Raab (GDR)
1985 Lech Piasecki (Pol)
1986 Uwe Ampler (GDR)
1987 Richard Vivean (Fra)
1989 Joachim Halupczok (Pol)

Women
Sprint
1980 Sue Reber (US)
1981 Sheila Ochowitz (US)
1982 Connie Paraskevin (US)
1983 Connie Paraskevin (US)
1984 Connie Paraskevin (US)
1985 Isabelle Nicoloso (Fra)
1986 Christa Rothenburger (GDR)
1987 Erika Salumiae (USSR)
1989 Erika Salumiae (USSR)

Individual Pursuit
1980 Nadezhda Kibardina (USSR)
1981 Nadezhda Kibardina (USSR)
1982 Rebecca Twigg (US)
1983 Connie Carpenter (US)
1984 Rebecca Twigg (US)
1985 Rebecca Twigg (US)
1986 Jeannie Longo (Fra)
1987 Rebecca Twigg-Whitehead (US)
1988 Jeannie Longo (Fra)
1989 Jeannie Longo (Fra)

Points Race
1988 Sally Hodge (GB)
1989 Jeannie Longo (Fra)

Road Team Time Trial
1987 USSR
1988 Italy
1989 USSR

Road Race
1980 Beth Heiden (US)
1981 Ute Enzenauer (FRG)
1982 Mandy Jones (GB)
1983 Marianne Berglund (Swe)
1985 Jeannie Longo (Fra)
1986 Jeannie Longo (Fra)
1987 Jeannie Longo (Fra)
1989 Jeannie Longo (Fra)

CYCLO CROSS
WORLD CHAMPIONS
(Since 1980)

Professional
1980 Roland Liboton (Bel)
1981 Johannes Stamsnidjer (Hol)
1982 Roland Liboton (Bel)
1983 Roland Liboton (Bel)
1984 Roaldn Liboton (Bel)
1985 Klaus-Peter Thaler (FRG)
1986 Albert Zweifel (Swi)
1987 Klaus-Peter Thaler (FRG)
1988 Pascal Richard (Swi)
1989 Danny De Bie (Bel)

Most Wins:
7 Eric de Vlaeminck (Bel) 1966, 1968-73

Amateur
1980 Fritz Saladin (Swi)
1981 Milos Fisera (Cze)
1982 Milos Fisera (Cze)
1983 Radomir Simunek (Cze)
1984 Radomir Simunek (Cze)
1985 Mike Kluge (FRG)
1986 Vito di Tano (Ita)
1987 Mike Kluge (FRG)
1988 K Camrda (Cze)
1989 Ondrej Glajza (Cze)

Most Wins:
5 Robert Vermiere (Bel) 1970-71, 1974-75, 1977

———— RECORDS ————

TOUR DE FRANCE
Fastest winning speed:
23.51mph/37.83kph Bernard Hinault, 1981
Longest Race:
3569 miles/5745 km 1926
Closest finishes:
8 sec (1989) Greg LeMond won from Laurent Fignon, 38 sec (1968) Jan Janssen won from Herman Van Springel

———— 1990 ————

Apr 8: Paris to Roubaix; *Apr 24-May 5:* Tour of Spain; *May 18-Jun 6:* Tour of Italy; *May 27-Jun 9:* Milk Race (Britain); *Jun 24:* National road race championships; *Jun 30-Jul 22* TOUR DE FRANCE; *Jul 27-Aug 4:* National track championships (Leicester); *Jul 29:* Wincanton Classic/World Cup series (Newcastle); *Jul 31-Aug 5:* Professional Tour of Britain; *Aug 20-26:* World track championships (Japan); *Sep 1-2:* World professional road race championships (Japan).

DARTS

1988-89

EMBASSY WORLD PROFESSIONAL CHAMPIONSHIP
Frimley Green, Surrey, Jan 6-14

QUARTER-FINALS
Jocky Wilson beat Mike Gregory 4-3; Bob Anderson beat Dave Whitcombe 4-3; Eric Bristow beat Peter Everson 4-3; John Lowe beat Dennis Hickling 4-0.

SEMI-FINALS
Wilson beat Anderson 5-4; Bristow beat John Lowe 5-1

FINAL
Wilson beat Bristow 6-4

BRITISH OPEN
London, Dec 30-31

Men
SEMI-FINALS
Martin Hurley beat Cliff Lazarenko 4-2; Brian Cairns beat Ray Battye 4-0

FINAL
Cairns beat Battye 4-2

Women
SEMI-FINALS
Kathy McCullough beat Dawn Linguard 3-1; Elsie Halligan beat Deta Hedman 3-1

FINAL
McCullough beat Halligan 3-2

NEWS OF THE WORLD TOURNAMENT
Dave Whitcombe beat Dennis Priestley 2-0

CHAMPIONS

(All winners British unless otherwise stated)

EMBASSY WORLD PROFESSIONAL CHAMPIONSHIP
Venues: 1978 Heart of the Midlands Night Club, Nottingham; 1979-85 Jollees, Longton, Stoke-on-Trent; 1986- Lakeside Country Club, Frimley Green, Surrey.

Year	Winner	Runner-up
1978	Leighton Rees	John Lowe
1979	John Lowe	Leighton Rees
1980	Eric Bristow	Bobby George
1981	Eric Bristow	John Lowe
1982	Jocky Wilson	John Lowe
1983	Keith Deller	Eric Bristow
1984	Eric Bristow	Dave Whitcombe
1985	Eric Bristow	John Lowe
1986	Eric Bristow	Dave Whitcombe
1987	John Lowe	Eric Bristow
1988	Bob Anderson	John Lowe
1989	Jocky Wilson	Eric Bristow

BRITISH OPEN
1975	Alan Evans
1976	Jack North
1977	John Lowe
1978	Eric Bristow
1979	Tony Brown
1980	Cliff Lazarenko
1981	Eric Bristow
1982	Jocky Wilson
1983	Eric Bristow
1984	John Cusnett
1985	Eric Bristow
1986	Eric Bristow
1987	Bob Anderson
1988	John Lowe
1989*	Brian Cairns

*Held December 1988

NEWS OF THE WORLD CHAMPIONSHIP
Winners since 1980
1980	Stefan Lord (Swe)
1981	John Lowe
1982	Roy Morgan
1983	Eric Bristow
1984	Eric Bristow
1985	Dave Lee
1986	Bobby George
1987	Mike Gregory
1988	Mike Gregory
1989	Dave Whitcombe

WOMEN'S DARTS
BRITISH OPEN
1979	Judy Campbell
1980	Linda Batten
1981	Ann Marie-Davies
1982	Maureen Flowers
1983	Sandy Earnshaw
1984	Ann Marie Davies
1985	Linda Batten
1986	Gwen Sutton
1987	Sharon Colclough
1988	Jane Stubbs
1989	Kathy McCullough

"What does an idiot like Bristow do? His language is disgusting. His gut is a disgrace. The people who get honours are civil servants for just doing their jobs, political appointments and now darts players."
Tory MP Terry Dicks congratulating Eric Bristow on his MBE

"I'm gutted. I have no idea why he got this."
John Lowe ditto

"There are a lot of knockers. The top nobs think the honours list is a closed shop. They think it should go to their own. It's nice to see an ordinary working lad get it."
Eric Bristow

"He's boring. All he talks about is his house and his car. Still, for a welder, he's done well."
Bristow on Lowe

"It couldn't happen to a nicer fella."
Bristow on losing world championship final to Jocky Wilson

"The piano helps me wind down. I played Debussy's Arabesque and Beethoven's Für Elise after the first two rounds on Friday."
Mark Day, 17, after winning the British Youth Darts Championship.

1990

Jan 5-13: Embassy World Professional Championship (Lakeside Country Club, Frimley Green)

EQUESTRIANISM

1989

(All winners GB unless otherwise stated)

SHOW JUMPING
European Championships
Rotterdam, Aug 16-20
Individual
1 John Whitaker on Next Milton
2 Michael Whitaker on Next Monsanta
3 Joss Lansink (Fra) on Optibeurs Felix
Team
1 Britain
2 France
3 Switzerland
John and Michael Whitaker from Yorkshire became the first brothers to finish 1, 2 at the Championships, an achievement that eluded both the d'Inzeos and the Schockemohles.

Volvo World Cup
Final standings
1 Ian Millar (Can) on Big Ben
2 John Whitaker on Next Milton
3 George Lindemann (US) on Jupiter

Silk Cut Derby
Hickstead, Aug 3-6
1 Nick Skelton on Burmah Apollo
2 Joe Turi on Country Classics
3 Philip Heffer on Viewpoint

King George V Gold Cup
NEC, Birmingham, Jun 17
1 Michael Whitaker on Next Didi
2 John Whitaker on Next Milton
3 Johannes Tops (Hol) on Activate

Queen Elizabeth II Cup
NEC, Birmingham, Jun 17
1 Janet Hunter on Everest Lisnamarrow
2 Liz Edgar on Everest Rapier
3 Veronique Whitaker on Cogshall's Sport On

THREE-DAY EVENT
European Championships
Burghley, Sep 7-10
Individual
1 Virginia Leng on Master Craftsman
2 Jane Thelwall on King's Jester
3 Lorna Clarke on Fearliath Mor
Leng became the first rider to win three titles. Lucinda Green (née Prior-Palmer) is the only other rider to win even two. Britain had the top four riders and won the team event very easily.
Team
1 Britain
2 Holland
3 Ireland

Badminton Three-Day Event
(Whitbread Trophy)
Badminton, May 4-7
1 Virginia Leng on Master Craftsman
2 Mary Thomson on King Boris
3 Mark Todd (NZ) on The Irishman

DRESSAGE
European Championships
Mondorf les Bains, Luxembourg, Aug 2-6
Individual
1 Nicole Uphoff (FRG) on Rembrandt

2 Margit Otto-Crépin (Fra) on Corlandus
3 Anna-Kathrin Lisenhoff (FRG) on Courage
Team
1 West Germany
2 USSR
3 Switzerland

CHAMPIONS

OLYMPIC GAMES
Show Jumping
Individual

	Rider	Horse
1900	Aime Haegeman (Bel)	Benton II
1912	Jean Cariou (Fra)	Mignon
1920	Tommaso Lequio (Ita)	Trebecco
1924	Alphonse Gemuseus (Swi)	Lucette
1928	Frantisek Ventura (Cze)	Eliot
1932	Takeichi Nishi (Jap)	Uranus
1936	Kurt Hasse (Ger)	Tora
1948	Humberto Cortes (Mex)	Arete
1952	Pierre d'Oriola (Fra)	Ali Baba
1956	Hans-Gunter Winkler (Ger)	Halla
1960	Raimondo d'Inzeo (Ita)	Posillipo
1964	Pierre d'Oriola (Fra)	Lutteur B
1968	William Steinkraus (US)	Snowbound
1972	Graziano Mancinelli (Ita)	Ambassador
1976	Alwin Schockemohle (FRG)	Warwick Rex
1980	Jan Kowalczyk (Pol)	Artemor
1984	Joe Fargis (US)	Touch of Class
1988	Pierre Durand (Fra)	Jappeloup

Team
1912	Sweden
1920	Sweden
1924	Sweden
1928	Spain
1932	No medals awarded
1936	Germany
1948	Mexico
1952	Britain
1956	West Germany
1960	West Germany
1964	West Germany
1968	Canada
1972	West Germany
1976	France
1980	USSR
1984	United States
1988	West Germany

Most gold medals
5 Hans-Gunter Winkler (Team 1956, 1960, 1964, 1972; Individual 1956)

Three-Day Event
Individual

	Rider	Horse
1912	Axel Nordlander (Swe)	Lady Artist
1920	Helmer Morner (Swe)	Germania
1924	Adolph van der Voort van Zijp (Hol)	Silver Piece
1928	Charles P de Mortanges (Hol)	Marcroix
1932	Charles P de Mortanges (Hol)	Marcroix
1936	Ludwig Stubbendorff (Ger)	Nurmi
1948	Bernard Chevallier (Fra)	Aiglonne
1952	Hans von Blixen-Finecke (Swe)	Jubal
1956	Petrus Kastenman (Swe)	Iluster

1960	Lawrence Morgan (US)	Salad Days
1964	Mauro Checcoli (Ita)	Surbean
1968	Jean-Jacques Guyon (Fra)	Pitou
1972	Richard Meade (GB)	Laurieston
1976	Edmund Coffin (US)	Bally-Cor
1980	Federico Roman (Ita)	Rossinan
1984	Mark Todd (NZ)	Charisma
1988	Mark Todd (NZ)	Charisma

Team

1912	Sweden
1920	Sweden
1924	Holland
1928	Holland
1932	United States
1936	Germany
1948	United States
1952	Sweden
1956	Britain
1960	Australia
1964	Italy
1968	Britain
1972	Britain
1976	United States
1980	USSR
1984	United States
1988	West Germany

Most gold medals

4 Charles Pahud de Mortanges (Team 1924, 1928; Individual 1928, 1932)

Dressage
Individual

	Rider	Horse
1912	Carl Bonde (Swe)	Emperor
1920	Janne Lundblad (Swe)	Uno
1924	Ernst Linder (Swe)	Piccolomini
1928	Carl von Langen (Ger)	Draufganger
1932	Xavier Lesage (Fra)	Taine
1936	Heinz Pollay (Ger)	Kronos
1948	Hans Moser (Swi)	Hummer
1952	Henri St Cyr (Swe)	Master Rufus
1956	Henri St Cyr (Swe)	Juli
1960	Sergey Filatov (USSR)	Absent
1964	Henri Chammartin (Swi)	Woermann
1968	Ivan Kizimov (USSR)	Ichor
1972	Liselott Linsenhoff (FRG)	Piaff
1976	Christine Stuckelberger (Swi)	Granat
1980	Elisabeth Theurer (Aut)	Mon Chérie
1984	Reiner Klimke (FRG)	Ahlerich
1988	Nicole Uphoff (FRG)	Rembrandt

Team

1928	Germany
1932	France
1936	Germany
1948	France
1952	Sweden
1956	Sweden
1960	Not held
1964	West Germany
1968	West Germany
1972	USSR
1976	West Germany
1980	USSR
1984	West Germany
1988	West Germany

Most gold medals

4 Henri St Cyr (Team 1952, 1956; Individual 1952, 1956)

Juan Samaranch, the IOC President, said Barcelona would almost certainly not be able to stage equestrianism at the 1992 Olympics because of the spread of African horse plague into Spain. At least 270 horses died during August 1989 alone. A decision on whether to switch the events or cancel them is expected in late 1990.

WORLD CHAMPIONSHIPS
Show Jumping
Individual

	Rider	Horse
1953	Francisco Goyoago (Spa)	Quorum
1954	Hans-Günter Winkler (FRG)	Halla
1955	Hans-Günter Winkler (FRG)	Halla
1956	Raimondo d'Inzeo (Ita)	Merano
1960	Raimondo d'Inzeo (Ita)	Gowran Girl
1966	Pierre d'Oriola (Fra)	Pomone
1970	David Broome (GB)	Beethoven
1974	Hartwig Steenken (FRG)	Simona
1978	Gerd Wiltfang (FRG)	Roman
1982	Norbert Koof (FRG)	Fire II
1986	Gail Greenhough (Can)	Mr T

Women

	Rider	Horse
1965	Marion Coakes (GB)	Stroller
1970	Janou Lefèbvre (Fra)	Rocket
1974	Janou Tissot (née Lefèbvre) (Fra)	Rocket

Team

1978	Britain
1982	France
1986	United States

Three-Day Event
Individual

	Rider	Horse
1966	Carlos Moratorio (Arg)	Chalon
1970	Mary Gordon-Watson (GB)	Cornishman V
1974	Bruce Davidson (US)	Irish Cap
1978	Bruce Davidson (US)	Might Tango
1982	Lucinda Green (GB)	Regal Realm
1986	Virginia Leng (GB)	Priceless

Team

1966	Ireland
1970	Britain
1974	United States
1978	Canada
1982	Britain
1986	Britain

Dressage
Individual

	Rider	Horse
1966	Josef Neckermann (FRG)	Mariano
1970	Yelena Petouchkova (USSR)	Pepel
1974	Reiner Klimke (FRG)	Mehmed
1978	Christine Stuckelberger (Swi)	Granat
1982	Reiner Klimke (FRG)	Ahlerich
1986	Anne Grethe Jensen (Den)	Marzog

Team

1966	West Germany
1970	USSR
1974	West Germany
1978	West Germany
1982	West Germany
1986	West Germany

EUROPEAN CHAMPIONSHIPS
Show Jumping
Individual

	Rider	Horse
1957	Hans-Günter Winkler (FRG)	Sonnenglanz
1958	Fritz Thiedemann (FRG)	Meteor
1959	Piero d'Inzeo (Ita)	Uruguay
1961	David Broome (GB)	Sunsalve
1962	David Barker (GB)	Mister Softee
1963	Graziano Mancinelli (Ita)	Rockette
1965	Hermann Schridde (FRG)	Dozent
1966	Nelson Pessoa (Bra)	Gran Geste
1967	David Broome (GB)	Mister Softee
1969	David Broome (GB)	Mister Softee
1971	Hartwig Steenken (FRG)	Simona

1973	Paddy McMahon (GB)	Penwood Forge Mill
1975	Alwin Schockemohle (FRG)	Warwick
1977	Johan Heins (Hol)	Seven Valleys
1979	Gerhard Wiltfang (FRG)	Roman
1981	Paul Schockemohle (FRG)	Deister
1983	Paul Schockemohle (FRG)	Deister
1985	Paul Schockemohle (FRG)	Deister
1987	Pierre Durand (Fra)	Jappeloup
1989	John Whitaker (GB)	Next Milton

Women

	Rider	Horse
1957	Pat Smythe (GB)	Flanagan
1958	Giulia Serventi (Ita)	Doly
1959	Ann Townsend (GB)	Bandit
1960	Susan Cohen (GB)	Clare Castle
1961	Pat Smythe (GB)	Flanagan
1962	Pat Smythe (GB)	Flanagan
1963	Pat Smythe (GB)	Flanagan
1966	Janou Lefèbvre (Fra)	Kenavo
1967	Kathy Kusner (US)	Untouchable
1968	Anneli Drummond-Hay (GB)	Merely-a-Monarch
1969	Iris Kellett (Ire)	Morning Light
1971	Ann Moore (GB)	Psalm
1973	Ann Moore (GB)	Psalm

Team

1975	West Germany
1977	Holland
1979	Britain
1981	West Germany
1983	Switzerland
1985	Britain
1987	Britain
1989	Britain

Three-Day Event

Individual

	Rider	Horse
1953	Lawrence Rook (GB)	Starlight
1954	Albert Hill (GB)	Crispin
1955	Frank Weldon (GB)	Kilbarry
1957	Sheila Willcox (GB)	High and Mighty
1959	Hans Schwarzenbach (Swi)	Burn Trout
1962	James Templar (GB)	M'Lord Connolly
1965	Marian Babirecki (Pol)	Volt
1967	Eddie Boylan (Ire)	Durlas Eile
1969	Mary Gordon-Watson (GB)	Cornishman V
1971	HRH Princess Anne (GB)	Doublet
1973	Aleksandr Yevdokimov (USSR)	Jeger
1975	Lucinda Prior-Palmer (GB)	Be Fair
1977	Lucinda Prior-Palmer (GB)	George
1979	Nils Haagensen (Den)	Monaco
1981	Hansueli Schmutz (Swi)	Oran
1983	Rachel Bayliss (GB)	Mystic Minstrel
1985	Virginia Holgate (GB)	Priceless
1987	Virginia Leng (née Holgate) (GB)	Night Cap
1989	Virginia Leng (GB)	Master Craftsman

Team

1953	Britain
1954	Britain
1955	Britain
1957	Britain
1959	West Germany
1962	USSR
1965	USSR
1967	Britain
1969	Britain
1971	Britain
1973	West Germany
1975	USSR

1977	Britain
1979	Ireland
1981	Britain
1983	Sweden
1985	Britain
1987	Britain
1989	Britain

Dressage

Individual

	Rider	Horse
1963	Henri Chammartin (Swi)	Wolfdietrich
1965	Henri Chammartin (Swi)	Wolfdietrich
1967	Reiner Klimke (FRG)	Dux
1969	Liselott Linsenhoff (FRG)	Piaff
1971	Liselott Linsenhoff (FRG)	Piaff
1973	Reiner Klimke (FRG)	Mehmed
1975	Christine Stuckelberger (Swi)	Granat
1977	Christine Stuckelberger (Swi)	Granat
1979	Elisabeth Theurer (Aut)	Mon Chérie
1981	Uwe Schulten-Baumer (FRG)	Madras
1983	Anne Grethe Jensen (Den)	Marzog
1985	Reiner Klimke (FRG)	Ahlerich
1987	Margrit Otto-Crepin (Fra)	Corlandus
1989	Nicole Uphoff (FRG)	Rembrandt

Team

1963	Britain
1965-89	West Germany

OTHER MAJOR SHOW JUMPING COMPETITIONS

British Derby

Hickstead

1961	Seamus Hayes (Ire)	Goodbye III
1962	Pat Smythe (GB)	Flanagan
1963	Nelson Pessoa (Bra)	Gran Geste
1964	Seamus Hayes (Ire)	Goodbye III
1965	Nelson Pessoa (Bra)	Gran Geste
1966	David Broome (GB)	Mister Softee
1967	Marion Coakes (GB)	Stroller
1968	Alison Westwood (GB)	The Maverick VII
1969	Anneli Drummond-Hay (GB)	Xanthos
1970	Harvey Smith (GB)	Mattie Brown
1971	Harvey Smith (GB)	Mattie Brown
1972	Hendrick Snoek (FRG)	Shirokko
1973	Alison Dawes (née Westwood) (GB)	Mr Banbury
1974	Harvey Smith (GB)	Salvador
1975	Paul Darragh (Ire)	Pele
1976	Eddie Macken (Ire)	Boomerang
1977	Eddie Macken (Ire)	Boomerang
1978	Eddie Macken (Ire)	Boomerang
1979	Eddie Macken (Ire)	Boomerang
1980	Michael Whitaker (GB)	Owen Gregory
1981	Harvey Smith (GB)	Sanyo Video
1982	Paul Schockemohle (FRG)	Deister
1983	John Whitaker (GB)	Ryan's Son
1984	John Ledingham (Ire)	Gabhran
1985	Paul Schockemohle (FRG)	Lorenzo
1986	Paul Schockemohle (FRG)	Next Deister
1987	Nick Skelton (GB)	Raffles
1988	Nick Skelton (GB)	Apollo
1989	Nick Skelton (GB)	Burmah Apollo

King George V Gold Cup

First held 1911. Winners since 1980

1980	David Bowen (GB)	Scorton
1981	David Broome (GB)	Mr Ross
1982	Michael Whitaker (GB)	Disney Way
1983	Paul Schockemohle (FRG)	Deister
1984	Nick Skelton (GB)	St James
1985	Malcolm Pyrah (GB)	Towerlands Anglezark
1986	John Whitaker (GB)	Next Ryan's Son
1987	Malcolm Pyrah (GB)	Towerlands Anglezark

| 1988 | Robert Smith (GB) | Brook Street Boysie |
| 1989 | Michael Whitaker (GB) | Next Didi |

Most wins
5 David Broome 1960, 1966, 1972, 1977, 1981

Queen Elizabeth II Cup
First held 1949. Winners since 1980

1980	Caroline Bradley (GB)	Tigre
1981	Liz Edgar (GB)	Everest Forever
1982	Liz Edgar (GB)	Everest Forever
1983	Jean Germany (GB)	Mandingo
1984	Veronique Whitaker (GB)	Next's Jingo
1985	Sue Pountain (GB)	Ned Kelly
1986	Liz Edgar (GB)	Everest Rapier
1987	Gillian Greenwood (GB)	Monsanta
1988	Janet Hunter (GB)	Everest Lisnamarrow
1989	Janet Hunter (GB)	Everest Lisnamarrow

Most wins
5 Liz Edgar 1977, 1979, 1981-82, 1986

Volvo World Cup
Inaugurated 1979

1979	Hugo Simon (Aut)	Gladstone
1980	Conrad Homfeld (US)	Balbuco
1981	Mike Matz (US)	Jet Run
1982	Melanie Smith (US)	Calypso
1983	Norman Dello Joio (US)	I Love You
1984	Mario Deslauriers (Can)	Aramis
1985	Conrad Homfeld (US)	Abdullah
1986	Leslie Burr-Lenehan (US)	McLain
1987	Katharine Burdsall (US)	The Natural
1988	Ian Millar (Can)	Big Ben
1989	Ian Millar (Can)	Big Ben

Nations Cup
(Gucci Cup)
Inaugurated 1947. Winners since 1980

1980	France
1981	West Germany
1982	West Germany
1983	Britain
1984	West Germany
1985	Britain
1986	Britain
1987	France
1988	France
1989	Britain

Three-Day Event
Badminton
(1956 event at Windsor)

1949	John Shedden (GB)	Golden Willow
1950	Tony Collings (GB)	Remus
1951	Hans Schwarzenbach (Swi)	Vae Victus
1952	Mark Darley (Ire)	Emily Little
1953	Lawrence Rook (GB)	Starlight
1954	Margaret Hough (GB)	Bambi
1955	Frank Weldon (GB)	Kilbarry
1956	Frank Weldon (GB)	Kilbarry
1957	Sheila Willcox (GB)	High and Mighty
1958	Sheila Willcox (GB)	High and Mighty
1959	Sheila Waddington (née Willcox) (GB)	Airs and Graces
1960	Bill Roycroft (Aus)	Our Solo
1961	Lawrence Morgan (Aus)	Salad Days
1962	Anneli Drummond-Hay (GB)	Merely-a-Monarch
1963	Susan Fleet (GB)	Gladiator#
1964	James Templer (GB)	M'Lord Connolly
1965	Eddie Boylan (Ire)	Durlas Eile
1966	Not held	

1967	Celia Ross-Taylor (GB)	Jonathan
1968	Jane Bullen (GB)	Our Nobby
1969	Richard Walker (GB)	Pasha
1970	Richard Meade (GB)	The Poacher
1971	Mark Phillips (GB)	Great Ovation
1972	Mark Phillips (GB)	Great Ovation
1973	Lucinda Prior-Palmer (GB)	Be Fair
1974	Mark Phillips (GB)	Columbus
1975	Cancelled after dressage	
1976	Lucinda Prior-Palmer (GB)	Wideawake
1977	Lucinda Prior-Palmer (GB)	George
1978	Jane Holderness-Roddam (née Bullen) (GB)	Warrior
1979	Lucinda Prior-Palmer (GB)	Killaire
1980	Mark Todd (NZ)	Southern Comfort
1981	Mark Phillips (GB)	Lincoln
1982	Richard Meade (GB)	Speculator III
1983	Lucinda Green (née Prior-Palmer) (GB)	Regal Realm
1984	Lucinda Green (GB)	Beagle Bay
1985	Virginia Holgate (GB)	Priceless
1986	Ian Stark (GB)	Sir Wattie
1987	cancelled	
1988	Ian Stark (GB)	Sir Wattie
1989	Virginia Leng (GB)	Master Craftsman

reduced to a One-Day Event because of the weather

Burghley Horse Trials

1961	Anneli Drummond-Hay (GB)	Merely-a-Monarch
1962	European Championship	
1963	Harry Freeman-Jackson (Ire)	St Finbar
1964	Richard Meade (GB)	Barberry
1965	Jeremy Beale (GB)	Victoria Bridge
1966	World Championship	
1967	Lorna Sutherland (GB)	Popadom
1968	Sheila Willcox (GB)	Fair and Square
1969	Gillian Watson (GB)	Shaitan
1970	Judy Bradwell (GB)	Don Camillo
1971	European Championship	
1972	Janet Hodgson (GB)	Larkspur
1973	Mark Phillips (GB)	Maid Marion
1974	World Championship	
1975	Aly Pattinson (GB)	Carawich
1976	Jane Holderness-Roddam (GB)	Warrior
1977	Lucinda Prior-Palmer (GB)	George
1978	Lorna Clarke (née Sutherland) (GB)	Greco
1979	Andrew Hoy (Aus)	Davy
1980	Richard Walker (GB)	John of Gaunt
1981	Lucinda Prior-Palmer (GB)	Beagle Bay
1982	Richard Walker (GB)	Ryan's Cross
1983	Virginia Holgate (GB)	Priceless
1984	Virginia Holgate (GB)	Night Cap
1985	European Championship	
1986	Virginia Leng (née Holgate) (GB)	Murphy Himself
1987	Mark Todd (NZ)	Wilton Fair
1988	Jane Thelwall (GB)	Kings Jester
1989	European Championship	

— 1990 —

May 3-6: Badminton Horse Trials (Badminton); May 31-Jun 3: Nations Cup meeting (Hickstead); Jun 14-17: Royal International Horse Show (NEC, Birmingham); Jul 24-Aug 5: World Equestrian Games (Stockholm); Aug 23-27: British Jumping Derby (Hickstead); Sep 6-9: Burghley Horse Trials (Burghley); Oct 1-6 Horse of the Year Show (Wembley); Dec 13-17: Olympia International championships (Olympia).

FENCING

1989

WORLD CHAMPIONSHIPS
Denver, Colorado, Jul 5-16

Men - Individual

FOIL
1 Alexander Koch (FRG)
2 Philippe Omnes (Fra)
3 Mauro Numa (Ita)

EPEE
1 Manuel Pereira (Spa)
2 Sandro Cumo (Ita)
3 Pavel Kolobkov (USSR)

SABRE
1 Grigory Kirienko (USSR)
2 Jaroslaw Koniusz (Pol)
3 Felix Becker (FRG)

Men - Team

FOIL
1 USSR
2 West Germany
3 France

EPEE
1 Italy
2 West Germany
3 Cuba

SABRE
1 USSR
2 West Germany
3 France

Women - Individual

FOIL
1 Olga Velitchko (USSR)
2 Anja Fichtel (FRG)
3 Zita Funkenhauser (FRG)

EPEE
1 Anja Straub (Swi)
2 Ute Schaeper (FRG)
3 Annalisa Coltori (Ita)

Women - Team

FOIL
1 West Germany
2 USSR
3 Italy

EPEE
1 Hungary
2 Italy
3 Switzerland

NATIONAL CHAMPIONSHIPS
All at the de Beaumont Centre, West Kensington

MEN'S FOIL
1 Donald McKenzie (Meadowbank)
2 David Seaman (Salle Goodall)
3 Austin Royle (Stockport)

MEN'S SABRE
1 Ian Williams (London Thames)
2 Tarek Yassir (London Thames)
3 Mark Slade (London Thames)

MEN'S EPEE
1 Hugh Kernohan (Boston)
2 Tony Perity (Boston)
3 Quentin Berriman (Boston)

WOMEN'S FOIL
1 Fiona McIntosh (Paul)
2 Linda Martin (Paul)
3 Amanda Ferguson (Ashton)

WOMEN'S EPEE
1 Penny Tomlinson (London Thames)
2 Alda Milner Barry (London Thames)
3 Teresa Purton (Gloucester)

The electric sabre was used for the first time at the Denver world championships, allowing the finals to be concluded in a rapid 2½ hours. Previously, sabre touches were called by five officials and often followed by lengthy arguments.

CHAMPIONS

OLYMPIC GAMES

Men

FOIL

	Individual	Team
1896	Emile Gravelotte (Fra)	-
1900	Emile Coste (Fra)	-
1904	Ramon Fonst (Cub)	Cuba
1908	Not held	
1912	Nedo Nadi (Ita)	-
1920	Nedo Nadi (Ita)	Italy
1924	Roger Ducret (Fra)	France
1928	Lucien Gaudin (Fra)	Italy
1932	Gustavo Marzi	France
1936	Giulio Gaudini (Ita)	Italy
1948	Jean Buhan (Fra)	France
1952	Christian d'Oriola (Fra)	France
1956	Christian d'Oriola (Fra)	Italy
1960	Viktor Zhdanovich (USSR)	USSR
1964	Egon Franke (Pol)	USSR
1968	Ion Drimba (Rom)	France
1972	Witold Woyda (Pol)	Poland
1976	Fabio Dal Zotto (Ita)	West Germany
1980	Vladimir Smirnov (USSR)	France
1984	Mauro Numa (Ita)	Italy
1988	Stefano Cerioni (Ita)	USSR

SABRE

	Individual	Team
1896	Jean Georgiadis (Gre)	-
1900	Georges de la Falaise (Fra)	-
1904	Manuel Diaz (Cub)	-
1908	Jeno Fuchs (Hun)	Hungary
1912	Jeno Fuchs (Hun)	Hungary
1920	Nedo Nadi (Ita)	Italy
1924	Sandor Posta (Hun)	Italy
1928	Odon Tersztyanszky (Hun)	Hungary
1932	Gyorgy Piller (Hun)	Hungary
1936	Endre Kabos (Hun)	Hungary

1948	Aladar Gerevich (Hun)	Hungary
1952	Pal Kovacs (Hun)	Hungary
1956	Rudolf Karpati (Hun)	Hungary
1960	Rudolf Karpati (Hun)	Hungary
1964	Tibor Pezsa (Hun)	USSR
1968	Jerzy Pawlowski (Pol)	USSR
1972	Viktor Sidiak (USSR)	Italy
1976	Viktor Krovopuskov (USSR)	USSR
1980	Viktor Krovopuskov (USSR)	USSR
1984	Jean-François Lamour (Fra)	Italy
1988	Jean-François Lamour (Fra)	Hungary

EPEE
First held 1900

	Individual	*Team*
1900	Ramon Fonst (Cub)	-
1904	Ramon Fonst (Cub)	-
1908	Gaston Alibert (Fra)	France
1912	Paul Anspach (Bel)	Belgium
1920	Armand Massard (Fra)	Italy
1924	Charles Delport (Bel)	France
1928	Lucien Gaudin (Fra)	Italy
1932	Giancarlo Cornaggia-Medici (Ita)	France
1936	Franco Riccardi (Ita)	Italy
1948	Luigi Cantone (Ita)	France
1952	Edoardo Mangiarotti (Ita)	Italy
1956	Carlo Pavesi (Ita)	Italy
1960	Giuseppe Delfino (Ita)	Italy
1964	Grigoriy Kriss (USSR)	Hungary
1968	Gyozo Kulcsar (Hun)	Hungary
1972	Csaba Fenyvesi (Hun)	Hungary
1976	Alexander Pusch (FRG)	Sweden
1980	Johan Harmenberg (Swe)	France
1984	Philippe Boisse (Fra)	W. Germany
1988	Arnd Schmitt (FRG)	France

Women

FOIL (only)

	Individual	*Team*
1924	Ellen Osiier (Den)	-
1928	Helene Mayer (Ger)	-
1932	Ellen Preis (Aut)	-
1936	Ilona Elek (Hun)	-
1948	Ilona Elek (Hun)	-
1952	Irene Camber (Ita)	-
1956	Gillian Sheen (GB)	-
1960	Heidi Schmid (W.Ger)	USSR
1964	Ildiko Ujlaki-Rejto (Hun)	Hungary
1968	Yelena Novikova (USSR)	USSR
1972	Antonella Ragno-Lonzi (Ita)	USSR
1976	Ildiko Schwarczenberger (Hun)	USSR
1980	Pascale Trinquet (Fra)	France
1984	Luan Jujie (Chn)	W.Germany
1988	Anja Fichtel (FRG)	W.Germany

WORLD CHAMPIONSHIPS
(in the 1980s)
Olympic champions are automatic world champions

Men

FOIL

	Individual	*Team*
1981	Vladimir Smirnov (USSR)	USSR
1982	Aleksandr Romankov (USSR)	USSR
1983	Aleksandr Romankov (USSR)	W.Germany
1985	Mauro Numa (Ita)	Italy
1986	Andrea Borella (Ita)	USSR
1987	Mathias Gey (FRG)	USSR
1989	Alexander Koch (FRG)	USSR

SABRE

1981	Mariusz Wodke (Pol)	Hungary
1982	Viktor Krovopuskov (USSR)	Hungary
1983	Vasiliy Etropolski (Bul)	USSR
1985	Gyorgy Nebald (Hun)	USSR
1986	Sergey Mindirgassov (USSR)	USSR
1987	Jean-Francois Lamour (Fra)	USSR
1989	Grigoriy Kirienko (USSR)	USSR

EPEE

1981	Zoltan Szekely (Hun)	USSR
1982	Jeno Pap (Hun)	France
1983	Ellmar Bormann (FRG)	France
1985	Phillippe Boisse (Fra)	W.Germany
1986	Philippe Riboud (Fra)	W.Germany
1987	Volker Fischer (FRG)	W.Germany
1989	Manuel Pereira (Spa)	Italy

Women

FOIL

1981	Cornelia Hanisch (FRG)	USSR
1982	Nalia Galiazova (USSR)	Italy
1983	Dorina Vaccoroni	Italy
1985	Cornelia Hanisch (FRG)	W.Germany
1986	Anja Fichtel (FRG)	USSR
1987	Elisabeta Tufan (Rom)	Hungary
1989	Olga Velitchko (USSR)	W.Germany

EPEE

1989	Anja Straub (Swi)	Hungary

———— FIXTURES 1990 ————

Feb 10: Men's National Epee Championship (de Beaumont Centre, London); *May 12-13:* Men's and Women's National Foil Championships (Sheffield); *May 26-27:* Women's National Epee Championships (de Beaumont Centre); *Jul 6-16:* World Championship (Lyon)

GAELIC SPORTS

1989

ALL-IRELAND HURLING CHAMPIONSHIP
Semi-finals
Antrim beat Offaly 4-15 (27) to 1-15 (18); Tipperary beat Galway 1-17 (20) to 2-11 (17)
Final
Croke Park, Dublin, Sep 3
Tipperary beat Antrim 4-29 (41) to 3-9 (18)

ALL-IRELAND GAELIC FOOTBALL CHAMPIONSHIP
Semi-finals
Cork beat Dublin 2-10 (16) to 1-9 (12); Mayo beat Tyrone 0-12 (12) to 1-6 (9)
Final
Croke Park, Dublin, Sep 17
Cork beat Mayo 0-17 (17) to 1-11 (14)

CHAMPIONS

ALL-IRELAND HURLING CHAMPIONS

1887	Tipperary (Tiobrad Arann)
1889	Dublin (Ath Cliath)
1890	Cork (Corcaigh)
1891	Kerry (Ciarraidhe)
1892	Cork (Corcaigh)
1893	Cork (Corcaigh)
1894	Cork (Corcaigh)
1895	Tipperary (Tiobrad Arann)
1896	Tipperary (Tiobrad Arann)
1897	Limerick (Luimneach)
1898	Tipperary (Tiobrad Arann)
1899	Tipperary (Tiobrad Arann)
1900	Tipperary (Tiobrad Arann)
1901	London Irish (Lonndain)
1902	Cork (Corcaigh)
1903	Cork (Corcaigh)
1904	Kilkenny (Cill Chainnigh)
1905	Kilkenny (Cill Chainnigh)
1906	Tipperary (Tiobrad Arann)
1907	Kilkenny (Cill Chainnigh)
1908	Tipperary (Tiobrad Arann)
1909	Kilkenny (Cill Chainnigh)
1910	Wexford (Loch Garman)
1911	Kilkenny (Cill Chainnigh)
1912	Kilkenny (Cill Chainnigh)
1913	Kilkenny (Cill Chainnigh)
1914	Clare (An Clar)
1915	Laois (Laois)
1916	Tipperary (Tiobrad Arann)
1917	Dublin (Ath Cliath)
1918	Limerick (Luimneach)
1919	Cork (Corcaigh)
1920	Dublin (Ath Cliath)
1921	Limerick (Luimneach)
1922	Kilkenny (Cill Chainnigh)
1923	Galway (Gaillimh)
1924	Dublin (Ath Cliath)
1925	Tipperary (Tiobrad Arann)
1926	Cork (Corcaigh)
1927	Dublin (Ath Cliath)
1928	Cork (Corcaigh)
1929	Cork (Corcaigh)
1930	Tipperary (Tiobrad Arann)
1931	Cork (Corcaigh)
1932	Kilkenny (Cill Chainnigh)
1933	Kilkenny (Cill Chainnigh)
1934	Limerick (Luimneach)
1935	Kilkenny (Cill Chainnigh)
1936	Limerick (Luimneach)
1937	Tipperary (Tiobrad Arann)
1938	Dublin (Ath Cliath)
1939	Kilkenny (Cill Chainnigh)
1940	Limerick (Luimneach)
1941	Cork (Corcaigh)
1942	Cork (Corcaigh)
1943	Cork (Corcaigh)
1944	Cork (Corcaigh)
1945	Tipperary (Tiobrad Arann)
1946	Cork (Corcaigh)
1947	Kilkenny (Cill Chainnigh)
1948	Waterford (Port Lairge)
1949	Tipperary (Tiobrad Arann)
1950	Tipperary (Tiobrad Arann)
1951	Tipperary (Tiobrad Arann)
1952	Cork (Corcaigh)
1953	Cork (Corcaigh)
1954	Cork (Corcaigh)
1955	Wexford (Loch Garman)
1956	Wexford (Loch Garman)
1957	Kilkenny (Cill Chainnigh)
1958	Tipperary (Tiobrad Arann)
1959	Waterford (Port Lairge)
1960	Wexford (Loch Garman)
1961	Tipperary (Tiobrad Arann)
1962	Tipperary (Tiobrad Arann)
1963	Kilkenny (Cill Chainnigh)
1964	Tipperary (Tiobrad Arann)
1965	Tipperary (Tiobrad Arann)
1966	Cork (Corcaigh)
1967	Kilkenny (Cill Chainnigh)
1968	Wexford (Loch Garman)
1969	Kilkenny (Cill Chainnigh)
1970	Cork (Corcaigh)
1971	Tipperary (Tiobrad Arann)
1972	Kilkenny (Cill Chainnigh)
1973	Limerick (Luimneach)
1974	Kilkenny (Cill Chainnigh)
1975	Kilkenny (Cill Chainnigh)
1976	Cork (Corcaigh)
1977	Cork (Corcaigh)
1978	Cork (Corcaigh)
1979	Kilkenny (Cill Chainnigh)
1980	Galway (Gaillimh)
1981	Offaly (Uibh Fhrili)
1982	Kilkenny (Cill Chainnigh)
1983	Kilkenny (Cill Chainnigh)
1984	Cork (Corcaigh)
1982	Offaly (Uibh Fhrili)
1986	Cork (Corcaigh)
1987	Galway (Gaillimh)
1988	Galway (Gaillimh)
1989	Tipperary (Tiobrad Arann)

Wins
26 Cork; 23 Tipperary, Kilkenny; 7 Limerick; 6 Dublin; 5 Wexford; 4 Galway; 2 Waterford, Offaly; 1 Kerry, London Irish, Clare, Laois

ALL-IRELAND GAELIC FOOTBALL CHAMPIONS

1887	Limerick (Luimneach)
1889	Tipperary (Tiobrad Arann)
1890	Cork (Corcaigh)
1891	Dublin (Ath Cliath)
1892	Dublin (Ath Cliath)
1893	Wexford (Loch Garmen)
1894	Dublin (Ath Cliath)
1895	Tipperary (Tiobrad Arann)
1896	Limerick (Luimneach)
1897	Dublin (Ath Cliath)
1898	Dublin (Ath Cliath)
1899	Dublin (Ath Cliath)
1900	Tipperary (Tiobrad Arann)
1901	Dublin (Ath Cliath)
1902	Dublin (Ath Cliath)
1903	Kerry (Ciarraidhe)
1904	Kerry (Ciarraidhe)
1905	Kildare (Cill Dara)
1906	Dublin (Ath Cliath)
1907	Dublin (Ath Cliath)
1908	Dublin (Ath Cliath)
1909	Kerry (Ciarraidhe)
1910	Louth (Lughbhaidh)
1911	Cork (Corcaigh)
1912	Louth (Lughbhaidh) ·
1913	Kerry (Ciarraidhe)
1914	Kerry (Ciarraidhe)
1915	Wexford (Loch Garman)
1916	Wexford (Loch Garman)
1917	Wexford (Loch Garman)
1918	Wexford (Loch Garman)
1919	Kildare (Cill Dara)
1920	Tipperary (Tiobrad Arann)
1921	Dublin (Ath Cliath)
1922	Dublin (Ath Cliath)
1923	Dublin (Ath Cliath)
1924	Kerry (Ciarraidhe)
1925	Galway (Gaillimh)
1926	Kerry (Ciarraidhe)
1927	Kildare (Cill Dara)
1928	Kildare (Cill Dara)
1929	Kerry (Ciarraidhe)
1930	Kerry (Ciarraidhe)
1931	Kerry (Ciarraidhe)
1932	Kerry (Ciarraidhe)
1933	Cavan (Cabhan)
1934	Galway (Gaillimh)
1935	Cavan (Cabhan)
1936	Mayo (Muigheo)
1937	Kerry (Ciarraidhe)
1938	Galway (Gaillimh)
1939	Kerry (Ciarraidhe)
1940	Kerry (Ciarraidhe)
1941	Kerry (Ciarraidhe)
1942	Dublin (Ath Cliath)
1943	Roscommon (Ros Comain)
1944	Roscommon (Ros Comain)
1945	Cork (Corcaigh)
1946	Kerry (Ciarraidhe)
1947	Cavan (Cabhan)
1948	Cavan (Cabhan)
1949	Meath (An Mhidhe)
1950	Mayo (Muigheo)
1951	Mayo (Muigheo)
1952	Cavan (Cabhan)
1953	Kerry (Ciarraidhe)
1954	Meath (An Mhidhe)
1955	Kerry (Ciarraidhe)
1956	Galway (Gaillimh)
1957	Louth (Lughbhaidh)
1958	Dublin (Ath Cliath)
1959	Kerry (Ciarraidhe)
1960	Down (An Dun)
1961	Down (An Dun)
1962	Kerry (Ciarraidhe)
1963	Dublin (Ath Cliath)
1964	Galway (Gaillimh)
1965	Galway (Gaillimh)
1966	Galway (Gaillimh)
1967	Meath (An Mhidhe)
1968	Down (An Dun)
1969	Kerry (Ciarraidhe)
1970	Kerry (Ciarraidhe)
1971	Offaly (Uibh Fhrili)
1972	Offaly (Uibh Fhrili)
1973	Cork (Corcaigh)
1974	Dublin (Ath Cliath)
1975	Kerry (Ciarraidhe)
1976	Dublin (Ath Cliath)
1977	Dublin (Ath Cliath)
1978	Kerry (Ciarraidhe)
1979	Kerry (Ciarraidhe)
1980	Kerry (Ciarraidhe)
1981	Kerry (Ciarraidhe)
1982	Offaly (Uibh Fhrili)
1983	Dublin (Ath Cliath)
1984	Kerry (Ciarraidhe)
1985	Kerry (Ciarraidhe)
1986	Kerry (Ciarraidhe)
1987	Meath (An Mhidhe)
1988	Meath (An Mhidhe)
1989	Cork (Corcaigh)

Wins

30 Kerry; **21** Dublin; **7** Galway; **5** Wexford, Cavan, Meath, Cork; **4** Tipperary, Kildare; **3** Louth, Mayo, Down, Offaly; **2** Limerick, Roscommon

ALL-IRELAND HURLING/GAELIC FOOTBALL 'DOUBLE'

1890 Cork   1895 Tipperary   1900 Tipperary

GOLF

A TIE AT THE BELFRY

For most of the world's leading players, the 1989 golf season reached its climax at The Belfry near Birmingham on a late September afternoon when Europe retained the Ryder Cup. The biennial match with the United States ended in a 14-14 tie, repeating the tie at Royal Birkdale 20 years earlier.

The circumstances, however, were vastly different. Then the Britain and Ireland team had been complete underdogs. Now Europe, winners of the trophy in 1985 and 1987, were competing on equal terms. For them, there was both relief and a tinge of disappointment about the result. Early on the final afternoon, when Europe was leading in just one of the the 12 singles matches, the Americans looked like heading for a comfortable win. Then Christy O'Connor jnr and José-Maria Canizares, the two least-regarded golfers in the European team, both scored magnificent last-hole victories; O'Connor promptly burst into tears. But the two last players, Nick Faldo and Ian Woosnam, both lost the opportunity to get the half-point Europe needed for outright victory; at the 18th Faldo followed a succession of equally distinguished players into the water and Curtis Strange, Woosnam's opponent, scored a magnificent birdie.

Tony Jacklin, Europe's captain for the past four Cups, confirmed afterwards that he would be giving up the job. Ray Floyd, the American captain, was asked what he had learned from the competition. "Probably never to accept the position again", he replied. The contest was again treated with enormous enthusiasm by all the players, the British golfing public, who made the occasion a sell-out well in advance, and the press.

"We Spank The Yanks", reported the *Daily Star*; only its most careful readers would be aware Europe had not actually won. The spectators were more sporting and avoided the wilder demonstrations of joy at American mistakes that marred the 1985 Cup; this was partly due to the absence of vantage points on the course which ensured that few of them could see anything.

MASTER FALDO

High tide for European golf had come in April when, one year after Sandy Lyle became Britain's first US Masters champion, Nick Faldo characteristically followed suit. It was a feature of the 1989 majors that for each winner - Faldo, Curtis Strange, Mark Calcavecchia and Payne Stewart - there was a shadow victor who had the tournament in his grasp and blew it.

Faldo was in a play-off against Scott Hoch (rhymes with choke, as everyone pointed out afterwards). At the 73rd Hoch had a putt of under two feet to win but he stared at the ball nervously and bent down to pick up some imaginary fluff, reminding some people of Doug Sanders at the 1970 British Open. Then he missed. Faldo had shared the lead with 49-year-old Lee Trevino after two rounds but then collapsed to a bad-tempered 77 to slide out of apparent contention. Sam Snead in 1952 was the last man to win the Masters with a 77 among his returns; but only Gary Player (64 in 1978) has ever beaten Faldo's last-round 65.

Faldo did honour to the green jacket in the succeeding weeks. He came home in May and won his first three European tournaments of the year - the PGA at Wentworth, with four sub-70 rounds; the Dunhill Masters at Woburn, where he began moderately but dined at Downing Street with President Bush and a 1913 cognac on the Thursday night and responded with two 65s and a 66; and the French Open at Chantilly, where he birdied the last hole from the lip of the bunker. That effectively was four in a row, since he won his last tournament of 1988, the Volvo Masters.

People were muttering nonsense about grand slams when Faldo returned to America for the US Open at Oak Hill in upstate New York. It took place in thoroughly English conditions of cold and rain but Faldo did not show. The British challenge came from Ian Woosnam who eventually finished joint second. But he never really looked like the winner. The man who did was Tom Kite, who was three strokes ahead in the final round and then hit the water at the fifth and triple-bogeyed. The winner was Curtis Strange, who became the first man to retain the title since Ben Hogan in 1951. Strange had a second-day 64 and then parred the first 15 holes on the final day while the others were collapsing. Kite finished equal ninth.

"From being a kid it has been my dream to leave a legacy. I want people to say 'Did you see Nick Faldo play?'."
Nick Faldo

"He's ruined the whole thing. He's put his foot in it. But then he's always doing that."
Alex Hay, Woburn managing director, after Faldo had won the tournament and complained about facilities for players' families

"Be patient. Keep smiling."
Caddie Andy Prodger's advice to Faldo at the Masters, on every page of the yardage chart

"The players' car park is too far away. The practice ground is no good. The place is full of kids. The weather is grotty and last year the courtesy car refused to bring my wife into town."
Mark James declining to compete in the Irish Open

"It gets to him, you know, all the pressure. The press, the telly and all the carry-on, it's a burden to bear. We thought he could bear it, but it turns out he's only human."
Alex Lyle on his son Sandy

The Open at Royal Troon produced marvellous weather but no kind of golfing challenge. Troon was tamed by the heatwave. Most of the time, there was no wind and the rough was less formidable than the fairways on some municipal courses. But the tournament was redeemed by a pulsating finish when Calcavecchia, the first US winner since 1983, won a play-off against the Australians Wayne Grady and Greg Norman. Grady and Norman both blew their chances, but from vastly different directions. Grady had led the tournament until he bogeyed the short 17th on the final round. His main rival was thought to be Tom Watson, returning to his best and most beautiful form. Watson had been gambled on by an army of supporters (and Watson himself, who slipped into a local betting shop) at prices up to 80-1 and was in contention all the way until he missed a tiddler at the seventh on the final day.

NORMAN'S CHARGE

Calcavecchia was close behind; but no one had considered Norman, 13th equal overnight, seven strokes back and starting his final round an hour and 40 minutes before the leaders. Norman birdied the first six holes and blazed to 64. Coming to the fourth and final hole of the play-off, the 18th, he was still thumping the ball a phenomenal distance; too far, it turned out. He found a bunker that in theory was out of range of anyone's driver. This was the third time Norman has lost a play-off of a major championship but perhaps the first time anyone has lost a major championship simply because they did not know their own strength.

Calcavecchia had intended to walk out of the tournament had his wife, back home heavily pregnant, gone into labour. She later gave birth to a girl named Brittney, one of the few children ever to be named after a golf tournament. Crowds at The Open were 164,000, the third highest in history. 200,000 are expected at St Andrews in 1990 but there are still no plans to make it all-ticket. The three Ozaki brothers from Japan all made the cut, a feat last achieved by the Whitcombe brothers in 1938 - Reg Whitcombe won that year. A women spectator was knocked unconscious by a ball hit by either Jet Ozaki or Nick Faldo; both blamed the other. Of the finishers, Bernhard Langer finished last and Severiano Ballesteros third last. Of the non-qualifiers, Arnold Palmer was rock-bottom with two 82s. In the qualifying tournaments, the R and A inserted new conditions requiring competitors to submit evidence of their ability. This was designed to prevent cheerful no-hopers coming along, even though the event is supposed to be open. Clemens Bayer, a German upholsterer, still entered the regional qualifier at Langley Park and took 105. "We made a booboo", said an R and A official.

The fourth major, the US PGA, was won by Payne Stewart, himself formerly known as Avis for so often coming second. Originally, he did not seem cured in 1989: he was ahead after 69 holes of the Masters and flattered then faltered at Troon as well. The loser this time was Mike Reid who led after both the second and third rounds and was still ahead - playing conservative but very capable golf - until he double bogeyed the 71st hole of the tournament, leaving Stewart, who had never got into the position to be nervous, as champion after a homeward nine of 31. Stewart, in keeping with his contract with the National Football League, was wearing plus-twos (knickers to the Americans) in club colours, on this occasion the blue, white and orange of the Chicago Bears. There was no provision to annul his title on grounds of taste. The first day of the tournament had given sentimentalists a pleasing contrast to the Open: Arnold Palmer took a 68, as did Jack Nicklaus.

MILLIGAN'S MOMENT

In August, Britain and Ireland's amateurs won the Walker Cup in Peachtree, Georgia. This was their first-ever win in America and meant that the three traditional Anglo-American trophies, the Ryder, Walker and Curtis Cups, all improbably rested on this side of the Atlantic. It was nearly an embarrassing failure. The British Isles team were 11-5 up and needed only 1 1/2 points from the final eight singles; they almost failed to get them. The Cup appeared to be lost when the last hope Jim Milligan was two down with three to play against the Americans' most experienced player, 45-year-old Jay Sigel. Milligan birdied the 16th, holed his pitch on the 17th and got his putt stone dead on the 18th to win.

The 1988 English amateur champion, Russell Claydon, had a stunning success in the Australian Masters at Huntingdale in February, when he came second to Greg Norman. Claydon had to pay his own fare and expenses and turn down the £23,000 prize to preserve his status. Claydon was then knocked out of the 1989 amateur championship by Ben Jackson, who caddied for him last year. Peter McEvoy was taken to the 10th extra hole, the 28th, in the Amateur by 18-year-old Drew Elliot, providing the longest match in the Championship since 1908. José-Maria Olazabal won a supposedly sudden-death play-off at the Dutch Open at the ninth extra hole, a European tour record. Olazabal beat Ronan Rafferty after missing an 18-inch putt; Rafferty, wanting a three-footer to win, sent that five foot past and missed again. The play-off equalled the record for a professional tournament set when Johnny Miller beat Ballesteros at Sun City in 1982.

Rafferty, after spending seven years being promising, mostly played more distinguished golf. He finally won his first European tour event: the Italian Open and just beat Olazabal in the final Order of Merit. Andrew Murray, who had never even led a tournament, won the European Open at Walton Heath; Murray has an arthritic condition and is struggling to continue playing at all.

At the US Masters Tom Watson overtook Nicklaus on the all-time money list - later Kite passed him; Nicklaus had led since overhauling Palmer in 1972. Greg Norman overtook Ballesteros on the world rankings list and regained his position as no.1 on August 20 after winning the International. The US PGA tour policy board rejected a plan to let overseas members cut down from 15 tournaments a year to 12. On-course betting returned to the European tour, with William Hill planning facilities at six tournaments in 1990. Head-to-head betting was barred.

The Australian Bob Emond took a 19 on a par-five at the Tournament Players Championship in Sydney, equalling the 20th century professional record held by Ray Ainsley of the US who tried to extricate his ball from a brook at Cherry Hills in 1938. At the US Open, four players - Doug Weaver, Mark Wiebe, Jerry Pate and Nick Price - had holes in one at the 6th between 8.15 and 10.05 on the second day. The odds against were between 332,000 to 1 and 8.7 million to one, depending who you asked. There had only been 17 holes in one at the previous 88 Opens.

"Sure, the purses are obscene...the average worker, let's say, makes $25,000 a year while a golfer makes $25,000 finishing 10th. Our values have departed somewhat."

Tom Watson

"Winning used to be the important thing. The money was nice to have, but it was not the most important thing. Today, the American player doesn't have that strong desire to win any more, he has the strong desire to win all this money."

Ray Floyd

"I couldn't be rational about my feelings right now. I played so poorly. I'm upset."
Arnold Palmer after two 82s at The Open, Jul 21

"I can remember over the last few years times when I've played in a major championship like this, and I'd walk through a group of younger players and they never looked up. Today they looked up."
Arnold Palmer after shooting 68 at the PGA, August 12

"Why would I want to be out there with all those young guns? No sense playing the flat bellies when you can play the round bellies."
Lee Trevino welcoming his 50th birthday and the Seniors tour

"You always have butterflies in your stomach but these butterflies are playing hockey."
Mike Reid, leader before the last round of the PGA Championship

"Believe me, I know how Mike feels. I've screwed up a few golf tournaments myself."
Payne Stewart, after winning the PGA

IMPROBABILITY DRIVE

The following round-up of holes in one is culled from various British newspapers and therefore must be true in every detail: Mark Alexander, aged six, of Marylebone, London became the youngest hole-in-oner in Britain. Playing with his dad and using a cut-down three wood (at the 109-yard sixth, Chessington, Surrey), Mark was totally unbothered and calmly went over and picked the ball out of the hole. Only the grown-ups got excited. Dorothy Huntley-Flint, the 90-year-old grandmother of Richard Branson, became the oldest woman to get one (the 13th, Barton-on-Sea, Dorset) easily eclipsing Marjorie Gait, 85, (Windwhistle, Somerset). There was also both Stan Durrant and his wife Madge (Thirsk and Northallerton), Stan for the fifth time; and Doug Sutton of Devon for the 10th time.

Hans Nielsen, captain of the Oxford Speedway team, reportedly had to give his wife Suzanne, a 36-handicapper, a Rolls-Royce to fulfil a rash promise after she managed it (the 130-yard fifth, Woodlands, Northamptonshire). Mark Law, 25, holed in one (Goring and Streatley, Oxon) and regretted it: it was a long-driving competition. Peter Hill and Peter Simner both got one while playing together (Cherry Lodge, Kent). Barry Baker, 16, did it on consecutive days at the same hole (the 182-yard 12th) at Reddish Vale, Stockport.

BOB EMOND'S 19: TOURNAMENT PLAYERS CHAMPIONSHIP, SYDNEY

1. hook into water;
2. penalty drop;
3. hit fairway;
4. found water;
5/6 . tried to hit out;
7. picked up for one-stroke penalty;
8. hit into water;
9. one-stroke penalty;
10/11. dropped and hit shoe for two-stroke penalty;
12. dropped and hit into water;
13. one-stroke penalty;
14 hit fringe of green;
15/16. two-stroke penalty for marking ball not on green;
17/18/19. putted out.

Golf Monthly launched a campaign to stop slow play, under the honorary chairmanship of Denis Thatcher. President Bush supported this campaign by playing what his doctor called "aerobic golf" near his holiday home in Maine; this included finishing one round in an hour and 51 minutes. However, it transpired that the President was not bothering with such details as counting wild tee shots. "Mr Bush fudges it from time to time," said Cape Arundel Golf Club professional Ken Raynor. "Some corners are cut. The game benefits from the President's interest." "He's not setting America's 20 million golfers a good example", grumbled Rich Skyzinski of the US Golf Association.

Melanie Boyce and Janette Harvey of Essex were banned for three years by the English Ladies' Golf Association for returning incorrect scores. Two burglars trying to rob a house on the edge of the Warley Park course in Essex were arrested by 24 off-duty policemen on a golf day. A sign appeared outside a house near a course in Kent offering "free-range golf balls for sale". Carol Lane, 43, of Harefield, Middlesex was granted a decree nisi from her husband Ken after 14 years. Mrs Lane described herself as "the original golf widow". She added: "Golf was his mistress. There was never another woman. I always knew where he was."

The National Golf Foundation said that in 1988 there were 23.4 million golfers in the US, up 40 per cent on 1985, who played 487 million rounds of golf. A quarter of them - and almost a third of the new golfers - were women. American visitors to Britain complained that some major British courses charged exorbitant fees, forced them to play off extremely forward tees and were sometimes less than overwhelmingly hospitable. 40 Japanese companies in Britain were offered one per cent each of Wentworth by the Chelsfield group, which bought the club in 1988. Members' fees - £500 before the takeover - will be £1700 in 1990. The South Korean tax authorities announced plans to charge capital gains tax on golf club memberships, which are sold like shares and can trade for up to £150,000.

Ping sued R and A and the USGA for 100 million dollars over the decision to ban their Eye-2 irons. The R and A's writ was thoughtfully handed to Michael Bonallack at the celebration dinner after the Walker Cup. A company in Boston, Massachusetts started testing a theory that golf balls would travel up to 40 yards further if frozen first to minus 196 degrees Centigrade. The company, Applied Cryogenics, were responding to countless enquiries from Japan. Dr Jeffrey Levine said "The Japanese do not seem to care about enhanced productivity or increased national GNP. They are on top of us all the time, sending us golf balls."

1989

THE MAJORS

US MASTERS

Augusta, Georgia, Apr 6-9
All from US unless otherwise stated

283	NICK FALDO (GB) 68-73-77-65
283	Scott Hoch 69-74-71-69

Faldo won play-off at 2nd extra hole

284	Greg Norman (Aus) 74-75-68-67
284	Ben Crenshaw 71-72-70-71
285	Seve Ballesteros (Spa) 71-72-73-69
286	Mike Reid 72-71-71-72
287	Jodie Mudd 73-76-72-66
288	Jeff Sluman 74-72-74-68
288	José-Maria Olazabal (Spa) 77-73-70-68
288	Chip Beck 74-76-70-68
289	Fred Couples 72-76-74-67
289	Mark O'Meara 74-71-72-72
289	Ken Green 74-69-73-73
290	Tom Watson 72-73-74-71
290	Paul Azinger 75-75-69-71
290	Don Pooley 70-77-76-67
290	Ian Woosnam (GB) 74-76-71-69
291	Jumbo Ozaki (Jap) 71-75-73-72
291	Tom Kite 72-72-72-75
291	Jack Nicklaus 73-74-73-71
291	Curtis Strange 74-71-74-72
291	Lee Trevino 67-74-81-69
291	David Frost (SA) 76-72-73-70
292	Payne Stewart 73-75-74-70
292	Tom Purtzer 71-76-73-72
293	Fuzzy Zoeller 76-74-69-74
293	Larry Mize 72-77-69-75
293	Lanny Wadkins 76-71-73-73
293	Bernhard Langer (FRG) 74-75-71-73
293	Steve Pate 76-75-74-68
294	Steve Jones 74-73-80-67
294	David Rummells 74-74-75-71
294	Mark Calcavecchia 74-72-74-74
296	Bruce Lietzke 74-75-79-68
296	Hubert Green 74-75-76-71
296	Peter Jacobsen 74-73-78-71
297	Bob Gilder 75-74-77-71
298	Charles Coody 76-74-76-72
298	Ray Floyd 76-75-73-74
298	Tommy Aaron 76-74-72-76
298	Scott Simpson 72-77-72-77
299	Dan Pohl 72-74-78-75

300	George Archer 75-75-75-75
300	Greg Twiggs 75-76-79-70
300	Mark McCumber 72-75-81-72
301	Mike Sullivan 76-74-73-78
301	Jay Haas 73-77-79-72
301	Bob Lohr 75-76-77-73
301	D A Weibring 72-79-74-76
302	Corey Pavin 74-74-78-76
304	Andy Bean 70-80-77-77
306	T C Chen (Tai) 71-75-76-84

Notables who failed to make the cut:
Andy North, Craig Stadler, Larry Nelson, Sandy Lyle, Gary Player, Bob Tway, Arnold Palmer

WHERE THEY FINISHED IN THE MAJORS, 1989

	Masters	US Open	Open	US PGA
Faldo	1	18=	11=	9=
Strange	18=	1	61=	2=
Calcavecchia	31=	61=	1	-
Stewart	24=	13=	8=	1
Woosnam	14=	2=	49=	6
Ballesteros	5=	43=	77=	12=
Norman	3=	33=	2=	12=
Watson	14=	46=	4	9=
Hoch	2	13=	-	7=

US OPEN

Rochester, New York, Jun 15-18
All from US unless otherwise stated

278	CURTIS STRANGE 74-64-73-70
279	Ian Woosnam (GB) 70-68-73-68
279	Chip Beck 71-69-71-68
279	Mark McCumber 70-68-72-69
280	Brian Claar 71-72-68-69
281	Jumbo Ozaki (Jap) 70-71-68-72
281	Scott Simpson 67-70-69-75
282	Peter Jacobsen 71-70-71-70
283	Paul Azinger 71-72-70-70
283	Hubert Green 69-72-74-68
283	José-Maria Olazabal (Spa) 69-72-70-72
283	Tom Kite 67-69-69-78
284	Payne Stewart 66-75-72-71
284	Mark Lye 71-69-72-72
284	Scott Hoch 70-72-70-72
284	Tom Pernice 67-75-68-74
284	Larry Nelson 68-73-68-75
285	Jay Don Blake 66-71-72-76
285	Nick Faldo (GB) 68-72-73-72
285	David Frost (SA) 73-72-70-70
286	Bill Glasson 73-70-70-73
286	Nolan Henke 75-69-72-70
286	Steve Elkington (Aus) 70-70-78-68
286	D A Weibring 70-74-73-69
286	Fred Couples 74-71-67-74
287	Robert Wrenn 74-71-73-69
287	Ray Floyd 68-74-74-71
287	Don Pooley 74-69-71-73
288	Hal Sutton 69-75-72-72
288	Emlyn Aubrey 69-73-73-73
288	Don Pohl 71-71-73-73
288	Scott Taylor 69-71-76-72
289	Mark Weibe 69-71-72-77
289	Joey Sindelar 67-77-74-71
289	Davis Love 71-74-73-71
289	Billy Mayfair 72-69-76-72
289	Dan Forsman 70-70-76-73
289	Brad Faxon 73-70-75-71
289	Isao Aoki (Jap) 70-70-75-74

289	Larry Mize 72-72-71-74
289	Edward Kirkby 70-70-73-76
289	Greg Norman (Aus) 72-68-73-76
290	Clark Dennis 72-72-72-74
290	Jack Nicklaus 67-74-74-75
290	Seve Ballesteros (Spa) 75-70-76-69
291	Steve Jones 69-75-77-70
291	John Mahaffey 77-68-74-72
291	Tom Watson 76-69-73-73
291	Richard Zokol (Can) 71-69-76-75
291	Ken Green 73-72-71-75
292	Steve Pate 74-69-73-76
292	Jodie Mudd 73-71-74-74
292	Tom Sieckmann 73-71-74-74
293	Ronnie Black 71-74-76-72
293	Hale Irwin 74-70-79-70
293	David Ogrin 73-72-73-75
293	Webb Heintzelman 72-70-75-76
293	Chris Perry 76-67-72-78
294	Clarence Rose 70-75-73-76
294	Bernhard Langer (FRG) 66-78-77-73
295	David Graham (Aus) 73-72-77-73
295	Mark Calcavecchia 74-70-74-77
296	Gregory Lescher 70-72-76-78
296	Tony Sills 72-72-71-81
296	Dan Halldorson (Can) 72-70-76-78
297	Bobby Wadkins 73-72-75-77
298	Ed Humenik 73-72-76-77
298	Dillard Pruitt 68-74-81-75
300	Doug Weaver 72-73-80-75
300	John Daly 74-67-80-79
301	Kurt Beck 68-73-83-77

Notables who failed to make the cut:
Lanny Wadkins, Ben Crenshaw, Andy North, Gary Player, Jerry Pate, Bob Tway, Fuzzy Zoeller, Sandy Lyle, Andy Bean, Lee Trevino

BRITISH OPEN

Royal Troon, Jul 20-23
All British unless otherwise stated

275	MARK CALCAVECCHIA (US) 71-68-68-68
275	Greg Norman (Aus) 69-70-72-64
275	Wayne Grady (Aus) 68-67-69-71
277	Tom Watson (US) 69-68-68-72
278	Jodie Mudd (US) 73-67-68-70
279	David Feherty 71-67-69-72
279	Fred Couples (US) 68-71-68-72
280	Eduardo Romero (Arg) 68-70-75-67
280	Paul Azinger (US) 68-73-67-72
280	Payne Stewart (US) 72-65-69-74
281	Mark McNulty (Zim) 75-70-70-66
281	Nick Faldo (GB) 71-71-70-69
282	Howard Clark 72-68-72-70
282	Philip Walton 69-74-69-70
282	Craig Stadler (US) 73-69-69-71
282	Roger Chapman 76-68-67-71
282	Mark James 69-70-71-72
282	Steve Pate (US) 69-70-70-73
283	Derrick Cooper 69-70-76-68
283	Don Pooley (US) 73-70-69-71
283	Tom Kite (US) 70-74-67-72
283	Larry Mize (US) 71-74-66-72
284	Davis Love (US) 72-70-73-69
284	Vijay Singh (Fij) 71-73-69-71
284	José Maria Olazabal (Spa) 68-72-69-75
285	Chip Beck (US) 75-69-68-73
285	Stephen Bennett 75-69-68-73
285	Scott Simpson (US) 73-66-72-74
285	Lanny Wadkins (US) 72-70-69-74
286	Gary Koch (US) 72-71-74-69
286	Brian Marchbank 69-74-73-70
286	Jack Nicklaus (US) 74-71-71-70
286	Peter Jacobsen (US) 71-74-71-70
286	Miguel Angel Martin (Spa) 68-73-73-72
286	Masashi Ozaki (Jap) 71-73-70-72

286	Mark Davis 77-68-67-74
286	Ian Baker-Finch (Aus) 72-69-70-75
286	Jeff Hawkes (SA) 75-67-69-75
287	Jeff Woodland (Aus) 74-67-75-71
287	Mike Harwood (Aus) 71-72-72-72
287	Tommy Armour (US) 70-71-72-74
288	José Rivero (Spa) 71-75-72-70
288	Mark O'Meara (US) 72-74-69-73
288	Lee Trevino (US) 68-73-73-74
288	Ray Floyd (US) 73-68-73-74
289	Sandy Lyle 73-73-71-72
289	Naomichi Ozaki (Jap) 71-71-69-78
289	Mark McCumber (US) 71-68-70-80
290	Ian Woosnam 74-72-73-71
290	Johnny Miller (US) 72-69-76-73
290	Christy O'Connor jnr (Ire) 71-73-72-74
291	Brett Ogle (Aus) 74-70-76-71
291	Ben Crenshaw (US) 73-73-74-71
291	Tateo Ozaki (Jap) 75-71-73-72
291	Mark Roe 74-71-73-73
291	Michael Allen (US) 74-67-76-74
291	Emmanuel Dussart (Fra) 76-68-73-74
291	Tony Johnstone (Zim) 71-71-74-75
291	Richard Boxall 74-68-73-76
291	Gene Sauers (US) 70-73-72-76
292	Paul Hoad 72-71-77-72
292	Mike Reid (US) 74-72-73-73
292	Curtis Strange (US) 70-74-74-74
292	Bob Tway (US) 76-70-71-75
292	Ronan Rafferty 70-72-74-76
292	David Graham (Aus) 74-72-69-77
292	Wayne Stephens 66-72-76-78
292	Ken Green (US) 75-71-68-78
293	Russell Claydon 70-74-74-75
293	Luis Carbonetti (Arg) 71-72-74-76
293	Sandy Stephen 71-74-71-77
294	Colin Gillies 72-74-74-74
295	Brad Faxon (US) 72-72-75-76
295	Peter Teravainen (US) 72-73-72-78
296	Emlyn Aubrey (US) 72-73-73-78
297	Martin Sludds 72-74-73-78
299	Robert Karlsson (Swe) 75-70-76-78
299	Seve Ballesteros (Spa) 72-73-76-78
301	Gavin Levenson (SA) 69-76-77-79
309	Bernhard Langer (FRG) 71-73-83-82

Notables who failed to make the cut:
Sam Torrance, Larry Nelson, Tom Weiskopf, Brian Barnes, Fuzzy Zoeller, Andy Bean, Gary Player, Eamonn Darcy, Ken Brown, Tony Jacklin, Arnold Palmer

TROON STATISTICS

Most consecutive birdies: **Greg Norman 6 (holes 1-6, round 4)**

Most consecutive pars: **Mark McCumber 13 (holes 5-17, round 3)**

Most birdies: **Mark Calcavecchia 23**

Most pars: **Lanny Wadkins 55**

Most 2s: **Mark Calcavecchia, Johnny Miller 6**

Most 3s: **Davis Love III 26**

Most 4s: **David Feherty 45**

Most birdies: **Mark Calcavecchia 23**

Most pars: **Lanny Wadkins 55**

Source: Golf Monthly

US PGA CHAMPIONSHIP

Kemper Lakes, Aug 10-13
All from US unless otherwise stated

276	PAYNE STEWART 74-66-69-67
277	Andy Bean 70-67-74-66
277	Curtis Strange 70-68-70-69
277	Mike Reid 66-67-70-74
278	Dave Rummells 68-69-69-72
279	Ian Woosnam (GB) 68-70-70-71
280	Craig Stadler 71-64-72-73
280	Scott Hoch 69-69-69-73
281	Nick Faldo (GB) 70-73-69-69
281	Ed Fiori 70-67-75-69
281	Tom Watson 67-69-74-71
282	Greg Norman (Aus) 74-71-67-70
282	Jim Gallagher jnr 73-69-68-72
282	Mark Weibe 71-70-69-72
282	Mike Sullivan 76-66-67-73
282	Seve Ballesteros (Spa) 72-70-66-74
283	Chris Perry 67-70-70-76
283	Isao Aoki (Jap) 72-71-65-75
283	Ben Crenshaw 68-72-72-71
283	Davis Love 73-69-72-69
283	Blaine McCallister 71-72-70-70
283	Buddy Gardner 72-71-70-70
283	Larry Mize 73-71-68-71
284	Jeff Sluman 75-70-69-70
284	Dan Pohl 71-69-74-70
284	Tommy Armour 69-71-72-72
285	David Frost (SA) 70-74-69-72
285	Tim Simpson 69-70-73-73
285	Jack Nicklaus 68-72-73-72
285	Mike Hulbert 70-71-72-72
285	Peter Jacobsen 70-70-73-72
285	Brian Tennyson 71-69-72-73
285	Howard Twitty 72-71-68-74
286	Don Pooley 70-71-72-73
286	Bob Gilder 73-74-71-68
286	Chip Beck 73-71-69-73
286	Tom Kite 67-73-72-74
286	Loren Roberts 69-71-72-74
286	Ian Baker-Finch (Aus) 74-68-70-74
286	Leonard Thompson 66-69-73-78
287	Bob Lohr 75-69-69-74
287	Steve Elkington (Aus) 69-75-71-72
287	Steve Pate 70-72-74-71
287	David Edwards 69-72-72-74
287	Bill Briton 75-67-71-74
288	Larry Nelson 71-74-68-75
288	Bruce Lietzke 70-72-73-73
288	Nick Price (Zim) 70-72-72-74
288	Wayne Grady (Aus) 70-75-72-71
288	Ray Floyd 73-71-70-74
289	Steve Jones 71-74-71-73
289	Kenny Perry 71-74-70-74
290	Clarence Rose 74-71-72-73
290	Scott Simpson 70-74-75-71
290	Phil Blackmar 68-75-75-72
290	Tom Purtzer 69-73-74-74
290	Doug Tewell 73-69-72-76
291	Andy North 69-75-77-70
291	Gene Sauers 76-68-75-72
291	Brad Bryant 70-70-72-79
292	Gary Koch 71-72-77-72
292	Bernhard Langer (FRG) 74-71-75-72
293	Greg Twiggs 71-73-74-75
293	Arnold Palmer 68-74-81-70
294	Mark McCumber 70-73-74-77
295	Hubert Green 69-73-76-77
296	Jodie Mudd 71-70-80-75
287	Dave Stockton 76-69-75-77
299	Ronnie Black 73-70-74-82
307	Curt Byrum 73-71-76-87

Notables who failed to make the cut:
Hal Sutton, Fred Couples, Fuzzy Zoeller, José-Maria Olazabal, Lanny Wadkins, Bob Tway, Lee Trevino, John Mahaffey, Paul Azinger, David Graham

US PGA TOUR
All winners from US unless stated

Mony Tournament of Champions
San Diego, California, Jan 8
279 Steve Jones: 282 Jay Haas, David Frost (SA)

Bob Hope Chrysler Classic
Palm Springs, California, Jan 15
343 Steve Jones; 343 Sandy Lyle (GB), Paul Azinger
Jones won play-off at 1st extra hole

Phoenix Open
Phoenix, Arizona, Jan 22
263 Mark Calcavecchia; 270 Chip Beck; 271 Scott Hoch, Paul Azinger, Bill Glasson

AT & T Pebble Beach National Pro-Am
Pebble Beach, California, Jan 29
277 Mark O'Meara; 278 Tom Kite; 280 Sandy Lyle (GB), Nick Price (SA), Jim Carter

Nissan Los Angeles Open
Riviera CC, California, Feb 5
272 Mark Calcavecchia; 273 Sandy Lyle (GB); 274 Hale Irwin

Hawaiian Open
Honolulu, Hawaii, Feb 12
197 Gene Sauers; 198 Dave Ogrin; 199 Dave Rummells
Rain reduced play to 54 holes

Sherson Lehman Hutton Open
San Diego, California, Feb 19
271 Greg Twiggs, 273 Steve Elkington (Aus), Mark O'Meara, Brad Faxon

Doral Ryder Open
Miami, Florida, Feb 26
275 Billy Glasson; 276 Fred Couples; 278 Mark Calcavecchia, Curtis Strange, Bruce Lietzke

Honda Classic
Palm Springs, Florida, Mar 5
266 Blaine McCallister; 270 Payne Stewart; 271 Curtis Strange, Steve Pate

The Nestle Invitational
Orlando, Florida, Mar 12
278 Tom Kite; 278 Davis Love; 279 Curtis Strange
Kite won play-off at 2nd extra hole

The Players Championship
Ponte Vedra, Florida, Mar 19
279 Tom Kite; 280 Chip Beck; 281 Bruce Lietzke

USF&G Classic
New Orleans, Louisiana, Mar 26
274 Tim Simpson; 276 Hal Suton, Greg Norman (Aus)

Houston Open
The Woodlands, Texas, Apr 2
280 Mike Sullivan; 281 Craig Stadler; 282 Severiano Ballesteros (Spa), Mike Donaldson, Mike Reid

US Masters
Augusta, Georgia, Apr 9
283 Nick Faldo (GB); 283 Scott Hoch; 284 Greg Norman (Aus), Ben Crenshaw
Faldo won play-off at 2nd extra hole

MCI Heritage Classic
Harbour Town, S.Carolina, Apr 16
199 Payne Stewart; 202 Kenny Perry; 204 Mark McCumber
Play curtailed to 54 holes

K-Mart Greater Greensboro Open
Forest Oaks, Apr 23
277 Ken Green; 279 John Huston; 281 Ed Fiori

Las Vegas International
Las Vegas, Nevada, Apr 30
336 Scott Hoch; 336 Robert Wrenn; 337 Craig Stadler, Gil Morgan
Hoch won play-off at 5th extra hole

GTE Byron Nelson Golf Classic
Dallas, Texas, May 7
265 Jodie Mudd, 265 Larry Nelson; 266 Mark O'Meara
Mudd won play-off at first extra hole

Memorial Tournament
Muirfield Village, Ohio, May 14
277 Bob Tway; 279 Fuzzy Zoeller; 281 Payne Stewart

Colonial National Invitational
Fort Worth, Texas, May 21
270 Ian Baker-Finch (Aus); 274 David Edwards; 276 David Frost (SA), Tim Simpson

Bell South Atlanta Classic
Marietta, Georgia, May 28
278 Scott Simpson; 278 Bob Tway; 279 Jay Don Blake, Davis Love
Simpson won play-off

Kemper Open
Potomac, Maryland, Jun 4
268 Tom Byrum; 273 Tommy Armour III, Jim Thorpe, Billy Ray Brown

Manufacturers Hanover Westchester Classic
Harrison, New York, Jun 11
277 Wayne Grady (Aus), Ronnie Black; 278 Tom Watson, Clarence Rose
Grady won play-off at 1st extra hole

US Open
Oak Hill, Rochester, New York, Jun 18
278 Curtis Strange; 279 Ian Woosnam (GB), Chip Beck, Mark McCumber

Canadian Open
Glen Abbey, Ontario, Jun 25
271 Steve Jones; 273 Clark Burroughs, Mark Calcavecchia, Mike Hulbert

Beatrice Western Open
Oak Brook, Illinois, Jul 2
275 Mark McCumber, Peter Jacobsen; 276 Paul Azinger
McCumber won play-off at 1st extra hole

Cannon Greater Hartford Open
Cromwell, Connecticut, Jul 9
267 Paul Azinger; 268 Wayne Levi; 270 Dave Rummells

Anheuser-Busch Classic
Williamsburg, Virginia, Jul 16
268 Mike Donald, Tim Simpson, Hal Sutton
Donald won play-off at 4th extra hole

Hardee's Golf Classic
Coal Valley, Illinois, Jul 23
268 Curt Byrum; 269 Brian Tennyson, Bill Britton

Buick Open
Grand Blanc, Michigan, Jul 30
273 Leonard Thompson; 274 Payne Stewart, Billy Andrade, Doug Tewell

Federal Express St Jude Golf Classic
Germantown, Tennessee, Aug 6
272 John Mahaffey; 275 Hubert Green, Bob Tway, Bernhard Langer (FRG), Bob Gilder

PGA Championship,
Kemper Lakes, Illinois, Aug 13
276 Payne Stewart; 277 Andy Bean, Curtis Strange, Mike Reid

The International
Castle Pines, Colorado, Aug 20
+13 Greg Norman (Aus); +11 Clarence Rose; +9 Chip Beck (*modified stableford*)

NEC World Series of Golf
Akron, Ohio, Aug 27
276 David Frost (SA), Ben Crenshaw; 278 Payne Stewart
Frost won play-off at 2nd extra hole

Greater Milwaukee Open
Franklin, Wisconsin, Sep 3
269 Greg Norman (Aus); 272 Andy Bean; 273 Mark Lye, Ted Schulz

B.C.Open
Endicott, New York, Sep 10
268 Mike Hulbert, Bob Estes; 269 Steve Elkington (Aus)
Hulbert won play-off at 1st extra hole

Bank of Boston Classic
Sutton, Massachusetts, Sep 17
271 Blaine McCallister; 272 Brad Faxon; 273 Dan Pooley, Mark Calcavecchia, Chris Perry

EUROPEAN PGA TOUR
All GB and Ireland unless otherwise stated

Tenerife Open
Golf Del Sur, Feb 26
275 José-Maria Olazabal (Spa); 278 David Gilford, José-Maria Canizares (Spa)

Karl Litten Desert Classic
Dubai, Mar 5
277 Mark James; 277 Peter O'Malley (Aus); 280 Paul Broadhurst
James won play-off at 1st extra hole

Renault Open de Baleares
Santa Ponsa, Majorca, Mar 12
279 Ove Sellberg (Swe); 281 José-Maria Olazabal (Spa), Mark McNulty (Zim), Phillip Parkin

Massimo Dutti Catalan Open
Pals, Costa Blanca, Spain, Mar 19
279 Mark Roe; 280 Jose-Maria Olazabal (Spa), Gordon Brand Jnr, Colin Montgomerie

AGF Open
La Grande Motte, Montpelier, Mar 27
277 Mark James; 280 Mark Mouland; 281 Bryan Norton (US)

Volvo Open
Is Molas, Sardinia, Apr 2
276 Vijay Singh (Fij); 279 Peter Fowler (Aus); 283 Bill Longmuir, Gordon Brand

Jersey European Airways Open
La Moye, Apr 9
281 Christy O'Connor, Jr; 281 Dennis Durnian; 282 Paul Broadhurst, Mats Lanner (Swe)
O'Connor won play-off at 1st extra hole

Credit Lyonnais Cannes Open
Cannes, Apr 16
207 Paul Broadhurst; 208 Brett Ogle (Aus), Jimmy Heggerty, Peter Senior (Aus)
Play reduced to 54 holes due to flooding

Cepsa Madrid Open
Puerta de Hierro, Madrid, Apr 23
272 Severiano Ballesteros (Spa); 273 Howard Clark; 275 Philip Walton

Peugeot Spanish Open
Valencia, Apr 30
281 Bernhard Langer (FRG); José-Maria Canizares (Spa), Paul Carrigill

Epson Grand Prix (Match Play)
St Pierre, Chepstow, May 7
1st: Severiano Ballesteros (Spa); 2nd: Dennis Durnian 3rd: Des Smyth

Volvo Belgian Open
Waterloo, May 14
273 Gordon J Brand; 277 Kevin Dickens; 278 Mark Davis

Lancia Italian Open
Monticello, May 21
273 Ronan Rafferty; 274 Sam Torrance; 275 Magnus Persson (Swe)

Volvo PGA Championship
Wentworth, May 29
272 Nick Faldo; 274 Ian Woosnam; 276 Craig Parry (Aus)

Dunhill British Masters
Woburn, Jun 4
267 Nick Faldo; 271 Ronan Rafferty; 276 Christy O'Connor Jr; Ove Sellberg (Swe); Mike Harwood (Aus)

Wang Four Stars National Pro-Celebrity
Moor Park, Jun 11
273 Craig Parry (Aus), Ian Woosnam; 274 Mike Harwood (Aus), David Gilford

NM English Open
The Belfry, Jun 18
279 Mark James, 280 Craig Parry (Aus), Sam Torrance, Eamonn Darcy

Carrolls Irish Open
Portmarnock, Jun 25
278 Ian Woosnam; Philip Walton; 282 Brett Ogle (Aus), Mark McNulty (SA), Ronan Rafferty
Woosnam won play-off at 1st extra hole

Peugeot French Open
Chantilly, Jul 2
273 Nick Faldo; 274 Bernhard Langer (FRG), Hugh Baiocchi (SA), Mark Roe

Torras Monte Carlo Open
Monte Carlo, Jul 9
261 Mark McNulty (Zim); 267 Jeff Hawkes (SA), José-Maria Canizares (Spa)

Bell's Scottish Open
Gleneagles, Jul 15
272 Michael Allen (US); 274 Ian Woosnam, José-Maria Olazabal (Spa)

118th British Open
Royal Troon, Jul 23
275 Mark Calcavecchia (US), Greg Norman (Aus), Wayne Grady (Aus); 277 Tom Watson (US)
Calcavecchia won play-off over 4 holes

KLM Dutch Open
Kennemer, Jul 30
277 José-Maria Olazabal (Spa); Roger Chapman, Ronan Rafferty
Olazabal won play-off at 9th extra hole

Scandinavian Enterprise Open
Drottningholm, nr Stockholm; Aug 6
268 Ronan Rafferty; 270 Mike Allen (US); 274 Peter Senior (Aus)

Benson & Hedges International
Fulford, York, Aug 13
272 Gordon Brand Jr; 273 Derrick Cooper; 274 Malcolm Mackenzie

PLM Open
Bokskogens, Sweden, Aug 20
271 Mike Harwood (Aus): 272 Peter Senior (Aus); 273 Sam Torrance

German Open
Frankfurt, Aug 27
266 Craig Parry (Aus); Mark James; 267 Michael Allen (US)
Parry won play-off at 2nd extra hole

Ebel European Masters Swiss Open
Crans-sur-Sierre, Sep 3
266 Severiano Ballesteros (Spa); 268 Craig Parry (Aus); 269 Stephen Bennett

Panasonic European Open
Walton Heath, Sep 10
277 Andrew Murray; 278 Frank Nobilo (NZ); 280 Sam Torrance

Lancome Trophy
St Nom-la-Breteche, France, Sep 17
266 Eduardo Romero (Arg); 267 José-Maria Olazabal (Spa), Bernhard Langer (FRG)

Sony World Rankings
(at Sep 17 1989)
Figures in brackets are 1986/88 average positions
1 (2) Greg Norman (Aus); 2 (1) Severiano Ballesteros (Sp); 3 (4) Nick Faldo (GB); 4 (5) Curtis Strange (US); 5 (9) Mark Calcavecchia (US); 6 (6) Ian Woosnam (GB); 7 (19) Payne Stewart (US); 8 (13) Tom Kite (US); 9 (15) José-Maria Olazabal (Sp); 10 (14) Chip Beck (US); 11 (12) Masashi Ozaki (Jap); 12 (3) Sandy Lyle (GB); 13 (8) Paul Azinger (US);14 (11) David Frost (SA) 15 (20) Fred Couples (US) 16 (7) Ben Crenshaw (US); 17 (23) Mark McCumber (US); 18 (16) Bernhard Langer (FRG); 19 (17) Tom Watson (Sco); 20 (18) Larry Nelson (US)

European Tour: Volvo Order of Merit
(at Sep 17 1989)
Figures are 1989 earnings in thousands of £ sterling.
Figures in brackets are 1988 final position
1 (9) Ronan Rafferty (NI) 264; 2 (3) José Maria Olazabal (Sp) 242; 3 (24) Craig Parry (Aus) 232; 4 (8) Mark James (Eng) 213; 5 (1) Severiano Ballesteros (Sp) 202; 6 (4) Ian Woosnam (Wal) 193; 7 (2) Nick Faldo (Eng) 188; 8 (51) Sam Torrance (Sco) 158; 9 (6) Mark McNulty (Zim) 157; 10 (11) Gordon Brand Jr (Sco) 155.

OTHER EVENTS

RYDER CUP
The Belfry, Sutton Coldfield, Sep 22-24
Day One
Foursomes
(European names first)
Nick Faldo and Ian Woosnam halved with Tom Kite and Curtis Strange; Howard Clark and Mark James lost to Lanny Wadkins and Payne Stewart 1 hole; Seve Ballesteros and José-Maria Olazabal halved with Tom Watson and Chip Beck; Bernhard Langer and Ronan Rafferty lost to Mark Calcavecchia and Ken Green 2 & 1
Fourballs
Sam Torrance and Gordon Brand Jr beat Curtis Strange and Paul Azinger 1 hole; Howard Clark and Mark James beat Fred Couples and Lanny Wadkins 3 & 2; Nick Faldo and Ian Woosnam beat Mark Calcavecchia and Mark McCumber 2 holes; Seve Ballesteros and José-Maria Olazabal beat Tom Watson and Mark O'Meara 6 & 5
First Day Score: EUROPE 5 UNITED STATES 3
Day Two
Foursomes
Nick Faldo and Ian Woosnam beat Lanny Wadkins and Payne Stewart 3 & 2; Gordon Brand Jr and Sam Torrance lost to Chip Beck and Paul Azinger 4 & 3; Christy O'Connor and Ronan Rafferty lost to Mark Calcavecchia and Ken Green 3 & 2; Severiano Ballesteros and José-Maria Olazabal beat Tom Kite and Curtis Strange 1 hole
Fourballs
Nick Faldo and Ian Woosnam lost to Chip Beck and Paul Azinger 2 & 1; Bernhard Langer and José-Maria Canizares lost to Tom Kite and Mark McCumber 2 & 1; Howard Clark and Mark James beat Payne Stewart and Curtis Strange; Severiano Ballesteros and José-Maria Olazabal beat Mark Calcavecchia and Ken Green 4 & 2
Second Day Score: EUROPE 9 UNITED STATES 7
Day Three
Singles
Severiano Ballesteros lost to Paul Azinger 1 hole; Bernhard Langer lost to Chip Beck 3 & 1; José-Maria Olazabal beat Payne Stewart 1 hole; Ronan Rafferty beat Mark Calcavecchia 1 hole; Howard Clark lost to Tom Kite

8 & 7; Mark James beat Mark O'Meara 3 & 2; Christy O'Connor beat Fred Couples 1 hole; José-Maria Canizares beat Ken Green 1 hole; Gordon Brand Jr lost to Mark McCumber 1 hole; Sam Torrance lost to Tom Watson 3 & 1; Nick Faldo lost to Lanny Wadkins 1 hole; Ian Woosnam lost of Curtis Strange 2 holes
Final Score: EUROPE 14 UNITED STATES 14
Europe retained Cup as holders

Best Overall Performances

	P	W	H	L
José-Maria Olazabal (Eur)	5	4	1	0
Seve Ballesteros (Eur)	5	3	1	1
Chip Beck (US)	5	3	1	1
Mark James (Eur)	4	3	0	1
Paul Azinger (US)	4	3	0	1
Tom Kite (US)	4	2	1	1
Nick Faldo (Eur)	5	2	1	2
Ian Woosnam (Eur)	5	2	1	2

Tom Kite's 8 and 7 win over Howard Clark was the biggest since cup matches were first played over 18 holes in 1961.

UP FOR THE CUP

"Let's go over there and kick some butt."
Tom Watson

"And don't come back without the Cup."
President Bush

"On those closing holes the pressure was incredible, and anyone can crack, even the Americans."
Tony Jacklin, Europe captain

"We had three boys in the row hit it in the water and you can't have that in a world-class competition."
Ray Floyd, US captain

"It is wonderful for Europe, wonderful for America, but mostly wonderful for golf."
Severiano Ballesteros on the tie

"A credit to human nature. I love you all."
Tony Jacklin on the Ryder cup crowd

"Big-mouth Yanks get their own butt kicked."
Headline in Daily Star

WALKER CUP
Peachtree, Atlanta, Georgia, Aug 16-17
FULL RESULTS
Foursomes
(US names first)
Robert Gamez & Doug Martin beat Russell Claydon & Darren Prosser 3 & 2; Danny Yates & Phil Mickelson halved with Stephen Dodd & Garth McGimpsey; Greg Lesher & Jay Sigel lost to Peter McEvoy & Eoghan O'Connell 6 & 5; David Eger & Kevin Johnson lost to Jim Milligan & Andrew Hare 2 & 1; Robert Gamez& Doug Martin halved with Peter McEvoy & Eoghan O'Connell; David Eger & Kevin Johnson lost to Jim Milligan & Andrew Hare 2 & 1; Greg Lesher & Jay Sigel lost to Russell Claydon & Craig Cassells 3 & 2; Danny Yates & Phil Mickelson lost to Stephen Dodd & Garth McGimpsey 2 & 1

Singles
Eric Meeks halved with Stephen Dodd; Robert Gamez beat Jim Milligan 7 & 6; Doug Martin lost to Russell Claydon 5 & 4; Ralph Howe lost to Eoghan O'Connell 5 & 4; Danny Yates lost to Peter McEvoy 2 & 1; Phil Mickleson beat Garth McGimpsey 4 & 2; Greg Lesher lost to Craig Cassells 1 hole; Jay Sigel halved with Neil Roderick halved; Robert Gamez beat Stephen Dodd 1 hole; Doug Martin halved with Andrew Hare halved; Greg Lesher beat Russell Claydon 3 & 2; Danny Yates beat Peter McEvoy 4 & 3; Phil Mickelson halved with Eoghan O'Connell; David Eger beat Neil Roderick 4 & 2; Kevin Johnson beat Craig Cassells 4 & 2; Jay Sigel halved with Jim Milligan
FINAL SCORE: UNITED STATES 11½ GREAT BRITAIN & IRELAND 12½

Best Overall Performances
	P	W	L	H
Robert Gamez (US)	4	3	0	1
Eoghan O'Connell (GB)	4	2	0	2
Andrew Hare (GB)	3	2	0	1
Peter McEvoy (GB)	4	2	1	1
Jim Milligan (GB)	4	2	1	1
Craig Cassells (GB)	3	2	1	0
Russell Claydon (GB)	4	2	2	0

TRUSTHOUSE FORTE PGA SENIORS
West Hill, Surrey, Jun 15-18
277 Neil Coles; 281 Peter Butler; 282 Alec Bickerdike

VOLVO SENIORS BRITISH OPEN
Turnberry, Jul 27-30
269 Bob Charles (NZ); 276 Bill Casper (US); 279 Bryant Hiskey (US)

THE AMATEUR CHAMPIONSHIP
Royal Birkdale, Jun 5-10
Stephen Dodd (Brynhill) beat Craig Cassells (Murcar) 5 & 3

US AMATEUR CHAMPIONSHIP
Merion, Ohio, Aug 22-27
Chris Patton beat Danny Green 3 & 1

BRABAZON TROPHY
Hoylake, May 19-21
293 Craig Rivett (SA) & Neil Roderick (GB) (shared title); 294 J P Price (GB), Andy Hare (GB), G Hay (GB)

PRESIDENT'S PUTTER
Rye, Jan 5-8
Mark Froggatt beat Jamie Warman 3 & 2

SUNNINGDALE FOURSOMES
Sunningdale, Mar 20-23
Andrew Hare (Sleaford) and Russell Claydon (Gog Magog) [scr] beat Julie Wade (Folkestone) & Vicki Thomas (Pennard) [10] 4 & 3

HALFORD HEWITT CUP
Deal, Apr 6-9
Eton beat Shrewsbury 3-2

WOMEN'S GOLF: THE MAJORS

NABISCO DINAH SHORE
Mission Hills, California, Mar 30-Apr 2
279 Julie Inkster; 284 Tammie Green, JoAnne Carner; 287 Betsy King, Jody Rosenthal

DU MAURIER CLASSIC
Beaconsfield, Montreal, Jun 29-Jul 2
279 Tammie Green; 280 Pat Bradley, Betsy King

MAZDA LPGA CHAMPIONSHIP
Mason, Ohio, May 18-21
274 Nancy Lopez; 277 Ayako Okamoto (Jap); 278 Susan Sanders

US WOMEN'S OPEN
Indianwood, Michigan, Jul 13-16
278 Betsy King; 282 Nancy Lopez; 282 Pat Bradley, Penny Hammel

OTHER WOMEN'S EVENTS

BRITISH WOMEN'S OPEN
Ferndown, Aug 3-6
274 Jane Geddes (US); 276 Florence Descampe (Bel); 278 Marie-Laure de Lorenzi (Fra)

LPGA WORLD CHAMPIONSHIP
Lake Lanier Islands, Georgia, Aug 24-27
275 Betsy King; 278 Pat Bradley, Patty Sheehan; 279 Laura Davies (GB), Beth Daniel

CHAMPIONS

BRITISH OPEN
Year	Winner	Score	Venue	Runner(s)-up/Score
1860	Willie Park, Snr	174	Prestwick	Tom Morris Snr 176
1861	Tom Morris, Snr	163	Prestwick	Willie Park 167
1862	Tom Morris, Snr	163	Prestwick	Willie Park 176
1863	Willie Park, Snr	168	Prestwick	Tom Morris Snr 170
1864	Tom Morris, Snr	167	Prestwick	Andrew Strath 169
1865	Andrew Strath	162	Prestwick	Willie Park 164
1866	Willie Park, Snr	169	Prestwick	David Park 171
1867	Tom Morris, Snr	170	Prestwick	Willie Park 172
1868	Tom Morris, Jnr	157	Prestwick	Bob Andrew 159
1869	Tom Morris, Jnr	154	Prestwick	Tom Morris Snr 157
1870	Tom Morris, Jnr	149	Prestwick	Bob Kirk, David Strath 161
1872	Tom Morris, Jnr	166	Prestwick	David Strath 169
1873	Tom Kidd	179	St Andrews	Jamie Anderson 180
1874	Mungo Park	159	Musselburgh	Tom Morris Jnr 161
1875	Willie Park, Snr	166	Prestwick	Bob Martin 168
1876	Bob Martin	176	St Andrews	David Strath 176
(Martin awarded title as Strath refused play-off)				
1877	Jamie Anderson	160	Musselburgh	Bob Pingle 162
1878	Jamie Anderson	157	Prestwick	Bob Kirk 157
1879	Jamie Anderson	170*	St Andrews	Andrew Kirkaldy 170
1880	Robert Ferguson	162	Musselburgh	Peter Paxton 167
1881	Robert Ferguson	170	Prestwick	Jamie Anderson 173

1882	Robert Ferguson	171	St Andrews	Willie Fernie 174
1883	Willie Fernie	159*	Musselburgh	Bob Ferguson 159
1884	Jack Simpson	160	Prestwick	William Fernie, Doublas Rolland 164
1885	Bob Martin	171	St Andrews	Archie Simpson, David Ayton 172
1886	David Brown	157	Musselburgh	Willie Campbell 159
1887	Willie Park, Jnr	161	Prestwick	Bob Martin 162
1888	Jack Burns	171	St Andrews	David Anderson, Ben Sayers 172
1889	Willie Park, Jnr	155*	Musselburgh	Andrew Kirkaldy 155
1890	John Ball	164	Prestwick	Willie Fernie, Archie Simpson 167
1891	Hugh Kirkaldy	166	St Andrews	Willie Fern, Andrew Kirkaldy 168
1892	Harold H. Hilton	305	Muirfield	John Ball Jnr, James Kirkaldy, Sandy Herd 308
1893	Willie Auchterlonie	322	Prestwick	Johnny Laidlay 324
1894	John H. Taylor	326	Sandwich	Douglas Rolland 331
1895	John H.Taylor	322	St Andrews	Sandy Herd 326
1896	Harry Vardon	316*	Muirfield	John H Taylor 316
1897	Harold H.Hilton	314	Hoylake	James Braid 315
1898	Harry Vardon	307	Prestwick	Willie park 308
1899	Harry Vardon	310	Sandwich	Jack White 315
1900	John H Taylor	309	St Andrews	Harry Vardon 317
1901	James Braid	309	Muirfield	Harry Vardon 312
1902	Sandy Herd	307	Hoylake	Harry Vardon, James Braid 308
1903	Harry Vardon	300	Prestwick	Tom Vardon 306
1904	Jack White	296	Sandwich	James Braid, John H Taylor 297
1905	James Braid	318	St Andrews	John H Taylor, R Jones 323
1906	James Braid	300	Muirfield	John H Taylor 304
1907	Arnaud Massy (Fra)	312	Hoylake	John H Taylor 314
1908	James Braid	291	Prestwick	Tom Ball 299
1909	John H Taylor	295	Deal	James Braid 299
1910	James Braid	299	St Andrews	Sandy Herd 303
1911	Harry Vardon	303*	Sandwich	Arnaud Massy 303
1912	Ted Ray	295	Muirfield	Harry Vardon 299
1913	John H Taylor	304	Hoylake	Ted Ray 312
1914	Harry Vardon	306	Prestwick	John H Taylor 309
1920	George Duncan	303	Deal	Sandy Herd 305
1921	Jock Hutchison (US)	296*	St Andrews	Roger H Wethered 296
1922	Walter Hagen (US)	300	Sandwich	George Duncan, Jim Barnes (US) 301
1923	Arthur Havers	295	Troon	Walter Hagen (US) 296
1924	Walter Hagen (US)	301	Hoylake	Ernest R Whitcombe 302
1925	Jim Barnes (US)	300	Prestwick	Archie Compston 301
1926	Bobby Jones (US)	291	Royal Lytham	Al Watrous (US) 293
1927	Bobby Jones (US)	285	St Andrews	Aubrey Boomer, Fred Robson 291
1928	Walter Hagen (US)	292	Sandwich	Gene Sarazen (US) 294
1929	Walter Hagen (US)	292	Muirfield	John Farrell (US) 298
1930	Bobby Jones (US)	291	Hoylake	Leo Deigel (US), Macdonald Smith (US) 293
1931	Tommy Armour (US)	296	Carnoustie	Jose Jurado (Arg) 297
1932	Gene Sarazen (US)	283	Prince's	Macdonald Smith (US) 288
1933	Densmore Shute (US)	292*	St Andrews	Craig Wood (US) 292
1934	Henry Cotton	283	Sandwich	Sid F Brews (SA) 288
1935	Alfred Perry	283	Muirfield	Alfred Padgham 287
1936	Alfred Padgham	287	Hoylake	Jimmy Adams 288
1937	Henry Cotton	290	Carnoustie	Reg Whitcombe 292
1938	Reg Whitcombe	295	Sandwich	Jimmy Adams 297
1939	Dick Burton	290	St Andrews	Johnny Bulla (US) 292
1946	Sam Snead (US)	290	St Andrews	Bobby Locke (SA), Johnny Bulla (US) 294
1947	Fred Daly	293	Hoylake	Reg Horne, Frank Stranahan (US) 294
1948	Henry Cotton	284	Muirfield	Fred Daly 289
1949	Bobby Locke (SA)	283*	Sandwich	Harry Bradshaw 283
1950	Bobby Locke (SA)	279	Troon	Roberto de Vicenzo (Arg) 281
1951	Max Faulkner	285	Portrush	Tony Cerda (Arg) 287
1952	Bobby Locke (SA)	287	Royal Lytham	Peter Thomson (Aus) 288
1953	Ben Hogan (US)	282	Carnoustie	Frank Stranahan (US) 286
1954	Peter Thomson (Aus)	283	Royal Birkdale	Sid Scott, Dai Rees, Bobby Locke (SA) 284
1955	Peter Thomson (Aus)	281	St.Andrews	Johnny Fallon 283
1956	Peter Thomson (Aus)	286	Hoylake	Flory van Donck (Bel) 289
1957	Bobby Locke (SA)	279	St Andrews	Peter Thomson (Aus) 282
1958	Peter Thomson (Aus)	278*	Royal Lytham	David Thomas 278
1959	Gary Player (SA)	284	Muirfield	Flory van Donck (Bel), Fred Bullock 286
1960	Kel Nagle (Aus)	278	St Andrews	Arnold Palmer (US) 279
1961	Arnold Palmer (US)	284	Royal Birkdale	Dai Rees 285
1962	Arnold Palmer (US)	276	Troon	Kel Nagle (Aus) 282
1963	Bob Charles (NZ)	277*	Royal Lytham	Phil Rodgers (US) 277
1964	Tony Lema (US)	279	St Andrews	Jack Nicklaus (US) 284
1965	Peter Thomson (Aus)	285	Royal Birkdale	Christy O'Connor, Brian Huggett 287
1966	Jack Nicklaus (US)	282	Muirfield	David Thomas, Doug Sanders (US) 283

1967	Roberto de Vicenzo (Arg)	278	Hoylake	Jack Nicklaus (US) 280
1968	Gary Player (SA)	289	Carnoustie	Jack Nicklaus (US), Bob Charles (NZ) 291
1969	Tony Jacklin	280	Royal Lytham	Bob Charles (NZ) 282
1970	Jack Nicklaus (US)	283*	St Andrews	Doug Sanders (US) 283
1971	Lee Trevino (US)	278	Royal Birkdale	Lu Liang Huan (Tai) 279
1972	Lee Trevino (US)	278	Muirfield	Jack Nicklaus (US) 279
1973	Tom Weiskopf (US)	276	Troon	Neil Coles 279
1974	Gary Player (SA)	282	Royal Lytham	Peter Oosterhuis 286
1975	Tom Watson (US)	279*	Carnoustie	Jack Newton (Aus) 279
1976	Johnny Miller (US)	279	Royal Birkdale	Jack Nicklaus (US), Seve Ballesteros (Spa) 285
1977	Tom Watson (US)	268	Turnberry	Jack Nicklaus (US) 269
1978	Jack Nicklaus (US)	281	St.Andrews	Simon Owen (NZ), Ben Crenshaw (US), Ray Floyd (US), Tom Kite (US) 283
1979	Seve Ballesteros (Spa)	283	Royal Lytham	Jack Nicklaus (US), Ben Crenshaw (US) 286
1980	Tom Watson (US)	271	Muirfield	Lee Trevino (US) 275
1981	Bill Rogers (US)	276	Sandwich	Bernhard Langer (FRG) 280
1982	Tom Watson (US)	284	Royal Troon	Peter Oosterhuis, Nick Price (SA) 285
1983	Tom Watson (US)	275	Royal Birkdale	Hale Irwin (US), Andy Bean (US) 276
1984	Seve Ballesteros (Spa)	276	St Andrews	Bernhard Langer (FRG), Tom Watson (US) 278
1985	Sandy Lyle	282	Sandwich	Payne Stewart (US) 283
1986	Greg Norman (Aus)	280	Turnberry	Gordon Brand Jnr 285
1987	Nick Faldo	279	Muirfield	Paul Azinger (US), Rodger Davis (Aus) 280
1988	Seve Ballesteros (Spa)	273	Royal Lytham	Nick Price (Zim) 275
1989	Mark Calcavecchia (US)	275*	Royal Troon	Greg Norman (Aus), Wayne Grady (Aus) 275

*denotes won after play-off

British Open Records

Most wins
6 Harry Vardon; 5 James Braid, John H.Taylor, Peter Thomson, Tom Watson,
4 Willie Park, Tom Morris, Snr, Tom Morris, Jnr, Walter Hagen, Bobby Locke
Lowest 72 hole total: 268 Tom Watson, Turnberry 1977
Lowest 18 hole total: 63 Mark Hayes, Turnberry 1977; Isao Aoki, Muirfield 1980;
Greg Norman, Turnberry 1986
Oldest winner: 46y 99d Tom Morris, Snr, 1867
Youngest Winner: 17y 161d Tom Morris, Jnr, 1868

ROUND-BY ROUND LEADERS IN THE OPEN

	1	2	3	4
1980 *Muirfield* par 71	Tom Watson (US)/ 68 Lee Trevino (US)	Trevino 135	Watson 202	Watson 271
1981 *Sandwich* par 71	Nick Job (GB)/ 70 Vicente Fernandez (Arg)	Bill Rogers (US) 138	Rogers 205	Rogers 271
1982 *Royal Troon* par 72	Bobby Clampett (US) 67	Clampett 133	Clampett 211	Watson 284
1983 *Royal Birkdale* par 71	Craig Stadler (US) 64	Stadler 134	Watson 205	Watson 275
1984 *St Andrews* par 72	Bill Longmuir (GB)/ 67 Greg Norman (Aus)/ Peter Jacobsen (US)	Ian Baker-Finch (Aus) 134	Baker-Finch/ 205 Watson	Severiano Ballesteros (Sp) 276
1985 *Sandwich* par 70	Christy O'Connor Jnr 64 (Ire)	David Graham (Aus)/ Sandy Lyle 139	Graham/ 209 Bernhard Langer (FRG)	Lyle 282
1986 *Turnberry* par 70	Ian Woosnam (GB) 70	Greg Norman (Aus) 137	Norman 211	Norman 280
1987 *Muirfield* par 71	Rodger Davis (Aus) 64	Paul Azinger (US) 136	Azinger 207	Nick Faldo (GB) 270
1988 *Royal Lytham* par 71	Ballesteros 67	Nick Price (SA) 137	Price 206	Ballesteros 273
1989 *Royal Troon* par 72	Wayne Stephens (GB) 66	Wayne Grady (Aus) 135	Grady 204	Mark Calcavecchia (US) 275

THE OTHER MAJORS

	US OPEN		US PGA		US MASTERS	
1895	Horace Rawlins	173	–		–	
1896	James Foulis	152	–		–	
1897	Joe Lloyd	162	–		–	
1898	Fred Herd	328	–		–	
1899	Willie Smith	315	–		–	
1900	Harry Vardon	313	–		–	
1901	Willie Anderson	331*	–		–	
1902	Laurie Auchterlonie	307	–		–	
1903	Willie Anderson	307*	–		–	
1904	Willie Anderson	303	–		–	
1905	Willie Anderson	314	–		–	
1906	Alex Smith	295	–		–	
1907	Alex Ross	302	–		–	
1908	Fred McLeod	322*	–		–	
1909	George Sargent	290	–		–	
1910	Alex Smith	298*	–		–	
1911	John McDermott	307*	–		–	
1912	John McDermott	294	–		–	
1913	Francis Ouimet	304*	–		–	
1914	Walter Hagen	290	–		–	
1915	Jerome Travers	297	–		–	
1916	Charles Evans Jnr	286	Jim Barnes	1 up	–	
1919	Walter Hagen	301*	Jim Barnes	6 & 5	–	
1920	Ted Ray (GB)	295	Jock Hutchison	1 up	–	
1921	Jim Barnes	289	Walter Hagen	3 & 2	–	
1922	Gene Sarazen	288	Gene Sarazen	4 & 3	–	
1923	Bobby Jones	296*	Gene Sarazen	1 up	–	
1924	Cyril Walker	297	Walter Hagen	2 up	–	
1925	Willie Macfarlane	291*	Walter Hagen	6 & 5	–	
1926	Bobby Jones	293	Walter Hagen	5 & 3	–	
1927	Tommy Armour	301*	Walter Hagen	1 up	–	
1928	Johnny Farrell	294*	Leo Diegel	6 & 5	–	
1929	Bobby Jones	294*	Leo Diegel	6 & 4	–	
1930	Bobby Jones	287	Tommy Armour	1 up	–	
1931	Billy Burke	292*	Tom Creavy	2 & 1	–	
1932	Gene Sarazen	286	Olin Outra	4 & 3	–	
1933	Johnny Goodman	287	Gene Sarazen	5 & 4	–	
1934	Olin Dutra	293	Paul Runyan	1 up	Horton Smith	284
1935	Sam Parks Jnr	299	Johnny Revolta	5 & 4	Gene Sarazen	282*
1936	Tony Manero	282	Densmore Shute	3 & 2	Horton Smith	285
1937	Ralph Guldahl	281	Densmore Shute	1 up	Byron Nelson	283
1938	Ralph Guldahl	284	Paul Runyan	8 & 7	Henry Picard	285
1939	Byron Nelson	284*	Henry Picard	1 up	Ralph Guldahl	279
1940	Lawson Little	287	Byron Nelson	1 up	Jimmy Demaret	280
1941	Craig Wood	284	Vic Ghezzi	1 up	Craig Wood	280
1942	–		Sam Snead	2 & 1	Byron Nelson	280*
1944	–		Bob Hamilton	1 up	–	
1945	–		Byron Nelson	4 & 3	–	
1946	Lloyd Mangrum	284*	Ben Hogan	6 & 4	Herman Keiser	282
1947	Lew Worsham	282*	Jim Ferrier	2 & 1	Jimmy Demaret	281
1948	Ben Hogan	276	Ben Hogan	7 & 6	Claude Harmon	279
1949	Cary Middlecoff	286	Sam Snead	3 & 2	Sam Snead	282
1950	Ben Hogan	287*	Chandler Harper	4 & 3	Jimmy Demaret	283
1951	Ben Hogan	287	Sam Snead	7 & 6	Ben Hogan	280
1952	Julius Boros	281	Jim Turnesa	1 up	Sam Snead	286
1953	Ben Hogan	283	Walter Burkemo	2 & 1	Ben Hogan	274
1954	Ed Furgol	284	Chick Harbert	4 & 3	Sam Snead	289*
1955	Jack Fleck	287	Doug Ford	4 & 3	Cary Middlecoff	279
1956	Cary Middlecoff	281	Jack Burke	3 & 2	Jack Burke Jnr	289
1957	Dick Mayer	282	Lionel Hebert	2 & 1	Doug Ford	282
1958	Tommy Bolt	283	Dow Finsterwald	276	Arnold Palmer	284
1959	Billy Casper	282	Bob Rosburg	277	Art Wall Jnr	284
1960	Arnold Palmer	280	Jay Hebert	281	Arnold Palmer	282

	US OPEN		US PGA		US MASTERS	
1961	Gene Littler	281	Jerry Barber	277*	Gary Player (SA)	280
1962	Jack Nicklaus	283*	Gary Player (SA)	278	Arnold Palmer	280*
1963	Julius Boros	293*	Jack Nicklaus	279	Jack Nicklaus	286
1964	Ken Venturi	278	Bobby Nichols	271	Arnold Palmer	276
1965	Gary Player (SA)	282*	Dave Marr	280	Jack Nicklaus	271
1966	Billy Casper	278*	Al Geiberger	280	Jack Nicklaus	288*
1967	Jack Nicklaus	275	Don January	281*	Gay Brewer	280
1968	Lee Trevino	275	Julius Boros	281	Bob Goalby	277
1969	Orville Moody	281	Ray Floyd	276	George Archer	281
1970	Tony Jacklin (GB)	281	Dave Stockton	279	Billy Casper	279*
1971	Lee Trevino	280*	Jack Nicklaus	281	Charles Coody	279
1972	Jack Nicklaus	290	Gary Player (SA)	281	Jack Nicklaus	286
1973	Johnny Miller	279	Jack Nicklaus	277	Tommy Aaron	283
1974	Hale Irwin	287	Lee Trevino	276	Gary Player (SA)	278
1975	Lou Graham	287*	Jack Nicklaus	276	Jack Nicklaus	276
1976	Jerry Pate	277	Dave Stockton	281	Ray Floyd	271
1977	Hubert Green	278	Lanny Wadkins	282*	Tom Watson	276
1978	Andy North	285	John Mahaffey	276*	Gary Player (SA)	277
1979	Hale Irwin	284	David Graham (Aus)	272*	Fuzzy Zoeller	280*
1980	Jack Nicklaus	272	Jack Nicklaus	274	Seve Ballesteros (Spa)	275
1981	David Graham (Aus)	273	Larry Nelson	273	Tom Watson	280
1982	Tom Watson	282	Ray Floyd	272	Craig Stadler	284*
1983	Larry Nelson	280	Hal Sutton	274	Seve Ballesteros (Spa)	280
1984	Fuzzy Zoeller	276*	Lee Trevino	273	Ben Crenshaw	277
1985	Andy North	279	Hubert Green	278	Bernhard Langer (FRG)	282
1986	Ray Floyd	279	Bob Tway	276	Jack Nicklaus	279
1987	Scott Simpson	277	Larry Nelson	287	Larry Mize	285*
1988	Curtis Strange	278	Jeff Sluman	272	Sandy Lyle (GB)	281
1989	Curtis Strange	278	Payne Stewart	276	Nick Faldo (GB)	283*

* denotes won after a play-off

Most Majors
18 Jack Nicklaus (6 Masters; 5 US PGA; 4 US Open; 3 British Open)
11 Walter Hagen (5 US PGA; 4 British Open; 2 US Open)
9 Ben Hogan (4 US Open; 2 Masters; 2 US PGA, 1 British Open)
9 Gary Player (3 British Open; 3 Masters; 2 US PGA; 1 US Open)
8 Tom Watson (5 British Open; 2 Masters; 1 US Open)

MOST MAJORS IN THE 1980s
Players
5 Tom Watson (US)
4 Seve Ballesteros (Spa)
3 Jack Nicklaus (US)
3 Larry Nelson (US)
2 Raymond Floyd (US)
2 Nick Faldo (GB)
2 Sandy Lyle (GB)
2 Curtis Strange (US)
Nations
29 United States
4 Spain
4 Great Britain
2 Australia
1 West Germany

RYDER CUP

United States versus Great Britain 1927-71; Great Britain and Ireland 1973-77;
versus Europe 1979- . Since 1963 played over three days.

		Running Scores			Captains	
	Venue	Day 1	Day 2	Day 3	GB/Europe	United States
		GB US	GB US			
1927	Worcester, Massachusetts	1 – 3	2½ – 9½	–	Ted Ray	Walter Hagen
1929	Moortown, Yorks	1½ – 2½	7 - 5	–	George Duncan	Walter Hagen
1931	Scioto, Ohio	1 – 3	3 – 9	–	Charles Whitcombe	Walter Hagen
1933	Southport and Ainsdale	2½ – 1½	6½ – 5½	–	John H Taylor	Walter Hagen
1935	Ridgewood, New Jersey	1 – 3	3 – 9	–	Charles Whitcombe	Walter Hagen
1937	Southport and Ainsdale	1½ – 2½	4 – 8	–	Charles Whitcombe	Walter Hagen*
1947	Portland, Oregan	0 – 4	1 – 11	–	Henry Cotton	Ben Hogan
1949	Ganton, Yorks	3 – 1	5 – 7	–	Charles Whitcombe*	Ben Hogan*
1951	Pinehurst, North Carolina	1 – 3	2½ – 9½	–	Arthur Lacey*	Sam Snead
1953	Wentworth, Surrey	1 – 3	5½ – 6½	–	Henry Cotton*	Lloyd Mangrum
1955	Thunderbird, Calif.	1 – 3	4 – 8	–	Dai Rees	Chick Harbert
1957	Lindrick Club, Yorks	1 – 3	7½ – 4½	–	Dai Rees	Jack Burke
1959	Elorado CC, California	1½ – 2½	3½ – 8½	–	Dai Rees	Sam Snead
1961	Royal Lytham & St Annes	2 – 6	9½ – 14½	–	Dai Rees	Jerry Barber
1963	Atlanta, Georgia	2 – 6	4 – 23	9 – 23	Johnny Fallon*	Arnold Palmer
1965	Royal Birkdale, Southport	4 – 4	7 – 9	12½ – 19½	Harry Weetman*	Byron Nelson*
1967	Houston, Texas	2½ – 5½	3 – 13	8½ – 23½	Dai J Rees*	Ben Hogan*
1969	Royal Birkdale, Southport	4½ – 3½	8 – 7½	16 – 16	Eric Brown*	Sam Snead*
1971	St Louis, Missouri	4½ – 3½	6 – 12½	13½ – 18½	Eric Brown*	Jay Hebert*
1973	Muirfield, Scotland	5½ – 2½	8 – 8	13 – 19	Bernard Hunt*	Jack Burke*
1975	Laurel Valley, Pennsylvania	1½ – 6½	3½ – 12½	11 – 21	Bernard Hunt*	Arnold Palmer*
1977	Royal Lytham & St Annes	1½ – 3½	2½ – 7½	7½ – 12½	Brian Huggett*	Dow Finsterwald*
		Eur US	Eur US	Eur US		
1979	Greenbrier, West Virginia	2½ – 5½	7½ – 8½	11 – 17	John Jacobs*	Billy Casper*
1981	Walton Heath GC, Surrey	4½ – 3½	5½ – 10½	9½ – 18½	John Jacobs*	Dave Marr*
1983	PGA National GC, Florida	4½ – 3½	8 – 8	13½ – 14½	Tony Jacklin*	Jack Nicklaus*
1985	The Belfry, Sutton Coldfield	3½ – 4½	9 – 7	16½ – 11½	Tony Jacklin*	Lee Trevino*
1987	Muirfield Village, Columbus	6 – 2	10½ – 5½	15 – 13	Tony Jacklin*	Jack Nicklaus*
1989	The Belfry, Sutton Coldfield	5 – 3	9 – 7	14 – 14	Tony Jacklin*	Raymond Floyd*

Denotes non-playing captain

WORLD MATCH-PLAY CHAMPIONSHIP

Sponsors: Piccadilly 1964-76, Colgate 1977-8, Suntory 1979-

1964 Arnold Palmer (US) beat Neil Coles (GB) 2 & 1
1965 Gary Player (SA) beat Peter Thomson (Aus) 3 & 2
1966 Gary Player (SA) beat Jack Nicklaus (US) 6 & 4
1967 Arnold Palmer (US) beat Peter Thomson (Aus) 1 up
1968 Gary Player (SA) beat Bob Charles (NZ) 1 up
1969 Bob Charles (NZ) beat Gene Littler (US) 37th
1970 Jack Nicklaus (US) beat Lee Trevino (US) 2 & 1
1971 Gary Player (SA) beat Jack Nicklaus (US) 5 & 4
1972 Tom Weiskopf (US) beat Lee Trevino (US) 4 & 3
1973 Gary Player (SA) beat Graham Marsh (Aus) 40th
1974 Hale Irwin (US) beat Gary Player (SA) 3 & 1
1975 Hale Irwin (US) beat Al Geiberger (US) 4 & 2

1976   David Graham (Aus) beat Hale Irwin (US) 38th
1977   Graham Marsh (Aus) beat Ray Floyd (US) 5 & 3
1978   Isoa Aoki (Jap) beat Simon Owen (NZ) 3 & 2
1979   Bill Rogers (US) beat Isao Aoki (Jap) 1 up
1980   Greg Norman (Aus) beat Sandy Lyle (GB) 1 up
1981   Seve Ballesteros (Spa) beat Ben Crenshaw (US) 1 up
1982   Seve Ballesteros (Spa) beat Sandy Lyle (GB) 37th
1983   Greg Norman (Aus) beat Nick Faldo (GB) 3 & 2
1984   Seve Ballesteros (Spa) beat Bernhard Langer (FRG) 2 & 1
1985   Seve Ballesteros (Spa) beat Bernhard Langer (FRG) 6 & 5
1986   Greg Norman (Aus) beat Sandy Lyle (GB) 2 & 1
1987   Ian Woosnam (GB) beat Sandy Lyle (GB) 1 up
1988   Sandy Lyle (GB) beat Nick Faldo (GB) 2 & 1
1989   Nick Faldo (GB) beat Ian Woosnam (GB) 1 up

Most wins
5 Gary Player; 4 Severiano Ballesteros; 3 Greg Norman; 2 Arnold Palmer, Hale Irwin

TOP MONEY WINNERS OF THE 1980s

	UNITED STATES	$		*EUROPE*	£
1980	Tom Watson	530,808		Greg Norman	74,829
1981	Tom Kite	375,698		Bernhard Langer	95,991
1982	Craig Stadler	446,462		Sandy Lyle	86,141
1983	Hal Sutton	426,668		Nick Faldo	140,761
1984	Tom Watson	476,260		Bernhard Langer	160,883
1985	Curtis Strange	542,321		Sandy Lyle	199,020
1986	Greg Norman	653,296		Seve Ballesteros	259,275
1987	Curtis Strange	925,941		Ian Woosnam	439,075
1988	Curtis Strange	1,147,644		Seve Ballesteros	502,000
1989	Tom Kite	1,395,278		Ronan Rafferty	400,311

WORLD CUP
(Formerly the Canada Cup)

1953	Argentina
1954	Australia
1955	United States
1956	United States
1957	Japan
1958	Ireland
1959	Australia
1960	United States
1961	United States
1962	United States
1963	United States
1964	United States
1965	South Africa
1966	United States
1967	United States
1968	Canada
1969	United States
1970	Australia
1971	United States
1972	Taiwan
1973	United States
1974	South Africa
1975	United States
1976	Spain
1977	Spain
1978	United States
1979	United States
1980	Canada
1981	Not held
1982	Spain
1983	United States
1984	Spain
1985	Canada
1986	Not held
1987	Wales
1988	United States

Most wins
Team: 17 United States; 4 Spain; 3 Australia, Canada; 2 South Africa
Played on winning Teams: 6 Jack Nicklaus, Arnold Palmer; 4 Sam Snead
Individual title: 3 Jack Nicklaus (US) 1963-64, 1971; 2 Stan Leonard (Can) 1954, 1959; Roberto de Vicenzo (Arg) 1962, 1970; Johnny Miller (US) 1973, 1975, Gary Player (SA) 1965, 1977

WALKER CUP

Year	Venue	Winners	Score
1922	Long Island, New York	US	8 – 4
1923	St Andrews, Scotland	US	6½ – 5½
1924	Garden City, New York	US	9 – 3
1926	St Andrews, Scotland	US	6½ – 5½
1928	Chicago GC, Illinois	US	11 – 1
1930	Royal St George's, England	US	10 – 2
1932	Brookline, Massachusetts	US	9½ – 2½
1934	St Andrews, Scotland	US	9½ – 2½
1936	Pine Valley, New Jersey	US	10½ – 1½
1938	St Andrews, Scotland	GB	7½ – 4½
1947	St Andrews, Scotland	US	8 – 4
1949	Winged Foot, New York	US	10 – 2
1951	Royal Birkdale, England	US	7½ – 4½
1953	Kittansett, Massachusetts	US	9 – 3
1955	St Andrews, Scotland	US	10 – 2
1957	Minikhada, Minnesota	US	8½ – 3½
1959	Muirfield, Scotland	US	9 – 3
1961	Seattle, Washington	US	11 – 1
1963	Turnberry, Scotland	US	14 – 10
1965	Baltimore, Maryland	Drawn	12 – 12
1967	Royal St George's, England	US	15 – 9
1969	Milwaukee, Wisconsin	US	13 – 11
1971	St Andrews, Scotland	GB	13 – 11
1973	Brookline, Massachusetts	US	14 – 10
1975	St Andrews, Scotland	US	15½ – 8½
1977	Shinnecock Hills, New York	US	16 – 8

1979	Muirfield, Scotland	US	15½ – 8½
1981	Cypress Point, California	US	15 – 9
1983	Royal Liverpool, England	US	13½ – 10½
1985	Pine Valley, Philadelphia	US	13 – 11
1987	Sunningdale, England	US	16½ – 7½
1989	Peachtree, Georgia	GB	12½ – 11½

Wins
28 United States; 3 Great Britain; 1 Drawn

THE AMATEUR CHAMPIONSHIP
Winners since 1980. All British unless otherwise stated

1980	Duncan Evans
1981	Philippe Ploujoux (Fra)
1982	Martin Thompson
1983	Andrew Parkin
1984	José-Maria Olazabal (Spa)
1985	Garth McGimpsey

1986	David Curry
1987	Paul Mayo
1988	Christian Hardin (Swe)
1989	Stephen Dodd

US AMATEUR CHAMPIONSHIP
Winners (all US) since 1980

1980	Hal Sutton
1981	Nathaniel Crosby
1982	Jay Sigel
1983	Jay Sigel
1984	Scott Verplank
1985	Sam Randolph
1986	Buddy Alexander
1987	Billy Mayfair
1988	Eric Meeks
1989	Chris Patton

WOMEN'S MAJORS
Winners since 1980

	US Open	US LPGA	du Maurier	Nabisco Dinah Shaw
1980	Amy Alcott	Sally Little	Pat Bradley	–
1981	Pat Bradley	Donna Caponi	Jan Stephenson	–
1982	Janet Alex	Jan Stephenson	Sandra Haynie	–
1983	Jan Stephenson (Aus)	Patty Sheehan	Hollis Stacey	Amy Alcott
1984	Hollis Stacey	Patty Sheehan	Julie Inkster	Julie Inkster
1985	Kathy Baker	Nancy Lopez	Pat Bradley	Alice Miller
1986	Jane Geddes	Pat Bradley	Pat Bradley	Pat Bradley
1987	Laura Davies (GB)	Jane Geddes	Jody Rosenthal	Betsy King
1988	Liselotte Nuemann (Swe)	Sherri Turner	Sally Little	Amy Alcott
1989	Betsy King	Nancy Lopez	Tammie Green	Julie Inkster

BRITISH WOMEN'S OPEN CHAMPIONSHIP
Winners since 1980

1980	Debbie Massey (US)
1981	Debbie Massey (US)
1982	Marta Figueras-Dotti (Spa)
1983	
1984	Ayako Okamoto (Jap)
1985	Betsy King (US)
1986	Laura Davies (GB)
1987	Alison Nicholas (GB)
1988	Corinne Dibnah (Aus)
1989	Jane Geddes (US)

1990

THE MAJORS
Apr 5-8: THE MASTERS (Augusta, Georgia); *Jun 14-17:* US OPEN (Medinah, Illinois); *Jul 19-22:* THE OPEN (St Andrews); *Aug 9-12:* US PGA Championship (Shoal Creek, Alabama)

OTHER TOURNAMENTS
Jan 4-7: Mony Tournament of Champions (Carlsbad, California); *Jan 11-14:* Northern Telecom Tucson Open (Tucson, Arizona); *Jan 17-21:* Bob Hope Chrysler Classic (La Quinta, California); *Jan 25-28:* Phoenix Open (Scottdale, Arizona); Feb 1-4: Tenerife Open (Del Sur); AT & T Pro-Am (Pebble Beach, California); *Feb 8-11:* European tournament (TBA); Hawaiian Open (Honolulu, USA); *Feb 15-18:* European Tournament (TBA); Shearson Lehman Hutton Open (La Jolla, California); *Feb 22-25:* Desert Classic/ETPD Tournament; Nissan Los Angeles Open (Pacific Palisades, California); *Mar 1-4* Mediterranean Open; Doral Ryder Open (Miami, Florida); *Mar 8-11:* Open de Balearas (Mallorca); Honda Classic (Coral Springs, Florida); *Mar 15-18:* US Tournament

Players' Championship (Ponte Vedra, Florida); Catalan Open (Spain); *Mar 22-25:* Volvo Open (Italy); Nestle Invitational (Orlando, Florida); *Mar 29-Apr 1:* European Tournament (TBA); Independent Insurance Agent Open (The Woodlands, Texas); *Apr 5-8:* Jersey Open (La Moye); Deposit Guaranty Golf Classic (Hattiesburg, Mississippi); *Apr 12-15:* Cannes Open (France); Heritage Classic (Hilton Head Island, South Carolina); *Apr 19-22:* Madrid Open (Spain); Greater Greensboro Open (Greensboro, North Carolina); *Apr 26-29:* Spanish Open (TBA); USF and G Classic (New Orleans, Louisiana); *May 3-6:* Benson and Hedges International (St Mellion); Byron Nelson Classic (Irving, Texas); *May 5-6:* Berkshire Trophy (The Berkshire); *May 10-13:* Belgian Open (Brussels); Memorial Tournament (Dublin, Ohio); *May 17-20:* Italian Open (TBA); South Western Bell Colonial (Fort Worth, Texas); *May 18-20:* Brabazon Trophy (Burnham and Berrow); *May 24-27:* South Atlanta Classic (Marietta, Georgia); *May 25-28:* Volvo PGA Championship (Wentworth); *May 30-31:* Lagonda Trophy (Camberley Heath); *May 30-Jun 1:* English Open seniors' championship (Bridgnorth and Enville); *May 31-Jun 3:* Dunlop British Masters (Woburn); Kemper Open (Potomac, Maryland); *Jun 4-9:* Amateur championship (Muirfield and Luffness New); *Jun 7-10:* Scandinavian Open (Drottningholm, Sweden); Western Open (Oak Brook, Illinois); *Jun 12-16:* British women's amateur championship (Dunbar); *Jun 13-16:* International European amateur championship (Denmark); *Jun 14-17:* Wang National Pro-Celebrity (Moor Park); *Jun 21-24:* Carroll's Irish Open (Portmarnock); Buick Classic (Rye, New York); *Jun 22-23:* Lytham Trophy (Royal Lytham & St Annes); *Jun 28-Jul 1:* French Open (TBA); Greater Hartford Open (Cromwell, Connecticut); *Jul 4-7:* Monte Carlo Open (Mont Agel); *Jul 5-8:* Anheuser-Busch Golf Classic (Williamsburg, Virginia); *Jul 11-14:* Bell's Scottish Open; *Jul 12-15:* Bank of Boston Classic (Sutton, Massachusetts); *Jul 26-29:* KLM Dutch Open (TBA); Buick Open (Grand Blanc, Michigan); *Jul 28-29 (or Jul 31-Aug 1):* Curtis Cup (Somerset Hills, New

Jersey); *Jul 26-29:* Volvo Seniors' British Open; European event (TBA); *Jul 30-Aug 4:* English amateur championship (Woodhall Spa); *Aug 2-5:* PLM Open (Bokskogen, Sweden); St Jude Classic (Memphis, Tennessee); *Aug 8-10:* British seniors' amateur championship (The Berkshire); *Aug 9-17:* British Boys' championships and internationals (Hunstanton); *Aug 9-12:* Murphy's Cup (Fulford, York); *Aug 14-17:* British Girls' championship (Penrith); *Aug 16-19:* NM English Open (TBA); The International (Castle Rock, Colorado); *Aug 23-26:* German Open (TBA); World Series of Golf (Akron, Ohio); Chattanooga Classic (Chattanooga, Tennessee); *Aug 30-Sep 2:* European Masters/Swiss Open (Crans-sur-Sierre); Greater Milwaukee Open (Franklin, Wisconsin); *Sep 6-9:* Panasonic European Open (Walton Heath); Hardee's Golf Classic (Coal Valley, Illinois); *Sep 12-14:* Home Internationals, men (Conwy); *Sep 13-16:* Lancome Trophy (St Nom La Breteche, France); Canadian Open (Oakville, Ontario); *Sep 20-23:* Suntory World Match Play (Wentworth); BMW International Open (TBA); BC Open (Edicott, New York); *Sep 27-30:* Epson Grand Prix (St Pierre, Chepstow); Southern Open (Columbus, Georgia); *Oct 4-7:* German Masters; Texas Open (San Antonio, Texas); *Oct 10-14:* Las Vegas Invitational (Las Vegas, Nevada); *Oct 11-14:* Dunhill Cup (St Andrews); Austrian Open; *Oct 17-20:* Walt Disney World/Oldsmobile Classic (Lake Buena Vista, Florida); *Oct 18-21:* Portuguese Open/Tournament Players' Championship; Women's World Cup (Russley, New Zealand); *Oct 25-28:* Volvo Masters (TBA); Nabisco Championship (Houston, Texas); *Nov 1-4:* Four Tours World championship of Golf (Japan); *Nov 7-10:* Isuzu Kapalua International (Maui, Hawaii); *Nov 15-18:* European Tournament (TBA); *Nov 16-18:* RMCC Invitational hosted by Greg Norman (Thousand Oaks, California); *Nov 24-25:* Skins Game (La Quinta, California); *Nov 29-Dec 2:* JC Penney Classic (Largo, Florida); *Dec 6-9:* Team Championship (Wellington, Florida)

FUTURE VENUES OF MAJOR TOURNAMENTS
1991
The Open – Royal Birkdale; US Open – Hazeltine National, Chaska, Minnesota; US PGA – Crooked Stick Golf Club, Carmel, Indiana
1992
The Open – Muirfield; US Open – Pebble Beach, California; US PGA – Bellerive Country Club, Creve Coeur, Missouri

GREYHOUND RACING

1989

DAILY MIRROR GREYHOUND DERBY
Wimbledon, Jun 24
480 metres
1 Lartigue Note (Trap 2) evens fav
2 Kilcannon Bullet (Trap 6) 2-1
3 Castleivy Mick (Trap 1) 10-1
4 Early Vocation (Trap 5) 10-1
5 Cooladine Style (Trap 3) 25-1
6 Catsrock Rocket (Trap 4) 7-1
Time: 28.79s
Trainer: Ger McKenna, Ireland

THE BBC GREYHOUND TELEVISION TROPHY
Catford, Apr 12
850 metres
1 Proud To Run (Trap 4) 4-5f
2 Catunda Flame (Trap 2) 6-1
3 Jet Streamer (Trap 5) 10-1
Time: 55.25s

GRAND NATIONAL
Hall Green, Apr 1
474 metres Hurdles
1 Lemon Chip (Trap 5) Evens f
2 Blazing Home (Trap 1) 3-1
3 Gismo Pasha (Trap 6) 9-1
Time: 29.64s

CHAMPIONS

GREYHOUND DERBY
At White City 1927-84, except 1940 at Harringay; at Wimbledon 1985 – . Raced over 500yd 1927, 525yd 1928-74, 500m 1975-85, 480m 1986-

		Price	Trap	Time
1927	Entry Badge	1-4f	5	29.01s
1928	Doher Ash	5-1	1	30.48s
1929	Mick the Miller	4-7f	4	29.96s
1930	Mick the Miller	4-9f	1	30.24s
1931	Seldom Lad	7-2	4	30.04s
1932	Wild Woolley	5-2	6	29.72s
1933	Future Cutlet	6-1	3	29.80s
1934	Davesland	3-1	4	29.81s
1935	Greta Ranee	4-1	3	30.18s
1936	Fine Jubilee	10-11f	3	29.48s
1937	Wattle Bark	5-2	6	29.26s
1938	Lone Keel	9-4	3	29.62s
1939	Highland Rum	2-1jf	6	29.35s
1940	G.R. Archduke	100-7	1	29.66s
1945	Ballyhennessy Seal	Evens f	1	29.56s
1946	Mondays News	5-1	3	29.24s
1947	Trev's Perfection	4-1	2	28.95s
1948	Priceless Border	1-2f	1	28.78s
1949	Narrogar Ann	5-1	2	28.95s
1950	Ballymac Ball	7-2	4	28.72s
1951	Ballylanigan Tanist	11-4	1	28.62s
1952	Endless Gossip	Evens f	6	28.50s
1953	Daws Dancer	10-1	5	29.20s
1954	Paul's Fun	8-15f	3	28.84s
1955	Rushton Mack	5-1	2	28.97s
1956	Dunmore King	7-2	3	29.22s
1957	Ford Spartan	Evens f	1	28.84s
1958	Pigalle Wonder	4-5f	1	28.65s

1959	Mile Bush Pride	Evens f	4	28.76s
1960	Duleek Dandy	25-1	4	29.15s
1961	Palm's Printer	2-1	1	28.84s
1962	The Grand Canal	2-1f	5	29.09s
1963	Lucky Boy Boy	Evens f	1	29.00s
1964	Hack Up Chieftain	20-1	1	28.92s
1965	Chittering Clapton	5-2	6	28.82s
1966	Faithful Hope	8-1	3	28.52s
1967	Tric-Trac	9-2	1	29.00s
1968	Camira Flash	100-8	4	28.89s
1969	Sand Star	5-4f	4	28.76s
1970	John Silver	11-4	2	29.01s
1971	Dolores Rocket	11-4	2	28.74s
1972	Patricia's Hope	7-1	5	28.55s
1973	Patricia's Hope	7-2	5	28.68s
1974	Jimsun	20-1	2	28.76s
1975	Tartan Khan	25-1	2	29.57s
1976	Mutts Silver	6-1	4	29.38s
1977	Balliniska Band	Evens f	5	29.16s
1978	Lacca Champion	6-4f	3	29.42s
1979	Sarah's Bunny	3-1	6	29.53s
1980	Indian Joe	13-8jf	6	29.68s
1981	Parkdown Jet	4-5f	6	29.57s
1982	Laurie's Panther	6-4f	1	29.60s
1983	I'm Slippy	6-1	4	29.40s
1984	Whisper Wishes	7-4f	4	29.43s
1985	Pagan Swallow	9-1	5	29.04s
1986	Tico	6-4jf	5	28.69s
1987	Signal Spark	14-1	4	28.83s
1988	Hit the Lid	3-1	6	28.53s
1989	Lartigue Note	Evens f	2	28.79s

BBC TELEVISION TROPHY
First Run 1956. Raced at various tracks and distances
Winners since 1980:

	(Venue)	Winner
1980	(Wembley)	Tread Fast
1981	(Perry Barr)	Decoy Boom
1982	(Belle Vue)	Alfa My Son
1983	(Walthamstow)	Sandy Lane
1984	(Wimbledon)	Weston Prelude
1985	(Wolverhampton)	Scurlogue Champ
1986	(Brough Park)	Scurlogue Champ
1987	(Oxford)	Glenowen Queen
1988	(Hall Green)	Minnie's Siren
1989	(Catford)	Proud To Run

Most wins: **2** Scurlogue Champ

1990

In 1990 the traditional pattern of 10 Classics will be scrapped and replaced by a set-up of 10 Group One races. The Oaks, the Scurry and the Laurels have been demoted to Group Two status and replaced by the Essex Vase, the Regency and the TV Trophy.

FIXTURES
Group One finals
Mar 30: Grand National (474m) Hall Green, Birmingham; April: TV Trophy tba; May 4: Essex Vase (400m) Romford; May 17: Regency (740m) Hove; May 19: Scottish Derby (500m) Shawfield, Glasgow; Jun 23: GREYHOUND DERBY (480m) Wimbledon; Sep 22: Gold Collar (555m) Catford; Sep 29: Cesarewitch (815m) Belle Vue, Manchester; Oct 13: Grand Prix (640m) Walthamstow; Nov 16: St Leger (655m) Wembley.

GYMNASTICS

1989

EUROPEAN CHAMPIONSHIPS
Men
Stockholm, May 6-7
Combined
1 Igor Korobchinsky (USSR) 58.100
2 Valentin Mogilnyi (USSR) 58.050
3 Holger Behrendt (GDR) 57.850
Floor
1 Igor Korobchinsky (USSR) 9.750
2 Cristian Brezeanu (Rom) 9.725
3 Holger Behrendt (GDR) 9.687
Pommel Horse
1 Valentin Mogilnyi (USSR) 9.837
2 Andreas Wecker (GDR) 9.737
3 Kalofer Hristozov (Bul) 9.700
Rings
1 Holger Behrendt (GDR) 9.850
2 Vitali Marinitch (GDR) 9.812
3 Andreas Aguilar (FRG) 9.800
Vault
1 Valentin Mogilnyi (USSR) 9.793
2 Gyula Takacs (Hun) 9.750
3 Marius Gherman (Rom) 9.712
Parallel Bars
1 Kalofer Hristozov (Bul) 9.837
2 Andreas Wecker (GDR) 9.775
3 Valentin Mogilnyi (USSR) 9.762
High Bars
1 Andreas Wecker (GDR) 9.862
2 Vitali Marinitch (GDR) & Nicusor Pascu (Rom) 9.850
(tied)
Women
Brussels, May 21-23
Combined
1 Svetlana Boginskaya (USSR) 39.862
2 Daniela Silivas (Rom) 39.849
3 Olga Strayeva (USSR) 39.612
Vault
1 Svetlana Boginskaya (USSR) 9.962
2 Milena Mavaodeyeva (Bul) 9.924
3 Cristina Bontas (Rom) 9.906
Beam
1 Gabriela Potorac (Rom) & Olessia Doudnik (USSR) 9.975 (tied)
3 Daniela Silivas (Rom) 9.962
Asymmetrical Bars
1 Henrietta Onodi (Hun) 9.962
2 Daniela Silivas (Rom) & Olga Strayeva (USSR) 9.950
(tied)
Floor
1 Svetlana Boginskaya (USSR) & Daniela Silivas (Rom) 10.000 (tied)
3 Christina Bontas (Rom) & Henrietta Onodi (Hun) 9.962 (tied)

BRITISH CHAMPIONSHIPS
Chesterfield, Mar 17
Men
Overall
1 James May (Bristol) 110.65
2 Paul Bowler (Manchester) 107.55
3 Neil Thomas (Liverpool) 106.45

Apparatus Champions:

Floor	Neil Thomas 18.950
Pommel horse	James May 18.250
Rings	James May 18.450
Vault	Neil Thomas 19.050
Parallel bars	James May 18.650
High Bar	James May 18.375

Women
Overall
1 Lisa Grayson (Redcar) 73.425
2 Lisa Shaw (Trent) 73.325
3 Joanna Prescott (Trent) 73.000
Apparatus Champions:

Vault	Lisa Shaw 19.250
Asymmetrical bars	Lisa Grayson 18.600
Beam	Joanna Prescott 18.050
Floor	Lorna Mainwaring 18.950

RHYTHMIC GYMNASTICS

EUROPEAN JUNIOR CHAMPIONSHIPS
Tenerife, Jun 15-18
Overall
1 Todorova Dimitrinka (Bulgaria) 39.2
2 Mila Marinova (Bulgaria) 39.1
3 Kristina Klukavichute (Bulgaria) 39.05
Team
1 Bulgaria 39.325
2 USSR 39.300
3 Spain 39.125

BRITISH RHYTHMIC CHAMPIONSHIPS
Bletchley, Jan 14
1 Alitia Sands (Coventry) 37.05
2 Gabrielle Yorath (Leeds) 35.85
3 Joanne Bisley (Coventry) 34.80

CHAMPIONS

OLYMPIC GAMES
Men
Combined

1900	Gustave Sandras (Fra)
1904	Julius Lenhart (Aut)
1908	Alberto Braglia (Ita)
1912	Alberto Braglia (Ita)
1920	Giorgio Zampori (Ita)
1924	Leon Stukelj (Yug)
1928	Georges Miez (Sui)
1932	Romeo Neri (Ita)
1936	Alfred Schwarzmann (Ger)
1948	Veikko Huhtanen (Fin)
1952	Viktor Chukarin (USSR)
1956	Viktor Chukarin (USSR)
1960	Boris Shakhlin (USSR)
1964	Yukio Endo (Jap)
1968	Sawao Kato (Jap)
1972	Sawao Kato (Jap)
1976	Nikolay Andrianov (USSR)
1980	Aleksandr Ditiatin (USSR)
1984	Koji Gushiken (Jap)
1988	Vlademir Artemov (USSR)

Floor

1932	Istvan Pelle (Hun)

1936	Georges Miez (Swi)
1948	Ferenc Pataki (Hun)
1952	William Thoresson (Swe)
1956	Valentin Muratov (USSR)
1960	Nobuyuki Aihara (Jap)
1964	Franco Menichelli (Ita)
1968	Sawao Kato (Jap)
1972	Nikolay Andrianov (USSR)
1976	Nikolay Andrianov (USSR)
1980	Roland Brückner (GDR)
1984	Li Ning (Chn)
1988	Sergey Kharikov (USSR)

Parallel Bars

1896	Alfred Flatow (Ger)
1904	George Eyser (US)
1924	August Güttinger (Swi)
1928	Ladislav Vacha (Cze)
1932	Romeo Neri (Ita)
1936	Konrad Frey (Ger)
1948	Michael Reusch (Swi)
1952	Hans Eugster (Swi)
1956	Viktor Chukarin (USSR)
1960	Boris Shakhlin (USSR)
1964	Yukio Endo (Jap)
1968	Akinori Nakayama (Jap)
1972	Sawao Kato (Jap)
1976	Sawao Kato (Jap)
1980	Aleksandr Tkachev (USSR)
1984	Bart Conner (US)
1988	Vlademir Artemov (USSR)

Pommel Horse

1896	Louis Zutter (Swi)
1904	Anton Heida (US)
1924	Josef Wilhelm (Swi)
1928	Hermann Hanggi (Swi)
1932	István Pelle (Hun)
1936	Konrad Frey (Ger)
1948	Paavo Aaltonen (Fin)
	Veikko Huhtanen (Fin) &
	Heikki Savolainen (Fin)
1952	Viktor Chukarin (USSR)
1956	Boris Shakhlin (USSR)
1960	Eugen Ekman (Fin) &
	Boris Shakhlin (USSR)
1964	Miroslav Cerar (Yug)
1968	Miroslav Cerar (Yug)
1972	Viktor Klimenko (USSR)
1976	Zoltán Magyar (Hun)
1980	Zoltán Magyar (Hun)
1984	Li Ning (Chn) &
	Peter Vidmar (US)
1988	Lyubomir Gueraskov (Bul)
	Zsolt Borkai (Hun) &
	Dmitri Belozerchev (USSR)

Rings

1896	Ioannis Mitropoulos (Gre)
1904	Hermann Glass (US)
1924	Francesco Martino (Ita)
1928	Leon Skutelj (Yug)
1932	George Gulack (US)
1936	Alois Hudec (Cze)
1948	Karl Frei (Swi)
1952	Grant Shaginyan (USSR)
1956	Albert Azaryan (USSR)
1960	Albert Azaryan (USSR)
1964	Takuji Hayata (Jap)
1968	Akinori Nakayama (Jap)
1972	Akinori Nakayama (Jap)
1976	Nikolay Andrianov (USSR)
1980	Aleksandr Ditiatin (USSR)
1984	Koji Gushiken (Jap) &
	Li Ning (Chn)
1988	Holger Behrendt (GDR) &
	Dmitri Belozerchev

Horizontal Bar

1896	Hermann Weingärtner (Ger)
1904	Anton Heida (US) &
	Edward Hennig (US)
1924	Leon Stukelj (Yug)
1928	Georges Miez (Swi)
1932	Dallas Bixler (US)
1936	Aleksanteri Saarvala (Fin)
1948	Josef Stadler (Swi)
1952	Jack Günthard (Swi)
1956	Takashi Ono (Jap)
1960	Takashi Ono (Jap)
1964	Boris Shakhlin (USSR)
1968	Mikhail Voronin (USSR) &
	Akinori Nakayama (Jap)
1972	Mitsuo Tsukahara (Jap)
1976	Mitsuo Tsukahara (Jap)
1980	Stoyan Deltchev (Bul)
1984	Shinji Morisue (Jap)
1988	Vladimir Artemov (USSR) &
	Valeri Lyukine (USSR)

Vault

1896	Carl Schumann (Ger)
1904	Anton Heida (US) &
	George Eyser (US)
1924	Frank Kriz (US)
1928	Eugen Mack (Swi)
1932	Savino Guglielmetti (Ita)
1936	Alfred Schwarzmann (Ger)
1948	Paavo Aaltonen (Fin)
1952	Viktor Chukarin (USSR)
1956	Helmuth Bantz (Ger) &
	Valentin Muratov (USSR)
1960	Takashi Ono (Jap) &
	Boris Shakhlin (USSR)
1964	Haruhiro Yamashita (Jap)
1968	Mikhail Voronin (USSR)
1972	Klaus Köste (GDR)
1976	Nikolay Andrianov (USSR)
1980	Nikolay Andrianov (USSR)
1984	Lou Yun (Chn)
1988	Lou Yun (Chn)

Team

1904	United States
1908	Sweden
1912	Italy
1920	Italy
1924	Italy
1928	Switzerland
1932	Italy
1936	Germany
1948	Finland
1952	USSR
1956	USSR
1960	Japan
1964	Japan
1968	Japan
1972	Japan
1976	Japan
1980	USSR
1984	United States
1988	USSR

Women

Combined

1952	Maria Gorokhovskaya (USSR)
1956	Larissa Latynina (USSR)
1960	Larissa Latynina (USSR)
1964	Vera Cáslavská (Cze)
1968	Vera Cáslavská (Cze)
1972	Lyudmila Tourischeva (USSR)
1976	Nadia Comaneci (Rom)
1980	Yelena Davydova (USSR)
1984	Mary Lou Retton (US)
1988	Yelena Shoushounova (USSR)

Asymmetrical Bars

1952	Margit Korondi (Hun)
1956	Agnes Keleti (Hun)
1960	Polina Astakhova (USSR)
1964	Polina Astakhova (USSR)
1968	Vera Cáslavská (Cze)
1972	Karin Janz (GDR)
1976	Nadia Comaneci (Rom)
1980	Maxi Gnauck (GDR)
1984	Ma Yanhong (Chn) &
	Julianne McNamara (US)
1988	Daniela Silivas (Rom)

Beam

1952	Nina Bocharova (USSR)
1956	Agnes Keleti (Hun)
1960	Eva Bosakova (Cze)
1964	Vera Cáslavská (Cze)
1968	Natalya Kuchinskaya (USSR)
1972	Olga Korbut (USSR)
1976	Nadia Comaneci (Rom)
1980	Nadia Comaneci (Rom)
1984	Simona Pauca (Rom) &
	Ecaterina Szabo (Rom)
1988	Daniela Silivas (Rom)

Floor

1952	Agnes Keleti (Hun)
1956	Larissa Latynina (USSR) &
	Agnes Keleti (Hun)
1960	Larissa Latynina (USSR)
1964	Larissa Latynina (USSR)
1968	Larissa Petrik (USSR) &
	Vera Cáslavská (Cze)
1972	Olga Korbut (USSR)
1976	Nelli Kim (USSR)
1980	Nelli Kim (USSR) &
	Nadia Comaneci (Rom)
1984	Ecaterina Szabo (Rom)
1988	Daniela Silivas (Rom)

Vault

1952	Yekaterina Kalinchuk (USSR)
1956	Larissa Latynina (USSR)
1960	Margarita Nikolayeva (USSR)
1964	Vera Cáslavská (Cze)
1968	Vera Cáslavská (Cze)
1972	Karin Janz (GDR)
1976	Nelli Kim (USSR)
1980	Natalya Shaposhnikova (USSR)
1984	Ecaterina Szabo (Rom)
1988	Svetlana Boginskaya (USSR)

Team

1928	Netherlands
1932	not held
1936	Germany
1948	Czechoslovakia
1952	USSR
1956	USSR
1960	USSR
1964	USSR
1968	USSR
1972	USSR
1976	USSR
1980	USSR
1984	Romania
1988	USSR

Rhythmic Gymnastics

1984	Fung Lori (Can)
1988	Marina Lobatch (USSR)

MOST OLYMPIC MEDALS

Total medals		Gold medals
18*	Larissa Latynina (USSR)	9
15	Nikolay Andrianov (USSR)	7
13	Boris Shakhlin (USSR)	7
13	Takashi Ono (Jap)	5
12	Sawao Kato (Jap)	8
11	Viktor Chukarin (USSR)	7
11	Vera Cáslavská (Cze)	7

Most in any sport

WORLD CHAMPIONSHIPS

(First held 1903)

Men

Combined (post-war winners)

1950	Walter Lehmann (Swi)
1954	Viktor Chukarin (USSR)
1958	Boris Shakhlin (USSR)
1962	Yuriy Titov (USSR)
1966	Mikhail Voronin (USSR)
1970	Eizo Kenmotsu (Jap)
1974	Shigeru Kasamatsu (Jap)
1978	Nikolay Andrianov (USSR)
1979	Aleksandr Ditiatin (USSR)
1981	Yuriy Korolev (USSR)
1983	Dmitri Belozerchev (USSR)
1985	Yuriy Korolev (USSR)
1987	Dmitri Belozerchev (USSR)

Individual Disciplines

Winners since 1981

Floor

1981	Yuriy Korolev (USSR) &
	Li Yuejiu (Chn)
1983	Tong Fei (Chn)
1985	Tong Fei (Chn)
1987	Lou Yun (Chn)

Vault

1981	Ralf-Peter Hemmann (GDR)
1983	Artur Akopian (USSR)
1985	Yuriy Korolev (USSR)
1987	Slvio Kroll (GDR) &
	Lou Yun (Chn)

Rings

1981	Aleksandr Ditiatin (USSR)
1983	Dmitriy Belozerchev (USSR) &
	Koji Gushiken (Jap)
1985	Li Ning (Chn) & Yuriy Korolev (USSR)
1987	Yuriy Korolev (USSR)

Pommel Horse

1981	Michael Nikolay (GDR) &
	Li Xiaoping (Chn)
1983	Dmitriy Belozerchev (USSR)
1985	Valentin Mogilnyi (USSR)
1987	Dmitri Belozerchev (USSR) &
	Zsolt Borkai (Hun)

Team

1981	USSR
1983	China
1985	USSR
1987	USSR

High Bar

1981	Aleksandr Tkachev (USSR)
1983	Dmitri Belozerchev (USSR)

1985   Tong Fei (Chn)
1987   Dmitri Belozerchev (USSR)

Parallel Bars
1981   Aleksandr Ditiatin (USSR) &
        Koji Gushiken (Jap)
1983   Vladimir Artemov (USSR) &
        Lou Yun (Chn)
1985   Silvio Kroll (GDR) &
        Valentin Mogilnyi (USSR)
1987   Vlademir Artemov (USSR)

Women
Combined (post-war winners)
1950   Helena Rakoczy (Pol)
1954   Galina Roudiko (USSR)
1958   Larissa Latynina (USSR)
1962   Larissa Latynina (USSR)
1966   Vera Cáslavská (Cze)
1970   Lyudmila Tourischeva (USSR)
1974   Lyudmila Tourischeva (USSR)
1978   Yelena Mukhina (USSR)
1979   Nelli Kim (USSR)
1981   Olga Bicherova (USSR)
1983   Natalya Yurchenko (USSR)
1985   Oksana Omelianchuk (USSR) &
        Yelena Shoushounova (USSR)
1987   Aurelia Dobre (Rom)

Individual Disciplines
Winners since 1981
Vault
1981   Maxi Gnauck (GDR)
1983   Boriana Stoyanova (Bul)
1985   Yelena Shoushounova (USSR)
1987   Yelena Shoushounova (USSR)

Beam
1981   Maxi Gnauck (GDR)
1983   Olga Mostepanova (USSR)
1985   Daniela Silivas (Rom)
1987   Aurelia Dobre (Rom)

Floor
1981   Natalya Ilyenko (USSR)
1983   Ecaterina Szabo (Rom)
1985   Oksana Omeliantchuk (USSR)
1987   Yelena Shoushounova (USSR) &
        Daniela Silivas (Rom)

Asymmetrical Bars
1981   Maxi Gnauck (GDR)
1983   Maxi Gnauck (GDR)
1985   Gabriela Fahnrich (GDR)
1987   Daniela Silivas (Rom) &
        Doerte Thumler (GDR)

Team (post-war)
1950   Sweden
1954   USSR
1958   USSR
1962   USSR
1966   Czechoslovakia
1970   USSR
1974   USSR
1978   USSR
1979   Romania
1981   USSR
1983   USSR
1985   USSR
1987   Romania

EUROPEAN CHAMPIONS
(Inaugurated 1955)
Combined winners only

Men
1955   Boris Shakhlin (USSR)
1957   Joachim Blume (Spa)
1959   Yuriy Titov (USSR)
1961   Miroslav Cerar (Yug)
1963   Miroslav Cerar (Yug)
1965   Franco Menichelli (Ita)
1967   Mikhail Voronin (USSR)
1969   Mikhail Voronin (USSR)
1971   Viktor Klimenko (USSR)
1973   Viktor Klimenko (USSR)
1975   Nikolay Andrianov (USSR)
1977   Vladimir Markelov (USSR)
1979   Stoyan Deltchev (Bul)
1981   Aleksandr Tkachev (USSR)
1983   Dmitriy Belozerchev (USSR)
1985   Dmitriy Belozerchev (USSR)
1987   Valeriy Lyukin (USSR)
1989   Igor Korobchinsky (USSR)

Women
1955   not held
1957   Larissa Latynina (USSR)
1959   Natalie Kot (Pol)
1961   Larissa Latynina (USSR)
1963   Mirjana Bilic (Yug)
1965   Vera Cáslavská (Cze)
1967   Vera Cáslavská (Cze)
1969   Karin Janz (GDR)
1971   Lyudmila Tourischeva (USSR) &
        Tamara Lazakovich (USSR)
1973   Lyudmila Tourischeva (USSR)
1975   Nadia Comaneci (Rom)
1977   Nadia Comaneci (Rom)
1979   Nadia Comaneci (Rom)
1981   Maxi Gnauck (GDR)
1983   Olga Bicherova (USSR)
1985   Yelena Shoushounova (USSR)
1987   Daniela Silivas (Rom)
1989   Svetlana Boginskaya (USSR)

——————— 1990 ———————

Jan 19   Gold Top Champions Cup (Royal Albert Hall,
            London);
Feb 27-28   USSR Display (Cardiff);
Mar 3-5   USSR Display (Alexandra Palace or
            Wembley Arena);
Mar 17-18   British School team championships
            (Gloucester Leisure Centre);
Apr 7   Champions All International (NEC,
            Birmingham);
Jun 9   Nat-West Bank Display (Crystal Palace);
Jun 23   British Girls' championships (Crystal Palace);
July   Weetabix National championships (Crystal
            Palace);
Oct 27-28   British National Championships (TBA);
Nov 17   Rhythmic International (Wembley Conference
            Centre);
Dec 15-16   Kraft International (Wembley or Alexandra
            Palace).

HOCKEY

1989

CHAMPIONS TROPHY
West Berlin, Jun 10-18
Holland 2 Great Britain 0
Australia 4 Pakistan 3
India 3 West Germany 2
West Germany 2 Great Britain 1
Australia 3 India 2
Holland 3 Pakistan 2
Australia 2 Great Britain 1
Holland 2 West Germany 1
Pakistan 1 India 0
Holland 4 India 1
Pakistan 2 Great Britain 1
Australia 1 West Germany 1
Great Britain 2 India 1
Australia 2 Holland 1
West Germany 4 Pakistan 1

FINAL TABLE
	P	W	D	L	F	A	Pts
1 Australia	5	4	1	0	12	8	9
2 Holland	5	4	0	1	12	6	8
3 West Germany	5	2	1	2	10	8	5
4 Pakistan	5	2	0	3	9	12	4
5 Great Britain	5	1	0	4	5	9	2
6 India	5	1	0	4	7	12	2

EUROPEAN CLUBS CUP
Men
Mulheim, May 15
Uhlenhorst (FRG) beat Atletico Terrassa (Spa) 2-0
Women
The Hague, May 15
Amsterdam (holders) beat Glasgow Western 3-2

POUNDSTRETCHER NATIONAL LEAGUE
(Inaugurated 1989)
First Division
	P	W	D	L	F	A	Pts
1 Southgate	15	10	4	1	52	12	34
2 Havant	15	11	1	3	26	8	34
3 Hounslow	15	9	2	4	41	23	29
4 O Loughtonians	15	7	7	1	37	19	28
5 Indian Gymkhana	15	8	3	4	21	18	27
6 Bromley	15	6	5	4	23	19	23
7 Teddington	15	7	2	6	24	23	23
8 East Grinstead	15	6	4	5	22	14	22
9 Slough	15	6	4	5	21	23	22
10 Welton	15	6	2	7	27	33	20
11 Stourport	15	5	4	6	27	25	19
12 ISCA	15	6	0	9	20	37	18
13 Harborne	15	4	2	9	18	36	14
14 Wakefield	15	3	4	8	14	29	13
15 Cambridge City	15	3	1	11	12	32	10
16 Warrington	15	0	1	14	10	44	1

Southgate were six points behind at the winter break but beat Hounslow 5-0 in their final match to overtake Havant.

POUNDSTRETCHER CUP FINALS
First Division
Hounslow beat Southgate 4-3 on penalties after drawing 2-2
Second Division
Cannock beat Reading 4-3

NATIONWIDE ANGLIA HA CUP FINAL
Chigwell, Mar 12
Hounslow beat Bromley 2-1

ROYAL BANK HA INDOOR CUP FINAL
Crystal Palace, Feb 24
St Albans beat East Grinstead 3-1

WOMEN'S NATIONAL CLUB CHAMPIONSHIP
Southampton, Apr 23
Ealing beat Sutton Coldfield 1-0

CHAMPIONS

OLYMPIC GAMES
First contested 1908
Men
1908	England
1920	Great Britain
1928	India
1932	India
1936	India
1948	India
1652	India
1956	India
1960	Pakistan
1964	India
1968	Pakistan
1972	West Germany
1976	New Zealand
1980	India
1984	Pakistan
1988	Great Britain

Most wins: 8 India
Women
First contested 1980
1980	Zimbabwe
1984	Holland
1988	Australia

WORLD CUP
Men
1971	Pakistan
1973	Holland
1975	India
1978	Pakistan
1982	Pakistan
1986	Australia

Women
1974	Holland
1976	West Germany
1978	Holland
1981	West Germany
1983	Holland
1986	Holland

WOMEN'S WORLD CHAMPIONSHIP
1975	England
1979	Holland

EUROPEAN CLUBS CUP
Men
1971	Frankfurt 1880 (FRG)
1972	Frankfurt 1880 (FRG)

1973 Frankfurt 1880 (FRG)
1974 Frankfurt 1880 (FRG)
1975 Frankfurt 1880 (FRG)
1976 Southgate (Eng)
1977 Southgate (Eng)
1978 Southgate (Eng)
1979 Klein Zwitserland (Hol)
1980 Slough (Eng)
1981 Klein Zwitserland (Hol)
1982 Dinamo Alma-Ata (USSR)
1983 Dinamo Alma-Ata (USSR)
1984 TG 1846 Frankental (FRG)
1985 Atletico Tarrasa (Spa)
1986 Kampong Utrecht (Hol)
1987 Bloemendaal (Hol)
1988 Uhlenhorst (FRG)
1989 Uhlenhorst (FRG)
Women
1974 Harvetschuder Hamburg (FRG)
1975 Amsterdam (Hol)
1976 Amsterdam (Hol)
1977 Amsterdam (Hol)
1978 Amsterdam (Hol)
1979 Amsterdam (Hol)
1980 Amsterdam (Hol)
1981 Amsterdam (Hol)
1982 Amsterdam (Hol)
1983 HGC Wassenaar (Hol)
1984 HGC Wassenaar (Hol)
1985 HGC Wassenaar (Hol)
1986 HGC Wassenaar (Hol)
1987 HGC Wassenaar (Hol)
1988 Amsterdam (Hol)
1989 Amsterdam (Hol)

ENGLISH LEAGUE CHAMPIONS
(Known as National League from 1989)
Men
1975 Bedfordshire Eagles
1976 Slough
1977 Southgate
1978 Southgate
1979 ISCA
1980 Slough
1981 Slough
1982 Slough
1983 Slough
1984 Neston
1985 East Grinstead
1986 East Grinstead
1987 Slough
1988 Southgate
1989 Southgate

ENGLISH WOMEN'S CHAMPIONS
1979 Chelmsford
1980 Norton
1981 Sutton Coldfield
1982 Slough
1983 Slough
1984 Sheffield
1985 Ipswich
1986 Slough
1987 Ealing
1988 Ealing
1989 Ealing

HOCKEY ASSOCIATION (HA) CUP
Men
1972 Hounslow
1973 Hounslow
1974 Southgate
1975 Southgate
1976 Nottingham
1977 Slough
1978 Guildford
1979 Slough
1980 Slough
1981 Slough
1982 Southgate
1983 Neston
1984 East Grinstead
1985 Southgate
1986 Southgate
1987 Southgate
1988 Southgate
1989 Hounslow

Veryan Pappin, who won an Olympic gold when he came on for the last 27 seconds of the final in Seoul, had the medal stolen from a parked car in High Wycombe, Bucks

━━━━━━━ **1990** ━━━━━━━

Men: *Feb 12-23:* WORLD CUP (Lahore); *Mar 2-4:* 1st European Indoor Cup (Amiens); *Apr 8:* HA Cup final (tba); *May 6:* League Cup finals (Luton); *May 12-13:* County Championship finals (Sheffield); *Aug 16-24:* Six Nations Tournament (Amstelveen, Holland)

Women: *Feb 23-25:* 1st European club indoor championship (Groningen, Holland); *Mar 24:* England v Netherlands (Wembley); *Mar 30-Apr 1:* Home Countries Tournament (Aberdeen); *Apr 20-22:* National club championship finals (Bournemouth); *May 2-13:* WORLD CUP (Sydney).

HORSE RACING

THE GREY EMINENCE

Two horses dominated British racing in 1989. One was a son of Blushing Groom, owned by an Arab oil sheikh, Hamdan Al-Maktoum, and priceless by the end of summer. The other was a grey gelding owned by a movie scriptwriter who had seen him looking scraggy and forlorn in his father's field.

Nashwan's storming classic victories give rise to comparisons with the greatest post-war thoroughbreds. But of the two, the gelding did far more to capture the public imagination. The combination of Desert Orchid's distinctive looks, jumping class and sheer racing impertinence made him the equine personality of the decade. And he won the Cheltenham Gold Cup on a day which for sheer sentiment may not have been surpassed on a racecourse this century. He not only won but, as became his custom, got home in a stirring finish when everything seemed against him.

There was sentiment attached to Nashwan's classic wins too, not so much because of the horse - brilliant though he was - but because of the trainer: Dick Hern, 69, who has been in a wheelchair since a hunting accident five years ago, underwent open-heart surgery last autumn and was told in March by the Queen - or at any rate her representative - that he was being given notice to quit his Royal-owned yard at West Ilsley to make way for a younger, fitter man: Willie Hastings-Bass. No public explanation was given and even informed opinion was bewildered: "Merciless", said Richard Baerlein in *The Guardian*.

So when Nashwan won the 2,000 the Newmarket unsaddling enclosure saw the nearest a British racecourse is ever likely to get to an anti-Royalist demonstration. Hern was cheered to the echo. Nashwan had won brilliantly from the front; his time was the fastest of the 38 electrically-clocked 2,000s and he was immediately backed down to 2-1 Derby favourite. His success reflected another Royal blunder: Nashwan, like Unfuwain, is out of Height of Fashion, the mare sold by the Queen to help finance the purchase of West Ilsley. This was Hern's first win in the 2,000 since Brigadier Gerard in 1971, who was also the last colt to win without a preparatory race. Lord Carnarvon, the Queen's racing manager and the man generally blamed for Hern's eviction, described the Press's coverage of the affair as "appalling" but again declined to explain why. Hern, maintaining the habit of a lifetime, loyally said as little as possible and was rewarded with a compromise: an offer to share West Ilsley with Hastings-Bass for one year only in 1990, which he accepted. He still had to make five lads redundant: "It goes against the grain," he said.

THE YEAR OF NASHWAN

"He's the best horse I've ever trained."
Dick Hern, trainer of Nashwan (and Brigadier Gerard and Troy and Henbit and...)

"I would think you could ride him down the side of a house."
Dick Hern, asked if Nashwan would like Epsom's undulations

"Horse racing's immortality panel, wherever in the celestial spheres that hard-nosed bunch may be sitting, can withhold their nod from Nashwan no longer."
Hugh McIlvanney, the Observer, after the Eclipse Stakes

"I fell in love with Nashwan when I stood within six feet - and in awe - of his powerful physique and majestic bearing in the pre-parade ring at Newmarket on 2,000 Guineas day. I was in raptures just minutes later, as I stood on the stand and watched unveiled the most perfect action I have ever witnessed in a thoroughbred."
Tony Morris, Racing Post

"We've seen only one horse to compare with him, and that was Sea Bird."
Lester Piggott

"That Nashwan is not being given the chance to complete his Triple Crown is one of the tragedies of the modern approach to racing. Such an unsporting gesture would never have attracted such muted criticism 10 years ago."
Richard Baerlein, The Observer

From then on, the horse took centre stage. Many observers were already making comparisons with the great post-war classic winners. And at Epsom, the remaining doubters were routed when Nashwan won the Derby as brilliantly as Shergar eight years earlier. He took on Cacoethes, his rival in the betting, with two furlongs to go and swept past him for a five-length win. The only puzzle was that the best of the rest was not Cacoethes or any other of the fancied runners but Clive Brittain's Terimon, a 500-1 shot and the highest priced placed horse in the 210 Derbys. Hern was asked if he would now buy Lord Carnarvon a celebration drink. He said it was an unfair question.

Nashwan went on to win the Eclipse - again by five lengths, again devastatingly and again from an outsider, this time the 200-1 pacemaker Opening Verse. Toiling behind were the stars of the two previous generations, Indian Skimmer and Warning. He took the King George at Ascot too, but this time only by a neck from Cacoethes and not in especially fast time. The Triple Crown - last won by Nijinsky in 1970 - seemed at his mercy but after much dithering, Sheikh Hamdan opted to send him to the Prix Niel at Longchamp the next day instead, to the disappointment of the Doncaster executive and all romantics of the turf. Angus Gold, the Sheikh's racing manager, cited the poor record of Leger winners in the Arc. There followed a disastrous weekend for both the St Leger and Nashwan. The Classic was postponed a week and shifted to Ayr after two accidents proved that the course at Doncaster had subsided during the dry summer. And Nashwan could finish only third at Longchamp. He missed the Arc, which was won by the more ordinary Carroll House, and was sent to stud, honour not quite satisfied.

The only comparable three-year-old colt over the classic distances was Old Vic, (owned by Hamdan's brother Sheikh Mohammed and trained by Henry Cecil) who became the first British-trained horse ever to win the Prix du Jockey Club. Old Vic also had a magnificent win in the Irish Derby which made Steve Cauthen the first jockey ever to win the world's four great Derbies - English, French, Irish and Kentucky. He was supposed to meet Nashwan in the King George but just as racing purists began to salivate, Old Vic - as happens so often in these cases - went lame. The Maktoum family's dominance was not in doubt. "Their enormous strength", wrote Richard Baerlein, "makes the old Aga Khan's domination in the 1920s and 30s seem insignificant."

In the 1000 Guineas, Sheikh Mohammed even managed to own three of the first four, including the winner Musical Bliss. When the family were beaten in a classic, it took another mega-millionaire to do it: the Aga Khan. Walter Swinburn cast aside Musical Bliss to ride Aliysa in The Oaks and got it right - or appeared to have done.

Aliysa's dope test proved positive when a derivative of camphor was discovered and the result was cast into doubt pending the Jockey Club's ruling.

Richard Burridge, Desert Orchid's owner, provided rather more of a role model for hopeful owners. And his devotion to his horse and its welfare gave his success a touching quality far removed from the business air of the Flat. Desert Orchid's personality suffused the whole jumping season.

"Something remarkable is happening when he visits a racecourse," wrote Brough Scott in the Sunday Times. "It is almost too good to last." Burridge seemed to think that too. On Gold Cup morning, there was snow and the going turned so swampy that Burridge comtemplated withdrawing his horse. Then when the 25-1 shot Yahoo jumped the last in front, it seemed as though the great grey was beaten. But Desert Orchid responded to his jockey Simon Sherwood, to the crowd, and his own remarkable courage and sense of occassion, to win by 1 1/2 lengths. There was extraordinary jubilation in the paddock, with even the bookmakers pretending they did not mind losing money. Meanwhile, almost unnoticed, Desert's Orchid's main rival Ten Plus lay by the third-last fence with a broken fetlock and had to be destroyed.

This win was Desert Orchid's eighth in a row after Simon Sherwood had replaced Colin Brown as the jockey in April 1988 and his 27th in all. The horse's earlier triumphs had included the King George VI and a stunning win from near-certain defeat over Pegwell Bay at Sandown on February 4. "You don't mind losing to him so much", said Pegwell's Bay trainer Tim Forster. All this helped build the legend and set the scene for the Gold Cup. Sherwood retired after the season and his partnership with the great horse ended abruptly in April with a fall at Liverpool.

In the Champion Hurdle, Beech Road at 50-1 became the longest-priced winner ever (equalling Kirriemuir 1965). Two months earlier, Beech Road would have not been a billion to one. The screens were put round him preparatory to shooting after a bad fall in a Cheltenham chase. Luckily, the horse jumped up in time to make it clear he was only winded. The Grand National was won by Little Polveir, who switched stables from John Edwards to Beech Road's trainer, Toby Balding, only five weeks beforehand. Two outsiders, Seeandem and Brown Trix, were killed at Becher's Brook and a month later the Jockey Club approved changes to the fence, regrading the slope and partly filling in the ditch in an attempt to head off criticism about safety without spoiling the spectacle. A record £56 million was bet on the race in Britain alone, £1 a head.

PIPE AND SCUDAMORE TRIUMPHANT

The rest of the jumping season was dominated, to a staggering extent, by two men: Martin Pipe and Peter Scudamore, who established a moral and statistical stranglehold on the sport that no one ever believed possible. Scudamore rode 221 winners, beating Jonjo O'Neill's record by 72. Pipe trained 208, which beat his own record by 79. The pair of them combined for 158 winners, and they left all their rivals breathless and a little bitter. No flat jockey had passed 200 winners since Sir Gordon Richards in 1952. Over the jumps it was assumed to be out of the question.

Scudamore's strike rate was 33 per cent, Pipe's 37, but when the one rode for the other it rose to a phenomenal 44 per cent, an astonishing record. And there were fences in the way. Pipe's hurdlers did seem to have a habit of hitting these harder than other horses and getting away with it; and many of his horses ran the same way, making the pace and sticking with it.

Security was very tight at Pipe's stables, at Nicholashayne on the Devon-Somerset border, and he was not especially forthcoming with the press. This led to dark speculation about exactly how he did it and dark rumours circulated, the most lurid of which depicted Nicholashayne as a sort of Transylvanian castle. The truth appeared to be that Pipe, by using the newest technology to determine when horses were at their peak, had transformed the art of training into something closer to science. This would have made him highly successful even in flat racing. In jumping, with its traditions of rustic casualness, it made him a phenomenon.

THE RECORD SMASHERS

PETER SCUDAMORE

221 winners

50th winner Oct 29

100th winner Dec 20 - previous fastest Jonjo O'Neill Feb 8 1978

150th winner (breaking O'Neill's record) Feb 7

1000th career winner Feb 14 - third man in NH history after Stan Mellor and John Francome. Mellor took 20 seasons, Francome 15, Sucdamore 11.

200th winner Apr 27 - last 200 on flat, Sir Gordon Richards 231 in 1952

MARTIN PIPE

208 winners

50th winner Oct 29

100th winner Dec 29 - previous fastest Michael Dickinson Mar 8 1983

130th winner (breaking his own record) Feb 6

Beats Michael Dickinson's prize money record, £358,837, Feb 18

200th winner May 19

There was also a good deal of luck. The mildest winter in memory caused a minimum of cancellations and a maximum of opportunity. And Scudamore remained happily injury-free, while his rivals had the usual run of jumping troubles: Chris Grant broke a leg, Phil Tuck broke an arm.... three of Scudamore's top seven rivals all managed to get injured in the space of 24 hours in December. Scudamore was even fortunate when he did fall badly. At Cheltenham on January 3 he was catapulted out of the saddle on Tarconey but landed on top of a padded wing. There was a lot of skill too. Scudamore was especially brilliant on Bonanza Boy, when he won the Racing Post Chase at Kempton from nowhere.

RECORDS AND RETIREMENTS

Several trainers, all of whom had been part of the jumping scene seemingly forever, faded out: Fred Winter, champion eight times, finally sold his Uplands yard to his former assistant Charlie Brooks; Monica Dickinson, whose son Michael - now in America - had once looked as unstoppable as Pipe, retired to end the dynasty; so did Neville Crump, 78, who had started in 1937, and Mercy Rimell, whose father-in-law had begun training at Kinnersley in 1924. After 35 years the highly successful flat trainer Jeremy Tree, 63, also decided to retire. Pat Rohan, after 30 years, opted for the Gulf to train for the Amir of Bahrain.

PIPEMAN OF THE YEAR

"It is quite possible that there will never be a combination of circumstances like this season's - the dominance he has held over his rivals, the help he's received from a great jockey, the freedom his stable has enjoyed from epidemics, and the mild weather. This really might be a record which will last forever."
Paul Haigh, Racing Post, on Martin Pipe

"Many professional observers would like to know why it is that his horses so often make the running. And why do they often kick the hurdles out of the way and yet experience no obvious immediate discomfort? Is it really true, as former employees have testified, that no one is allowed in the Nicholashayne stables after 5 pm each day other than the trainer, the head lad and the vet?"
Private Eye on Pipe

"Unsubstantiated rubbish."
Pipe on Private Eye

"Jealousy has long been racing's bestselling sin. Indulging in it demeans us all. On all known evidence Martin Pipe is something uncomfortably close to genius. It's high time to be proud of him."
Racing Post

"He's a genius. It's a privilege to ride for him."
Peter Scudamore on Pipe

"Peter's been a great rider for a long time, indeed the only difference this winter had been the quality of the horses he has has to ride, and more important the number of them."
Oliver Sherwood, trainer, on Scudamore

"I'll have to find him a really bad novice chaser to find out just how good he is."
Jonjo O'Neill, trainer, on Scudamore

"In some ways you have to say he has improved some horses."
Monica Dickinson, trainer, on Pipe

"They don't run because they are non-runners."
Pipe conducting public relations

At Royal Ascot Pat Eddery rode eight winners, equalling Pigott's 20th-century record (1965 and 1975) though short of Fred Archer's 12 (1878). That gave Eddery the edge on his rivals on the jockey's table and he maintained his lead over Steve Cauthen into the autumn. The newest, though not youngest, riding star Ray Cochrane, 33, was appointed Guy Harwood's stable jockey. Greville Starkey, sacked after 14 years, decided to retire. Frankie Dettori, only 18, took over Cochrane's job with Luca Cumani. Willie Shoemaker, 57, made a farewell European tour before his planned retirement from the saddle in February 1990. He had 22 rides during his last stint in Britain and two wins.

Corey Roberts, 17, a stable lad with Captain JH Wilson, applied for a licence to give Britain the not quite unprecented novelty of a black jockey. The rider Gareth Charles-Jones, 28, whose wife Jessica was paralysed in a fall in 1988, learned that he had lung cancer.

In America there was a genuine attempt on the triple crown. Sunday Silence, a colt who had been put up for auction as both a yearling and a two-year-old and failed to sell either time, won both the Kentucky Derby and The Preakness and came to New York and the final leg, the Belmont, as 4-5 favourite. There was a five million dollar bonus for the treble. But this time Sunday Silence's great rival Easy Goer, only nosed out in the Preakness, burst through and cut him down by eight lengths. Sunday Silence's great trainer, Charlie Whittingham, 76, walked sadly away - aware that one racing achievement is now bound to elude him. "You're in New York now, Charlie," jeered the crowd. In Canada, With Approval did win the local version of the triple crown, the first to do so in 26 years.

GUILTY SECRETS

All over the racing world, time-honoured skullduggery continued, sometimes with new variations. A Chicago jockey, Geary Louviere was banned for life when a buzzer - used to startle horses into action - fell out of his breeches after he had ridden a winner. In Western Australia, Peter Hall was banned for 10 years after a similar offence. Three Hong Kong jockeys were given 18 months in jail after being found guilty of pulling their mounts in return for money from the textile tycoon Yuan Loong Yang's Shanghai Syndicate. Yang escaped jail. The Australian jockey Rod Staples, given immunity from prosecution to testify in the case, said in court that 90 per cent of his rides in Hong Kong were non-triers.

Traces of cocaine were found in horses trained by several US trainers, including two of the most successful, D Wayne Lukas and Laz Barrera. The cases were dismissed for lack of evidence. In France, the trainer Georges Mikhailides was banned for a year after traces of steroids showed up on a runner at Saint-Cloud, the third positive test on one of his runners in four months. Another French trainer, John Fellows, was fined 80,000 francs (£7,000) when steroids showed up. A third, Jean-François Bernard, was fined 30,000 francs after a test on his filly Chess Mistress proved positive to human urine. It belonged to the filly's lad who became impatient when the horse failed to produce a sample.

The Australian Supreme Court held that the jockey Malcolm Johnston was responsible for the injuries caused to another rider Glen Frazier in a fall 11 years earlier. Johnston was ordered to pay £60,000 and jockeys went on strike over who should pay the liability insurance.

Vaguely Noble, the 1968 Arc winner, died in Kentucky aged 24. The mare Park Top, winner of the 1969 King George, died at the same age. Secretariat, the 1973 US triple crown winner, died aged 19. Sagace, winner of the 1984 Arc, died aged only nine. The popular mare Triptych died aged seven after galloping into a night-watchman's truck. Monksfield, twice champion hurdler, died after breaking a leg at stud.

Indiana became the 43rd US State to legalise pari-mutuel betting. Racing restarted in Macao, in the South China Sea, after a 48-year gap. In Britain, all-weather tracks at Lingfield and Southwell were under construction in preparation for an autumn opening which would make the flat season last all year, providing further opportunities for poor horses, rich bookmakers and demented punters. The satellite TV service for betting shops SIS spread nationwide and Extel, the providers of the traditional staid commentaries, retired defeated on June 30. The Big Four bookmakers became the Big Three when Sears, owners of William Hill, sold out to Grand Met, owners of Mecca. Grand Met then sold the whole caboodle to Brent Walker for £685 million. The publicans' daily, the *Morning Advertiser*, abolished its racing pages after 40 years: "Modern entrepreneurial publicans," said the paper's managing editor, "are not interested in racing, but in running pubs profitably."

Other people did seem interested in racing. Aggregate attendances at Royal Ascot were the highest ever: 221,341 including 73,535 on the Thursday. An astonishing 25,000 attended the Spring Bank Holiday Monday meeting at Cartmel. In Ireland 100,000 attended the five-day fiesta at Galway with betting estimated at about £IR 8 million. The betting shock of the year came at Garden State Park, New Jersey when a horse called Sal's Needle, beaten a total of 141 lengths in his first four career outings, romped home and paid pari-mutuel odds of 347-1. A horse called Frank Harris, named after the Victorian philanderer, showed his namesake's tendencies and had to have a bucket of water thrown over him after winning at Newmarket. He was gelded.

1989

THE CLASSICS
General Accident 1000 Guineas
Newmarket, May 4

1 Musical Bliss	Walter Swinburn	7-2
2 Kerrera	Pat Eddery	9-1
3 Aldbourne	Paul Hamblett	20-1
4 Ensconse	Ray Cochrane	7-4f
5 Pass the Peace	Tommy Quinn	7-2
6 Bequest	Greville Starkey	10-1
7 Muhubub	Richard Hills	16-1

Trainer: Michael Stoute, Newmarket
Owner: Sheikh Mohammed
Time: 1m 42.69s
Distance: ¾ length

General Accident 2000 Guineas
Newmarket, May 6

1 Nashwan	Willie Carson	3-1f
2 Exbourne	Cash Asmussen	10-1
3 Danehill	Pat Eddery	9-1
4 Markofdistinction	Ray Cochrane	4-1
5 Monsagem	Steve Cauthen	20-1
6 Lunar Mover	Paul Eddery	50-1
7 Pure Genius	Greville Starkey	20-1
8 Zayyani	Billy Newnes	9-1
9 Saratogan	John Reid	7-2
10 Sharp N'Early	Brian Rouse	100-1
11 Shaadi	Walter Swinburn	5-1
12 Greensmith	Michael Hills	100-1
13 Mon Tresor	Michael Roberts	40-1
14 Travelling Tryst	Tony Ives	200-1

Trainer: Dick Hern, West Ilsley
Owner: Hamdan Al-Maktoum
Time: 1m 36.44s
(Fastest time since introduction of electric timing at Newmarket in 1952)
Distance: 1 length

Ever Ready Derby
Epsom, Jun 7

1 Nashwan	Willie Carson	5-4f
2 Terimon	Michael Roberts	500-1
3 Cacoethes	Greville Starkey	3-1
4 Ile de Nisky	George Duffield	20-1
5 Mill Pond	Pat Eddery	16-1
6 Gran Alba	Brian Rouse	80-1
7 Classic Fame	John Reid	33-1
8 Torjoun	Ray Cochrane	11-1
9 Flockton's Own	Richard Hills	500-1
10 Prince of Dance	Steve Cauthen	11-2
11 Warrshan	Walter Swinburn	13-1
12 Polar Run	Tony Clark	250-1

Trainer: Dick Hern, West Ilsley
Owner: Hamdan Al-Maktoum
Time: 2m 34.90s
Distance: 5 lengths
(The only other horse priced above 100-1 to be placed in the Derby was Black Tommy, 200-1 second in 1857).

Gold Seal Oaks
Epsom, Jun 10

1 Aliysa	Walter Swinburn	11-10f
2 Snow Bride	Steve Cauthen	13-2
3 Roseate Tern	Willie Carson	25-1
4 Mamaluna	Greville Starkey	50-1
5 Knoosh	John Reid	16-1
6 Tessla	Paul Eddery	7-1
7 Musical Bliss	Michael Roberts	4-1
8 Always On A Sunday	Brent Thomson	10-1
9 Rambushka	Pat Eddery	16-1

Trainer: Michael Stoute, Newmarket
Owner: Aga Khan
Time: 2m 34.22s
Distance: 3 lengths

"Someone suggested that the Jockey Club Race Planning Committee consisted of a table and four chairs - and I bet they've got woodworm."
Jenny Pitman, trainer

"Owning a racehorse is probably the most expensive way of getting on to a racecourse for nothing."
Clement Freud, The Times

"My advice to the working public is this: don't bet, don't race, don't expect any treatment of fairness."
Fallen racehorse owner Terry Ramsden

"The bookmakers are screwing every punter to the ground. You would be better off burning your money."
Barney Curley, trainer

Footnote to readers of the Racing Post point-to-point annual: "We describe the Talybont as being better run than many in Wales. Please scrub."
Iain Mackenzie, Racing Post

"There is a young lady from Warwickshire waiting to take entries behind the main tent."
Announcement at Worcestershire point-to-point. Chaddesley Corbett

Overheard at Fontwell: "No dear, it's the jockeys who are amateurs, not the horses."
Letter in Sporting Life from R.M. Warner of Surrey

St.Leger
Ayr, Sep 23

1	Michelozzo	Steve Cauthen	6-4f
2	Sapience	Kevin Fallon	15-1
3	Roseate Tern	Willie Carson	5-2
4	Terimon	Mark Birch	7-2
5	Blazing Torch	Michael Hills	100-1
6	N C Owen	Franco Dettori	12-1
7	Alphabel	Tony Cruz	14-1
8	Skisurf	John Lowe	250-1

Trainer: Henry Cecil, Newmarket
Owner: Charles St George
Time: 3m 20.72s
Distance: 8 lengths

MOST SUCCESSFUL JOCKEYS IN ENGLISH CLASSICS IN THE 1980s

		Derby	Oaks	1000	2000	Leger
9	**Willie Carson**	2	2	-	3	2
8	**Steve Cauthen**	2	2	1	-	3
6	**Walter Swinburn**	2	2	1	1	-
6	**Lester Piggott**	1	2	1	1	1
4	**Pat Eddery**	1	-	-	2	1
3	**Ray Cochrane**	1	1	1	-	-
3	**Freddie Head**	-	-	2	1	-
2	**Greville Starkey**	-	-	-	2	-
2	**Joe Mercer**	-	-	-	-	2
1	**Christy Roche**	1	-	-	-	-
1	**Billy Newnes**	-	1	-	-	-
1	**Brian Rouse**	-	-	1	-	-
1	**John Reid**	-	-	1	-	-
1	**Philip Robinson**	-	-	1	-	-
1	**Gary Moore**	-	-	1	-	-
1	**Paul Cook**	-	-	-	-	1

IRISH CLASSICS
Airlie Coolmore 2000 Guineas
The Curragh, May 20

1	Shaadi	Walter Swinburn	7-2
2	Great Commotion	Willie Carson	10-1
3	Distant Relative	Michael Hills	25-1

Trainer: Michael Stoute, Newmarket

Goffs 1000 Guineas
The Curragh, May 27

1	Ensconce	Ray Cochrane	13-8f
2	Aldbourne	Paul Hamblett	10-1
3	Run to Jenny	Paul Eddery	33-1

Trainer: Luca Cumani, Newmarket

Budweiser Derby
The Curragh, Jul 2

1	Old Vic	Steve Cauthen	4-11f
2	Observation Post	Willie Carson	12-1
3	Ile de Nisky	Pat Eddery	5-1

Trainer: Henry Cecil, Newmarket

Kildangan Oaks
The Curragh, Jul 16

1	Alydaress	Michael Kinane	7-4
2	Aliya	Walter Swinburn	4-7f
3	Petite Ile	Ron Quinton	14-1

Trainer: Henry Cecil, Newmarket

Jefferson Smurfit Memorial St.Leger
The Curragh, Sep 23

1	Petite Ile	Ron Quinton	3-1f
2	Tyrone Bridge	Buster Parnell	8-1
3	Lazaz	Walter Swinburn	6-1

Trainer: John Oxx, Ireland

FRENCH CLASSICS
Poule d'Essai des Poulains (2000 Guineas)
Longchamp, May 7

1	Kendor	Maurice Philliperon
2	Goldneyev	G Guignard
3	Ocean Falls	Cash Asmussen

Trainer: R Touflan, France

Poule d'Essai des Pouliches (1000 Guineas)
Longchamp, May 14

1	Pearl Bracelet	Alfred Gibert
2	Pass the Peace	Tommy Guinn
3	Golden Opinion	Cash Asmussen

Trainer: R Wojtowiez, France

Prix du Jockey Club (Derby)
Chantilly, June 4

1	Old Vic	Steve Cauthen
2	Dancehall	Cash Asmussen
3	Galetto	Eric Legrix

Trainer: Henry Cecil, Newmarket

Prix du Diane (Oaks)
Chantilly, June 11

1	Lady In Silver	Tony Cruz
2	Louveterie	Cash Asmussen
3	Premier Amour	Dominic Boeuf

Trainer: R Wojtowiez, France

US TRIPLE CROWN
Kentucky Derby
Churchill Downs, May 6

1	Sunday Silence	Pat Valenzuela
2	Easy Goer	Pat Day
3	Awe Inspiring	Craig Perrett

Trainer: Charlie Whittingham

Preakness Stakes
Pimlico, Maryland, May 20

1	Sunday Silence	Pat Valenzuela
2	Easy Goer	Pat Day
3	Rock Point	Chris Antley

Trainer: Charlie Whittingham

Belmont Stakes
Belmont Park, New York, Jun 10

1	Easy Goer	Pat Day
2	Sunday Silence	Pat Valenzuela
3	Le Voyageur	Randy Romero

Trainer: Shug McGaughey

THE BIG HANDICAPS

	Winner	*Trainer*	*Jockey*
Doncaster, Mar 31 1m			
William Hill LINCOLN HANDICAP	FACT FINDER	Reg Akehurst	Tyrone Williams 20-1
Chester, May 10 2 1/4m+			
Ladbroke CHESTER CUP	GREY SALUTE	John Jenkins	Pat Eddery 7-1
Ascot, Jun 21 1m			
ROYAL HUNT CUP	TRUE PANACHE	Jeremy Tree	Pat Eddery 5-1f
Ascot, Jun 23 6f			
WOKINGHAM STAKES	MAC'S FIGHTER	Bill O'Gorman	Cash Asmussen 16-1
Newcastle, Jul 1 2m			
Newcastle Brown Ale			
NORTHUMBERLAND PLATE	ORPHEUS	Guy Harwood	Richard Fox 4-1jf
York, Jul 15 1 1/4m+			
JOHN SMITH'S MAGNET CUP	ICONA	Michael Stoute	Tony Ives 12-1
Goodwood, Jul 25 6f			
William Hill STEWARDS' CUP	VERY ADJACENT	Geoff Lewis	Dale Gibson 12-1
Goodwood, Jul 27 1m			
SCHWEPPES GOLDEN MILE	SAFAWAN	Michael Stoute	Willie Carson 11-2
York, Aug 23 1 3/4m			
Tote EBOR HANDICAP	SAPIENCE	Jimmy Fitzgerald	Pat Eddery 15-2
Ayr, Sep 22			
AYR GOLD CUP	JOVEWORTH	Michael O'Neill	Jimmy Fortune 50-1

TWO-YEAR-OLD RACES

Ascot, Jun 20 6f			
COVENTRY STAKES	ROCK CITY	Richard Hannon	Willie Carson 9-1
Ascot, Jun 21 5f fillies			
QUEEN MARY STAKES	DEAD CERTAIN	David Elsworth	Steve Cauthen 8-1
Ascot, Jun 22 5f			
NORFOLK STAKES	PETILLANTE	Alex Scott	Richard Hills 10-1
Newmarket, Jul 11 6f fillies			
Hillsdown CHERRY HINTON STAKES	CHIMES OF FREEDOM	Henry Cecil	Steve Cauthen 4-9f
Newmarket, Jul 12 6f			
Anglia TV JULY STAKES	ROCK CITY	Richard Hannon	Willie Carson 7-4
Goodwood, Jul 26 6f			
Scottish Equitable RICHMOND STAKES	CONTRACT LAW	Willie Jarvis	Bruce Raymond 7-1
York, Aug 23 6f			
Scottish Equitable GIMCRACK STAKES	ROCK CITY	Richard Hannon	Willie Carson 1-2f
York, Aug 24 6f fillies			
Pacemaker Update LOWTHER STAKES	DEAD CERTAIN	David Elsworth	Steve Cauthen 5-4f

THREE-YEAR-OLD RACES

Newbury, Apr 15 1m			
S & F GREENHAM STAKES	ZAYYANI	Fulke Johnson-Houghton	Billy Newnes 6-1
Newmarket, Apr 19 7f			
Ladbroke EUROPEAN FREE HANDICAP	DANEHILL	Jeremy Tree	Pat Eddery 6-1
Newmarket, Apr 20 1m			
Heidseck CRAVEN STAKES	SHAADI	Michael Stoute	Walter Swinburn 5-2f
Sandown, Apr 29 1 1/4m			
Guardian CLASSIC TRIAL	OLD VIC	Henry Cecil	Steve Cauthen 4-9f
Chester, May 9 1 1/2m+			
Dalham CHESTER VASE	OLD VIC	Henry Cecil	Steve Cauthen 6-4
Lingfield, May 13 1 1/2m			
Calor DERBY TRIAL	CACOETHES	Guy Harwood	Greville Starkey 5-2
Lingfield, May 13 1 1/2m			
Marley OAKS TRIAL	ALIYSA	Michael Stoute	Walter Swinburn 4-7f
York, May 17 1 1/2m			
William Hill DANTE STAKES	TORJOUN	Luca Cumani	Ray Cochrane 6-1
Goodwood, May 24 1 1/4m			
NM PREDOMINATE STAKES	WARRSHAN	Michael Stoute	Walter Swinburn 7-2
Ascot, Jun 20 1m			
ST JAMES'S PALACE STAKES	SHAADI	Michael Stoute	Walter Swinburn 6-4f
Ascot, Jun 20 1 1/2m			
KING EDWARD VII STAKES	CACOETHES	Guy Harwood	Pat Eddery 8-13f
Ascot, Jun 20 7f			
JERSEY STAKES	ZILZAL	Michael Stoute	Walter Swinburn 10-11f
Ascot, Jun 21			
CORONATION STAKES	GOLDEN OPINION	André Fabré	Cash Asmussen 7-2f
Ascot, Jun 22 1 1/2m fillies			
RIBBLESDALE STAKES	ALYDARESS	Henry Cecil	Steve Cauthen 4-1

Goodwood, Jul 25 1 1/2m

GORDON STAKES	WARRSHAN	Michael Stoute	Walter Swinburn 3-1

York, Aug 23 1 1/2m

GREAT VOLTIGEUR STAKES	ZALAZL	Henry Cecil	Steve Cauthen 7-4

York, Aug 23 1 1/2m fillies

Aston Upthorpe YORKSHIRE OAKS	ROSEATE TERN	Dick Hern	Willie Carson 11-2

OTHER MAJOR RACES

Newbury, Apr 15 1 1/2m

Lanes End JOHN PORTER STAKES	UNFUWAIN	Dick Hern	Willie Carson 4-9f

Ascot, Apr 22 2m

Insulpak SAGARO STAKES	TRAVEL MYSTERY	Martin Pipe	Ray Cochrane 9-1

Newmarket, May 5 1 1/2m

GA JOCKEY CLUB STAKES	UNFUWAIN	Dick Hern	Willie Carson 5-6f

Chester, May 11 1m 5ft+

ORMONDE STAKES	MOUNTAIN KINGDOM	Clive Brittain	Steve Cauthen 4-6f

York, May 17 1 3/4m

Coloroll YORKSHIRE CUP	MOUNTAIN KINGDOM	Clive Brittain	Steve Cauthen 2-1f

Newbury, May 19 1m

Juddmonte LOCKINGE STAKES	MOST WELCOME	Geoff Wragg	Paul Eddery 9-1

Sandown, May 29 2m

Mappin & Webb HENRY II STAKES	SADEEM	Guy Harwood	Greville Starkey 9-2

Epsom, Jun 8 1 1/2m

Hanson CORONATION CUP	SHERIFF'S STAR	Lady Herries	Ray Cochrane 11-4f

Ascot, Jun 22

CORK AND ORRERY STAKES	DANEHILL	Jeremy Tree	Willie Carson 11-8f

Ascot, Jun 22 2 1/2m

ASCOT GOLD CUP	SADEEM	Guy Harwood	Willie Carson 8-11f

Ascot, Jun 23 1 1/2m

HARDWICKE STAKES	ASSATIS	Guy Harwood	Pat Eddery 4-11f

Ascot, Jun 23 5f

KING'S STAND STAKES	INDIAN RIDGE	David Elsworth	Steve Cauthen 9-4f

Sandown, Jul 8 1 1/4m

Coral ECLIPSE STAKES	NASHWAN	Dick Hern	Willie Carson 2-5f

Newmarket, Jul 11, 1 1/2m

PRINCESS OF WALES'S STAKES	CARROLL HOUSE	Michael Jarvis	Walter Swinburn 10-1

Newmarket, Jul 13 6f

Carroll Foundation JULY CUP	CADEAUX GENEREUX	Alex Scott	Paul Eddery 10-1

Ascot, Jul 22 1 1/2m

KING GEORGE VI and QUEEN ELIZABETH Diamond Stakes	NASHWAN	Dick Hern	Willie Carson 2-9f

Goodwood, Jul 26 1m

Swettenham Stud SUSSEX STAKES	ZILZAL	Michael Stoute	Walter Swinburn 5-2

Goodwood, Jul 27 2m 5f

GOODWOOD CUP	MAZZACANO	Guy Harwood	Pat Eddery 15-2

Newbury, Aug 12 1m 5f+

Walmac GEOFFREY FREER STAKES	IBN BEY	Paul Cole	Richard Quinn 9-2

York, Aug 22 1 1/4m+

Juddmonte INTERNATIONAL STAKES	ILE DE CHYPRE	Guy Harwood	Tony Clark 16-1

York, Aug 24 5f

William Hill SPRINT CHAMPIONSHIP	CADEAUX GENEREUX	Alex Scott	Pat Eddery 11-10f

Goodwood, Aug 26 1m

Beefeater Gin CELEBRATION MILE	DISTANT RELATIVE	Barry Hills	Michael Hills 2-1

Doncaster, Sep 14 2 1/4m

DONCASTER CUP	WELD	William Jarvis	Willie Carson 1-5f

Ascot, Sep 30 1m

QUEEN ELIZABETH II STAKES	ZILZAL	Michael Stoute	Walter Swinburn Evens f

OVERSEAS RACES

Maisons-Lafitte, Jul 23, 5f+, 2y-o

PRIX ROBERT PAPIN	OZONE FRIENDLY	Barry Hills	Pat Eddery 49-10

Deauville, Aug 13

PRIX DU HARAS	POLISH PRECEDENT	André Fabré	Cash Asmussen 2-5f

Deauville, Aug 20, 2-y-o

PRIX MORNY	MACHIAVELLIAN	François Boutin	Freddie Head 9-10f

Phoenix Park, Sep 2 1 1/4m

EBF PHOENIX CHAMPION STAKES	CARROLL HOUSE	Michael Jarvis	Michael Kinane 5-1

Longchamp, Sep 3 1m

PRIX DU MOULIN	POLISH PRECEDENT	Andre Fabre	Cash Asmussen 2-5f

Arlington, Illinois, Sep 3 1m 2f

ARLINGTON MILLION	STEINLEN	D.Wayne Lukas	Jose Santos 53-10

Longchamp, Sep 10 2-y-o 7f

PRIX DE LA SALAMANDRE	MACHIAVELLIAN	François Boutin	Freddie Head 7-10f

NATIONAL HUNT RACING
Waterford Crystal Champion Hurdle
Cheltenham, Mar 14

1	Beech Road	Richard Guest	50-1
2	Celtic Chief	Graham McCourt	6-1
3	Celtic Shot	Peter Scudamore	8-1
4	Floyd	Simon Sherwood	14-1
5	Vagador	Mark Perrett	20-1
6	Mole Board	Hywel Davies	20-1
7	Kribensis	Richard Dunwoody	11-8f
8	Cloughtaney	Mr William Mullins	33-1
9	Chatam	John Lower	14-1
10	Condor Pan	Tommy Carmody	16-1
11	Wishlon	Ian Shoemark	40-1
12	Grey Salute	Stephen Smith-Eccles	10-1
f	Chesham Squire	Graham Bradley	66-1
f	Cashew King	Trevor Wall	100-1
f	Sprowston Boy	Dermot Browne	100-1

Trainer: Toby Balding, Fyfield
Owner: Tony Geake
Distance: 2 lengths

TOTE CHELTENHAM GOLD CUP
Cheltenham, Mar 16

1	Desert Orchid	Simon Sherwood	5-2f
2	Yahoo	Tom Morgan	25-1
3	Charter Party	Richard Dunwoody	14-1
4	Bonanza Boy	Peter Scudamore	15-2
5	West Tip	Peter Hobbs	66-1
6	Golden Freeze	Mark Pitman	16-1
f	Carvill's Hill	Ken Morgan	5-1
f	Ten Plus	Kevin Mooney	11-2
f	The Thinker	Chris Grant	15-2
f	Slalom	Jimmy White	33-1
r	Cavvie's Clown	Russ Arnott	8-1
pu	Pegwell Bay	Carl Llewellyn	25-1
bd	Ballyhane	Richard Rowe	33-1

Trainer: David Elsworth, Whitsbury
Owner: Richard Burridge
Distance: 1 1/2 lengths

SEAGRAM GRAND NATIONAL
Aintree, Apr 8

1	Little Polveir	Jimmy Frost	28-1
2	West Tip	Richard Dunwoody	12-1
3	The Thinker	Simon Sherwood	10-1
4	Lastofthebrownies	Tommy Carmody	16-1
5	Durham Edition	Chris Grant	15-2
6	Monamore	Graham McCourt	20-1
7	Gala's Image	Neale Doughty	18-1
8	Bonanza Boy	Peter Scudamore	10-1
9	Team Challenge	Michael Bowlby	30-1
10	Newnham	Mr Simon Andrews	50-1
11	The Thirsty Farmer	L Kelp	100-1
12	Attitude Adjuster	Niall Madden	25-1
13	Sidbury Hill	Kevin Mooney	100-1
14	Mr Baker	M Moran	100-1

The following horses fell, refused or were brought down:

f	1st Cerimau	Peter Hobbs	80-1
f	2nd Cranlome	K O'Brien	66-1
r	2nd BobTisdall	Jimmy White	25-1
f	6th Dixton House	Tom Morgan	7-1f
f	6th Sergeant Sprite	Tom Taaffe	50-1
f	6th Seeandem	L Cusack	100-1
f	6th Brown Trix	Mr D Pitcher	300-1
f	6th Hettinger	Ray Goldstein	300-1
bd	6th Sir Jest	Michael Hammond	40-1
f	11th Friendly Henry	Hywell Davies	66-1
f	11th Stearsby	Brendan Powell	14-1
f	11th Perris Valley	B Sheridan	16-1
r	15th Smartside	Mr A Hambly	300-1
f	16th Mr Chris	Brian Storey	200-1
pu	18th Beamwam	Mr D Naylor-Leyland	100-1

f	19th Gainsay	Mark Pitman	25-1
r	19th Queensway Boy	Allen Webb	50-1
f	20th Smart Tar	Carl Llewellyn	18-1
pu	21st Numerate	Tarnya Davies	100-1
pu	21st Mearlin	Simon McNeill	300-1
pu	23rd Polar Nomad	A Merrigan	80-1
pu	23rd Kersil	Andy Orkney	300-1
pu	25th Bartres	Graham Bradley	33-1
pu	28th Memberson	Mr G Upton	33-1
pu	28th Mithras	Robert Stronge	66-1
r	28th Rausal	David Tegg	50-1

Trainer: Toby Balding, Fyfield
Owner: Edward Harvey
Time: 10m 06.9s
Distance: 7 lengths   40 ran

IF THEY COULD TALK

" **Highland Wedding was a good horse but he was a bastard. Little Polveir is a really nice horse, one anybody would be happy to get up on.**"
Toby Balding, trainer, on his two Grand National winners, 1969 and 1989

"**You don't have to be opposed to jump racing in general or the Grand National in particular to want to ask whether the situation has now become unacceptable.**"
Racing Post editorial on the deaths at Becher's

"**There's no need for these Arthur Daleys to sit in the Winchester pub and make a bet on this disgusting sport.**"
Richard Cottrell, Tory MP, on The Grand National

"**If the welfare of the Thoroughbred was paramount we would not race two-year-olds at all and the Classics would be for four-year-olds, genuinely mature adults instead of schoolboys. But pigs will be flying first.**"
John Oaksey, Racing Post

"**In their way, horses have to be braver than us. We can choose what we do for a living.**"
Peter Scudamore

NATIONAL HUNT TABLES 1988-89
Jockeys

		Mounts	Wins
1	Peter Scudamore	664	221
2	Mark Dwyer	458	92
3	Richard Dunwoody	671	91
4	Graham McCourt	426	86
5	Simon Sherwood	317	68
6	Brendan Powell	581	64

Trainers

		Runners	Winners	Prize money
1	Martin Pipe	566	208	£589,460
2	David Elsworth	255	54	£359,990
3	Toby Balding	371	59	£312,924
4	Josh Gifford	384	63	£292,624
5	John Edwards	402	78	£245,785
6	Arthur Stephenson	547	90	£236,074

OTHER BIG JUMP RACES
Steeplechases
Haydock, Jan 21 3m

PETER MARSH CHASE	BISHOP'S YARN	Toby Balding	Richard Guest 13-2

Cheltenham, Mar 14 2m

ARKLE CHALLENGE TROPHY	WATERLOO BOY	David Nicholson	Richard Dunwoody 20-1

Cheltenham, Mar 15 2m

QUEEN MOTHER CHAMPION CHASE	BARNBROOK AGAIN	David Elsworth	Simon Sherwood 7-4f

Cheltenham, Mar 15 3m

Sun Alliance CHASE	ENVOPAK TOKEN	Josh Gifford	Peter Hobbs 16-1

Cheltenham, Mar 16 3m 1f

Ritz Club NH HANDICAP CHASE	DIXTON HOUSE	John Edwards	Tom Morgan 13-2

Liverpool, Apr 6, 3m 1f

MARTELL CUP	YAHOO	John Edwards	Tom Morgan 13-2

Sandown, Apr 29, 3m 5f+

33rd Whitbread GOLD CUP	BROWN WINDSOR	Nicky Henderson	Mark Bowlby 12-1

HURDLES
Newbury, Feb 11 2m 100y hcap

TOTE GOLD TROPHY	GREY SALUTE	John Jenkins	Richard Dunwoody 8-1

Wincanton, Feb 23 2m

KINGWELL HURDLE	FLOYD	David Elsworth	Richard Dunwoody 8-1

Cheltenham, Mar 14 3m1f

Waterford Crystal STAYERS' HURDLE	RUSTLE	Nicky Henderson	Mark Bowlby 4-1

Cheltenham, Mar 15 2 1/2m

Sun Alliance NOVICES' HURDLE	SAYFARS LAD	Martin Pipe	Mark Perrett 12-1

Cheltenham, Mar 16 2m

Daily Express TRIUMPH HURDLE	IKDAM	Richard Holder	Neil Coleman 66-1

Liverpool, Apr 7 2m

ANNIVERSARY HURDLE	VAYRUA	Guy Harwood	Mark Perrett 12-1

Liverpool, Apr 8 2 1/2m

Sandeman AINTREE HURDLE	BEECH ROAD	Toby Balding	Richard Guest 10-1

Haydock, May 1 2m

Swinton Insurance HANDICAP HURDLE	STATE JESTER	Bill Elsey	John Quinn 14-1

IRISH RACING
Leopardstown, Jan 14

Ladbrooke Handicap Hurdle	REDUNDANT PAL	Paddy Mullins	Pat Kavanagh 16-1

Fairyhouse, Mar 27 3m

Jameson IRISH GRAND NATIONAL	MAID OF MONEY	John Fowler	Anthony Powell 10-1

CHAMPIONS

THE ENGLISH CLASSICS

	1000 Guineas	2000 Guineas	Derby	Oaks	St Leger
1776	-	-	-	-	Allabaculia
1777	-	-	-	-	Bourbon
1778	-	-	-	-	Hollandaise
1779	-	-	-	Bridget	Tommy
1780	-	-	Diomed	Tetoum	Ruler
1781	-	-	Young Eclipse	Faith	Serina
1782	-	-	Assassin	Ceres	Imperatrix
1783	-	-	Saltram	Maid of the Oaks	Phenomenon
1784	-	-	Sergeant	Stella	Omphale
1785	-	-	Aimwell	Trifle	Cowslip
1786	-	-	Noble	Yellow Filly	Paragon
1787	-	-	Sir Peter Teazle	Annette	Spadille
1788	-	-	Sir Thomas	Nightshade	Young Flora
1789	-	-	Skyscraper	Tag	Pewett
1790	-	-	Rhadamanthus	Hippolyta	Ambidexter
1791	-	-	Eager	Portia	Young Traveller
1792	-	-	John Bull	Volante	Tartar
1793	-	-	Waxy	Caelia	Ninety-Three
1794	-	-	Daedalus	Hermione	Beningbrough
1795	-	-	Spread Eagle	Platina	Hambletonian
1796	-	-	Didelot	Pasiot	Ambrosio
1797	-	-	(unnamed colt)	Nike	Lounger
1798	-	-	Sir Harry	Bellissima	Symmetry
1799	-	-	Archduke	Bellina	Cockfighter
1800	-	-	Champion	Ephemera	Champion
1801	-	-	Eleanor	Eleanor	Quiz
1802	-	-	Tyrant	Scotia	Orville
1803	-	-	Ditto	Theophania	Remembrancer

	1000 Guineas	2000 Guineas	Derby	Oaks	St Leger
1804	-	-	Hannibal	Pelisse	Sancho
1805	-	-	Cardinal Beaufort	Meteora	Staveley
1806	-	-	Paris	Bronze	Fyldener
1807	-	-	Election	Briseis	Paulina
1808	-	-	Pan	Morel	Petronius
1809	-	Wizard	Pope	Maid of Orleans	Ashton
1810	-	Hephestion	Whalebone	Oriana	Octavian
1811	-	Trophonius	Phantom	Sorcery	Soothsayer
1812	-	Cwrw	Octavius	Manuella	Otterington
1813	-	Smolensko	Smolensko	Music	Altisidora
1814	Charlotte	Olive	Blucher	Medora	William
1815	Unnamed filly	Tigris	Whisker	Minuet	Fihlo da Puta
1816	Rhoda	Nectar	Prince Leopod	Landscape	The Duchess
1817	Neva	Manfred	Azor	Neva	Ebor
1818	Corinne	Interpreter	Sam	Corinne	Reveller
1819	Catgut	Antar	Tiresias	Shoveler	Antonio
1820	Rowena	Pindarrie	Sailor	Caroline	St Patrick
1821	Zeal	Reginald	Gustavus	Augusta	Jack Spigot
1822	Whizgig	Pastille	Moses	Pastille	Theodore
1823	Zinc	Nicolo	Emilius	Zinc	Barefoot
1824	Cobweb	Schahriar	Cedric	Cobweb	Jerry
1825	Tontine	Enamel	Middleton	Wings	Memnon
1826	Problem	Devise	Lapdog	Lilias	Tarrare
1827	Arab	Turcoman	Mameluke	Gulnare	Matilda
1828	Zoe	Cadland	Cadland	Turquoise	The Colonel
1829	Young Mouse	Patron	Frederick	Green Mantle	Rowton
1830	Charlotte West	Augustus	Priam	Variation	Birmingham
1831	Galantine	Riddlesworth	Spaniel	Oxygen	Chorister
1832	Galata	Archibald	St.Giles	Galata	Margrave
1833	Tarantella	Clearwell	Dangerous	Vespa	Rockingham
1834	May-Day	Glencoe	Plenipotentiary	Pussy	Touchstone
1835	Preserve	Ibrahim	Mundig	Queen of Trumps	Queen of Trumps
1836	Destiny	Bay Middleton	Bay Middleton	Cyprian	Elis
1837	Chapeau D'Espange	Achmet	Phosphorus	Miss Letty	Mango
1838	Barcarolle	Grey Momus	Amato	Industry	Don John
1839	Cara	The Corsair	Bloomsbury	Deception	Charles the Twelth
1840	Crucifix	Crucifix	Little Wonder	Crucifix	Launcelot
1841	Potentia	Ralph	Coronation	Ghunznee	Satirist
1842	Firebrand	Meteor	Attila	Our Nell	The Blue Bonnet
1843	Extempore	Cotherstone	Cotherstone	Poison	Nutwith
1844	Sorella	The Ugly Buck	Orlando	The Princess	Foig a Ballagh
1845	Picnic	Idas	The Merry Monarch	Refraction	The Baron
1846	Mendicant	Sir Tatton Sykes	Pyrrhus the First	Mendicant	Sir Tatton Sykes
1847	Clementina	Conyngham	Cossack	Miami	VanTromp
1848	Canezou	Flatcatcher	Surplice	Cymba	Surplice
1849	The Flea	Nunnykirk	The Flying Dutchman	Lady Evelyn	The Flying Dutchman
1850	Lady Orford	Pitsford	Voltigeur	Rhedycina	Voltigeur
1851	Aphrodite	Hernandez	Teddington	Iris	Newminster
1852	Kate	Stockwell	Daniel O'Rourke	Songstress	Stockwell
1853	Mentmore Lass	West Australian	West Australian	Catherine Hayes	West Australian
1854	Virage	The Hermit	Andover	Mincemeat	Knight of St George
1855	Habena	Lord of the Isles	Wild Dayrell	Marchioness	Saucebox
1856	Manganese	Fazzoletto	Ellington	Mincepie	Warlock
1857	Imperieuse	Vedette	Blink Bonny	Blink Bonny	Imperieuse
1858	Governess	Fitzroland	Beadsman	Governess	Sunbeam
1859	Mayonaise	Promised Land	Musjid	Summerside	Gamester
1860	Sagitta	The Wizard	Thormanby	Butterfly	St Albans
1861	Nemesis	Diophantus	Kettledrum	Brown Duchess	Caller Ou
1862	Hurricane	The Marquis	Caractacus	Fue de Joie	The Marquis
1863	Lady Augusta	Macaroni	Macaroni	Queen Bertha	Lord Clifden
1864	Tomato	General Peel	Blair Athol	Fille de L'Air	Blair Athol
1865	Siberia	Gladiateur	Gladiateur	Regalia	Gladiateur
1866	Repulse	Lord Lyon	Lord Lyon	Tormentor	Lord Lyon
1867	Achievement	Vauban	Hermit	Hippia	Achievement
1868	Formosa	Moslem} Formosa} (dead heat)	Blue Gown	Formosa	Formosa
1869	Scottish Queen	Pretender	Pretender	Brigantine	Pero Gomez
1870	Hester	Macgregor	Kingcraft	Gamos	Hawthornden
1871	Hannah	Bothwell	Favonius	Hannah	Hannah
1872	Reine	Prince Charlie	Cremorne	Reine	Wenlock
1873	Cecilia	Gang Forward	Doncaster	Marie Stuart	Marie Stuart
1874	Apology	Atlantic	Gearge Frederick	Apology	Apology

	1000 Guineas	2000 Guineas	Derby	Oaks	St Leger
1875	Spinaway	Camballo	Galopin	Spinaway	Craig Millar
1876	Camelia	Petrarch	Kisber	Enguerrande } Camelia } dead heat	Petrarch
1877	Belpheobe	Chamant	Silvio	Placida	Silvio
1878	Pilgrimage	Pilgrimage	Sefton	Jannette	Jannette
1879	Wheel of Fortune	Charibert	Sir Bevys	Wheel of Fortune	Rayon d'Or
1880	Elizabeth	Petronel	Bend Or	Jenny Howlet	Robert the Devil
1881	Thebais	Peregrine	Iroquois	Thebais	Iroquois
1882	St Marguerite	Shotover	Shotover	Geheimniss	Dutch Oven
1883	Hauteur	Galliard	St Blaise	Bonny Jean	Ossian
1884	Busybody	Scot Free	St Gatien	Busybody	The Lambkin
1885	Farewell	Paradox	Melton } Harvester } dead heat	Lonely	Melton
1886	Miss Jummy	Ormonde	Ormonde	Miss Jummy	Ormonde
1887	Reve d'Or	Enterprise	Merry Hampton	Reve d'Or	Kilwarlin
1888	Briarroot	Ayrshire	Ayrshire	Seabreeze	Seabreeze
1889	Minthe	Enthusiast	Donovan	L'Abbesse de Jouarre	Donovan
1890	Semolina	Surefoot	Sainfoin	Memoir	Memoir
1891	Mimi	Common	Common	Mimi	Common
1892	La Fleche	Bona Vista	Sir Hugo	La Fleche	La Fleche
1893	Siffleuse	Isinglass	Isinglass	Mrs Butterwick	Isinglass
1894	Amiable	Ladas	Ladas	Amiable	Throstle
1895	Galeottia	Kirkconnel	Sir Visto	La Sagesse	Sir Visto
1896	Thais	St Frusquin	Persimmon	Canterbury Pilgrim	Persimmon
1897	Chelandry	Galtee More	Galtee More	Limasol	Galtee More
1898	Nun Nicer	Disraeli	Jeddah	Airs and Graces	Wildfowler
1899	Sibola	Flying Fox	Flying Fox	Musa	Flying Fox
1900	Winifreda	Diamond Jubilee	Diamond Jubilee	La Roche	Diamond Jubilee
1901	Aida	Handicapper	Volodyovski	Caps and Bells II	Doricles
1902	Sceptre	Sceptre	Ard Patrick	Sceptre	Sceptre
1903	Quintessence	Rock Sand	Rock Sand	Our Lassie	Rock Sand
1904	Pretty Polly	St Amant	St Amant	Pretty Polly	Pretty Polly
1905	Cherry Lass	Vedas	Cicero	Cherry Lass	Challacombe
1906	Flair	Gorgos	Spearmint	Keystone II	Troutbeck
1907	Witch Elm	Slieve Gallion	Orby	Glass Doll	Wool Winder
1908	Rhodora	Norman III	Signorinetta	Signorinetta	Your Majesty
1909	Electra	Minoru	Minoru	Perola	Bayardo
1910	Winkipop	Neil Gow	Lemberg	Rosedrop	Swynford
1911	Atmah	Sunstar	Sunstar	Cherimoya	Prince Palatine
1912	Tagalie	Sweeper II	Tagalie	Mirska	Tracery
1913	Jest	Louvis	Aboyeur	Jest	Night Hawk
1914	Princess Dorrie	Kennymore	Durbar II	Princess Dorrie	Black Jester
1915	Vaucluse	Pommern	Pommern	Snow Marten	Pommern
1916	Canyon	Clarissimus	Fifinella	Fifinella	Hurry On
1917	Diadem	Gay Crusader	Gay Crusader	Sunny Jane	Gay Crusader
1918	Ferry	Gainsborough	Gainsborough	My Dear	Gainsborough
1919	Roseway	The Panther	Grand Parade	Bayuda	Keysoe
1920	Cinna	Tetratema	Spion Kop	Charlebelle	Caligula
1921	Bettina	Criag an Eran	Humorist	Love in Idleness	Polemarch
1922	Silver Urn	St Louis	Captain Cuttle	Pogrom	Royal Lancer
1923	Tranquil	Ellangowan	Papyrus	Brownhylda	Tranquil
1924	Plack	Diophon	Sansovino	Straitlace	Salmon-Trout
1925	Saucy Sue	Manna	Manna	Saucy Sue	Solario
1926	Pillion	Colorado	Coronach	Short Story	Coronach
1927	Cresta Run	Adam's Apple	Call Boy	Beam	Book Law
1928	Scuttle	Flamingo	Fellstead	Toboggan	Fairway
1929	Taj Mah	Mr Jinks	Trigo	Pennycomequick	Trigo
1930	Fair Isle	Diolite	Blenheim	Rose of England	Singapore
1931	Four Course	Cameronian	Cameronian	Brulette	Sandwich
1932	Kandy	Orwell	April the Fifth	Udaipur	Firdaussi
1933	Betty Brown	Rodosto	Hyperion	Chatelaine	Hyperion
1934	Campanula	Colombo	Windsor Lad	Light Brocade	Windsor Lad
1935	Mesa	Bahram	Bahram	Quashed	Bahram
1936	Tide-Way	Pay Up	Mahmoud	Lovely Rosa	Boswell
1937	Exhibitionist	Le Ksar	Mid-day Sun	Exhibitionist	Chulmleigh
1938	Rockfel	Pasch	Bois Roussel	Rockfel	Scottish Union
1939	Galatea II	Blue Peter	Blue Peter	Galatea II	
1940	Godiva	Djebel	Pont l'Eveque	Godiva	Turkhan
1941	Dancing Time	Lambert Simnel	Owen Tudor	Commotion	Sun Castle
1942	Sun Chariot	Big Game	Watling Street	Sun Chariot	Sun Chariot
1943	Herringbone	Kingsway	Straight Deal	Why Hurry	Herringbone

	1000 Guineas	2000 Guineas	Derby	Oaks	St Leger
1944	Picture Play	Garden Path	Ocean Swell	Hycilla	Tehran
1945	Sun Stream	Court Martial	Dante	Sun Stream	Chamossaire
1946	Hypericum	Happy Knight	Airborne	Steady Aim	Airborne
1947	Imprudence	Tudor Minstel	Pearl Diver	Imprudence	Sayajirao
1948	Queenpot	My Babu	My Love	Masaka	Black Tarquin
1949	Musidora	Nimbus	Nimbus	Musidora	Ridge Wood
1950	Camaree	Palestine	Galcador	Asmena	Scratch II
1951	Belle of All	Ki Ming	Arctic Prince	Neasham Belle	Talma II
1952	Zabara	Thunderhead II	Tulyar	Frieze	Tulyar
1953	Happy Laughter	Nearula	Pinza	Ambiguity	Premonition
1954	Festoon	Darius	Never Say Die	Sun Cap	Never Say Die
1955	Meld	Our Babu	Phil Drake	Meld	Meld
1956	Honeylight	Gilles de Retz	Lavandin	Sicarelle	Cambremer
1957	Rose Royale II	Crepello	Crepello	Carrozza	Ballymoss
1958	Bella Paola	Pall Mall	Hard Ridden	Bella Paola	Alcide
1959	Petite Etoile	Taboun	Parthia	Petite Etoile	Cantelo
1960	Never Too Late	Martial	St. Paddy	Never Too Late	St Paddy
1961	Sweet Solera	Rockavon	Psidium	Sweet Solera	Aurelius
1962	Abermaid	Privy Councillor	Larkspur	Monade	Hethersett
1963	Hula Dancer	Only for Life	Relko	Noblesse	Ragusa
1964	Pourparler	Baldric II	Santa Claus	Homeward Bound	Indiana
1965	Night Off	Niksar	Sea Bird II	Long Look	Provoke
1966	Glad Rags	Kashmir II	Charlottown	Valoris	Sodium
1967	Fleet	Royal Palace	Royal Palace	Pia	Ribocco
1968	Caergwrle	Sir Ivor	Sir Ivor	La Lagune	Ribero
1969	Full Dress II	Right Tack	Blakeney	Sleeping Partner	Intermezzo
1970	Humble Duty	Nijinsky	Nijinsky	Lupe	Nijinsky
1971	Altesse Royale	Brigadier Gerard	Mill Reef	Altesse Royale	Athens Wood
1972	Waterloo	High Top	Roberto	Ginevra	Boucher
1973	Mysterious	Mon Fils	Morston	Mysterious	Peleid
1974	Highclere	Nonoalco	Snow Knight	Polygamy	Bustino
1975	Nocturnal Spree	Bolkonski	Grundy	Juliette Marny	Bruni
1976	Flying Water	Wollow	Empery	Pawneese	Crow
1977	Mrs McArdy	Nebbiolo	The Minstrel	Dunfermline	Dunfermline
1978	Enstone Spark	Roland Gardens	Shirley Heights	Fari Salinia	Julio Mariner
1979	One in a Million	Tap On Wood	Troy	Scintillate	Son of Love
1980	Quick as Lightning	Known Fact	Henbit	Bireme	Light Cavalry
1981	Fairy Footsteps	To-Agori-Mou	Shergar	Blue Wind	Cut Above
1982	On the House	Zino	Golden Fleece	Time Charter	Touching Wood
1983	Ma Biche	Lomond	Teenoso	Sun Princess	Sun Princess
1984	Pebbles	El Gran Senor	Secreto	Circus Plume	Commanche Run
1985	Oh So Sharp	Shaheed	Slip Anchor	Oh So Sharp	Oh So Sharp
1986	Midway Lady	Dancing Brave	Shahrastani	Midway Lady	Moon Madness
1987	Miesque	Don't Forget Me	Reference Point	Unite	Reference Point
1988	Ravinella	Doyoun	Kahyasi	Diminuendo	Minster Son
1989	Musical Bliss	Nashwan	Nashwan	Aliysa	Michelozzo

Horses underlined won more than one classic

FASTEST TIMES FOR THE ENGLISH CLASSICS

Derby: 2m 33.80s Mahmoud (1936) HT
2m 33.84s Kahyasi (1988) ET
Oaks: 2m 34.21s Time Charter (1982) ET
1000 Guineas: 1m 36.85s Oh So Sharp (1985) ET
2000 Guineas: 1m 35.80s My Babu (1948) HT
St Leger: 3m 01.60s Coronach (1926) HT
3m 01.60s Windsor Lad (1934) HT

HT=Hand Timed, ET=Electronically Timed

THE TRIPLE CROWN: 2,000 GUINEAS, DERBY AND ST LEGER

Horse	Year	Jockey(s)
West Australian	1853	Frank Butler
Gladiateur	1865	Harry Grimshaw
Lord Lyon	1866	Harry Custance 2, R. Thomas 1
Ormonde	1886	Fred Archer 2, George Barrett 1
Common	1891	George Barrett
Isinglass	1893	Tommy Loates
Galtee More	1897	Charlie Wood
Flying Fox	1899	Morny Cannon
Diamond Jubilee	1900	Herbert Jones
Rock Sand	1903	Danny Maher 2, J Martin
Pommern	1915	Steve Donoghue
Gay Crusader	1917	Steve Donoghue
Gainsborough	1918	Joe Childs
Bahram	1935	Freddie Fox 2, Charlie Smirke 1
Nijinsky	1970	Lester Piggott

GRAND NATIONAL WINNERS (1836-1919)

1836 The Duke	1857 Emigrant	1878 Shifnal	1899 Manifesto
1837 The Duke	1858 Little Charley	1879 The Liberator	1900 Ambush II
1838 Sir William	1859 Half Caste	1800 Empress	1901 Grudon
1839 Lottery	1860 Anatis	1881 Woodbrook	1902 Shannon Lass
1840 Jerry	1861 Jealousy	1882 Seaman	1903 Drumcree
1841 Charity	1862 Huntsman	1883 Zoedone	1904 Moifaa
1842 Gay Lad	1863 Emblem	1884 Voluptuary	1905 Kirkland
1843 Vanguard	1864 Emblematic	1885 Roquefort	1906 Ascetic's Silver
1844 Discount	1865 Alcibiade	1886 Old Joe	1907 Eremon
1845 Cureall	1866 Salamander	1887 Gamecock	1908 Rubio
1846 Pioneer	1867 Cortolvin	1888 Playfair	1909 Lutteur III
1847 Matthew	1868 The Lamb	1889 Frigate	1910 Jenkinstown
1848 Chandler	1869 The Colonel	1890 Ilex	1911 Glenside
1849 Peter Simple	1870 The Colonel	1891 Come Away	1912 Jerry M
1850 Abd-el-Kader	1871 The Lamb	1892 Father O'Flynn	1913 Covetcoat
1851 Abd-el-Kader	1872 Casse Tete	1893 Cloister	1914 Sunloch
1852 Miss Mowbray	1873 Disturbance	1894 Why Not	1915 Ally Sloper
1853 Peter Simple	1874 Reugny	1895 Wild Man from Borneo	1916 Vermouth
1854 Bourton	1875 Pathfinder	1896 Soarer	1917 Ballymacad
1855 Wanderer	1876 Regal	1897 Manifesto	1918 Poethlyn
1856 Freetrader	1877 Austerlitz	1898 Drogheda	1919 Poethlyn

GRAND NATIONAL AND OTHER BIG RACE WINNERS SINCE 1920

Grand National	Cheltenham Gold Cup	Champion Hurdle	Arc de Triomphe	Irish Derby
1920 Troytown	-	-	Comrade	He Goes
1921 Shaun Spadah	-	-	Ksar	Ballyheron
1922 Music Hall	-	-	Ksar	Spike Island
1923 Sergeant Murphy	-	-	Parth	Waygood
1924 Master Robert	Red Splash	-	Massine	Zodiac/Haine
1925 Double Chance	Balinode	-	Priori	Zionist
1926 Jack Horner	Koko	-	Biribi	Embargo
1927 Sprig	Thrown In	Blaris	Mon Talisman	Knight of the Grail
1928 Tipperary Tim	Patron Saint	Brown Jack	Kantar	Baytown
1929 Gregalach	Easter Hero	Royal Falcon	Ortello	Kopi
1930 Shaun Goilin	Easter Hero	Brown Tony	Motrico	Rock Star
1931 Grakle	-	-	Pearl Cap	Sea Serpent
1932 Forbra	Golden Miller		Motrico	Dastur
1933 Kellsboro' Jack	Golden Miller	Insurance	Crapom	Harninero
1934 Golden Miller	Golden Miller	Chenango	Brantome	Primero/Patriot King
1935 Reynoldstown	Golden Miller	Lion Courage	Samos	Museum
1936 Reynoldstown	Golden Miller	Victor Norman	Corrida	Raeburn
1937 Royal Mail	-	Free Fare	Corrida	Phidias
1938 Battleship	Morse Code	Our Hope	Eclair au Chocolat	Rosewell
1939 Workman	Brendan's Cottage	Africa Sister	-	Mondragon
1940 Bogskar	Roman Hackle	Solford	-	Turkhan
1941 -	Poet Prince	Seneca	La Pacha	Sol Oriens
1942 -	Medoc II	Forestation	Djebel	Windsor Slipper
1943 -	-	-	Verso II	The Phoenix
1944 -	-	-	Ardan	Slide On
1945 -	Red Rower	Brains Trust	Nikellora	Piccadilly
1946 Lovely Cottage	Prince Regent	Distel	Caracella	Bright News
1947 Caughoo	Fortina	National Spirit	Le Paillon	Sayajirao
1948 Sheila's Cottage	Cottage Rake	National Spirit	Migoli	Nathoo
1949 Russian Hero	Cottage Rake	Hatton's Grace	Coronation	Hindostan
1950 Freebooter	Cottage Rake	Hatton's Grace	Tantieme	Dark Warrior
1951 Nickel Coin	Silver Fame	Hatton's Grace	Tantieme	Fraise du Bois II
1952 Teal	Mont Tremblant	Sir Ken	Nuccio	Thirteen of Diamonds
1953 Early Mist	Knock Hard	Sir Ken	La Sorellina	Chamier
1954 Royal Tan	Four Ten	Sir Ken	Sica Boy	Zarathustra
1955 Quare Times	Gay Donald	Clair Soleil	Ribot	Panaslipper
1956 E.S.B.	Limber Hill	Doorknocker	Ribot	Talgo
1957 Sundew	Linwell	Merry Deal	Oreso	Ballymoss
1958 Mr. What	Kerstin	Bandalore	Ballymoss	Sindon
1959 Oxo	Roddy Owen	Fare Time	Saint Crespin	Fidalgo
1960 Merryman II	Pas Seul	Another Flash	Puissant Chef	Chamour
1961 Nicolaus Silver	Saffron Tartan	Eborneezer	Molvedo	Your Highness
1962 Kilmore	Mandarin	Anzio	Soltikoff	Tambourine II
1963 Ayala	Mill House	Winning Fair	Exbury	Ragusa
1964 Team Spirit	Arkle	Magic Court	Prince Royal II	Santa Claus
1965 Jay Trump	Arkle	Kirriemuir	Sea Bird II	Meadow Court
1966 Anglo	Arkle	Salmon Spray	Bon Mot	Sodium
1967 Foinavon	Woodland Venture	Saucy Kit	Topyo	Ribocco
1968 Reg Alligator	Fort Leney	Persian War	Vaguely Noble	Ribero

Grand National	Cheltenham Gold Cup	Champion Hurdle	Arc de Triomphe	Irish Derby
1969 Highland Wedding	What a Myth	Persian War	Levmoss	Prince Regent
1970 Gay Trip	L'Escargot	Persian War	Sassafras	Nijinsky
1971 Specify	L'Escargot	Bula	Mill Reef	Irish Ball
1972 Well To Do	Glencaraig Lady	Bula	San San	Steel Pulse
1973 Red Rum	The Dikler	Comedy of Errors	Rheingold	Weaver's Hall
1974 Red Rum	Captain Christy	Lanzarote	Allez France	English Prince
1975 L'Escargot	Ten Up	Comedy of Errors	Star Appeal	Grundy
1976 Rag Trade	Royal Frolic	Night Nurse	Ivanjica	Malacate
1977 Red Rum	Davy Lad	Night Nurse	Alleged	The Minstrel
1978 Lucius	Midnight Court	Monksfield	Alleged	Shirley Heights
1979 Rubstic	Alverton	Monksfield	Three Troikas	Troy
1980 Ben Nevis	Master Smudge	Sea Pigeon	Detroit	Tyrnavos
1981 Aldaniti	Little Owl	Sea Pigeon	Gold River	Shergar
1982 Grittar	Silver Buck	For Auction	Akiyda	Assert
1983 Corbiere	Bregawn	Gaye Brief	All Along	Shareef Dancer
1984 Hallo Dandy	Burrough Hill Lad	Dawn Run	Sagace	El Gran Senor
1985 Last Suspect	Forgive N'Forget	See You Then	Rainbow Quest	Law Society
1986 West Tip	Dawn Run	See You Then	Dancing Brave	Shahrastani
1987 Maori Venture	The Thinker	See You Then	Trempolino	Sir Harry Lewis
1988 Rhyme N'Reason	Charter Party	Celtic Shot	Tony Bin	Kahyasi
1989 Little Polveir	Desert Orchid	Beech Road	Carroll House	Old Vic

DERBY WINNERS OF THE 1980s

	Jockey	Price	Distance	Time	Trainer	Owner
1980 Henbit	Willie Carson	7-1	3/4 l	2m 34.77s	Dick Hern	Etti Plesch
1981 Shergar	Walter Swinburn	10-11	10l	2m 22.21s	Michael Stoute	HH Aga Khan
1982 Golden Fleece	Pat Eddery	3-1	3l	2m 34.27s	Vincent O'Brien	Robert Sangster
1983 Teenoso	Lester Piggott	9-2	3l	2m 49.07s	Geoffrey Wragg	Eric Moller
1984 Secreto	Christy Roche	14-1	sh	2m 39.12s	David O'Brien	Luigi Miglietti
1985 Slip Anchor	Steve Cauthen	9-4	7l	2m 36.23s	Henry Cecil	Lord H de Walden
1986 Shahrastani	Walter Swinburn	11-2	1/2 l	2m 37.13s	Michael Stoute	HH Aga Khan
1987 Reference Point	Steve Cauthen	6-4	11/2l	2m 33.90s	Henry Cecil	Louise Freedman
1988 Kahyasi	Ray Cochrane	11-1	11/2l	2m 33.84s	Luca Cumani	HH Aga Khan
1989 Nashwan	Willie Carson	5-4	5l	2m 34.90s	Dick Hern	Hamdan al Maktoum

GRAND NATIONAL WINNERS OF THE 1980s

Horse	Age/Weight	Jockey	Price	Trainer	Owner
1980 Ben Nevis	12-10-12	Mr Charlie Fenwick	40-1	Tim Forster	Redmond Stewart
1981 Aldaniti	11-10-13	Bob Champion	10-1	Josh Gifford	Nick Embiricos
1982 Grittar	9-11-5	Mr Dick Saunders	7-1	Frank Gilman	Frank Gilman
1983 Corbiere	8-11-4	Ben De Haan	13-1	Mrs Jenny Pitman	Brian Burroughs
1984 Hallo Dandy	10-10-2	Neale Doughty	13-1	Gordon Richards	Richard Shaw
1985 Last Suspect	11-10-5	Hywel Davies	50-1	Tim Forster	Duchess of Westminster
1986 West Tip	9-10-11	Richard Dunwoody	15-2	Michael Oliver	Peter Luff
1987 Maori Venture	11-10-13	Steve Knight	28-1	Andy Turnell	Jim Joel
1988 Rhyme n' Reason	9-10-11	Brendon Powell	10-1	David Elsworth	Juliet Reed
1989 Little Polveir	12-10-3	Jimmy Frost	28-1	Toby Balding	Edward Harvey

HORSES KILLED IN THE GRAND NATIONAL AFTER 1960

1963	Avenue Neuilly	Valentine's	9th	1979	Kintal	Chair	15th
1967	Vulcano	First ditch	3rd		Alverton	Becher's	22nd
1968	Champion Prince	Water	16th	1983	Duncreggan	Canal Turn	8th
1970	Racoon	First ditch	3rd	1884	Earthstopper	collapsed after race	
1973	Grey Sombrero	Chair	15th	1987	Dark Ivy	Becher's	6th
1975	Land Lark	Chair	15th	1989	Seeandem	Becher's	6th
	Beau Bob	Becher's	22nd		Brown Trix	Becher's	6th
1977	Winter Rain	Becher's	6th				
	Zeta's Son	Valentine's	25th	**Source:** *Racing Post*			

CHAMPION FLAT RACE JOCKEYS 1840-1945

Year	Jockey	Wins	Year	Jockey	Wins	Year	Jockey	Wins
1840	Elnathan Flatman	50	1875	Fred Archer	172	1912	Frank Wootton	118
1841	Elnathan Flatman	68	1876	Fred Archer	207	1913	Danny Maher	115
1842	Elnathan Flatman	42	1877	Fred Archer	218	1914	Steve Donoghue	129
1843	Elnathan Flatman	60	1878	Fred Archer	229	1915	Steve Donoghue	62
1844	Elnathan Flatman	64	1879	Fred Archer	197	1916	Steve Donoghue	43
1845	Elnathan Flatman	81	1880	Fred Archer	120	1917	Steve Donoghue	42
1846	Elnathan Flatman	81	1881	Fred Archer	220	1918	Steve Donoghue	66
1847	Elnathan Flatman	89	1882	Fred Archer	210	1919	Steve Donoghue	129
1848	Elnathan Flatman	104	1883	Fred Archer	232	1920	Steve Donoghue	143
1849	Elnathan Flatman	94	1884	Fred Archer	241	1921	Steve Donoghue	141
1850	Elnathan Flatman	88	1885	Fred Archer	246	1922	Steve Donoghue	102
1851	Elnathan Flatman	78	1886	Fred Archer	170	1923	Steve Donoghue &	
1852	Elnathan Flatman	92	1887	Charlie Wood	151		Charlie Elliott	89
1853	John Wells	86	1888	Fred Barrett	108	1924	Charlie Elliott	106
1854	John Wells	82	1889	Tommy Loates	167	1925	Gordon Richards	118
1855	George Fordham	70	1890	Tommy Loates	147	1926	Tommy Weston	95
1856	George Fordham	108	1891	Morny Cannon	137	1927	Gordon Richards	164
1857	George Fordham	84	1892	Morny Cannon	182	1928	Gordon Richards	148
1858	George Fordham	91	1893	Tommy Loates	222	1929	Gordon Richards	135
1859	George Fordham	118	1894	Morny Cannon	167	1930	Freddy Fox	129
1860	George Fordham	146	1895	Morny Cannon	184	1931	Gordon Richards	145
1861	George Fordham	106	1896	Morny Cannon	164	1932	Gordon Richards	190
1862	George Fordham	166	1897	Morny Cannon	145	1933	Gordon Richards	259
1863	George Fordham	103	1898	Otto Madden	161	1934	Gordon Richards	212
1864	Harry Grimshaw	164	1899	Sam Loates	160	1935	Gordon Richards	217
1865	George Fordham	142	1900	Lester Reiff	143	1936	Gordon Richards	174
1866	S Kenyon	123	1901	Otto Madden	130	1937	Gordon Richards	216
1867	George Fordham	143	1902	Willie Lane	170	1938	Gordon Richards	200
1868	George Fordham	110	1903	Otto Madden	154	1939	Gordon Richards	155
1869	George Fordham	95	1904	Otto Madden	161	1940	Gordon Richards	68
1870	W Gray &		1905	Elijah Wheatley	124	1941	Harry Wragg	71
	Charlie Maidment	76	1906	Billy Higgs	149	1942	Gordon Richards	67
1871	George Fordham &		1907	Billy Higgs	146	1943	Gordon Richards	65
	Charlie Maidment	86	1908	Danny Maher	139	1944	Gordon Richards	88
1872	Tommy Cannon	87	1909	Frank Wootton	165	1945	Gordon Richards	104
1873	Harry Constable	110	1910	Frank Wootton	137			
1874	Fred Archer	147	1911	Frank Wootton	187			

CHAMPION FLAT RACE JOCKEYS, TRAINERS AND OWNERS 1946-88

	Jockey		Apprentice		Trainer	£	Owner	£
1946	Gordon Richards	212	Joe Sime	40	Frank Butters	56,140	HH Aga Khan	24,118
1947	Gordon Richards	269	Dennis Buckle	20	Fred Darling	65,313	HH Aga Khan	44,020
1948	Gordon Richards	224	Dennis Buckle	25	Noel Murless	66,542	HH Aga Khan	46,393
1949	Gordon Richards	261	Willie Snaith	31	Frank Butters	71,721	HH Aga Khan	68,916
1950	Gordon Richards	201	Lester Piggott	52	Charles Semblat	57,044	Marcel Boussac	57,044
1951	Gordon Richards	227	Lester Piggott	51	Jack Jarvis	56,397	Marcel Boussac	39,339
1952	Gordon Richards	231	Joe Mercer	26	Marcus Marsh	92,093	HH Aga Khan	92,518
1953	Gordon Richards	191	Joe Mercer	61	Jack Jarvis	71,546	Victor Sassoon	58,579
1954	Doug Smith	129	Eddie Hide	53	Cecil Boyd-Rochfort	65,326	HM The Queen	40,993
1955	Doug Smith	168	Philip Robinson	46	Cecil Boyd-Rochfort	74,424	Lady Zia Wernher	46,345
1956	Doug Smith	155	Eddie Hide	75	Charles Elsey	61,621	Maj L Holliday	39,327
1957	Scobie Breasley	173	Greville Starkey	45	Noel Murless	116,898	HM The Queen	62,211
1958	Doug Smith	165	Peter Boothman	37	Cecil Boyd-Rochfort	84,186	John McShain	63,264
1959	Doug Smith	157	Bobby Elliott	27	Noel Murless	145,727	H H Aly Khan	100,668
1960	Lester Piggott	170	Bobby Elliott	39	Noel Murless	118,327	Victor Sassoon	90,069
1961	Scobie Breasley	171	Brian Lee	52	Noel Murless	95,972	Maj L Holliday	39,227
1962	Scobie Breasley	179	Bruce Raymond	13	Dick Hern	70,206	Maj L Holliday	70,206
1963	Scobie Breasley	176	David Yates	24	Paddy Prendergast	125,294	Jim Mullion	68,882
1964	Lester Piggott	140	Paul Cook	46	Paddy Prendergast	128,102	Mrs H Jackson	98,270
1965	Lester Piggott	166	Paul Cook	62	Paddy Prendergast	75,323	Jean Ternynck	65,301
1966	Lester Pigott	191	Sandy Barclay	71	Vincent O'Brien	123,848	Lady Zia Wernher	78,075
1967	Lester Piggott	117	Ernie Johnson	39	Noel Murless	256,899	Jim Joel	120,925
1968	Lester Piggott	139	David Coates & Richard Dicey	40	Noel Murless	141,508	Raymond Guest	97,075
1969	Lester Piggott	163	Clive Eccleston	41	Arthur Budgett	105,349	David Robinson	92,553
1970	Lester Piggott	162	Phillip Waldron	59	Noel Murless	199,524	Chas Engelhard	182,059
1971	Lester Piggott	162	Pat Eddery	71	Ian Balding	157,488	Paul Mellon	138,786
1972	Willie Carson	132	R Edmondson	42	Dick Hern	206,767	Mrs Jean Hislop	155,190
1973	Willie Carson	163	Stephen Perks	41	Noel Murless	132,984	Nelson B Hunt	124,771
1974	Pat Eddery	148	Alan Bond	40	Peter Walwyn	206,445	Nelson B Hunt	147,244

1975	Pat Eddery	164	Alan Bond	66	Peter Walwyn	382,527	Carlo Vittandi	209,492
1976	Pat Eddery	162	David Dineley	54	Henry Cecil	261,301	Dan Wildenstein	244,500
1977	Pat Eddery	176	Jimmy Bleasdale	67	Vincent O'Brien	439,124	Robert Sangster	348,023
1978	Willie Carson	182	Kevin Darley	70	Henry Cecil	382,812	Robert Sangster	160,405
1979	Joe Mercer	164	Philip Robinson	51	Henry Cecil	683,971	Michael Sobell	339,751
1980	Willie Carson	165	Philip Robinson	59	Dick Hern	831,964	Simon Weinstock	236,332
1981	Lester Piggott	179	Bryn Crossley	45	Michael Stoute	723,786	HH Aga Khan	441,654
1982	Lester Piggott	188	Billy Newnes	57	Henry Cecil	872,614	Robert Sangster	397,749
1983	Willie Carson	159	Michael Hills	39	Dick Hern	549,598	Robert Sangster	461,488
1984	Steve Cauthen	130	Tommy Quinn	62	Henry Cecil	551,939	Robert Sangster	395,901
1985	Steve Cauthen	195	Gary Carter & Willie Ryan	37	Henry Cecil	1,148,206	Shk Mohammed	1,082,502
1986	Pat Eddery	177	Gary Carter	34	Michael Stoute	1,266,807	Shk Mohammed	830,121
1987	Steve Cauthen	197	Gary Bardwell	27	Henry Cecil	1,882,116	Shk Mohammed	1,232,240
1988	Pat Eddery	183	Gary Bardwell	39	Henry Cecil	1,186,122	Shk Mohammed	1,143,343

CHAMPION NATIONAL HUNT JOCKEYS & TRAINERS SINCE 1946

	Jockey		Trainer	£
1946	Fred Rimell	54	Tom Rayson	9,933
1947	Jack Dowdeswell	58	Fulke Walwyn	11,115
1948	Bryan Marshall	66	Fulke Walwyn	16,790
1949	Tim Molony	60	Fulke Walwyn	15,563
1950	Tim Molony	95	Peter Cazalet	18,427
1951	Tim Molony	83	Fred Rimell	18,381
1952	Tim Molony	99	Neville Crump	19,377
1953	Fred Winter	121	Vincent O'Brien	15,515
1954	Dick Francis	76	Vincent O'Brien	14,274
1955	Tim Molony	67	Ryan Price	13,888
1956	Fred Winter	74	Charlie Hall	15,807
1957	Fred Winter	80	Neville Crump	18,495
1958	Fred Winter	82	Fulke Walwyn	23,013
1959	Tim Brookshaw	83	Ryan Price	26,550
1960	Stan Mellor	68	Peter Cazalet	22,270
1961	Stan Mellor	118	Fred Rimell	34,811
1962	Stan Mellor	80	Ryan Price	40,950
1963	Josh Gifford	70	Keith Piggott	23,091
1964	Josh Gifford	94	Fulke Walwyn	67,129
1965	Terry Biddlecombe	114	Peter Cazalet	36,153
1966	Terry Biddlecombe	102	Ryan Price	42,267
1967	Josh Gifford	122	Ryan Price	41,222
1968	Josh Gifford	82	Denys Smith	37,944
1969	Bob Davies & Terry Biddlecombe	77 77	Fred Rimell	38,344
1970	Bob Davies	91	Fred Rimell	61,864
1971	Graham Thorner	74	Fred Winter	60,739
1972	Bob Davies	89	Fred Winter	62,396
1973	Ron Barry	125	Fred Winter	79,066
1974	Ron Barry	94	Fred Winter	101,782
1975	Tommy Stack	82	Fred Winter	74,205
1976	John Francome	96	Fred Rimell	111,740
1977	Tommy Stack	97	Fred Winter	85,202
1978	Jonjo O'Neill	149	Fred Winter	145,915
1979	John Francome	95	Peter Easterby	150,746
1980	Jonjo O'Neill	115	Peter Easterby	218,258
1981	John Francome	105	Peter Easterby	236,867
1982	John Francome & Peter Scudamore	120 120	Michael Dickinson	296,028
1983	John Francome	106	Michael Dickinson	358,837
1984	John Francome	131	Michael Dickinson	266,146
1985	John Francome	101	Fred Winter	218,978
1986	Peter Scudamore	91	Nicky Henderson	162,234
1987	Peter Scudamore	123	Nicky Henderson	162,234
1988	Peter Scudamore	132	David Elsworth	344,210
1989	Peter Scudamore	221	Martin Pipe	589,460

US RACING
Triple Crown

The following horses have all won the Triple Crown:

Horse	Year	Jockey
Sir Barton	1919	John Loftus
Gallant Fox	1930	Earl Sande
Omaha	1935	W Saunders
War Admiral	1937	C Kurtsinger
Whirlaway	1941	Eddie Arcaro
Count Fleet	1943	Johnny Longden
Assault	1946	W Mehrtens
Citation	1948	Eddie Arcaro
Secretariat	1973	Ron Turcotte
Seattle Slew	1977	Jean Cruguet
Affirmed	1978	Steve Cauthen

Breeder's Cup

	Sprint	Mile	Juvenile	Juvenile Fillies
1984	Ellio	Royal Heroine	Chief's Crown	Outstandingly
1985	Precisionist	Cozzene	Tasso	Twilight Ridge
1986	Smile	Last Tycoon	Capote	Brave Raj
1987	Very Subtle	Miesque	Success Express	Epitome
1988	Gulch	Miesque	Is It True?	Open Mind

	Distaff	Classic	Turf
1984	Princess Rooney	Wild Again	Lashkari
1985	Life's Magic	Proud Truth	Pebbles
1986	Lady's Secret	Skywalker	Manila
1987	Sacahuista	Ferdinand	Theatrical
1988	Personal Ensign	Alysheba	Great Communicator

AUSTRALIAN RACING
Melbourne Cup

(Winners since 1980)

1980	Beldale Ball
1981	Just a Dash
1982	Gurner's Lane
1983	Kiwi
1984	Black Night
1985	What a Nuisance
1986	At Talaq
1987	Kensei
1988	Empire Rose

RECORDS

Highest race speed: 43.26 mph by Big Racket over 1/4 mile carrying 114 lb at Mexico City, Feb 5 1945. **Most wins** *Horse:* 137 Galgo jr, Puerto Rico, 1930-36. *Jockey:* 8796 and counting Bill Shoemaker 1949-Jun 1989: 4870. *Jockey in Britain:* Sir Gordon Richards 1920-1954; 4349 (5200+ worldwide) Lester Piggott 1948-1985.

1990

BIG RACES

Mar 13-15	National Hunt Festival (Cheltenham).
Mar 22	Flat season commences (Doncaster).
Apr 7	Grand National (Liverpool).
Apr 17-19	Craven Meeting (Newmarket).

May 3	One Thousand Guineas (Newmarket).
May 5	Two Thousand Guineas (Newmarket).
Jun 6	Derby (Epsom).
Jun 9	Oaks (Epsom).
Jun 19-22	Royal Ascot.
Jul 10-12	July Meeting (Newmarket).
Jul 28	King George VI and Queen Elizabeth Diamond Stakes (Ascot).
Jul 31-Aug 4	Glorious Goodwood Meeting.
Aug 21-23	August Ebor Meeting (York).
Sep 15	St Leger (Doncaster).
Sep 19-22	Ayr Western Meeting.
Sep 27-29	Ascot Festival Meeting
Oct 3-6	Cambridgeshire Meeting (Newmarket).
Oct 7	Prix de l'Arc de Triomphe (Longchamp, Paris, France).
Oct 18-20	Newmarket Houghton meeting.
Nov 10	Final Flat meeting of 1990 season (Doncaster).

FULL RACING FIXTURES 1990

Jan 1:	Catterick; Cheltenham, Devon and Exeter, Leicester, Windsor, Southwell (AWT)
Jan 2:	Ayr, Cheltenham, SOUTHWELL (AWT)
Jan 3:	Ayr, Sedgefield, Lingfield (AWT)
Jan 4:	Nottingham, LINGFIELD (AWT)
Jan 5:	Edinburgh, Southwell, Folkestone, Haydock
Jan 6:	Haydock, Market Rasen, Sandown, SOUTHWELL (AWT)
Jan 8:	Wolverhampton, Chepstow, Lingfield (AWT)
Jan 9:	Leicester, Newton Abbot, LINGFIELD (AWT)
Jan 10:	Kelso, Plumpton, Southwell (AWT)
Jan 11:	Wincanton, SOUTHWELL (AWT)
Jan 12:	Wetherby, Edinburgh, Ascot, Lingfield (AWT)
Jan 13:	Newcastle, Market Rasen, Ascot, Warwick, LINGFIELD (AWT)
Jan 15:	Carlisle, Fontwell, Southwell (AWT)
Jan 16:	Sedgefield, Folkestone, Worcester, SOUTHWELL (AWT)
Jan 17:	Ludlow, Windsor, Lingfield (AWT)
Jan 18:	Newton Abbot, LINGFIELD (AWT)
Jan 19:	Catterick, Kempton, Towcester, Southwell (AWT)
Jan 20:	Haydock, Catterick, Warwick, Kempton, SOUTHWELL (AWT)
Jan 22:	Edinburgh, Leicester, Lingfield (AWT)
Jan 23:	Nottingham, Chepstow, LINGFIELD (AWT)
Jan 24:	Sedgefield, Wolverhampton, Southwell (AWT)
Jan 25:	Huntingdon, Taunton, SOUTHWELL (AWT)
Jan 26:	Ayr, Doncaster, Wincanton, Lingfield (AWT)
Jan 27:	Ayr, Doncaster, Cheltenham, LINGFIELD (AWT)
Jan 29:	Plumpton, Southwell (AWT)
Jan 30:	Sedgefield, Leicester, SOUTHWELL (AWT)
Jan 31:	Hereford, Windsor, Lingfield (AWT)
Feb 1:	Towcester, LINGFIELD(AWT)
Feb 2:	Kelso, Bangor-on-Dee
Feb 3:	Wetherby, Chepstow, Stratford, Sandown, SOUTHWELL (AWT)
Feb 5:	Wolverhampton, Fontwell, Lingfield (AWT)
Feb 6:	Carlisle, Warwick, LINGFIELD (AWT)
Feb 7:	Ludlow, Ascot, Southwell (AWT)
Feb 8:	Huntingdon, Wincanton, SOUTHWELL (AWT)
Feb 9:	Ayr, Sedgefield, Newbury, Lingfield (AWT)
Feb 10:	Ayr, Uttoxeter, Catterick, Newbury, Lingfield (AWT)
Feb 12:	Nottingham, Plumpton, Southwell (AWT)
Feb 13:	Newton Abbot, Towcester, SOUTHWELL (AWT)
Feb 14:	Worcester, Folkestone, Lingfield (AWT)
Feb 15:	Leicester, Sandown, Taunton, Lingfield (AWT),
Feb 16:	Edinburgh, Fakenham, Sandown, Southwell (AWT)
Feb 17:	Newcastle, Nottingham, Chepstow, Windsor, SOUTHWELL (AWT)
Feb 19:	Wolverhampton, Fontwell, Lingfield (AWT)
Feb 20:	Sedgefield, Huntingdon, LINGFIELD (AWT)
Feb 21:	Catterick Bridge, , Warwick, Southwell (AWT)
Feb 22:	Folkestone, Wincanton, SOUTHWELL (AWT)
Feb 23:	Kelso, Kempton, Lingfield (AWT)
Feb 24:	Doncaster, Stratford, Kempton, Edinburgh, LINGFIELD (AWT)
Feb 26:	Doncaster, Leicester, Southwell (AWT)
Feb 27:	Nottingham, Plumpton, SOUTHWELL (AWT)
Feb 28:	Wetherby, Worcester, Lingfield (AWT)
Mar 1:	Ludlow, LINGFIELD (AWT)
Mar 2:	Haydock, Newbury, Southwell (AWT)
Mar 3:	Haydock, Hereford, Newbury, Market Rasen, SOUTHWELL (AWT)
Mar 5:	Leicester, Windsor, Lingfield (AWT)
Mar 6:	Sedgefield, Warwick, LINGFIELD (AWT)

Mar 7: Catterick Bridge, Bangor-on-Dee, Southwell (AWT)
Mar 8: Wincanton, Stratford, SOUTHWELL (AWT)
Mar 9: Carlisle, Market Rasen, Lingfield (AWT), Grand Military (Sandown)
Mar 10: Ayr, Chepstow, Doncaster, LINGFIELD (AWT), Grand Military (Sandown)
Mar 12: Ayr, Plumpton
Mar 13: Sedgefield, N.H. Meeting (Cheltenham)
Mar 14: N.H. Meeting (Cheltenham), Newton Abbot
Mar 15: Hexham, N.H. Meeting (Cheltenham)
Mar 16: Fakenham, Lingfield, Wolverhampton
Mar 17: Newcastle, Uttoxeter, Chepstow, Lingfield
Mar 19: Newcastle, Wolverhampton
Mar 20: Nottingham, Fontwell Park
Mar 21: Kelso, Worcester
Mar 22: DONCASTER, Towcester, Devon & Exeter
Mar 23: DONCASTER, Ludlow, Newbury
Mar 24: DONCASTER, Bangor-on-Dee, Newbury, Hexham
Mar 26: LEICESTER, FOLKESTONE, Hexham
Mar 27: LEICESTER, Royal Artillery (Sandown)
Mar 28: CATTERICK, Worcester
Mar 29: NEWCASTLE, Taunton
Mar 30: BEVERLEY, Plumpton, Wincanton
Mar 31: BEVERLEY, Southwell, Ascot, WARWICK

Apr 2: FOLKESTONE, Ludlow, NOTTINGHAM
Apr 3: HAMILTON, Sedgefield
Apr 4: HAMILTON, Huntingdon
Apr 5: BRIGHTON, Liverpool
Apr 6: Liverpool, Devon & Exeter, KEMPTON
Apr 7: Liverpool, Hereford, LINGFIELD (AWT)
Apr 9: Kelso, WOLVERHAMPTON
Apr 10: PONTEFRACT, WOLVERHAMPTON, Fontwell
Apr 11: RIPON, Worcester, Ascot
Apr 12: RIPON, Southwell, Taunton
Apr 14: Carlisle, Southwell, KEMPTON, HAYDOCK, Towcester, Newton Abbot, NEWCASTLE, Plumpton
Apr 16: Carlisle, Fakenham, Chepstow, NEWCASTLE, KEMPTON, Hereford, Wetherby, Huntingdon, Newton Abbot, Market Rasen, Plumpton, NOTTINGHAM, Wincanton, Towcester, Uttoxeter, WARWICK
Apr 17: NEWMARKET, Wetherby, Chepstow, Uttoxeter, WARWICK
Apr 18: AYR, Cheltenham, PONTEFRACT, NEWMARKET
Apr 19: AYR (MIXED), Cheltenham, NEWMARKET
Apr 20: Ayr, NEWBURY, THIRSK
Apr 21: NEWBURY, Bangor-on-Dee, Ayr, Stratford, THIRSK
Apr 23: EDINBURGH, BRIGHTON
Apr 24: EPSOM, Perth, Sedgefield
Apr 25: CATTERICK, EPSOM, Perth
Apr 26: BEVERLEY, Ludlow, †Wincanton, Perth
Apr 27: CARLISLE, Southwell, SANDOWN
Apr 28: SANDOWN (MIXED), LEICESTER, Hexham, RIPON, Market Rasen, Uttoxeter, †Worcester
Apr 30: †WINDSOR, WOLVERHAMPTON, †Hexham, PONTEFRACT

May 1: REDCAR, NOTTTINGHAM, †Ascot, BATH
May 2: ASCOT, †Cheltenham, Kelso
May 3: NEWMARKET, †Sedgefield, †Newton Abbot, SALISBURY
May 4: HAMILTON, NEWMARKET, Newton Abbot
May 5: HAYDOCK, Hereford, †Hexham, NEWMARKET, THIRSK
May 7: DONCASTER, Ludlow, Devon & Exeter, HAYDOCK (MIXED), Southwell, Fontwell, KEMPTON Towcester, Newcastle, WARWICK
May 8: CHESTER, Chepstow, †FOLKESTONE, SALISBURY
May 9: SALISBURY CHESTER, †Wetherby, †Worcester, †SANDOWN
May 10: CARLISLE, CHESTER, †Huntingdon, †Uttoxeter
May 11: BEVERLEY, LINGFIELD, †Stratford, CARLISLE, †Taunton
May 12: BEVERLEY, Bangor-on Dee, BATH, LINGFIELD, †Warwick, †Newcastle, † Market Rasen
May 14: HAMILTON, WOVERHAMPTON , †WINDSOR
May 15: YORK, †NOTTINGHAM, †BRIGHTON, †Towcester, Newton Abbot
May 16: †KEMPTON, Worcester, †Perth, YORK, †Newton Abbot
May 17: Perth, †Huntingdon, YORK
May 18: THIRSK, NEWMARKET, NEWBURY, †Stratford
May 19: †HAMILTON, NEWMARKET, †LINGFIELD, THIRSK, †SOUTHWELL, NEWBURY, †Warwick
May 21: EDINBURGH, WOLVERHAMPTON, BATH, †United Hunts Meeting (Folkestone)
May 22: BEVERLEY, SALISBURY
May 23: GOODWOOD, Hereford
May 24: CATTERICK, GOODWOOD
May 25: HAYDOCK, Towcester, †PONTEFRACT, Sedgefield
May 26: KEMPTON , †SOUTHWELL, Cartmel, DONCASTER, †WARWICK, †LINGFIELD, HAYDOCK, Hexham
May 28: CHEPSTOW, Fakenham, Cartmel, DONCASTER, Hereford, Devon & Exeter, †Hexham, Huntingdon, Fontwell, REDCAR, LEICESTER, SANDOWN, Wetherby, Uttoxeter
May 29: REDCAR, LEICESTER, †SANDOWN, †Uttoxeter

May 30:   BRIGHTON, Cartmel, †RIPON
May 31:   CARLISLE, BRIGHTON
Jun 1:   HAMILTON, NOTTINGHAM, †GOODWOOD, †Stratford
Jun 2:   EDINBURGH, †Market Rasen, LINGFIELD, Stratford
Jun 4:   †EDINBURGH, LEICESTER, REDCAR
Jun 5:   YARMOUTH, FOLKESTONE
Jun 6:   †BEVERLEY, YARMOUTH, EPSOM
Jun 7:   BEVERLEY, EPSOM
Jun 8:   CATTERICK, SOUTHWELL, EPSOM, †HAYDOCK †GOODWOOD
Jun 9:   †CARLISLE, †LEICESTER, EPSOM, HAYDOCK
Jun 11:   PONTEFRACT, NOTTINGHAM, †BRIGHTON
Jun 12:   PONTEFRACT, GOODWOOD
Jun 13:   BEVERLEY, †KEMPTON, †HAMILTON, NEWBURY
Jun 14:   HAMILTON, †CHEPSTOW, NEWBURY
Jun 15:   †DONCASTER, SOUTHWELL, †GOODWOOD, YORK, SANDOWN
Jun 16:   YORK, †NOTTINGHAM, BATH, †LINGFIELD, SANDOWN
Jun 18:   EDINBURGH, †WOLVERHAMPTON, BRIGHTON, †WINDSOR
Jun 19:   THIRSK, ROYAL ASCOT
Jun 20:   RIPON, ROYAL ASCOT
Jun 21:   RIPON, ROYAL ASCOT
Jun 22:   AYR, SOUTHWELL, ROYAL ASCOT, REDCAR
Jun 23:   AYR, †WARWICK, ASCOT, REDCAR, †LINGFIELD
Jun 25:   EDINBURGH, NOTTINGHAM, †WINDSOR
Jun 26:   YARMOUTH, BRIGHTON, †NEWBURY
Jun 27:   CARLISLE, †CHESTER, †KEMPTON, SALISBURY
Jun 28:   CARLISLE, SALISBURY
Jun 29:   DONCASTER, NEWMARKET, †BATH, †NEWCASTLE, †GOODWOOD, LINGFIELD
Jun 30:   †DONCASTER, NEWMARKET, CHEPSTOW, NEWCASTLE, WARWICK, †LINGFIELD
Jul 2:   EDINBURGH, †WOLVERHAMPTON, †WINDSOR, PONTEFRACT
Jul 3:   CHEPSTOW, FOLKESTONE
Jul 4:   †CATTERICK, WARWICK, YARMOUTH
Jul 5:   CATTERICK, YARMOUTH, †BRIGHTON, †HAYDOCK
Jul 6:   †BEVERLEY, SOUTHWELL, SANDOWN, HAYDOCK
Jul 7:   BEVERLEY, †NOTTINGHAM, BATH, HAYDOCK, SANDOWN
Jul 9:   EDINBURGH, LEICESTER, †WINDSOR, †RIPON
Jul 10:   PONTEFRACT, NEWMARKET
Jul 11:   †REDCAR, NEWMARKET, BATH, †KEMPTON
Jul 12:   †HAMILTON , NEWMARKET, †CHEPSTOW, KEMPTON
Jul 13:   †HAMILTON, †CHESTER, LINGFIELD, YORK, WARWICK
Jul 14:   AYR, CHESTER, LINGFIELD, YORK, †SOUTHWELL, SALISBURY
Jul 16:   AYR, WOLVERHAMPTON , †WINDSOR, †BEVERLEY
Jul 17:   AYR, †LEICESTER, †FOLKESTONE, BEVERLEY
Jul 18:   CATTERICK, YARMOUTH, †SANDOWN, †HAMILTON
Jul 19:   CATTERICK, †CHEPSTOW, †HAMILTON, SANDOWN
Jul 20:   †AYR, †NEWMARKET, NEWBURY, THIRSK
Jun 21:   AYR, NEWMARKET, †LINGFIELD, RIPON, †SOUTHWELL, NEWBURY
Jul 23:   AYR, †NOTTINGHAM, BATH, †WINDSOR
Jul 24:   †REDCAR, YARMOUTH, FOLKESTONE
Jul 25:   †DONCASTER, YARMOUTH, †SANDOWN, REDCAR
Jul 26:   DONCASTER, BRIGHTON
Jul 27:   CARLISLE, ASCOT, †PONTEFRACT
Jul 28:   HAMILTON, †SOUTHWELL, ASCOT, NEWCASTLE, †WARWICK
Jul 30:   NEWCASTLE, †WOLVERHAMPTON, LINGFIELD, †WINDSOR
Jul 31:   BEVERLEY, †LEICESTER, GOODWOOD
Aug 1:   CATTERICK, †SOUTHWELL, GOODWOOD
Aug 2:   YARMOUTH, GOODWOOD
Aug 3:   Bangor-on-Dee, †EDINBURGH, GOODWOOD, THIRSK, †NEWMARKET
Aug 4:   THIRSK, †Market Rasen, GOODWOOD, NEWMARKET, Newton Abbot, †WINDSOR
Aug 6:   RIPON, †NOTTINGHAM, Newton Abbot
Aug 7:   REDCAR, †NOTTINGHAM, BRIGHTON
Aug 8:   PONTEFRACT, BRIGHTON, †KEMPTON, Devon & Exeter
Aug 9:   †Uttoxeter, PONTEFRACT, BRIGHTON, DEVON & EXETER
Aug 10:   †HAYDOCK , Market Rasen, Plumpton, REDCAR, †NEWMARKET
Aug 11:   HAYDOCK, NEWMARKET, †LINGFIELD , REDCAR, †SOUTHWELL, †Worcester
Aug 13:   †THIRSK, †LEICESTER, WINDSOR, Worcester
Aug 14:   †CATTERICK, YARMOUTH, BATH, Devon & Exeter, †Fontwell Park
Aug 15:   BEVERLEY, SOUTHWELL, †FOLKESTONE, SALISBURY
Aug 16:   BEVERLEY, SOUTHWELL, Newton Abbot, SALISBURY
Aug 17:   †HAYDOCK, SOUTHWELL, NEWBURY, Perth
Aug 18:   †LINGFIELD, Bangor-on-Dee, Perth, RIPON, NEWBURY, †Market Rasen, †WOLVERHAMPTON
Aug 20:   HAMILTON, WINDSOR
Aug 21:   YORK, FOLKESTONE
Aug 22:   YORK, YARMOUTH, Fontwell Park
Aug 23:   YORK, YARMOUTH, †SALISBURY, NEWMARKET, Devon & Exeter, GOODWOOD

Aug 25: GOODWOOD, Hereford, Cartmel, NEWCASTLE, Market Rasen, †WINDSOR, NEWMARKET
Aug 27: CHEPSTOW, Huntingdon, Cartmel, NEWCASTLE, Southwell, Newton Abbot, Ripon, Warwick, Plumpton,WOLVERHAMPTON, SANDOWN
Aug 28: RIPON, Newton Abbot
Aug 29: REDCAR, BRIGHTON, Newton Abbot
Aug 30: LINGFIELD, Worcester
Aug 31: THIRSK, CHESTER, SANDOWN
Sep 1: RIPON, CHESTER, SANDOWN, Hereford
Sep 3: Hexham, NOTTINGHAM
Sep 4: Pontefract, BRIGHTON, Sedgefield
Sep 5: YORK, Fontwell
Sep 6: YORK, Newton Abbot, SALISBURY
Sep 7: HAYDOCK, Hereford, KEMPTON, Newton Abbot
Sep 8: HAYDOCK, SOUTHWELL, KEMPTON, THIRSK, Stratford-on-Avon
Sep 10: HAMILTON, WOLVERHAMPTON
Sep 11: CARLISLE, LEICESTER, LINGFIELD
Sep 12: DONCASTER, Devon & Exeter
Sep 13: DONCASTER, FOLKESTONE
Sep 14: DONCASTER, Huntingdon, GOODWOOD
Sep 15: DONCASTER, Bangor-on-Dee, CHEPSTOW, Worcester, GOODWOOD
Sep 17: EDINBURGH, LEICESTER, BATH, Plumpton
Sep 18: SANDOWN, YARMOUTH, Sedgefield
Sep 19: AYR (Western), YARMOUTH, Devon & Exeter, BEVERLEY, SANDOWN
Sep 20: AYR (Western), LINGFIELD, Uttoxeter, BEVERLEY, YARMOUTH,
Sep 21: AYR (Western), SOUTHWELL, NEWBURY, Worcester
Sep 22: AYR (Western), NEWBURY, Market Rasen, CATTERICK, Worcester
Sep 24: NOTTINGHAM, FOLKESTONE, HAMILTON
Sep 25: PONTEFRACT, NOTTINGHAM, KEMPTON, Sedgefield
Sep 26: BRIGHTON, Ludlow, Perth, Southwell
Sep 27: Perth, ASCOT, Taunton
Sep 28: HAYDOCK, ASCOT, REDCAR
Sep 29: ASCOT, Stratford, Carlisle, HAYDOCK, REDCAR
Oct 1: BATH, Southwell, Carlisle, WOLVERHAMPTON, Fontwell
Oct 2: NEWCASTLE, WOLVERHAMPTON, BRIGHTON, Devon & Exeter
Oct 3: SALISBURY, Cheltenham, Perth, NEWMARKET
Oct 4: Cheltenham, LINGFIELD, NEWMARKET
Oct 5: GOODWOOD, NEWMARKET, Hexham
Oct 6: NEWMARKET, Kelso, Chepstow, Uttoxeter, GOODWOOD, Worcester
Oct 8: PONTEFRACT, WARWICK
Oct 9: REDCAR, WARWICK, FOLKESTONE, Newton Abbot
Oct 10: HAYDOCK, Towcester, Plumpton, YORK
Oct 11: HAYDOCK, Wincanton, YORK
Oct 12: Carlisle, ASCOT, Market Rasen
Oct 13: Ayr, Bangor-on-Dee, ASCOT, YORK, Southwell, Warwick
Oct 15: AYR, LEICESTER, Fontwell
Oct 16: AYR, LEICESTER, CHEPSTOW, Sedgefield
Oct 17: REDCAR, Cheltenham, WOLVERHAMPTON, Wetherby
Oct 18: Hexham, NEWMARKET, Taunton, Uttoxeter
Oct 19: CATTERICK, Ludlow, NEWMARKET
Oct 20: CATTERICK, NEWMARKET, Kempton, Kelso, Southwell, Stratford
Oct 22: FOLKESTONE, Fakenham, NOTTINGHAM
Oct 23: CHESTER, CHEPSTOW, NOTTINGHAM, Plumpton
Oct 24: EDINBURGH, CHESTER, Ascot, Newcastle
Oct 25: PONTEFRACT, NEWBURY, Southwell, Wincanton
Oct 26: DONCASTER, Hereford, Devon & Exeter, Newbury
Oct 27: NEWBURY, Huntingdon, Catterick Bridge, DONCASTER
Oct 29: LEICESTER, BATH, LINGFIELD
Oct 30: REDCAR, LEICESTER, Fontwell, SALISBURY
Oct 31: EDINBURGH, YARMOUTH, Newbury
Nov 1: NEWMARKET, Kempton, Stratford
Nov 2: Sedgefield, LINGFIELD (AWT), Bangor-on-Dee, NEWMARKET, Wetherby,
Nov 3: Wetherby, NEWMARKET, Chepstow, Southwell (AWT), Sandown, Worcester
Nov 5: NEWCASTLE, Wolverhamton, Plumpton
Nov 6: HAMILTON PARK, Hereford, Devon & Exeter, Nottingham
Nov 7: Kelso, SOUTHWELL (AWT), Newbury
Nov 8: Uttoxeter, LINGFIELD (AWT), Wincanton
Nov 9: DONCASTER, Cheltenham, Hexham, Market Rasen
Nov 10: DONCASTER, Cheltenham, Windsor
Nov 12: FOLKESTONE, Wolverhampton, Carlisle
Nov 13: Sedgefield, SOUTHWELL (AWT)
Nov 14: Worcester, Kempton
Nov 15: Ayr, Towcester, Lingfield (AWT), Taunton
Nov 16: Ayr, Huntingdon, Ascot
Nov 17: Ayr, Warwick, Ascot, Catterick

Nov 19:	Bangor-on-Dee, Windsor, Leicester
Nov 20:	Wetherby, SOUTHWELL (AWT), Wolverhampton
Nov 21:	Haydock, Plumpton, Kelso
Nov 22:	Haydock, Ludlow, LINGFIELD (AWT), Wincanton
Nov 23:	Sedgefield, Leicester, Newbury
Nov 24:	Newcastle, Market Rasen, Newbury, Towcester (R)
Nov 26:	Catterick, Nottingham, Folkestone
Nov 27:	Huntingdon, Newton Abbot, Stratford
Nov 28:	Hexham, Hereford
Nov 29:	Carlisle, Warwick, Lingfield (AWT), Taunton
Nov 30:	Bangor-on-Dee, Sandown, SOUTHWELL (AWT)
Dec 1:	Wetherby, Nottingham, Chepstow, Sandown
Dec 3:	Kelso, Worcester
Dec 4:	Newcastle, Leicester, Fontwell
Dec 5:	Catterick, Huntingdon, Ludlow, Southwell (AWT)
Dec 6:	Uttoxeter, Taunton, Windsor, LINGFIELD (AWT)
Dec 7:	Doncaster, Cheltenham, Devon & Exeter
Dec 8:	Doncaster, Cheltenham, Lingfield, Towcester
Dec 10:	Edinburgh, Warwick
Dec 11:	Sedgefield, Plumpton
Dec 12:	Haydock Park, Worcester,
Dec 13:	Haydock Park, SOUTHWELL (AWT)
Dec 14:	Catterick Bridge, Fakenham, Hereford
Dec 15:	Edinburgh, Nottingham, Ascot, LINGFIELD (AWT)
Dec 18:	Folkestone, Southwell (AWT)
Dec 19:	Bangor-on-Dee, Lingfield (AWT)
Dec 20:	Kelso, Towcester
Dec 21:	Hexham, Ludlow, Uttoxeter
Dec 22:	Edinburgh, Hereford, Chepstow, Lingfield
Dec 26:	Sedgefield, Huntingdon, Kempton, Wetherby, Market Rasen, Newton Abbot, Wolverhampton, Wincanton
Dec 27:	Wetherby, Wolverhampton, Kempton, LINGFIELD (AWT), Taunton
Dec 28:	Carlisle, Stratford, Fontwell
Dec 29:	Newcastle, Newbury, Folkestone, Warwick, SOUTHWELL (AWT)
Dec:31:	Catterick, Leicester, Plumpton

© *The Jockey Club 1989*
† Evening Meeting,
(AWT) = All-weather track. Flat meetings in capitals. National Hunt in upper and lower case.

ICE HOCKEY

1989

■ **Sergei Priakin of the Soviet Wings Ice Hockey team signed a $150,000-a-year contract with Calgary Flames. He was the first player given permission from the Soviet Ice Hockey Federation to play in the NHL. The New Jersey Devils signed two Soviet players, Viacheslav Fetisov and Sergei Starikov.**

WORLD CHAMPIONSHIPS
Stockholm, Sweden, Apr 15-May 1

MEDAL ROUND RESULTS
Canada 5 Sweden 3
USSR 1 Czechoslovakia 0
Czechoslovakia 2 Sweden 1
USSR 5 Canada 3
Canada 4 Czechoslovakia 3
USSR 5 Sweden 1

FINAL POSITIONS
1 USSR	3	3	0	0	11	4	6
2 Canada	3	2	0	1	12	11	4
3 Czechoslovakia	3	1	0	2	5	6	2
4 Sweden	3	0	0	3	5	12	0

In qualifying game Romania beat New Zealand 50-1

HEINEKEN BRITISH CHAMPIONSHIP
Wembley, Apr 22-23

SEMI-FINALS
AYR BRUINS beat Durham Wasps 12-6; NOTTINGHAM PANTHERS beat Whitley Warriors 8-6

FINAL
NOTTINGHAM PANTHERS beat Ayr Bruins 6-3

NATIONAL HOCKEY LEAGUE
FINAL STANDINGS
Wales Conference
Patrick Division

	P	W	L	T	Pts	GF	GA
Washington	80	41	29	10	92	305	259
Pittsburgh	80	40	33	7	87	347	349
NY Rangers	80	37	35	8	82	310	307
Philadelphia	80	36	36	8	80	307	285
New Jersey	80	27	41	12	66	281	325
NY Islanders	80	28	47	5	61	265	325

Play-offs
Philadelphia beat Washington 4-2
Pittsburgh beat New York Rangers 4-0
Divisional Final
Philadelphia beat Pittsburgh 4-3

Adams Division

	P	W	L	T	Pts	GF	GA
Montreal	80	53	18	9	115	315	218
Boston	80	37	29	14	88	289	256
Buffalo	80	38	35	7	83	291	299
Hartford	80	37	38	5	79	299	290
Quebec	80	27	46	7	61	269	342

Play-offs
Montreal beat Hartford 4-0
Boston beat Buffalo 4-1
Divisional Final
Montreal beat Boston 4-1
Wales Conference Final
Montreal beat Philadelphia 4-2

Campbell Conference
Norris Division

	P	W	L	T	Pts	GF	GA
Detroit	80	34	34	12	80	313	316
St Louis	80	33	35	12	78	275	285
Minnesota	80	27	37	16	70	258	278
Chicago	80	27	41	12	66	297	335
Toronto	80	28	46	6	62	259	242

Play-offs
Chicago beat Detroit 4-2
St Louis beat Minnesota 4-1
Divisional Final
Chicago beat St Louis 4-1
Smythe Division

	P	W	L	T	Pts	GF	GA
Calgary	80	54	17	9	117	354	226
Los Angeles	80	42	31	7	91	376	335
Edmonton	80	38	34	8	84	325	306
Vancouver	80	33	39	8	74	251	253
Winnipeg	80	26	42	12	64	300	355

Play-offs
Calgary beat Vancouver 4-3
Los Angeles beat Edmonton 4-3
Divisional Final
Calgary beat Los Angeles 4-0
Campbell Conference Final
Calgary beat Chigago 4-1

STANLEY CUP
Game 1: Calgary Flames 3 Montreal Canadiens 2
Game 2: Montreal Canadiens 4 Calgary Flames 2
Game 3: Montreal Canadiens 4 Calgary Flames 3 (OT)
Game 4: Calgary Flames 4 Montreal Canadiens 2
Game 5: Calgary Flames 3 Montreal Canadiens 2
Game 6: Calgary Flames 4 Montreal Canadiens 2
Calgary won best-of-seven series 4-2

Conn Smythe Trophy for MVP award in play-offs:
Al Macinnis (Calgary)
NHL MVP award:
Wayne Gretzky (Los Angeles) - record ninth time

CHAMPIONS

OLYMPIC GAMES
1920	Canada
1924	Canada
1928	Canada
1932	Canada
1936	Great Britain
1948	Canada
1952	Canada
1956	USSR
1960	United States
1964	USSR
1968	USSR
1972	USSR
1976	USSR
1980	United States
1984	USSR
1988	USSR

Most wins:
7 USSR, 6 Canada

WORLD CHAMPIONSHIPS

1920	Canada
1924	Canada
1928	Canada
1930	Canada
1931	Canada
1932	Canada
1933	United States
1934	Canada
1935	Canada
1936	Great Britain
1937	Canada
1938	Canada
1939	Canada
1947	Czechoslovakia
1948	Canada
1949	Czechoslovakia
1950	Canada
1951	Canada
1952	Canada
1953	Sweden
1954	USSR
1955	Canada
1956	USSR
1957	Sweden
1958	Canada
1959	Canada
1960	United States
1961	Canada
1962	Sweden
1963	USSR
1964	USSR
1965	USSR
1966	USSR
1967	USSR
1968	USSR
1969	USSR
1970	USSR
1971	USSR
1972	Czechoslovakia
1973	USSR
1974	USSR
1975	USSR
1976	Czechoslovakia
1977	Czechoslovakia
1978	USSR
1979	USSR
1980	United States
1981	USSR
1982	USSR
1983	USSR
1984	USSR
1985	Czechoslovakia
1986	USSR
1987	Sweden
1988	USSR
1989	USSR

Most wins:
23 USSR; 19 Canada

STANLEY CUP

(First contested 1893)

Post-war winners:

1944-45	Toronto Maple Leafs
1945-46	Montreal Canadiens
1946-47	Toronto Maple Leafs
1947-48	Toronto Maple Leafs
1948-49	Toronto Maple Leafs
1949-50	Detroit Red Wings
1950-51	Toronto Maple Leafs
1951-52	Detroit Red Wings
1952-53	Montreal Canadiens
1953-54	Detroit Red Wings
1954-55	Detroit Red Wings
1955-56	Montreal Canadiens
1956-57	Montreal Canadiens
1957-58	Montreal Canadiens
1958-59	Montreal Canadiens
1959-60	Montreal Canadiens
1960-61	Chicago Blackhawks
1961-62	Toronto Maple Leafs
1962-63	Toronto Maple Leafs
1963-64	Toronto Maple Leafs
1964-65	Montreal Canadiens
1965-66	Montreal Canadiens
1966-67	Toronto Maple Leafs
1967-68	Montreal Canadiens
1968-69	Montreal Canadiens
1969-70	Boston Bruins
1970-71	Montreal Canadiens
1971-72	Boston Bruins
1972-73	Montreal Canadiens
1973-74	Philadelphia Flyers
1974-75	Philadelphia Flyers
1975-76	Montreal Canadiens
1976-77	Montreal Canadiens
1977-78	Montreal Canadiens
1978-79	Montreal Canadiens
1979-80	New York Islanders
1980-81	New York Islanders
1981-82	New York Islanders
1982-83	New York Islanders
1983-84	Edmonton Oilers
1984-85	Edmonton Oilers
1985-86	Montreal Canadiens
1986-87	Edmonton Oilers
1987-88	Edmonton Oilers
1988-89	Calgary Flames

Most wins:
23 Montreal Canadiens; **11** Toronto Maple Leafs; **7** Detroit Red Wings; **6** Ottawa Senators; **5** Montreal Victorias, Boston Bruins

HEINEKEN BRITISH CHAMPIONSHIP

1982	Dundee Rockets
1983	Dundee Rockets
1984	Dundee Rockets
1985	Fife Flyers
1986	Murrayfield Racers
1987	Durham Wasps
1988	Durham Wasps
1989	Nottingham Panthers

━━━━ 1990 ━━━━

Mar 23-Apr 1: World Championships, Pool C (Hungary); *Mar 29-Apr 9:* World Championships, Pool B (Megeve and St Gervais, (France); *Apr 16-May 2:* World Championships, Pool A (Berne and Freiborg, Switzerland); *Apr 21-22:* Heineken Championship finals (Wembley Arena)

JUDO

1989

CHAMPIONS

EUROPEAN CHAMPIONSHIPS
Helsinki, May 11-15

Men

Open
Juha Salonen (Fin) beat F Moller (GDR)

Heavyweight/Over 95kg
Rafal Kuback (Pol) beat T Muller (GDR)

Half-heavy/Under 95kg
Koba Kurtanidze (USSR) beat Jiri Sosna (Cze)

Middle/Under 86kg
Fabien Canu (Fra) beat V Boudiukin (USSR)

Half-middle/Under 78kg
Bachir Varayev (USSR) beat Frank Wieneke (FRG)

Lightweight/Under 71kg
Jorma Korhonen (Fin) beat Bertalan Hatjos (Hun)

Half-light/Under 65kg
Bruno Carabetta (Fra) beat S Kosmynin (USSR)

Extra-light/Under 60kg
Amirin Totikashvili (USSR) beat Petr Sedivak (Cze)

Women

Open
Angelique Seriese (Hol) beat M Maksymow (Pol)

Heavyweight/Over 72kg
Angelique Seriese (Hol) beat A Akerblom (Fin)

Half-heavy/Under 72kg
Ingrid Berghmans (Bel) beat E Karlsson (Swe)

Middle/Under 65kg
Emanuel Pierantozzi (Ita) beat Alexandra Schreiber (FRG)

Half-middle/Under 61kg
Catherine Fleury (Fra) beat L Sindlerova (Cze)

Lightweight/Under 56kg
Catherine Arnaud (Fra) beat M Gontowicz (Pol)

Half-light/Under 52kg
Jaana Ronkainen (Fin) beat Dominique Brun (Fra)

Extra-light/Under 48kg
Cecile Nowak (Fra) beat Karen Briggs (GB)

BRITISH OPEN CHAMPIONSHIPS
Crystal Palace, Apr 8-9
Winners
Men

Heavyweight/Over 95kg:	Elvis Gordon (GB)
Half-heavy/Under 95kg:	Nicholas Kokotaylo (GB)
Middle/Under 86kg:	Densign White (GB)
Half-middle/Under 78kg:	Marc Vallot (Bel)
Lightweight/Under 71kg:	Stephen Ravenscroft (GB)
Half-light/Under 65kg:	Franck Decroix (Fra)
Extra-light/Under 60kg:	Carl Finney (GB)

Women

Heavyweight/Over 75kg:	Rigina Sigmund (FRG)
Half-heavy/Under 72kg:	Ingrid Berghmans (Bel)
Middleweight/Under 66kg:	Rowena Sweatman (GB)
Half-middle/Under 61kg:	Diane Bell (GB)
Lightweight/Under 56kg:	Nicole Flagothier (Bel)
Half-light/Under 52kg:	Sharon Rendle (GB)
Extra-light/Under 48kg:	Karen Briggs (GB)

OLYMPIC GAMES
Open

1964	Anton Geesink (Hol)
1972	Willem Ruska (Hol)
1976	Haruki Uemura (Jap)
1980	Dietmar Lorenz (GDR)
1984	Yasuhiro Yamashita (Jap)

Heavyweight/Over 95kg

1964	Isao Inokuma (Jap)
1972	Willem Ruska (Hol)
1976	Sergey Novikov (USSR)
1980	Angelo Parisi (Fra)
1984	Hitoshi Saito (Jap)
1988	Hitoshi Saito (Jap)

Half-heavyweight/Under 95kg

1972	Shota Chochoshvili (USSR)
1976	Kazuhiro Ninomiya (Jap)
1980	Robert Van de Walle (Bel)
1984	Hyeung-Zoo Ha (SKo)
1988	Aurelio Miguel (Bra)

Middleweight/Under 86kg

1964	Isao Okano (Jap)
1972	Shinobu Sekine (Jap)
1976	Isamu Sonoda (Jap)
1980	Jürg Röthlisberger (Swi)
1984	Peter Seisenbacher (Aut)
1988	Peter Seisenbacher (Aut)

Half-middleweight/Under 78kg

1980	Shota Khabareli (USSR)
1984	Frank Weineke (FRG)
1988	Waldemar Legien (Pol)

Lightweight/Under 71kg

1964	Takehide Nakatani (Jap)
1972	Toyokazu Nomura (Jap)
1976	Vladimir Nevzorov (USSR)
1980	Ezio Gamba (Ita)
1984	Byeong-Kuen Ahn (SKo)
1988	Marc Alexandre (Fra)

Half-lightweight/Under 65kg

1972	Takao Kawaguchi (Jap)
1976	Hector Rodriguez (Cub)
1980	Nikolay Solodukhin (USSR)
1984	Yoshiyuki Matsuoka (Jap)
1988	Lee Kyung-Keun (SKo)

Extra-lightweight/Under 60kg

1980	Thierry Rey (Fra)
1984	Shinji Hosokawa (Jap)
1988	Kim Jae-Yup (SKo)

WORLD CHAMPIONSHIPS
Men

Open

1956	Shokichi Natsui (Jap)
1958	Koji Sone (Jap)
1961	Anton Geesink (Hol)
1965	Isao Inokuma (Jap)
1967	Matsuo Matsunaga (Jap)
1969	Masatoshi Shinomaki (Jap)

'71 Masatoshi Shinomaki (Jap)
'73 Kazuhiro Ninomiya (Jap)
'75 Haruki Uemura (Jap)
'79 Sumio Endo (Jap)
'81 Yasuhiro Yamashita (Jap)
'83 Hitoshi Saito (Jap)
'85 Yoshimi Masaki (Jap)
'87 N Ogawa (Jap)

Heavyweight/Over 95kg
'65 Anton Geesink (Hol)
'67 Willem Ruska (Hol)
'69 Shuji Suma(Jap)
'71 Willem Ruska (Hol)
'73 Chonufuhe Tagaki (Jap)
'75 Sumio Endo (Jap)
'79 Yasuhiro Yamashita (Jap)
'81 Yasuhiro Yamashita (Jap)
'83 Yasuhiro Yamashita (Jap)
'85 Yong-Chul Cho (SKo)
'987 Grigori Vertichev (USSR)

Half-heavyweight/Under 95kg
'967 Nobuyuki Sato (Jap)
'969 Fumio Sasahara (Jap)
'971 Fumio Sasahara (Jap)
'973 Nobuyuki Sato (Jap)
'975 Jean-Luc Rouge (Fra)
'979 Tengiz Khubuluri (USSR)
'981 Tengiz Khubuluri (USSR)
'983 Valerily Divisenko (USSR)
'985 Hitoshi Sugai (Jap)
'987 Hitoshi Sugai (Jap)

Middleweight/Under 86kg
'979 Detlef Ultsch (GDR)
'981 Bernard Tchoullouyan (Fra)
'983 Detlef Ultsch (GDR)
'985 Peter Seisenbacher (Aut)
'987 Fabien Canu (Fra)

Half-middleweght/Under 78kg
'965 Isao Okano (Jap)
'967 Eiji Maruki (Jap)
'969 Isamu Sonoda (Jap)
'971 Shozo Fujii (Jap)
'973 Shozo Fujii (Jap)
'975 Shozo Fujii (Jap)
'979 Shozo Fujii (Jap)
'981 Neil Adams (GB)
'983 Nobutoshi Hikage (Jap)
'985 Nobutoshi Hikage (Jap)
'987 Hirotaka Okada (Jap)

Lightweight/Under 71kg
'967 Hiroshi Minatoya (Jap)
'969 Hiroshi Minatoya (Jap)
'971 Hizashi Tsuzawa (Jap)
'973 Kazutoyo Nomura (Jap)
'975 Vladimir Nevzorov (USSR)
'979 Kyoto Katsuki (Jap)
'981 Chong-Hak Park (SKo)
'983 Hidetoshi Nakanishi (Jap)
'985 Byeong-Kuen Ahn (SKo)
'987 Mike Swain (US)

Half-lightweight/Under 65kg
'965 Hiroshi Minatoya (Jap)
'967 Takosumi Shigeoka (Jap)
'969 Yoshio Sonoda (Jap)
'971 Takao Kawaguchi (Jap)
'973 Yoshiharu Minami (Jap)
'975 Yoshiharu Minami (Jap)
'979 Nikolai Soludukhin (USSR)
'981 Katsuhiko Kashiwazaki (Jap)

1983 Nikolai Soludukhin (USSR)
1985 Yuriy Sokolov (USSR)
1987 Yosuke Yamamoto (Jap)

Extra-lightweight/Under 60kg
1979 Thierry Ray (Fra)
1981 Yasuhiko Moriwaki (Jap)
1983 Khazret Tletseri (USSR)
1985 Shinji Hosokawa (Jap)
1987 Kim Jae-Yup (SKo)

Women
Open
1980 Ingrid Berghmans (Bel)
1982 Ingrid Berghmans (Bel)
1984 Ingrid Berghmans (Bel)
1986 Ingrid Berghmans (Bel)
1987 Fenglian Gao (Chn)

Heavyweight/Over 72kg
1980 Margarita de Cal (Ita)
1982 Natalina Lupino (Fra)
1984 Maria-Teresa Motta (Ita)
1986 Fenglian Gao (Chn)
1987 Fenglian Gao (Chn)

Half-heavyweight/Under 72kg
1980 Jocelyn Triadou (Fra)
1982 Barbara Classen (FRG)
1984 Ingrid Berghmans (Bel)
1986 Irene de Kok (Hol)
1987 Irene de Kok (Hol)

Middleweight/Under 66kg
1980 Edith Simon (Aut)
1982 Brigitte Deydier (Fra)
1984 Brigitte Deydier (Fra)
1986 Brigitte Deydier (Fra)
1987 Aleaxandra Schreiber (FRG)

Half-middleweight/Under 61kg
1980 Anita Staps (Hol)
1982 Martine Rothier (Fra)
1984 Natasha Hernandez (Ven)
1986 Diane Bell (GB)
1987 Diane Bell (GB)

Lightweight/Under 56kg
1980 Gerda Winkelbauer (Aut)
1982 Beatrice Rodriguez (Fra)
1984 Ann-Maria Burns (US)
1986 Ann Hughes (GB)
1987 Catherine Arnaud (Fra)

Half-lightweight/Under 52kg
1980 Edith Hrovat (Aut)
1982 Loretta Doyle (GB)
1984 Kaori Yamaguchi (Jap)
1986 Dominique Brun (Fra)
1987 Sharon Rendle (GB)

Extra-lightweight/Under 48kg
1980 Jane Bridge (GB)
1982 Karen Briggs (GB)
1984 Karen Briggs (GB)
1986 Karen Briggs (GB)
1987 Z Li (Chn)

1990

Apr 7-8: British Open Championships (Crystal Palace); *May 10-13:* Senior European Championship (Wurzburg, West Germany); *Oct 27-28:* European Team Championships (Yugoslavia); *Nov 15-18:* Junior European Championships (Istanbul)

LACROSSE

―――――――――――――――― **1989** ――――――――――――――――

WOMEN'S LACROSSE

WORLD CUP
WACA Ground, Perth, Australia, Aug 23-Sep 10

Round Robin Matches

	Aus	Can	Eng	Sco	USA	Wal
Australia	–	6-4	3-8	4-1	2-1	9-3
Canada	4-6	–	3-13	5-4	2-17	11-4
England	8-3	13-3	–	7-1	2-3	8-4
Scotland	1-4	4-5	1-7	–	5-10	5-3
USA	1-2	17-2	3-2	10-5	–	18-5
Wales	3-9	4-11	4-8	3-5	5-18	–

Table

		P	W	D	L	F	A	Pts
1	United States	5	4	0	1	49	16	8
2	England	5	4	0	1	38	14	8
3	Australia	5	4	0	1	24	17	8
4	Canada	5	2	0	3	25	44	4
5	Scotland	5	1	0	4	16	29	2
6	Wales	5	0	0	5	19	51	0

Play-off Matches
Final
United States beat England 6-5
3rd/4th Places
Australia beat Canada 10-1
5th/6th Places
Scotland beat Wales 5-3

HOME INTERNATIONAL SERIES
Champions: England

HATTERSLEY SALVER
1 East 2 Combined Universities 3 South

SAC CLUBS & COLLEGES TROPHY
Centaur beat Berkshire Wanderers 4-1

NATIONAL SCHOOLS CHAMPIONSHIP
Queen Anne School, Caversham beat Wycombe Abbey School 2-0

MEN'S LACROSSE

AVON INSURANCE NORTHERN SENIOR FLAGS
Didsbury
Stockport beat Cheadle 9-8 (aet)

SOUTHERN SENIOR FLAGS
Hampstead beat London University 17-16

BRINE NORTHERN LEAGUE
Champions: Mellor

ENGLISH CLUB CHAMPIONSHIP (IROQUOIS CUP)
Stockport beat Hampstead 20-7

―――――――――――― **CHAMPIONS** ――――――――――――

MEN'S WORLD CHAMPIONSHIP
(First held 1967)
1967	United States
1974	United States
1978	Canada
1982	United States
1986	United States

WOMEN'S WORLD CUP
1982	United States
1986	Australia
1989	United States

IROQUOIS CUP
(English Men's Club Championship, first contested 1890)
Winners since 1980:
1980	South Manchester
1981	Cheadle
1982	Sheffield University
1983	Sheffield University
1984	Cheadle
1985	Cheadle
1986	Heaton Mersey
1987	Stockport
1988	Mellor
1989	Stockport

Most wins:
17 Stockport; 11 South Manchester; 10 Old Hulmeians, Mellor; 7 Old Waconians; 6 Heaton Mersey; 5 Cheadle

―――――――――――――――― **1990** ――――――――――――――――

Mar 17: AEWLA Schools' championship (London); Apr 7-8: England Trials, women; Apr 28-29: AEWLA Clubs and Colleges Tournament, women (Merton); May 4: England v England Reserves, women (Crystal Palace); May 5: Wales v Scotland, women (TBA); May 12: Scotland v England, women (TBA); May 19: England v Wales, women (TBA).

MODERN PENTATHLON

1989

MEN'S WORLD CHAMPIONSHIP
Budapest, Sep 3
Individual
1 Laszlo Fabian (Hun) 5654 pts
2 Attila Mizser (Hun) 5616 pts
3 P Blazek (Cze) 5615 pts
Team
1 Hungary 16,651 pts
2 USSR 16,388 pts
3 Czechoslovakia 15,986 pts

WOMEN'S WORLD CHAMPIONSHIP
Wiener Nieustat, Austria, Aug 6
Individual
1 Lori Norwood (US) 5315 pts
2 Iren Kovacs (Hun) 5222 pts
3 Caroline Delemer (Fra) 5198 pts
Team
1 Poland 15,260 pts
2 United States 15,128 pts
3 Italy 14,845 pts

MEN'S BRITISH CHAMPIONSHIP
Milton Keynes, Jul 16
Individual
1 Graham Brookhouse 5813 pts
2 Dominic Mahoney 5707 pts
3 Richard Phelps 5675 pts
Team
1 Spartan MPC 16,579 pts
2 Army 'A' 16,451 pts

WOMEN'S BRITISH CHAMPIONSHIP
Wantage, May 28
Individual
1 Teresa Purton 5321 pts
2 Alison Holington 5134 pts
3 Mandy Flaherty 5119 pts
Team
1 Pegasus 12,070 pts
2 Wessex Wyvern 10,500 pts
3 West Norfolk 9700 pts

CHAMPIONS

WORLD CHAMPIONSHIPS
(Not held in Olympic years)
Men - Individual
1981 Janusz Pyciak-Peciak (Pol)
1982 Daniele Masala (Ita)
1983 Anatoliy Starostin (USSR)
1985 Attila Mizser (Hun)
1986 Carlo Massullo (Ita)
1987 Joel Bouzou (Fra)
1989 Laszlo Fabian (Hun)
Men - Team
1981 Poland
1982 USSR
1983 USSR
1985 USSR
1986 Italy
1987 Hungary
1989 Hungary

Women - Individual
1981 Anne Ahlgren (Swe)
1982 Wendy Norman (GB)
1983 Lynn Chernobrywy (Can)
1984 Svetlana Jakovleva (USSR)
1985 Barbara Kotowska (Pol)
1986 Irina Kisselyeva (USSR)
1987 Irina Kisselyeva (USSR)
1988 Dorota Idzi (Pol)
1989 Lori Norwood (US)
Women - Team
1981 Great Britain
1982 Great Britain
1983 Great Britain
1984 USSR
1985 Poland
1986 France
1987 USSR
1988 Poland
1989 Poland

OLYMPIC GAMES
Men Only
Individual
1912 Gosta Lilliehook (Swe)
1920 Gustaf Dryssen (Swe)
1924 Bo Lindman (Swe)
1928 Sven Thofelt (Swe)
1932 Johan Oxenstierna (Swe)
1936 Gotthardt Handrick (Ger)
1948 Willie Grut (Swe)
1952 Lars Hall (Swe)
1956 Lars Hall (Swe)
1960 Ferenc Nemeth (Hun)
1964 Ferenc Torok (Hun)
1968 Bjorn Ferm (Swe)
1972 Andras Balczo (Hun)
1976 Janusz Pyciak-Peciak (Pol)
1980 Anatoly Starostin (USSR)
1984 Daniele Masala (Ita)
1988 Janos Martinek (Hun)
Team
1952 Hungary
1956 USSR
1960 Hungary
1964 USSR
1968 Hungary
1972 USSR
1976 Great Britain
1980 USSR
1984 Italy
1988 Hungary

1990

Apr 8-11	Senior International (Aldershot);
May 12-13	National Triathlon Championship (Milton Keynes);
May 25-27	British Women's Championship (Wantage);
Jun 8-10	British Men's Championship
Jul 25-29	Men's World Championship (Finland)
Aug 23-26	Women's World Championship (Sweden).

MOTOR CYCLING

E ddie Lawson became world 500cc motor cycling champion in 1989 for the fourth time in six years. He was the first man ever to retain the title on a different machine, having switched from Yamaha to Honda. The season produced a long duel between the teams with Lawson battling for the title with his old Californian buddy Wayne Rainey.

Rainey led until August but then, at the Swedish Grand Prix at Anderstorp, crashed – inches from Lawson's back wheel. Lawson only won four races but never finished lower than fifth. At 31, he dismissed suggestions of retirement and said he would be trying for a fifth title in 1990. In contrast, the Texan Kevin Schwantz won six grands prix on his Suzuki – including the first in Japan, the last in Brazil and, with a spectacular ride, the British Grand Prix at Donington. Schwantz's intermittent brilliance, however, was marred by accidents and breakdowns, and he was beaten into fourth place overall. Two Australians, Wayne Gardner, the 1987 champion, and Kevin Magee, both broke legs at the US Grand Prix. Magee broke his doing a lap of honour, after finishing fourth.

Steve Webster and Tony Hewitt from Yorkshire became world sidecar champions for the third successive year; Spanish riders won the three remaining categories. Taru Rinne, 20, of Finland began competing in the 125cc class to become the only woman in grand prix motor cycling. Five competitors were killed at the Isle of Man TT races – Phil Hogg, John Mulcahy, Marco Frattorelli, Phil Miller and Steve Henshaw – bringing the death toll since 1911 to 151.

———— 1989 ————

WORLD CHAMPIONSHIP GRANDS PRIX
500cc
Japanese GP
Suzuka, Mar 26
1 Kevin Schwantz (US) Suzuki 98.41mph/158.34kph
2 Wayne Rainey (US) Yamaha
3 Eddie Lawson (US) Honda

Australian GP
Philip Island, Apr 9
1 Wayne Gardner (Aus) Honda 103.06mph/165.82kph
2 Wayne Rainey (US) Yamaha
3 Christian Sarron (Fra) Yamaha

United States GP
Laguna Seca, Calif, Apr 16
1 Wayne Rainey (US) Yamaha 89.43mph/143.89kph
2 Kevin Schwantz (US) Suzuki
3 Eddie Lawson (US) Honda

Spanish GP
Jerez, Apr 30
1 Eddie Lawson (US) Honda 85.43mph/137.46kph
2 Wayne Rainey (US) Yamaha
3 Niall Mackenzie (GB) Yamaha

Italian GP
Misano, May 14
1 Pier Chili (Ita) Honda 72.36mph/116.27kph
2 Simon Buckmaster (GB) Honda
3 Michael Rudroff (FRG) Honda

West German GP
Hockenheim, May 28
1 Wayne Rainey (US) Yamaha 122.46mph/197.04kph
2 Eddie Lawson (US) Honda
3 Michael Doohan (Aus) Honda

Austrian GP
Salzburg, Jun 4
1 Kevin Schwantz (US) Suzuki 118.62mph/190.86kph
2 Eddie Lawson (US) Honda

3 Wayne Rainey (US) Yamaha

Yugoslav GP
Rijeka, Jun 11
1 Kevin Schwantz (US) Suzuki 110.06mph/177.09kph
2 Wayne Rainey (US) Yamaha
3 Eddie Lawson (US) Honda

Dutch GP
Assen, Jun 24
1 Wayne Rainey (US) Yamaha 104.60mph/168.30kph
2 Eddie Lawson (US) Honda
3 Christian Sarron (Fra) Yamaha

Belgian GP
Spa Francorchamps, Jul 2
1 Eddie Lawson (US) Honda 104.69mph/168.45kph
2 Kevin Schwantz (US) Suzuki
3 Wayne Rainey (US) Yamaha

French GP
Le Mans, Jul 16
1 Eddie Lawson (US) Honda 95.20mph/153.18kph
2 Kevin Schwantz (US) Suzuki
3 Wayne Rainey (US) Yamaha

British GP
Donington Park, Aug 6
1 Kevin Schwantz (US) Suzuki 94.21mph/151.58kph
2 Eddie Lawson (US) Honda
3 Wayne Rainey (US) Yamaha

Swedish GP
Anderstorp, Aug 13
1 Eddie Lawson (US) Honda 96.83mph/155.80kph
2 Christian Sarron (Fra) Yamaha
3 Wayne Gardner (Aus) Honda

Czechoslovak GP
Brno, Aug 20
1 Kevin Schwantz (US) Suzuki 95.62mph/153.85kph
2 Eddie Lawson (US) Honda
3 Wayne Rainey (US) Yamaha

Brazilian GP
Golania, Sep 17
1 Kevin Schwantz (US) Suzuki 97.91mph/157.54kph
2 Eddie Lawson (US) Honda
3 Wayne Rainey (US) Yamaha

FINAL CHAMPIONSHIP POSITIONS
1 Eddie Lawson (US) Honda 228pts
2 Wayne Rainey (US) Yamaha 210.5pts
3 Christian Sarron (Fra) Yamaha 165.5pts
4 Kevin Schwantz (US) Suzuki 162.5pts
5 Kevin Magee (Aus) Honda 138.5pts
6 Pier Chili (Ita) Honda 122.7pts

THE OTHER WORLD CHAMPIONS
250cc
1 Sito Pons (Spa) Honda 262pts
2 Reinhold Roth (FRG) Honda 190pts
3 Jacques Cornu (Swi) Honda 187pts

125cc
1 Alex Criville (Spa) Cobas 166pts
2 Hans Spaan (Hol) Honda 152pts
3 Ezio Gianola (Ita) Honda 138pts

80cc
1 Champi Herreros (Spa) Derbi 90pts
2 Stefan Dorflinger (Swi) Krauser 80pts
3 Peter Oetti (FRG) Krause 75pts

Sidecars
1 Steve Webster/Tony Hewitt (GB) LCR Krauser 145pts
2 Egbert Streuer/Geral de Haas (Hol) LCR Krauser 134pts
3 Rolf Biland/Kurt Waltisperg (Swi) LCR Yamaha 127pts

ISLE OF MAN TT RACES
Supersport 600
1 Steve Hislop (Honda) 112.58mph
2 Dave Leach (Yamaha)
3 Jim Whitham (Honda)

Supersport 400
1 Eddie Laycock (Suzuki) 105.27mph
2 Graeme McGregor (Suzuki)
3 Barry Woodland (Yamaha)

TT Formula One
1 Steve Hislop (Honda) 119.36mph
2 Brian Morrison (Honda)
3 Nick Jefferies (Yamaha)
(Hislop became first man to lap TT course at 120 mph)

Sidecar TT (I)
1 Dave Molyneux/Colin Hardman (Yamaha) 104.56mph
2 Kenny Howles/Steve Pointer (Yamaha)
3 Neil Smith/Dave Wood (Yamaha)

125cc TT
1 Robert Dunlop (Honda) 102.58mph
2 Ian Lougher (Honda)
3 Carl Fogarty (Honda)

750cc Production TT
1 Carl Fogarty (Honda) 114.68mph
2 Dave Leach (Yamaha)
3 Steve Hislop (Honda)

Sidecar TT (II)
1 Mick Boddice/Chas Birks (Yamaha) 107.17mph
2 Dennis Brown/Bill Nelson (Yamaha)
3 Dave Molyneux/Colin Hardman (Yamaha)

1300cc Production TT
1 Dave Leach (Yamaha) 115.61mph
2 Nick Jefferies (Yamaha)
3 Alan Batson (Yamaha)

Junior TT
1 Johnny Rea (Yamaha) 112.12mph
2 Eddie Laycock (Yamaha)
3 Steve Hazlett (EMC)

Senior TT
1 Steve Hislop (Honda) 118.23mph
2 Nick Jefferies (Yamaha)
3 Graeme McGregor (Honda)

MEN WHO HAVE WON THREE ISLE OF MAN TT RACES IN ONE WEEK

Mike Hailwood 1961
Lightweight 125cc; Lightweight 250cc; Senior TT
Mike Hailwood 1967
Lightweight 250cc; Junior TT; Senior TT
Joey Dunlop 1985
Formula One; Junior TT; Senior TT
Joey Dunlop 1988
Formula One; Junior TT; Senior TT
Steve Hislop 1989
Supersport 600; Formula One; Senior TT

MOTO CROSS
World 500cc Championship
1 Dave Thorpe (GB) 358pts
2 Jeff Leisk (Aus) 293pts
3 Eric Geboers (Bel) 279pts
World Team Championship
1 United States 4pts
2 Italy 11pts
3 Great Britain 15pts

——— CHAMPIONS ———

WORLD CHAMPIONS

1949		
125cc	Nello Pagani (Ita)	Mondial
250cc	Bruno Ruffo (Ita)	Guzzi
350cc	Freddie Frith (GB)	Velocette
500cc	Leslie Graham (GB)	AJS
Sidecar	Eric Oliver (GB)	Norton
1950		
125cc	Bruno Ruffo (Ita)	Mondial
250cc	Dario Ambrosini (Ita)	Benelli
350cc	Bob Foster (GB)	Velocette
500cc	Umberto Masetti (Ita)	Gilera
Sidecar	Eric Oliver (GB)	Norton
1951		
125cc	Carlo Ubbiali (Ita)	Mondial
250cc	Bruno Ruffo (Ita)	Guzzi
350cc	Geoff Duke (GB)	Norton
500cc	Geoff Duke (GB)	Norton
Sidecar	Eric Oliver (GB)	Norton
1952		
125cc	Cecil Sandford (GB)	MV
250cc	Enrico Lorensetti (Ita)	Guzzi
350cc	Geoff Duke (UK)	Norton
500cc	Umberto Masetti (Ita)	Gilera
Sidecar	Cyril Smith (GB)	Norton
1953		
125cc	Werner Haas (FRG)	NSU
250cc	Werner Haas (FRG)	NSU
350cc	Fergus Anderson (GB)	Guzzi
500cc	Geoff Duke (GB)	Gilera
Sidecar	Eric Oliver (GB)	Norton

1954		
125cc	Rupert Hollaus (Aut)	NSU
250cc	Werner Haas (FRG)	NSU
350cc	Fergus Anderson (GB)	Guzzi
500cc	Geoff Duke (GB)	Gilera
Sidecar	Wilhelm Noll (FRG)	BMW

1955		
125cc	Carlo Ubbiali (Ita)	MV
250cc	Herman Muller (FRG)	NSU
350cc	Bill Lomas (GB)	Guzzi
500cc	Geoff Duke (GB)	Gilera
Sidecar	Wilhelm Faust (FRG)	BMW

1956		
125cc	Carlo Ubbiali (Ita)	MV
250cc	Carlo Ubbiali (Ita)	MV
350cc	Bill Lomas (GB)	Guzzi
500cc	John Surtees (GB)	MV
Sidecar	Wilhelm Noll (FRG)	BMW

1957		
125cc	Tarquinio Provini (Ita)	Mondial
250cc	Cecil Sandford (GB)	Mondial
350cc	Keith Campbell (Aus)	Guzzi
500cc	Libero Liberati (Ita)	Gilera
Sidecar	Fritz Hillebrand (FRG)	BMW

1958		
125cc	Carlo Ubbiali (Ita)	MV
250cc	Tarquinio Provini (Ita)	MV
350cc	John Surtees (GB)	MV
500cc	John Surtees (GB)	MV
Sidecar	Walter Schneider (FRG)	BMW

1959		
125cc	Carlo Ubbiali (Ita)	MV
250cc	Carlo Ubbiali (Ita)	MV
350cc	John Surtees (GB)	MV
500cc	John Surtees (GB)	MV
Sidecar	Walter Schneider (FRG)	BMW

1960		
125cc	Carlo Ubbiali (Ita)	MV
250cc	Carlo Ubbiali (Ita)	MV
350cc	John Surtees (GB)	MV
500cc	John Surtees (GB)	MV
Sidecar	Helmut Fath (FRG)	BMW

1961		
125cc	Tom Phillis (Aus)	Honda
250cc	Mike Hailwood (GB)	Honda
350cc	Gary Hocking (Rho)	MV
500cc	Gary Hocking (Rho)	MV
Sidecar	Max Deubel (FRG)	BMW

1962		
50cc	Ernst Degner (FRG)	Suzuki
125cc	Luigi Taveri (Swi)	Honda
250cc	Jim Redman (Rho)	Honda
350cc	Jim Redman (Rho)	Honda
500cc	Mike Hailwood (GB)	MV
Sidecar	Max Deubel (FRG)	BMW

1963		
50cc	Hugh Anderson (NZ)	Suzuki
125cc	Hugh Anderson (NZ)	Suzuki
250cc	Jim Redman (Rho)	Honda
350cc	Jim Redman (Rho)	Honda
500cc	Mike Hailwood (GB)	MV
Sidecar	Max Deubel (FRG)	BMW

1964		
50cc	Hugh Anderson (NZ)	Suzuki
125cc	Luigi Taveri (Swi)	Honda
250cc	Phil Read (GB)	Yamaha
350cc	Jim Redman (Rho)	Honda
500cc	Mike Hailwood (GB)	MV
Sidecar	Max Deubel (FRG)	BMW

1965		
50cc	Ralph Bryans (Ire)	Honda
125cc	Hugh Anderson (NZ)	Suzuki
250cc	Phil Read (GB)	Yamaha
350cc	Jim Redman (Rho)	Honda
500cc	Mike Hailwood (GB)	MV
Sidecar	Fritz Scheidegger (Swi)	BMW

1966		
50cc	Hans-Georg Anscheidt (FRG)	Suzuki
125cc	Luigi Taveri (Swi)	Honda
250cc	Mike Hailwood (GB)	Honda
350cc	Mike Hailwood (GB)	Honda
500cc	Giacomo Agostini (Ita)	MV
Sidecar	Fritz Scheidegger (Swi)	BMW

1967		
50cc	Hans-Georg Anscheidt (FRG)	Suzuki
125cc	Bill Ivy (GB)	Yamaha
250cc	Mike Hailwood (GB)	Honda
350cc	Mike Hailwood (GB)	Honda
500cc	Giacomo Agostini (Ita)	MV
Sidecar	Klaus Enders (FRG)	BMW

1968		
50cc	Hans-Georg Anscheidt (FRG)	Suzuki
125cc	Phil Read (GB)	Yamaha
250cc	Phil Read (GB)	Yamaha
350cc	Giacomo Agostini (Ita)	MV
500cc	Giacomo Agostini (Ita)	MV
Sidecar	Helmut Fath (FRG)	URS

1969		
50cc	Angel Nieto (Spa)	Derbi
125cc	Dave Simmonds (GB)	Kawasaki
250cc	Kel Carruthers (Aus)	Benelli
350cc	Giacomo Agostini (Ita)	MV
500cc	Giacomo Agostini (Ita)	MV
Sidecar	Klaus Enders (FRG)	BMW

1970		
50cc	Angel Nieto (Spa)	Derbi
125cc	Dieter Braun (FRG)	Suzuki
250cc	Rod Gould (GB)	Yamaha
350cc	Giacomo Agostini (Ita)	MV
500cc	Giacomo Agostini (Ita)	MV
Sidecar	Klaus Enders (FRG)	BMW

1971		
50cc	Jan de Vries (Hol)	Kreidler
125cc	Angel Nieto (Spa)	Derbi
250cc	Phil Read (GB)	Yamaha
350cc	Giacomo Agostini (Ita)	MV
500cc	Giacomo Agostini (Ita)	MV
Sidecar	Horst Owesle (FRG)	Munch

1972		
50cc	Angel Nieto (Spa)	Derbi
125cc	Angel Nieto (Spa)	Derbi
250cc	Jarno Saarinen (Fin)	Yamaha
350cc	Giacomo Agostini (Ita)	MV
500cc	Giacomo Agostini (Ita)	MV
Sidecar	Klaus Enders (FRG)	BMW

1973		
50cc	Jan de Vries (Hol)	Kreidler
125cc	Kent Andersson (Swe)	Yamaha
250cc	Dieter Braun (FRG)	Yamaha
350cc	Giacomo Agostini (Ita)	MV
500cc	Phil Read (GB)	MV
Sidecar	Klaus Enders (FRG)	BMW

1974		
50cc	Henk van Kessel (Hol)	Kreidler
125cc	Kent Andersson (Swe)	Yamaha
250cc	Walter Villa (Ita)	H-Davidson
350cc	Giacomo Agostini (Ita)	Yamaha
500cc	Phil Read (GB)	MV
Sidecar	Klaus Enders (FRG)	Busch BMW

1975		
50cc	Angel Nieto (Spa)	Kreidler
125cc	Paolo Pileri (Ita)	Morbidelli
250cc	Walter Villa (Ita)	H-Davidson
350cc	Johnny Cecotto (Ven)	Yamaha
500cc	Giacomo Agostini (Ita)	Yamaha
Sidecar	Rolf Steinhausen (FRG)	Konig
1976		
50cc	Angel Nieto (Spa)	Bultaco
125cc	Pier-Paolo Bianchi (Ita)	Morbidelli
250cc	Walter Villa (Ita)	H-Davidson
350cc	Walter Villa (Ita)	H-Davidson
500cc	Barry Sheene (GB)	Suzuki
Sidecar	Rolf Steinhausen (FRG)	Busch Konig
1977		
50cc	Angel Nieto (Spa)	Bultaco
125cc	Pier-Paolo Bianchi (Ita)	Morbidelli
250cc	Mario Lega (Ita)	Morbidelli
350cc	Takazumi Katayama (Jap)	Yamaha
500cc	Barry Sheene (GB)	Suzuki
750cc	Steve Baker (US)	Yamaha
F1	Phil Read (GB)	Honda
Sidecar	George O'Dell (GB)	Yamaha
1978		
50cc	Ricardo Tormo (Spa)	Bultaco
125cc	Eugenio Lazzarini (Ita)	MBA
250cc	Kork Ballington (SA)	Kawasaki
350cc	Kork Ballington (SA)	Kawasaki
500cc	Kenny Roberts (US)	Yamaha
750cc	Johnny Cecotto (Ven)	Yamaha
F1	Mike Hailwood (GB)	Ducati
Sidecar	Rolf Biland (Swi)	Yamaha
1979		
50cc	Eugenio Lazzarini (Ita)	Kreidler
125cc	Angel Nieto (Spa)	Morbidelli
250cc	Kork Ballington (SA)	Kawasaki
350cc	Kork Ballington (SA)	Kawasaki
500cc	Kenny Roberts (US)	Yamaha
750cc	Patrick Pons (Fra)	Yamaha
F1	Ron Haslam (GB)	Honda
Sidecar	Rolf Biland (Swi)	Yamaha
1980		
50cc	Eugenio Lazzarini (Ita)	Kreidler
125cc	Pier-Paolo Bianchi (Ita)	MBA
250cc	Anton Mang (FRG)	Kawasaki
350cc	John Ekerold (SA)	Yamaha
500cc	Kenny Roberts (US)	Yamaha
F1	Graeme Crosby (NZ)	Suzuki
Sidecar	Jock Taylor (GB)	Yamaha
1981		
50cc	Ricardo Tormo (Spa)	Bultaco
125cc	Angel Nieto (Spa)	Minarelli
250cc	Anton Mang (FRG)	Kawasaki
350cc	Anton Mang (FRG)	Kawasaki
500cc	Marco Lucchinelli (Ita)	Suzuki
F1	Graeme Crosby (NZ)	Suzuki
Sidecar	Rolf Biland (Swi)	Yamaha
1982		
50cc	Stefan Dorflinger (Swi)	MBA
125cc	Angel Nieto (Spa)	Garelli
250cc	Jean-Louis Tournadre (Fra)	Yamaha
350cc	Anton Mang (FRG)	Kawasaki
500cc	Franco Uncini (Ita)	Suzuki
F1	Joey Dunlop (Ire)	Honda
Sidecar	Werner Schwarzel (FRG)	Yamaha
1983		
50cc	Stefan Dorflinger (Swi)	Kreidler
125cc	Angel Nieto (Spa)	Garelli

250cc	Carlos Lavado (Ven)	Yamaha
500cc	Freddie Spencer (US)	Honda
F1	Joey Dunlop (Ire)	Honda
Sidecar	Rolf Biland (Swi)	Yamaha
1984		
80cc	Stefan Dorflinger (Swi)	Zundapp
125cc	Angel Nieto (Spa)	Garelli
250cc	Christian Sarron (Fra)	Yamaha
500cc	Eddie Lawson (US)	Yamaha
F1	Joey Dunlop (Ire)	Honda
Sidecar	Egbert Streuer (Hol)	Yamaha
1985		
80cc	Stefan Dorflinger (Swi)	Krauser
125cc	Fausto Gresini (Ita)	Garelli
250cc	Freddie Spencer (US)	Honda
500cc	Freddie Spencer (US)	Honda
F1	Joey Dunlop (Ire)	Honda
Sidecar	Egbert Streuer (Hol)	Yamaha
1986		
80cc	Jorge Martinez (Spa)	Derbi
125cc	Luca Cadalora (Ita)	Garelli
250cc	Carlos Lavado (Ven)	Yamaha
500cc	Eddie Lawson (US)	Yamaha
F1	Joey Dunlop (Ire)	Honda
Sidecar	Egbert Streuer (Hol)	Yamaha
1987		
80cc	Jorge Martinez (Spa)	Derbi
125cc	Fausto Gresini (Ita)	Garelli
250cc	Anton Mang (FRG)	Honda
500cc	Wayne Gardner (Aus)	Honda
F1	Virginio Ferrari (Ita)	Yamaha
Sidecar	Steve Webster (GB)	LCR Krauser
1988		
80cc	Jorge Martinez (Spa)	Derbi
125cc	Jorge Martinez (Spa)	Derbi
250cc	Sito Pons (Spa)	Honda
500cc	Eddie Lawson (US)	Yamaha
F1	Carl Fogarty (GB)	Honda
Sidecar	Steve Webster (GB)	LCR Krauser
1989		
80cc	Champi Herreros (Spa)	Derbi
125cc	Alex Criville (Spa)	Cobas
250cc	Sito Pons (Spa)	Honda
500cc	Eddie Lawson (US)	Honda
Sidecar	Steve Webster (GB)	LCR Krauser

— 1990 —

FIXTURES

(subject to confirmation)

Mar 25: Japanese Grand Prix (Suzuka); *Apr 1:* Australian Grand Prix (Philip Island); *Apr 8:* US Grand Prix (Laguna Seca, California); *Apr 29:* Spanish Grand Prix (Jarama); *May 20:* Italian Grand Prix (Misano); *May 27:* West German Grand Prix (Nurburgring); *May 28-Jun 8:* TT races (Isle of Man); *Jun 10:* Austrian Grand Prix (Salzburg); *Jun 17:* Yugoslav Grand Prix (Rijeka); *Jun 30:* Dutch Grand Prix (Assen); *Jul 8:* Belgian Grand Prix (Spa Francorchamps); *Jul 15:* French Grand Prix (Magny Cours); *Jul 29:* Brazilian Grand Prix (Rio de Janeiro); *Aug 5:* BRITISH GRAND PRIX (Donington Park); *Aug 12:* Swedish Grand Prix (Anderstorp); *Aug 26:* Czechoslovak Grand Prix (Brno); *Sep 2:* Hungarian Grand Prix (Budapest); *Sep 30:* TT Formula 1 World Championship final round (Donington Park).

MOTOR RACING & RALLYING

A lain Prost, driving a McLaren, became the 1989 world champion but only after a battle for the championship against his team-mate Ayrton Senna, which reached unprecedented levels of bitterness off the track as well as on it, while everyone outside the McLaren team was merely a spectator.

After 27 Grand Prix victories with McLaren, Prost quit in July and two months later signed for Ferrari. At Monza the McLaren mechanics reportedly put a plate of spaghetti in Prost's car, which was a gesture of anger not a joke. That day, Prost said that no one at McLaren cared about him, that his engine was less powerful than Senna's and that if he complained, he was just told to stop moaning. Jean-Marie Balestre, president of the ruling body FISA, supported Prost and said he had clearly been given an inferior car.

The bizarre part is that through all this Prost was actually leading the Championship; he was driving with great consistency while his team-mate/enemy had regular problems completing races. Senna, having won three consecutive grand-prix – San Marino, Monaco and Mexico – early on, once again appeared in total command: Bernie Ecclestone, the head of the Formula One Constuctors' Association, called for a form of handicapping in which successful drivers would be forced to make compulsory pit stops. But thereafter, though Senna dominated the practice sessions, he had a series of mishaps in the races themselves.

He won again in Germany and Belgium; but Prost won in the US, France, Britain and Italy and collected a string of second places. In Montreal, Senna was ahead and then broke down with only three laps to go. In Phoenix, he passed Jim Clark's record of 33 pole positions but had electrical problems in the race itself and Prost won again. At Le Castellet, where Prost won two days after announcing his departure from McLaren, Senna had transmission trouble after only 100 yards. At Monza, where Prost's bitterness spilled over, Senna was leading by 20 seconds with nine laps to go when an engine blow-out let Prost in. Prost clinched the title after the Japanese Grand Prix; he and Senna collided, Senna went on to win but was disqualified.

Nigel Mansell's first season with Ferrari was a strange mixture. During tests at Paul Ricard in January, his car burst into flames - "At the moment we have a mountain to climb," he said sadly. Ten weeks later, the car's seven-speed gearbox worked stunningly well. Mansell seized the lead from Riccardo Patrese round a 140 mph corner and drove brilliantly to victory in a race in which Britons took four of the first seven places.

But when the circuit moved on to Imola, with Italian - and British - expectations sky-high, Mansell developed gearbox trouble and his team-mate Gerhard Berger had what in the old days would undoubtedly have been a fatal crash. Mansell's further adventures included regular transmission trouble, a disqualification in Montreal for rejoining the race illegally, a thrilling win over Senna in Hungary and then a one race ban and 50,000 dollar fine in Portugal after an extraordinary set of events: an infringement of rules at a pit stop, a refusal to respond to a black flag (which he says he never saw) and then a collision with Senna: "I am at a loss for words," said Ron Dennis of McLaren.

Mansell signed for 1990 with Ferrari while Berger and Prost swapped teams but John Bernard, the former McLaren designer, resigned as Ferrari's technical director after three turbulent years. Enrique Scalabrone of Williams was signed to replace him. Prost, Senna and Mansell were all expected to earn 10 million dollars each for just signing their 1990 contracts, 10 times the amount Jody Scheckter made as world champion in 1979. The former champion Emerson Fittipaldi, 42, won a million dollars himself by winning the Indy 500. Jochen Mass, Stanley Dickens and Manuel Reuter won Le Mans to give Mercedes its first win since 1952.

Riccardo Patrese made up for other disappointments by winning the Formula One drivers' annual ski week. Johnny Herbert, the British Benetton driver, finished fifth in the US Grand Prix but a local firm reportedly refused him a hire car because he was under 25. At a meeting at Oulton Park the programme suggested that spectators call at the Enquiry Office to collect "emergency massages".

1989

FORMULA ONE WORLD CHAMPIONSHIP
Brazilian GP
Rio de Janeiro, Mar 26
1 Nigel Mansell (GB)   Ferrari
  115.30mph/185.52kph
2 Alain Prost (Fra)   McLaren
3 Mauricio Gugelmin (Bra) March
4 Johnny Herbert (GB)   Benetton
5 Derek Warwick (GB)   Arrows
6 Alessandro Nannini (Ita) Benetton
Pole Position: Senna (Bra) McLaren
Championship leaders:
1 Mansell 9pts; 2 Prost 6pts; 3 Gugelmin 4pts

San Marino GP
Imola, Apr 23
1 Ayrton Senna (Bra)   McLaren
  126.21mph/203.07kph
2 Alain Prost (Fra)   McLaren
3 Alessandro Nannini (Ita) Benetton
4 Thierry Boutsen (Bel)   Williams
5 Derek Warwick (GB)   Arrows
6 Jonathan Palmer (GB)   Tyrrell
Pole Position: Senna
Championship leaders:
1 Prost 12pts; 2 Mansell 9pts & Senna 9pts

Monaco GP
Monte Carlo, May 7
1 Ayrton Senna (Bra)   McLaren
  84.15mph/135.40kph
2 Alain Prost (Fra)   McLaren
3 Stefan Modena (Ita)   Brabham
4 Alex Caffi (Ita)   Dallara
5 Michele Alboreto (Ita)   Tyrrell
6 Martin Brundle (GB)   Brabham
Pole Position: Senna
Championship leaders:
1 Prost & Senna 18pts; 3 Mansell 9pts

Mexican GP
Mexico City, May 28
1 Ayrton Senna (Bra)   McLaren
  119.96mph/193.02kph
2 Riccardo Patrese (Ita)   Williams
3 Michele Alboreto (Ita)   Tyrrell
4 Alessandro Nannini (Ita) Benetton
5 Alain Prost (Fra)   McLaren
6 Gabrielle Tarquini (Ita) AGS
Pole Position: Senna
Championship leaders:
1 Senna 27pts; 2 Prost 20pts; 3 Mansell 9pts

United States GP
Phoenix, Jun 4
1 Alain Prost (Fra)   McLaren
  87.37mph/140.60kph
2 Riccardo Patrese (Ita)   Williams
3 Eddie Cheever (US)   Arrows
4 Christian Danner (FRG)   Rial
5 Johnny Herbert (GB)   Benetton
6 Thierry Boutsen (Bel)   Williams
Pole Position: Senna
Championship leaders:
1 Prost 29pts; 2 Senna 27pts; 3 Patrese 12pts

Canadian GP
Montreal, Jun 18
1 Thierry Boutsen (Bel)   Williams
  93.02mph/149.67kph
2 Riccardo Patrese (Ita)   Williams
3 Andrea de Cesaris (Ita) Dallara

4 Nelson Piquet (Bra)   Lotus
5 René Arnoux (Fra)   Ligier
6 Alex Caffi (Ita)   Dallara
Pole Position: Prost
Championship leaders:
1 Prost 29pts; 2 Senna 27pts; 3 Patrese 18pts

French GP
Le Castellet, Jul 9
1 Alain Prost (Fra)   McLaren
  116.14mph/186.87kph
2 Nigel Mansell (GB)   Ferrari
3 Riccardo Patrese (Ita)   Williams
4 Jean Alesi (Fra)   Tyrrell
5 Stefan Johannsson (Swe) Onyx
6 Olivier Grouillard (Fra) Ligier
Pole Position: Prost
Championship leaders:
1 Prost 38pts; 2 Senna 27pts; 3 Patrese 22pts

British GP
Silverstone, Jul 16
1 Alain Prost (Fra)   McLaren
  143.69mph/231.20kph
2 Nigel Mansell (GB)   Ferrari
3 Alessandro Nannini (Ita) Benetton
4 Nelson Piquet (Bra)   Lotus
5 Pierluigi Martini (Ita) Minardi
6 Luis Sala (Spa)   Minardi
Pole Position: Senna
Championship leaders:
1 Prost 47pts; 2 Senna 27pts; 3 Patrese 22pts

German GP
Hockenheim, Jul 30
1 Ayrton Senna (Bra)   McLaren
  140.35mph/225.83kph
2 Alain Prost (Fra)   McLaren
3 Nigel Mansell (GB)   Ferrari
4 Riccardo Patrese (Ita)   Williams
5 Nelson Piquet (Bra)   Lotus
6 Derek Warwick (GB)   Arrows
Pole Position: Senna
Championship leaders:
1 Prost 53pts; 2 Senna 36pts; 3 Patrese & Mansell 25pts

Hungarian GP
Budapest, Aug 13
1 Nigel Mansell (GB)   Ferrari
  104.50mph/167.20kph
2 Ayrton Senna (Bra)   McLaren
3 Thierry Boutsen (Bel)   Williams
4 Alain Prost (Fra)   McLaren
5 Eddie Cheever (US)   Arrows
6 Nelson Piquet (Bra)   Lotus
Pole Position: Patrese
Championship leaders:
1 Prost 56pts; 2 Senna 42pts; 3 Mansell 34pts

Belgian GP
Spa, Aug 27
1 Ayrton Senna (Bra)   McLaren
  113.49mph/181.58kph
2 Alain Prost (Fra)   McLaren
3 Nigel Mansell (GB)   Ferrari
4 Thierry Boutsen (Bel)   Williams
5 Alessandro Nannini (Ita) Benetton
6 Derek Warwick (GB)   Arrows
Pole Position: Senna
Championship leaders:
1 Prost 62pts; 2 Senna 51pts; 3 Mansell 38pts

Italian GP

Monza, Sep 10
1 Alain Prost (Fra) — McLaren
144.26mph/232.12kph
2 Gerhard Berger (Aut) — Ferrari
3 Thierry Boutsen (Bel) — Williams
4 Riccardo Patrese (Ita) — Williams
5 Jean Alesi (Fra) — Tyrrell
6 Martin Brundle (GB) — Brabham
Pole Position: Senna
Championship leaders:
1 Prost 71pts; 2 Senna 51pts; 3 Mansell 38pts

Portuguese GP

Estoril, Sep 24
1 Gerhard Berger (Aut) — Ferrari
2 Alain Prost (Fra) — McLaren
3 Stefan Johannsson (Swe) — Onyx
4 Alessandro Nannini (Ita) — Benetton
5 Pierluigi Martini (Ita) — Minardi
6 Jonathan Palmer (GB) — Tyrrell
Pole Position: Senna
Championship leaders:
1 Prost 75pts; 2 Senna 51pts; 3 Mansell 38pts

WORLD SPORTSCAR CHAMPIONSHIP

Suzuka, Japan, Apr 9
1 Jean-Louis Schlesser (Fra) and Mauro Baldi (Ita),
Mercedes
Dijon, France May 21
1 Bob Wollek (Fra) and Frank Jellinski (FRG), Porsche
Jarama, Spain, Jun 25
1 Jochen Mass (FRG) and Jean-Louis Schlesser (Fra),
Mercedes
Brands Hatch, Jul 23
1 Mauro Baldi (Ita) and Kenny Acheson (GB), Mercedes
Nürburgring, West Germany, Aug 20
1 Jean-Louis Schlesser (Fra) and Jochen Mass (FRG),
Mercedes
Donington Park, Sep 3
1 Jean-Louis Schlesser (Fra) and Jochen Mass (FRG),
Mercedes
Spa, Belgium, Sep 17
1 Mauro Baldi (Ita) and Kenny Acheson (GB), Mercedes

FIA FORMULA 3000 CHAMPIONSHIP

Silverstone, Apr 9
1 Thomas Danielsson (Swe), Reynard-Cosworth
Vallelunga, Italy, May 1
1 Martin Donnelly (GB), Reynard-Mugen
Pau, France, May 15
1 Jean Alesi (Fra), Reynard-Mugen
Jerez, Spain, Jun 4
1 Erik Bernard (Fra), Lola-Mugen
Enna, Italy, Jul 16
1 Andrea Chiesa (Swi), Reynard-Ford
Brands Hatch, Aug 20
1 Martin Donnelly (GB), Reynard-Mugen
Birmingham, Aug 28
1 Jean Alesi (Fra), Reynard-Mugen
Spa, Belgium
1 Jean Alesi (Fra), Reynard-Mugen

OTHER MAJOR RESULTS

Daytona 24 Hours

Daytona Beach, Florida, Feb 5
1 John Andretti (US), Derek Bell (GB), Bob Wollek (Fra);
Porsche 621 laps at 92.01mph/147.40kph
2 Price Cobb (US), John Nielson (Den), Jan Lammers
(Hol), Andy Wallace (GB); Jaguar
3 Walter Brun (Swi), Hans Stuck (FRG), Oscar Larrauri
(Arg), Doc Bundy (US); Porsche

Daytona 500

Daytona Beach, Florida, Feb 19
1 Darrell Waltrip (US), Chevrolet Monte Carlo
148.47mph/238.89kph
2 Ken Schrader (US), Chevrolet Monte Carlo
3 Dale Earnhardt (US), Chevrolet Monte Carlo

Indianapolis 500

Indianapolis, May 28
1 Emerson Fittipaldi (Bra), Penske-Chevrolet
167.58mph/269.64kph
2 Al Unser Jr (US), Lola-Chevrolet
3 Raul Boesel (Bra), Lola-Judd

Le Mans 24 Hour Race

June 10/11
1 Jochen Mass (FRG), Manuel Reuter (FRG), Stanley
Dickens (Swe) Sauber-Mercedes 389 laps; avge speed:
137.49mph/219.99kph; Distance covered: 5,265km
2 Mauro Baldi (Ita), Ken Acheson (GB), Gianfranco
Brancatelli (Ita) Suaber-Mercedes
3 Hans Stuck (FRG), Bob Wollek (Fra), Porsche 962-Joest

"With Ferrari, everything is possible."
Gazetta Dello Sport *correspondent on
Mansell's win in Rio*

**"I'm not disputing that he's a great driver. But
he is not a phenomenon, no way. Three or
four other current drivers in his car would
do exactly the same job. At times they
would do it with a little more style."**
Nigel Mansell on Ayrton Senna

**"There's nothing to say between Prost and
me any more. We only communicate
through an engineer."**
Ayrton Senna

**"I accept most things but I won't be treated
like an imbecile."**
Alain Prost on his relations with McLaren

**"Winning or not winning a world
championship is not so important. It is
only a transient moment in life."**
Ayrton Senna

RALLYING 1989

WORLD CHAMPIONSHIP

Swedish Rally

Jan 5-8
1 Ingvar Carlsson (Swe) 4h 58m 15s Mazda
2 Per Eklund (Swe) 4h 59m 18s Lancia
3 Kenneth Eriksson (Swe) 4h 59m 57s Toyota

Monte Carlo Rally

Jan 20-27
1 Miki Biasion (Ita) 7h 13m 27s Lancia
2 Didier Auriol (Fra) 7h 19m 54s Lancia
3 Bruno Saby (Fra) 7h 21m 08s Lancia

Portuguese Rally

Feb 28-Mar 5
1 Miki Biasion (Ita) 6h 47m 01s Lancia
2 Markku Alen (Fin) 6h 57m 19s Lancia
3 Alessandro Fiorio (Ita) 7h 10m 19s Lancia

Safari Rally
Mar 25-30
1 Miki Biasion (Ita) 6h 55m 27s Lancia
2 Mike Kirkland (Ken) 8h 16m 11s Nissan
3 Stig Blomqvist (Swe) 9h 17m 39s Volkswagen

Tour of Corsica
Apr 21-27
1 Didier Auriol (Fra) 7h 12m 39s Lancia
2 François Chatriot (Fra) 7h 14m 36s BMW
3 Juha Kankunnen (Fin) 7h 16m 29s Toyota

Acropolis Rally
May 27-Jun 1
1 Miki Biasion (Ita) 7h 31m 43s Lancia
2 Didier Auriol (Fra) 7h 33m 41s Lancia
3 Alessandro Fiorio (Ita) 7h 35m 14s Lancia

New Zealand Rally
Jul 13-16
1 Inqvar Carlsson (Swe) 6h 59m 55s Mazda
2 R Millen (US) 7h 02m 37s Mazda
3 Malcolm Wilson (GB) 7h 03m 24s Vauxhall

Argentina Rally
Aug 2-6
1 Mikael Ericsson (Swe) 7h 06m 00s Lancia
2 Alessandro Fiorio (Ita) 7h 08m 26s Lancia
3 Jorge Recalde (Arg) 7h 19m 00s Lancia

Australian Rally
Sept 14-17
1 Juha Kankunnen (Fin) 5h 32m 09s Toyota
2 Kenneth Eriksson (Swe) 5h 33m 16s Toyota
3 Markku Alen (Fin) 5h 34m 22s Lancia

--- CHAMPIONS ---

FORMULA ONE WORLD CHAMPIONSHIP
World Champion Drivers

Year	Winner	Car	Runner-up	Third
1950	Giuseppe Farina (Ita)	Alfa Romeo	Juan Manuel Fangio (Arg)	Luigi Fagioli (Ita)
1951	Juan Manuel Fangio (Arg)	Alfa Romeo	Alberto Ascari (Ita)	Jose Gonzalez (Arg)
1952	Alberto Ascari (Ita)	Ferrari	Giuseppe Farina (Ita)	Piero Taruffi (Ita)
1953	Alberto Ascari (Ita)	Ferrari	Juan Manuel Fangio (Arg)	Giuseppe Farina (Ita)
1954	Juan Manuel Fangio (Arg)	Maserati/Mercedes	Jose Gonzalez (Arg)	Mike Hawthorn (GB)
1955	Juan Manuel Fangio (Arg)	Mercedes-Benz	Stirling Moss (GB)	Eugenio Castellotti (Ita)
1956	Juan Manuel Fangio (Arg)	Lancia-Ferrari	Stirling Moss (GB)	Peter Collins (GB)
1957	Juan Manuel Fangio (Arg)	Maserati	Stirling Moss (GB)	Luigi Musso (Ita)
1958	Mike Hawthorn (GB)	Ferrari	Stirling Moss (GB)	Tony Brooks (GB)
1959	Jack Brabham (Aus)	Cooper-Climax	Tony Brooks (GB)	Stirling Moss (GB)
1960	Jack Brabham (Aus)	Cooper-Climax	Bruce McLaren (NZ)	Stirling Moss (GB)
1961	Phil Hill (US)	Ferrari	Wolfgang Von Trips (FRG)	Stirling Moss (GB)
1962	Graham Hill (GB)	BRM	Jim Clark (GB)	Bruce McLaren (NZ)
1963	Jim Clark (GB)	Lotus-Climax	Graham Hill (GB)	Richie Ginther (US)
1964	John Surtees (GB)	Ferrari	Graham Hill (GB)	Jim Clark (GB)
1965	Jim Clark (GB)	Lotus-Climax	Graham Hill (GB)	Jackie Stewart (GB)
1966	Jack Brabham (Aus)	Brabham-Repco	John Surtees (GB)	Jochen Rindt (Aut)
1967	Denny Hulme (NZ)	Brabham-Repco	Jack Brabham (Aus)	Jim Clark (GB)
1968	Graham Hill (GB)	Lotus-Ford	Jackie Stewart (GB)	Denny Hulme (NZ)
1969	Jackie Stewart (GB)	Matra-Ford	Jacky Ickx (Bel)	Bruce McLaren (NZ)
1970	Jochen Rindt (Aut)	Lotus-Ford	Jacky Ickx (Bel)	Clay Regazzoni (Swi)
1971	Jackie Stewart (GB)	Tyrrell-Ford	Ronnie Peterson (Swe)	François Cevert (Fra)
1972	Emerson Fittipaldi (Bra)	Lotus-Ford	Jackie Stewart (GB)	Denny Hulme (NZ)
1973	Jackie Stewart (GB)	Tyrrell-Ford	Emerson Fittipaldi (Bra)	Ronnie Peterson (Swe)
1974	Emerson Fittipaldi (Bra)	McLaren-Ford	Clay Regazzoni (Swi)	Jody Scheckter (SA)
1975	Niki Lauda (Aut)	Ferrari	Emerson Fittipaldi (Bra)	Carlos Reutemann (Arg)
1976	James Hunt (GB)	McLaren-Ford	Niki Lauda (Aut)	Jody Scheckter (SA)
1977	Niki Lauda (Aut)	Ferrari	Jody Scheckter (SA)	Mario Andretti (US)
1978	Mario Andretti (US)	Lotus-Ford	Ronnie Peterson (Swe)	Carlos Reutemann (Arg)
1979	Jody Scheckter (SA)	Ferrari	Gilles Villeneuve (Can)	Alan Jones (Aus)
1980	Alan Jones (Aus)	Williams-Ford	Nelson Piquet (Bra)	Carlos Reutemann (Arg)
1981	Nelson Piquet (Bra)	Brabham-Ford	Carlos Reutemann (Arg)	Alan Jones (Aus)
1982	Keke Rosberg (Fin)	Williams-Ford	Didier Pironi (Fra)	John Watson (GB)
1983	Nelson Piquet (Bra)	Brabham-BMW	Alain Prost (Fra)	René Arnoux (Fra)
1984	Niki Lauda (Aut)	McLaren-TAG	Alain Prost (Fra)	Elio de Angelis (Ita)
1985	Alain Prost (Fra)	McLaren-TAG	Michele Alboreto (Ita)	Keke Rosberg (Fin)
1986	Alain Prost (Fra)	McLaren-TAG	Nigel Mansell (GB)	Nelson Piquet (Bra)
1987	Nelson Piquet (Bra)	Williams-Honda	Nigel Mansell (GB)	Ayrton Senna (Bra)
1988	Ayrton Senna (Bra)	McLaren-Honda	Alain Prost (Fra)	Gerhard Berger (Aut)
1989				

Most titles: 5 Fangio; **3** Brabham, Stewart, Lauda, Piquet; **2** Clark, Ascari, Graham Hill, Fittipaldi, Prost

Constructors' Cup

1958 Vanwall	1959 Cooper-Climax	1960 Cooper-Climax	1961 Ferrari	1962 BRM
1963 Lotus-Climax	1964 Ferrari	1965 Lotus-Climax	1966 Brabham-Repco	1967 Brabham-Repco
1968 Lotus-Ford	1969 Matra-Ford	1970 Lotus-Ford	1971 Tyrrell-Ford	1972 Lotus-Ford
1973 Lotus-Ford	1974 McLaren-Ford	1975 Ferrari	1976 Ferrari	1977 Ferrari
1978 Lotus-Ford	1979 Ferrari	1980 Williams-Ford	1981 Williams-Ford	1982 Ferrari
1983 Ferrari	1984 McLaren-Porsche	1985 McLaren-TAG	1986 Williams-Honda	1987 Williams-Honda
1988 McLaren-Honda				

Most titles: 8 Ferrari; **7** Lotus (5 Lotus-Ford; 2 Lotus-Climax); **4** Williams (2 Williams-Ford; 2 Williams-Honda); **4** McLaren (1 McLaren-TAG; 1 McLaren-Ford; 1 McLaren-Honda; 1 McLaren-Porsche)

HIGHEST PLACED BRITONS IN THE FORMULA ONE WORLD CHAMPIONSHIP

1976	James Hunt	1st
1977	James Hunt	5th
1978	John Watson	6th
1979	John Watson	9th
1980	John Watson	jt. 10th
1981	John Watson	6th
1982	John Watson	jt. 2nd
1983	John Watson	jt. 6th
1984	Derek Warwick	7th
1985	Nigel Mansell	6th
1986	Nigel Mansell	2nd
1987	Nigel Mansell	2nd
1988	Derek Warwick	jt. 7th

THE RACE WINNERS

(up to and including Sep 1989)

ALBORETO, Michele (5)
1982 Las Vegas; 1983 Detroit (both Tyrrell); 1984 Belgian; 1985 Canadian, German (all Ferrari)

ANDRETTI, Mario (12)
1971 South African (Ferrari); 1976 Japanese; 1977 United States (West), Spanish, French, Italian; 1978 Argentine, Belgian, Spanish, French, German, Dutch (all Lotus)

ARNOUX, René (7)
1980 Brazilian, South African; 1982 French, Italian (all Renault); 1983 Canadian, German, Dutch (all Ferrari)

ASCARI, Alberto (13)
1951 German, Italian; 1952 Belgian, French, British, German, Dutch, Italian; 1953 Argentine, Dutch, Belgian, British, Swiss (all Ferrari)

BAGHETTI, Giancarlo (1)
1961 French (Ferrari)

BANDINI, Lorenzo (1)
1964 Austrian (Ferrari)

BELTOISE, Jean-Pierre (1)
1972 Monaco (BRM)

BERGER, Gerhard (5)
1986 Mexican (Benetton); 1987 Japanese, Australian; 1988 Italian; 1989 Portuguese (all Ferrari)

BONNIER, Jo (1)
1959 Dutch (BRM)

BOUTSEN, Thierry (1)
1989 Canadian (Williams)

BRABHAM, Jack (14)
1959 Monaco, British; 1960 Dutch, Belgian, French, British, Portuguese (all Cooper); 1966 French, British, Dutch, German; 1967 French, Canadian; 1970 South African (all Brabham)

BRAMBILLA, Vittorio (1)
1975 Austrian (March)

BROOKS, Tony (6)
1957 British*; 1958 Belgian, German, Italian (all Vanwall); 1959 French, German (both Ferrari)

CEVERT, François (1)
1971 United States (Tyrrell)

CLARK, Jim (25)
1962 Belgian, British, United States; 1963 Belgian, Dutch, French, British, Italian, Mexican, South African; 1964 Dutch, Belgian, British; 1965 South African, Belgian, French, British, Dutch, German; 1966 United States; 1967 Dutch, British, United States, Mexican; 1968 South African (all Lotus)

COLLINS, Peter (3)
1956 Belgian, French (both Lancia-Ferrari); 1958 British (Ferrari)

DE ANGELIS, Elio (2)
1982 Austrian; 1985 San Marino (both Lotus)

DEPAILLER, Patrick (2)
1978 Monaco (Tyrrell); 1979 Spanish (Ligier)

FAGIOLI, Luigi (1)
1951 French* (Alfa Romeo)

FANGIO, Juan Manuel (24)
1950 Monaco, Belgian, French; 1951 Swiss, French, Spanish (all Alfa Romeo); 1953 Italian (Maserati); 195 Argentine, Belgian (both Maserati), French, German, Swiss, Italian; 1955 Argentine, Belgian, Dutch, Italian (all Mercedes-Benz); 1956 Argentine*, British, German (all Lancia-Ferrari); 1957 Argentine, Monaco, French, German (all Maserati)

FARINA, Giuseppe (5)
1950 British, Swiss, Italian; 1951 Belgian (all Alfa Romeo); 1953 German (Ferrari)

FITTIPALDI, Emerson (14)
1970 United States; 1972 Spanish, Belgian, British, Austrian, Italian; 1973 Argentine, Brazilian, Spanish (all Lotus); 1974 Brazilian, Belgian, Canadian; 1975 Argentine, British (all McLaren)

GETHIN, Peter (1)
1971 Italian (BRM)

GINTHER, Richie (1)
1965 Mexican (Honda)

GONZALEZ, José Froilan (2)
1951 British; 1954 British (both Ferrari)

GURNEY, Dan (4)
1962 French (Porsche); 1964 French, Mexican (both Brabham); 1967 Belgian (Eagle)

HAWTHORN, Mike (3)
1953 French; 1954 Spanish; 1958 French (all Ferrari)

HILL, Graham (14)
1962 Dutch, German, Italian, South African; 1963 Monaco, United States; 1964 Monaco, United States; 1965 Monaco, United States (all BRM); 1968 Spanish, Monaco, Mexican; 1969 Monaco (all Lotus)

HILL, Phil (3)
1960 Italian; 1961 Belgian, Italian (all Ferrari)

HULME, Denny (8)
1967 Monaco, German (both Brabham); 1968 Italian, Canadian; 1969 Mexico; 1972 South African; 197 Swedish; 1974 Argentine (all McLaren)

HUNT, James (10)
1975 Dutch (Hesketh); 1976 Spanish, French, German, Dutch, Canadian, United States; 1977 British, United States, Japanese (all McLaren)

ICKX, Jacky (8)
1968 French (Ferrari); 1969 German, Canadian (both Brabham); 1970 Austrian, Canadian, Mexican; 197 Dutch; 1972 German (all Ferrari)

IRELAND, Innes (1)
1961 United States (Lotus)

JABOUILLE, Jean-Pierre (2)
1979 French; 1980 Austrian (both Renault)

JONES, Alan (12)
1977 Austrian (Shadow); 1979 German, Austrian, Dutch, Canadian; 1980 Argentine, French, British, Canadian, United States; 1981 United States (West), Las Vegas (all Williams)

LAFFITE, Jacques (6)
1977 Swedish; 1979 Argentine, Brazilian; 1980 German (all Ligier); 1981 Austrian, Canadian (both Talbot-Ligier)

LAUDA, Niki (25)
1974 Spanish, Dutch; 1975 Monaco, Belgian, Swedish, French, United States; 1976 Brazilian, South African, Belgian, Monaco, British; 1977 South African, German, Dutch (all Ferrari); 1978 Swedish, Italian (both Brabham); 1982 United States (West), British; 1984 South African, French, British, Austrian, Italian; 1985 Dutch (all McLaren)

McLAREN, Bruce (4)
1959 United States; 1960 Argentine; 1962 Monaco (all Cooper); 1968 Belgian (McLaren)

MANSELL, Nigel (15)
1985 European, South African; 1986 Belgian, Canadian, French, British, Portuguese; 1987 San Marino, French, British, Austrian, Spanish, Mexican (all Williams); 1989 Brazilian, Hungarian (Ferrari)

MASS, Jochen (1)
1975 Spanish§ (McLaren)

MOSS, Stirling (16)
1955 British (Mercedes-Benz); 1956 Monaco, Italian (both Maserati); 1957 British*, Pescara, Italian (all Vanwall); 1958 Argentine (Cooper), Dutch, Portuguese, Moroccan (all Vanwall) 1959 Portuguese, Italian (Cooper); 1960 Monaco, United States; 1961 Monaco, German (all Lotus)

MUSSO, Luigi (1)
1956 Argentine* (Lancia-Ferrari)

NILSSON, Gunnar (1)
1977 Belgian (Lotus)

PACE, Carlos (1)
1975 Brazilian (Brabham)

PATRESE, Riccardo (2)
1982 Monaco; 1983 South African (both Brabham)

PETERSON, Ronnie (10)
1973 French, Austrian, Italian, United States; 1974 Monaco, French, Italian (all Lotus); 1976 Italian (March); 1978 South African, Austrian (both Lotus)

PIRONI, Didier (3)
1980 Belgian (Ligier); 1982 San Marino, Dutch (both Ferrari)

PIQUET, Nelson (20)
1980 United States (West), Dutch, Italian; 1981 Argentine, San Marino, German; 1982 Canadian; 1983 Brazilian, Italian, European; 1984 Canadian, Detroit; 1985 French (all Brabham); 1986 Brazilian, German, Hungarian, Italian; 1987 German, Hungarian, Italian (all Williams)

PROST, Alain (39)
1981 French, Dutch, Italian; 1982 South African, Brazilian; 1983 French, Belgian, British, Austrian (all Renault); 1984 French, San Marino, Monaco§, German, Dutch, European, Portuguese; 1985 Brazilian, Monaco, British, Austrian, Italian; 1986 San Marino, Monaco, Austrian, Australian; 1987 Brazilian, Belgian, Portuguese; 1988 Brazilian, Monaco, Mexican, French, Portuguese, Spanish, Australian; 1989 United States, French, British, Italian (all McLaren)

REGAZZONI, Clay (5)
1970 Italian; 1974 German; 1975 Italian; 1976 United States (West) (all Ferrari); 1979 British (Williams)

REUTEMANN, Carlos (12)
1974 South African, Austrian, United States; 1975 German (all Brabham); 1977 Brazilian; 1978 Brazilian, United States (West), British, United States (all Ferrari); 1980 Monaco; 1981 Brazilian, Belgian (all Williams)

REVSON, Peter (2)
1973 British, Canadian (both McLaren)

RINDT, Jochen (6)
1969 United States; 1970 Monaco, Dutch, French, British, German (all Lotus)

RODRIGUEZ, Pedro (2)
1967 South African (Cooper); 1970 Belgian (BRM)

ROSBERG, Keke (5)
1982 Swiss; 1983 Monaco; 1984 Dallas; 1985 Detroit, Australian (all Williams)

SCARFIOTTI, Ludovico (1)
1966 Italian (Ferrari)

SCHECKTER, Jody (10)
1974 Swedish, British; 1975 South African; 1976 Swedish (all Tyrrell); 1977 Argentine, Monaco, Canadian (all Wolf); 1979 Belgian, Monaco, Italian (all Ferrari)

SENNA, Ayrton (19)
1985 Portuguese, Belgian; 1986 Spanish, Detroit; 1987 Monaco, United States (all Lotus); 1988 San Marino, Canadian, United States, British, German, Hungarian, Belgian, Japanese; 1989 San Marino, Monaco, Mexican, German, Belgian (all McLaren)

SIFFERT, Jo (2)
1968 British (Lotus); 1971 Austrian (BRM)

STEWART, Jackie (27)
1965 Italian; 1966 Monaco (both BRM); 1968 Dutch, German, United States; 1969 South African, Spanish, Dutch, French, British, Italian (all Matra); 1970 Spanish (March); 1971 Spanish, Monaco, French, British, German, Canadian; 1972 Argentine, French, Canadian, United States; 1973 South African, Belgian, Monaco, Dutch, German (all Tyrrell)

SURTEES, John (6)
1963 German; 1964 German, Italian; 1966 Belgian (all Ferrari); 1967 Italian (Honda)

TAMBAY, Patrick (2)
1982 German; 1983 San Marino (both Ferrari)

TARUFFI, Piero (1)
1952 Swiss (Ferrari)

TRINTIGNANT, Maurice (2)
1955 Monaco (Ferrari); 1958 Monaco (Cooper)

VILLENEUVE, Gilles (6)
1978 Canadian; 1979 South African, United States (West), United States; 1981 Monaco, Spanish (all Ferrari)

VON TRIPS, Wolfgang (2)
1961 Dutch, British (both Ferrari)

WATSON, John (5)
1976 Austrian (Penske); 1981 British; 1982 Belgian, Detroit; 1983 United States West (all McLaren)

* denotes shared drive
§ only half points awarded
Figures in brackets () indicate total wins

Most wins in a season
8 Ayrton Senna (Bra) 1988; **7** Jim Clark (GB) 1963, Alain Prost (Fra)1984, 1988; **6** Alberto Ascari (Ita) 1952, Juan Manuel Fangio (Arg) 1954, Jim Clark (GB) 1965, Jackie Stewart (GB) 1969, 1971, James Hunt (GB) 1976, Mario Andretti (US) 1978, Nigel Mansell (GB) 1987
Most successive wins
9 Alberto Ascari (Ita) 1952-3; 5 Jack Brabham (Aus) 1960, Jim Clark (GB) 1965
Most pole positions
39 Ayrton Senna (Bra); **33** Jim Clark (GB); **29** Juan Manuel Fangio (Arg); **24** Niki Lauda (Aut), Nelson Piquet (Bra)

THE LEADING GRAND PRIX WINNERS OF THE 1980s

Drivers

39	**Alain Prost (Fra)**
20	**Nelson Piquet (Bra)**
19	**Ayrton Senna (Bra)**
15	**Nigel Mansell (GB)**
8	**Niki Lauda (Aut)**
7	**Alan Jones (Aus)**
5	**René Arnoux (Fra)**
5	**Michele Alboreto (Ita)**
5	**Keke Rosberg (Fin)**
5	**Gerhard Berger (Aut)**

Cars

55	**McLaren**
36	**Williams**
18	**Ferrari**
15	**Brabham**
14	**Renault**
8	**Lotus**
4	**Ligier/Talbot-Ligier**

Excluding Japanese, Spanish and Australian Grand Prix 1989

CARS

Race Wins
97 Ferrari 1951-89; 79 Lotus 1960-87, McLaren 1968-89; 41 Williams 1979-89; 35 Brabham 1964-85; 23 Tyrrell 1971-83; 17 BRM 1959-72; 16 Cooper 1958-67; 15 Renault 1979-83; 10 Alfa Romeo 1950-51; 9 Mercedes-Benz 1954-55; Maserati 1953-57; Vanwall 1957-58; Matra 1968-69; 8 Ligier 1977-81; 3 Wolf 1970-76; 3 March 1970-76; 2 Honda 1965-67; 1 Porsche 1962; Eagle 1967; Hesketh 1975; Penske 1976; Shadow 1977; Benetton 1986

Most wins in a season
15 McLaren-Honda 1988; 12 McLaren-Porsche 1984; 9 Williams-Honda 1986, 1987, McLaren-Honda 1989 (to Italian GP); 8 Lotus-Ford 1978; 7 Ferrari 1952, 1953; Lotus-Climax 1963; Tyrrell-Ford 1971; Lotus-Ford 1973

Most successive wins
14 Ferrari 1952-3; 11 McLaren-Honda 1988; 9 Alfa Romeo 1950-51; 8 McLaren-TAG 1984-85

ENGINES

Wins
154 Ford; 97 Ferrari; 51 Honda; 40 Climax; 26 Porsche/TAG; 21 Renault; 18 BRM; 12 Alfa Romeo; 11 Maserati, Offenhauser; 9 BMW, Mercedes-Benz, Vanwall; 8 Repco; 3 Matra; 1 Weslake

BRITISH GRAND PRIX WINNERS

1950-54, 1956, 1958, 1960, 1963, 1965, 1967, 1969, 1971, 1973, 1975, 1977, 1979, 1981, 1983, 1985, 1987, 1988, 1989 at Silverstone; 1955, 1957, 1959, 1961-62 at Aintree; 1964, 1966, 1968, 1970, 1972, 1974, 1976, 1978, 1980, 1982, 1984, 1986 at Brands Hatch

1950	Giuseppe Farina (Ita)	Alfa Romeo
1951	Jose Froilan Gonzalez (Arg)	Ferrari
1952	Alberto Ascari (Ita)	Ferrari
1953	Alberto Ascari (Ita)	Ferrari
1954	Jose Froilan Gonzalez (Arg)	Ferrari
1955	Stirling Moss (GB)	Mercedes-Benz
1956	Juan Manuel Fangio (Arg)	Lancia-Ferrari
1957	Stirling Moss (GB) & Tony Brooks (GB)	Vanwall
1958	Peter Collins (GB)	Ferrari
1959	Jack Brabham (Aus)	Cooper-Climax
1960	Jack Brabham (Aus)	Cooper-Climax
1961	Wolfgang Von Trips (FRG)	Ferrari
1962	Jim Clark (GB)	Lotus-Climax
1963	Jim Clark (GB)	Lotus-Climax
1964	Jim Clark (GB)	Lotus-Climax
1965	Jim Clark (GB)	Lotus-Climax
1966	Jack Brabham (Aus)	Brabham-Repco
1967	Jim Clark (GB)	Lotus-Ford
1968	Jo Siffert (Swi)	Lotus-Ford
1969	Jackie Stewart (GB)	Matra-Ford
1970	Jochen Rindt (Aut)	Lotus-Ford
1971	Jackie Stewart (GB)	Tyrrell-Ford
1972	Emerson Fittipaldi (Bra)	Lotus-Ford
1973	Peter Revson (US)	McLaren-Ford
1974	Jody Scheckter (SA)	Tyrrell-Ford
1975	Emerson Fittipaldi (Bra)	McLaren-Ford
1976	Niki Lauda (Aut)	Ferrari
1977	James Hunt (GB)	McLaren-Ford
1978	Carlos Reutemann (Arg)	Ferrari
1979	Clay Regazzoni (Swi)	Williams-Ford
1980	Alan Jones (Aus)	Williams-Ford
1981	John Watson (GB)	McLaren-Ford
1982	Niki Lauda (Aut)	McLaren-Ford
1983	Alain Prost (Fra)	Renault
1984	Niki Lauda (Aut)	McLaren-TAG
1985	Alain Prost (Fra)	McLaren-TAG
1986	Nigel Mansell (GB)	Williams-Honda
1987	Nigel Mansell (GB)	Williams-Honda
1988	Ayrton Senna (Bra)	McLaren-Honda
1989	Alain Prost (Fra)	McLaren-Honda

WORLD SPORTSCAR CHAMPIONS

Inaugurated for types in 1953. A drivers' championship was introduced in 1981

Drivers

1981	Bob Garretson (US) Porsche
1982	Jacky Ickx (Bel) Porsche
1983	Jacky Ickx (Bel) Porsche
1984	Stefan Bellof (FRG) Porsche
1985	Derek Bell (GB) & Hans Stuck (FRG) Porsche
1986	Derek Bell (GB) & Hans Stuck (FRG) Porsche
1987	Raul Boesel (Bra) Jaguar
1988	Martin Brundle (GB) Jaguar

Cars

1953	Ferrari	1974	Matra-Simca
1954	Ferrari	1975	Alfa Romeo
1955	Mercedes-Benz	1976	Porsche
1956	Ferrari	1977	Porsche
1957	Ferrari	1978	Porsche
1958	Ferrari	1979	Porsche
1959	Aston Martin	1980	Lancia
1960	Ferrari	1981	Porsche
1961	Ferrari	1982	Porsche
1962-67	Not held	1983	Porsche
1968	Ford	1984	Porsche
1969	Porsche	1985	Rothmans-Porsche
1970	Porsche	1986	Brun Motorsport
1971	Porsche	1987	Silk Cut Jaguar
1972	Ferrari	1988	Silk Cut Jaguar
1973	Matra-Simca		

FIA FORMULA 3000 INTERNATIONAL CHAMPIONSHIP

Inaugurated 1985

1985	Christian Danner (FRG) March-Smith
1986	Ivan Capelli (Ita) March-Mader
1987	Stefano Modena (Ita) March-Cosworth
1988	Roberto Moreno (Bra) Reynard-Nicholson
1989	Jean Alesi (Fra) Reynard-Mugen

LE MANS 24 HOUR RACE

First held 1923
Winners since 1980

1980	Jean-Pierre Jaussaud/Jean Rondeau (Fra) Rondeau-Cosworth
1981	Derek Bell (GB)/Jacky Ickx (Bel) Porsche
1982	Derek Bell (GB)/Jacky Ickx (Bel) Porsche
1983	Hurley Haywood/Al Holbert (both US)/Vern Schuppan (Aut) Porsche
1984	Klaus Ludwig (FRG)/Henri Pescarolo (Fra) Porsche
1985	Paulo Barillo (Ita)/Klaus Ludwig/John Winter (both FRG) Porsche
1986	Derek Bell (GB)/Al Holbert (US)/Hans Stuck (FRG) Porsche
1987	Derek Bell (GB)/Al Holbert (US)/Hans Stuck (FRG) Porsche
1988	Jan Lammers (Hol)/Johnny Dumfries/Andy Wallace (both GB) Jaguar
1989	Stanley Dickens (Swe)/Jochen Mass/Manuel Reuter (both FRG) Mercedes

Most wins
6 Jacky Ickx 1969, 1975-77, 1981-82; 5 Derek Bell 1975, 1981-82, 1986-87; 4 Olivier Gendebien (Bel) 1958, 1960-62, Henri Pescarolo 1972-74, 1984

INDIANAPOLIS 500

First held 1911
Winners since 1980. US unless otherwise stated

1980	Johnny Rutherford	Chaparral
1981	Bobby Unser	Penske
1982	Gordon Johncock	Wildcat
1983	Tom Sneva	March

1984	Rick Mears	March
1985	Danny Sullivan	March
1986	Bobby Rahal	March
1987	Al Unser	March
1988	Rick Mears	Penske
1989	Emerson Fittipaldi (Bra)	Penske

Most wins
4 A J Foyt 1961, 1964, 1967, 1977; Al Unser 1970-71, 1978, 1987; 3 Louis Meyer 1928, 1933, 1936, Mauri Rose 1941, 1947-48, Bobby Unser 1968, 1975, 1981; Johnny Rutherford 1974, 1976, 1980, Rick Mears 1979, 1984, 1988

DAYTONA 500
First held 1959
Winners sincer 1980. All winners US

1980	Buddy Baker Oldsmobile
1981	Richard Petty Buick
1982	Bobby Allison Buick
1983	Cale Yarborough Pontiac
1984	Cale Yarborough Chevrolet
1985	Bill Elliott Ford
1986	Geoff Bodine Chevrolet
1987	Bill Elliott Ford
1988	Bobby Allison Buick
1989	Darrell Waltrip Chevrolet

Most wins
7 Richard Petty 1964, 1966, 1971, 1973-74, 1979, 1981; 4 Cale Yarborough 1968, 1977, 1983-84; 3 Bobby Allison 1979, 1982, 1988

RALLYING

MONTE CARLO RALLY
Inaugurated 1911
Winners since 1980

1980	Walter Rohrl (FRG) Fiat
1981	Jean Ragnotti (Fra) Renault
1982	Walter Rohrl (FRG) Opel
1983	Walter Rohrl (FRG) Opel
1984	Walter Rohrl (FRG) Audi
1985	Ari Vatanen (Fin) Peugeot
1986	Henri Toivonen (Fin) Lancia
1987	Miki Biasion (Ita) Lancia
1988	Bruno Saby (Fra) Lancia
1989	Miki Biasion (Ita) Lancia

Most wins
4 Sandro Munari (Ita) 1972, 1975-77; Walter Rohrl (FRG); 3 Jean Trevoux (Fra) 1939, 1949, 1951

LOMBARD RAC RALLY
Inaugurated 1951
Winners since 1980

1980	Henri Toivonen (Fin) Talbot
1981	Hannu Mikkola (Fin) Audi
1982	Hannu Mikkola (Fin) Audi
1983	Stig Blomqvist (Swe) Audi
1984	Ari Vatanen (Fin) Peugeot
1985	Henri Toivonen (Fin) Lancia
1986	Timo Salonen (Fin) Peugeot
1987	Juha Kankkunen (Fin) Lancia
1988	Markku Alen (Fin) Lancia

Most wins
4 Hannu Mikola (Fin) 1978-79, 1981-82; 3 Erik Carlsson (Swe) 1960-62, Timo Makinen (Fin) 1973-75.

SAFARI RALLY
Inaugurated 1953
Winners since 1980

1980	Shekhar Mahta (Ken) Datsun
1981	Shekhar Mahta (Ken) Datsun
1982	Shekhar Mahta (Ken) Datsun
1983	Ari Vatanen (Fin) Opel
1984	Bjorn Waldegard (Swe) Toyota
1985	Juha Kankunen (Fin) Toyota
1986	Bjorn Waldegard (Swe)Toyota
1987	Hanu Mikkola (Fin) Audi
1988	Miki Biasion (Ita) Lancia
1989	Miki Biasion (Ita) Lancia

Most wins
5 Shekhar Mehta 3 Joginder Singh 1965, 1974, 1976

WORLD RALLY CHAMPIONS
Drivers

1977	Sandro Munari (Ita)
1978	Markhu Alen (Fin)
1979	Bjorn Waldegaard (Swe)
1980	Walter Rohrl (FRG)
1981	Ari Vatanen (Fin)
1982	Walter Rohrl (FRG)
1983	Hannu Mikkola (Fin)
1984	Stig Blomqvist (Swe)
1985	Timo Salonen (Fin)
1986	Juha Kankunen (Fin)
1987	Juha Kankunen (Fin)
1988	Miki Biasion (Ita)

1990

(all dates provisional)

FORMULA ONE GRAND PRIX
Mar 11: United States (Phoenix); *Mar 25:* Brazilian (Rio de Janeiro); *Apr 8:* San Marino (Imola); *May 27:* Monaco (Monte Carlo); *June 10:* Canadian (Montreal); *Jun 24:* Mexican (Mexico City); *Jul 8:* Frech (Le Castellet); *Jul 15:* BRITISH (Silverstone); *Jul 29:* West German (Hockenheim); *Aug 12:* Hungarian (Budapest); *Aug 26:* Belgian (Spa); *Sep 9:* Italian (Monza); *Sep 23:* Portuguese (Estoril); *Sep 30:* Spanish (Jerez); *Oct 21:* Japanese (Suzuka); *Nov 4:* Australian (Adelaide).

OTHER DATE
May 27: Indianapolis 500 (Indianapolis)

WORLD SPORTS CAR CHAMPIONSHIP
Mar 25: Australian (tba); *Apr 8:* Japanese (Suzuka); *Apr 29:* Spanish (Jarama/Jerez); *May 27:* Italian (Monza); *Jun 3:* Belgian (Spa); *Jun 16-17:* Le Mans 24-hour race (Le Mans); *Jul 1:* German (Nurburgring/Hockenheim); *Aug ?:* French (Magny Cours/Le Castellet); *Aug 19:* British (Donington Park); *Sep 9:* Canadian (Montreal); *Sep 23:* United States (tba); *Oct 7:* Mexican (Mexico City).

RALLYING
Jan 19-26: Monte Carlo Rally; *Feb 9-13:* Swedish Rally; *Mar 6-11:* Portuguese Rally; *Apr 12-16:* Safari Rally (Kenya); *Jun 2-7:* Acropolis Rally (Greece); *Jun 29-Jul 4:* New Zealand Rally; *Aug 22-27:* Rally of 1000 Lakes (Finland); *Sep 13-17:* Australian Rally; *Oct 7-13:* Italian Rally; *Oct 27-Nov 2:* Ivory Coast Rally; *Nov 25-29:* Lombard RAC Rally (based in Harrogate).

NATIONAL RALLY CHAMPIONSHIP
Jun 27: Mazda Winter Rally; *Mar 10:* Skip Brown Rally; *Apr 7:* Granite City Rally (Aberdeen); *May 19:* Manx National Rally; *Jun 16:* Kerridge Severn Valley Rally; *Jul 7:* Kayel Graphics Rally; *Sep 1:* Cumbria Rally; *Sep 29:* Trackrod Forest Rally.

NETBALL

1989

ENGLISH COUNTIES LEAGUE
First Division

	P	W	D	L	F	A	Pts
1 Birmingham	7	7	0	0	356	276	35
2 Essex Met	7	6	0	1	305	265	31
3 Surrey	7	5	0	2	386	334	27
4 Herts	7	4	0	3	343	325	23
5 Beds	7	3	0	4	227	258	19
6 Hants North	7	2	0	5	249	282	15
7 Kent	7	1	0	6	262	318	10
8 East Essex	7	0	0	7	252	373	5

Second Division

	P	W	D	L	F	A	Pts
1 Middlesex	7	7	0	0	294	247	35
2 Cheshire	7	5	1	1	296	251	29
3 Gloucester	7	5	0	2	320	269	27
4 South Yorks	7	3	1	3	290	282	21
5 South Staffs	7	2	1	4	278	198	17
6 Warwicks	7	2	0	5	239	272	15
7 Derbys	7	1	1	5	251	282	13
8 Worcs	7	1	0	6	243	316	11

Northern Division champs: Humberside
Midland Division champs: Northants
Southern Division champs: South Bucks
After play-off Derbys retained Division 2 place and Northants were promoted in place of Worcs.

NATIONAL CLUBS COMPETITION
Bournemouth, May 13
Linden (Birmingham) beat Hirondelles (Surrey) 47-39

EVIAN INTER COUNTIES TOURNAMENT
Anerley, London, Apr 15-16
Seniors
Birmingham beat Hertfordshire 15-13

Under-21
Kent beat Surrey 13-12

CHAMPIONS

WORLD CHAMPIONSHIPS
First held 1963
1963 Australia
1967 New Zealand
1971 Australia
1975 Australia
1979 Australia, New Zealand and
     Trinidad &Tobago (all shared the title)
1983 Australia
1987 New Zealand

ENGLISH COUNTIES LEAGUE
(Formerly National League)
1985 Birmingham
1986 Birmingham
1987 Birmingham
1988 Surrey
1989 Birmingham

1990

Feb 3: Scotland v England, seniors and under-21 (Kelvin Hall, Glasgow);
Feb 17: England v Wales, seniors and under-21 (Poole);
Mar 4: UK and Ireland under-18 tournament (Perth);
Apr 21-22: Inter-Counties Tournament (Anerley, London);
May 5: National League play-offs;
May 12: National Clubs final; *Jun:* England tour to Australia.

ORIENTEERING

1989

WORLD CHAMPIONSHIP
Skovde, Sweden, Aug 12-20
Men – Individual
1 Petter Thoresen (Nor) 1h 36m 16s
2 Kent Olsson (Swe) 1h 39m 26s
3 Havard Tveite (Nor) 1h 39m 58s
Men – Team
1 Norway 4h 06m 01s
2 Sweden 4h 09m 04s
3 Finland 4h 10m 22s
Women – Individual
1 Marita Skogum (Swe) 1h 04m 06s
2 Jajana Galikova (Cze) 1h 05m 30s
3 Alida Abola (USSR) 1h 08m 13s
Women – Team
1 Sweden 3h 43m 46s
2 Czechoslovakia 3h 44m 1s
3 Finland 3h 47m 35s

TSB BRITISH CHAMPIONSHIPS
Starpost, Berkshire, May 13
Men
Steve Hale (Perth)
Women
Yvette Hague (Edinburgh University)

TSB JAN KJELLSTROM INTERNATIONAL FESTIVAL
Longleat/Stourhead, Mar 24-27
Men
Hakan Eriksson (Sweden)
Women
Karen Parker (Manchester)

CHAMPIONS

WORLD CHAMPIONSHIPS
Inaugurated 1966
Men – Individual
1966   Age Hadler (Nor)
1968   Karl Johansson (Swe)
1970   Stig Berge (Nor)
1972   Age Hadler (Nor)
1974   Bernt Frilen (Swe)
1976   Egil Johansen (Nor)
1978   Egil Johansen (Nor)
1979   Oyvin Thon (Nor)
1981   Oyvin Thon (Nor)

1983   Morten Berglia (Nor)
1985   Kari Sallinen (Fin)
1987   Kent Olsson (Swe)
1989   Peter Thoresen (Nor)
Men – Team
1966   Sweden
1968   Sweden
1970   Norway
1972   Sweden
1974   Sweden
1976   Sweden
1978   Norway
1979   Sweden
1981   Norway
1983   Norway
1985   Norway
1987   Norway
1989   Norway
Women – Individual
1966   Ulla Lindqvist (Swe)
1968   Ulla Lindqvist (Swe)
1970   Ingrid Hadler (Nor)
1972   Sarolta Monspart (Hun)
1974   Mona Norgaard (Den)
1976   Lia Veijalainen (Fin)
1978   Anne Berit Eid (Nor)
1979   Outi Bergonstrom (Fin)
1981   Annichen Kringstad (Nor)
1983   Annichen Kringstad-Svensson (Swe)
1985   Annichen Kringstad-Svensson (Swe)
1987   Arja Hannus (Swe)
1989   Marita Skogum (Swe)
Women – Team
1966   Sweden
1968   Norway
1970   Sweden
1972   Finland
1974   Sweden
1976   Sweden
1978   Finland
1979   Finland
1981   Sweden
1983   Sweden
1985   Sweden
1987   Norway
1989   Sweden

1990

Mar 24-25: British Championships (Sheffield);
Apr 13-16: Jan Kjellstrom Festival (Perth).

POLO

1989

WORLD CUP
Berlin, Aug 20
Final
United States beat Great Britain 7-6
Third-place Play-off
Argentina beat Chile 16-2

COWDRAY PARK CUP
Cowdray Park, Jul 24-30
Semi-finals
Cowdray Park beat Hildon House 8-4
Giscours beat Chopendoz 7½-7
Final
Giscours beat Cowdray Park 10-7

BRITISH OPEN (Davidoff Gold Cup)
Cowdray Park, Jul 17
Tramontana beat Cowdray Park 13-8

TOP HANDICAP PLAYERS IN BRITAIN IN 1989
10 Goals Carlos Cracida (Mex), Gonzalo Heguy, Horacio Heguy, Gonzalo Fieres, Ernesto Trotz (all Arg)
9 Goals Luis Lalor, Pablo Diaz Alberdi, Hector Crotto (All Arg), Gabriel Donoso (Chi), Howard Hipwood (Eng), Owen Rinehart (US)

CHAMPIONS

WORLD CUP
Inaugurated 1987
| 1987 | Argentina |
| 1989 | United States |

COWDRAY PARK CUP
Inaugurated 1956
1956	Los Indios
1957	Windsor Park
1958	Cowdray Park
1959	Casarejo
1960	Casarejo
1961	Cowdray Park
1962	Cowdray Park
1963	La Vulchi
1964	Jersey Lilies
1965	Jersey Lilies
1966	Windsor Park
1967	Woolmers Park
1968	Pimms
1969	Windsor Park
1970	Boca Raton
1971	Pimms
1972	Pimms
1973	Stowell Park
1974	Stowell Park
1975	Greenhill Farm
1976	Stowell Park
1977	Foxcote
1978	Stowell Park
1979	Songhai
1980	Stowell Park
1981	Falcons
1982	Southfield
1983	Falcons
1984	Southfield
1985	Maple Leafs
1986	Tramontona
1987	Tramontona
1988	Tramontona
1989	Giscours

OLYMPIC GAMES
Dropped after 1936
1900	Great Britain
1908	Great Britain
1920	Great Britain
1924	Argentina
1936	Argentina

RACKETS

1989

CELESTION AMATEUR DOUBLES
Queen's Club, Feb 1-12
John Prenn & James Male beat Willie Boone & Charles Hue-Williams 15-16 18-13 15-5 15-11 15-4

PROFESSIONAL SINGLES
Queen's Club, Feb 1-12
Neil Smith beat Shannon Hazell 15-12 15-4 14-17 8-15 15-7

RANK XEROX UNIVERSITY MATCH
Queen's Club, Feb 28
Oxford beat Cambridge 2-1

CELESTION OPEN SINGLES
Queen's Club, Mar 3-19
James Male beat Neil Smith 15-11 2-15 15-8 9-15 15-4 15-6

CELESTION OPEN DOUBLES
Queen's Club, Apr 4-16
John Prenn & James Male beat Neil Smith & Shannon Hazell 12-15 0-15 16-14 15-6 15-10 15-12

CHAMPIONS

WORLD CHAMPIONS
Organised on a challenge basis. All winners British unless otherwise stated.
Winners
1820	Robert Mackay
1825	Thomas Pittman
1834	John Pittman
1838	John Lamb
1846	L C Mitchell
1860	Francis Erwood
1862	William Hart Dyke
1863	Henry Gray
1866	William Gray
1876	H B Fairs
1878	Joseph Gray
1887	Peter Latham
1903	J Jamsetjhi (Ind)
1911	Charles Williams
1913	Jock Soutar (US)
1929	Charles Williams
1937	David Milford
1947	James Dear
1954	Geoffrey Atkins
1972	William Surtees (US)
1973	Howard Angus
1974	William Surtees (US)
1981	John Prenn
1984	Willie Boone
1986	John Prenn

REAL TENNIS

1989

GEORGE WIMPEY PROFESSIONALS' DOUBLES
Canford, Jan 6-8
Lachlan Deuchar & Jerome Fletcher beat Chris & Steve Ronaldson 2-6 6-3 6-2

GEORGE WIMPEY LADIES' OPEN DOUBLES
Canford, Jan 6-8
Sally Jones & Alex Warren-Piper beat Katrina Allen & Penny Fellows 6-2 6-3

HENRY LEAF CUP
Queen's Club, Jan 22
Radley beat Wellington 3-0

BATHURST CUP
Mar 23-29
Elimination Round:
Great Britain beat France 5-0; United States beat Australia 3-2
Final: Great Britain beat United States 3-2

RANK XEROX PROFESSIONAL SINGLES
Maidenhead, May 10-14
Chris Ronaldson beat Lachlan Deuchar 2-6 6-5 6-5 6-4

CHAMPIONS

WORLD CHAMPIONS
Organised on a challenge basis

Men
1740	Clerge (Fra)
1765	Raymond Masson (Fra)
1785	Joseph Barcellon (Fra)
1816	Marchesio (Ita)
1819	Phillip Cox (GB)
1829	Edmond Barre (Fra)
1862	Edmund Tomkins (GB)
1871	George Lambert (GB)
1885	Tom Pettitt (US)
1890	Charles Saunders (GB)
1895	Peter Latham (GB)
1905	Cecil Fairs (GB)
1907	Peter Latham (GB)
1908	Cecil Fairs (GB)
1912	Fred Covey (GB)
1914	Jay Gould (US)
1916	Fred Covey (GB)
1928	Pierre Etchebaster (Fra)
1955	James Dear (GB)
1957	Albert Johnson (GB)
1959	Northrup Knox (US)
1969	Pete Bostwick (US)
1972	Jimmy Bostwick (US)
1976	Howard Angus (GB)
1981	Chris Ronaldson (GB)
1987	Wayne Davies (Aus)

Women
First held 1985, contested biennially
1985	Judy Clarke (Aus)
1987	Judy Clarke (Aus)

ROWING

1989

WORLD CHAMPIONSHIPS
Bled, Yugoslavia, Sep 2-10

Men

Single Sculls
1 Thomas Lange (GDR) 6m 58.14s
2 Vaclav Chalupa (Cze) 7m 01.05s
3 Yuri Yanson (USSR) 7m 01.31s

Double Sculls
1 Lars Bjoeness/Rol Bent Thorsen (Nor) 6m 23.40s
2 Nicolaas Riens/Ronald Florijn (Hol) 6m 24.68s
3 Arnold Jonke/Christoph Zerbst (Aut) 6m 25.80s

Quadruple Sculls
1 Holland 6m 03.99s
2 Italy 6m 04.26s
3 Sweden 6m 05.66s

Coxless Pairs
1 Thomas Jung/Uwe Kellner (GDR) 6m 39.95s
2 Steve Redgrave/Simon Berrisford (GB) 6m 42.84s
3 Karl Sinzinger/Hermann Baver (Aut) 6m 43.40s

Coxed Pairs
1 Carmine & Giuseppe Abbagnale (Ita) 6m 54.81s
2 Dragos Neagu/Ioan Snep (Rom) 6m 56.90s
3 Milan Jansa/Robert Krazovec (Yug) 6m 57.97s

Coxless Fours
1 East Germany 6m 06.94s
2 United States 6m 07.92s
3 New Zealand 6m 08.63s

Coxed Fours
1 Romania 6m 14.90s
2 Czechoslovakia 6m 17.37s
3 Great Britain 6m 17.57s

Eights
1 West Germany 5m 43.88s
2 East Germany 5m 45.70s
3 Great Britain 5m 47.01s

Lightweight Single Sculls
1 Frans Goebel (Hol) 7m 17.07s
2 Wim van Balleghem (Bel) 7m 20.03s
3 Alwin Otten (FRG) 7m 21.80s

Lightweight Double Sculls
1 Christoph Schmoezler & Walter Rantasa (Aut) 7m 33.03s
2 Jose Maria de Marco & Fernando Climent (Spa) 7m 03.53s
3 Petr Kovac & Yibor Groeppel (Cze) 7m 04.68s

Lightweight Quadruple Sculls
1 West Germany 6m 04.78s
2 Switzerland 6m 07.24s
3 France 6m 07.50s

Lightweight Coxless Fours
1 West Germany 6m 28.70s
2 Italy 6m 32.36s
3 Great Britain 6m 34.35s

Lightweight Eights
1 Italy 5m 47.95s
2 Denmark 5m 49.38s
3 West Germany 5m 51.15s

Women

Single Sculls
1 Elizabeta Lipa (Rom) 7m 27.96s
2 Birgit Peter (GDR) 7m 31.47s
3 Katalin Sarlos (Hun) 7m 34.15s

Double Sculls
1 Jana Sorgers & Beate Schramm (GDR) 7m 01.71s
2 Veronika Cochela & Elisabeta Lipa (Rom) 7m 07.32s
3 Magdalena Gueorguieva & P Alexandrova (Bul) 7m 11.55s

Quadruple Sculls
1 East Germany 6m 16.62s
2 USSR 6m 22.39s
3 Bulgaria 6m 23.63s

Coxless Pairs
1 Kathrin Haaker & Judith Zeidler (GDR) 7m 26.97s
2 Doina Balan & M Gurelea (Rom) 7m 30.70s
3 S Werremeier & I Althoff (FRG) 7m 31.13s

Coxless Fours
1 East Germany 6m 45.81s
2 China 6m 48.45s
3 Romania 6m 50.58s

Eights
1 Romania 6m 07.92s
2 East Germany 6m 08.19s
3 China 6m 11.84s

Lightweight Single Sculls
1 Kris Karlson (US) 8m 01.12s
2 Rita De Fauw (Bel) 8m 03.14s
3 Laurien Vermulst (Hol) 8m 04.78s

Lightweight Double Sculls
1 Cary Beth Sands & Kris Karlson (US) 7m 11.04s
2 Phillipa Baker & Linda De Jong (NZ) 7m 13.70s
3 Christiane Weber & Alrun Urbach (FRG) 7m 14.94s

Lightweight Coxless Fours
1 China 7m 01.70s
2 Great Britain 7m 04.88s
3 West Germany 7m 06.12s

BOAT RACE
Putney to Mortlake, Mar 25
Oxford University beat Cambridge University by 2 1/2 lengths (8 secs). Time: 18m 27s
Crews
Oxford
Cox: A R M Norrish (Kingston Coll/University)
Stroke: R J Thorp (Shrewsbury/St Johns)
No 7:   J W C Searle (Hampton/Christ Church)
No 6:   M Gaffney (US Naval Academy/Hertford)
No 5:   G Dillon (Becket, King's College London/Oriel)
No 4:   C A Maclennan (Camp Hill/Keble)
No 3:   G C Cheveley (Tonbridge/Pembroke)
No 2:   P F Gleeson (St Martins, Brentwood/Hertford)
Bow: C B Blanchard (KCS/Oriel)
Cambridge
Cox: L Weiss (Harvard/Emmanuel)
Stroke: G R Pooley (Berkhamsted/Imperial College/LMBC)
No 7:   J R Garman (Shrewsbury/LMBC)
No 6:   N R T Justicz (Brown, USA/Sidney Sussex)
No 5:   T J B Backhouse (Winchester/Magdalene)
No 4:   M J Brittin (Hampton/Robinson)
No 3:   P M Mant (Cheltenham/Selwyn)
No 2:   M J K Smith (Shrewsbury/Magdalene)
Bow: R Clarke (Stourport HS/Fitzwilliam)

Reserve Race Isis (Oxford) beat Goldie (Cambridge) by just over 1 length.

WOMEN'S BOAT RACE
Reverse Henley course, Mar 19
Cambridge University beat Oxford University by 5 secs (no time taken)
Reserve Race Osiris (Oxford) beat Blondie (Cambridge) by 1¼ lengths.

150TH HENLEY ROYAL REGATTA
Jun 28-Jul 3

Ladies Plate
Notts County RA 'A' beat Harvard University (US) by ⅔ length. 6m 11s (record)
after a re-run following objection

Visitors' Cup
Isis BC 'A' beat Durham University by 5 lengths. 6m 50s (record)

Thames Cup
University of London beat Ridley College by 3½ lengths. 6m 24s

Special Schools' Race
Bedford Modern beat St Pauls by ¾ length. 4m 33s

Prince Philip Cup
University of London beat Levski Spartak (Bul) by 4 lengths. 6m 51s (equals record)

Wyfold Cup
Leander Club 'A' beat Notts County RA 'B' by 1⅔ lengths. 6m 32s (record)

Britannia Cup
Leander Club beat Lea RC 'A' by 2 lengths. 6m 53s (record)

Stewards' Cup
University of London/Oxford University beat Nautilus RC by 2⅔ lengths. 6m 28s (record)

Grand Challenge Cup
RC Hansa Dortmund (FRG) beat Dinamo (USSR) by 3 lengths. 5m 59s (record)

Princess Elizabeth Cup
Hampton School beat Shiplake College by 1 length. 6m 27s (record)

Queen Mother Cup
SC Eridanea/SC Firenze (Ita) beat Kubanj Krasnodar (USSR) by 3¼ lengths. 6m 15s (record)

Silver Goblets & Nickalls'
Simond Berrisford/Steve Redgrave (Leander Club) beat Volker Grabow/Guido Grabow (RC Witten, FRG) easily, 7m 09s (record)

Diamond Sculls
Vaclav Chalupa (Dukla Praha, Cze) beat Kajetaw Broniewski (AZS-AWF Warszawa, Pol) by 1 length, 7m 23s

Double Sculls
Ronald Floryn (Die Lethe, Hol)/Nicolaas Rienks (Okeanos, Hol) beat P Luzek/I Gruza (Dukla Praha, Cze) by 5 lengths. 7m 04s

——— CHAMPIONS ———

OLYMPIC GAMES
Men
Single Sculls
1900	Henri Barrelet (Fra)
1904	Frank Greer (US)
1908	Harry Blackstaffe (GB)
1912	William Kinnear (GB)
1920	John Kelly Snr (US)
1924	Jack Beresford Jr (GB)
1928	Henry Pearce (Aus)
1932	Henry Pearce (Aus)
1936	Gustav Schäfer (Ger)
1948	Mervyn Wood (Aus)
1952	Yuriy Tyukalov (USSR)
1956	Vyacheslav Ivanov (USSR)
1960	Vyacheslav Ivanov (USSR)
1964	Vyacheslav Ivanov (USSR)
1968	Henri Jan Wienese (Hol)
1972	Yuriy Malishev (USSR)
1976	Pertti Karppinen (Fin)
1980	Pertti Karppinen (Fin)
1984	Pertti Karppinen (Fin)
1988	Thomas Lange (GDR)

Double Sculls
1904	John Mulcahy/William Varley (US)
1920	Paul Costello/John Kelly (US)
1924	Paul Costello/John Kelly (US)
1928	Paul Costello/Charles McIlvaine (US)
1932	William Garrett Gilmore/Kenneth Myers (US)
1936	Jack Beresford/Leslie Southwood (GB)
1948	Richard Burnell/Herbert Bushnell (GB)
1952	Tranquilo Capozzo/Eduardo Guerrero (Arg)
1956	Aleksandr Berkutov/Yuriy Tyukalov (USSR)
1960	Vaclav Kozak/Pavel Schmidt (Cze)
1964	Boris Dubrovsky/Oleg Tyurin (USSR)
1968	Anatoliy Sass/Aleksandr Timoshinin (USSR)
1972	Gennadiy Korshikov/Aleksandr Timoshinin (USSR)
1976	Alf Hansen/Frank Hansen (Nor)
1980	Joachim Dreifke/Klaus Kroppelien (GDR)
1984	Bradley Lewis/Paul Enquist (US)
1988	Ronald Florjin/Nicolaas Rienks (Hol)

Coxless Pairs
1904	Robert Farnam/Joseph Ryan (US)
1908	John Fenning/Gordon Thomson (GB)
1924	Antonie Beijnen/Wilhelm Rosingh (Hol)
1928	Kurt Moeschter/Bruno Muller (Ger)
1932	Lewis Clive/Arthur Edwards (GB)
1936	Willie Eichorn/Hugo Strauss (Ger)
1948	George Laurie/John Wilson (GB)
1952	Charles Logg/Thomas Price (US)
1956	James Fifer/Duvall Hecht (US)
1960	Valentin Boreyko/Oleg Golovanov (USSR)
1964	George Hungerford/Roger Jackson (Can)
1968	Heinz-Jürgen Bothe/Jorg Lucke (GDR)
1972	Siegfried Brietzke/Wolfgang Mager (GDR)
1976	Bernd Landvoigt/Jorg Landvoigt (GDR)
1980	Bernd Landvoigt/Jorg Landvoigt (GDR)
1984	Petru Iosub/Valer Toma (Rom)
1988	Andrew Holmes/Steven Redgrave (GB)

Coxed Pairs
1900	Holland
1906	Italy
1920	Italy
1924	Switzerland
1928	Switzerland
1932	United States
1936	Germany
1948	Denmark
1952	France
1956	United States
1960	West Germany
1964	United States
1968	Italy
1972	East Germany
1976	East Germany
1980	East Germany
1984	Italy
1988	Italy

Quadruple Sculls
1976	East Germany
1980	East Germany
1984	West Germany
1988	Italy

Coxless Fours

1904	United States
1908	Great Britain
1924	Great Britain
1928	Great Britain
1932	Great Britain
1936	Germany
1948	Italy
1952	Yugoslavia
1956	Canada
1960	United States
1964	Denmark
1968	East Germany
1972	East Germany
1976	East Germany
1980	East Germany
1984	New Zealand
1988	East Germany

Coxed Fours

1900	Germany
1900†	France
1912	Germany
1920	Switzerland
1924	Switzerland
1928	Italy
1932	Germany
1936	Germany
1948	United States
1952	Czechoslovakia
1956	Italy
1960	West Germany
1964	West Germany
1968	New Zealand
1972	West Germany
1976	USSR
1980	East Germany
1984	Great Britain
1988	East Germany

† *There were two finals in 1900*

Eights

1900	United States
1904	United States
1908	Great Britain
1912	Great Britain
1920	United States
1924	United States
1928	United States
1932	United States
1936	United States
1948	United States
1952	United States
1956	United States
1960	Germany
1964	United States
1968	West Germany
1972	New Zealand
1976	East Germany
1980	East Germany
1984	Canada
1988	West Germany

Women

Single Sculls

1976	Christine Scheiblich (GDR)
1980	Sanda Toma (Rom)
1984	Valeria Racila (Rom)
1988	Jutta Behrendt (GDR)

Double Sculls

1976	Svetla Otzetova/Zdravka Yordanova (Bul)
1980	Yelena Khlopsteva/Larisa Popova (USSR)
1984	Marioara Popescu/Elisabeta Oleniuc (Rom)
1988	Birgit Peter/Martina Schroeter (GDR)

Coxless Pairs

1976	Stoyanka Grouitcheva/Siika Kelbetcheva (Bul)
1980	Cornelia Klier/Ute Steindorf (GDR)
1984	Rodica Arba/Elena Horvat (Rom)
1988	Rodica Arba/Olga Homeghi (Rom)

Quadruple Sculls

1976	East Germany
1980	East Germany
1984	Romania
1988	East Germany

Coxed Fours

1976	East Germany
1980	East Germany
1984	Romania
1988	East Germany

Eights

1976	East Germany
1980	East Germany
1984	United States
1988	East Germany

WORLD CHAMPIONSHIPS

First held for men 1962, and for women 1974. Not held in Olympic years. Winners in heavyweight classes since 1981:

Men

Single Sculls

1981	Peter-Michael Kolbe (FRG)
1982	Rudiger Reiche (GDR)
1983	Peter-Michael Kolbe (FRG)
1985	Pertti Karppinen (Fin)
1986	Peter-Michael Kolbe (FRG)
1987	Thomas Lange (GDR)
1989	Thomas Lange (GDR)

Double Sculls

1981	Klaus Kroppelien/Joachim Dreifke (GDR)
1982	Alf Hansen/Rolf Thorsen (Nor)
1983	Thomas Lange/Uwe Heppner (GDR)
1985	Thomas Lange/Uwe Heppner (GDR)
1986	Alberto Belgori/Igor Pescialli (Ita)
1987	Danayl Yordanov/Vassil Radev (Bul)
1989	Lars Bjoeness/Rol Bent Thorsen (Nor)

Coxless Pairs

1981	Yuriy Pimenov/Nikolay Pimenov (USSR)
1982	Magnus Grepperud/Sverre Loken (Nor)
1983	Carl Ertel/Ulf Sauerbrey (GDR)
1985	Nikolay Pimenov/Yuriy Pimenov (USSR)
1986	Nikolay Pimenov/Yuriy Pimenov (USSR)
1987	Andrew Holmes/Steven Redgrave (GB)
1989	Thomas Jung/Uwe Kellner (GDR)

Coxed Pairs

1981	Italy
1982	Italy
1983	East Germany
1985	Italy ·
1986	Great Britain
1987	Italy
1989	Italy

Coxless Fours

1981	USSR
1982	Switzerland
1983	West Germany
1985	West Germany
1986	United States
1987	East Germany
1989	East Germany

Coxed Fours

1981	East Germany
1982	East Germany
1983	New Zealand
1985	USSR

1986	East Germany
1987	East Germany
1989	Romania

Quadruple Sculls
1981	East Germany
1982	East Germany
1983	West Germany
1985	Canada
1986	USSR
1987	USSR
1989	Holland

Eights
1981	USSR
1982	New Zealand
1983	New Zealand
1985	USSR
1986	Australia
1987	United States
1989	West Germany

Women
Single Sculls
1981	Sanda Toma (Rom)
1982	Irina Fetissova (USSR)
1983	Jutta Hampe (GDR)
1985	Cornelia Linse (GDR)
1986	Jutta Hampe (GDR)
1987	Magdalena Georgieva (Bul)
1989	Elisabeta Lipa (Rom)

Double Sculls
1981	Margarita Kokarevitha/Antonina Makhina (USSR)
1982	Yelena Braticko/Antonina Makhina (USSR)
1983	Jutta Scheck/Martina Schroter (GDR)
1985	Sylvia Schurabe/Martina Schroter (GDR)
1986	Sylvia Schurabe/Beate Schramm (GDR)
1987	Steska Madina/Violeta Ninova (Bul)
1989	Jana Sorgers/Beate Schramm (GDR)

Coxless Pairs
1981	Sigrid Anders/Iris Rudoph (GDR)
1982	Silvia Frohlich/Marita Sandig (GDR)
1983	Silvia Frohlich/Marita Sandig (GDR)
1985	Rodica Arba/Elena Florea (Rom)
1986	Rodica Arba/Olga Homeghi (Rom)
1987	Rodica Arba/Olga Homeghi (Rom)
1989	Kathrin Haaker/Judith Zeidler (GDR)

Quadruple Sculls
1981	USSR
1982	USSR
1983	USSR
1985	East Germany
1986	East Germany
1987	East Germany
1989	East Germany

Coxed Fours
1981	USSR
1982	USSR
1983	East Germany
1985	East Germany
1986	Romania
1987	Romania
1989	–

Coxless Fours
1986	United States
1987	–
1989	East Germany

Eights
1987	Romania
1989	Romania

UNIVERSITY BOAT RACE
Cambridge wins (69):
1836, 1839-41, 1845-46, 1849, 1856, 1858, 1860, 1870-74, 1876, 1879, 1884, 1886-89, 1899-1900, 1902-04, 1906-08, 1914, 1920-22, 1924-36, 1939, 1947-51, 1953, 1955-58, 1961-62, 1964, 1968-73, 1975, 1986
Oxford wins (65):
1829, 1842, 1849, 1852, 1854, 1857, 1859, 1861-69, 1875, 1878, 1880-83, 1885, 1890-98, 1901, 1905, 1909-13, 1923, 1937-38, 1946, 1952, 1954, 1959-60, 1963, 1965-67, 1974, 1976-85, 1987-89
There was a dead-heat in 1877
Fastest Time: 16 min 45 sec, Oxford (1984)
Biggest winning margin: 20 lengths, Cambridge (1900)
Most winning boats: 6 – Boris Rankov (Oxford) 1978-83

HENLEY ROYAL REGATTA
Diamond Sculls
Inaugurated 1884. Winners since 1980
1980	Riccardo Ibarra (Arg)
1981	Chris Baillieu (GB)
1982	Chris Baillieu (GB)
1983	Steven Redgrave (GB)
1984	Chris Baillieu (GB)
1985	Steven Redgrave (GB)
1986	Bjarne Eltang (Den)
1987	Peter-Michael Kolbe (FRG)
1988	Hamish McGlashan (Aus)
1989	Vaclav Chalupa (Cze)

Most wins
6 Guy Nickalls (1888-91, 1893-94), Stuart Mackenzie 1957-62; **5** A A Casamajor 1855-58, 1861, J Lowndes 1879-83

Grand Challenge Cup
First held 1839. Winners since 1980
1980	Charles River RA (US)
1981	Oxford University/Thames Tradesmen (GB)
1982	Leander/London RC (GB)
1983	London RC/University of London (GB)
1984	Leander/London RC (GB)
1985	Harvard University (US)
1986	Nautilus (GB)
1987	Soviet Army (USSR)
1988	Leander/University of London (GB)
1989	RC Hansa Dortmund (FRG)

Most wins
31 Leander Club 1840, 1875, 1880, 1891-94, 1896, 1898-1901, 1903-05, 1913, 1922, 1924-26, 1929, 1932, 1934, 1946, 1949, 1952-53, 1975†, 1982†, 1984†, 1988†
(† Boat shared with either Thames Tradesmen, London RC or University of London)

═══════ 1990 ═══════

Mar 31: Oxford v Cambridge, University Boat Race (Putney to Mortlake) 16.30hrs;

Jun 21-25: National championships (Holme Pierrepont, Nottingham);

Jul 4-8: Henley Royal Regatta (Henley-on-Thames);

Oct 27-Nov 4: World championships (Tasmania).

RUGBY LEAGUE

THE STAR WIDNES

Five days into 1989, rugby league scored possibly its greatest triumph yet against rugby union when Jonathan Davies, perhaps the most talked-about RU player of his generation, deserted Llanelli, Wales and the chance of the Lions captaincy to join Widnes. Davies became the 154th Welsh international to switch codes. Nothing on the field quite matched the drama of this news, long rumoured and long denied. Davies's decision was apparently influenced by the fate of Mark Ring, who rejected a lucrative move to Hull Kingston Rovers and immediately got injured; he was also annoyed by the offhand attitude of Welsh officials at his last training session.

The Widnes coach Doug Laughton cheekily named Davies in his squad for the John Player final before he actually signed. In the event, Davies watched Widnes lose from the stands while everyone watched him. He didn't quite have the immediate impact on the field of his new team-mate Martin Offiah, who scored 60 tries in the season and reached 100 in his RL career in 80 games, and a record 17½ months. But Davies's move encouraged yet more well-known Welshmen to think about migration. Widnes themselves later signed Paul Moriarty from Swansea and Jonathan Griffiths moved from Llanelli to St Helens.

Widnes went on to retain the Championship after the fixture list threw up a remarkable finale: a winner-take-all home game with Wigan, who were only one point behind and still in with a chance of the grand slam. However, Widnes scored four tries in 12 minutes either side of half-time to win 32-18 even though their Tongan star, Emosi Koloto, was sent off. The game took place the day after the Hillsborough disaster and at the time any sporting triumph round Merseyside seemed hollow. Widnes also retained the Premiership, with an 18-10 win over Hull at Old Trafford.

For much of the season, Castleford had high hopes of a first Championship. They were unbeaten for 12 games up to early January and they led the table until March 18. Their coach Darryl van der Velde had Ten Commandments posted on the dressing room wall including "Winners make commitments. Losers make promises". Alas, Castleford's promise faded badly and they finished fifth. Widnes beat them 36-4 on March 30 and captured the lead, which they clung on to despite Wigan's late surge, which included 12 successive wins.

Just about everything else went to Wigan, including the Challenge Cup for the second year running. They recorded the biggest win in the final since 1960, 27-0 over St Helens, after a game dominated by Ellery Hanley. Wigan's coach, Graham Lowe, resigned afterwards to spend more time with his family in Queensland after winning 11 trophies with the club in three years. St Helens reacted by putting 13 of their squad up for transfer. The Leeds-Widnes quarter-final had been watched by Headingley's first full house (26,282) since the 1960s.

Leigh easily won the Second Division and, just as easily, Runcorn Highfield came bottom. Runcorn also lost 92-2 to Wigan in the JPS Trophy, using nine amateurs because their players had gone on strike. Their coach, Bill Ashurst, a 41-year-old born-again Christian, came on as substitute and 11 minutes later was sent off for head-butting. Joe Lydon of Wigan was given a nine-month suspended prison sentence for head-butting a 15-year-old fan at St Helens. Lydon believed the boy had been shouting abuse and told the court he had caught his injured finger in the boy's clothing: "My immediate reaction was to free myself using my head."

Fulham advertised in *The Times* for sponsors under the heading "Attention Sporting Angels". Hull Kingston Rovers and York left their traditional homes, Craven Park and Wigginton Road, for new stadia and a profit from developers. Chorley Borough moved south to share Altrincham FC's ground, changing their name to Trafford Borough; a new Chorley club was admitted to the League. Mansfield Marksmen also moved south to become Nottingham City. Wigan and Warrington briefly went west to play in Milwaukee; 16,500 people turned up but the NFL did not visibly quake.

The New South Wales Rugby League launched a million-pound promotional campaign using the well-known RL figure Tina Turner. In New Zealand, Jamie Kahakura, 26, played stand-off for Whakaki in the Gisborne-East Coast competition before being banned for being female.

1988-89

STONES BITTER CHAMPIONSHIP
Division One

			P	W	D	L	F	A	Pts	Av. Home Attendance
1	(1)	WIDNES	26	20	1	5	726	345	41	8,648
2	(3)	WIGAN	26	19	0	7	543	434	38	14,543
3	(5)	LEEDS	26	18	0	8	530	380	36	12,060
4	(10)	HULL	26	17	0	9	427	355	34	6,804
5	(7)	CASTLEFORD	26	15	2	9	601	480	32	6,580
6	(P)	FEATHERSTONE R	26	13	1	12	482	545	27	4,379
7	(2)	ST HELENS	26	12	1	13	513	529	25	9,514
8	(4)	BRADFORD N	26	11	1	14	545	518	23	4,969
9	(P)	WAKEFIELD T	26	11	1	14	413	540	23	5,151
10	(11)	SALFORD	26	11	0	15	469	526	22	5,470
11	(6)	WARRINGTON	26	10	0	16	456	455	20	4,893
12	(P)	*OLDHAM*	26	8	1	17	462	632	17	5,759
13	(8)	*HALIFAX*	26	6	1	19	335	535	13	8,022
14	(9)	*HULL KR*	26	6	1	19	408	636	13	5,298

LEADING SCORERS 1988-89

Tries
60 Martin Offiah (Widnes)
29 Ellery Hanley (Wigan)
24 Les Quirk (St Helens)
24 Grant Anderson (Castleford)

Goals
129 Martin Ketteridge (Castleford)
118 David Hobbs (Bradford N)
113 Paul Loughlin (St Helens)

Points
289 Andy Currier (Widnes)
271 David Hobbs (Bradford N)
270 Martin Ketteridge (Castleford)

Results: Division One

	BN	C	F	HA	HU	HKR	L	O	STH	S	WT	WAR	WID	WIG
Bradford N	x	6-20	23-32	30-18	32-20	38-14	10-18	30-10	12-16	42-18	8-28	15-4	16-16	17-21
Castleford	38-20	x	14-14	30-0	16-23	38-20	38-0	22-19	46-12	38-12	38-14	23-16	22-24	4-17
Featherstone R	20-48	20-26	x	21-17	25-22	28-6	18-32	18-14	13-12	22-18	14-15	15-14	10-22	19-24
Halifax	26-14	21-12	4-24	x	6-14	12-12	20-23	0-12	40-8	21-12	20-22	4-16	26-20	16-20
Hull	28-10	8-18	4-14	24-4	x	26-2	14-12	11-8	21-12	12-6	10-16	10-8	23-16	18-28
Hull KR	24-22	32-30	15-30	12-4	12-15	x	13-18	34-6	22-30	18-24	38-18	7-17	13-16	18-19
Leeds	10-7	32-18	36-18	34-12	6-13	21-8	x	48-4	32-0	18-16	28-16	8-22	14-30	22-14
Oldham	14-30	34-18	40-18	12-14	9-7	30-16	22-28	x	22-26	23-22	24-8	16-2	16-35	21-27
St Helens	23-16	14-14	10-31	50-16	9-20	29-0	15-6	58-12	x	30-14	30-14	30-16	16-44	11-18
Salford	33-18	18-20	8-12	22-4	6-18	24-14	6-24	38-20	22-4	x	18-8	25-18	15-12	24-16
Wakefield T	14-23	26-8	19-12	27-10	2-11	6-12	14-12	12-12	21-14	18-36	x	14-10	14-28	25-20
Warrington	22-23	20-26	30-22	33-4	20-14	60-24	8-10	32-30	14-25	18-6	30-18	x	8-18	4-13
Widnes	12-22	36-4	58-2	5-4	38-6	43-6	8-20	38-14	29-22	50-8	40-12	32-4	x	32-18
Wigan	20-13	12-20	14-10	26-12	20-35	32-16	16-8	40-18	14-7	28-18	34-12	26-10	10-24	x

Division Two

			P	W	D	L	F	A	Pts	Av. Home Attendance
1	(R)	**LEIGH**	28	26	0	2	925	338	52	2,346
2	(9)	**BARROW**	28	21	1	6	726	326	43	1,594
3	(5)	**SHEFFIELD E**	28	19	1	8	669	362	39	838
4	(6)	YORK	28	17	1	10	585	383	35	2,021
5	(R)	SWINTON	28	16	2	10	621	482	34	1,435
6	(16)	DONCASTER	28	17	0	11	599	464	34	1,906
7	(13)	WHITEHAVEN	28	15	2	11	522	378	32	1,310
8	(8)	KEIGHLEY	28	16	0	12	551	525	32	961
9	(18)	ROCHDALE H	28	15	0	13	655	677	30	1,027
10	(14)	BRAMLEY	28	14	1	13	600	514	29	1,004
11	(11)	CARLISLE	28	14	1	13	512	441	29	678
12	(20)	BATLEY	28	13	3	12	461	416	29	924
13	(15)	DEWSBURY	28	13	0	15	518	626	26	772
14	(17)	HUNSLET	28	12	1	15	473	540	25	947
15	(17)	FULHAM	28	10	0	18	464	650	20	588
16	(4)	CHORLEY B	28	9	1	18	408	533	19	512
17	(10)	WORKINGTON T	28	9	1	18	365	549	19	774
18	(19)	HUDDERSFIELD B	28	9	1	18	400	615	19	1,114
19	(7)	MANSFIELD M	28	4	1	23	308	769	9	560
20	(12)	RUNCORN H	28	2	1	25	224	998	5	298

LEADING SCORERS 1988-89

Tries	*Goals*	*Points*
34 Barrie Ledger (Leigh)	148 Mark Aston (Sheffield E)	307 Mark Aston (Sheffield E)
32 Derek Bate (Swinton)	117 Chris Johnson (Leigh)	279 Chris Johnson (Leigh)
28 Peter Lister (Bramley)	115 Dean Marwood (Barrow)	
28 Darryl Powell (Sheffield E)	110 David Noble (Doncaster)	

SILK CUT CHALLENGE CUP

PRELIMINARY ROUND

Barrow Island 11 THATTO HEATH 18; LEEDS 32 Hunslet 6; Milford 0 SWINTON 36; WAKEFIELD T 18 Bramley 10; West Hull 2 DONCASTER 48; YORK 35 Workington T 8

FIRST ROUND

Hull 4 CASTLEFORD 7; BARROW 38 Huddersfield B 16; CARLISLE 58 Mansfield M 1; CHORLEY B 8 Thatto Heath 4; Dewsbury 9 OLDHAM 40; Doncaster 6 WIGAN 38; Fulham 10 BRADFORD N 28; Rochdale 24 HULL KR 28; Runcorn 8 KEIGHLEY 28; Salford 14 WIDNES 18; SHEFFIELD E 23 Leigh 17; Swinton 5 ST HELENS 16; WAKEFIELD T 3 Batley 4; Whitehaven 0 FEATHERSTONE R 32; York 9 LEEDS 28

SECOND ROUND

Bradford Northern 4 WIGAN 17; Castleford 18 WIDNES 32; HULL KINGSTON ROVERS 28 Chorley 4; LEEDS 24 Carlisle 4; ST HELENS 28 Barrow 6; Sheffield Eagles 20 OLDHAM 32; Wakefield Trinity 4 FEATHERSTONE ROVERS 10; WARRINGTON 56 Keighley 7

THIRD ROUND

Oldham 4 WIGAN 12; Hull Kingston Rovers 4 WARRINGTON 30; Leeds 4 WIDNES 24; ST HELENS 32 Featherstone Rovers 3

SEMI-FINALS

ST HELENS 16 Widnes 14 (at Central Park, Wigan. Att: 17,119); Warrington 6 WIGAN 13 (at Maine Road, Manchester. Att: 26,529)

FINAL

WIGAN 27 St Helens 0
Wembley, Apr 29
T: K.Iro(2), Hanley, Gregory, Hampson
G: Lydon(3)
DG: Gregory
Wigan: Hampson, A Iro, K Iro, Bell, Lydon, Edwards, Gregory, Lucas, Kiss (Betts), Shelford, Platt, Potter (Goodway), Hanley
St Helens: Connolly, O'Connor, Veivers, Loughlin (Bloor), Quirk, Cooper, Holding, Burke, Groves, Forber, Dwyer (Evans), Haggerty (Dwyer), Vautin
Referee: R.F. Tennant (Castleford)
Attendance: 78,000

PREMIERSHIP FINALS

Old Trafford, May 14
Attendance: 40,194

STONES BITTER PREMIERSHIP

Widnes 18 Hull 10

2ND DIVISION PREMIERSHIP

Sheffield Eagles 43 Swinton 18

JOHN PLAYER SPECIAL TROPHY FINAL

Burnden Park: Wigan 12 Widnes 6 Att: 20,709

JOHN SMITH'S YORKSHIRE CUP FINAL

Elland Road: Leeds 33 Castleford 12 Att: 23,000

GRUNHALLE LAGER LANCASHIRE CUP FINAL

Knowsley Road: Wigan 22 Salford 17 Att: 19,167

CIS CHARITY SHIELD

Anfield: Widnes 27 Wigan 22

WORLD CUP FINAL

Eden Park, Auckland. New Zealand 12 Australia 25 Att: 48,000

WHITBREAD TEST MATCHES

1st Test Wigan: Great Britain 26 France 10 Att: 8,266
2nd Test Avignon: France 8 Great Britain 30 Att: 12,000

SYDNEY GRAND FINAL

Sydney: Canberra 19 Balmain 14

THE TRAIL FROM WALES

The following Welsh RU internationals have all joined the professional game in the 1980s:

Tommy David, Pontypridd to Cardiff City, 1981-82

Steve Fenwick, Bridgend to Cardiff City, 1981-82

Paul Ringer, Llanelli to Cardiff City, 1981-82

Brynmor Williams, Swansea to Cardiff City, 1982-83

Rob Ackerman, Cardiff to Whitehaven, 1985-86

Terry Holmes, Cardiff to Bradford N, 1985-86

Gary Pearce, Llanelli to Hull, 1986-87

Stuart Evans, Neath to St Helens, 1987-88

David Bishop, Pontypool to Hull KR, 1988-89

Adrian Hadley, Cardiff to Salford 1988-89

Jonathan Davies, Llanelli to Widnes, 1988-89

Jonathan Griffiths, Llanelli to St Helens 1988-89

Paul Moriarty, Swansea to Widnes, 1988-89

AWARDS:

Man of Steel Ellery Hanley (Wigan)
Coach of the Year Graham Lowe (Wigan)
First Division Player of the Year David Hulme (Widnes)
Second Division Player of the Year Darryl Powell (Sheffield E)
Young Player of the Year Paul Newlove (Featherstone R)

CHAMPIONS

	Challenge Cup	Premiership	Championship (1)	Div.1 (2)	Regal Trophy (3)
Barrow	1955				
Batley	1897, 1898, 1901		1924		
Bradford Northern	1906*, 1944, 1947 1949	1978		1980, 1981	1975, 1980
Broughton R	1902, 1911				
Castleford	1935, 1969, 1970 1986				1977
Dewsbury	1912, 1943		1973		
Featherstone R	1967, 1973, 1983			1977	
Halifax	1903, 1904, 1931, 1939, 1987		1907, 1965	1986	1972
Huddersfield	1913, 1915, 1920, 1933, 1945, 1953		1912, 1913, 1915, 1929, 1930, 1949 1962		
Hull	1914, 1982		1920, 1921, 1936, 1956, 1958	1983	1982
Hull Kingston R	1980	1981, 1984	1923, 1925	1979, 1984, 1985	1985
Hunslet	1908, 1934		1908, 1938		
Leeds	1910, 1923, 1932, 1936, 1941, 1942, 1957, 1968, 1977, 1978	1975, 1979	1961, 1969, 1972		1973, 1984
Leigh	1921, 1971		1906	1982	
Oldham	1899, 1925, 1927		1910, 1911, 1957		
Rochdale Hornets	1922				
St Helens	1956, 1961, 1966, 1972, 1976	1976, 1977, 1985	1932, 1953, 1959, 1966, 1970, 1971	1975	1988
Salford	1938		1914, 1933, 1937, 1939	1974, 1976	
Swinton	1900, 1926, 1928		1927, 1928, 1931 1935		
Wakefield Trinity	1909, 1946, 1960, 1962, 1963		1967, 1968		
Warrington	1905, 1907, 1950, 1954, 1974	1986	1948, 1954, 1955	1981	1974, 1978,
Widnes	1930, 1937, 1964, 1975, 1979, 1981, 1984	1980, 1982, 1983, 1988, 1989		1978, 1988, 1989	1976, 1979
Wigan	1924, 1929, 1948, 1951, 1958, 1959, 1965, 1985, 1988, 1989	1987	1909, 1922, 1926, 1934, 1946, 1947, 1950, 1952, 1960	1987	1983,1986, 1987,1989
Workington T	1952		1951		

* As Bradford
(1) Championship Play-off 1907-72
(2) Division One 1974-89
(3) Formerly John Player Special Trophy

OTHER COMPETITIONS
Division Two
(Since 1973-74)
1974 Bradford Northern; **1975** Huddersfield; **1976** Barrow; **1977** Hull; **1978** Leigh; **1979** Hull; **1980** Featherstone Rovers; **1981** York; **1982** Oldham; **1983** Fulham; **1984** Barrow; **1985** Swinton; **1986** Leigh; **1987** Hunslet; **1988** Oldham; **1989** Leigh

LANCASHIRE COUNTY CUP
Wins:
20 Wigan 1906, 1909-10, 1913, 1923, 1929, 1939, 1947-52, 1967, 1972, 1974, 1986-89; **10** St Helens 1927, 1954, 1961-65, 1968-69, 1985; **9** Oldham 1908, 1911, 1914, 1920, 1925, 1934, 1957-59; **8** Warrington 1922, 1930, 1933, 1938, 1960, 1966, 1981, 1983; **6** Widnes 1946, 1975-77, 1979-80; **5** Salford 1932, 1935-37, 1973; **4** Leigh 1953, 1956, 1971, 1982; Swinton 1926, 1928, 1940, 1970; **3** Rochdale Hornets 1912, 1915, 1919; **2** Barrow 1955, 1984; **1** Workington Town 1978

YORKSHIRE COUNTY CUP
Wins:
17 Leeds 1922, 1929, 1931, 1933, 1935-36, 1938, 1959, 1969, 1971, 1973-74, 1976-77, 1980-81, 1989; **12** Huddersfield 1910, 1912, 1914-15, 1919-20, 1927, 1932, 1939, 1951, 1953, 1958; **11** Bradford Northern 1907, 1941-42, 1944, 1946, 1949-50, 1954, 1966, 1979, 1988; **9** Wakefield Trinity 1911, 1925, 1947-48, 1952, 1957, 1961-62, 1965; **7** Hull KR 1921, 1930, 1967-68, 1972, 1975, 1986; **5** Halifax 1909, 1945, 1955-56, 1964, Hull 1924, 1970, 1983-85; **3** Castleford 1978, 1982, 1987, Dewsbury 1926, 1928, 1943, Hunslet 1906, 1908, 1963, York 1923, 1934, 1937; **2** Featherstone Rovers 1940, 1960; **1** Batley 1913
(Years indicate second half of season.)

CHARITY SHIELD
Winners:
1985 Wigan; **1986** Halifax; **1987** Wigan; **1988** Widnes; **1989** Widnes

WORLD CUP
Wins:
6 Australia 1957, 1968, 1970, 1975*, 1977, 1988; **3** Great Britain 1954, 1960, 1972
* Known as The International Championship

SYDNEY PREMIERSHIP
Wins:
20 South Sydney 1908-09, 1914, 1918, 1925-29, 1931-32, 1950-51, 1953-55, 1967-68, 1970-71; **15** St George 1941, 1949, 1956-66, 1977, 1979; **11** Balmain 1915-17, 1919-20, 1924, 1939, 1944, 1946-47, 1969; Eastern Suburbs 1911-13, 1923, 1935-37, 1940, 1945, 1974-75

CLUBS WHO HAVE JOINED AND LEFT THE RUGBY LEAGUE SINCE THE WAR
1945	**In** Workington Town
	Out St Helens Recs, Leigh
1946	**In** Leigh
1948	**In** Whitehaven
1951	**In** Cardiff, Doncaster
1952	**Out** Cardiff
1954	**In** Blackpool Borough
1955	**Out** Belle Vue Rangers
1963	**Out** Bradford Northern
1964	**In** Bradford Northern (*)
1980	**In** Fulham
1981	**In** Cardiff City, Carlisle
1983	**In** Kent Invicta
1984	**In** Mansfield Marksmen, Sheffield Eagles
1985	**Out** Southend (formerly Kent Invicta), Bridgend (formerly Cardiff City)
1989	**In** Chorley

(*) Bradford Northern disbanded after 13 matches of the 1963-64 season but were re-formed for the start of the 1964-65 season.

LANCE TODD/HARRY SUNDERLAND WINNERS
(Since 1976)

	Lance Todd*	Harry Sunderland†
1976	Geoff Pimblett	George Nicholls
	St Helens	*St Helens*
1977	Steve Pitchford	Geoff Pimblett
	Leeds	*St Helens*
1978	George Nicholls	Bob Haigh
	St Helens	*Bradford Northern*
1979	Dave Topliss	Kevin Dick
	Wakefield Trinity	*Leeds*
1980	Brian Lockwood	Mal Aspey
	Hull Kingston Rovers	*Widnes*
1981	Mick Burke	Len Casey
	Widnes	*Hull Kingston Rovers*
1982	Eddie Cunningham	Mick Burke
	Widnes	*Widnes*
1983	David Hobbs	Tony Myler
	Featherstone Rovers	*Widnes*
1984	Joe Lydon	John Dorahy
	Widnes	*Hull Kingston Rovers*
1985	Brett Kenny	Harry Pinner
	Wigan	*St Helens*
1986	Bob Beardmore	Les Boyd
	Castleford	*Warrington*
1987	Graham Eadie	Joe Lydon
	Halifax	*Wigan*
1988	Andy Gregory	David Hulme
	Wigan	*Widnes*
1989	Ellery Hanley	Alan Tait
	Wigan	*Widnes*

* Man of match in Challenge Cup Final
† Man of match in Premiership Final

AWARDS
Man of Steel
1978	George Nicholls (St Helens)
1979	Doug Laughton (Widnes)
1980	George Fairbairn (Wigan)
1981	Ken Kelly (Warrington)
1982	Mick Morgan (Oldham)
1983	Allan Agar (Featherstone R)
1984	Joe Lydon (Widnes)
1985	Ellery Hanley (Bradford N)
1986	Gavin Miller (Hull KR)
1987	Ellery Hanley (Wigan)
1988	Martin Offiah (Widnes)
1989	Ellery Hanley (Wigan)

1st Division Player of the Year
1978	George Nicholls (St Helens)
1979	Mick Adams (Widnes)
1980	Mick Adams (Widnes)
1981	Ken Kelly (Warrington)
1982	Steve Norton (Hull)
1983	Keith Mumby (Bradford N)
1984	Joe Lydon (Widnes)
1985	Ellery Hanley (Bradford N)
1986	Gavin Miller (Hull KR)
1987	Andy Gregory (Wigan)
1988	Steve Hampson (Wigan)
1989	David Hulme (Widnes)

Coach of the Year
1978	Frank Myler (Widnes)
1979	Doug Laughton (Widnes)
1980	Peter Fox (Bradford N)
1981	Billy Benyon (Warrington)
1982	Arthur Bunting (Hull)
1983	Arthur Bunting (Hull)
1984	Tommy Dawes (Barrow)
1985	Roger Millward (Hull KR)
1986	Chris Anderson (Halifax)
1987	Graham Lowe (Wigan)
1988	Doug Laughton (Widnes)
1989	Graham Lowe (Wigan)

Most Awards:
4 Ellery Hanley (3 Man of Steel, 1 Div. 1), Fred Lindop (4 Referee of Year); 3 Joe Lydon (Man of Steel, Div. 1, Young Player of Year), Shaun Edwards (3 Young Player of Year).

———— RECORDS ————

ALL FIRST-CLASS MATCHES
Single Game Records
Biggest win: 119-2 Huddersfield v Swinton Park Rangers (Challenge Cup) 1914; **Most tries in a match:** 11 George Henry West, Hull Kingston Rovers v Brookland Rovers (Challenge Cup) 1905; **Most goals in a match:** 22 Jim Sullivan, Wigan v Flimby & Fothergill (Challenge Cup), 1925;

Most points in a match: 53 George Henry West (as above)

Season Records
Most tries: 80 Albert Rosenfeld (Huddersfield) 1913-14; **Most goals:** 221 David Watkins (Salford) 1972-3; **Most points:** 496 (194 goals, 36 tries) Lewis Jones (Leeds) 1956-7

Career Records
Most tries: 796 Brian Bevan (Warrington & Blackpool Borough) 1946-64; **Most goals:** 2,859 Jim Sullivan (Wigan) 1921-46; **Most points:** 6,220 Neil Fox (Wakefield Trinity, Bradford Northern, Hull Kingston Rovers, York, Bramley, Huddersfield) 1956-79; **Most appearances:** 921 Jim Sullivan (Wigan) 1921-46; **Most consecutive club appearances:** 239 Keith Elwell (Widnes) May 1977-Sep 1982; **Most consecutive games scoring points:** 92 David Watkins (Salford) Aug 1972-Apr 1974

INTERNATIONAL MATCHES
Most appearances: 60 Jim Sullivan, Wales, Great Britain & Other Nationalities, 1921-39; **Most tries:** 45 Mick Sullivan, Great Britain & England 1954-63; **Most goals:** 160 Jim Sullivan; **Most points:** 329 Jim Sullivan; **Biggest win:** 70-8 Australia v Papua New Guinea, 1988

———— 1990 ————

Jan 13: Regal Trophy Final; *Jan 21:* Under-21 international, France v Britain (Villeneuve); *Jan 28:* Challenge Cup First Round; *Feb 11:* Challenge Cup Second Round; *Feb 16:* Under-21 international, Britain v France (tba); *Feb 25:* Challenge Cup Third Round; *Mar 10* and *Mar 31:* Challenge Cup semi-finals; *Apr 7:* Test match Britain v France (tba); *Apr 28:* Silk Cut CHALLENGE CUP FINAL (Wembley); *May 13:* Premiership Final (Old Trafford).

RUGBY UNION

THE COMEBACK OF THE YEAR

The traditional British ability to win the last battle came out in remarkable fashion when Finlay Calder's Lions, having been humiliated in the opening Test in Australia, came back stunningly to take the series. Calder reportedly resigned after the defeat. They won the Second Test in Brisbane with two late tries, then went back to Sydney with renewed confidence for the decider. Even then, Australia were 12-9 up but suddenly the great David Campese made a terrible pass and Ieuan Evans pounced on it to score.

However, there were times in the series when the ball seemed irrelevant. It was an exceptionally butch tour. There was a lot of punching on the field and a great many words off it, none of them involving the Test match referee, René Hourquet, who spoke no English. The Australians sent a video-nasty of the Second Test incidents to the four home unions. The Lions hardly protested innocence when accused of brutality; they just claimed they were adopting Australian tactics.

Mike Teague, the Gloucester flanker, was voted man of the series, having been left out of the original Test team and coming close to drowning (along with David Young) during a boating excursion on the Barron River in North Queensland. The excitement of the tour helped secure the future of the Lions - despite the loss of South Africa as a destination - but they will now go abroad at four-yearly intervals instead of three, with New Zealand scheduled for 1993.

The euphoria was hardly dampened by the news from New Zealand, where the All-Blacks won five internationals - two against France, two against Argentina and a 24-12 win in the Bledisloe Cup against Australia - to remind everyone who really dominates world rugby.

This took their unbeaten run to 17 since losing to France in 1986, equalling their records of 1961-4 and 1965-70.

After the Lions tour, a "World XV", paid either £18 a day expenses or £35,000 blood money depending on who you believe, turned up in South Africa managed by Willie-John McBride, who said they were all there just to play rugby. Members of the Cape Malay Traditional singers composed a song in honour of the head of South African Rugby, Dr Danie Craven, which was performed at Newlands as part of the matchday entertainment. Demonstrations against the tour were banned by the South African Government.

The Party included 10 Welshmen among the players and six Welsh Rugby Union committeemen among the hangers-on. Mike Hall, one of the 10, was evicted from his flat by his anti-apartheid landlord. Clive Rowlands, the Welsh Rugby Union president, and David East, secretary for only eight months, resigned in protest at their colleagues' attitude - though Rowlands' resignation lasted only 24 hours.

ENCORE UNE FOIS

France won the Five Nations Championship for the fourth successive year (a tie with Scotland in 1986 followed by three outright wins). This was the result expected before the competition began, but not on the final morning when England only needed to beat Wales to be champions. However, Wales beat England in the Arms Park mud, extending England's winless sequence there to 26 years, which was the compensation the Welsh wanted for a year of humiliation after the 1988 Triple Crown which included defeat by everyone except Western Samoa.

England started disappointingly with a draw in the Calcutta Cup, when they had all the possession but could do nothing with it. They then won a bruising battle in Dublin ("Any player pausing for a micro-second to assess his options," wrote Stephen Jones in the *Sunday Times*, "was likely to wake up 10 minutes later") and their forwards were sufficiently fired up to dominate France and beat them at Twickenham for the first time in 10 years.

Wales, having lost Jonathan Davies to the officially-paid game before the tournament began, were in a hopeless state; in December they had even lost at home to Romania (an almost identical Romanian side later lost 58-3 to England), and their 31-12 defeat in Paris was their heaviest in the Championship since 1924. But when England are at the Arms Park, normal form disappears, and Wales won.

The game of the Championship was the eight-try bonanza between Scotland and Ireland; six of the tries came in just 25 minutes before half-time: "Hogmanay, Burns Night and St Patrick's Day all rolled into one," said David Irvine of *The Guardian*. Later, though, the Scots had a humiliation greater than anything Wales had suffered when a near full-strength team went down 28-24 to Japan. Wisely, Scotland had decided not to count it as a full international.

"We need a modesty which recognises that the All Blacks practise the most intelligent game in the world. France needs the discipline and vigour of the world champions."
Jacques Fouroux, French coach

" I have no doubt that the static game which has been played by so many European sides during the past decade is finished. And yet Fouroux continues with this policy. He is taking France backwards."
Pierre Villepreux

Pierre Villepreux (coaching England): "If you get tired, just say OK, Pierre." England players: "OK Pierre."

"The English are mentally inferior rugby-wise. They feel inferior and they play inferior." *Brian Thomas, Neath coach*

"The dead hand of committees is everywhere."
Defector Jonathan Davies on the Welsh Rugby Union

"I didn't want to be treated like a star - a human being would have done."
Defector Paul Moriarty, ditto

"Matters have reached such depths of duplicity that if the Welsh Rugby Union was a publicly-owned commercial concern, it would surely have been put into liquidation and a receiver called in".
Clem Thomas, the Observer, *after the row over South Africa.*

"When did he ever REALLY run for Wales the way Bennett and John used to? I saw him running backwards quite a bit."
Bobby Windsor on Davies.

"Look here, England have just played a match against Romania. That's an oppressive place, but I haven't had one single letter of protest about that. Why is it that you chaps always get so emotional about South Africa?"
Dudley Wood, RFU secretary to Frank Keating of The Guardian.

EARLY BATH

The English club season was dominated yet again by Bath and they made sure of winning the First Division on March 11, six weeks before their final game. From April 2 1988 to February 17 1989 Bath went unbeaten for 40 games before losing 18-12 to Gloucester at Kingsholm. With a weakened team, Bath later lost 17-13 at home to Newport and, idling, went down 15-12 to Leicester the week before they met again in the Cup Final.

When it mattered, though, there was only one winner. Bath left it late but a try by Stuart Barnes two minutes from time gave them the trophy for the fifth time in six years. Bath also signed a new £150,000 sponsorship deal to develop training facilities, talked of expanding their fixture list to play the best clubs overseas and generally exuded an air of efficiency and ambition that in any other sport could safely be called professional. Not in rugby: indeed the RFU called in officials from Bath (and Sale) for a "chat" about the amateur regulations. Dusty Hare retired after the final, disappointed by Leicester's failure, but with a record of 7,177 points in first-class rugby.

Welsh rugby was dominated by Llanelli and Neath. Llanelli won the Merit Table but Neath finished the season with a world points record of 1917 including 345 tries. Their season ended amid acrimony with the resignation of the coaching staff over a sponsorship dispute. Neath also beat Llanelli in the Welsh Cup final, but that was controversial as well: Mark Jones stamped on Laurence Delaney of Llanelli and became the first man in 18 finals to be sent off, though only into the sin bin. Pontypool, beaten only twice the previous season, lost 19 games. "What we need," said their coach John Perkins plaintively, "is a few hairy-arsed forwards."

Rugby's popularity reached new peaks. England's two home internationals were over-subscribed by 140,000 and the RFU announced plans to build a new £10m North Stand with 20,000 seats in time for the 1991 World Cup, the first stage of a major redevelopment. Even the Varsity match (which Oxford won 27-7, their biggest margin since 1909) had its biggest crowd in 23 years, 53,000, and the derided County Championship final attracted a record 27,500. Le Pontet, who won the French rugby league and cup double in 1988, even reversed all usual trends by switching to rugby union. Dudley Wood, secretary of the RFU, said this seemed to be against International Board rules but added: "Still, I suppose the French have always been a law unto themselves."

Simon van Oppen, who broke his spine eight years ago playing rugby as a 16-year-old at Bedford School, lost his action against the school in the Court of Appeal for failing to insure him.

The match at Whitby on Corby's Northern tour was called off after 47 minutes when the referee concluded that several Corby players were too drunk to continue; Whitby were leading 80-0. Mrs Christine Kenyon marched on to the pitch during a match between Aretians Thirds and Bristol Saracens to argue with her husband Mike. She dumped his kit bag and pet dog at his feet. Husband, wife and dog were all sent off by the referee.

1989

LIONS TOUR OF AUSTRALIA 1989

Perth, Jun 10
WESTERN AUSTRALIA 0
LIONS 44
T: Mullin (3), Evans, White, Underwood (2), Moore, S Hastings C: Dods (4)

Melbourne, Jun 14
AUSTRALIA 'B' 18
T: Knox, Niuqila, Tuynman, Penalty Try C: Knox
LIONS 23
T: Jeffrey (2), Armstrong C: G Hastings P: G Hastings (3)

Brisbane, June 17
QUEENSLAND 15
P: Lynagh (4) DG: Lynagh
LIONS 19
T: Jones P: G Hastings (3) DG: Chalmers (2)

Cairns, Jun 21
QUEENSLAND 'B' 6
P: Palm (2)
LIONS 30
T: Oti, Robinson, Smith, Dooley C: Andrew (4)
P: Dods (2)

North Sydney, Jun 24
NEW SOUTH WALES 21
T: Roebuck C: Roebuck P: Roebuck (5)
LIONS 23
T: G Hastings, Norster P: G Hastings (2)
DG: Chalmers (3)

June 27
NEW SOUTH WALES 'B' 19
T: Burke (2) C: Patterson P: Patterson (3)
LIONS 39
T: Armstrong, Underwood (2), S Hastings, Hall (2), Sole
C: Dods (4) P: Dods

Sydney, Jul 1
FIRST TEST
AUSTRALIA 30
T: Walker, Gourley, Maguire, Martin C: Lynagh (4)
P: Lynagh DG: Lynagh
BRITISH LIONS 12
P: Hastings (2), Chalmers DG: Chalmers

Teams - Australia: G J Martin; A S Niuqila, D Maguire, L F Walker, D I Campese; M P Lynagh, N C Farr-Jones; C P Lillicrap (M N Hartill), T A Lawton (N I McBain), D Crowley, S A G Cutler, W A Campbell, J S Miller, S R Gourley, S N Tuynman.

Lions: A G Hastings; I C Evans, M R Hall, B J Mullin, R Underwood; C M Chalmers, R N Jones; D M B Sole, B C Moore, D Young, P J Ackford, R L Norster, D B White, F Calder, D Richards.

Canberra, Jul 4
AUSTRALIAN CAPITAL TERRITORY 25
T: Alchin (2), Doyle C: Pini (2) P: Pini (3)
LIONS 41
T: Dooley, Hall, Armstrong, S Hastings, Pen, Try
C: Dods (3) P: Dods (5)

Brisbane, Jul 8, SECOND TEST
AUSTRALIA   12
T: Martin C: Lynagh P: Lynagh (2)
BRITISH LIONS   19
T: G Hastings, Guscott C: Andrew P: G Hastings,
Andrew DG: Andrew

Teams – **Australia:** G J Martin; D I Campese, D Maguire,
L F Walker, I Williams; M P Lynagh, N C Farr-Jones;
M N Hartill, T A Lawton, D Crowley, S A Cutler,
W A Campbell, S R Gourley, J S Miller, S N Tuynman.

Lions: A G Hastings; I C Evans, S Hastings, J C Guscott,
R Underwood; C R Andrew, R N Jones; D M B Sole,
B C Moore, D Young, P J Ackford, W A Dooley, M C
Teague, F Calder, D Richards.

Sydney, Jul 15, THIRD TEST
AUSTRALIA   18
T: Williams C: Lynagh P: Lynagh (4)
British Lions   19
T: Evans P: G Hastings (5)

Teams – **Australia:** G J Martin; D I Campese, D J Maguire,
L F Walker, I M Williams; M P Lynagh, N C Farr-Jones;

M N Hartill, T A Lawton, D Crowley, S A G Cutler,
W A Campbell, S R Gourley, J S Miller, S N Tuynman.
Lions: A G Hastings; I C Evans, S Hastings, J C Guscott,
R Underwood; C R Andrew, R N Jones; D M B Sole,
B C Moore, D Young, P J Ackford, W A Dooley,
M C Teague, F Calder, D Richards.

Newcastle, Jul 19
NEW SOUTH WALES COUNTRY XV   13
T: I Tonkin P: Macfarlane (3)
LIONS   72
T: Mullin (3), Armstrong (2), Jeffrey (2), Devereux,
Chalmers, Chilcott, Robinson, Clement, Dods, Smith C:
Dods (8)

Brisbane, Jul 23
ANZAC XV   15
T: Williams C: Lynagh P: Lynagh (3)
LIONS   19
T: Mullin, Devereux C: G Hastings
P: G Hastings DG: Chalmers, G Hastings

LIONS TOURS

To Australia and New Zealand

Year	Tour Captain	Full Tour Record						Test Record					
		P	W	D	L	F	A	P	W	D	L	F	A
1888	Robert Seddon (Eng) (a)	35	27	6	2	292	98	-					
1899*	Matthew Mullineaux (Eng)	21	18	0	3	333	90	4	3	0	1	38	23
1904	Darky Bedell-Sivright (Sco)	19	16	1	2	287	84	4	3	0	1	53	12
1908	Arthur Harding (Wal)	26	16	1	9	323	201	3	0	1	2	8	64
1930	Doug Prentice (Eng)	28	20	0	8	624	318	5	1	0	4	39	59
1950	Karl Mullen (Ire)	29	22	1	6	570	214	6	2	1	3	63	43
1959	Ronnie Dawson (Ire)	31	25	0	6	756	336	6	3	0	3	83	66
1966	Michael Campbell-Lamerton (Sco)	33	22	3	8	502	329	6	2	0	4	74	87
1971	John Dawes (Wal)	26	23	1	2	580	231	4	2	1	1	48	42
1977§	Phil Bennett (Wal)	26	21	0	5	617	320	4	1	0	3	41	54
1983#	Cieran Fitzgerald (Ire)	18	12	0	6	478	276	4	0	0	4	26	78
1989*	Finlay Calder (Sco)	12	11	0	1	360	192	3	2	0	1	50	60

To South Africa

Year	Tour Captain	P	W	D	L	F	A	P	W	D	L	F	A
1891	Bill Maclagan (Sco)	19	19	0	0	224	3	3	3	0	0	11	0
1896	John Hammond (Eng)	21	19	1	1	310	45	4	3	0	1	34	16
1903	Mark Morrison (Sco)	22	11	3	8	231	138	3	0	2	1	10	18
1910	Tom Smyth (Ire)	24	13	3	8	290	236	3	1	0	2	23	38
1924	Ronald Cove-Smith (Eng)	21	9	3	9	175	155	4	0	1	3	15	43
1938	Sam Walker (Ire)	23	17	0	6	407	272	3	1	0	2	36	61
1955	Robin Thompson (Ire)	24	18	1	5	418	271	4	2	0	2	49	75
1962	Arthur Smith (Sco)	24	15	4	5	351	208	4	0	1	3	20	48
1968	Tom Kiernan (Ire)	20	15	1	4	377	181	4	0	3	1	38	61
1974	Willie John McBride (Ire)	22	21	1	0	729	207	4	3	1	0	79	34
1980	Bill Beaumont (Eng)	18	15	0	3	401	244	4	1	0	3	68	77

* To Australia only; § To New Zealand & Fiji; # To New Zealand only
(a) Seddon killed in a drowning accident during tour. Replaced as skipper by Arthur Stoddart

---

TOUR SUMMARY
P 12; W 11; D 0; L 1; For 360; Against 192

Appearances
9 S Hastings (1); 8 Underwood (1), Evans (1), Ackford,
Young (1), Sole (1); 7 Jones, Moore, G Hastings, Chalmers
(1), Mullin (1); 6 Calder, Richards, Guscott, Dooley, Hall,
Teague, Norster, White, Robinson, Griffiths (1), Andrew
(1); 5 Dods, Armstrong, Smith, Chilcott, Jeffrey,
Devereux; 4 Lenihan; 3 Oti; 2 Clement (1); 1 Dean

*Figures in brackets indicate appearances as replacement
Dean (after 25 minutes of the first game) and Oti returned
home early through injury.*

Scorers
Tries
7 Mullin; 5 Armstrong; 4 Underwood, Jeffrey;
3 S Hastings, Hall; 2 Dooley, G Hastings, Evans, Smith,
Robinson, Devereux; 1 White, Moore, Jones, Oti, Sole,
Norster, Guscott, Chalmers, Chilcott, Clement, Dods, Pen.
try
Conversions
19 Dods; 5 Andrew; 2 G Hastings
Penalty Goals
17 G Hastings; 8 Dods; 1 Chalmers, Andrew
Dropped Goals
7 Chalmers; 1 Andrew, G Hastings

Points
66 Dods, G Hastings; **28** Chalmers, Mullin; **20** Armstrong; **16** Underwood, Andrew, Jeffrey; **12** Hall, S Hastings; **8** Dooley, Evans, Smith, Robinson, Devereux; **4** White, Moore, Jones, Oti, Sole, Norster, Guscott, Chilcott, Clement, Pen. try

The Squad

ENGLAND
P J Ackford (Harlequins)
C R Andrew (Wasps)
replacement for Dean, June 15
W A Dooley (Preston Grasshoppers)
G J Chilcott (Bath)
J C Guscott (Bath)
B C Moore (Nottingham)
C Oti (Wasps)
D Richards (Leicester)
R A Robinson (Bath)
M C Teague (Gloucester)
R Underwood (Leicester and RAF)

IRELAND
D G Lenihan (Cork Constitution)
B J Mullin (London Irish)
P M Dean (St Mary's College)
S J Smith (Ballymena)

SCOTLAND
G Armstrong (Jedforest)
F Calder, capt (Stewart's/Melville FP)
C M Chalmers (Melrose)
P W Dods (Gala)
G Hastings (London Scottish)
S Hastings (Watsonians)
J Jeffrey (Kelso)
D M B Sole (Edinburgh Academicals)
D B White (London Scottish)

WALES
A Clement (Swansea)
replacement for Oti, July 3
J A Devereux (Bridgend)
I C Evans (Llanelli)
M Griffiths (Bridgend)
M R Hall (Cambridge U and Bridgend)
R N Jones (Swansea)
R L Norster (Cardiff)
D Young (Cardiff)

INTERNATIONAL CHAMPIONSHIP

Murrayfield, Jan 21
SCOTLAND   23
T: Armstrong, White, Chalmers   C: Dods;   P: Dods (2);
DG: Chalmers
WALES   7
T: Hall; P: Bowen

Lansdowne Road, Jan 21
IRELAND   21
T: Mullin;   C: Kiernan;   P: Kiernan (5)
FRANCE   26
T: Lagisquet (2), Lafond, Blanco   C: Lafond (2);
P: Lafond (2)

Twickenham, Feb 4
ENGLAND   12
P: Andrew (2), Webb (2)
SCOTLAND   12
T: Jeffrey;   C: Dods: P: Dods (2)

Cardiff, Feb 4
WALES   13
T: M.Jones;   P: Thorburn (3)
IRELAND   19
T: Manion, Dean;   C: Kiernan   P: Kiernan (3)

"To me, basically, it's open warfare. They've set the rules. They've set the standards. As far as I'm concerned, if the officials aren't going to control it, we're going to have to do something about it."
Nick Farr-Jones, Australian captain.

"In the past the Australians have always talked about the moaning poms while adopting a macho image themselves. All we have done is adopt the southern hemisphere style and they don't like it."
Roger Uttley, Lions coach

"They ought to know we'll whack 'em back."
Steve Cutler, Australian lock

"If that is the price of winning, they can have it. What a tragedy if someone ends up with their brains scrambled from a deliberate kick to the head. In two years who is going to remember the Ballymore Test score anyway? It was a zoo out there."
Tom Lawton, Australian hooker after Second Test

"Perhaps significantly, three members of the aggressive and dominant British pack are of the constabulary. They did to the Wallabies what they do to the Pakistanis and punks back home."
Harris on Saturday, The Australian

"Nowadays it appears international rugby entails an acceptable level of violence encouraged by official silence."
Robert Armstrong, The Guardian

"It's been for all to see a classic case of 'whingeing Wallabies."
Nigel Starmer-Smith, Rugby World

"We must stop the spectre of grown men behaving immaturely."
Sandy Sanders, President of the RFU

"For five minutes we played well."
Finlay Calder, Lions captain, after the First Test

"I wrote to my wife at lunchtime and said I was retiring. I'd better get back to the hotel and get the letter out of the post."
Flinlay Calder, after the Second Test

"I feel like retiring."
David Campese, Australian wing, after the Third Test.

Paris, Feb 18
FRANCE   31
T: Blanco (2), Berbizier, Dintrans
C: Lafond (3)   P: Lafond (2)   DG: Mesnel
WALES   12
P: Thorburn (4)

Lansdowne Road, Feb 18
IRELAND 3
P: Kiernan
ENGLAND 16
T: Moore, Richards C: Andrew P: Andrew (2)

Murrayfield, Mar 4
SCOTLAND 37
T: Tukalo (3), Jeffrey, Cronin C: Dods (4) P: Dods (3)
IRELAND 21
T: Mullin (2), Dunlea C: Kiernan (3) P: Kiernan

Twickenham, Mar 4
ENGLAND 11
T: Carling, Robinson P: Andrew
FRANCE 0

Cardiff, Mar 18
WALES 12
T: Hall C: Thorburn P: Thorburn (2)
ENGLAND 9
P: Andrew (2) DG: Andrew

Paris, Mar 18
FRANCE 19
T: Berbizier, Blanco, Lagisquet C: Berot (2) P: Berot
SCOTLAND 3
P: Dods

Final Table

	P	W	D	L	F	A	Pts
France	4	3	0	1	76	47	6
England	4	2	1	1	48	27	5
Scotland	4	2	1	1	75	59	5
Ireland	4	1	0	3	64	92	2
Wales	4	1	0	3	44	82	2

ENGLAND IN ROMANIA
Bucharest, May 13
ROMANIA 3
P: Ignat
ENGLAND 58
T: Oti (4), Guscott (3), Richards, Probyn.
C: Hodgkinson (8) P: Hodgkinson DG: Andrew
*This was England's biggest-ever international win.
Hodgkinson's 19 points on debut was an England record.*

FRANCE IN NEW ZEALAND
Christchurch, Jun 17
NEW ZEALAND 25
T: Wright (2), A.Whetton C: Fox (2) P: Fox (3)
FRANCE 17
T: Blanco (2), Cecilion C: Berot P: Berot

Auckland, Jul 1
NEW ZEALAND 34
T: A. Whetton, Stanley, Deans, Fitzpatrick C: Fox (3)
P: Fox (4)
FRANCE 20
T: Rouge-Thomas, Cecilion P: Blanco (4)

BLEDISLOE CUP
Auckland, Aug 5
NEW ZEALAND 24
T: Gallagher, Loe C: Fox (2) P: Fox (4)
AUSTRALIA 12
T: Campese C: Lynagh P: Lynagh (2)
*Michael Lynagh was the top international points scorer
after this game with 429. Grant Fox became the first New
Zealander to pass 300, with 302. David Campese reached
a record 33 tries.*

TOSHIBA COUNTY CHAMPIONSHIP
Semi-finals
Redruth: Cornwall 13 Warwickshire 10
Blackheath: Durham 10 Kent 6
Final, Twickenham, Apr 1
Durham 13 Cornwall 9

PILKINGTON CUP
3rd Round
ASPATRIA 6 Moseley 3; BATH 82 Oxford 9; Bedford 3
NOTTINGHAM 6; Blackheath 6 WATERLOO 13;
BRISTOL 13 Orrell 7; Brixham 4 GLOUCESTER 28;
Gosforth 9 WAKEFIELD 29; HAVANT 9 Exeter 3;
HEREFORD 10 Tynedale 6; Liverpool St Helens 6
LEICESTER 37; LONDON IRISH 14 Berry Hill 3;
LONDON SCOTTISH 16 Saracens 0; RICHMOND 6
Northampton 0; ROSSLYN PARK 18 Plymouth Albion 0;
Rugby 3 HARLEQUINS 25; WASPS 33 Durham City 3
4th Round
BATH 48 Hereford 0; BRISTOL 45 London Irish 16;
GLOUCESTER 19 Waterloo 16; HARLEQUINS 22
London Scottish 6; Richmond 9 NOTTINGHAM 12;
Rosslyn Park 9 LEICESTER 23; WAKEFIELD 18 Havant
10; WASPS 39 Aspatria 7
5th Round
BATH 14 Bristol 12; HARLEQUINS 15 Nottingham 9;
LEICESTER 22 Wasps 18; Wakefield 13 GLOUCESTER
28
Semi-finals
Gloucester 3 BATH 6; Harlequins 7 LEICESTER 16
Final, Twickenham, Apr 29
BATH 10 Leicester 6
T: Barnes, P: Hare (2)
(2) P: BarnesAtt: 59,300 (World record for a club match)

SCHWEPPES WELSH CUP
5th Round
CARDIFF 24 Aberavon Quins 15; Ebbw Vale 6
ABERTILLERY 17; GLAMORGAN WANDERERS 18
Taffs Well 4; Glynneath 9 BRIDGEND 42; LLANHARAN
17 South Wales Police 10; NEATH 47 Blaina 12; Newport
3 NEWBRIDGE 7; Pontypridd 11 LLANELLI 26
6th Round
LLANELLI 22 Bridgend 13; Glamorgan Wanderers 0
NEATH 38; Llanharan 13 CARDIFF 25; NEWBRIDGE
12 Abertillery 9
Semi-finals
Cardiff 12 NEATH 19; LLANELLI 26 Newbridge 24
Final, Cardiff, May 6
NEATH 14   Llanelli 13
T: Jones, P: Williams,   T: Evans, P: Stephens (2),
B: Williams, C: Thorburn   DG: Stephens

SAVE & PROSPER MIDDLESEX SEVENS
Twickenham, May 6
Harlequins 18 Rosslyn Park 12

HOSPITALS CUP
Richmond, Mar 8
St Mary's 20 The London 9

CATHAY PACIFIC HONG KONG SEVENS
Hong Kong, Apr 2
New Zealand 22-10 Australia

COURAGE LEAGUE TABLES

League 1 / Full Playing Record

			P	W	D	L	F	A	Pts	P	W	D	L	F	A
1	(4)	BATH	11	10	0	1	263	98	20	42	35	2	5	1263	511
2	(5)	Gloucester	11	7	1	3	215	112	15	44	34	1	9	1028	525
3	(2)	Wasps	11	7	1	3	206	138	15	35	20	2	13	791	560
4	(8)	Nottingham	11	6	1	4	142	122	13	43	25	3	15	825	522
5	(6)	Orrell	11	6	1	4	148	157	13	44	29	2	13	956	546
6	(1)	Leicester	11	6	1	4	189	199	13	38	28	1	9	918	573
7	(9)	Bristol	11	6	0	5	188	117	12	45	30	2	13	1138	556
8	(3)	Harlequins	11	5	0	6	194	184	10	31	19	1	13	561	497
9	(P)	Rosslyn Park	11	5	0	6	172	208	10	35	20	0	15	710	561
10	(7)	Moseley	11	3	0	8	113	242	6	43	21	1	21	766	837
11	(10)	*Waterloo*	11	1	1	9	120	235	3	40	24	1	15	914	579
12	(P)	*Llverpool St.H*	11	1	0	10	116	254	2	37	13	3	21	546	657

League 2 / Full Playing Record

			P	W	D	L	F	A	Pts	P	W	D	L	F	A
1	(3)	SARACENS	11	11	0	0	288	80	22	34	25	1	8	722	448
2	(5)	BEDFORD	11	6	2	3	141	187	14	40	19	2	19	649	696
3	(12)	Northampton	11	6	1	4	165	131	13	40	19	1	20	733	627
4	(R)	Sale	11	5	2	4	195	152	12	39	20	4	15	784	560
5	(R)	Coventry	11	6	0	5	150	143	12	40	13	1	26	528	817
6	(8)	London Irish	11	5	2	4	194	222	12	34	18	2	4	761	662
7	(4)	Headingley	11	5	1	5	179	136	11	44	28	2	14	999	562
8	(11)	Blackheath	11	4	1	6	181	144	9	33	17	1	15	581	358
9	(6)	Richmond	11	4	1	6	112	216	9	31	13	2	16	419	553
10	(10)	Gosforth	11	4	0	7	176	246	8	40	21	1	18	732	652
11	(7)	*London Scots*	11	3	1	7	146	160	7	31	13	3	15	458	464
12	(9)	*London Welsh*	11	1	1	9	125	235	3	35	8	2	25	502	898

League 3

			P	W	D	L	F	A	Pts
1	(3)	PLYMOUTH ALB	11	11	0	0	311	89	22
2	(P)	RUGBY	11	10	0	1	268	99	20
3	(1)	Wakefield	11	9	0	2	282	114	18
4	(2)	W.Hartlepool	11	5	1	5	164	133	11
5	(10)	Nuneaton	11	5	0	6	178	214	10
6	(4)	Sheffield	11	4	1	6	170	182	9
7	(5)	Vale of Lune	11	4	1	6	120	145	9
8	(P)	Askeans	11	4	1	6	141	215	9
9	(9)	Exeter	11	4	0	7	142	180	8
10	(6)	Fylde	11	4	0	7	136	181	8
11	(7)	Met. Police	11	4	0	7	130	275	8
12	(8)	Maidstone	11	0	0	11	74	289	0

BATH'S MEMORABLE SEASON

Courage Championship

Harlequins (a)	**WON 26-9**
Gloucester (h)	**WON 19-9**
Rosslyn Park (a)	**WON 19-9**
Bristol (h)	**WON 16-9**
Moseley (a)	**WON 38-0**
Orrell (h)	**WON 36-12**
Wasps (h)	**WON 16-6**
Liverpool St Helens (a)	**WON 21-7**
Nottingham (h)	**WON 22-16**
Waterloo (h)	**WON 38-9**
Leicester (a)	**LOST 12-15**

Pilkington Cup

3rd Round:	**Oxford (h)**	**WON 82-9**
4th Round:	**Hereford (h)**	**WON 48-0**
Quarter-final:	**Bristol (h)**	**WON 14-12**
Semi-final:	**Gloucester (a)**	**WON 6-3**
Final:	**Leicester (n)**	**WON 10-6**

All the Other Champions

Area League North:	ROUNDHAY
Area League South:	LYDNEY
London Division 1:	BASINGSTOKE
London 2 North:	CHESHUNT
London 2 South:	OLD ALLEYNIANS
London 3 North-East:	ETON MANOR*
London 3 North-West:	FINCHLEY
London 3 South-East:	OLD COLFEIANS
London 3 South-West:	ALTON
North 1:	KENDAL
North 2:	BRADFORD & BINGLEY
North-West 1:	WIGAN
North-West 2:	COCKERMOUTH
North-East 1:	ROTHERHAM*
North-East 2:	YORK
Midlands 1:	WALSALL*
Midlands 2 West:	SUTTON COLDFIELD
Midlands 2 East;	LEIGHTON BUZZARD
East Midlands/Leics:	TOWCESTRIANS
North Midlands:	CAMP HILL
Notts/Lincs/Derbys:	SCUNTHORPE
Staffs/Warwicks:	KERESLEY
South-West 1:	CLIFTON

South-West 2:   MATSON
Western Counties: GORDON LODGE
Southern Counties: BANBURY
Cornwall/Devon: PENRYN
Gloucs/Somerset: OLD CULVERHAYS*
Bucks/Oxon: CHILTERN
Berks/Dorset/Wilts: BRACKNELL
* Won division with 100% record - 10 wins out of 10

WALES
Whitbread Merit Table (unofficial)

		P	W	D	L	F	A	%	Full Playing Record					
									P	W	D	L	F	A
1	Llaneli	25	23	0	2	796	388	92.00	50	41	0	9	1578	780
2	Neath	28	24	0	4	1069	276	85.71	50	46	0	4	1917	471
3	Newbridge	28	23	1	4	673	390	83.92	48	38	2	8	1197	625
4	Bridgend	31	25	0	6	645	377	80.64	53	40	1	12	1243	673
5	Pontypridd	31	23	1	7	905	407	75.80	45	33	1	11	1280	596
6	Swansea	24	15	0	9	500	371	62.49	44	30	0	14	1110	701
7	Cardiff	21	12	2	7	411	384	61.9	44	26	4	14	1075	773
8	Abertillery	29	16	0	13	542	494	55.17	50	30	0	20	1022	693
9	Maesteg	32	14	3	15	470	516	48.43	50	27	3	20	903	766
10	Newport	29	13	0	16	595	602	44.82	49	27	1	21	1066	927
11	Pontypool	32	14	0	18	527	627	43.75	48	24	1	23	886	853
12	Ebbw Vale	32	14	0	18	438	688	43.75	48	23	2	23	737	939
13	South Wales Police	26	8	0	18	433	566	30.76	51	24	1	26	964	919
14	Glam Wanderers	28	8	0	20	436	511	28.57	49	25	1	23	968	785
15	Cross Keys	31	7	2	22	349	756	25.80	50	22	2	26	715	1018
16	Aberavon	31	7	1	23	378	660	24.19	46	14	1	31	663	894
17	Tredegar	25	4	0	21	283	685	16.00	48	16	1	31	627	1032
18	Penarth	25	1	0	24	253	958	4.00	44	9	0	35	519	1348

MONTHLY AWARDS
September: NEATH; October: PONTYPRIDD; December: NEATH; January: NEWBRIDGE; March: NEATH; April: PONTYPRIDD

SCOTLAND
McEwan's Club Championship
First Division

		P	W	D	L	F	A	Pts	Full Playing Record					
1	Kelso	13	10	0	3	357	111	20	32	21	0	11	763	349
2	Boroughmuir	13	9	2	2	314	145	20	36	28	2	6	969	407
3	Hawick	13	10	0	3	280	161	20	34	23	0	11	701	418
4	Edinburgh Acs	13	8	2	3	242	127	18	34	19	3	12	698	430
5	Heriot's FP	13	9	0	4	301	196	18	31	21	1	9	772	475
6	Jedforest	13	8	1	4	270	164	17	32	22	2	8	786	445
7	Selkirk	13	7	1	5	175	153	15	33	21	1	11	586	393
8	West of Scotland	13	5	1	7	164	263	11	32	15	1	16	477	567
9	Stewart's Melville	13	5	1	7	168	278	11	35	16	1	18	511	731
10	Melrose	12	5	0	7	208	162	10	31	20	0	10	725	378
11	Ayr	13	4	1	8	202	271	9	36	19	1	16	711	548
12	Glasgow High Kelvinside	13	3	1	9	144	258	7	27	13	1	13	498	416
13	Glasgow Academicals	12	2	0	10	112	225	4	31	10	1	20	457	532
14	Watsonians	13	0	0	13	97	520	0	29	3	0	26	282	935

RUGBY CHAMPIONS

Year	Winners	Grand Slam	Triple Crown	Year	Winners	Grand Slam	Triple Crown
1883	England	-	England	1898	-	-	-
1884	England	-	England	1899	Ireland	-	Ireland
1885	-	-	-	1900	Wales	-	Wales
1886	England	-	-	1901	Scotland	-	Scotland
	Scotland	-	-	1902	Wales	-	Wales
1887	Scotland	-	-	1903	Scotland	-	Scotland
1888	-	-	-	1904	Scotland	-	-
1889	-	-	-	1905	Wales	-	Wales
1890	England	-	-	1906	Ireland	-	-
	Scotland	-	-		Wales	-	-
1891	Scotland	-	Scotland	1907	Scotland	-	Scotland
1892	England	-	England	1908	Wales	Wales	Wales
1893	Wales	-	Wales	1909	Wales	Wales	Wales
1894	Ireland	-	Ireland	1910	England	-	-
1895	Scotland	-	Scotland	1911	Wales	Wales	Wales
1896	Ireland	-	-	1912	England	-	-
1897	-	-	-		Ireland		

Year	Winners	Grand Slam	Triple Crown	Year	Winners	Grand Slam	Triple Crown
1913	England	England	England	1958	England	-	-
1914	England	England	England	1959	France	-	-
1920	England	-	-	1960	France	-	England
	Scotland				England		
	Wales			1961	France	-	-
1921	England	England	England	1962	France	-	-
1922	Wales	-	-	1963	England	-	-
1923	England	England	England	1964	Scotland	-	-
1924	England	England	England		Wales		
1925	Scotland	Scotland	Scotland	1965	Wales	-	Wales
1926	Scotland	-	-	1966	Wales	-	-
	Ireland			1967	France	-	-
1927	Scotland	-	-	1968	France	France	-
	Ireland			1969	Wales	-	Wales
1928	England	England	England	1970	Wales	-	-
1929	Scotland	-	-		France		
1930	England	-	-	1971	Wales	Wales	Wales
1931	Wales	-	-	1972	-	-	-
1932	England	-	-	1973	Quintuple tie	-	-
	Wales	-	-	1974	Ireland	-	-
	Ireland			1975	Wales	-	-
1933	Scotland	-	Scotland	1976	Wales	Wales	Wales
1934	England	-	England	1977	France	France	Wales
1935	Ireland	-	-	1978	Wales	Wales	Wales
1936	Wales	-	-	1979	Wales	-	Wales
1937	England	-	England	1980	England	England	England
1938	Scotland	-	Scotland	1981	France	France	-
1939	England	-	-	1982	Ireland	-	Ireland
	Wales			1983	France	-	-
	Ireland				Ireland		
1947	Wales	-	-	1984	Scotland	Scotland	Scotland
	England			1985	Ireland	-	Ireland
1948	Ireland	Ireland	Ireland	1986	France	-	-
1949	Ireland	-	Ireland		Scotland		
1950	Wales	Wales	Wales	1987	France	France	-
1951	Ireland	-	-	1988	Wales	-	Wales
1952	Wales	Wales	Wales		France		
1953	England	-	-	1989	France	-	-
1954	England	-	England				
	Wales						
	France				**WINS**		
1955	Wales	-	-	32 Wales	8 Wales	17 Wales	
	France			27 England	8 England	15 England	
1956	Wales	-	-	20 Scotland	4 France	9 Scotland	
1957	England	England	England	18 Ireland	2 Scotland	6 Ireland	
				17 France	1 Ireland		

THE INTERNATIONAL CHAMPIONSHIP IN THE 1980S

	ENG V IRE	SCO V ENG	ENG V WAL	IRE V SCO	IRE V WAL
1980	24-9	18-30	9-8	22-15	21-7
1982	15-16	9-9	17-7	21-12	20-12
1984	12-9	18-6	15-24	9-32	9-18
1986	25-20	33-6	21-18	9-10	12-19
1988	35-3	6-9	3-11	22-18	9-12
	IRE V ENG	**ENG V SCO**	**WAL V ENG**	**SCO V IRE**	**WAL V IRE**
1981	6-10	23-17	21-19	10-9	9-8
1983	25-15	12-22	13-13	13-15	23-9
1985	13-10	10-7	24-15	15-18	9-21
1987	17-0	21-12	19-12	16-12	11-15
1989	3-16	12-12	12-9	37-21	13-19
	WAL V SCO	**FRA V ENG**	**FRA V IRE**	**SCO V FRA**	**WAL V FRA**
1980	17-6	13-17	19-18	22-14	18-9
1982	18-34	15-27	22-9	16-7	22-12
1984	9-15	32-18	25-12	21-12	16-21
1986	22-15	29-10	29-9	18-17	15-23
1988	25-20	10-9	25-6	23-12	9-10
	SCO V WAL	**ENG V FRA**	**IRE V FRA**	**FRA V SCO**	**FRA V WAL**
1981	15-6	12-16	13-19	16-9	19-15
1983	15-19	15-19	22-16	19-15	16-9
1985	21-25	9-9	15-15	11-3	14-3
1987	21-14	15-19	13-19	28-22	16-9
1989	23-7	11-0	21-26	19-3	31-12

WORLD CUP
Inaugurated 1987
1987 New Zealand 29 France 9

COUNTY CHAMPIONSHIPS
1889 Yorkshire
1890 Yorkshire
1891 Lancashire
1892 Yorkshire
1893 Yorkshire
1894 Yorkshire
1985 Yorkshire
1896 Yorkshire
1897 Kent
1898 Northumberland
1899 Devon
1900 Durham
1901 Devon
1902 Durham
1903 Durham
1904 Kent
1905 Durham
1906 Devon
1907 Devon & Durham (shared)
1908 Cornwall
1909 Durham
1910 Gloucestershire
1911 Devon
1912 Devon
1913 Gloucestershire
1914 Midlands
1915-19 Not held
1920 Gloucestershire
1921 Gloucestershire
1922 Gloucestershire
1923 Somerset
1924 Cumberland
1925 Leicestershire
1926 Yorkshire
1927 Kent
1928 Yorkshire
1929 Middlesex
1930 Gloucestershire
1931 Gloucestershire
1932 Gloucestershire
1933 Hampshire
1934 East Midlands
1935 Lancashire
1936 Hampshire
1937 Gloucestershire
1938 Lancashire
1939 Warwickshire
1940-46 Not held
1947 Lancashire
1948 Lancashire
1949 Lancashire
1950 Cheshire
1951 East Midlands
1952 Middlesex
1953 Yorkshire
1954 Middlesex
1955 Lancashire
1956 Middlesex
1957 Devon
1958 Warwickshire
1959 Warwickshire
1960 Warwickshire
1961 Cheshire
1962 Warwickshire
1963 Warwickshire
1964 Warwickshire
1965 Warwickshire
1966 Middlesex

1967 Surrey & Durham
1968 Middlesex
1969 Lancashire
1970 Staffordshire
1971 Surrey
1972 Gloucestershire
1973 Lancashire
1974 Gloucestershire
1975 Gloucestershire
1976 Gloucestershire
1977 Lancashire
1978 North Midlands
1979 Middlesex

Finals of the 1980s

1980	Lancashire	21	Gloucestershire	15
1981	Northumberland	15	Gloucestershire	6
1982	Lancashire	7	North Midlands	3
1983	Gloucestershire	19	Yorkshire	7
1984	Gloucestershire	36	Somerset	18
1985	Middlesex	12	Notts, Lincs, Derbys	9
1986	Warwickshire	16	Kent	6
1987	Yorkshire	22	Middlesex	7
1988	Lancashire	23	Warwickshire	18
1989	Durham	13	Cornwall	9

Most wins: 15 Gloucestershire; **13** Lancashire;
11 Yorkshire; **9** Warwickshire; **8** Durham (including two shared), Middlesex; **7** Devon (including one shared)

PILKINGTON CUP
Formerly John Player Cup

1972	Gloucester	17	Moseley	6
1973	Coventry	27	Bristol	15
1974	Coventry	26	London Scottish	6
1975	Bedford	28	Rosslyn Park	12
1976	Gosforth	23	Rosslyn Park	14
1977	Gosforth	27	Waterloo	11
1978	Gloucester	6	Leicester	3
1979	Leicester	15	Moseley	12
1980	Leicester	21	London Irish	9
1981	Leicester	22	Gosforth	15
1982	Gloucester	12	Moseley	12 (shared)
1983	Bristol	28	Leicester	22
1984	Bath	10	Bristol	9
1985	Bath	24	London Welsh	15
1986	Bath	25	Wasps	17
1987	Bath	19	Wasps	12
1988	Harlequins	28	Bristol	22
1989	Bath	10	Leicester	6

Most wins: 5 Bath; **3** Leicester, Gloucester (including one shared)

SCHWEPPES WELSH CUP

1972	Neath	15	Llanelli	9
1973	Llanelli	30	Cardiff	7
1974	Llanelli	12	Aberavon	10
1975	Llanelli	15	Aberavon	6
1976	Llanelli	15	Swansea	4
1977	Newport	16	Cardiff	15
1978	Swansea	13	Newport	9
1979	Bridgend	18	Pontypridd	12
1980	Bridgend	15	Swansea	9
1981	Cardiff	14	Bridgend	6
1982	Cardiff *	12	Bridgend	12
1983	Pontypool	18	Swansea	6
1984	Cardiff	24	Neath	19
1985	Llanelli	15	Cardiff	14
1986	Cardiff	28	Newport	21
1987	Cardiff	16	Swansea	15 aet
1988	Llanelli	28	Neath	13
1989	Neath	14	Llanelli	13

* Winners on most tries rule
Most wins: 6 Llanelli; **5** Cardiff

UNIVERSITY MATCH
Results in the 1980s

1980	Cambridge	13	Oxford	9
1981	Cambridge	9	Oxford	9
1982	Cambridge	20	Oxford	13
1983	Cambridge	20	Oxford	9
1984	Cambridge	32	Oxford	6
1985	Oxford	7	Cambridge	6
1986	Oxford	15	Cambridge	10
1987	Cambridge	15	Oxford	10
1988	Oxford	27	Cambridge	7

Wins: 48 Cambridge; **46** Oxford; **13** Drawn

MIDDLESEX SEVENS
Finals of the 1980s

1980	Richmond	34	Rosslyn Park	18
1981	Rosslyn Park	16	London Welsh	14
1982	Stewart's Melville FP	34	Richmond	12
1983	Richmond I	20	London Welsh	13
1984	London Welsh	34	Heriot's FP	18
1985	Wasps	25	Nottingham	6
1986	Harlequins	18	Nottingham	10
1987	Harlequins	22	Rosslyn Park	6
1988	Harlequins	20	Bristol	18
1989	Harlequins	18	Rosslyn Park	12

Most wins: 12 Harlequins; **9** Richmond; **8** London Welsh; **6** London Scottish; **5** St Mary's Hospital, Loughborough College; **4** Rosslyn Park

COURAGE CLUBS CHAMPIONSHIP
Formerly National Merit Tables

	League 1	League 2	League 3
1985-6	Gloucester	Orrell	
1986-7	Bath	Waterloo	Vale of Lune
1987-8	Leicester	Rosslyn Park	Wakefield
1988-9	Bath	Saracens	Plymouth Alb

CATHAY PACIFIC-HONG KONG BANK SEVENS

1976	Cantabrians
1977	Fiji
1978	Fiji
1979	Australia
1980	Fiji
1981	Barbarians
1982	Australia
1983	Australia
1984	Fiji
1985	Australia

1986	New Zealand
1987	New Zealand
1988	Australia
1989	New Zealand

——— 1990 ———

Jan 20: ENGLAND V IRELAND (Twickenham); WALES V FRANCE (Cardiff).

Jan 27: RFU Cup third round; WELSH CUP FIFTH Round.

Feb 3: FRANCE V ENGLAND (Paris); IRELAND V SCOTLAND (Dublin).

Feb 10: RFU Cup fourth round.

Feb 17: ENGLAND V WALES (Twickenham); SCOTLAND V FRANCE (Murrayfield).

Feb 24: RFU and Welsh Cups quarter-finals.

Mar 3: WALES V SCOTLAND (Cardiff); FRANCE V IRELAND (Paris); TOSHIBA COUNTY Championship semi-finals.

Mar 14: UAU Final (Twickenham).

Mar 17: SCOTLAND v ENGLAND (Murrayfield).

Mar 24: IRELAND v WALES (Dublin). RFU Cup semi-finals.

Mar 31-

Apr 1: Hong Kong Sevens.

Apr 7: County Championship final; Welsh Cup semi-finals.

May 5: RFU Cup final (Twickenham); Welsh Cup final (Cardiff).

May 12: Middlesex sevens (Twickenham).

May 24: France v Romania.

COURAGE LEAGUE FIRST DIVISION FIXTURES 1990

Jan 13: Bath v Bedford; Harlequins v Rosslyn Park; Leicester v Gloucester; Moseley v Nottingham; Saracens v Bristol; Wasps v Orrell.

Mar 10: Bedford v Wasps; Bristol v Leicester; Gloucester v Harlequins; Nottingham v Bath; Orrell v Moseley; Rosslyn Park v Saracens.

Mar 31: Bristol v Wasps; Gloucester v Orrell; Harlequins v Nottingham; Leicester v Moseley; Rosslyn Park v Bedford; Saracens v Bath.

April 28: Bath v Leicester; Bedford v Bristol; Moseley v Harlequins; Nottingham v Gloucester; Orrell v Rosslyn Park; Wasps v Saracens.

SHOOTING

━━━ 1989 ━━━

NATIONAL RIFLE ASSOCIATION MEETING
Bisley, Jul 8-22
Winners of major titles:

Queen's Prize
Jeremy Thompson, Central Bankers

Land Rover Grand Aggregate
Simon Belither, Uppingham Vets

Daily Telegraph Challenge Cup
Richard Hind, Nottinghamian

Daily Mail Cup
Phillip Hobson, Royal Navy

Save and Prosper St George's Vase
Jeremy Thompson, Central Bankers

Prince of Wales Prize
Jeremy Thompson, Central Bankers

Mackinnon Trophy
Canada

Chancellor's Trophy
Cambridge University

Duke of Cambridge Trophy
Richard Hind, Nottinghamian

Senior County Championship
Essex

National Trophy
England

━━━ CHAMPIONS ━━━

OLYMPIC GAMES
Men
Free Pistol
1896	Sumner Paine (US)
1900	Conrad Röderer (Swi)
1908	Paul van Asbroeck (Bel)
1912	Alfred Lane (US)
1920	Karl Frederick (US)
1936	Torsten Ullmann (Swe)
1948	Edwin Vazquez Cam (Per)
1952	Huelet Benner (US)
1956	Pentti Linnosvuo (Fin)
1960	Aleksey Gushchin (USSR)
1964	Väinö Markkanen (Fin)
1968	Grigory Kossykh (USSR)
1972	Ragnar Skanaker (Swe)
1976	Uwe Potteck (GDR)
1980	Aleksandr Melentyev (USSR)
1984	Xu Haifeng (Chn)
1988	Sorin Babii (Rom)

Rapid Fire Pistol
1896	Jean Phrangoudis (Gre)
1900	Maurice Larrouy (Fra)
1912	Alfred Lane (US)
1920	Guilherme Paraense (Bra)
1924	Henry Bailey (US)
1932	Renzo Morigi (Ita)
1936	Cornelius van Oyen (Ger)
1948	Károly Takács (Hun)
1952	Károly Takács (Hun)
1956	Stefan Petrescu (Rom)

1960	William McMillan (US)
1964	Pentti Linnosvuo (Fin)
1968	Jozef Zapedzki (Pol)
1972	Jozef Zapedzki (Pol)
1976	Norbert Klaar (GDR)
1980	Corneliu Ion (Rom)
1984	Takeo Kamachi (Jap)
1988	Afanasi Kouzmine (USSR)

Trap
1900	Roger de Barbarin (Fra)
1908	Walter Ewing (Can)
1912	James Graham (US)
1920	Mark Arie (US)
1924	Gyula Halasy (Hun)
1952	George Généréux (Can)
1956	Galliano Rossini (Ita)
1960	Ion Dumitrescu (Rom)
1964	Ennio Mattarelli (Ita)
1968	Bob Braithwaite (GB)
1972	Angelo Scalzone (Ita)
1976	Don Haldeman (US)
1980	Luciano Giovanetti (Ita)
1984	Luciano Giovanetti (Ita)
1988	Dmitri Monakov (USSR)

Running Game Target
1900	Louis Debray (Fra)
1972	Yakov Zhelezniak (USSR)
1976	Aleksandr Gazov (USSR)
1980	Igor Sokolov (USSR)
1984	Li Yuwei (Chn)
1988	Tor Heiestad (Nor)

Small Bore Rifle (Prone)
1908	A.A. Carnell (GB)
1912	Frederick Hird (US)
1920	Lawrence Nuesslein (US)
1924	Pierre Coquelin de Lisle (Fra)
1932	Bertil Rönnmark (Swe)
1936	Willy Rögeberg (Nor)
1948	Arthur Cook (US)
1952	Iosif Sarbu (Rom)
1956	Gerald Ouellette (Can)
1960	Peter Kohnke (FRG)
1964	László Hammerl (Hun)
1968	Jan Kurka (Cze)
1972	Ho-Jun Li (NKo)
1976	Karl-Heinz Smieszek (FRG)
1980	Karoly Varga (Hun)
1984	Edward Etzel (US)
1988	Miroslav Varga (Cze)

Small Bore Rifle (Three Position)
1952	Erling Kongshaug (Nor)
1956	Anatoliy Bogdanov (USSR)
1960	Viktor Shamburkin (USSR)
1964	Lones Wigger (US)
1968	Bernd Klingner (FRG)
1972	John Writer (US)
1976	Lanny Bassham (US)
1980	Viktor Vlasov (USSR)
1984	Malcolm Cooper (GB)
1988	Malcolm Cooper (GB)

Skeet
1968	Yevgeniy Petrov (USSR)
1972	Konrad Wirnhier (FRG)
1976	Josef Panacek (Cze)
1980	Hans Kjeld Rasmussen (Den)
1984	Matthew Dryke (US)
1988	Axel Wegner (GDR)

Air Rifle
1984　Philippe Heberle (Fra)
1988　Goran Maksimovic (Yug)

Air Pistol
1988　Taniou Kiriakov (Bul)

Women

Sport Pistol
1984　Linda Thom (Can)
1988　Nino Saluokvadze (USSR)

Small Bore Rifle (Three position)
1984　Wu Xiaoxuan (Chn)
1988　Silvia Sperber (FRG)

Air Rifle
1984　Pat Spurgin (US)
1988　Irina Chilova (USSR)

Air Pistol
1988　Jasna Sekaric (Yug)

Most Olympic Medals

11 Carl Osburn (US)
8 Konrad Stäheli (Swi)
8 Otto Olsen (Nor)

QUEEN'S PRIZE
Principal event at the NRA meeting at Bisley every July.
Winners in the 1980s (All British unless otherwise stated):
1980　Alain Marion (Can)
1981　Geoffrey Ayling (Aus)
1982　Lindsay Peden
1983　Alain Marion (Can)
1984　David Richards
1985　John Bloomfield
1986　Geoffrey Cox
1987　Andrew Tucker
1988　John Pugsley
1989　Jeremy Thompson

SNOOKER

S teve Davis became world champion for the third year running and the sixth time in all, crushing John Parrott 18–3 in a final so one-sided that even British TV viewers seemed to lose interest. Davis won £105,000, taking his season's winnings past £650,000, and thus ended the season dominating the sport, which is how he started it. There was a dramatic semi-final when Davis had to fight off a comeback from Stephen Hendry (who recovered from 2–10 to 9–12), but overall it was a dullish Championship which touched bottom when Eddie Charlton beat Cliff Thorburn in the first round at 2.40 am with 50 people present, several asleep.

Davis won five tournaments before the New Year, but briefly lost form in mid-season and all kinds of strange things occurred. Doug Mountjoy, 46, won two tournaments in seven weeks including the UK Open, having won only two matches the previous season; he gave the credit to his coach Frank Callan: "Without that guy I'm nothing". Tony Meo won a tournament having been 200-1 in the betting. And then, after 5½ winless years, Alex Higgins, roared on by the crowd like a matador, beat four of the world's top seven to take the Irish Masters. He was limping heavily after Higginsishly falling 26 ft from the window of his girlfriend's flat. Less than 24 hours after his win, Higgins was knocked out of the World Championship in a qualifying game by Darren Morgan.

The long-running feud between Barry Hearn and the governing body, the WPBSA, continued and Tennents, the UK Open sponsors, withdrew, in apparent annoyance. The Association were unable to find a new sponsor and Hearn, barred from the hospitality room last year, took over as tournament director. A game at Wembley between Terry Griffiths and Silvino Francisco ended with a 5-1 win for Griffiths, as a surprisingly large number of people had predicted; bookmakers declined to pay out and this was said to be the fourth time controversy of this sort had involved Francisco. Snooker continued to attempt expansion overseas but at the European Open in Deauville the attendance went as low as six and Eugene Hughes was mistaken for a waiter by a patron of the casino next door. The magazine *Nature* theorised that the Moon was formed when a large chunk of the earth broke off after being hit by massive space debris, which, if true, would make snooker the first cosmic game.

1988-89

EMBASSY WORLD PROFESSIONAL CHAMPIONSHIP
Crucible Theatre, Sheffield

FIRST ROUND
STEVE DAVIS beat Steve Newbury 10 – 5; JIMMY WHITE beat Dene O'Kane 10 – 5; STEVE DUGGAN beat Cliff Wilson 10 – 1; JOHN VIRGO beat Darren Morgan 10 – 4; MIKE HALLETT beat Doug Mountjoy 10 – 7; DAVID ROE beat Tony Knowles 10 – 6; JOHN PARROTT beat Steve James 10 – 9; DENNIS TAYLOR beat Eugene Hughes 10 – 3; EDDIE CHARLTON beat Cliff Thorburn 10 – 9; TERRY GRIFFITHS beat Bob Chaperon 10 – 6; TONY MEO beat Joe Johnson 10 – 5; SILVINO FRANCISCO beat Joe O'Boye 10 – 5; WILLIE THORNE beat Paddy Browne 10 – 5; WAYNE JONES beat Neal Foulds 10 – 9; STEPHEN HENDRY beat Gary Wilkinson 10 – 9; DEAN REYNOLDS beat Peter Francisco 10 – 7.

SECOND ROUND
STEVE DAVIS beat Steve Duggan 13 – 3; JIMMY WHITE beat John Virgo 13 – 12; MIKE HALLETT beat David Roe 13 – 12; JOHN PARROTT beat Dennis Taylor 13 – 10; TERRY GRIFFITHS beat Silvino Francisco 13 – 9; TONY MEO beat Eddie Charlton 13 – 8; DEAN REYNOLDS beat Wayne Jones 13 – 3; STEPHEN HENDRY beat Willie Thorne 13 – 4.

QUARTER-FINALS
STEVE DAVIS beat Mike Hallett 13 – 3; STEPHEN HENDRY beat Terry Griffiths 13 – 5; JOHN PARROTT beat Jimmy White 13 – 7; TONY MEO beat Dean Reynolds 13 – 9

SEMI-FINALS
STEVE DAVIS beat Stephen Hendry 16 – 9; JOHN PARROTT beat Tony Meo 16 – 7

FINAL
STEVE DAVIS beat John Parrott 18 – 3
(Players underlined beat higher–ranked players)
Highest breaks:
143 Darren Morgan 142 Tony Meo 141 Stephen Hendry

OTHER RANKING TOURNAMENTS
Fidelity Unit Trusts International
Trentham Gardens, Stoke-on-Trent
Steve Davis beat Jimmy White 12 – 6
Highest Break: 136 Dean Reynolds

Rothmans Grand Prix
Hexagon Theatre, Reading
Steve Davis beat Alex Higgins 10 – 6
Highest Break: 139 Dean Reynolds

BCE Canadian Masters
Minkler Auditorium, Toronto
Jimmy White beat Steve Davis 9 – 4
Highest Break: 132 Dennis Taylor

Tennents UK Open
Guildhall, Preston
Doug Mountjoy beat Stephen Hendry 16 – 12
Highest Break: 139 David Roe

Mercantile Credit Classic
Norbreck Castle Hotel, Blackpool
Doug Mountjoy beat Wayne Jones 13 – 11
Highest Break: 143 Nigel Gilbert

ICI European Open
Deauville Casino, France
John Parrott beat Terry Griffiths 9 – 8
Highest Break: 147 Alain Robidoux

Anglian British Open
Derby Assembly Rooms
Tony Meo beat Dean Reynolds 13 – 6
Highest Break: 140 Mark Johnston-Allen

OTHER PROFESSIONAL FINALS 1988 – 89
Canadian Professional:
Alain Robidoux beat Jim Wych 8 – 4
Australian Professional:
John Campbell beat Robbie Foldvari 9 – 7
New Zealand Masters:
Stephen Hendry beat Mike Hallett 6 – 1
Dubai Duty Free Masters:
Neal Foulds beat Steve Davis 5 – 4
LEP: Hong Kong Masters:
Jimmy White beat Neal Foulds 6 – 3
Fosters Professional:
Mike Hallett beat Stephen Hendry 8 – 5
LEP Matchroom Trophy:
Steve Davis beat Dennis Taylor 10 – 7
Everest World Match-Play:
Steve Davis beat John Parrott 9 – 5
Norwich Union Grand Prix:
Steve Davis beat Jimmy White 5 – 4
Benson & Hedges Masters:
Stephen Hendry beat John Parrott 9 – 6
Scottish Professionals:
John Rea beat Murdo Macleod 9 – 7
English Professional:
Mike Hallett beat John Parrott 9 – 7
Welsh Professional:
Doug Mountjoy beat Terry Griffiths 9 – 6
Irish Professional:
Alex Higgins beat Jack McLaughlin 9 – 7
Benson & Hedges Irish Masters:
Alex Higgins beat Stephen Hendry 9 – 8
Fersina Windows World Cup:
England beat Rest of the World 9 – 8
Matchroom League:
1st: Steve Davis 2nd John Parrott
Continental Airlines London Masters:
Stephen Hendry beat John Parrott 4 – 2

━━━ CHAMPIONS ━━━

WORLD PROFESSIONAL CHAMPIONSHIP
(Embassy World Professional Championship since 1976)
All winners British unless otherwise stated

1927	Joe Davis	20 – 11	Tom Dennis
1928	Joe Davis	16 – 13	Fred Lawrence
1929	Joe Davis	19 – 14	Tom Dennis
1930	Joe Davis	25 – 12	Tom Dennis
1931	Joe Davis	25 – 21	Tom Dennis
1932	Joe Davis	30 – 19	Clark McConachy (NZ)
1933	Joe Davis	25 – 18	Willie Smith
1934	Joe Davis	25 – 23	Tom Newman
1935	Joe Davis	25 – 20	Willie Smith
1936	Joe Davis	34 – 27	Horace Lindrum (Aus)
1937	Joe Davis	32 – 29	Horace Lindrum (Aus)
1938	Joe Davis	37 – 24	Sidney Smith
1939	Joe Davis	43 – 30	Sidney Smith
1940	Joe Davis	37 – 36	Fred Davis
1946	Joe Davis	78 – 67	Horace Lindrum (Aus)
1947	Walter Donaldson	82 – 63	Fred Davis
1948	Fred Davis	84 – 61	Walter Donaldson
1949	Fred Davis	80 – 65	Walter Donaldson
1950	Walter Donaldson	51 – 46	Fred Davis
1951	Fred Davis	58 – 39	Walter Donaldson
1952	Horace Lindrum	94 – 49	Clark McConachy (NZ)

Professional Match-Play Championship

1952	Fred Davis	38 – 35	Walter Donaldson
1953	Fred Davis	37 – 34	Walter Donaldson
1954	Fred Davis	39 – 21	Walter Donaldson
1955	Fred Davis	37 – 34	John Pulman
1956	Fred Davis	38 – 35	John Pulman
1957	John Pulman	39 – 34	Jackie Rea

Challenge Matches

1964	John Pulman	19 – 16	Fred Davis
1964	John Pulman	40 – 33	Rex Williams
1965	John Pulman	37 – 36	Fred Davis
1965	John Pulman	25 – 22	Rex Williams
1965	John Pulman	39 – 12	Freddie van Rensburg (SA)
1966	John Pulman	5 – 2	Fred Davis
1968	John Pulman	39 – 34	Eddie Charlton (Aus)

1969	John Spencer	37 – 24	Gary Owen
1970	Ray Reardon	37 – 33	John Pulman
1971*	John Spencer	37 – 29	Warren Simpson (Aus)
1972	Alex Higgins	37 – 32	John Spencer
1973	Ray Reardon	38 – 32	Eddie Charlton (Aus)
1974	Ray Reardon	22 – 12	Graham Miles
1975	Ray Reardon	31 – 30	Eddie Charlton (Aus)
1976	Ray Reardon	27 – 16	Alex Higgins
1977	John Spencer	25 – 21	Cliff Thorburn (Can)
1978	Ray Reardon	25 – 18	Perrie Mans (SA)
1979	Terry Griffiths	24 – 16	Dennis Taylor
1980	Cliff Thorburn (Can)	18 – 16	Alex Higgins
1981	Steve Davis	18 – 12	Doug Mountjoy
1982	Alex Higgins	18 – 15	Ray Reardon
1983	Steve Davis	18 – 6	Cliff Thorburn (Can)
1984	Steve Davis	18 – 16	Jimmy White
1985	Dennis Taylor	18 – 17	Steve Davis
1986	Joe Johnson	18 – 12	Steve Davis
1987	Steve Davis	18 – 14	Joe Johnson
1988	Steve Davis	18 – 11	Terry Griffiths
1989	Steve Davis	18 – 3	John Parrott

*Played November 1970

RANKING TOURNAMENT WINNERS
Fidelity Unit Trusts International
1981– 84 Jameson International; 1985 Goya International; 1986 BCE International; 1987 Fidelity Unit Trusts International

1982	Tony Knowles
1983	Steve Davis
1984	Steve Davis
1985	Cliff Thorburn (Can)
1986	Neal Foulds
1987	Steve Davis
1988	Steve Davis
1989	Steve Davis

Rothmans Grand Prix
1982–83 Professional Players' Tournament; 1984– Rothmans Grand Prix

1982	Ray Reardon
1983	Tony Knowles

1984   Dennis Taylor
1985   Steve Davis
1986   Jimmy White
1987   Stephen Hendry
1988   Steve Davis

Mercantile Credit Classic
1984 Lada Classic; 1985– Mercantile Credit Classic
1984   Steve Davis
1985   Willie Thorne
1986   Jimmy White
1987   Steve Davis
1988   Steve Davis
1989   Doug Mountjoy

United Kingdom Open
1984 – 85 Coral UK Open; 1986 – 88 Tennents UK Open
1984   Steve Davis
1985   Steve Davis
1986   Steve Davis
1987   Steve Davis
1988   Doug Mountjoy

British Open
1985–87 Dulux British Open; 1988 MIM Britannia British Open; 1989 Anglian British Open
1985   Silvino Francisco (SA)
1986   Steve Davis
1987   Jimmy White
1988   Stephen Hendry
1989   Tony Meo

BCE Canadian Masters
1988   Jimmy White

ICI European Open
1989   John Parrott

SUMMARY OF RANKING TOURNAMENT WINS

		WC	FU	RP	MC	UK	BO	CM	ED
20	Steve Davis	6	4	2	3	4	1	–	–
5	Ray Reardon	4	–	1	–	–	–	–	–
4	Jimmy White	–	–	1	1	–	1	1	–
2	Cliff Thorburn	1	1	–	–	–	–	–	–
2	Dennis Taylor	1	–	1	–	–	–	–	–
2	Tony Knowles	–	1	1	–	–	–	–	–
2	Stephen Hendry	–	–	1	–	–	1	–	–
2	Doug Mountjoy	–	–	–	1	1	–	–	–
1	John Spencer	1	–	–	–	–	–	–	–
1	Terry Griffiths	1	–	–	–	–	–	–	–
1	Alex Higgins	1	–	–	–	–	–	–	–
1	Joe Johnson	1	–	–	–	–	–	–	–
1	Neal Foulds	–	1	–	–	–	–	–	–
1	Willie Thorne	–	–	–	1	–	–	–	–
1	Silvino Francisco	–	–	–	–	–	1	–	–
1	Tony Meo	–	–	–	–	–	1	–	–
1	John Parrott	–	–	–	–	–	–	–	1

WC – Embassy World Professional Championship;
FU – Fidelity Unit Trusts International;
RP – Rothmans Grand Prix;
MC – Mercantile Credit Classic;
UK – United Kingdom Open;
BO – British Open;
CM – BCE Canadian Masters;
EO – ICI European Open

OTHER MAJOR TOURNAMENTS

Pot Black
1969   Ray Reardon
1970   John Spencer
1971   John Spencer
1972   Eddie Charlton (Aus)
1973   Eddie Charlton (Aus)
1974   Graham Miles
1975   Graham Miles
1976   John Spencer
1977   Perrie Mans (SA)
1978   Doug Mountjoy
1979   Ray Reardon
1980   Eddie Charlton (Aus)
1981   Cliff Thorburn (Can)
1982   Steve Davis
1983   Steve Davis
1984   Terry Griffiths
1985   Doug Mountjoy
1986   Jimmy White
Discontinued

Benson & Hedges Masters
1975   John Spencer
1976   Ray Reardon
1977   Doug Mountjoy
1978   Alex Higgins
1979   Perrie Mans (SA)
1980   Terry Griffiths
1981   Alex Higgins
1982   Steve Davis
1983   Cliff Thorburn (Can)
1984   Jimmy White
1985   Cliff Thorburn (Can)
1986   Cliff Thorburn (Can)
1987   Dennis Taylor
1988   Steve Davis
1989   Stephen Hendry

Coral UK Championship
Sponsored by Coral since 1978
1977   Patsy Fagan
1978   Doug Mountjoy
1979   John Virgo
1980   Steve Davis
1981   Steve Davis
1982   Terry Griffiths
1983   Alex Higgins
Became a ranking event in 1984

Benson & Hedges Irish Masters
1978   John Spencer
1979   Doug Mountjoy
1980   Terry Griffiths
1981   Terry Griffiths
1982   Terry Griffiths
1983   Steve Davis
1984   Steve Davis
1985   Jimmy White
1986   Jimmy White
1987   Steve Davis
1988   Steve Davis
1989   Alex Higgins

Winfield Australian Masters
1979   Ian Anderson (Aus)
1980   John Spencer
1981   Tony Meo
1982   Steve Davis
1983   Cliff Thorburn (Can)
1984   Tony Knowles
1985   Tony Meo
1986   Dennis Taylor
1987   Stephen Hendry
Discontinued

Fersina Windows World Cup
Previously sponsored by four different firms
1979 Wales (Griffiths, Reardon, Mountjoy)
1980 Wales (Griffiths, Reardon, Mountjoy)
1981 England (S. Davis, Taylor, Spencer)
1982 Canada (Thorburn, Stevens, Werbeniuk)
1983 England (Knowles, Meo, S.Davis)
1984 Not held
1985 All-Ireland (Higgins, Taylor, Hughes)
1986 Ireland 'A' (Higgins, Taylor, Hughes)
1987 Ireland 'A' (Higgins, Taylor, Hughes)
1988 England (S.Davis, Foulds, White)
1989 England (S.Davis, Foulds, White)

Lada Classic
1980 John Spencer
1981* Steve Davis
1982 Terry Griffiths
1983 Steve Davis
* Played in December 1980
Became a ranking event in 1984

Welsh Professional Championship
1980 Doug Mountjoy
1981 Ray Reardon
1982 Doug Mountjoy
1983 Ray Reardon
1984 Doug Mountjoy
1985 Terry Griffiths
1986 Terry Griffiths
1987 Doug Mountjoy
1988 Terry Griffiths
1989 Doug Mountjoy

Yamaha International Masters
1981 Steve Davis
1982 Steve Davis
1983 Ray Reardon
1984 Steve Davis

English Professional Championship
1981 Steve Davis
1982–4 Not held
1985 Steve Davis
1986 Tony Meo
1987 Tony Meo
1988 Dean Reynolds
1989 Mike Hallett

Langs Scottish Masters
1981 Jimmy White
1982 Steve Davis
1983 Steve Davis
1984 Steve Davis
1985 Cliff Thorburn (Can)
1986 Cliff Thorburn (Can)
1987 Joe Johnson
Discontinued

Jameson International
1981 Steve Davis
Became a ranking event in 1982

Scottish Professional Championship
1981 Ian Black
1982 Eddie Sinclair
1983 Murdo Macleod
1984 Not held
1985 Murdo Macleod
1986 Stephen Hendry
1987 Stephen Hendry
1988 Stephen Hendry
1989 John Rea

Irish Professional Championship
1982 Dennis Taylor
1983 Alex Higgins
1984 Not held
1985 Dennis Taylor
1986 Dennis Taylor
1987 Dennis Taylor
1988 Jack McLaughlin
1989 Alex Higgins

Fosters World Doubles Championship
1982 – 86 Hofmeister World Doubles; 1987 Fosters World Doubles
1982 Steve Davis/Tony Meo
1983 Steve Davis/Tony Meo
1984 Alex Higgins/Jimmy White
1985 Steve Davis/Tony Meo
1986 Steve Davis/Tony Meo
1987 Mike Hallett/Stephen Hendry
Discontinued

Canadian Professional Championship
1983 Kirk Stevens
1984 Cliff Thorburn
1985 Cliff Thorburn
1986 Cliff Thorburn
1987 Cliff Thorburn
1988 Alain Robidoux

Australian Professional Championship
1984 Eddie Charlton
1985 John Campbell
1986 Warren King
1987 Warren King
1988 John Campbell

Everest World Match–Play Championship
1988 Steve Davis

OFFICIAL MAXIMUM BREAKS
22 Jan 1955 Joe Davis (Exhibition)
22 Dec 1965 Rex Williams (Exhibition)
11 Jan 1982 Steve Davis (Lada Classic)
23 Apr 1983 Cliff Thorburn (Embassy W/Champs)
28 Jan 1984 Kirk Stevens (B & H Masters)
17 Nov 1987 Willie Thorne (Tennents UK Champs)
20 Feb 1988 Tony Meo (Matchroom League)
24 Sep 1988 Alain Robidoux (European Open)
18 Feb 1989 John Rea (Scottish Pro Champs)
8 Mar 1989 Cliff Thorburn (Matchroom League)

WORLD AMATEUR CHAMPIONS
1963 Gary Owen
1966 Gary Owen
1968 David Taylor
1970 Johnathan Barron
1972 Ray Edmonds
1974 Ray Edmonds
1976 Doug Mountjoy
1978 Cliff Wilson
1980 Jimmy White
1982 Terry Parsons
1984 O B (Omprakash) Agrawal (Ind)
1985 Paul Mifsud (Mal)
1986 Paul Mifsud (Mal)
1987 Darren Morgan
1988 James Wattana (Tha)

STEVE DAVIS IN THE 1980s

1980: Coral UK Championship

1981: Embassy World Professional Championship; Coral UK Championship; World Cup; Lada Classic; Yamaha Masters; English Professional Championship; Jameson International

1982: Pot Black; Benson & Hedges Masters; Winfield Australian Masters; Yamaha Masters; Langs Scottish Masters; World Doubles Championship

1983: Embassy World Professional Championship; Jameson International; Pot Black; Benson & Hedges Irish Masters; World Cup; Lada Classic; Lang Scottish Masters; World Doubles Championship

1984: Embassy World Professional Championship; Jameson International; Lada Classic; Coral UK Open; Benson & Hedges Irish Masters; Yamaha Masters; Langs Scottish Masters

1985: Rothmans Grand Prix; Coral UK Open; English Professional Championship; World Doubles Championship

1986: Tennents UK Open; Dulux British Open; World Doubles Championship

1987: Embassy World Professional Championship; Fidelity Unit Trusts International; Mercantile Credit Classic; Tennents UK Open; Benson & Hedges Irish Masters

1988: Embassy World Professional Championship; Fidelity Unit Trusts International; Rothmans Grand Prix; Mercantile Credit Classic; Benson & Hedges Masters; Benson & Hedges Irish Masters; World Cup; Everest World Match–Play

1989: Embassy World Professional Championship; World Cup

"I am a patient man and an optimist and I believe it won't come to that. But if it gets completely intolerable you won't see us any more. We are both proud men of independent means."
Barry Hearn threatening to quit organised snooker along with Steve Davis

"I'm not bent. I barely even play cards for penny stakes."
Silvino Francisco, Daily Mirror, Jan 25

"There are a million things wrong with snooker, but the matches are straight."
Clive Everton, Independent Mar 3

"I feel a bit, well, poncy. I've caught myself talking about 'my publisher' once or twice. That goes down really well in Romford."
Barry Hearn, on writing a novel

"They are gentlemen compared to that madman."
Patricia Hammond on the experience of being a neighbour both to the Kray brothers and Alex Higgins, Time Out, Mar 15

"I couldn't care less about the fans. I'm a professional snooker player and I'm playing to win. If the fans don't like it, they can lump it."
Eddie Charlton, after beating Cliff Thorburn in Sheffield at 2.40 am

"It is my best performance and I have reached a standard which I didn't think possible."
Steve Davis after the World Championship final, Daily Telegraph, May 2

"I played like a slow puncture."
John Parrott, ditto, the Sun, May 2

1990

Jan 2–14 : Mercantile Credit Classic (Norbreck Castle Hotel, Blackpool);

Jan 19–20 : Overseas Ranking Tournament (to be announced);

Jan 22–29: Embassy World Professional Championship qualifying matches (Norbreck Castle Hotel, Blackpool);

Feb 11–14 : Benson & Hedges Masters (Wembley Conference Centre);

Feb 18–Mar 4 British Open (Derby Assembly Rooms);

Mar 6–17: Overseas Ranking Tournament (to be announced);

Mar 20–23: Fersina World Cup (International Centre, Bournemouth);

Mar 7–Apr 1: Benson & Hedges Irish Masters (Goff's, Kill, Co.Kildare):

Apr 13–29: Embassy World Professional Championship (Crucible Theatre, Sheffield)

SPEEDWAY

1989

WORLD CHAMPIONSHIPS
Individual
Munich, Sep 2
1 Hans Nielsen (Oxford/Denmark) 15pts
2 Simon Wigg (Oxford/England) 12pts
3 Jeremy Doncaster (Reading/England) 12pts
4 Erik Gundersen (Cradley Heath/Denmark) 11pts
5 Kevin Tatum (Coventry/England) 10pts
6 Andy Smith (Bradford/England) 10pts
Pairs
Leszno, Poland, Aug 5
1 Denmark (Erik Gundersen/Hans Nielsen) 48pts
3 Sweden (Jimmy Nilsen/Per Jonsson) 44pts
3 England (Paul Thorp/Kevin Tatum) 37pts
Team
Bradford, Sep 17
1 England 48pts
  (Jeremy Doncaster/Kevin Tatum/Simon Wigg/Paul Thorp)
2 Denmark 34pts
3 Sweden 30pts

Long Track
Marianske Lazne, Czechoslovakia, Aug 20
1 Simon Wigg (Oxford/England) 38pts
2 Ales Dryml (Cze) 37pts
3 Karl Maier (FRG) 33pts

BRITISH LEAGUE RIDERS' CHAMPIONSHIP
Belle Vue, Oct 1
1 Shawn Moran (Belle Vue) 15pts
2 Hans Nielsen (Oxford) 14pts
3 Brian Karger (Swindon) 14pts

NATIONAL LEAGUE RIDERS' CHAMPIONSHIP
Coventry, Sep 9
1 Mark Loram (Ipswich) 14pts
2 Kenny McKinna (Glasgow) 12pts
3 David Blackburn (Berwick) 11pts

CHAMPIONS

WORLD CHAMPIONS

	Individual	Pairs	Team	Long Track
1936	Lionel Van Praag (Aus)	–	–	–
1937	Jack Milne (US)	–	–	–
1938	Bluey Wilkinson (Aus)	–	–	–
1949	Tommy Price (Eng)	–	–	–
1950	Freddie Williams (Wal)	–	–	–
1951	Jack Young (Aus)	–	–	–
1952	Jack Young (Aus)	–	–	–
1953	Freddie Williams (Wal)	–	–	–
1954	Ronnie Moore (NZ)	–	–	–
1955	Peter Craven (Eng)	–	–	–
1956	Ove Fundin (Swe)	–	–	–
1957	Barry Briggs (NZ)	–	–	–
1958	Barry Briggs (NZ)	–	–	–
1959	Ronnie Moore (NZ)	–	–	–
1960	Ove Fundin (Swe)	–	Sweden	–
1961	Ove Fundin (Swe)	–	Poland	–
1962	Peter Craven (Eng)	–	Sweden	–
1963	Ove Fundin (Swe)	–	Sweden	–
1964	Barry Briggs (NZ)	–	Sweden	–
1965	Bjorn Knutsson (Swe)	–	Poland	–
1966	Barry Briggs (NZ)	–	Poland	–
1967	Ove Fundin (Swe)	–	Sweden	–
1968	Ivan Mauger (NZ)	–	Great Britain	–
1969	Ivan Mauger (NZ)	–	Poland	–
1970	Ivan Mauger (NZ)	New Zealand (Moore/Mauger)	Sweden	–
1971	Ole Olsen (Den)	Poland (Szczakiel/Wyglenda)	Great Britain	Ivan Mauger (NZ)
1972	Ivan Mauger (NZ)	England (Wilson/Betts)	Great Britain	Ivan Mauger (NZ)
1973	Jerzy Szczakiel (Pol)	Sweden (Michanek/Jansson)	Great Britain	Ole Olsen (Den)
1974	Anders Michanek (Swe)	Sweden (Michanek/Sjosten)	England	Egon Muller (FRG)
1975	Ole Olsen (Den)	Sweden (Michanek/Jansson)	England	Egon Muller (FRG)
1976	Peter Collins (Eng)	England (Simmons/Louis)	Australia	Egon Muller (FRG)
1977	Ivan Mauger (NZ)	England (Simmons/Collins)	England	Anders Michanek (Swe)
1978	Ole Olsen (Den)	England (Simmons/Kennett)	Denmark	Egon Muller (FRG)
1979	Ivan Mauger (NZ)	Denmark (Olsen/Nielsen)	New Zealand	Alois Weisbock (FRG)
1980	Michael Lee (Eng)	England (Jessup/Collins)	England	Karl Maier (FRG)
1981	Bruce Penhall (US)	United States (Penhall/Schwartz)	Denmark	Michael Lee (Eng)
1982	Bruce Penhall (US)	United States (Sigalos/Schwartz)	United States	Karl Maier (FRG)
1983	Egon Muller (FRG)	England (Carter/Collins)	Denmark	Shawn Moran (US)]
1984	Erik Gundersen (Den)	England (Collins/Morton)	Denmark	Erik Gundersen (Den)
1985	Erik Gundersen (Den)	Denmark (Gundersen/Knudsen)	Denmark	Simon Wigg (Eng)

1986	Hans Nielsen (Den)	Denmark (Gundersen/Nielsen)	Denmark	Erik Gundersen (Den)
1987	Hans Nielsen (Den)	Denmark (Gundersen/Nielsen)	Denmark	Karl Maier (FRG)
1988	Erik Gundersen (Den)	Denmark (Gundersen/Nielsen)	Denmark	Karl Maier (FRG)
1989	Hans Nielsen (Den)	Denmark (Gundersen/Nielsen)	England	Simon Wigg (Eng)

Most Wins

Individual   6 Ivan Mauger; 5 Ove Fundin; 4 Barry Briggs; 3 Ole Olsen

Pairs   – Team: 7 England; 6 Denmark; 3 Sweden
     – Ind: 5 Erik Gundersen (Den); 4 Peter Collins (Eng), Hans Nielsen (Den)

Team   – Team: 8 Denmark; 6 Sweden; 5 England; 4 Britain
     – Ind: 7 Hans Nielsen (Den), Erik Gundersen (Den); 6 Ove Fundin (Swe)

Long Track: 4 Egon Muller (FRG), Karl Maier (FRG)

BRITISH SPEEDWAY LEAGUE

Champions since formation of two divisions in 1968.
Known as British League and National League since 1968

	British League	National League
1968	Coventry	Belle Vue Colts
1969	Poole	Belle Vue Colts
1970	Belle Vue	Canterbury
1971	Belle Vue	Eastbourne
1972	Belle Vue	Crewe
1973	Reading	Boston
1974	Exeter	Birmingham
1975	Ipswich	Birmingham
1976	Ipswich	Newcastle
1977	White City	Eastbourne
1978	Coventry	Canterbury
1979	Coventry	Mildenhall
1980	Reading	Rye House
1981	Cradley Heath	Middlesbrough
1982	Belle Vue	Newcastle
1983	Cradley Heath	Newcastle
1984	Ipswich	Long Eaton
1985	Oxford	Ellesmere Port
1986	Oxford	Eastbourne
1987	Coventry	Eastbourne
1988	Coventry	Hackney

Most Titles

Division One/British League
10 Belle Vue; 8 Wembley; 7 Wimbledon; 3 Coventry

BRITISH LEAGUE RIDERS' CHAMPIONSHIP

1965	Barry Briggs (Swindon)
1966	Barry Briggs (Swindon)
1967	Barry Briggs (Swindon)
1968	Barry Briggs (Swindon)
1969	Barry Briggs (Swindon)
1970	Barry Briggs (Swindon)
1971	Ivan Mauger (Belle Vue)
1972	Ole Olsen (Wolverhampton)
1973	Ivan Mauger (Exeter)
1974	Peter Collins (Belle Vue)
1975	Peter Collins (Belle Vue)
1976	Ole Olsen (Coventry)
1977	Ole Olsen (Coventry)
1978	Ole Olsen (Coventry)
1979	John Louis (Ipswich)
1980	Les Collins (Leicester)
1981	Kenny Carter (Halifax)
1982	Kenny Carter (Halifax)
1983	Erik Gundersen (Cradley Heath)
1984	Chris Morton (Belle Vue)
1985	Erik Gundersen (Cradley Heath)
1986	Hans Nielsen (Oxford)
1987	Hans Nielsen (Oxford)
1988	Jan Pedersen (Cradley Heath)
1989	Shawn Moran (Belle Vue)

NATIONAL LEAGUE RIDERS' CHAMPIONSHIP

1968	Graham Plant (Teesside)
1969	Geoff Ambrose (Crayford)
1970	Dave Jessup (Eastbourne)
1971	John Louis (Ipswich)
1972	Phil Crump (Crewe)
1973	Arthur Price (Boston)
1974	Carl Glover (Boston)
1975	Laurie Etheridge (Crayford)
1976	Joe Owen (Newcastle)
1977	Colin Richardson (Eastbourne)
1978	Steve Koppe (Canterbury)
1979	Ian Gledhill (Stoke)
1980	Wayne Brown (Berwick)
1981	Mike Ferreira (Canterbury)
1982	Joe Owen (Newcastle)
1983	Steve McDermott (Berwick)
1984	Ian Barney (Peterborough)
1985	Neil Middleditch (Arena Essex)
1986	Paul Thorp (Stoke)
1987	Andrew Silver (Arena Essex)
1988	Troy Butler (Milton Keynes)
1989	Mark Loram (Ipswich)

NATIONAL LEAGUE PAIRS CHAMPIONSHIP

1975	Newcastle
1976	Ellesmere Port
1977	Boston
1978	Ellesmere Port
1979	Milton Keynes
1980	Middlesbrough
1981	Canterbury
1982	Weymouth
1983	Weymouth
1984	Stoke
1985	Ellesmere Port
1986	Edinburgh
1987	Mildenhall
1988	Stoke
1989	Stoke

SQUASH

1989

WOMEN'S WORLD CHAMPIONSHIP
Warmond, Holland, Mar 5-12

Singles

QUARTER-FINALS
Martine Le Moignan (GB) beat Robyn Lambourne (Aus) 9-7 9-2 9-2; Liz Irving (Aus) beat Michelle Martin (Aus) 9-7 9-6 10-8; Susan Devoy (NZ) beat Danielle Drady (Aus) 10-8 6-9 9-1 9-7; Sarah Fitzgerald (Aus) beat Alison Cumings (GB) 6-9 9-7 9-1 3-9 10-8

SEMI-FINALS
Le Moignan beat Fitzgerald 9-4 9-5 0-9 5-9 9-1; Devoy beat Irving 5-9 10-9 9-6 9-2
3rd Place
Irving beat Fitzgerald 9-5 9-2 9-1

FINAL
Le Moignan beat Devoy (NZ) 4-9 9-4 10-8 10-8

Team

QUARTER-FINALS
England beat Scotland 3-0; New Zealand beat Canada 3-0; Australia beat Holland 3-0; West Germany beat Ireland 3-1

SEMI-FINALS
England beat New Zealand 2-1; Australia beat West Germany 3-0

FINAL
England beat Australia 2-0
Final Standings; 1 England; 2 Australia; 3 New Zealand; 4 West Germany; 5 Ireland; 6 Scotland

HI-TEC BRITISH OPEN
Wembley, Apr 12-17

QUARTER-FINALS
Men
Jahangir Khan (Pak) beat Umar Hayat Khan (Pak) 9-0 9-2 9-0; Rodney Martin (Aus) beat Chris Dittmar (Aus) 10-9 9-7 2-9 9-1; Ross Norman (NZ) beat B Martin (Aus) 9-7 10-9 9-6; Chris Robertson (Aus) beat Jansher Khan (Pak) 9-4 9-6 9-0

SEMI-FINALS
Jahangir Khan beat Norman 9-0 6-9 9-3 9-4; Rodney Martin beat Robertson 5-9 9-10 9-4 9-2 9-5

FINAL
Jahangir Khan beat Rodney Martin 9-2 3-9 9-5 0-9 9-2

Women

QUARTER-FINALS
Susan Devoy (NZ) beat Robyn Lambourne (Aus) 9-6 9-1 9-1; Liz Irving (Aus) beat R Best (RoI) 9-6 9-2 9-5; Martine Le Moignan (GB) beat Michelle Martin (Aus) 9-3 9-4 9-2; Danielle Drady (Aus) beat Sarah Fitzgerald (Aus) 9-6 9-1 9-5

SEMI-FINALS
Le Moignan beat Drady 4-9 9-6 9-7 9-6; Devoy beat Irving 9-4 9-7 3-9 9-2

FINAL
Devoy beat Le Moignan 8-10 10-8 9-3 9-6

EUROPEAN TEAM CHAMPIONSHIPS
Helsinki, Apr 26-29

FINALS
Men
1st-2nd places: England beat Sweden 4-1
3rd-4th places: Finland beat West Germany 4-1
5th-6th places: Holland beat Spain 5-0
Women
1st-2nd places: England beat Ireland 3-0
3rd-4th places: Holland beat Sweden 3-0
5th-6th places: Finland beat West Germany 3-0

WORLD RANKINGS
(Summer1989)
Men
1 Jahangir Khan (Pak)
2 Jansher Khan (Pak)
3 Chris Dittmar (Aus)
4 Rodney Martin (Aus)
5 Chris Robertson (Aus)
Women
1 Susan Devoy (NZ)
2 Lisa Opie (GB)
3 Martine Le Moignan (GB)
4 Liz Irving (Aus)
5 Michelle Martin (Aus)

CHAMPIONS

WORLD OPEN CHAMPIONSHIP
(Not held 1978)
Men

1976	Geoff Hunt (Aus)
1977	Geoff Hunt (Aus)
1979	Geoff Hunt (Aus)
1980	Geoff Hunt (Aus)
1981	Jahangir Khan (Pak)
1982	Jahangir Khan (Pak)
1983	Jahangir Khan (Pak)
1984	Jahangir Khan (Pak)
1985	Jahangir Khan (Pak)
1986	Ross Norman (NZ)
1987	Jansher Khan (Pak)
1988	Jahangir Khan (Pak)

Women

1976	Heather McKay (Aus)
1979	Heather McKay (Aus)
1981	Rhonda Thorne (Aus)
1983	Vicki Cardwell (Aus)
1985	Susan Devoy (NZ)
1987	Susan Devoy (NZ)
1989	Martine Le Moignan (GB)

WOMEN'S WORLD TEAM CHAMPIONSHIP

1979	Great Britain
1981	Australia
1983	Australia
1985	England
1987	England
1989	England

WORLD AMATEUR/ISRF CHAMPIONSHIPS

From 1987 a Team competition only

Individual

1967	Geoff Hunt (Aus)
1969	Geoff Hunt (Aus)
1971	Geoff Hunt (Aus)
1973	Cam Nancarrow (Aus)
1975	Kevin Shawcross (Aus)
1977	Maqsood Ahmed (Pak)
1979	Jahangir Khan (Pak)
1981	Steve Bowditch (Aus)
1983	Jahangir Khan (Pak)
1985	Jahangir Khan (Pak)

Team

1967	Australia
1969	Australia
1971	Australia
1973	Australia
1975	Great Britain
1977	Pakistan
1979	Great Britain
1981	Pakistan
1983	Pakistan
1985	Pakistan
1987	Pakistan

BRITISH OPEN CHAMPIONSHIPS

First held in 1922 for women; 1930 for men.
Post-war winners

Men

1946	Mahmoud Karim (Egy)
1947	Mahmoud Karim (Egy)
1948	Mahmoud Karim (Egy)
1949	Mahmoud Karim (Egy)
1950	Hashim Khan (Pak)
1951	Hashim Khan (Pak)
1952	Hashim Khan (Pak)
1953	Hashim Khan (Pak)
1954	Hashim Khan (Pak)
1955	Hashim Khan (Pak)
1956	Roshan Khan (Pak)
1957	Hashim Khan (Pak)
1958	Azam Khan (Pak)
1959	Azam Khan (Pak)
1960	Azam Khan (Pak)
1961	Azam Khan (Pak)
1962	Mohibullah Khan (Pak)
1963	Abdel AbouTaleb (Egy)
1964	Abdel AbouTaleb (Egy)
1965	Abdel AbouTaleb (Egy)
1966	Abdel AbouTaleb (Egy)
1967	Jonah Barrington (GB)
1968	Jonah Barrington (GB)
1969	Geoff Hunt (Aus)
1970	Jonah Barrington (GB)
1971	Jonah Barrington (GB)
1972	Jonah Barrington (GB)
1973	Jonah Barrington (GB)
1974	Geoff Hunt (Aus)
1975	Qamar Zaman (Pak)
1976	Geoff Hunt (Aus)
1977	Geoff Hunt (Aus)
1978	Geoff Hunt (Aus)
1979	Geoff Hunt (Aus)
1980	Geoff Hunt (Aus)
1981	Geoff Hunt (Aus)
1982	Jahangir Khan (Pak)
1983	Jahangir Khan (Pak)
1984	Jahangir Khan (Pak)
1985	Jahangir Khan (Pak)
1986	Jahangir Khan (Pak)
1987	Jahangir Khan (Pak)
1988	Jahangir Khan (Pak)
1989	Jahangir Khan (Pak)

Most wins

8 Geoff Hunt, Jahangir Khan; **7** Hashim Khan; **6** Abdel Fattah Amr Bey, Jonah Barrington

Women

1947	Joan Curry (GB)
1948	Joan Curry (GB)
1949	Joan Curry (GB)
1950	Janet Morgan (GB)
1951	Janet Morgan (GB)
1952	Janet Morgan (GB)
1953	Janet Morgan (GB)
1954	Janet Morgan (GB)
1955	Janet Morgan (GB)
1956	Janet Morgan (GB)
1957	Janet Morgan (GB)
1958	Janet Morgan (GB)
1959	Not held
1960	Sheila Macintosh (GB)
1961	Fran Marshall (GB)
1962	Heather Blundell (Aus)
1963	Heather Blundell (Aus)
1964	Heather Blundell (Aus)
1965	Heather Blundell (Aus)
1966	Heather McKay (née Blundell) (Aus)
1967	Heather McKay (Aus)
1968	Heather McKay (Aus)
1969	Heather McKay (Aus)
1970	Heather McKay (Aus)
1971	Heather McKay (Aus)
1972	Heather McKay (Aus)
1973	Heather McKay (Aus)
1974	Heather McKay (Aus)
1975	Heather McKay (Aus)
1976	Heather McKay (Aus)
1977	Heather McKay (Aus)
1978	Susan Newman (Aus)
1979	Barbara Wall (Aus)
1980	Vicki Hoffman (Aus)
1981	Vicki Hoffman (Aus)
1982	Vicki Cardwell (née Hoffman)(Aus)
1983	Vicki Cardwell (Aus)
1984	Susan Devoy (NZ)
1985	Susan Devoy (NZ)
1986	Susan Devoy (NZ)
1987	Susan Devoy (NZ)
1988	Susan Devoy (NZ)
1989	Susan Devoy (NZ)

Most wins:

16 Heather McKay; **9** Janet Morgan; **6** Margot Lumb, Susan Devoy

---

1990

Jan 11-15: World Young Masters Invitation (East Grinstead); *Feb 15-18:* European Junior Team Championship (Ghent, Belgium); *Feb 19-25:* Welsh Open (Cardiff); *Mar 28-31:* Prince Rainier Cup (Monte Carlo); *Apr 14-23:* British Open (Wembley Conference Centre); *May 2-6:* European Team Championship (Zurich).

SWIMMING

Adrian Moorhouse, Britain's Olympic gold medallist, continued his run of triumphs when he won his fourth successive European gold medal – equalling Michael Gross – at the 19th European Championships in Bonn and broke the world 100m breaststroke record in the heat. He was the first British swimmer to set a world record for 13 years, since David Wilkie in the 200m breaststroke at the 1976 Olympics. Nick Gillingham then equalled the record in that event but had his name in the books for only two days: Mike Barrowman surpassed him at the Pan-Pacific Games, where US swimmers broke four records in a day.

Mark Spitz, winner of seven golds at the 1972 Olympics, announced plans to enter the 100-metres butterfly in 1992, when he will be 42. Former Olympic medallist Sharron Davies, 26, made a comeback and qualified for the Commonwealth Games by finishing 6th in the individual medley in Bonn. She retired after Moscow, 1980, and made her decision while commentating in Seoul: "I just kept wishing I was in the water." Vicki Keith of Canada became the first person to cross the English Channel using the butterfly stroke. It took her 23 hours 33 minutes, compared to the freestyle record of 7 hours 40 minutes. Audrey Scott, hon. sec. of the Channel Swimming Association, said of those who make the attempt: "They are all mad."

1989

EUROPEAN CHAMPIONSHIPS
Bonn, West Germany, Aug 12-20

Men
50 Metres Freestyle
1 Vladimir Tkachenko (USSR) 22.64s
2 Evgeneyev Kotriaga (USSR) 22.67s
3 Nils Rudolph (GDR) 22.76s

100 Metres Freestyle
1 Giorgio Lamberti (Ita) 49.24s
2 Juriy Bashkatov (USSR) 50.13s
3 Raimundos Mazhoulis (USSR) 50.15s

200 Metres Freestyle
1 Giorgio Lamberti (Ita) 1m 46.69s
2 Artur Wojdat (Pol) 1m 47.96s
3 Anders Holmertz (Swe) 1m 48.06s

400 Metres Freestyle
1 Artur Wojdat (Pol) 3m 47.78s
2 Stefan Pfeiffer (FRG) 3m 48.68s
3 Maruis Podkoscielny (Pol) 3m 49.29s

1500 Metres Freestyle
1 Jorg Hoffmann (GDR) 15m 01.52s
2 Stefan Pfeiffer (FRG) 15m 01.93s
3 Maruis Podkoscielny (Pol) 15m 19.29s

100 Metres Butterfly
1 Rafal Sukala (Pol) 54.47s
2 Bruno Gutzeit (Fra) 54.50s
3 Martin Herrmann (FRG) 54.54s

200 Metres Butterfly
1 Tamas Darnyi (Hun) 1m 58.87s
2 Rafal Szukala (Pol) 2m 00.62s
3 Kozelj Matijaz (Yug) 2m 00.73s

100 Metres Breaststroke
1 Adrian Moorhouse (GB) 1m 01.71s
2 Dmitri Volkov (USSR) 1m 01.94s
3 Nick Gillingham (GB) 1m 02.12s

200 Metres Breaststroke
1 Nick Gillingham (GB) 2m 12.90s
2 Gary O'Toole (Ire) 2m 15.73s
3 Joszef Szabo (Hun) 2m 16.05s

100 Metres Backstroke
1 Martin Lopez-Zubero (Spa) 56.44s
2 Sergey Zabolotnov (USSR) 56.45s
3 Dirk Richter (GDR) 56.52s

200 Metres Backstroke
1 Stefano Battistelli (Ita) 1m 59.96s
2 Vladimir Selkov (USSR) 2m 00.02s
3 Tino Weber (GDR) 2m 00.54s

200 Metres Individual Medley
1 Tamas Darnyi (Hun) 2m 01.03s
2 Raik Hannemann (GDR) 2m 03.07s
3 Josef Hladky (FRG) 2m 03.21s

400 Metres Individual Medley
1 Tamas Darnyi (Hun) 4m 15.25s
2 Patrick Kuehl (GDR) 4m 16.08s
3 Stefano Battistelli (Ita) 4m 19.13s

4 x 100 Metres Freestyle Relay
1 West Germany 3m 19.68s
2 France 3m 19.73s
3 Sweden 3m 19.76s

4 x 200 Metres Freestyle Relay
1 Italy 7m 15.39s
2 West Germany 7m 17.38s
3 East Germany 7m 17.79s

4 x 100 Metres Medley Relay
1 USSR 3m 41.44s
2 France 3m 43.09s
3 Italy 3m 43.14s

Diving – Platform
1 Georgy Chogovadze (USSR) 639.69pts
2 Jan Hempel (GDR) 578.43s
3 Vladimir Timoshini (USSR) 572.40s

Diving – Springboard
1 Albin Killat (FRG) 672.75pts
2 Alexandr Gladshenko (USSR) 666.42pts
3 Jan Hempel (GDR) 663.84pts

Water Polo
1 West Germany (10-9)
2 Yugoslavia
3 Italy

Women

50 Metres Freestyle
1 Catherine Plewinski (Fra) 25.63s
2 Daniela Hunger (GDR) 25.64s
3 Katrin Meissner (GDR) 25.87s

100 Metres Freestyle
1 Katrin Meissner (GDR) 55.38s
2 Manuela Stellmach (GDR) 55.40s
3 Marianne Muis (Hol) 55.61s

200 Metres Freestyle
1 Manuela Stellmach (GDR) 1m 58.93s
2 Marianne Muis (Hol) 1m 59.96s
3 Mette Jacobsen (Den) 2m 00.35s

400 Metres Freestyle
1 Anke Moehring (GDR) 4m 05.84s
2 Heike Freidrich (GDR) 4m 10.14s
3 Manuela Melchorri (Ita) 4m 10.89s

800 Metres Freestyle
1 Anke Moehring (GDR) 8m 23.99s
2 Astrid Strauss (GDR) 8m 28.24s
3 Irene Dalby (Nor) 8m 28.59s

100 Metres Butterfly
1 Catherine Plewinski (Fra) 59.08s
2 Jacqueline Jakob (GDR) 1m 00.42s
3 Kathleen Nord (GDR) 1m 00.81s

200 Metres Butterfly
1 Kathleen Nord (GDR) 2m 09.33s
2 Jacqueline Jakob (GDR) 2m 10.94s
3 Mette Jacobsen (Den) 2m 12.63s

100 Metres Breaststroke
1 Susanne Boernike (GDR) 1m 09.55s
2 Tanya Dangalakova (Bul) 1m 09.65s
3 Manuela Dalla Valle (Ita) 1m 10.39s

200 Metres Breaststroke
1 Susanne Boernike (GDR) 2m 27.77s
2 Brigitte Becue (Bel) 2m 29.94s
3 Elena Volkova (USSR) 2m 29.95s

100 Metres Backstroke
1 Kristin Otto (GDR) 1m 01.86s
2 Krisztina Egerszegi (Hun) 1m 02.44s
3 Anja Eichorst (GDR) 1m 03.10s

200 Metres Backstroke
1 Dagmar Hase (GDR) 2m 12.46s
2 Krisztina Egerszegi (Hun) 2m 12.61s
3 Kristin Otto (GDR) 2m 14.29s

200 Metres Individual Medley
1 Daniela Hunger (GDR) 2m 13.26s
2 Marianne Muis (Hol) 2m 15.85s
3 Mildred Muis (Hol) 2m 17.23s

400 Metres Individual Medley
1 Daniela Hunger (GDR) 4m 41.82s
2 Krisztina Egerszegi (Hun) 4m 44.75s
3 Grit Mueller (GDR) 4m 46.06s

4 x 100 Metres Freestyle Relay
1 East Germany 3m 42.46s
2 Holland 3m 43.66s
3 West Germany 3m 46.15s

4 x 200 Metres Freestyle Relay
1 East Germany 7m 58.54s
2 Holland 8m 08.00s
3 Italy 8m 10.49s

4 x 100 Metres Medley Relay
1 East Germany 4m 07.40s
2 Italy 4m 10.78s
3 Holland 4m 11.53s

Diving – Platform
1 Ute Wetzig (GDR) 403.35pts
2 Inga Afonina (USSR) 400.83pts
3 Jana Eichler (GDR) 395.55pts

Diving – Springboard
1 Marina Babkova (USSR) 514.23pts
2 Britta Baldus (GDR) 510.72pts
3 S Alexeyeva (USSR) 486.09pts

Water Polo
1 Holland (14-11)
2 Hungary
3 France

Synchronised Solo
1 Kristina Falasinidi (USSR)
2 Karine Schuler (Fra)
3 Karin Singer (Swi)

Synchronised Duet
1 Karine Schuler/Marianne Aeschbacher (Fra)
2 Maria Cherneyeva/Elena Foshevskaya (USSR)
3 Karin Singer/Edith Boss (Swi)

MEDAL TABLE
(Leading Positions)

		Gold	Silver	Bronze	Total
1	East Germany	16	10	11	38
2	USSR	5	8	4	22
3	Italy	4	1	6	11
4	France	3	4	1	9
5	West Germany	3	3	3	9
6	Hungary	3	4	1	8
7	Holland	1	4	3	9
8	Poland	2	2	2	6
9	Great Britain	2	0	1	3
10	Spain	1	0	0	1

PAN-PACIFIC CHAMPIONSHIPS
Tokyo, August

Men

50 Metres Freestyle
1 Tom Jager (US) 22.12s
2 Andrew Baildon (Aus) 22.54s
3 Steve Crocker (US) 22.78s

100 Metres Freestyle
1 Brent Lang (US) 49.56s
2 Andrew Baildon (Aus) 50.03s
3 Doug Gjersten (US) 50.11s

200 Metres Freestyle
1 Doug Gjertsen (US) 1m 49.09s
2 John Olsen (US) 1m 49.47s
3 Turlough O'Hare (Can) 1m 50.23s

400 Metres Freestyle
1 Turlough O'Hare (Can) 3m 52.89s
2 Dan Jorgensen (US) 3m 53.85s
3 Paul Robinson (US) 3m 55.04s

1500 Metres Freestyle
1 Glenn Housman (Aus) 15m 06.00s
2 Lars Jorgensen (US) 15m 14.45s
3 Michael McKenzie (Aus) 15m 21.52s

100 Metres Backstroke
1 Jeff Rouse (US) 56.34s
2 Scot Johnson (US) 56.52s
3 Mark Tewksbury (Can) 56.65s

200 Metres Backstroke
1 Don Veatch (US) 2m 01.27s
2 Gary Anderson (Can) 2m 02.34s
3 Paul Kingsman (NZ) 2m 03.14s

100 Metres Breaststroke
1 Richard Korhammer (US) 1m 02.95s
2 Rich Schroeder (US) 1m 03.09s
3 Chen Jianhong (Chn) 1m 03.19s

200 Metres Breaststroke
1 Mike Barrowman (US) 2m 13.09s
2 Nelson Diebel (US) 2m 14.94s
3 Jon Cleveland (Can) 2m 15.76s

100 Metres Butterfly
1 Anthony Nesty (Sur) 53.80s
2 Wade King (US) 53.86s
3 Mark Henderson (US) 54.13s

200 Metres Butterfly
1 Melvin Stewart (US) 1m 59.40s
2 Dave Wharton (US) 1m 59.56s
3 Anthony Mosse (NZ) 2m 00.03s

200 Metres Medley
1 Dave Wharton (US) 2m 00.11s
2 Ron Karnaugh (US) 2m 02.83s
3 Gary Anderson (Can) 2m 03.19s

400 Metres Medley
1 Dave Wharton (US) 4m 16.14s
2 Eric Namesnik (US) 4m 17.02s
3 Raymond Brown (Aus) 4m 23.61s

4 x 50 Metres Medley Relay
1 United States 1m 39.22s
2 China 1m 42.08s
3 Australia 1m 42.16s

4 x 100 Metres Medley Relay
1 United States 3m 39.27s
2 Canada 3m 43.42s
3 Australia 3m 46.75s

4 x 100 Metres Freestyle Relay
1 United States 3m 17.75s
2 Australia 3m 22.39s
3 Canada 3m 24.23s

Women

50 Metres Freestyle
1 Jenny Thompson (US) 25.85s
2 Yang Wenyi (Chn) 25.95s
3 Ann Leigh Fetter (US) 25.96s

100 Metres Freestyle
1 Yong Zhuan (Chn) 55.68s
2 Jenny Thompson (US) 55.84s
3 Nicole Halslett (US) 55.99s

200 Metres Freestyle
1 Patricia Noall (Can) 2m 00.87s
2 Mitzi Kremer (US) 2m 01.18s
3 Yong Zhuan (Chn) 2m 01.44

400 Metres Freestyle
1 Janet Evans (US) 4m 04.53s
2 Jane Skillman (US) 4m 11.46s
3 Janelle Elford (Aus) 4m 12.57s

800 Metres Freestyle
1 Janet Evans (US) 8m 16.22s
2 Janelle Elford (Aus) 8m 21.16s
3 Julie Kole (US) 8m 23.46s

1500 Metres Freestyle
1 Janelle Elford (Aus) 16m 10.58s
2 Barbara Metz (US) 16m 27.44s
3 Julie Kole (US) 16m 28.25s

100 Metres Backstroke
1 Lea Loveless (US) 1m 02.69s
2 Nicole Livingstone (Aus) and
  Anne Mahoney (US) 1m 03.52s (dead-heat)

200 Metres Backstroke
1 Dede Trimble (US) 2m 13.76s
2 Anna Simcic (NZ) 2m 14.21s
3 Nicole Livingstone (Aus) 2m 14.22s

100 Metres Breaststroke
1 Keltie Dugan (Can) 1m 09.79s
2 Tracey McFarlane (US) 1m 09.81s
3 Mary Ellen Blanchard (US) 1m 11.08s

200 Metres Breaststroke
1 Mary Ellen Blanchard (US) 2m 23.02s
2 Nathalie Giguere (Can) 2m 23.12s
3 Tracey McFarlane (US) 2m 23.13s

100 Metres Butterfly
1 Qian Hong (Chn) 1m 00.45s
2 Wang Xiaohong (Chn) 1m 00.81s
3 Jenna Johnson (US) 1m 01.01s

200 Metres Butterfly
1 Rie Shito (Jap) 2m 11.29s
2 Julia Gorman (US) 2m 11.45s
3 Wang Xiaohong (Chn) 2m 11.55s

200 Metres Medley
1 Lin Li (Chn) 2m 14.69s
2 Summer Sanders (US) 2m 16.09s
3 Michelle Griglione (US) 2m 16.77s

400 Metres Medley
1 Janet Evans (US) 4m 39.38s
2 Lin Li (Chn) 4m 45.69s
3 Donna Proctor (Aus) 4m 45.99s

4 x 50 Metres Medley Relay
1 United States 1m 53.28s
2 China 1m 54.78s
3 Australia 1m 55.10s

4 x 100 Metres Medley Relay
1 United States 4m 09.93s
2 Australia and China 4m 11.54s (dead-heated)

4 x 100 Metres Freestyle Relay
1 United States 3m 43.63s
2 Canada 3m 47.80s
3 China 3m 47.94s

TSB NATIONAL CHAMPIONSHIPS
Coventry, Jul 13-16

Men
50 Metres Freestyle:
23.87s Mike Fibbens (Barnet Copthall)
100 Metres Freestyle:
51.68s Mike Fibbens (Barnet Copthall)
200 Metres Freestyle:
1m 53.34s Jonathan Broughton (City of Leeds)
400 Metres Freestyle:
3m 58.84s Campbell McNeil (Paisley)
1500 Metres Freestyle:
15m 44.19s Kevin Boyd (Borough of S.Tyneside)
100 Metres Backstroke:
58.52s Gary Binfield (Maxwell)
200 Metres Backstroke:
2m 05.26s Gary Binfield (Maxwell)
100 Metres Breaststroke:
1m 03.31s Adrian Moorhouse (City of Leeds)
200 Metres Breaststroke:
2m 18.45s Nick Gillingham (City of Birmingham)
100 Metres Butterfly:
55.33s David Parker (City of Coventry)
200 Metres Butterfly:
2m 05.08s Alastair Quinn (Sale)
200 Metres Medley:
2m 06.05s Grant Robins (Portsmouth Northsea)
400 Metres Medley:
4m 26.45s Paul Brew (Kelly College)
Club Freestyle Relay:
3m 30.14s City of Leeds
Club Medley Relay:
3m 49.27s City of Leeds

Women
50 Metres Freestyle:
26.49s Caroline Woodcock (Haywards Heath)
100 Metres Freestyle:
58.21s Karen Pickering (Ipswich)
200 Metres Freestyle:
2m 05.23s Joanna Coull (City of Birmingham)
400 Metres Freestyle:
4m 22.37s Karen Mellor (City of Sheffield)
800 Metres Freestyle:
8m 53.39s Karen Mellor (City of Sheffield)

100 Metres Backstroke:
1m 04.70s Katharine Read (Barnet Copthall)
200 Metres Backstroke:
2m 16.11s Katharine Read (Barnet Copthall)
100 Metres Breaststroke:
1m 11.55s Suki Brownsdon (Wigan Wasps)
200 Metres Breaststroke:
2m 35.01s Suki Brownsdon (Wigan Wasps)
100 Metres Butterfly:
1m 02.05s Madelaine Scarborough (Portsmouth Northsea)
200 Metres Butterfly:
2m 15.24s Samantha Purvis (Wigan Wasps) and Madelaine
Scarborough (Portsmouth Northsea) dead-heated
200 Metres Medley:
2m 19.29s Sharron Davies (Bracknell)
400 Metres Medley:
4m 51.91s Suki Brownsdon (Wigan Wasps)
Club Freestyle Relay:
3m 58.54s City of Birmingham
Club Medley Relay:
4m 27.29s Wigan Wasps

——— CHAMPIONS ———

OLYMPIC CHAMPIONS
Men
50 Metres Freestyle
1988   Matt Biondi (US) 22.39s
100 Metres Freestyle
1896	Alfred Hajos (Hun) 1m 22.2s
1904	Zoltan von Halmay (Hun) 1m 22.08s
1908	Charles Daniels (US) 1m 05.6s
1912	Duke Kahanamoku (US) 1m 03.4s
1920	Duke Kahanamoku (US) 1m 01.4s
1924	Johnny Weissmuller (US) 59.0s
1928	Johnny Weissmuller (US) 58.6s
1932	Yasuji Miyazaki (Jap) 58.2s
1936	Ferenc Csik (Hun) 57.6s
1948	Walter Ris (US) 57.3s
1952	Clarke Scholes (US) 57.4s
1956	Jon Henricks (Aus) 55.4s
1960	John Devitt (Aus) 55.2s
1964	Don Schollander (US) 53.4s
1968	Mike Wenden (Aus) 52.2s
1972	Mark Spitz (US) 51.22s
1976	Jim Montgomery (US) 49.99s
1980	Jörg Woithe (GDR) 50.4s
1984	Rowdy Gaines (US) 49.80s
1988	Matt Biondi (US) 48.63s

200 Metres Freestyle
1900	Frederick Lane (Aus) 2m 25.2s
1904	Charles Daniels (US) 2m 44.2s
1968	Mike Wenden (Aus) 1m 55.2s
1972	Mark Spitz (US) 1m 52.78s
1976	Bruce Furniss (US) 1m 50.29s
1980	Sergey Koplyakov (USSR) 1m 49.81s
1984	Michael Gross (FRG) 1m 47.44s
1988	Duncan Armstrong (Aus) 1m 47.25s

400 Metres Freestyle
1896	Paul Neumann (Aut) 8m 12.6s (500m)
1904	Charles Daniels (US) 6m 16.2s
1908	Henry Taylor (GB) 5m 36.8s
1912	George Hodgson (Can) 5m 24.4s
1920	Norman Ross (US) 5m 26.8s
1924	Johnny Weissmuller (US) 5m 04.2s
1928	Albeto Zorilla (Arg) 5m 01.6s
1932	Buster Crabbe (US) 4m 48.4s
1936	Jack Medica (US) 4m 44.5s
1948	William Smith (US) 4m 41.0s
1952	Jean Boiteux (Fra) 4m 30.7s
1956	Murray Rose (Aus) 4m 27.3s
1960	Murray Rose (Aus) 4m 18.3s
1964	Don Schollander (US) 4m 12.2s
1968	Mike Burton (US) 4m 09.0s
1972	Brad Cooper (Aus) 4m 00.27s
1976	Brian Goodell (US) 3m 51.93s
1980	Vladimir Salnikov (USSR) 3m 51.31s
1984	George Dicarlo (US) 3m 51.23s
1988	Uwe Dassler (GDR) 3m 46.95s

1500 Metres Freestyle
1896	Alfred Hajos (Hun) 18m 22.2s (1200m)
1900	John Jarvis (GB) 13m 40.2s (1000m)
1904	Emil Rausch (Ger) 27m 18.2s (1 Mile)
1908	Henry Taylor (GB) 22m 48.4s
1912	George Hodgson (Can) 22m 00.0s
1920	Norman Ross (US) 22m 23.2s
1924	Andrew Charlton (Aus) 20m 06.6s
1928	Arne Borge (Swe) 19m 51.8s
1932	Kusuo Kitamura (Jap) 19m 12.4s
1936	Noboru Terada (Jap) 19m 13.7s
1948	James McLane (US) 19m 18.5s
1952	Ford Konno (US) 18m 30.0s
1956	Murray Rose (Aus) 17m 58.9s
1960	John Konrads (Aus) 17m 19.6s
1964	Bob Windle (Aus) 17m 01.7s
1968	Mike Burton (US) 16m 38.9s
1972	Mike Burton (US) 15m 52.58s
1976	Brian Goodell (US) 15m 02.40s
1980	Vladimir Salnikov (USSR) 14m 58.27s
1984	Michael O'Brien (US) 15m 05.20s
1988	Vladimir Salnikov (USSR) 15m 00.40s

100 Metres Backstroke
1904	Walter Brack (Ger) 1m 16.8s
1908	Arno Bieberstein (Ger) 1m 24.6s
1912	Harry Hebner (US) 1m 21.2s
1920	Warren Kealoha (US) 1m 15.2s
1924	Warren Kealoha (US) 1m 13.2s
1928	George Kojac (US) 1m 08.2s
1932	Masaji Kiyokawa (Jap) 1m 08.6s
1936	Adolf Kiefer (US) 1m 05.9s
1948	Allen Stack (US) 1m 06.4s
1952	Yoshinobu Oyakawa (US) 1m 05.4s
1956	David Thiele (Aus) 1m 02.2s
1960	David Thiele (Aus) 1m 01.9s
1968	Roland Matthes (GDR) 58.7s
1972	Roland Matthes (GDR) 56.58s
1976	John Naber (US) 55.49s
1980	Bengt Baron (Swe) 56.53s
1984	Rick Carey (US) 55.79s
1988	Daichi Suzuki (Jap) 55.05s

200 Metres Backstroke
1900	Ernst Hoppenberg (Ger) 2m 47.0s
1964	Jed Graef (US) 2m 10.3s
1968	Roland Matthes (GDR) 2m 09.6s
1972	Roland Matthes (GDR) 2m 02.82s
1976	John Naber (US) 1m 59.19s
1980	Sandor Wladar (Hun) 2m 01.93s
1984	Rick Carey (US) 2m 00.23s
1988	Igor Polianski (USSR) 1m 59.37s

100 Metres Breaststroke
1968	Don McKenzie (US) 1m 07.7s
1972	Nobutaka Taguchi (Jap) 1m 04.94s
1976	John Hencken (US) 1m 03.11s
1980	Duncan Goodhew (GB) 1m 03.34s
1984	Steve Lundquist (US) 1m 01.65s
1988	Adrian Moorhouse (GB) 1m 02.04s

200 Metres Breaststroke
1908	Frederick Holman (GB) 3m 09.2s
1912	Walter Bathe (Ger) 3m 01.8s
1920	Häken Malmroth (Swe) 3m 04.4s
1924	Robert Skelton (US) 2m 56.5s
1928	Yoshiyuki Tsuruta (Jap) 2m 48.8s
1932	Yoshiyuki Tsuruta (Jap) 2m 45.4s
1936	Tetsuo Hamuro (Jap) 2m 41.5s

1948	Joseph Verdeur (US) 2m 39.3s
1952	John Davies (Aus) 2m 34.4s
1956	Masaru Furukawa (Jap) 2m 34.7s
1960	William Mulliken (US) 2m 37.4s
1964	Ian O'Brien (Aus) 2m 27.8s
1968	Felipe Munoz (Mex) 2m 28.7s
1972	John Hencken (US) 2m 21.55s
1976	David Wilkie (GB) 2m 15.11s
1980	Robertas Zhulpa (USSR) 2m 15.85s
1984	Victor Davis (Can) 2m 13.34s
1988	Jozef Szabo (Hun) 2m 13.52s

100 Metres Butterfly

1968	Doug Russell (US) 55.9s
1972	Mark Spitz (US) 54.27s
1976	Matt Vogel (US) 54.35s
1980	Pär Arvidsson (Swe) 54.92s
1984	Michael Gross (FRG) 53.08s
1988	Anthony Nesty (Sur) 53.0s

200 Metres Butterfly

1956	William Yorzyk (US) 2m 19.3s
1960	Mike Troy (US) 2m 12.8s
1964	Kevin Berry (Aus) 2m 06.6s
1968	Carl Robie (US) 2m 08.7s
1972	Mark Spitz (US) 2m 00.70s
1976	Mike Bruner (US) 1m 59.23s
1980	Sergey Fesenko (USSR) 1m 59.76s
1984	Jon Sieben (Aus) 1m 57.04s
1988	Michael Gross (FRG) 1m 56.94s

200 Metres Individual Medley

1968	Charles Hickcox (US) 2m 12.0s
1972	Gunnar Larsson (Swe) 2m 07.17s
1984	Alex Baumann (Can) 2m 01.42s
1988	Tamas Darnyi (Hun) 2m 02.15s

400 Metres Individual Medley

1964	Richard Roth (US) 4m 45.4s
1968	Charles Hickcox (US) 4m 48.4s
1972	Gunnar Larsson (Swe) 4m 31.98s
1976	Rod Strachan (US) 4m 23.68s
1980	Aleksandr Sidorenko (USSR) 4m 22.89s
1984	Alex Baumann (Can) 4m 17.41s
1988	Tamas Darnyi (Hun) 4m 14.75s

4 x 100 Metres Freestyle Relay

1964	United States 3m 33.2s
1968	United States 3m 31.7s
1972	United States 3m 26.42s
1984	United States 3m 19.03s
1988	United States 3m 16.53s

4 x 200 Metres Freestyle Relay

1908	Great Britain 10m 55.6s
1912	Australasia 10m 11.6s
1920	United States 10m 04.4s
1924	United States 9m 53.4s
1928	United States 9m 36.2s
1932	Japan 8m 58.4s
1936	Japan 8m 51.5s
1948	United States 8m 46.0s
1952	United States 8m 31.1s
1956	Australia 8m 23.6s
1960	United States 8m 10.2s
1964	United States 7m 52.1s
1968	United States 7m 52.3s
1972	United States 7m 35.78s
1976	United States 7m 23.22s
1980	USSR 7m 23.50s
1984	United States 7m 15.69s
1988	United States 7m 12.51s

4 x 100 Metres Medley Relay

1960	United States 4m 05.4s
1964	United States 3m 58.4s
1968	United States 3m 54.9s
1972	United States 3m 48.16s
1976	United States 3m 42.22s

1980	Australia 3m 45.70s
1984	United States 3m 39.30s
1988	United States 3m 36.93s

Springboard Diving

1908	Albert Zürner (Ger)
1912	Paul Günther (Ger)
1920	Louis Kuehn (US)
1924	Albert White (US)
1928	Peter Desjardins (US)
1932	Michael Galitzen (US)
1936	Richard Degener (US)
1948	Bruce Harlan (US)
1952	David Browning (US)
1956	Robert Clotworthy (US)
1960	Gary Tobian (US)
1964	Kenneth Sitzberger (US)
1968	Bernard Wrightson (US)
1972	Vladimir Vasin (USSR)
1976	Phil Boggs (US)
1980	Aleksandr Portnov (USSR)
1984	Greg Louganis (US)
1988	Greg Louganis (US)

Platform Diving

1904	George Sheldon (US)
1908	Hjalmar Johansson (Swe)
1912	Erik Adlerz (Swe)
1920	Clarence Pinkston (US)
1924	Albert White (US)
1928	Peter Desjardins (US)
1932	Harold Smith (US)
1936	Marshall Wayne (US)
1948	Samuel Lee (US)
1952	Samuel Lee (US)
1956	Joaquin Capilla Perez (Mex)
1960	Robert Webster (US)
1964	Robert Webster (US)
1968	Klaus Dibiasi (Ita)
1972	Klaus Dibiasi (Ita)
1976	Klaus Dibiasi (Ita)
1980	Falk Hoffmann (GDR)
1984	Greg Louganis (US)
1988	Greg Louganis (US)

Women

50 Metres Freestyle

1988	Kristin Otto (GDR) 25.49s

100 Metres Freestyle

1912	Fanny Durack (Aus) 1m 22.2s
1920	Etheleda Bleibtrey (US) 1m 13.6s
1924	Ethel Lackie (US) 1m 12.4s
1928	Albina Osipowich (US) 1m 11.0s
1932	Helene Madison (US) 1m 06.8s
1936	Hendrika Mastenbroek (Hol) 1m 05.9s
1948	Greta Andersen (Den) 1m 06.3s
1952	Katalin Szöke (Hun) 1m 06.8s
1956	Dawn Fraser (Aus) 1m 02.0s
1960	Dawn Fraser (Aus) 1m 01.2s
1964	Dawn Fraser (Aus) 59.5s
1968	Jan Henne (US) 1m 00.0s
1972	Sandra Neilson (US) 58.59s
1976	Kornelia Ender (GDR) 55.65s
1980	Barbara Krause (GDR) 54.79s
1984	Nancy Hogshead (US) & Carrie Steinseifer (US) 55.92s
1988	Kristin Otto (GDR) 54.93s

200 Metres Freestyle

1968	Debbie Meyer (US) 2m 10.5s
1972	Shane Gould (Aus) 2m 03. 56s
1976	Kornelia Ender (GDR) 1m 59.26s
1980	Barbara Krause (GDR) 1m 58.33s
1984	Mary Wayte (US) 1m 59.23s
1988	Heike Friedrich (GDR) 1m 57.65s

400 Metres Freestyle
1920	Ethelda Bleibtrey (US)	4m 34.0s (300m)
1924	Martha Norelius (US)	6m 02.2s
1928	Martha Norelius (US)	5m 42.8s
1932	Helene Madison (US)	5m 28.5s
1936	Hendrika Mastenbroek (Hol)	5m 26.4s
1948	Ann Curtis (US)	5m 17.8s
1952	Valeria Gyenge (Hun)	5m 12.1s
1956	Lorraine Crapp (Aus)	4m 54.6s
1960	Chris von Saltza (US)	4m 50.6s
1964	Virginia Duenkel (US)	4m 43.3s
1968	Debbie Meyer (US)	4m 31.8s
1972	Shane Gould (Aus)	4m 19.04s
1976	Petra Thümer (GDR)	4m 09.89s
1980	Ines Diers (GDR)	4m 08.76s
1984	Tiffany Cohen (US)	4m 07.10s
1988	Janet Evans (US)	4m 03.85s

800 Metres Freestyle
1968	Debbie Mayer (US)	9m 24.0s
1972	Keena Rothhammer (US)	8m 53.68s
1976	Petra Thümer (GDR)	8m 37.14s
1980	Michelle Ford (Aus)	8m 28.90s
1984	Tiffany Cohen (US)	8m 24.95s
1988	Janet Evans (US)	8m 20.20s

100 Metres Backstroke
1924	Sybil Bauer (US)	1m 23.2s
1928	Maria Braun (Hol)	1m 22.0s
1932	Eleanor Holm (US)	1m 19.4s
1936	Nida Senff (Hol)	1m 18.9s
1948	Karen Harup (Den)	1m 14.4s
1952	Joan Harrison (SA)	1m 14.3s
1956	Judy Grinham (GB)	1m 12.9s
1960	Lynn Burke (US)	1m 09.3s
1964	Cathy Ferguson (US)	1m 07.7s
1968	Kaye Hall (US)	1m 06.2s
1972	Melissa Belote (US)	1m 05.78s
1976	Ulrike Richter (GDR)	1m 01.83s
1980	Rica Reinisch (GDR)	1m 00.86s
1984	Theresa Andrews (US)	1m 02.55s
1988	Kristin Otto (GDR)	1m 00.89s

200 Metres Backstroke
1968	Pokey Watson (US)	2m 24.8s
1972	Melissa Belote (US)	2m 19.19s
1976	Ulrike Richter (GDR)	2m 13.43s
1980	Rica Reinisch (GDR)	2m 11.77s
1984	Jolanda de Rover (Hol)	2m 12.38s
1988	Krisztina Egerszegi (Hun)	2m 09.29s

100 Metres Breaststroke
1968	Djurdjica Bjedov (Yug)	1m 15.8s
1972	Catherine Carr (US)	1m 13.58s
1976	Hennelore Anke (GDR)	1m 11.16s
1980	Ute Geweniger (GDR)	1m 10.22s
1984	Petra Van Staveren (Hol)	1m 09.88s
1988	Tania Dangalakova (Bul)	1m 07.95s

200 Metres Breaststroke
1924	Lucy Morton (GB)	3m 33.2s
1928	Hilde Schrader (Ger)	3m 12.6s
1932	Claire Dennis (Aus)	3m 06.3s
1936	Hideko Maehata (Jap)	3m 03.6s
1948	Petronella van Vliet (Hol)	2m 57.2s
1952	Eva Szekely (Hun)	2m 51.7s
1956	Ursula Happe (FRG)	2m 53.1s
1960	Anita Lonsbrough (GB)	2m 49.5s
1964	Galina Prozumenschikova (USSR)	2m 46.4s
1968	Sharon Wichman (US)	2m 44.4s
1972	Beverley Whitfield (Aus)	2m 41.71s
1976	Marina Koshevaya (USSR)	2m 33.35s
1980	Lina Kachushite (USSR)	2m 29.54s
1984	Anne Ottenbrite (Can)	2m 30.38s
1988	Silke Hoerner (GDR)	2m 26.71s

100 Metres Butterfly
1956	Shelley Mann (US)	1m 11.0s
1960	Carolyn Schuler (US)	1m 09.5s
1964	Sharon Stouder (US)	1m 04.7s
1968	Lynette McClements (Aus)	1m 05.0s
1972	Mayumi Aoki (Jap)	1m 03.34s
1976	Kornelia Ender (GDR)	1m 00.13s
1980	Caren Metschuck (GDR)	1m 00.42s
1984	Mary T. Meagher (US)	59.26s
1988	Kristin Otto (GDR)	59.00s

200 Metres Butterfly
1968	Ada Kok (Hol)	2m 24.7s
1972	Karen Moe (US)	2m 15.57s
1976	Andrea Pollack (GDR)	2m 11.41s
1980	Ines Geissler (GDR)	2m 10.44s
1984	Mary T. Meagher (US)	2m 06.90s
1988	Kathleen Nord (GDR)	2m 09.51s

200 Metres Individual Medley
1968	Claudia Kolb (US)	2m 24.7s
1972	Sharon Gould (Aus)	2m 23.07s
1984	Tracy Caulkins (US)	2m 12.64s
1988	Daniela Hunger (GDR)	2m 16.23s

400 Metres Individual Medley
1964	Donna De Varona (US)	5m 18.7s
1968	Claudia Kolb (US)	5m 08.5s
1972	Gail Neall (Aus)	5m 02.97s
1976	Ulrike Tauber (GDR)	4m 42.77s
1980	Petra Schneider (GDR)	4m 36.29s
1984	Tracy Caulkins (US)	4m 39.24s
1988	Janet Evans (US)	4m 37.36s

4 x 100 Metres Freestyle Medley
1912	Great Britain	5m 52.8s
1920	United States	5m 11.6s
1924	United States	4m 58.8s
1928	United States	4m 47.6s
1932	United States	4m 38.0s
1936	Netherlands	4m 36.0s
1948	United States	4m 29.2s
1952	Hungary	4m 24.4s
1956	Australia	4m 17.1s
1960	United States	4m 08.9s
1964	United States	4m 03.8s
1968	United States	4m 02.5s
1972	United States	3m 55.19s
1976	United States	3m 44.82s
1980	East Germany	3m 42.71s
1984	United States	3m 43.43s
1988	East Germany	3m 40.63s

4 x 100 Metres Medley Relay
1960	United States	4m 41.1s
1964	United States	4m 33.9s
1968	United States	4m 28.3s
1972	United States	4m 20.75s
1976	East Germany	4m 07.95s
1980	East Germany	4m 06.67s
1984	United States	4m 08.34s
1988	East Germany	4m 03.74s

Springboard Diving
1920	Aileen Riggin (US)
1924	Elizabeth Becker (US)
1928	Helen Meany (US)
1932	Georgia Coleman (US)
1936	Marjorie Gestring (US)
1948	Victoria Draves (US)
1952	Pat McCormick (US)
1956	Pat McCormick (US)
1960	Ingrid Krämer (GDR)
1964	Ingrid Engel (née Krämer) (GDR)
1968	Sue Gossick (US)
1972	Micki King (US)
1976	Jennifer Chandler (US)
1980	Irina Kalinina (USSR)
1984	Sylvie Bernier (Can)
1988	Goa Min (Chn)

Platform Diving

1912	Greta Johansson (Swe)
1920	Stefani Fryland-Clausen (Den)
1924	Caroline Smith (US)
1928	Elizabeth Pinkston (US)
1932	Dorothy Poynton (US)
1936	Dorothy Hill (née Poynton) (US)
1948	Victoria Draves (US)
1952	Pat McCormick (US)
1956	Pat McCormick (US)
1960	Ingrid Krämer (GDR)
1964	Lesley Bush (US)
1968	Milena Duchkova (Cze)
1972	Ulrika Knape (Swe)
1976	Elena Vaytsekhovskaya (USSR)
1980	Martina Jäschke (GDR)
1984	Zhou Jihong (Chn)
1988	Xu Yanmei (Chn)

Synchronised - Solo

1984	Tracie Ruiz (US)
1988	Carolyn Waldo (Can)

Synchronised - Duet

1984	Candy Costie & Tracie Ruiz (US)
1988	Michelle Cameron & Carolyn Waldo (Can)

WORLD CHAMPIONS
Men
50 Metres Freestyle
1986	Tom Jager (US) 22.49s

100 Metres Freestyle
1973	Jim Montgomery (US) 51.70s
1975	Andrew Coan (US) 51.25s
1978	David McCagg (US) 50.24s
1982	Jorg Woithe (GDR) 50.18s
1986	Matt Biondi (US) 48.94s

200 Metres Freestyle
1973	Jim Montgomery (US) 1m 53.02s
1975	Tim Shaw (US) 1m 51.04s
1978	William Forrester (US) 1m 51.02s
1982	Michael Gross (FRG) 1m 49.84s
1986	Michael Gross (FRG) 1m 47.92s

400 Metres Freestyle
1973	Rick DeMont (US) 3m 58.18s
1975	Tim Shaw (US) 3m 54.88s
1978	Vladimir Salnikov (USSR) 3m 51.94s
1982	Vladimir Salnikov (USSR) 3m 51.30s
1986	Rainer Henkel (FRG) 3m 50.05s

1500 Metres Freestyle
1973	Steve Holland (Aus) 15m 31.85s
1975	Tim Shaw (US) 15m 28.92s
1978	Vladimir Salnikov (USSR) 15m 03.99s
1982	Vladimir Salnikov (USSR) 15m 01.77s
1986	Rainer Henkel (FRG) 15m 05.31s

100 Metres Backstroke
1973	Roland Matthes (GDR) 57.47s
1975	Roland Matthes (GDR) 58.15s
1978	Robert Jackson (US) 56.36s
1982	Dirk Richter (GDR) 55.95s
1986	Igor Polianski (USSR) 55.58s

200 Metres Backstroke
1973	Roland Matthes (GDR) 2m 01.87s
1975	Zoltan Verraszto (Hun) 2m 05.05s
1978	Jesse Vassallo (US) 2m 02.16s
1982	Rick Carey (US) 2m 00.82s
1986	Igor Polianski (USSR) 1m 58.78s

100 Metres Breaststroke
1973	John Hencken (US) 1m 04.02s
1975	David Wilkie (GB) 1m 04.26s
1978	Walter Kusch (GDR) 1m 03.56s
1982	Steve Lundquist (US) 1m 02.75s
1986	Victor Davis (Can) 1m 02.71s

200 Metres Breaststroke
1973	David Wilkie (GB) 2m 19.28s
1975	David Wilkie (GB) 2m 18.23s
1978	Nick Nevid (US) 2m 18.37s
1982	Victor Davis (Can) 2m 14.77s
1986	Jozsef Szabo (Hun) 2m 14.27s

100 Metres Butterfly
1973	Bruce Robertson (Can) 55.69s
1975	Greg Jagenburg (US) 55.63s
1978	Joe Bottom (US) 54.30s
1982	Matt Gribble (US) 53.88s
1986	Pablo Morales (US) 53.54s

200 Metres Butterfly
1973	Robin Backhaus (US) 2m 03.32s
1975	William Forrester (US) 2m 01.95s
1978	Michael Bruner (US) 1m 59.38s
1982	Michael Gross (FRG) 1m 58.85s
1986	Michael Gross (FRG) 1m 56.53s

200 Metres Individual Medley
1973	Gunnar Larsson (Swe) 2m 08.36s
1975	Andras Hargitay (Hun) 2m 07.72s
1978	Graham Smith (Can) 2m 03.65s
1982	Aleksey Sidorenko (USSR) 2m 03.30s
1986	Tamas Darnyi (Hun) 2m 01.57s

400 Metres Individual Medley
1973	Andras Hargitay (Hun) 4m 31.11s
1975	Andras Hargitay (Hun) 4m 32.57s
1978	Jesse Vassallo (US) 4m 20.05s
1982	Ricardo Prado (Bra) 4m 19.78s
1986	Tamas Darnyi (Hun) 4m 18.98s

4 x 100 Metres Freestyle Relay
1973	United States 3m 27.18s
1975	United States 3m 24.85s
1978	United States 3m 19.74s
1982	United States 3m 19.26s
1986	United States 3m 19.89s

4 x 200 Metres Freestyle Relay
1973	United States 7m 33.22s
1975	West Germany 7m 39.44s
1978	United States 7m 20.82s
1982	United States 7m 21.09s
1986	East Germany 7m 15.91s

4 x 100 Metres Medley Relay
1973	United States 3m 49.49s
1975	United States 3m 49.0s
1978	United States 3m 44.63s
1982	United States 3m 40.84s
1986	United States 3m 41.25s

Springboard Diving
1973	Phil Boggs (US)
1975	Phil Boggs (US)
1978	Phil Boggs (US)
1982	Greg Louganis (US)
1986	Greg Louganis (US)

Platform Diving
1973	Klaus Dibiasi (Ita)
1975	Klaus Dibiasi (Ita)
1978	Greg Louganis (US)
1982	Greg Louganis (US)
1986	Greg Louganis (US)

Women
50 Metres Freestyle
1986	Tamara Costache (Rom) 25.28s

100 Metres Freestyle
1973	Kornelia Ender (GDR) 57.54s
1975	Kornelia Ender (GDR) 56.50s
1978	Barbara Krause (GDR) 55.68s
1982	Birgit Meineke (GDR) 55.79s
1986	Kristin Otto (GDR) 55.05s

200 Metres Freestyle
1973 Keena Rothhammer (US) 2m 04.99s
1975 Shirley Babashoff (US) 2m 02.50s
1978 Cynthia Woodhead (US) 1m 58.53s
1982 Annemarie Verstappen (Hol) 1m 59.53s
1986 Heike Friedrich (GDR) 1m 58.26s

400 Metres Freestyle
1973 Heather Greenwood (US) 4m 20.28s
1975 Shirley Babashoff (US) 4m 16.87s
1978 Tracey Wickham (Aus) 4m 06.28s
1982 Carmela Schmidt (GDR) 4m 08.98s
1986 Heike Friedrich (GDR) 4m 07.45s

800 Metres Freestyle
1973 Novella Calligaris (Ita) 8m 52.97s
1975 Jenny Turrall (Aus) 8m 44.75s
1978 Tracey Wickham (Aus) 8m 24.94s
1982 Kim Linehan (US) 8m 27.48s
1986 Astrid Strauss (GDR) 8m 28.24s

100 Metres Backstroke
1973 Ulrike Richter (GDR) 1m 05.42s
1975 Ulrike Richter (GDR) 1m 03.30s
1978 Linda Jezek (US) 1m 02.55s
1982 Kristin Otto (GDR) 1m 01.30s
1986 Betsy Mitchell (US) 1m 01.74s

200 Metres Backstroke
1973 Melissa Belote (US) 2m 20.52s
1975 Birgit Treiber (GDR) 2m 15.46s
1978 Linda Jezek (US) 2m 11.93s
1982 Cornelia Sirch (GDR) 2m 09.91s
1986 Cornelia Sirch (GDR) 2m 11.37s

100 Metres Breaststroke
1973 Renate Vogel (GDR) 1m 13.74s
1975 Hannalore Anke (GDR) 1m 12.72s
1978 Julia Bogdanova (USSR) 1m 10.31s
1982 Ute Geweniger (GDR) 1m 09.14s
1986 Sylvia Gerasch (GDR) 1m 08.11s

200 Metres Breaststroke
1973 Renate Vogel (GDR) 2m 40.01s
1975 Hannalore Anke (GDR) 2m 37.25s
1978 Lina Kachushite (USSR) 2m 31.42s
1982 Svetlana Varganova (USSR) 2m 28.82s
1986 Silke Hoerner (GDR) 2m 27.40s

100 Metres Butterfly
1973 Kornelia Ender (GDR) 1m 02.53s
1975 Kornelia Ender (GDR) 1m 01.24s
1978 Mary-Joan Pennington (US) 1m 00.20s
1982 Mary T. Meagher (US) 59.41s
1986 Kornelia Gressler (GDR) 59.51s

200 Metres Butterfly
1973 Rosemarie Kother (GDR) 2m 13.76s
1975 Rosemarie Kother (GDR) 2m 13.82s
1978 Tracy Caulkins (US) 2m 09.87s
1982 Ines Geissler (GDR) 2m 08.66s
1986 Mary T. Meagher (US) 2m 08.41s

200 Metres Individual Medley
1973 Angela Hubner (GDR) 2m 20.51s
1975 Kathy Heddy (US) 2m 19.80s
1978 Tracy Caulkins (US) 2m 14.07s
1982 Petra Schneider (GDR) 2m 11.79s
1986 Kristin Otto (GDR) 2m 15.56s

400 Metres Individual Medley
1973 Gudrun Wegner (GDR) 4m 57.31s
1975 Ulrike Tauber (GDR) 4m 52.76s
1978 Tracy Caulkins (US) 4m 40.83s
1982 Petra Schneider (GDR) 4m 36.10s
1986 Kathleen Nord (GDR) 4m 43.75s

4 x 100 Metres Freestyle Relay
1973 East Germany 3m 52.45s
1975 East Germany 3m 49.37s
1978 United States 3m 43.43s
1982 East Germany 3m 43.97s
1986 East Germany 3m 40.57s

4 x 200 Metres Freestyle Relay
1986 East Germany 7m 59.33s

4 x 100 Metres Medley Relay
1973 East Germany 4m 16.84s
1975 East Germany 4m 14.74s
1978 United States 4m 08.21s
1982 East Germany 4m 05.88s
1986 East Germany 4m 04.82s

Springboard Diving
1973 Christine Kohler (GDR)
1975 Irina Kalinina (USSR)
1978 Irina Kalinina (USSR)
1982 Megan Meyer (US)
1986 Gao Min (Chn)

Platform Diving
1973 Ulrike Knape (Swe)
1975 Janet Ely (US)
1978 Irina Kalinina (USSR)
1982 Wendy Wyland (US)
1986 Lin Chen (Chn)

Synchronised – Solo
1973 Teresa Andersen (US)
1975 Gail Buzonas (US)
1978 Helen Vanderburg (Can)
1982 Tracie Ruiz (US)
1986 Carolyn Waldo (Can)

Synchronised – Duet
1973 United States
1975 United States
1978 Canada
1982 Canada
1986 Canada

Synchronised – Team
1973 United States
1975 United States
1978 United States
1982 Canada
1986 Canada

WORLD RECORDS
(As at Oct 6, 1989)

Men
50 Metres Freestyle:
22.12s Tom Jager (US), Tokyo, Aug 20, 1989
100 Metres Freestyle:
48.42s Matt Biondi (US), Austin, Texas, Aug 10, 1988
200 Metres Freestyle:
1m 46.69s Giorgio Lamberti (Ita), Bonn, Aug 15, 1989
400 Metres Freestyle:
3m 46.95s Uwe Dassler (GDR), Seoul, Sep 23, 1988
1500 Metres Freestyle:
14m 54.76s Vladimir Salnikov (USSR), Moscow, Feb 22, 1983
100 Metres Backstroke:
54.51s David Berkoff (US), Seoul, Sep 24, 1988
200 Metres Backstroke:
1m 58.14s Igor Polianski (USSR), Erfurt, GDR, Mar 3, 1985
100 Metres Breaststroke:
1m 01.49s Adrian Moorhouse (GB), Bonn, Aug 16, 1989
200 Metres Breaststroke:
2m 12.89s Mike Barrowman (US), Tokyo, Aug 20, 1989
100 Metres Butterfly:
52.84s Pablo Morales (US), Orlando, Florida, Jun 23, 1986
200 Metres Butterfly:
1m 56.24s Michael Gross (FRG), Hannover, Jun 28, 1986
200 Metres Medley:
2m 00.11s Dave Wharton (US), Tokyo, Aug 20, 1989
400 Metres Medley:
4m 14.75s Tamas Darnyi (Hun), Seoul, Sep 21, 1988
4 x 100 Metres Free Relay:
3m 16.53s United States, Seoul, Sep 23, 1988

4 x 200 Metres Free:
7m 12.51s United States, Seoul, Sep 21, 1988
4 x 100 Metres Medley:
3m 36.93s United States, Seoul, Sep 25, 1988

Women

50 Metres Freestyle:
24.98s Yang Wenyi (Chn), Guangzhou, China, Apr 10, 1988
100 Metres Freestyle:
54.73s Kristin Otto (GDR), Madrid, Aug 19, 1986
200 Metres Freestyle:
1m 57.55s Heike Friedrich (GDR), East Berlin, Jun 18, 1986
400 Metres Freestyle:
4m 03.85s Janet Evans (US), Seoul, Sep 22, 1988
800 Metres Freestyle:
8m 16.22s Janet Evans (US), Tokyo, Aug 20, 1989
100 Metres Backstroke:
1m 00.59s Ina Kleber (GDR), Moscow, Aug 24, 1984
200 Metres Backstroke:
2m 08.60s Betsy Mitchell (US), Orlando, Florida, Jun 27, 1986
100 Metres Breaststroke:
1m 07.91s Silke Hoerner (GDR), Strasbourg, Aug 21, 1987
200 Metres Breaststroke:
2m 26.71s Silke Hoerner (GDR), Seoul, Sep 21, 1988
100 Metres Butterfly:
57.93s Mary Meagher (US), Milwaukee, Wisconsin, Aug 16, 1981
200 Metres Butterfly:
2m 05.96s Mary Meagher (US), Milwaukee, Wisconsin, Aug 13, 1981

200 Metres Medley:
2m 11.73s Ute Geweniger (GDR), East Berlin, Jul 4, 1981
400 Metres Medley:
4m 36.10s Petra Schneider (GDR), Guayaquil, Ecuador, Aug 1, 1982
4 x 100 Metres Free:
3m 40.57s East Germany, Madrid, Aug 19, 1986
4 x 200 Metres Free:
7m 55.47s East Germany, Strasbourg, Aug 18, 1987
4 x 100 Metres Medley:
4m 03.69s East Germany, Moscow, Aug 24, 1984

Other World Records broken or equalled in 1989
Men: 200 Metres Breaststroke: 2m 12.90s Mike Barrowman (US) Los Angeles, Aug 3; 2m 12.90s Nick Gillingham (GB) Bonn, Aug 18

1990

Feb 23-25:	British Grand Prix meeting (Leicester);
Mar 16-18:	British Grand Prix meeting (Southampton);
May 26-28:	British Grand Prix finals (Leeds);
Jul 26-29:	ASA National championships (Crystal Palace);
Jul 30-Aug 4:	ASA National age group championships (Leeds);
Nov 15-18:	ASA National winter championships (Coventry).

TABLE TENNIS

1989

MEN'S WORLD TEAM CHAMPIONSHIP
(Swaythling Cup)
Dortmund, Apr 4
Final
Sweden beat China 5-0
3rd Place Play-off
North Korea beat USSR 5-3

WOMEN'S WORLD TEAM CHAMPIONSHIP
(Corbillion Cup)
Dortmund, Apr 4
Final
China beat South Korea 3-0
3rd Place Play-off
Hong Kong beat Hungary 3-0

WORLD CHAMPIONSHIPS
Dortmund, Mar 29-Apr 9
Men's Singles
Quarter-finals
Andrzej Grubba (Pol) beat Kim Taek-Soo (SKo) 21-18 21-19 21-15; Jorgen Persson (Swe) beat Xu Zengcai (Chn) 21-11 21-16 17-21 15-21 21-18; Yu Shentong (Chn) beat Jiang Jialiang (Chn) 22-20 18-21 21-16 21-18; Jan-Over Waldner (Swe) beat Tibor Klampar (Hun) 21-19 11-21 21-18 22-20
Semi-finals
Jan Ove Waldner beat Andrzej Grubba 16-21 21-16 21-19 21-17; Jorgen Persson beat Yu Shentong 11-21 21-10 21-9 21-11
Final
Jan-Ove Waldner beat Jorgen Persson 21-17 21-18 20-22 18-21 21-10

Women's Singles
Quarter-finals
Hyun Jung-Hwa (SKo) beat Chen Zihe (Chn) 21-18 17-21 21-14 21-16; Chen Jing (Chn) beat Kyoko Uchiyama (Jap) 21-10 21-9 21-16; Qiao Hong (Chn) beat Wang Xiaoming (Fra) 21-16 21-12 21-14; Li Bun-Hui (NKo) beat Li Huifen (Chn) 12-21 21-19 21-12 21-13
Semi-finals
Qiao Hong beat Hyun Jung-Hwa 21-13 21-15 21-17; Li Bun-Hui beat Chen Jing 21-17 22-20 21-13
Final
Qiao Hong beat Li Bun-Hui 21-15 21-12 11-21 21-16

Men's Doubles
Semi-finals
Joerg Rosskopf/Steffen Fetzner (FRG) beat Chen Longcan/Wei Qingguang (Chn) 11-21 21-12 21-17; Lesek Kucharski (Pol)/Zoran Kalinic (Yug) beat Teng Yi/Hui Jun (Chn) 22-24 21-17 21-14
Final
Rosskopf/Fetzner beat Kucharski/Kalinic 18-21 21-17 21-19

Women's Doubles
Semi-finals
Chen Jing/Hu Xiaoxing (Chn) beat Li Jun/Ding Yaping (Chn) 21-14 22-24 21-10; Qiao Hong/Deng Yaping (Chn) beat Gao Jun/Liu Wei (Chn) 23-25 21-13 23-21
Final
Qiao Hong/Deng Yaping beat Chen Jing/Hu Xiaoxing 21-18 21-19

Mixed Doubles
Semi-finals
Yoo Nam-Kyu/Hyun Jung-Hwa (SKo) beat Chen Longcan/Chen Jing (Chn) 16-21 21-18 21-12; Zoran

Kalinic/Gordana Perkucin (Yug) Chen Zhibin/Gao Jun (Chn) 21-12 21-14
Final
Yoo Nam-Kyu/Hyun Jung-Hwa beat Kalinic/Perkucin 21-17 21-13

COMMONWEALTH CHAMPIONSHIPS
Cardiff, Mar 19-26
Men's Singles
Alan Cooke (Eng) beat Atanda Musa (Nig) 21-13 21-17 21-13
Women's Singles
Chai Po Wa (HK) beat Chan Tan Lui (HK) 21-16 21-15 21-8
Men's Doubles
Skylet Andrew/Nicky Mason (Eng) beat Atanda Musa/Titus Omotara (Nig) 21-14 21-18
Women's Doubles
Chai Po Wa/Chan Tan Lui (HK) beat Kerri Tepper/Wendy Hughes (Aus)
Mixed Doubles
Liu Fuk Man/Chan Tan Lui (HK) beat Skylet Andrew/Fiona Elliot (Eng) 21-12 21-19

CHAMPIONS

MEN'S WORLD TEAM CHAMPIONSHIP
Swaythling Cup

1927	Hungary
1928	Hungary
1929	Hungary
1930	Hungary
1931	Hungary
1932	Czechoslovakia
1933	Hungary
1934	Hungary
1935	Hungary
1936	Austria
1937	United States
1938	Hungary
1939	Czechoslovakia
1940-46	Not held
1947	Czechoslovakia
1948	Czechoslovakia
1949	Hungary
1950	Czechoslovakia
1951	Czechoslovakia
1952	Hungary
1953	England
1954	Japan
1955	Japan
1956	Japan
1957	Japan
1959	Japan
1961	China
1963	China
1965	China
1967	Japan
1969	Japan
1971	China
1973	Sweden
1975	China
1977	China
1979	Hungary
1981	China

1983	China
1985	China
1987	China
1989	Sweden

Most wins
12 Hungary

WOMEN'S WORLD TEAM CHAMPIONSHIP
Corbillon Cup

1934	Germany
1935	Czechoslovakia
1936	Czechoslovakia
1937	United States
1938	Czechoslovakia
1939	Germany
1940-46	Not held
1947	England
1948	England
1949	United States
1950	Romania
1951	Romania
1952	Japan
1953	Romania
1954	Japan
1955	Romania
1956	Romania
1957	Japan
1959	Japan
1961	Japan
1963	Japan
1965	China
1967	Japan
1969	USSR
1971	Japan
1973	South Korea
1975	China
1977	China
1979	China
1981	China
1983	China
1985	China
1987	China
1989	China

Most wins
9 China

WORLD CHAMPIONSHIPS
Men's Singles

1927	Roland Jacobi (Hun)
1928	Zoltan Mechlovits (Hun)
1929	Fred Perry (Eng)
1930	Victor Barna (Hun)
1931	Miklos Szabados (Hun)
1932	Victor Barna (Hun)
1933	Victor Barna (Hun)
1934	Victor Barna (Hun)
1935	Victor Barna (Hun)
1936	Standa Kolar (Cze)
1937	Richard Bergmann (Aut)
1938	Bohumil Vana (Cze)
1939	Richard Bergmann (Aut)
1940-46	Not held
1947	Bohumil Vana (Cze)
1948	Richard Bergmann (Eng)
1949	Johnny Leach (Eng)
1950	Richard Bergmann (Eng)
1951	Johnny Leach (Eng)
1952	Hiroji Satoh (Jap)
1953	Ferenc Sido (Hun)
1954	Ichiro Ogimura (Jap)
1955	Toshiaki Tanaka (Jap)
1956	Ichiro Ogimura (Jap)
1957	Toshiaki Tanaka (Jap)

1959	Jung-Kuo-tuan (Chn)
1961	Chuang Tse-tung (Chn)
1963	Chuang Tse-tung (Chn)
1965	Chuang Tse-tung (Chn)
1967	Nobuhiko Hasegawa (Jap)
1969	Shigeo Ito (Jap)
1971	Stellan Bengtsson (Swe)
1973	Hsi En-Ting (Chn)
1975	Istvan Jonyer (Hun)
1977	Mitsuru Kohno (Jap)
1979	Seiji Ono (Jap)
1981	Guo Yue-Hua (Chn)
1983	Guo Yue-Hua (Chn)
1985	Jiang Jialiang (Chn)
1987	Jiang Jialiang (Chn)
1989	Jan-Ove Waldner (Swe)

Most wins
5 Victor Barna

Women's Singles

1927	Maria Mednyanszky (Hun)
1928	Maria Mednyanszky (Hun)
1929	Maria Mednyanszky (Hun)
1930	Maria Mednyanszky (Hun)
1931	Maria Mednyanszky (Hun)
1932	Anna Sipos (Hun)
1933	Anna Sipos (Hun)
1934	Marie Kettnerova (Cze)
1935	Marie Kettnerova (Cze)
1936	Ruth Aarons (US)
1937	-
1938	Trudi Pritzi (Aut)
1939	Vlasha Depetrisova (Cze)
1940-46	Not held
1947	Gizi Farkas (Hun)
1948	Gizi Farkas (Hun)
1949	Gizi Farkas (Hun)
1950	Angelica Rozeanu (Rom)
1951	Angelica Rozeanu (Rom)
1952	Angelica Rozeanu (Rom)
1953	Angelica Rozeanu (Rom)
1954	Angelica Rozeanu (Rom)
1955	Angelica Rozeanu (Rom)
1956	Timo Okawa (Jap)
1957	Fujie Eguchi (Jap)
1959	Kimiyo Matsuzaki (Jap)
1961	Chiu Chung-Hui (Chn)
1963	Kimiyo Matsuzaki (Jap)
1965	Naoko Fukazu (Jap)
1967	Sachiko Morisawa (Jap)
1969	Toshiko Kowada (Jap)
1971	Lin Hui-Ching (Chn)
1973	Hu Yu-Lan (Chn)
1975	Pak Yung-Sun (NKo)
1977	Pak Yung-Sun (NKo)
1979	Ge Hsin-Ai (Chn)
1981	Tong Ling (Chn)
1983	Cao Yan-Hua (Chn)
1985	Cao Yan-Hua (Chn)
1987	He Zhili (Chn)
1989	Qiao Hong (Chn)

Most wins
6 Angelica Rozeanu

Men's doubles
Winners since 1970

1971	I Jonyer/T Klampar (Hun)
1973	Stellan Bengtsson/Kjell Johansson (Swe)
1975	Gabor Gergely/Istvan Jonyer (Hun)
1977	Li Zhenshi/Liang Geliang (Chn)
1979	Dragutin Surbek/Anton Stipancic (Yug)
1981	Cai Zhen-Hua/Li Zhen-Shi (Chn)
1983	Dragutin Surbek/Zoran Kalinic (Yug)
1985	Mikael Appelgren/Ulf Carlsson (Swe)

1987   Chen Longcan/Wei Quingguang (Chn)
1989   Joerg Rosskopf/Steffen Fetzner (FRG)
Most wins
8 Barna (Hun) 1929-35, 1939

Women's Doubles
Winners since 1970
1971   Cheng Min-Chih/Lin Hui-Ching (Chn)
1973   Maria Alexandru (Rom)/Miho Hamada (Jap)
1975   Maria Alexandru (Rom)/Shoko Takashima (Jap)
1977   Pak Yong Ok (NKo)/Yang Yin (Chn)
1979   Zhang Li/Zhang Deijing (Chn)
1981   Zhang Deijing/Cao Yanhua (Chn)
1983   Shen Jianping/Dai Lili (Chn)
1985   Dai Lili/Geng Lijuan (Chn)
1987   Yang Young-Ja/Hyun Jung-Hua (SKo)
1989   Qiao Hong/Deng Yaping (Chn)
Most wins
7 Maria Mednyanszky (Hun) 1928, 1930-35

Mixed doubles
Winners since 1970
1971   Lin Hui-Ching/Chang Shih-Lin (Chn)
1973   Liang Geliang/Li Li (Chn)
1975   Anna Ferdman/Stanislav Gomozkov (USSR)
1977   Claudia Bergeret/Jacques Secretin (FRA)
1979   Liang Geliang/Ge Zinai (Chn)
1981   Huang Junquin/Xie Saike (Chn)
1983   Ni Xialin/Guo Yue-Hua (Chn)

1985   Cao Yan-Hua/Cai Zhenhua (Chn)
1987   Hui Jun/Geng Lijuan (Chn)
1989   Hyun Jung-Hua/Yoo Nam-Kyu (SKo)
Most wins
6 Maria Mednyanszky (Hun) 1927-28, 1930-31, 1933-34.

OLYMPIC GAMES
First included 1988
Men's Singles
1988   Yoo Nam-Kyu (SKo)
Women's Singles
1988   Chen Jing (Chn)
Men's Doubles
1988   Chen Longcan/Wei Qingguang(Chn)
Women's Doubles
1988   Hyun Jung-Hwa (SKo)/Yang Young-Ja (SKo)

—————— **1990** ——————

Jan 4-7: English Open (Manchester), Jan 23: Yugoslavia v England, European Super League; Feb 3-4 European Top 12; Feb 13 England v Czechoslovakia, European Super League (Bude); Mar 6 England v West Germany, European Super League (Bexleyheath); Apr 8-16 European Championships; May 5-6 National championships.

TENNIS

━━━━ DOUBLE DEUTSCH ━━━━

O n the same cool afternoon, the two young West Germans who grew up within five miles of each other outside Heidelberg - 21-year-old Boris Becker and 20-year-old Steffi Graf - won the two Wimbledon singles titles, giving Germany an unprecedented double triumph. Two months later, at the US Open, they did it again. Becker's triumph at Flushing Meadow over Ivan Lendl proved that he could win on a surface other than grass and gave him a new status of mastery in the game. For three hours 51 minutes Becker and Lendl slugged it out in the tennis match of the year on a day of fearsome heat and humidity. Becker emerged triumphant.

Afterwards, the computer still ranked Lendl No.1. But few believed the computer any more. People began to talk of Becker as the player of the 1990s, but there were already youngsters beginning to emerge to whom both Becker and Graf appeared a bit fogeyish. The two French Open champions were both 17 - Michael Chang and Arantxa Sanchez - and threatened to be formidable tennis powers in the very near future. There are others.

The men's year had started with Lendl in awesome form. He won the Australian Open by beating Miloslav Mecir 6-2 6-2 6-2, the most one-sided final in the tournament since 1940. From then until the French Open he won 33 matches out of 35, winning four titles: and he was proceeding with his customary efficiency in Paris when he met the then little-known 17-year-old American Michael Chang in the last 16. Chang flummoxed Lendl by slipping in lobs and, at one point, an underarm serve. He went on to win the tournament and gave the credit to Jesus. He later complained that all this money he was winning was no use to him; he had no car or girlfriend to spend it on, only his hobby of aquariums - and now he was famous, people kept giving him fish.

Chang's arrival at Wimbledon provided a fresh and innocent diversion; the other rising American Andre Agassi declined to attend. However, Chang went out to Tim Mayotte and the decisive contest was once again Becker-Lendl. They met in the semi-finals and Lendl's determination to win Wimbledon - which is turning into a magnificent obsession - almost carried him through. He had gone ahead, one set all and 3-0, when a shower arrived and gave Becker a chance to regroup mentally. He made it in five sets and went on to reverse the 1988 final with ease; Stefan Edberg had an off-day. Lendl said he intends to miss the French Open in 1990 to prepare for Wimbledon.

With one aberration, women's tennis was more predictable. Steffi Graf once again bestrode the sport but narrowly failed to repeat her 1988 grand slam. She won three of the four comfortably enough but was stunned in the Paris final by 17-year-old Arantxa Sanchez of Spain who shouted "Vamos" after her winners and fought back from 5-3 down in the final set. Graf was suffering from the after-effects of a bad pizza. Nonetheless, this defeat provided one indication that Graf might not win every women's tennis tournament between now and the millennium. Another was the rise of Monica Seles, a 15-year-old grunting Yugoslav, who gave Graf a hard time in the French semi-finals. And on the distant horizon, there was 13-year-old Jennifer Capriati, an Evert clone from Florida who won the under-18s at the US Open and was picked for the Wightman Cup. Sanchez charmed everyone with her winning smile, her proficient but original use of English and her mature range of shots. Before Wimbledon she tacked her mother's maiden name, Vicario, on to hers so her mum did not feel left out. Seles baffled doctors by growing two inches between Wimbledon and the US.

TEARS AND TANTRUMS

Much of the year was taken up with a farewell to Chris Evert. She said it would probably be her last Wimbledon. At the US Open, she really did call it a day after 1,304 career victories, 157 titles and 18 Grand Slam singles titles, and turned the tournament into a sentimental jamboree. Evert declined to go quietly and she played magnificently to beat Seles 6-0 6-2 but her attempt to reach her 18th US semi-final in 19 years foundered against Zina Garrison. "A tear came to my eye," the winner said. Everyone else was in floods. Evert said she would have won two more Wimbledons but for love: her ex, Jimmy Connors, turned up at her 1975 semi-final against Billie-Jean King with the actress Susan George and she was too livid to concentrate. In 1978 she could only think of John Lloyd and not of Martina Navratilova, whom she was playing.

CHRIS EVERT

Total Tournament Wins: **157 (all-time record)**

Career Wins: **1,304 (Navratilova 1,196)**

Grand Slam wins:

Wimbledon (3): 1974, 1976, 1981

US Open (6): 1975-78, 1980, 1982
In the 19 US Opens since 1971 she has won the title six times, been runner-up three times and reached eight other semi-finals.

French Open (7): 1974-75, 1979-80, 1983, 1985-86

Australian Open (2): 1982, 1984
She won at least one Grand Slam event every year 1974-86.

Longest Streak: **125 consecutive matches won on clay 1973-79 (the longest sequence by any player on any surface). Between Mar-Sep 1974 she won a then world record 55 consecutive matches (all surfaces).**

Career Earnings: **$8,858,192 (Navratilova ($14,625,192)**

Was Ranked World No 1. as follows:
Nov 1975-Jul 1978
Jan-Mar 1979
Jun-Aug 1979
Nov 1980-Jun 1982
Oct-Nov 1985

Meetings with Martina Navratilova: **1973-88, played 80, won 37, lost 43**

Navratilova battled on, losing to Graf in the finals at both Wimbledon and Flushing in a manner that would once have been unthinkable and now seemed utterly inevitable. Graf said dismissively after the US Open that she had had a harder time in the semi-final against Gabriela Sabatini. "I know how to beat her," said Martina grimly. "I just wasn't able to do it."

At Wimbledon, of course, the tennis was only a fraction of the story. John McEnroe had threatened to drop his shorts on Centre Court if Chang won the title. That turned out to be one of the few imaginable McEnroe-related events that did not happen. It was a vintage year for Bratwatchers.

He fought back from two sets down for the first time in his life, against Darren Cahill. Scotland Yard investigated four death threats. Then he had air freshener sprayed in his face as he left Court 14 after a doubles match, and had a fourth round war with John Fitzgerald in which McEnroe complained about everything and Fitzgerald complained about McEnroe, saying his time-wasting was close to cheating. He did play the occasional bit of sublime tennis, mostly when he was at his angriest. And McEnroe was praised by both Leo Turner, the retiring chief locker attendant, as the only champion generous enough to buy all the attendants champagne, and eight-year-old Katie Watson, whom he comforted after she was knocked to the ground by a TV crew.

The most dramatic outburst of the fortnight, anyway, came not from McEnroe but from "Gentleman" Tim Mayotte who smashed his racket in fury during his quarter-final against Edberg when umpire John Frame mysteriously overruled a service line call at a vital stage of a tiebreak and declined to play a let.

"Should've, would've, could've. It's God's Way of torturing you when you lose."
Brad Gilbert

"As the years go by, it does seem that control and discipline within the game are diminishing."
Neale Fraser

"You may have seen the ball as good but I thought it was wide, and it would be tough to take a point like that."
Andre Agassi to the crowd at Indian Wells

"I've tried to talk to him, but 18-year-olds listen to what they want to hear."
John McEnroe on Agassi

"Andre Agassi was recently born again. Now, if he can only grow up."
Sports Illustrated

"I have to give Jesus Christ the credit for anything that has happened in my life".
Michael Chang

"Money is not one of those things that really appeals to me. Every time I touch money, I wash my hands because it's dirty... I really don't have anything to spend it on."
Michael Chang

"Becker has a spontaneity that Lendl can only marvel at, an elasticity that Lendl can only envy, a nonchalance that Lendl can only dream about. It's not that Lendl isn't a worthy champion; he has been that and more - an indefatigable competitor, the hardest-working man in the game, the ultimate systems analyst, a problem solver. He held the game in good hands. But Becker gave it wings."
Tony Kornheiser, Washington Post

"The British can field a better team than they have. I don't mean different players - same players but better prepared."
Marty Riessen, US Wightman Cup Coach

"The parents, coaches and LTA haven't the slightest idea of what tennis today is all about."
Sue Mappin, British Wightman Cup Coach

"There is too much pettiness and jealousy among the British players. They should be competitive and prove a point with their racket."
Warren Jacques, British team manager

Despite the hot English summer, much of Wimbledon took place in familiar conditions; the women's final had to be played on the Sunday because of rain. The price of a small bowl of strawberries rose to £1.65 but was cut to £1.50 after protests. A mouse stopped play on Court One; a sparrow on Centre Court. Boris Becker briefly wore a shirt with more blue and green than white to protest against the All-England Club's bossiness. On men's semi-final day the publicists for the film Batman successfully handed out their hats and T-shirts to spectators despite the club's edicts to the contrary. The great German triumph was missed by about half West Germany's TV viewers: Wimbledon, more interested in cash than publicity, sold the rights to a cable network instead of the traditional channel. In an attempt to stop touts, the All-England Club introduced a "white market"; but fewer than 100 of the 2,100 debenture-holders co-operated. A new issue of debentures for 1991-95 was offered to existing holders at £19,250 each. The total attendance at 400,288 was second only to 1988 (411,270) when the tournament was extended to a 14th day. The previous 13-day record was 400,032 in 1986.

The two champions did their best to cope with the problems of fame. Becker, it was revealed, has insured himself for £6 million (premium: £100,000) against the risk of kidnap. Graf received death threats accusing her of "killing the fun and joy" of tennis and a man who has pestered her for several years slashed his wrists in front of her.

BRITS VANQUISHED

British tennis players had no problem being famous. But one British male did stay in the Wimbledon singles until the first Saturday: Nick Fulwood reached the third round but then lost a seemingly winnable match against Paul Chamberlin. "I'd like to have seen a bit more spirit," said the British coach Warren Jacques. Sara Gomer had three match points against the No. 8 seed Pam Shriver but lost.

The 6ft 5in Chris Bailey managed to reach the last eight at Queen's Club and led Britain to a Davis Cup win over Finland, briefly encouraging hopes of a return to the world group. The team then had a promising home draw, which forced the clay court specialists of Argentina on to grass at Eastbourne. As ever, British hopes were soon clay. Bailey complained that the Eastbourne crowds did not get behind the team properly. "There are a lot of old biddies around," he said. A departing spectator suggested to a journalist that the headlines should be "No Sets Please, We're British". West Germany and Sweden reached the Davis Cup final, to be played in December, for the second successive year. The US women (13-year-old Capriati included) beat Britain 7-0 in the Wightman Cup, yet again. The former British women's No. 1 Annabel Croft signed to appear in a pantomime at Crawley with Roland Rat.

In February, Bjorn Borg went to hospital in Milan after taking an overdose of sleeping pills. After a number of learned articles appeared on the pressures of being a 32-year-old multi-millionaire has-been, everyone involved denied that Borg had attempted suicide; he just wanted to sleep. In July, Borg's fashion business, into which a fair chunk of his estimated £59 million fortune had gone, went bust. In September, he married an Italian pop star, Loredana Berte.

The year's other winners included Brad Gilbert, who won three Grand Prix titles in three weeks in August, the first man to do so since Becker in 1986; he also reached four successive finals, last achieved by Lendl in 1982. Then he had stomach trouble and lost in the first round of the US Open to Todd Witsken. The losers included Pat Cash, the 1987 Wimbledon champion, who severely damaged an achilles tendon playing the Japan Open in April; and the Austrian Thomas Muster who reached the finals of the Lipton Tournament in Key Biscayne, then was hit by a car two hours later, and put out for months with a damaged knee. "Thank God I'm alive," he said. There was also Pam Shriver, who was dumped as a doubles partner by Martina Navratilova after winning 74 tournaments out of 91 together. Shriver complained she was told by someone else. She also said she was having a mid-life crisis at 27, and was voted out of office ("A disgrace. These young kids in tennis don't have a clue" - Chris Evert) as vice-president of the Women's International Tennis Association. Meanwhile Jimmy Connors lost in the second round of Wimbledon to Dan Goldie, and in the French to Jay Berger who pays 50 dollars to buy old - fashioned metal rackets from his local supermarket.

━━━━ 1989 ━━━━

Underlined players beat seeds higher than themselves

THE ALL-ENGLAND CHAMPIONSHIPS
Wimbledon Jun 26-Jul 9

Men's Singles
Third Round
JOHN FITZGERALD (Aus) beat Jonas B Svenson (Swe) 6-4 6-4 7-6; MATS WILANDER (Swe) [4] beat Jason Stoltenberg (Aus) 6-3 6-3 6-3 CHRISTO VAN RENSBURG (SA) beat Brad Drewett (Aus) 6-3 2-6 2-6 6-2 10-8; JOHN McENROE (US) [5] beat Jim Pugh (US) 6-3 6-4 6-2; MICHAEL CHANG (US) [9] beat Michiel Schapers (Hol) 4-6 6-3 7-5 7-5; TIM MAYOTTE (US) [8] beat David Pate (US) 6-4 6-1 6-3; AMOS MANSDORF (Isr) [16] beat Greg Holmes (US) 6-2 6-4 6-2; STEFAN EDBERG (Swe) [2] beat Scott Davis (US) 6-3 6-4 4-6 6-2; AARON KRICKSTEIN (US) [13] beat Peter Kuhnen (FRG) 4-6 6-3 6-3 6-2; PETER LUNDGREN (Swe) beat Ken Flach (US) 6-3 6-2 6-7 6-3; DAN GOLDIE (US) beat Wally Masur (Aus) 7-6 7-6 3-6 7-6; PAUL CHAMBERLIN (US) beat Nick Fulwood (GB) 3-6 7-6 6-4 6-2; IVAN LENDL (Cze) [1] beat Tomas Carbonelli (Spa) 7-6 6-3 6-1; BORIS BECKER (FRG) [3] beat Jan Gunnarsson (Swe) 7-5 7-6 6-3; LEIF SHIRAS (US) beat Kevin Curren (US) [12] 4-6 6-3 5-7 7-6 6-3; SLOBODAN ZIVOJINOVIC (Yug) beat Miloslav Mecir (Cze) [7] 6-7 6-1 7-5 6-3

How the other seeds fell:
Jakob Hlasek (Swi) [6] lost to Thomas Hogstedt (Swe) (1st Round) 3-6 6-7 1-6; Jimmy Connors (US) [10] lost to Goldie (2nd Round) 6-7 7-5 4-6 2-6; Brad Gilbert (US) [11] lost to Fitzgerald (1st Round) 2-6 5-7 6-1 6-3 2-6; Andrei Chesnokov (USSR) [14] lost to Drewett (1st Round) 4-6 6-7 0-6

Fourth Round
BECKER beat Krickstein 6-4 6-4 7-5; EDBERG beat Mansdorf 6-4 6-3 6-2; LENDL beat Lundgren 1-6 7-6 6-2 6-4; McEnroe beat Fitzgerald 6-3 0-6 6-4 6-4; CHAMBERLIN beat Shiras 7-5 6-4 7-6; MAYOTTE beat Chang 6-3 6-1 6-3; GOLDIE beat Zivojinovic 6-4 6-4 7-6; WILANDER beat Van Rensburg 3-6 7-5 7-5 6-3

Quarter-finals
BECKER beat Chamberlin 6-1 6-2 6-0; EDBERG beat Mayotte 7-6 7-6 6-3; LENDL beat Goldie 7-6 7-6 6-0; McENROE beat Wilander 7-6 3-6 6-3 6-4

Semi-finals
BECKER beat Lendl 7-5 6-7 2-6 6-4 6-3; EDBERG beat McEnroe 7-5 7-6 7-6

Final
BECKER beat Edberg 6-0 7-6 6-4

TWO WEEKS IN SUMMER

"Quite simply, the more they drink, the more we profit. So make them drink."
Reported instructions to barmen in Wimbledon hospitality chalets

"I personally don't give a shit what you think about my double faults."   John McEnroe

"He's playing guys who have credibility and decency...decent sportsmen. They're trying their hardest - and he's going on with all this ridiculous nonsense."
John Fitzgerald on McEnroe

"A sour-grapes situation."
McEnroe on Fitzgerald

"Off the court, he's really very shy."
Ilie Nastase on McEnroe

"I could give you guys another pain in the butt and let my son come out here."
Jimmy Connors on his future plans

Journalist: "What do you have to do to win Wimbledon?"

Mats Wilander: "Improve my serve and then my volley and then my forehand and my backhand and my footwork. In that order."

"Emotionally you can compare him to Nastase. Like all artists, he has to bring something extra to his work. Germanic people are supposed to be stable and square, but you would think Boris was born in Naples. He will always live on his emotions."
Ion Tiriac, Becker's manager.

"I would love to be just a normal guy and do normal things."   Boris Becker

"I don't know what they carry in their shoulder bags these days. Gold, I think."
Leo Turner, Wimbledon chief locker-room attendant

"Only when we are grandfather and grandmother will people realise what we achieved."
Becker on the German double

"This isn't my last stand. I'm not Custer."
Martina Navratilova

" I'll be back next year, but it doesn't get any easier."
John McEnroe

"A colleague and his father went to the Wimbledon finals on Sunday. They gave two spare centre court tickets to an official booth selling returns for charity. When two men later sat down in the empty seats beside them, they naturally assumed they had bought their tickets from this booth. Hardly, said the two men. They had just paid £500 apiece for them in a Wimbledon car park."
Martin Fletcher, The Times

"During Wimbledon fortnight the BBC shows tennis every day for several hours... During the US Open the BBC apparently did not think it worthwhile paying to show any of the proceedings at all, not even the highlights of the finals. One might deduce from this that the BBC is under the impression that what the public wants to see is not the actual tennis being played but the Wimbledon courts - the grass, the stands and so on. In that case, why don't they sometimes broadcast programmes showing just the courts even when there are no players and spectators getting in the way?"
Letter in The Independent from Wilfred Beckerman of Oxford

Women's Singles

Third Round
JANA NOVOTNA (Cze) [10] beat Katrina Adams (US) 6-4 6-1; HANA MANDLIKOVA (Aus) [14] beat Donna Faber (US) 6-2 6-4; MARTINA NAVRATILOVA (US) [2] beat Nicole Provis (Aus) 6-0 6-3; LAURA GOLARSA (Ita) beat Louise Field (Aus) 6-4 7-6, PATTY FENDICK (US) beat Shaun Stafford (US) 2-6 6-1 6-3; GRETCHEN MAGERS (US) beat Pam Shriver (US) [8] 2-6 6-2 12-10; MARY JOE FERNANDEZ (US) [12] beat Catherine Tanvier (Fra) 4-6 6-2 6-4; JO-ANNE FAULL (Aus) beat Laura Gildemeister (Per) 6-3 7-6; CHRIS EVERT (US) [4] beat Anne Hobbs (GB) 6-4 6-1; STEFFI GRAF (FRG) [1] beat Anne Minter (Aus) 6-1 6-3; MONICA SELES (Yug) [11] beat Eva Svigerova (Cze) 6-4 6-3; CATARINA LINDQVIST (Swe) beat Natalya Zvereva (USSR) [9] 7-6 4-6 6-4; ARANTXA SANCHEZ VICARIO (Spa) [7] beat Raffaella Reggi (Ita) 4-6 6-3 7-5; ROS FAIRBANK (SA) beat Liz Smylie (Aus) 6-3 6-3 HELENA SUKOVA (Cze) [6] beat Claudia Khode-Kilsch (FRG) 4-6 6-3 6-3; LORI McNEIL (US) [15] beat Judith Wiesner (Aut) 5-7 6-2 6-4
How the other seeds fell:
Helen Kelesi (Can) [13] lost to Shaun Stafford (US) (1st Round) 6-7 5-7; Zina Garrison (US) [5] lost to Field (2nd Round) 6-1 2-6 5-7; Gabriela Sabatini (Arg) [3] lost to Fairbank (2nd Round) 4-6 3-6; Susan Sloane (US) [16] lost to Gildemeister (2nd Round) 3-6 5-7

Fourth Round
GRAF beat Seles 6-0 6-1; NAVRATILOVA beat Mandlikova 6-3 6-2;`EVERT beat Fendick 6-2 6-2; LINDQVIST beat Sukova 6-4 7-6; SANCHEZ beat McNeil 6-3 2-6 6-1; MAGERS beat Faull 6-7 6-1 6-0; GOLARSA beat Novotna 7-6 2-6 6-4; FAIRBANK beat Fernandez 6-4 2-6 6-0;

Quarter-finals
GRAF beat Sanchez 7-5 6-1; NAVRATILOVA beat Magers 6-1 6-2; EVERT beat Golarsa 6-3 2-6 7-5; LINDQVIST beat Fairbank 7-5 7-5

Semi-finals
GRAF beat Evert 6-2 6-1; NAVRATILOVA beat Lindqvist 7-6 6-1

Final
GRAF beat Navratilova 6-2 6-7 6-1

Men's Doubles

Final
JOHN FITZGERALD (Aus) & ANDERS JARRYD (Swe) beat Rick Leach and Jim Pugh (US) 3-6 7-6 6-4 7-6

Women's Doubles
Final
JANA NOVOTNA & HELENA SUKOVA (Cze) beat Larisa Savchenko and Natalya Zvereva (USSR) 6-1 6-2

Mixed Doubles
Final
JIM PUGH (US) & JANA NOVOTNA (Cze) beat Mark Kratzmann and Jenny Byrne (Aus) 6-4 5-7 6-4

The Other Finals
Ladies' Plate
Wendy White (US) beat Elna Reinach (SA) 6-3 6-4

Veterans' Singles
Tom Gullikson (US) beat Tim Gullikson (US) 7-5 6-3

Veterans' Doubles
Anand Amritraj & Vijay Amritraj (Ind) & Bob Lutz & Dick Stockton (US) 6-3 6-2

Junior Boys
Nicklas Kulti (Swe) beat Todd Woodbridge (Aus) 6-4 6-3

Junior Girls
Andrea Strnadova (Cze) beat Meredith McGrath (US) 6-2 6-3

Junior Boys' Doubles
Jared Palmer & Jonathan Stark (US) beat John-Laffnie de Jager & Wayne Ferreira (SA) 7-6 7-6

Junior Girls' Doubles
Jennifer Capriati & Meredith McGrath (US) beat Andrea Strnadova & Eva Sviglerova (Cze) 6-4 6-2

COUNTRIES THAT HAVE WON BOTH MEN'S AND WOMEN'S TITLES AT WIMBLEDON IN SAME YEAR

(Since 1922 when Challenge system abolished)

United States	1930, 1932, 1938-39, 1947-51, 1953, 1955, 1972, 1974-75, 1981-84
Australia	1965, 1970-71
France	1925
Great Britain	1934
West Germany	1989

AUSTRALIAN OPEN
Melbourne, Jan 16-29
Men's Singles
Fourth Round
IVAN LENDL (Cze) [2] beat Amos Mansdorf (Isr) [16] 7-6 7-4 6-2; THOMAS MUSTER (Aut) [11] beat Magnus Gustafsson (Swe) 6-3 6-2 7-5; STEFAN EDBERG (Swe) [4] beat Pat Cash (Aus) [13] 6-4 6-0 6-2; MILOSLAV MECIR (Cze) [9] beat Christo Van Rensburg (SAf) 6-4 6-1 6-0; JAN GUNNARSSON (Swe) beat Michiel Schapers (Hol) 7-6 6-16-2; JOHN McENROE (US) [7] beat Aaron Krickstein (US) [10] 7-6 6-2 6-3; JONAS SVENSSON (Swe) [14] beat Boris Becker (FRG) [3] 7-6 6-4 6-3; GORAN IVANISEVIC (Yug) beat Leonardo Lavelle (Mex) 3-6 3-6 6-3 6-4 6-1
Quarter-finals
LENDL beat McEnroe 7-6 6-2 7-6; MUSTER beat Edberg default; MECIR beat Ivanisevic (Yug) 7-5 6-0 6-3; GUNNARSSON beat Svensson 6-0 6-3 4-6 6-4
Semi-finals
LENDL beat Muster 6-2 6-4 5-7 7-5; MECIR beat Gunnarsson 7-5 6-2 6-2

Final
LENDL beat Mecir 6-2 6-2 6-2
Women's Singles
Fourth Round
STEFFI GRAF (FRG) [1] beat Nicole Provis (Aus) [16] 6-4 6-0; HELENA SUKOVA (Cze) [5] beat Catherine Tanvier (Fra) 7-5 6-4; BELINDA CORDWELL (NZ) beat Brenda Schultz (Hol) 6-3 6-2; GABRIELA SABATINI (Arg) [3] beat Raffaella Reggi (Ita) [13] 6-0 4-6 6-1; CATARINA LINDQVIST (Swe) beat Judith Wiesner (Aut) 7-5 6-2; CLAUDIA KOHDE-KILSCH (FRG) [8] beat Donna Faber (US) 6-3 6-3; ZINA GARRISON (US) [6] beat Cammy McGregor (US) 7-5 6-1; MARTINA NAVRATILOVA (US) [2] beat Hana Mandlikova (Aus) [15] 6-4 6-1
Quarter-finals
GRAF beat Kohde-Kilsch 6-2 6-3; SUKOVA beat Navratilova 6-2 3-6 9-7; CORDWELL beat Lindqvist 6-2 2-6 6-1; SABATINI beat Garrison 6-4 2-6 6-4
Semi-finals
GRAF beat Sabatini 6-3 6-0; SUKOVA beat Cordwell 7-6 4-6 6-2
Final
GRAF beat Sukova 6-4 6-4

Men's Doubles
Final
RICK LEACH & JIM PUGH (US) beat Darren Cahill and Mark Kratzmann (Aus) 6-4 6-4 6-4

Women's Doubles
Final
MARTINA NAVRATILOVA & PAM SHRIVER (US) beat Patty Fendick (US) and Jill Hetherington (Can) 3-6 6-3 6-2

Mixed Doubles
Final
JIM PUGH (US) & JAN ANOVOTNA (Cze) beat Sherwood Stewart and Zina Garrison (US) 6-3 6-4

FRENCH OPEN
Paris, May 29-Jun 11
Men's Singles
Fourth Round
MICHAEL CHANG (US) [15] beat Ivan Lendl (Cze) [1] 4-6 4-6 6-3 6-3 6-3; ROLAND AGENOR (Hai) beat Sergio Bruguera (Spa) 2-6 3-6 6-3 6-1 6-2; ANDREI CHESNOKOV (USSR) beat Jim Courier (US) 2-6 3-6 7-6 6-2 7-5; MATS WILANDER (Swe) [4] beat Lawson Duncan (US) 7-5 6-3 6-2; STEFAN EDBERG (SWE) [3] beat Goran Ivanisevic (Yug) 7-5 6-3 6-3; ALBERTO MANCINI (Arg) [11] beat Jakob Hlasek (Swi) [6] 6-4 6-4 4-6 2-6 6-4; BORIS BECKER (FRG) [2] beat Guillermo Perez-Roldan (Arg) [16] 3-6 6-4 6-2 4-6 7-5; JAY BERGER (US) beat Thierry Tulasne (Fra) 3-6 6-2 6-0 6-3
Quarter-finals
CHANG beat Agenor 6-4 2-6 6-4 7-6; CHESNOKOV beat Wilander 6-4 6-0 7-5; EDBERG beat Mancini 6-1 6-3 7-6; BECKER beat Berger 6-3 6-4 6-1
Semi-finals
CHANG beat Chesnokov 6-1 5-7 7-6 7-5; EDBERG beat Becker 6-3 6-4 5-7 3-6 6-2
Final
CHANG beat Edberg 6-1 3-6 4-6 6-4 6-2
Women's Singles
Fourth Round
STEFFI GRAF (FRG) [1] beat Silvia La Fratta (Ita) 6-2 6-1; ARANTXA SANCHEZ-VICARIO (Spa) [7] beat Amandi Coetzer (SA) 6-3 6-2; MONICA SELES (Yug) beat Jo-Anne Faull (Aus) 6-3 6-2; JANA NOVOTNA (Cze) [11] beat Sylvia Hanika (FRG) 6-1 6-4; CONCHITA MARTINEZ (Spa) [8] beat Katerina Maleeva (Bul) [9] 6-0 6-1; MARY JOE FERNANDEZ (US) [15] beat Gabriela Sabatini (Arg) [2] 6-4 6-4; HELEN KELESI (Can) [10] beat Ann Grossman (US) 6-1 6-2; MANUELA MALEEVA (Bul) [6] beat Janine Thompson (Aus) 7-6 6-2

Quarter-finals
GRAF beat Martinez 6-0 6-4; SANCHEZ-VICARIO beat Novotna 6-2 6-2; FERNANDEZ beat Kelesi 6-2 7-5; SELES beat Maleeva 6-3 7-5
Semi-finals
SANCHEZ-VICARIO beat Fernandez 6-2 6-2; GRAF beat Seles 6-3 3-6 6-3
Final
SANCHEZ-VICARIO beat Graf 7-6 3-6 7-5

Men's Doubles
Final
JIM GRABB & PATRICK McENROE (US) beat Mansur Bahrami (Irn) and Eric Winogradsky (Fra) 6-4 2-6 6-4 7-6

Women's Doubles
Final
LARISA SAVCHENKO & NATALYA ZVEREVA (USSR) beat Gabriela Sabatini (Arg) and Steffi Graf (FRG) 6-4 6-4

Mixed Doubles
Final
TOM NIJSSEN & MANON BOLLEGRAF (Hol) beat Horacio de la Pena (Arg) and Arantxa Sanchez Vicario (Spa) 6-3 6-7 6-2

UNITED STATES OPEN
Flushing Meadow, New York, Aug 28-Sep 10
Men's Singles
Fourth Round
IVAN LENDL (Cze) [1] beat Andrei Chesnokov (USSR) [16] 6-3 4-6 1-6 6-4 6-3; JIMMY CONNORS (US) [13] beat Stefan Edberg (Swe) [3] 6-2 6-3 6-1; ANDRE AGASSI (US) [6] beat Jim Grabb (USA) 6-1 7-5 6-3; TIM MAYOTTE (US) [9] beat Michael Chang (US) [7] 7-5 6-1 1-6 6-3; BORIS BECKER (FRG) [2] beat Mikael Pernfors (Swe) 5-7 6-3 6-2 6-1; YANNICK NOAH (Fra) beat Alberto Mancini (Arg) [10] 6-3 3-6 6-7 6-3 6-3; AARON KRICKSTEIN (US) [14] beat Paul Haarhuis (Hol) 6-2 6-4 7-5; JAY BERGER beat (US) [11] beat Pete Sampras (US) 7-5 6-2 6-1
Quarter-finals
BECKER beat Noah 6-3 6-3 6-2; LENDL beat Mayotte 6-4 6-0 6-1; KRICKSTEIN beat Berger 3-6 6-4 6-2 1-0 retired; AGASSI beat Connors 6-1 4-6 0-6 6-3 6-4
Semi-finals
BECKER beat Krickstein 6-4 6-3 6-4; LENDL beat Agassi 7-6 6-2 3-6 6-1
Final
BECKER beat Lendl 7-6 1-6 6-3 7-6

Women's Singles
Fourth Round
MARTINA NAVRATILOVA (US) [2] beat Regina Rajchrtova (Cze) 6-2 6-0; MANUELA MALEEVA (Bul) [7] beat Natalya Zvereva (USSR) [13] 6-2 6-0; ZINA GARRISON (US) [5] beat Donna Faber (US) 6-4 7-6; CHRIS EVERT (US) [4] beat Monica Seles (Yug) [12] 6-0 6-2; STEFFI GRAF (FRG) [1] beat Ros Fairbank (SA) 6-4 6-0; HELENA SUKOVA (Cze) [8] beat Larisa Savchenko (USSR) 4-6 6-1 6-2; GABRIELA SABATINI (Arg) [3] beat Conchita Martinez (Spa) [15] 6-1 6-1; ARANTXA SANCHEZ-VICARIO (Spa) [6] beat Barbara Paulus (Aut) 6-2 6-2
Quarter-finals
NAVRATILOVA beat Maleeva 6-0 6-0; GARRISON beat Evert 7-6 6-2; GRAF beat Sukova 6-1 6-1; SABATINI beat Sanchez-Vicario 3-6 6-4 6-1
Semi-finals
NAVRATILOVA beat Garrison 7-6 6-2; GRAF beat Sabatini 3-6 6-4 6-2
Final
GRAF beat Navratilova 3-6 7-5 6-1

Men's Doubles
Final
JOHN McENROE (US) & MARK WOODFORDE (Aus) beat Ken Flach & Robert Seguso (US) 6-4 4-6 6-3 6-3

Women's Doubles
Final
HANA MANDLIKOVA (Aus) & MARTINA NAVRATILOVA (US) beat Pam Shriver and Mary Joe Fernandez (US) 5-7 6-4 6-4

Mixed Doubles
Final
ROBIN WHITE & SHELBY CANNON (US) beat Meredith McGrath & Rick Leach (US) 3-6 6-2 7-5

OTHER MAJOR EVENTS 1989
Men
Rotterdam Grand Prix, *Rotterdam, Feb 12*
Jakob Hlasek (Swi) beat Anders Jarryd (Swe) 6-1 7-5
Volvo Indoor Champs, Memphis, *Tennessee, Feb 19*
Brad Gilbert (US) beat Johan Kriek (US) 6-2 6-2 retd
Stella Artois Indoor Champs, *Milan, Feb 19*
Boris Becker (FRG) beat Alexander Volkov (USSR) 6-1 6-2
Eagle Classic, Scottsdale, *Arizona, Mar 12*
Ivan Lendl (Cze) beat Stefan Edberg (Swe) 6-2 6-3
Champions Cup Indian Wells, *California, Mar 19*
Miloslav Mecir (Cze) beat Yannick Noah (Fra) 3-6 2-6 6-1 6-2 6-3
International Players Championship, *Key Biscayne, Florida, Apr 2*
Ivan Lendl (Cze) beat Thomas Muster (Aut), withdrew, injured
Japan Open, *Tokyo, Apr 23*
Stefan Edberg (Swe) beat Ivan Lendl (Cze) 6-3 2-6 6-4
Monte Carlo Open, *Monte Carlo, Apr 30*
Alberto Mancini (Arg) beat Boris Becker (FRG) 7-5 2-6 7-6 7-5
Tournament of Champions, *New York, May 8*
Ivan Lendl (Cze) beat Jamie Yzaga (Per) 6-2 6-1
German Open, *Hamburg, May 14*
Ivan Lendl (Cze) beat Horst Skoff (Aut) 6-4 6-1 6-3
Italian Open, *Rome, May 21*
Alberto Mancini (Arg) beat Andre Agassi (US) 6-3 4-6 2-6 7-6 6-1
Stella Artois Grass Court Champs, *Queen's Club, London, Jun 18*
Ivan Lendl (Cze) beat Christo Van Rensburg (SA) 4-6 6-3 6-4
Bristol Trophy, *Bristol, England, Jun 25*
Eric Jelen (FRG) beat Nick Brown (GB) 6-4 3-6 7-5
US Professional Champs, *Boston, Jul 17*
Andres Gomez (Ecu) beat Mats Wilander (Swe) 6-1 6-4
Washington DC Classic, *Washington, Jul 31*
Tim Mayotte (US) beat Brad Gilbert (US) 3-6 6-4 7-5
Volvo International, *Stratton Mountain, Vermont, Aug 6*
Brad Gilbert (US) beat Jim Pugh (US) 7-5 6-0
US Hardcourt Champs, *Indianapolis, Aug 13*
John McEnroe (US) beat Jay Berger (US) 6-4 4-6 6-4
Players International, *Montreal, Aug 20*
Ivan Lendl (Cze) beat John McEnroe (US) 6-1 6-3

Women
New South Wales Open, *Sydney, Jan 15*
Martina Naratilova (US) beat Catarina Linqvist (Swe) 6-2 6-4
Pan Pacific Tournament, *Tokyo, Feb 5*
Martina Navratilova (US) beat Lori McNeil (US) 6-7 6-3 7-6
Virginia Slims of Washington, *Feb 19*
Steffi Graf (FRG) beat Zina Garrison (US) 6-1 7-5
Virginia Slims of California, *Oakland, Feb 26*
Zina Garrison (US) beat Larisa Savchenko (USSR) 6-1 6-1
US Women's hardcourt Champs, *San Antonio, Texas; Mar 5*
Steffi Graf (FRG) beat Ann Henricksson (US) 6-1 6-4
Virginia Slims of Indian Wells, *California, Mar 12*
Manuela Maleeva (Bul) beat Jenny Byrne (Aus) 6-4 6-1
Virginia Slims of Florida, *Boca Raton, Mar 19*
Steffi Graf (FRG) beat Chris Evert (US) 4-6 6-2 6-3

Lipton International Players' Championship,
Key Biscayne, Florida, Apr 2
Gabriela Sabatini (Arg) beat Chris Evert (US) 6-1 4-6 6-2
Family Circle Cup, Hilton Head, *South Carolina, Apr 9*
Steffi Graf (FRG) beat Natalya Zvereva (USSR) 6-1 6-1
Bausch and Lomb Tournament, *Amelia Island, Florida,*
Apr 16
Gabriela Sabatini (Arg) beat Steffi Graf (FRG) 3-6 6-3 7-5
Tampa Women's Open, *Tampa, Florida, Apr 23*
Conchita Martinez (Spa) beat Gabriela Sabatini (Arg) 6-3
6-2
Virginia Slims of Houston, *Apr 30*
Monica Seles (Yug) beat Chris Evert (US) 3-6 6-1 6-4
Virginia Slims of Hamburg, *May 7*
Steffi Graf (FRG) beat Jana Novotna (Cze) default
Italian Open, *Rome, May 14*
Gabriela Sabatini (Arg) beat Arantxa Sanchez-Vicario
(Spa) 6-2 5-7 6-4
German Open, *Berlin, May 21*
Steffi Graf (FRG) beat Gabriela Sabatini (Arg) 6-3 6-1
Dow Classic, *Edgbaston, Jun 18*
Martina Navratilova (US) beat Zina Garrison (US) 7-6 6-3
Pilkington Glass Championship, *Eastbourne, Jun 24*
Martina Navratilova (US) beat Raffaella Reggi (Ita) 7-6 6-2
Great American Bank Classic, *San Diego, Aug 6*
Steffi Graf (FRG) beat Zina Garrison (US) 6-4 7-5
Virginia Slims of Los Angeles, *Manhattan Beach,*
California, Aug 13
Martina Navratilova (US) beat Gabriela Sabatini (Arg) 6-0
6-2
United Jersey Bank Classic, *Mahwah, New Jersey, Aug*
20
Steffi Graf (FRG) beat Andrea Temesvari (Hun) 7-5 6-2
Canadian Players Challenge, *Toronto, Aug 27*
Martina Navratilova (US) beat Arantxa Sanchez-Vicario
(Spa) 6-2 6-2

MEN'S RANKINGS

(after US Open, Sep 1989)

1 (2) Ivan Lendl (Cze); 2 (4) Boris Becker (FRG); 3 (5)
Stefan Edberg (Swe); 4 (11) John McEnroe (US); 5 (3)
Andre Agassi (US) 6 (30) Michael Chang (US); 7 (21) Brad
Gilbert (US); 8 (10) Tim Mayotte (US); 9 (8) Jakob Hlasek
(Swi); 10 (16) Thomas Muster (Aut); 11 (49) Alberto
Mancini (Arg); 12 (1) Mats Wilander (Swe); 13 (34) Jay
Berger (US); 14 (12) Yannick Noah (Fra); 15 (15) Aaron
Krickstein (US); 16 (7) Jimmy Connors (US); 17 (54)
Martin Jaite (Arg); 18 (14) Andrei Chesnokov (USSR); 19
(26) Amos Mansdorf (Isr); 20 (73) Uwe Steeb (FRG).

Figures in brackets are positions on Jan 1 1989

WOMEN'S RANKINGS

(after US Open, Sep 1989)

1 (1) Steffi Graf (FRG); 2 (2) Martina Navratilova (US); 3
(4) Gabriela Sabatini (Arg); 4 (18) Arantxa Sanchez-
Vicario (Spa); 5 (3) Chris Evert (US); 6 (9) Zina Garrison
(US); 7 (6) Manuela Maleeva (Bul); 8 (8) Helena Sukova
(Cze); 9 (5) Pam Shriver (US); 10 (86) Monica Seles
(Yug); 11 (45) Jana Novotna (Cze); 12 (40) Conchita
Martinez (Spa); 13 (15) Mary Joe Fernandez (US);14 (7)
Natalia Zvereva (USSR); 15 (29) Hana Mandlikova (Aus);
16 (11) Katerina Maleeva (Bul); 17 (42) Caterina Lindqvist
(Swe); 18 (19) Helen Kelesi (Can); 19 (62) Belinda
Cordwell (NZ); 20 (23) Raffaella Reggi (Ita).

Figures in brackets are positions on Nov 21 1988

She bustled this way and that, as if mounted
on castors and hurtling across a highly
polished floor."
*Rex Bellamy, The Times, on Arantxa Sanchez-
Vicario*

"I am very joyed. I am very exciting. I don't
have words to talk in."
*Arantxa Sanchez-Vicario, after winning the
French Open*

"I don't get many trophies. You get a cheque
and, if you're lucky, flowers. The cheques
pay the bills, the flowers wither away, and
all you've got left is memories."
Martina Navratilova

"Last year she was unbelievable. But I
believe she can be better still. She's
probably the best I've seen."
Chris Evert on losing to Graf at Wimbledon

"She is such a great player. I have wonderful
memories of watching her win Wimbledon
on the TV when I was a little girl. She has
meant so much to tennis. But I couldn't
take a chance."
Steffi Graf after beating Evert

"I know how to beat her. I just wasn't able to
do it."
Navratilova on Graf after the US Open

"I don't just think the no. 100 man in the
world would beat Steffi Graf; the no. 5000
would thrash her."   *Stefan Edberg*

"This is it. There are no more maybes, no
more depending upons, no more
probables."
Chris Evert, announcing her retirement

"Aw, I hope she gets pregnant and has little
Chrissies. I hope she gets stretchmarks
like the rest of us."
Evert fan at the US Open

"If you were looking for the future of
women's tennis you might have dallied a
while at the Grandstand Court on
Saturday to see a sturdy 13-year-old
named Jennifer Capriati demolish the top
seed in the 18-and-under draw, 6-1 6-1,
in 49 minutes. There's something eerily
familiar about Capriati. Maybe it's the
two-fisted backhand, or the demure little
grunt of the serve. Maybe it's the ponytail
or the South Florida address. Maybe it's
the fact that her first teacher was dad
Jimmy Evert, and her manager is son
John Evert and she looks a little like
daughter Jeannie Evert. Maybe it's that
she's got the instincts of an assassin."
*Tony Kornheiser, Washington Post, at the US
Open*

DAVIS CUP
World Group
Round One, *Feb 3-5*
France beat Isreal 4-1
Austria beat Australia 5-0
West Germany beat Indonesia 5-0
Czchoslovakia beat USSR 4-1
Yugoslavia beat Denmark 4-1
United States beat Paraguay 5-0
Spain beat Mexico 3-2
Sweden beat Italy 4-1
Quarter-finals
West Germany beat Czechoslovakia 3-2
Sweden beat Austria 3-2
United States beat France 3-0
Yugoslavia beat Spain 4-1
Semi-finals
West Germany beat United States 3-2
Sweden beat Yugoslavia 4-1
Final (Dec 15-17 1989)

BRITAIN IN THE DAVIS CUP
European Zone
Finland 1 Britain 4
Helsinki, May 5-7
(GB players first)

Jeremy Bates beat Ollie Rahnasto 6-1 6-2 7-5; Chris Bailey lost to Veli Paloheimo 1-6 2-6 6-4 6-7; Bates and Andrew Castle beat Paloheimo & Rahnasto 6-4 7-6 7-5; Bailey beat Rahnasto 6-4 7-6 7-5; Bates beat Paloheimo 6-2 7-5

World Group Qualifier
Britain 2 Argentina 3
Eastbourne, Jul 21-23
(GB players first)

Jeremy Bates beat Martin Jaite 6-2 6-7 6-3 1-6 7-5; Chris Bailey lost to Alberto Mancini 5-7 7-6 6-7 7-5 4-6; Andrew Castle & Nick Brown lost to Javier Frana & Gustavo Luza 6-7 4-6 3-6; Bailey lost to Jaite 6-7 3-6 5-7; Bates beat Mancini 5-0 (ret'd)

WIGHTMAN CUP
United States 7 Britain 0
Williamsburg, Virginia, Sep 14-16
(US names first)

Lori McNeil beat Jo Durie 7-5 6-1; Jennifer Capriati beat Clare Wood 6-0 6-0; Mary Jo Fernandez beat Sara Gomer 6-1 6-2; McNeil beat Gomer 6-4 6-2; Fernandez beat Durie 6-1 7-5; Fernandez and Betsy Nagelsen beat Gomer and Wood 6-2 7-6; McNeil and Patty Fendick beat Durie and Anne Hobbs 6-3 6-3

CHAMPIONS

THE ALL-ENGLAND CHAMPIONSHIPS, WIMBLEDON
Men's Singles
(Until 1922 defending champions played only one challenge match against the winners of the open competition)

1877	Spencer Gore (GB) beat W C Marshall (GB) 6-1 6-2 6-4
1878	Frank Hadow (GB) beat Spencer Gore (GB) 7-5 6-1 9-7
1879	Rev John Hartley (GB) beat St L Goold (GB) 6-2 6-4 6-2
1880	Rev John Hartley (GB) beat Herbert Lawford (GB) 6-3 6-2 2-6 6-3
1881	William Renshaw (GB) beat Rev John Hartley (GB) 6-0 6-1 6-1
1882	William Renshaw (GB) beat Ernest Renshaw (GB) 6-1 2-6 4-6 6-2 6-2
1883	William Renshaw (GB) beat Ernest Renshaw (GB) 2-6 6-3 6-3 4-6 6-3
1884	William Renshaw (GB) Herbert Lawford (GB) 6-0 6-4 9-7
1885	William Renshaw (GB) beat Herbert Lawford (GB) 7-5 6-2 4-6 7-5
1886	William Renshaw (GB) beat Herbert Lawford (GB) 6-0 5-7 6-3 6-4
1887	Herbert Lawford (GB) beat Ernest Renshaw (GB) 1-6 6-3 3-6 6-4 6-4
1888	Ernest Renshaw (GB) beat Herbert Lawford (GB) 6-3 7-5 6-0
1889	William Renshaw (GB) beat Ernest Renshaw (GB) 6-4 6-1 3-6 6-0
1890	Willoughby Hamilton (GB) beat William Renshaw (GB) 6-8 2-6 3-6 6-1 6-1
1891	Wilfred Baddeley (GB) beat Joshua Pim (GB) 6-4 1-6 7-5 6-0
1892	Wilfred Baddeley (GB) beat Joshua Pim (GB) 4-6 6-3 6-3 6-2
1893	Joshua Pim (GB) beat Wilfred Baddeley (GB) 3-6 6-1 6-3 6-2
1894	Joshua Pim (GB) beat Wilfred Baddeley (GB) 10-8 6-2 8-6
1895	Wilfred Baddeley (GB) beat W V Eaves (GB) 4-6 2-6 8-6 6-2 6-3
1896	Harold Mahoney (GB) beat Wilfred Baddeley (GB) 6-2 6-8 5-7 8-6 6-3
1897	Reginald Doherty (GB) beat Harold Mahoney (GB) 6-4 6-4 6-3
1898	Reginald Doherty (GB) beat Lawrence Doherty (GB) 6-3 6-3 2-6 7-5 6-1
1899	Reginald Doherty (GB) beat Arthur Gore (GB) 1-6 4-6 6-2 6-3 6-3
1900	Reginald Doherty (GB) beat Sidney Smith (GB) 6-8 6-3 6-1 6-2
1901	Arthur Gore (GB) beat Reginald Doherty (GB) 4-6 7-5 6-4 6-4
1902	Lawrence Doherty (GB) beat Arthur Gore (GB) 6-4 6-3 3-6 6-0
1903	Lawrence Doherty (GB) beat Frank Riseley (GB) 7-5 6-3 6-0
1904	Lawrence Doherty (GB) beat Frank Riseley (GB) 6-1 7-5 8-6
1905	Lawrence Doherty (GB) beat Norman Brookes (Aus) 8-6 6-2 6-4
1906	Lawrence Doherty (GB) beat Frank Riseley (GB) 6-4 6-2 6-3
1907	Norman Brookes (Aus) beat Arthur Gore (GB) 6-4 6-2 6-2
1908	Arthur Gore (GB) beat H Roper Barrett (GB) 6-3 6-2 4-6 3-6 6-4
1909	Arthur Gore (GB) beat Josiah Ritchie (GB) 6-8 1-6 6-2 6-2 6-2
1910	Tony Wilding (NZ) beat Arthur Gore (GB) 6-4 7-5 4-6 6-2
1911	Tony Wilding (NZ) beat H Roper Barrett (GB) 6-4 4-6 2-6 6-2 retired
1912	Tony Wilding (NZ) beat Arthur Gore (GB) 6-4 6-4 4-6 6-4
1913	Tony Wilding (NZ) beat M McLoughlin (US) 8-6 6-3 10-8
1914	Norman Brookes (Aus) beat Tony Wilding (NZ) 6-4 6-4 7-5
1919	Gerald Patterson (Aus) beat Norman Brookes (Aus) 6-3 7-5 6-2
1920	Bill Tilden (US) beat Gerald Patterson (Aus) 2-6 6-3 6-2 6-4

1921	Bill Tilden (US) beat Brian Norton (SA) 4-6 2-6 6-1 6-0 7-5
1922	Gerald Patterson (Aus) beat Randolph Lycett (GB) 6-3 6-4 6-2
1923	William Johnston (US) beat Frank Hunter (US) 6-0 6-3 6-1
1924	Jean Borotra (Fra) beat René Lacoste (Fra) 6-1 3-6 6-1 3-6 6-4
1925	René Lacoste (Fra) beat Jean Borotra (Fra) 6-3 6-3 4-6 8-6
1926	Jean Borotra (Fra) beat Howard Kinsey (US) 8-6 6-1 6-3
1927	Henri Cochet (Fra) beat Jean Borotra (Fra) 4-6 4-6 6-3 6-4 7-5
1928	René Lacoste (Fra) beat Henri Cochet (Fra) 6-1 4-6 6-4 6-2
1929	Henri Cochet (Fra) beat Jean Borotra (Fra) 6-4 6-3 6-4
1930	Bill Tilden (US) beat William Allison (US) 6-3 9-7 6-4
1931	Sidney Wood (US) beat Frank Shields (US) w.o.
1932	Ellsworth Vines (US) beat Bunny Austin (GB) 6-4 6-2 6-0
1933	Jack Crawford (Aus) beat Ellsworth Vines (US) 4-6 11-9 6-2 2-6 6-4
1934	Fred Perry (GB) beat Jack Crawford (Aus) 6-3 6-0 7-5
1935	Fred Perry (GB) beat Gottfried von Cramm (Ger) 6-2 6-4 6-4
1936	Fred Perry (GB) beat Gottfried von Cramm (Ger) 6-1 6-1 6-0
1937	Donald Budge (US) beat Gottfried von Cramm (Ger) 6-3 6-4 6-2
1938	Donald Budge (US) beat Bunny Austin (GB) 6-1 6-0 6-3
1939	Bobby Riggs (US) beat Ellwood Cooke (US) 2-6 8-6 3-6 6-3 6-2
1946	Yvon Petra (Fra) beat Geoffrey Brown (Aus) 6-2 6-4 7-9 5-7 6-4
1947	Jack Kramer (US) beat Tom Brown (US) 6-1 6-3 6-2
1948	Bob Falkenburg (US) beat John Bromwich (Aus) 7-5 0-6 6-2 3-6 7-5
1949	Ted Schroeder (US) beat Jaroslav Drobny (Cze) 3-6 6-0 6-3 4-6 6-4
1950	Budge Patty (US) beat Frank Sedgman (Aus) 6-1 8-10 6-2 6-3
1951	Dick Savitt (US) beat Ken McGregor (Aus) 6-4 6-4 6-4
1952	Frank Sedgman (Aus) beat Jaroslav Drobny (Egy) 4-6 6-2 6-3 6-2
1953	Vic Seixas (US) beat Kurt Nielson (Den) 9-7 6-3 6-4
1954	Jaroslav Drobny (Egy) beat Ken Rosewall (Aus) 13-11 4-6 6-2 9-7
1955	Tony Trabert (US) beat Kurt Nielsen (Den) 6-3 7-5 6-1
1956	Lew Hoad (Aus) beat Ken Rosewall (Aus) 6-2 4-6 7-5 6-4
1957	Lew Hoad (Aus) beat Ashley Cooper (Aus) 6-2 6-1 6-2
1958	Ashley Cooper (Aus) beat Neale Fraser (Aus) 3-6 6-3 6-4 13-11
1959	Alex Olmedo (US) beat Rod Laver (Aus) 6-4 6-3 6-4
1960	Neale Fraser (Aus) beat Rod Laver (Aus) 6-4 3-6 9-7 7-5
1961	Rod Laver (Aus) beat Chuck McKinley (US) 6-3 6-1 6-4
1962	Rod Laver (Aus) beat Marty Mulligan (Aus) 6-2 6-2 6-1
1963	Chuck McKinley (US) beat Fred Stolle (Aus) 9-7 6-1 6-4
1964	Roy Emerson (Aus) beat Fred Stolle (Aus) 6-4 12-10 4-6 6-3
1965	Roy Emerson (Aus) beat Fred Stolle (Aus) 6-2 6-4 6-4
1966	Manuel Santana (Spa) beat Dennis Ralston (US) 6-4 11-9 6-4
1967	John Newcombe (Aus) beat Wilhelm Bungert (FRG) 6-3 6-1 6-1
1968	Rod Laver (Aus) beat Tony Roche (Aus) 6-3 6-4 6-2
1969	Rod Laver (Aus) beat John Newcombe (Aus) 6-4 5-7 6-4 6-4
1970	John Newcombe (Aus) beat Ken Rosewall (Aus) 5-7 6-3 6-2 3-6 6-1
1971	John Newcombe (Aus) beat Stan Smith (US) 6-3 5-7 2-6 6-4 6-4
1972	Stan Smith (US) beat Ilie Nastase (Rom) 4-6 6-3 6-3 4-6 7-5
1973	Jan Kodes (Cze) beat Alex Metreveli (USSR) 6-1 9-8 6-3
1974	Jimmy Connors (US) beat Ken Rosewall (Aus) 6-1 6-1 6-4
1975	Arthur Ashe (US) beat Jimmy Connors (US) 6-1 6-1 5-7 6-4
1976	Bjorn Borg (Swe) beat Ilie Nastase (Rom) 6-4 6-2 9-7
1977	Bjorn Borg (Swe) beat Jimmy Connors (US) 3-6 6-2 6-1 5-7 6-4
1978	Bjorn Borg (Swe) beat Jimmy Connors (US) 6-2 6-2 6-3
1979	Bjorn Borg (Swe) beat Roscoe Tanner (US) 6-7 6-1 3-6 6-3 6-4
1980	Bjorn Borg (Swe) beat John McEnroe (US) 1-6 7-5 6-3 6-7 8-6
1981	John McEnroe (US) beat Bjorn Borg (Swe) 4-6 7-6 7-6 6-4
1982	Jimmy Connors (US) beat John McEnroe (US) 3-6 6-3 6-7 7-6 6-4
1983	John McEnroe (US) beat Chris Lewis (NZ) 6-2 6-2 6-2
1984	John McEnroe (US) beat Jimmy Connors (US) 6-1 6-1 6-2
1985	Boris Becker (FRG) beat Kevin Curren (US) 6-3 6-7 7-6 6-4
1986	Boris Becker (FRG) beat Ivan Lendl (Cze) 6-4 6-3 7-5
1987	Pat Cash (Aus) beat Ivan Lendl (Cze) 7-6 6-2 7-5
1988	Stefan Edberg (Swe) beat Boris Becker (FRG) 4-6 7-6 6-4 6-2
1989	Boris Becker (FRG) beat Stefan Edberg (Swe) 6-0 7-6 6-4

Women's Singles

1884	Maud Watson (GB) beat L Watson (GB) 6-8 6-3 6-3
1885	Maud Watson (GB) beat Blanche Bingley (GB) 6-1 7-5
1886	Blanche Bingley (GB) beat Maud Watson (GB) 6-3 6-3
1887	Lottie Dod (GB) beat Blanche Bingley (GB) 6-2 6-0
1888	Lottie Dod (GB) beat Blanche Hillyard (née Bingley) (GB) 6-3 6-3
1889	Blanche Hillyard (GB) beat Helen Rice (GB) 4-6 8-6 6-4
1890	Helen Rice (GB) beat M Jacks (GB) 6-4 6-1
1891	Lottie Dod (GB) beat Blanche Hillyard (GB) 6-2 6-1
1892	Lottie Dod (GB) beat Blanche Hillyard (GB) 6-1 6-1
1893	Lottie Dod (GB) beat Blanche Hillyard (GB) 6-8 6-1 6-4

1894	Blanche Hillyard (GB) beat L Austin (GB) 6-1 6-1
1895	Charlotte Cooper (GB) beat H Jackson (GB) 7-5 8-6
1896	Charlotte Cooper (GB) beat W H Pickering (GB) 6-2 6-3
1897	Blanche Hillyard (GB) beat Charlotte Cooper (GB) 5-7 7-5 6-2
1898	Charlotte Cooper (GB) beat L Martin (GB) 6-4 6-4
1899	Blanche Hillyard (GB) beat Charlotte Cooper (GB) 6-2 6-3
1900	Blanche Hillyard (GB) beat Charlotte Cooper (GB) 4-6 6-4 6-4
1901	Charlotte Sterry (GB) beat Blanche Hillyard (GB) 6-2 6-2
1902	Muriel Robb (GB) beat Charlotte Sterry (GB) 7-5 6-1
1903	Dorothea Douglass (GB) beat E W Thompson (GB) 4-6 6-4 6-2
1904	Dorothea Douglass (GB) beat Charlotte Sterry (GB) 6-0 6-3
1905	May Sutton (US) beat Dorothea Douglass (GB) 6-3 6-4
1906	Dorothea Douglass (GB) beat May Sutton (US) 6-3 9-7
1907	May Sutton (US) beat Dorothea Lambert Chambers (GB) 6-1 6-4
1908	Charlotte Sterry (GB) beat A M Morton (GB) 6-4 6-4
1909	Dora Boothby (GB) beat A M Morton (GB) 6-4 4-6 8-6
1910	Dorothea Lambert Chambers (GB) beat Dora Boothby (GB) 6-2 6-2
1911	Dorothea Lambert Chambers (GB) beat Dora Boothby (GB) 6-0 6-0
1912	Ethel Larcombe (GB) beat Charlotte Sterry (GB) 6-3 6-1
1913	Dorothea Lambert Chambers (GB) beat R J McNair (GB) 6-0 6-4
1914	Dorothea Lambert Chambers (GB) beat Ethel Larcombe (GB) 7-5 6-4
1919	Suzanne Lenglen (Fra) beat Dorothea Lambert Chambers (GB) 10-8 4-6 9-7
1920	Suzanne Lenglen (Fra) beat Dorothea Lambert Chambers (GB) 6-3 6-0
1921	Suzanne Lenglen (Fra) beat Elizabeth Ryan (US) 6-2 6-0
1922	Suzanne Lenglen (Fra) beat Molla Mallory (US) 6-2 6-0
1923	Suzanne Lenglen (Fra) beat Kathleen McKane (GB) 6-2 6-2
1924	Kathleen McKane (GB) beat Helen Wills (US) 4-6 6-4 6-4
1925	Suzanne Lenglen (Fra) beat Joan Fry (GB) 6-2 6-0
1926	Kathleen Godfree (GB) beat Lili d'Alvarez (Spa) 6-2 4-6 6-3
1927	Helen Wills (US) beat Lili d'Alvarez (Spa) 6-2 6-4
1928	Helen Wills (US) beat Lili d'Alvarez (Spa) 6-2 6-3
1929	Helen Wills (US) beat Helen Jacobs (US) 6-1 6-2
1930	Helen Moody (née Wills) (US) beat Elizabeth Ryan (US) 6-2 6-2
1931	Cilly Aussem (Ger) beat Hilda Krahwinkel (Ger) 7-2 7-5
1932	Helen Moody (US) beat Helen Jacobs (US) 6-3 6-1
1933	Helen Moody (US) beat Dorothy Round (GB) 6-4 6-8 6-3
1934	Dorothy Round (GB) beat Helen Jacobs (US) 6-2 5-7 6-3
1935	Helen Moody (US) beat Helen Jacobs (US) 6-3 3-6 7-5
1936	Helen Jacobs (US) beat Hilde Sperling (Ger) 6-2 4-6 7-5
1937	Dorothy Round (GB) beat Jadwiga Jedrzejowska (Pol) 6-2 2-6 7-5
1938	Helen Moody (US) beat Helen Jacobs (US) 6-4 6-0
1939	Alice Marble (US) beat Kay Stammers (GB) 6-2 6-0
1946	Pauline Betz (US) beat Louise Brough (US) 6-2 6-4
1947	Margaret Osborne (US) beat Doris Hart (US) 6-2 6-4
1948	Louise Brough (US) beat Doris Hart (US) 6-3 8-6
1949	Louise Brough (US) beat Margaret du Pont (US) 10-8 1-6 10-8
1950	Louise Brough (US) beat Margaret du Pont (US) 6-1 3-6 6-1
1951	Doris Hart (US) beat Shirley Fry (US) 6-1 6-0
1952	Maureen Connolly (US) beat Louise Brough (US) 7-5 6-3
1953	Maureen Connolly (US) beat Doris Hart (US) 8-6 7-5
1954	Maureen Connolly (US) beat Louise Brough (US) 6-2 7-5
1955	Louise Brough (US) beat Beverley Fleitz (US) 7-5 8-6
1956	Shirley Fry (US) beat Angela Buxton (GB) 6-3 6-1
1957	Althea Gibson (US) beat Darlene Hard (US) 6-3 6-2
1958	Althea Gibson (US) beat Angela Mortimer (GB) 8-6 6-2
1959	Maria Bueno (Bra) beat Darlene Hard (US) 6-2 6-3
1960	Maria Bueno (Bra) beat Sandra Reynolds (SA) 8-6 6-0
1961	Angela Mortimer (GB) beat Christine Truman (GB) 4-6 6-4 7-5
1962	Karen Susman (US) beat Vera Sukova (Cze) 6-4 6-4
1963	Margaret Smith (Aus) beat Billie Jean Moffitt (US) 6-3 6-4
1964	Maria Bueno (Bra) beat Margaret Smith (Aus) 6-4 7-9 6-3
1965	Margaret Smith (Aus) beat Maria Bueno (Bra) 6-4 7-5
1966	Billie Jean King (née Moffitt) (US) beat Maria Bueno (Bra) 6-3 3-6 6-1
1967	Billie Jean King (US) beat Ann Jones (GB) 6-3 6-4
1968	Billie Jean King (US) beat Judy Tegart (Aus) 9-7 7-5
1969	Ann Jones (GB) beat Billie Jean King (US) 3-6 6-3 6-2
1970	Margaret Court (née Smith) (Aus) beat Billie Jean King (US) 14-12 11-9
1971	Evonne Goolagong (Aus) beat Margaret Court (Aus) 6-4 6-1
1972	Billie Jean King (US) beat Evonne Goolagong (Aus) 6-3 6-3
1973	Billie Jean King (US) beat Chris Evert (US) 6-0 7-5
1974	Chris Evert (US) beat Olga Morozova (USSR) 6-0 6-4
1975	Billie Jean King (US) beat Evonne Cawley (née Goolagong) (Aus) 6-0 6-1
1976	Chris Evert (US) beat Evonne Cawley (Aus) 6-3 4-6 8-6
1977	Virginia Wade (GB) beat Betty Stove (Hol) 4-6 6-3 6-1
1978	Martina Navratilova (Cze) beat Chris Evert (US) 2-6 6-4 7-5

1979	Martina Navratilova (Cze) beat Chris Evert-Lloyd (US) 6-4 6-4
1980	Evonne Cawley (Aus) beat Chris Evert-Lloyd (US) 6-1 7-6
1981	Chris Evert-Lloyd (US) beat Hana Mandlikova (Cze) 6-2 6-2
1982	Martina Navratilova (US) beat Chris Evert-Lloyd (US) 6-1 3-6 6-2
1983	Martina Navratilova (US) beat Andrea Jaeger (US) 6-0 6-3
1984	Martina Navratilova (US) beat Chris Evert-Lloyd (US) 7-6 6-2
1985	Martina Navratilova (US) beat Chris Evert-Lloyd (US) 4-6 6-3 6-2
1986	Martina Navratilova (US) beat Hana Mandlikova (Cze) 7-6 6-3
1987	Martina Navratilova (US) beat Steffi Graf (FRG) 7-5 6-3
1988	Steffi Graf (FRG) beat Martina Navratilova (US) 5-7 6-2 6-1
1989	Steffi Graf (FRG) beat Martina Navratilova (US) 6-2 6-7 6-1

DOUBLES WINNERS OF THE 1980s
Men's Doubles

1980	Peter McNamara & Paul McNamee (Aus)
1981	Peter Fleming & John McEnroe (US)
1982	Peter McNamara & Paul McNamee (Aus)
1983	Peter Fleming & John McEnroe (US)
1984	Peter Fleming & John McEnroe (US))
1985	Heinz Gunthardt (Swi) & Balazs Taroczy (Hun)
1986	Joakim Nystrom & Mats Wilander (Swe)
1987	Ken Flach & Robert Seguso (US)
1988	Ken Flach & Robert Seguso (US)
1989	John Fitzgerald (Aus) & Anders Jarryd (Swe)

Women'sDoubles

1980	Kathy Jordan & Anne Smith (US)
1981	Martina Navratilova (Cze) & Pam Shriver (US)
1982	Martina Navratilova & Pam Shriver (US)
1983	Martina Navratilova & Pam Shriver (US)
1984	Martina Navratilova & Pam Shriver (US)
1985	Kathy Jordan (US) & Elizabeth Smylie (Aus)
1986	Martina Navratilova & Pam Shriver (US)
1987	Claudia Kohde-Kilsch (FRG) & Helena Sukova (Cze)
1988	Steffi Graf (FRG) & Gabriela Sabatini (Arg)
1989	Jana Novotna and Helena Sukova (Cze)

Mixed Doubles

1980	John Austin & Tracy Austin (US)
1981	Frew McMillan (SA) & Betty Stove (Hol)
1982	Kevin Curren (SA) & Anne Smith (US)
1983	John Lloyd (GB) & Wendy Turnbull (Aus)
1984	John Lloyd (GB) & Wendy Turnbull (Aus)

1985	Paul McNamee (Aus) & Martina Navratilova (US)
1986	Ken Flach & Kathy Jordan (US)
1987	Jeremy Bates & Jo Durie (GB)
1988	Sherwood Stewart & Zina Garrison (US)
1989	Jim Pugh (US) & Jana Novotna (Cze)

YOUNGEST WINNERS OF GRAND SLAM TITLES

Men

y	m			
17	3	Michael Chang	French Open	1989
17	7	Boris Becker	Wimbledon	1985
17	9	Mats Wilander	French Open	1982
17	*	Rodney Heath	Australian	1905
18		Bjorn Borg	French Open	1974

* exact birthdate unknown

Women

15	10	Lottie Dod	Wimbledon	1887
16	9	Tracy Austin	US Open	1979
16	11	Maureen Connolly	US Open	1951
17	6	Arantxa Sanchez	French Open	1989
17	10	May Sutton	Wimbledon	1905

Source: New York Times

THE OTHER GRAND SLAM SINGLES CHAMPIONS
Post-war winners
Men's Singles

	US Champs	French Champs	Australian Champs
1946	Jack Kramer (US)	Marcel Bernard (Fra)	John Bromwich (Aus)
1947	Jack Kramer (US)	Jozsef Asboth (Hun)	Dinny Pails (Aus)
1948	Ricardo Gonzales (US)	Frank Parker (US)	Adrian Quist (Aus)
1949	Ricardo Gonzales (US)	Frank Parker (US)	Frank Sedgman (Aus)
1950	Arthur Larsen (US)	Budge Patty (US)	Frank Sedgman (Aus)
1951	Frank Sedgman (US)	Jaroslav Drobny (Egy)	Dick Savitt (US)
1952	Frank Sedgman (US)	Jaroslav Drobny (Egy)	Ken McGregor (Aus)
1953	Tony Trabert (US)	Ken Rosewall (Aus)	Ken Rosewall (Aus)
1954	Vic Seixas (US)	Tony Trabert (US)	Mervyn Rose (Aus)
1955	Tony Trabert (US)	Tony Trabert (US)	Ken Rosewall (Aus)
1956	Ken Rosewall (Aus)	Lew Hoad (Aus)	Lew Hoad (Aus)
1957	Malcolm Anderson (Aus)	Sven Davidson (Swe)	Ashley Cooper (Aus)
1958	Ashley Cooper (Aus)	Mervyn Rose (Aus)	Ashley Cooper (Aus)
1959	Neale Fraser (Aus)	Nicola Pietrangeli (Ita)	Alex Olmedo (US)
1960	Neale Fraser (Aus)	Nicola Pietrangeli (Ita)	Rod Laver (Aus)
1961	Roy Emerson (Aus)	Manuel Santana (Spa)	Roy Emerson (Aus)
1962	Rod Laver (Aus)	Rod Laver (Aus)	Rod Laver (Aus)
1963	Raphael Osuna (Mex)	Roy Emerson (Aus)	Roy Emerson (Aus)
1964	Roy Emerson (Aus)	Manuel Santana (Spa)	Roy Emerson (Aus)
1965	Manuel Santana (Spa)	Fred Stolle (Aus)	Roy Emerson (Aus)
1966	Fred Stolle (Aus)	Tony Roche (Aus)	Roy Emerson (Aus)
1967	John Newcombe (Aus)	Roy Emerson (Aus)	Roy Emerson (Aus)
1968	Arthur Ashe (US)	Ken Rosewall (Aus)	Bill Bowrey (Aus)
Open*	Arthur Ashe (US)	-	-
1969	Stan Smith (US)	Rod Laver (Aus)	Rod Laver (Aus)

* Two championships held, one for amateurs only

US Champs	French Champs	Australian Champs
*Open** Rod Laver (Aus)		
1970 Ken Rosewall (Aus)	Jan Kodes (Cze)	Arthur Ashe (US)
1971 Stan Smith (US)	Jan Kodes (Cze)	Ken Rosewall (Aus)
1972 Ilie Nastase (Rom)	Andres Gimeno (Spa)	Ken Rosewall (Aus)
1973 John Newcombe (Aus)	Ilie Nastase (Rom)	John Newcombe (Aus)
1974 Jimmy Connors (US)	Bjorn Borg (Swe)	Jimmy Connors (US)
1975 Manuel Orantes (Spa)	Bjorn Borg (Swe)	John Newcombe (Aus)
1976 Jimmy Connors (US)	Adriano Panatta (Ita)	Mark Edmondson (Aus)
1977 Guillermo Vilas (Arg)	Guillermo Vilas (Arg)	Roscoe Tanner (US) (Jan)
		Vitas Gerulaitas (US) (Dec)
1978 Jimmy Connors (US)	Bjorn Borg (Swe)	Guillermo Vilas (Arg)
1979 John McEnroe (US)	Bjorn Borg (Swe)	Guillermo Vilas (Arg)
1980 John McEnroe (US)	Bjorn Borg (Swe)	Brian Teacher (US)
1981 John McEnroe (US)	Bjorn Borg (Swe)	Johan Kriek (SA)
1982 Jimmy Connors (US)	Mats Wilander (Swe)	Johan Kriek (SA)
1983 Jimmy Connors (US)	Yannick Noah (Fra)	Mats Wilander (Swe)
1984 John McEnroe (US)	Ivan Lendl (Cze)	Mats Wilander (Swe)
1985 Ivan Lendl (Cze)	Mats Wilander (Swe)	Stefan Edberg (Swe)
1986 Ivan Lendl (Cze)	Ivan Lendl (Cze)	
1987 Ivan Lendl (Cze)	Ivan Lendl (Cze)	Stefan Edberg (Swe)
1988 Mats Wilander (Swe)	Mats Wilander (Swe)	Mats Wilander (Swe)
1989 Boris Becker (FRG)	Michael Chang (US)	Ivan Lendl (Cze)

Women's Singles

US Champs	French Champs	Australian Champs
1946 Pauline Betz (US)	Margaret Osborne (US)	Nancye Bolton (Aus)
1947 Louise Brough (US)	Pat Todd (US)	Nancye Bolton (Aus)
1948 Margaret Du Pont (US)	Nelly Landry (Fra)	Nancye Bolton (Aus)
1949 Margaret Du Pont (US)	Margaret Du Pont (US)	Doris Hart (US)
1950 Margaret Du Pont (US)	Doris Hart (US)	Louise Brough (US)
1951 Maureen Connolly (US)	Shirley Fry (US)	Nancye Bolton (Aus)
1952 Maureen Connolly (US)	Doris Hart (US)	Thelma Long (Aus)
1953 Maureen Connolly (US)	Maureen Connolly (US)	Maureen Connolly (US)
1954 Doris Hart (US)	Maureen Connolly (US)	Thelma Long (Aus)
1955 Doris Hart (US)	Angela Mortimer (GB)	Beryl Penrose (Aus)
1956 Shirley Fry (US)	Althea Gibson (US)	Mary Carter (Aus)
1957 Althea Gibson (US)	Shirley Bloomer (GB)	Shirley Fry (US)
1958 Althea Gibson (US)	Zsuzsi Kormoczy (Hun)	Angela Mortimer (GB)
1959 Maria Bueno (Bra)	Christine Truman (GB)	Mary Reitano (Aus)
1960 Darlene Hard (US)	Darlene Hard (US)	Margaret Smith (Aus)
1961 Darlene Hard (US)	Ann Haydon (GB)	Margaret Smith (Aus)
1962 Margaret Smith (Aus)	Margaret Smith (Aus)	Margaret Smith (Aus)
1963 Maria Bueno (Bra)	Lesley Turner (Aus)	Margaret Smith (Aus)
1964 Maria Bueno (Bra)	Margaret Smith (Aus)	Margaret Smith (Aus)
1965 Margaret Smith (Aus)	Lesley Turner (Aus)	Margaret Smith (Aus)
1966 Maria Bueno (Bra)	Ann Jones (GB)	Margaret Smith (Aus)
1967 Billie Jean King (US)	Françoise Durr (Fra)	Nancy Richey (US)
1968 Margaret Court (Aus)	Nancy Richey (US)	Billie Jean King (US)
*Open** Virginia Wade (GB)		
1969 Margaret Court (Aus)	Margaret Court (Aus)	Margaret Court (Aus)
*Open** Margaret Court (Aus)		
1970 Margaret Court (Aus)	Margaret Court (Aus)	Margaret Court (Aus)
1971 Billie Jean King (US)	Evonne Goolagong (Aus)	Margaret Court (Aus)
1972 Billie Jean King (US)	Billie Jean King (US)	Virginia Wade (GB)
1973 Margaret Court (Aus)	Margaret Court (Aus)	Margaret Court (Aus)
1974 Billie Jean King (US)	Chris Evert (US)	Evonne Goolagong (Aus)
1975 Chris Evert (US)	Chris Evert (US)	Evonne Goolagong (Aus)
1976 Chris Evert (US)	Sue Barker (GB)	Evonne Cawley (Aus)
1977 Chris Evert (US)	Mimi Jauseovec (Yug)	Kerry Reid (Aus) (Jan)
		Evonne Cawley(Aus) (Dec)
1978 Chris Evert (US)	Virginia Ruzici (Rom)	Christine O'Neill (Aus)
1979 Tracy Austin (US)	Chris Evert-Lloyd (US)	Barbara Jordan (US)
1980 Chris Evert-Lloyd (US)	Chris Evert-Lloyd (US)	Hana Mandlikova (Cze)
1981 Tracy Austin (US)	Hana Mandlikova (Cze)	Martina Navratilova (US)
1982 Chris Evert-Lloyd (US)	Martina Navratilova (US)	Chris Evert-Lloyd (US)
1983 Martina Navratilova (US)	Chris Evert-Lloyd (US)	Martina Navratilova (US)
1984 Martina Navratilova (US)	Martina Navratilova (US)	Chris Evert-Lloyd (US)
1985 Hana Mandlikova (Cze)	Chris Evert-Lloyd (US)	Martina Navratilova (US)
1986 Martina Navratilova (US)	Chris Evert-Lloyd (US)	
1987 Martina Navratilova (US)	Steffi Graf (FRG)	Hana Mandlikova (Cze)
1988 Steffi Graf (FRG)	Steffi Graf (FRG)	Steffi Graf (FRG)
1989 Steffi Graf (FRG)	Arantxa Sanchez-Vicario (Spa)	Steffi Graf (FRG)

* Two championships held, one for amateurs only

WINNERS OF MOST GRAND SLAM SINGLES TITLES

Wimbledon
Men: 7 William Renshaw
Women: 8 Helen Wills-Moody; Martina Navratilova

US Championships
Men: 7 Bill Tilden; Dick Sears; Bill Larned
Women: 7 Molla Mallory; Helen Wills-Moody

French Open
Men: 6 Bjorn Borg
Women: 7 Chris Evert-Lloyd

Australian Open
Men: 6 Roy Emerson
Women: 11 Margaret Court (née Smith)

Overall
Men: 12 Roy Emerson
Women: 24 Margaret Court (née Smith)

GRAND SLAM WINNERS
(all four Grand Slam tournaments in one year)
Donald Budge 1938
Rod Laver 1962
Rod Laver 1969
Maureen Connolly 1953
Margaret Court 1970
Steffi Graf 1988

MOST GRAND SLAM TITLES IN THE 80s

(Singles only)

		W	US	FR	AUS
15	Martina Navratilova	6	4	2	3
9	Chris Evert-Lloyd	1	2	4	2
8	Steffi Graf	2	2	2	2
7	Ivan Lendl	-	3	3	1
7	Mats Wilander	-	1	3	3
6	John McEnroe	3	3	-	-
4	Boris Becker	3	1	-	-
4	Hana Mandlikova	-	1	1	2

MAIDEN/MARRIED NAMES OF WOMEN PLAYERS

Maiden Name	*Married Name*
Blanche Bingley	Blanche Hillyard
Evonne Goolagong	Evonne Cawley
Charlotte Cooper	Charlotte Sterry
Dorothea Douglass	Dorothea Lambert Chambers
Chris Evert	Chris Evert-Lloyd
Ann Haydon	Ann Jones
Kathleen McKane	Kathleen Godfree
Margaret Osborne	Margaret Du Pont
Margaret Smith	Margaret Court
Helen Wills	Helen Moody

DAVIS CUP

Challenge system 1900-72

1900	United States	British Isles	3-0
1901	Not held		
1902	United States	British Isles	3-2
1903	British Isles	United States	4-1
1904	British Isles	Belgium	5-0
1905	British Isles	United States	5-0
1906	British Isles	United States	5-0
1907	Australasia	British Isles	3-2
1908	Australasia	United States	3-2
1909	Australasia	United States	5-0
1910	Not held		
1911	Australasia	United States	5-0
1912	British Isles	Australasia	3-2
1913	United States	British Isles	3-2
1914	Australasia	United States	3-2
1915-18	Not held		
1919	Australasia	British Isles	4-1
1920	United States	Australasia	5-0
1921	United States	Japan	5-0
1922	United States	Australasia	4-1
1923	United States	Australasia	4-1
1924	United States	Australasia	5-0
1925	United States	France	5-0
1926	United States	France	4-1
1927	France	United States	3-2
1928	France	United States	4-1
1929	France	United States	3-2
1930	France	United States	4-1
1931	France	Britain	3-2
1932	France	United States	3-2
1933	Great Britain	France	3-2
1934	Great Britain	United States	4-1
1935	Great Britain	United States	5-0
1936	Great Britain	Australia	3-2
1937	United States	Britain	4-1
1938	United States	Australia	3-2
1939	Australia	United States	3-2
1940-45	Not held		
1946	United States	Australia	5-0
1947	United States	Australia	4-1
1948	United States	Australia	5-0
1949	United States	Australia	4-1
1950	Australia	United States	4-1
1951	Australia	United States	3-2
1952	Australia	United States	4-1
1953	Australia	United States	3-2
1954	United States	Australia	3-2
1955	Australia	United States	5-0
1956	Australia	United States	5-0
1957	Australia	United States	3-2
1958	United States	Australia	3-2
1959	Australia	United States	3-2
1960	Australia	Italy	4-1
1961	Australia	Italy	5-0
1962	Australia	Mexico	5-0
1963	United States	Australia	3-2
1964	Australia	United States	3-2
1965	Australia	Spain	4-1
1966	Australia	India	4-1
1967	Australia	Spain	4-1
1968	United States	Australia	4-1
1969	United States	Romania	5-0
1970	United States	West Germany	5-0
1971	United States	Romania	3-2
1972	United States	Romania	3-2
1973	Australia	United States	5-0
1974	South Africa	India	w.o.
1975	Sweden	Czechoslovakia	3-2
1976	Italy	Chile	4-1
1977	Australia	Italy	3-1
1978	United States	Britain	4-1
1979	United States	Italy	5-0
1980	Czechoslovakia	Italy	4-1
1981	United States	Argentina	3-1
1982	United States	France	4-1
1983	Australia	Sweden	3-2
1984	Sweden	United States	4-1
1985	Sweden	West Germany	3-2
1986	Australia	Sweden	3-2
1987	Sweden	India	5-0
1988	West Germany	Sweden	4-1

Most wins
28 United States
Since abolition of Challenge system:
5 United States; **4** Australia, Sweden

WIGHTMAN CUP
(Annual contest between ladies' teams from United States (US) and Britain (GB))

	Winners	Score		Winners	Score
1923	US	7-0	1961	US	6-1
1924	GB	6-1	1962	US	4-3
1925	GB	4-3	1963	US	6-1
1926	US	4-3	1964	US	5-2
1927	US	5-2	1965	US	5-2
1928	GB	4-3	1966	US	4-3
1929	US	4-3	1967	US	6-1
1930	GB	4-3	1968	GB	4-3
1931	US	5-2	1969	US	5-2
1932	US	4-3	1970	US	4-3
1933	US	4-3	1971	US	4-3
1934	US	5-2	1972	US	5-2
1935	US	4-3	1973	US	5-2
1936	US	4-3	1974	GB	6-1
1937	US	6-1	1975	GB	5-2
1938	US	5-2	1976	US	5-2
1939	US	5-2	1977	US	7-0
1940-45	Not held		1978	GB	4-3
1946	US	7-0	1979	US	7-0
1947	US	7-0	1980	US	5-2
1948	US	6-1	1981	US	7-0
1949	US	7-0	1982	US	6-1
1950	US	7-0	1983	US	6-1
1951	US	6-1	1984	US	5-2
1952	US	7-0	1985	US	7-0
1953	US	7-0	1986	US	7-0
1954	US	6-0*	1987	US	5-2
1955	US	6-1	1988	US	7-0
1956	US	5-2	1989	US	7-0
1957	US	6-1	**Wins**		
1958	GB	4-3	51 United States; 10 Great		
1959	US	4-3	Britain		
1960	GB	4-3	*One match not played		

GRAND PRIX MASTERS
Singles finals
1970 Stan Smith (US) beat Rod Laver (Aus)
       Round Robin series
1971 Ilie Nastase (Rom) beat Stan Smith (US)
       Round Robin series
1972 Ilie Nastase (Rom) beat Stan Smith (US)
       6-3 6-2 3-6 2-6 6-3
1973 Ilie Nastase (Rom) beat Tom Okker (Hol)
       6-3 7-5 4-6 6-3
1974 Guillermo Vilas (Arg) beat Ilie Nastase (Rom)
       7-6 6-2 3-6 3-6 6-4
1975 Ilie Nastase (Rom) beat Bjorn Borg (Swe)
       6-2 6-2 6-1
1976 Manuel Orantes (Spa) beat Wotjek Fibak (Pol)
       5-7 6-2 0-6 7-6 6-1
1977 (a)
1978 Jimmy Connors (US) beat Bjorn Borg (Swe)
       6-4 1-6 6-4
1979 John McEnroe (US) beat Arthur Ashe (US)
       6-7 6-3 7-5
1980 Bjorn Borg (Swe) beat Vitas Gerulaitis (US)
       6-2 6-2
1981 Bjorn Borg (Swe) beat Ivan Lendl (Cze)
       6-4 6-2 6-2
1982 Ivan Lendl (Cze) beat Vitas Gerulaitis (US)
       6-7 2-6 7-6 6-2 6-4
1983 Ivan Lendl (Cze) beat John McEnroe (US)
       6-4 6-4 6-2
1984 John McEnroe (US) beat Ivan Lendl (Cze)
       6-3 6-4 6-4
1985 John McEnroe (US) beat Ivan Lendl (Cze)
       7-5 6-0 6-4
1986 Ivan Lendl (Cze) beat Boris Becker (FRG)
       6-2 7-6 6-3

1987 Ivan Lendl (Cze) beat Mats Wilander (Swe)
       6-2 6-2 6-3
1988 Boris Becker (FRG) beat Ivan Lendl (Cze)
       5-7 7-6 3-6 6-2 7-6

(a) None held in 1977. Moved from late season to early season

Doubles Champions
1970 Stan Smith & Arthur Ashe (US)
1971-74 Not held
1975 Juan Gisbert & Manuel Orantes (Spa)
1976 Fred McNair & Sherwood Stewart (US)
1977 -
1978 Bob Hewitt & Frew McMillan (SA)
1979 Peter Fleming & John McEnroe (US)
1980 Peter Fleming & John McEnroe (US)
1981 Peter Fleming & John McEnroe (US)
1982 Peter Fleming & John McEnroe (US)
1983 Peter Fleming & John McEnroe (US)
1984 Peter Fleming & John McEnroe (US)
1985 Peter Fleming & John McEnroe (US)
1986 Anders Jarryd & Stefan Edberg (Swe)
1987 Miloslav Mecir & Tomas Smid (Cze)
1988 Rick Leach & Jim Pugh (US)

1990

Jan 1-7:	BP National championships (US); South Australian Men's Open championships.
Jan 8-14:	New South Wales Open
Jan 15-28:	AUSTRALIAN OPEN CHAMPIONSHIPS (Melbourne), New Zealand Open (Auckland).
Feb 2-4:	Davis Cup, World Group first round (in draw order) - West Germany v Netherlands, Argentina v Israel, New Zealand v Yugoslavia, Australia v France, Czechoslovakia v Switzerland, US v Mexico, Spain v Austria, Italy v Sweden.
Feb 12-18:	North American Indoor championships;
Feb 19-25:	US Professional Indoor championships, Stuttgart Classic (West Germany).
Feb 26-Mar 4:	Volvo Tennis/Indoor (US)
Mar 5-11:	Newsweek Champions Cup (US).
Mar 12-25:	Lipton International Players' championships (Key Biscayne, US);
Mar 30-Apr 1:	Davis Cup World Group second round;
Apr 2-8:	Orlando Classic (US).
Apr 9-15:	Japan and Asian Open (Tokyo).
Apr 22:	National TV Classic (US), Nice Open (France), China Open (Beijing).
Apr 23-29	Monte Carlo Open (Monaco).
Apr 30-May 6	BMW Open (Munich, West Germany).
May 4-6:	Davis Cup Euro/African Zone Group 1 second round, including Britain v Ireland or Romania.
May 7-13:	BMW German Open (Hamburg); US men's Clay Court championships.
May 14-20:	Italian men's Open championships (Rome); Yugoslav Open.
May 21-27:	Peugeot ATP World Team Cup (Dusseldorf, West Germany
May 28-Jun 10:	FRENCH OPEN CHAMPIONSHIPS (Paris).

Jun 11-17:	Stella Artois Grass Court championships (Queen's Club, London), Dow Classic, women (Edgbaston Priory).
Jun 18-23:	Bristol Trophy (Bristol), Pilkington Classic, women (Eastbourne).
Jun 25-Jul 8:	ALL ENGLAND CHAMPIONSHIPS (Wimbledon).
Jul 22-29:	Federation Cup (Atlantic City).
Jul 23-29:	Canadian Open championships (Montreal).
Jul 30-Aug 5:	Volvo Tennis (Los Angeles, US); Swedish Open (Bastad).
Aug 6-12:	Thriftway ATP championships (US); Czech Open championships.
Aug 27-Sep 9:	US OPEN CHAMPIONSHIPS (Flushing Meadow, New York).
Sep 21-23:	Davis Cup World Group (semi-finals).
Oct 22-28:	Stockholm Open (Sweden).
Oct 29-Nov 4:	Open de Paris (France).
Nov 5-11:	Kremlin Cup International Indoor championships (Moscow); Citibank Open (US).
Nov 6-11:	Silk Cut championships (Wembley).
Nov 12-18:	ATP finals (TBA).
Dec:	Davis Cup final.

VOLLEYBALL

1989

WOMEN'S EUROPEAN CHAMPIONSHIP
Stuttgart, Sep 2-10
Semi-finals
EAST GERMANY beat Romania 3-0: USSR beat Italy 3-0
Final
USSR beat East Germany 3-1
3rd Place Play-off
ITALY beat Romania 3-0
Final Placings
1 USSR; 2 East Germany; 3 Italy; 4 Romania; 5
Czechoslovakia; 6 West Germany; 7 Bulgaria; 8
Yugoslavia; 9 Poland; 10 France; 11 Turkey; 12 Finland

ROYAL BANK OF SCOTLAND NATIONAL CUP FINALS
Crystal Palace, Mar 11
Men
Malory CLC beat Star Aquila 3-2
Women
Britannia beat Sovereign Leasing Sale 3-2

ROYAL BANK OF SCOTLAND NATIONAL LEAGUE
Men's Division 1

		P	W	L	F	A	Pts
1	Malory CLC	22	19	3	60	26	38
2	Star Aquila	22	17	5	57	26	34
3	Hilton Leeds	22	16	6	55	31	32
4	Reebok Liverpool City	22	16	6	52	31	32
5	Speedwell Rucanor	22	15	7	55	32	30
6	Polonia	22	13	9	51	40	26
7	Staffordshire Moorlands	22	10	12	43	46	20
8	Time Out Spark	22	7	15	36	54	14
9	Poole	22	7	15	32	51	14
10	Redwood	22	7	15	30	51	14
11	Capital City	22	5	17	32	55	8*
12	Bradford	22	0	22	6	66	0

* 2 pts deducted

Women's Division 1

		P	W	L	F	A	Pts
1	Britannia	14	13	1	40	9	26
2	Brixton Knights	14	12	2	38	14	24
3	Sovereign Leasing Sale	14	10	4	35	19	20
4	Southsea Scorpions	14	6	8	26	30	12
5	Ashcombe Syenco	14	5	9	24	31	10
6	Hilton Leeds	14	5	9	22	32	10
7	NM Portsmouth	14	4	10	17	35	8
8	MGI Wessex	14	1	13	9	41	2

ENGLISH VOLLEYBALL ASSOCIATION CUP FINALS
Hemel Hempstead, May 6
Men
Eastway beat Solent 3-0
Women
Purbrook Park beat RTB (Liverpool) 3-0

NATWEST COUNTY CUP
Leeds, May 15
Merseyside beat Durham 2-0

NATWEST SUPERCUP
Manchester University, May 20
Men
Malory CLC beat Star Aquila 3-2

Women
Britannia beat Brixton Knights 3-0

WOMEN'S BRITISH CHAMPIONSHIP
Newtonabbey, Belfast, Jun 11
1 England; 2 Scotland; 3 N.Ireland; 4 R.of Ireland

CHAMPIONS

WORLD CHAMPIONSHIPS
Men
1949	USSR
1952	USSR
1956	Czechoslovakia
1960	USSR
1962	USSR
1966	Czechoslovakia
1970	East Germany
1974	Poland
1978	USSR
1982	USSR
1986	United States

Women
1952	USSR
1956	USSR
1960	USSR
1962	Japan
1966	Japan
1970	USSR
1974	Japan
1978	Cuba
1982	China
1986	China

OLYMPIC GAMES
Men
1964	USSR
1968	USSR
1972	Japan
1976	Poland
1980	USSR
1984	United States
1988	United States

Women
1964	Japan
1968	USSR
1972	USSR
1976	Japan
1980	USSR
1984	China
1988	USSR

EUROPEAN CHAMPIONSHIPS
Winners since 1981
Men
1981	USSR
1983	USSR
1985	USSR
1987	USSR
1989	Italy

Women
1981	Bulgaria
1983	USSR
1985	USSR
1987	East Germany
1989	USSR

WATER SKIING

━━━ 1989 ━━━ ━━━ CHAMPIONS ━━━

WORLD CHAMPIONSHIPS
West Palm Beach, Florida, Aug 30-Sep 4

Men
Overall
1 Patrice Martin (Fra) 2704.7 pts
2 Carl Roberge (US) 2698.8 pts
3 Bruce Neville (Aus) 2559.0 pts

Slalom
1 Andy Mapple (GB) 125.00 pts
2 Carl Roberge (US) 124.50 pts
3 John Battleday (GB) 116.50 pts

Jump
1 Geoff Carrington (Aus) 117.6m
2 Andrea Alessi (Ita) 115.7m
3 Bruce Neville (Aus) 115.7m

Tricks
1 Aymeric Benett (Fra) 10,980 pts
2 Patrice Martin (Fra) 10,230 pts
3 Cory Pickos (US) 9,790 pts

Women
Overall
1 Deena Mapple (US) 2745.4 pts
2 Ana Maria Carrasco (Ven) 2635.6 pts
3 Karen Neville (Aus) 2576.9 pts

Slalom
1 Kim Laskoff (US) 111.50 pts
2 Deena Mapple (US) 111.00 pts
3 Susi Graham (Can) 110.00 pts

Jump
1 Deena Mapple (US) 86.5m
2 Karen Morse (GB) 82.1m
3 Julie Shull (US) 81.6m

Tricks
1 Tawn Larsen (US) 16,130 pts
2 Natalya Rumiantsev (USSR) 14,980 pts
3 Britt Larsen (US) 14,300 pts

Team
1 United States 8,408 pts
2 Australia 7,880 pts
3 France 7,842 pts

BRITISH NATIONAL CHAMPIONSHIPS
Tallington, Lincs, Jul 15-16

Men
Overall: Paul Studd
Slalom: John Battleday
Tricks: John Battleday
Jump: Paul Studd

Women
Overall: Philippa Roberts
Slalom: Philippa Roberts
Tricks: Philippa Roberts
Jump: Karen Morse

WORLD CHAMPIONS
Men
Overall
1949	Christian Jourdan (Fra) & Guy de Clercq (Bel)
1950	Dick Pope jnr (US)
1953	Alfredo Mendoza (US)
1955	Alfredo Mendoza (US)
1957	Joe Cash (US)
1959	Chuck Stearns (US)
1961	Bruno Zaccardi (Ita)
1963	Billy Spencer (US)
1965	Roland Hillier (US)
1967	Mike Suyderhoud (US)
1969	Mike Suyderhoud (US)
1971	George Athans (Can)
1973	George Athans (Can)
1975	Carlos Suarez (Ven)
1977	Mike Hazelwood (GB)
1979	Joel McClintock (Can)
1981	Sammy Duvall (US)
1983	Sammy Duvall (US)
1985	Sammy Duvall (US)
1987	Sammy Duvall (US)
1989	Patrice Martin (Fra)

Women
Overall
1949	Willa Worthington (US)
1950	Willa Worthington-McGuire (US)
1953	Leah Marie Rawls (US)
1955	Willa Worthington-McGuire (US)
1957	Marina Doria (Swi)
1959	Vickie Van Hook (US)
1961	Sylvie Hulsemann (Lux)
1963	Jeanette Brown (US)
1965	Liz Allan (US)
1967	Jeanette Stewart-Wood (GB)
1969	Liz Allan (US)
1971	Christy Weir (US)
1973	Lisa St John (US)
1975	Liz Allan-Shetter (US)
1977	Cindy Todd (US)
1979	Cindy Todd (US)
1981	Karin Roberge (US)
1983	Ana Maria Carrasco (Ven)
1985	Karen Neville (Aus)
1987	Deena Brush (US)
1989	Deena Mapple (née Brush) (US)

Team
United States have won the team title at every world championship since the title was inaugurated in 1957.

━━━ 1990 ━━━

Sep 8-18: European Championship (Jersey).

WEIGHTLIFTING

1989

WORLD CHAMPIONSHIP
Athens, Sep 16-23

Flyweight (up to 52kg)
1 Ivan Ivanov (Bul) 272.5kg
2 He Zhuoqiang (Chn) 262.5kg
3 Traian Ciharean (Rom) 260kg

Bantamweight (up to 56kg)
1 Hafiz Suleimanov (USSR) 287.5kg
2 Liu Shoubin (Chn) 285kg
3 He Yinqgiang (Chn) 280kg

Featherweight (up to 60kg)
1 Naim Suleymanoglu (Tur) 317.5kg
2 Peshalov (Bul) 307.5kg
3 Attila Czanka (Rom) 305kg

Lightweight (up to 67.5kg)
1 Israil Militossian (USSR) 347.5kg
2 Ioto Iotov (Bul) 337.5kg
3 Kim Myong-Nam (NKo) 327.5kg

Middleweight (up to 75kg)
1 Altimarat Orazdurdiev (USSR) 362.5kg
2 Pablo Lara (Cub) 357.5kg
3 Chon Chou-lo (NKo) 355.0kg

Light-heavyweight (up to 82.5kg)
1 Kiril Kunev (Bul) 385kg
2 Plamen Bratiochev (Bul) 380kg
3 Ingo Steinhofel (GDR) 377.5kg

Middle-heavyweight (up to 90kg)
1 Anatoliy Khrapatiy (USSR) 415kg
2 Sergey Sirtsov (USSR) 407.5kg
3 Ivan Chakarov (Bul) 400kg

Up to 100kg
1 Peter Stefanov (Bul) 415kg
2 Nicu Vlad (Rom) 412.5kg
3 Pavel Kouznetsov (USSR) 400kg

Heavyweight (up to 110kg)
1 Stefan Botev (Bul) 427.5kg
2 Andrew Davies (GB) 395kg
3 Miroslaw Dabrowski (Pol) 382.5kg

Super-heavyweight (over 110kg)
1 Alexander Kurlovich (USSR) 460kg
2 Rizvan Guelishkanov (USSR) 432.5kg
3 Michael Schubert (GDR) 425kg

When the Championships were over, Hafiz Suleimanov, the Soviet winner of the bantamweight category, went to the Turkish Embassy in Athens with his trainer and asked to defect.

CHAMPIONS

OLYMPIC GAMES

Flyweight (up to 52kg)
1972	Zygmunt Smalcerz (Pol)
1976	Aleksandr Voronin (USSR)
1980	Kanybek Osmonoliev (USSR)
1984	Zeng Guoqiang (Chn)
1988	Sevdalim Marinov (Bul)

Bantamweight (up to 56kg)
1948	Joseph de Pietro (US)
1952	Ivan Udodov (USSR)
1956	Charles Vinci (US)
1960	Charles Vinci (US)

1964	Aleksey Vakhonin (USSR)
1968	Mohammad Nassiri (Irn)
1972	Imre Foldi (Hun)
1976	Norair Nurikyan (Bul)
1980	Daniel Nunez (Cub)
1984	Wu Shude (Chn)
1988	Oleg Mirzoian (USSR)

Featherweight (up to 60kg)
1920	Frans de Haes (Bel)
1924	Pierino Gabetti (Ita)
1928	Franz Andrysek (Aut)
1932	Raymond Suvigny (Fra)
1936	Anthony Terlazzo (US)
1948	Mahmoud Fayad (Egy)
1952	Rafael Chimishkyan (USSR)
1956	Isaac Berger (US)
1960	Yevgeniy Minayev (USSR)
1964	Yoshinobu Miyake (Jap)
1968	Yoshinobu Miyake (Jap)
1972	Norair Nurikyan (Bul)
1976	Nikolai Kolesnikov (USSR)
1980	Viktor Mazin (USSR)
1984	Chen Weiqiang (Chn)
1988	Naim Suleymanoglu (Tur)

Lightweight (up to 67.5kg)
1920	Alfred Neuland (Est)
1924	Edmond Decottignies (Fra)
1928	Kurt Helbig (Ger) &
	Hans Haas (Aut)
1932	René Duverger (Fra)
1936	Anwar M Mesbah (Egy) &
	Robert Fein (Aut)
1948	Ibrahim Shams (Egy)
1952	Tommy Kono (US)
1956	Igor Rybak (USSR)
1960	Viktor Bushuyev (USSR)
1964	Waldemar Baszanowski (Pol)
1968	Waldemar Baszanowski (Pol)
1972	Mukharbi Kirzhinov (USSR)
1976	Pyotr Korol (USSR)
1980	Yanko Rusev (Bul)
1984	Jing Yuan Yao (Chn)
1988	Joachim Kunz (GDR)

Middleweight (up to 75kg)
1920	Henri Gance (Fra)
1924	Carlo Galimberti (Ita)
1928	Roger François (Fra)
1932	Rudolf Ismayr (Ger)
1936	Khadr El Thouni (Egy)
1948	Frank Spellman (US)
1952	Peter George (US)
1956	Fyodor Bogdanovski (USSR)
1960	Aleksandr Kurinov (USSR)
1964	Hans Zdrazila (Cze)
1968	Viktor Kurentsov (USSR)
1972	Yordan Bikov (Bul)
1976	Yordan Mitkov (Bul)
1980	Asen Zlatev (Bul)
1984	Karl-Heinz Radschinsky (FRG)
1988	Borislav Guidikov (Bul)

Light-heavyweight (up to 82.5kg)
1920	Ernest Cadine (Fra)
1924	Charles Rigoulot (Fra)
1928	Said Nosseir (Egy)
1932	Louis Hostin (Fra)
1936	Louis Hostin (Fra)
1948	Stanley Stanczyk (US)
1952	Trofim Lomakin (USSR)

1956	Tommy Kono (US)
1960	Ireneusz Palinski (Pol)
1964	Rudolf Plyukfelder (USSR)
1968	Boris Selitsky (USSR)
1972	Leif Jenssen (Nor)
1976	Valeriy Shary (USSR)
1980	Yurik Vardanyan (USSR)
1984	Petre Becheru (Rom)
1988	Israil Arsamakov (USSR)

Middle-heavyweight (up to 90kg)
1952	Norbert Schemansky (US)
1956	Arkadiy Vorobyev (USSR)
1960	Arkadiy Vorobyev (USSR)
1964	Vladimir Golovanov (USSR)
1968	Kaarlo Kangasniemi (Fin)
1972	Andom Nikolov (Bul)
1976	David Rigert (USSR)
1980	Peter Baczako (Hun)
1984	Nicu Vlad (Rom)
1988	Anatoliy Khrapatu (USSR)

Up to 100 kg
1980	Ota Zaremba (Cze)
1984	Rolf Milser (FRG)
1988	Pavel Kouznetsov (USSR)

Heavyweight (up to 110kg)
1920	Filippo Bottino (Ita)
1924	Giuseppe Tonani (Ita)
1928	Josef Strassberger (Ger)
1932	Jaroslav Skobla (Cze)
1936	Josef Manger (Aut)
1948	John Davis (US)
1952	John Davis (US)
1956	Paul Anderson (US)
1960	Yuriy Vlasov (USSR)
1964	Leonid Zhabotinsky (USSR)
1968	Leonid Zhabotinsky (USSR)
1972	Jan Talts (USSR)
1976	Yuriy Zaitsev (USSR)
1980	Leonid Taranenko (USSR)
1984	Norberto Oberburger (Ita)
1988	Yuri Zakharevich (USSR)

Super-heavyweight (over 110kg)
1972	Vasiliy Alexeyev (USSR)
1976	Vasiliy Alexeyev (USSR)
1980	Sultan Rakhmanov (USSR)
1984	Dino Lukin (Aus)
1988	Alexandr Kurlovich (USSR)

WORLD CHAMPIONSHIPS
First held 1898, Not held in Olympic years
Winners since 1981

Flyweight (up to 52kg)
1981	Kanybek Osmonalyev (USSR)
1982	Stefan Leletko (Pol)
1983	Neno Terziyski (Bul)
1985	Sevdalim Marinov (Bul)
1986	Sevdalim Marinov (Bul)
1987	Sevdalim Marinov (Bul)
1989	Ivan Ivanov (Bul)

Bantamweight (up to 56kg)
1981	Anton Kodiabashev (Bul)
1982	Anton Kodiabashev (Bul)
1983	Oleg Mirzoyan (USSR)
1985	Neno Terziyski (Bul)
1986	Mitko Grablev (Bul)
1987	Neno Terziyski (Bul)
1989	Hafiz Suleimanov (USSR)

Featherweight (up to 60kg)
1981	Beloslav Manolov (Bul)
1982	Yurik Sarkisyan (USSR)
1983	Yurik Sarkisyan (USSR)
1985	Neum Shalamanov (Bul)
1986	Neum Shalamanov (Bul)
1987	Stefan Topourov (Bul)
1989	Naim Suleymanoglu (formerly Neum Shalamanov) (Tur)

Lightweight (up to 67.5kg)
1981	Jaochim Kunz (GDR)
1982	Piotr Mandra (Pol)
1983	Joachim Kunz (GDR)
1985	Mikhail Petrov (Bul)
1986	Mikhail Petrov (Bul)
1987	Mikhail Petrov (Bul)
1989	Israil Militossian (USSR)

Middleweight (up to 75kg)
1981	Yanko Rusev (Bul)
1982	Yanko Rusev (Bul)
1983	Alexandr Varbanov (Bul)
1985	Alexandr Varbanov (Bul)
1986	Alexandr Varbanov (Bul)
1987	Borislav Guidikov (Bul)
1989	Altimarat Orazdurdiev (USSR)

Light-heavyweight (up to 82.5kg)
1981	Yurik Vardanyan (USSR)
1982	Asen Zlatev (Bul)
1983	Yurik Vardanyan (USSR)
1985	Yurik Vardanyan (USSR)
1986	Asen Zlatev (Bul)
1987	Laszlo Barsi (Hun)
1989	Kiril Kunev (Bul)

Middle-heavyweight (up to 90kg)
1981	Blagoi Blagoyev (Bul)
1982	Blagoi Blagoyev (Bul)
1983	Blagoi Blagoyev (Bul)
1985	Viktor Solodov (USSR) & Anatoliy Khrapatiy (USSR)
1986	Anatoliy Khrapatiy (USSR)
1987	Anatoliy Khrapatiy (USSR)
1989	Anatoliy Khrapatiy (USSR)

Up to 100 kg
1981	Viktor Sots (USSR)
1982	Viktor Sots (USSR)
1983	Pavel Kouznetsov (USSR)
1985	Sandor Szanyi (Hun)
1986	Nicu Vlad (Rom)
1987	Pavel Kouznetsov (USSR)
1989	Peter Stefanov (Bul)

Heavyweight (up to 110kg)
1981	Valeriy Kravchuk (USSR)
1982	Sergey Arakelov (USSR)
1983	Vyacheslav Klokov (USSR)
1985	Yuriy Zakharevich (USSR)
1986	Yuriy Zakharevich (USSR)
1987	Yuriy Zakharevich (USSR)
1989	Stefan Botev (Bul)

Super-heavyweight (over 110kg)
1981	Anatoliy Pisarenko (USSR)
1982	Anatoliy Pisarenko (USSR)
1983	Anatoliy Pisarenko (USSR)
1985	Antonio Krastev (Bul)
1986	Antonio Krastev (Bul)
1987	Alexander Kurlovich (USSR)
1989	Alexander Kurlovich (USSR)

WINTER SPORTS

Marc Girardelli, the Italo-Austrian Swiss-based Luxemburgeois – a sort of one-man united Europe – dominated the 1988/89 ski season, winning the World Cup downhill and overall titles as well as the combined event at the World Championship in Vail, Colorado. But the Championship, the first in the US for 39 years, produced a large number of surprises including wins for an unknown 21-year-old West German, Hansjoerg Tauscher, in the downhill and the Swiss Martin Hangl, without a win for four years, in the super-giant slalom. The rush of unknowns encouraged American indifference to the competition and normal skiing continued at Vail as the events went on; but the Championship succeeded in its aim of selling Vail as a resort to Europe – and a lot of equipment to Americans.

Vreni Schneider, the Swiss shoemaker's daughter, dominated women's competitions. Despite her well-known loathing of downhill, she won 13 World Cup events, equalling Ingemar Stenmark's 78-79 total. Stenmark finished his World Cup career with his 86th win, in the Aspen giant slalom, a total which, now the sport has become more competitive, may never be beaten.

The British ski jumper and farceur Eddie Edwards failed to finish last in a World Cup event in Lake Placid, beating the Dutchman Gerrit Konijnenberg on "style". Edwards then rose to 78th out of 83, including non-finishers: "I kicked some butt," he said. However, a week later he broke his collarbone in practice. Tightened regulations are due to end Edwards' participation and the attendant diversion. The mildest European winter in memory provided horrible complications for skiing. But at the end of January there were reports of excellent snow and empty slopes not far away in Iran. The après-ski was said to be somewhat less inviting.

1989

ALPINE SKIING WORLD CHAMPIONSHIPS
Vail, Colorado, US, Jan 29-Feb 12

Men
Combined
1 Marc Girardelli (Lux)
2 Paul Accola (Swi)
3 Gunter Mader (Aut)

Downhill
1 Hansjoerg Tauscher (FRG)
2 Peter Muller (Swi)
3 Karl Alpiger (Swi)

Slalom
1 Rudi Nierlich (Aut)
2 Armin Bittner (FRG)
3 Marc Girardelli (Lux)
This was Ingemar Stenmark's last world championship race

Giant Slalom
1 Rudi Nierlich (Aut)
2 Helmut Mayer (Aut)
3 Pirmin Zurbriggen (Swi)

Super-Giant Slalom
1 Martin Hangl (Swi)
2 Pirmin Zurbriggen (Swi)
3 Tomas Cizman (Yug)

Women
Combined
1 Tamara McKinney (US)
2 Vreni Schneider (Swi)
3 Brigitte Oertli (Swi)

Downhill
1 Maria Walliser (Swi)
2 Karen Percy (Can)
3 Karin Dedler (FRG)

Slalom
1 Mateja Svet (Yug)
2 Vreni Schneider (Swi)
3 Tamara McKinney (US)

Giant Slalom
1 Vreni Schneider (Swi)
2 Carole Merle (Fra)
3 Christelle Guignard (Fra)

Super-Giant Slalom
1 Ulrike Maier (Aut)
2 Sigrid Wolf (Aut)
3 Michela Gerge (FRG)

ALPINE SKIING WORLD CUP
Men
Overall
1 Marc Girardelli (Lux) 407 pts
2 Pirmin Zurbriggen (Swi) 309 pts
3 Alberto Tomba (Ita) 189 pts

Downhill
1 Marc Girardelli (Lux) 139 pts
2 Helmut Hoeflehner (Aut) 112 pts
3 Daniel Mahrer (Swi) 102 pts

Slalom
1 Armin Bittner (FRG) 117 pts
2 Alberto Tomba (Ita) 112 pts
3 Marc Girardelli (Lux) and Ole Christian Furuseth (Nor) 106 pts

Giant Slalom
1 Ole Christian Furuseth (Nor) 82 pts *
2 Pirmin Zurbriggen (Swi) 82 pts
3 Rudolf Nierlich (Aut) 79 pts
* Won with more second places
Furuseth was the first Norwegian to win a World Cup title.

Super-Giant Slalom
1 Pirmin Zurbriggen (Swi) 62 pts
2 Lars-Boerje Eriksson (Swe) 51 pts
3 Franck Picard (Fra) 49 pts

Women
Overall
1 Vreni Schneider (Swi) 376 pts
2 Maria Walliser (Swi) 261 pts
3 Michela Figini (Swi) 248 pts

Downhill
1 Michela Figini (Swi) 176 pts
2 Maria Walliser (Swi) 142 pts
3 Michela Gerg (FRG) 81 pts

Slalom
1 Vreni Schneider (Swi) 175 pts
2 Monika Maierhofer (Aut) 85 pts
3 Tamara McKinney (US) 77 pts

Giant Slalom
1 Vreni Schneider (Swi) 165 pts
2 Mateja Svet (Yug) 106 pts
3 Maria Walliser (Swi) 87 pts

Super-Giant Slalom
1 Carole Merle (Fra) 75 pts
2 Sigrid Wolf (Aut) 71 pts
3 Anita Wachter (Aut) 56 pts

Nations Cup
1 Switzerland 2,305 pts
2 Austria 2,061 pts
3 West Germany 878 pts

Marc Girardelli in 1988-89 was the first person to win at all four disciplines in the same World Cup season. He won 1 Super-G race, 2 giant slaloms, 3 downhills and 1 slalom

---

CHAMPIONS

ALPINE SKIING

WORLD CUP
Men
Overall Champions
1967 Jean-Claude Killy (Fra); 1968 Jean-Claude Killy (Fra); 1969 Karl Schranz (Aut); 1970 Karl Schranz (Aut); 1971 Gustavo Theoni (Ita); 1972 Gustavo Theoni (Ita); 1973 Gustavo Theoni (Ita); 1974 Piero Gros (Ita); 1975 Gustavo Theoni (Ita); 1976 Ingemar Stenmark (Swe); 1977 Ingemar Stenmark (Swe); 1978 Ingemar Stenmark (Swe); 1979 Peter Luscher (Swi); 1980 Andreas Wenzel (Lie); 1981 Phil Mahre (US); 1982 Phil Mahre (US); 1983 Phil Mahre (US);1984 Pirmin Zurbriggen (Swi); 1985 Marc Girardelli (Lux); 1986 Marc Girardelli (Lux); 1987 Pirmin Zurbriggen (Swi); 1988 Pirmin Zurbriggen (Swi); 1989 Marc Girardelli (Lux)

	Downhill	Slalom	Giant Slalom	Super-Giant Slalom
1967	Jean Claude Killy (Fra)	Jean-Claude Killy (Fra)	Jean-Claude Killy (Fra)	-
1968	Gerhard Nenning (Aut)	Dumeng Giovanoli (Swi)	Jean-Claude Killy (Fra)	-
1969	Karl Schranz (Aut)	Alfred Matt (Aut)	Karl Schranz (Aut)	-
		Alain Penz (Fra)		
		Jean-Noel Augert (Fra)		
		Patrick Russel (Fra)		
1970	Karl Schranz (Aut)	Patrick Russel (Fra)	Gustavo Theoni (Ita)	-
	Karl Cordin (Aut)	Alain Penz (Fra)		
1971	Berhard Russi (Swi)	Jean-Noel Augert (Fra)	Gustavo Theoni (Ita)	-
			Patrick Russell (Fra)	
1972	Bernhard Russi (Swi)	Jean-Noel Augert (Fra)	Gustavo Theoni (Ita)	-
1973	Roland Collombin (Swi)	Gustavo Theoni (Ita)	Hans Hinterseer (Aut)	-
1974	Roland Collombin (Swi)	Gustavo Theoni (Ita)	Piero Gros (Ita)	-
1975	Franz Klammer (Aut)	Ingemar Stenmark (Swe)	Ingemar Stenmark (Swe)	-
1976	Franz Klammer (Aut)	Ingemar Stenmark (Swe)	Ingemar Stenmark (Swe)	-
1977	Franz Klammer (Aut)	Ingemar Stenmark (Swe)	Heini Hemmi (Swi)	-
1978	Franz Klammer (Aut)	Ingemar Stenmark (Swe)	Ingemar Stenmark (Swe)	-
1979	Peter Muller (Swi)	Ingemar Stenmark (Swe)	Ingemar Stenmark (Swe)	-
1980	Peter Muller (Swi)	Ingemar Stenmark (Swe)	Ingemar Stenmark (Swe)	-
1981	Harti Weirather (Aut)	Ingemar Stenmark (Swe)	Ingemar Stenmark (Swe)	-
1982	Steve Podborski (Can)	Phil Mahre (US)	Phil Mahre (US)	-
	Peter Muller (Swi)			
1983	Franz Klammer (Aut)	Ingemar Stenmark (Swe)	Phil Mahre (US)	-
1984	Urs Raber (Swi)	Marc Girardelli (Lux)	Ingemar Stenmark (Swe)	-
1985	Helmet Hoeflehner (Aut)	Marc Girardelli (Lux)	Marc Girardelli (Lux)	-
1986	Peter Wirnsberger (Aut)	Rok Petrovic (Yug)	Joel Gaspoz (Swi)	Markus Wasmeier (FRG)
1987	Pirmin Zurbriggen (Swi)	Bojan Krizaj (Yug)	Pirmin Zurbriggen (Swi)	Pirmin Zurbriggen (Swi)
1988	Pirmin Zurbriggen (Swi)	Alberto Tomba (Ita)	Alberto Tomba (Ita)	Pirmin Zurbriggen (Swi)
1989	Marc Girardelli (Lux)	Armin Bittner (FRG)	Ole Furuseth (Nor)	Pirmin Zurbriggen (Swi)

Women
Overall Champions
1967 Nancy Greene (Can); 1968 Nancy Greene (Can); 1969 Gertrud Gabl (Aut); 1970 Michele Jacot (Fra); 1971 Annemarie Moser-Proll (Aut); 1972 Annemarie Moser-Proll (Aut); 1973 Annemarie Moser-Proll (Aut); 1974 Annemarie Moser-Proll (Aut); 1975 Annemarie Moser-Proll (Aut); 1976 Rosi Mittermaier (FRG); 1977 Lise-Marie Morerod (Swi); 1978 Hanni Wenzel (Lie); 1979 Annemarie Moser-Proll (Aut); 1980 Hanni Wenzel (Lie); 1981 Marie-Therese Nadig (Swi); 1982 Erika Hess (Swi); 1983 Tamara McKinney (US); 1984 Erika Hess (Swi); 1985 Michela Figini (Swi); 1986 Maria Walliser (Swi); 1987 Maria Walliser (Swi); 1988 Michela Figini (Swi); 1989 Vreni Schneider (Swi)

	Downhill	Slalom	Giant Slalom
1967	Marielle Goitschell (Fra)	Marielle Goitschell (Fra) Annie Famose (Fra)	Nancy Greene (Can)
1968	Isabelle Mir (Fra) Olga Pall (Aut)	Annie Famose (Fra)	Nancy Greene (Can)
1969	Wiltrud Drexel (Aut)	Gertrud Gabl (Aut)	Marilyn Cochran (US)
1970	Isabelle Mir (Fra)	Ingrid Laforgue (Fra)	Michele Jacot (Fra) Francoise Macchi (Fra)
1971	Annemarie Moser-Proll (Aut)	Britt Laforgue (Fra) Betsy Clifford (Can)	Annemarie Moser-Proll (Aut)
1972	Annemarie Moser-Proll (Aut)	Britt Laforgue (Fra)	Annemarie Moser-Proll (Aut)
1973	Annemarie Moser-Proll (Aut)	Patricia Emonet (Fra)	Monika Kaserer (Aut)
1974	Annemarie Moser-Proll (Aut)	Christa Zechmeister (FRG)	Hanni Wenzel (Lie)
1975	Annemarie Moser-Proll (Aut)	Lise-Marie Morerod (Swi)	Annemarie Moser-Proll (Aut)
1976	Brigette Habersatter-Totschnig (Aut)	Lise-Marie Morerod (Swi)	Rosi Mittermaier (FRG)
1977	Brigette Habersatter-Totschnig (Aut)	Lise-Marie Morerod (Swi)	Lise-Marie Morerod (Swi)
1978	Annemarie Moser-Proll (Aut)	Hanni Wenzel (Lie)	Lise-Marie Morerod (Swi)
1979	Annemarie Moser-Proll (Aut)	Regina Sackl (Aut)	Christa Kinshoffer (Aut)
1980	Marie-Therese Nadig (Swi)	Perrine Pelen (Fra)	Hanni Wenzel (Lie)
1981	Marie-Therese Nadig (Swi)	Erika Hess (Swi)	Tamara McKinney (US)
1982	Cecile Gros-Gaudenier (Fra)	Erika Hess (Swi)	Irene Epple (FRG)
1983	Doris De Agostini (Swi)	Erika Hess (Swi)	Tamara McKinney (US)
1984	Maria Walliser (Swi)	Tamara McKinney (US)	Erika Hess (Swi)
1985	Michela Figini (Swi)	Erika Hess (Swi)	Michela Figini (Swi) Marina Kiehl (FRG)
1986	Maria Walliser (Swi)	Roswitha Steiner (Aut)	Vreni Schneider (Swi)
1987	Michela Figini (Swi)	Corinne Schmidhauser (Swi)	Maria Walliser (Swi) Vreni Schneider (Swi)
1988	Michela Figini (Swi)	Roswitha Steiner (Aut)	Mateja Svet (Yug)
1989	Michela Figini (Swi)	Vreni Schneider (Swi)	Vreni Schneider (Swi)

Super-Giant Slalom
(Instituted 1986)
1986 Marina Kiehl (FRG); 1987 Maria Walliser (Swi); 1988 Michela Figini (Swi); 1989 Carole Merle (Fra)
Most World Cup race wins:
86 Ingemar Stenmark; **62** Annemarie Moser-Proll
Most Race wins in one season
13 Ingemar Stenmark; 1978-79, Vreni Schneider, 1988-89; **12** Jean-Claude Killy, 1966-67; **11** Annemarie Moser-Proll, 1972-73; Pirmin Zurbriggen 1986-87

NATIONS CUP
(Team prize at World Cup)
1967-68, 1970-72 France; 1969, 1973-82 Austria; 1983-89 Switzerland

ALPINE SKIING WORLD CHAMPIONSHIPS
(Post-war winners)
Men
Combined
1954 Stein Eriksen (Nor); 1956 Toni Sailer (Aut); 1958 Toni Sailer (Aut); 1960 Guy Perillat (Fra); 1962 Karl Schranz (Aut); 1964 Ludwig Leitner (FRG); 1966 Jean-Claude Killy (Fra); 1968 Jean-Claude Killy (Fra); 1970 Bill Kidd (US); 1972 Gustavo Theoni (Ita); 1974 Franz Klammer (Aut); 1976 Gustavo Theoni (Ita); 1978 Andrea Wenzel (Lie); 1980 Phil Mahre (US); 1982 Michel Vion (Fra); 1985 Pirmin Zurbriggen (Swi); 1987 Marc Girardelli (Lux); 1989 Marc Girardelli (Lux)

	Downhill	Slalom	Giant Slalom	Super-Giant Slalom
1950	Zeno Colo (Ita)	Georges Schneider (Swi)	Zeno Colo (Ita)	-
1954	Christian Pravda (Aut)	Stein Eriksen (Nor)	Stein Eriksen (Nor)	-
1958	Toni Sailer (Aut)	Josef Rieder (Aut)	Toni Sailer (Aut)	-
1962	Karl Schranz (Aut)	Charles Bozon (Fra)	Egon Zimmermann (Aut)	-
1966	Jean-Claude Killy (Fra)	Carlo Senoner (Ita)	Guy Perillat (Fra)	-
1970	Bernhard Russi (Swi)	Jean-Noel Augert (Fra)	Karl Schranz (Aut)	-
1974	David Zwilling (Aut)	Gustavo Theoni (Ita)	Gustavo Theoni (Ita)	-
1978	Josef Walcher (Aut)	Ingemar Stenmark (Swe)	Ingemar Stenmark (Swe)	-
1982	Harti Weirather (Aut)	Ingemar Stenmark (Swe)	Steve Mahre (US)	-
1985	Pirmin Zurbriggen (Swi)	Jonas Nilsson (Swe)	Markus Wasmaier (FRG)	-

| 1987 | Peter Muller (Swi) | Frank Worndl (FRG) | Pirmin Zurbriggen (Swi) | Pirmin Zurbriggen (Swi) |
| 1989 | Hansjoerg Tauscher (FRG) | Rudolf Nierlich (Aut) | Rudolf Nierlich (Aut) | Martin Hangl (Swi) |

Women
Combined
1954 Ida Schopfer (Swi); 1956 Madeleine Berthod (Swi); 1958 Frieda Danzer (Swi); 1960 Anne Heggtveit (Can); 1962 Marielle Goitschel (Fra); 1964 Marielle Goitschel (Fra); 1966 Marielle Goitschel (Fra); 1968 Nancy Greene (Can); 1970 Michele Jacot (Fra); 1972 Annemarie Moser-Proll (Aut); 1974 Fabienne Serrat (Fra); 1976 Rosi Mittermaier (FRG); 1978 Annemarie Moser-Proll (Aut); 1980 Hanni Wenzel (Lie); 1982 Erika Hess (Swi); 1985 Erika Hess (Swi); 1987 Erika Hess (Swi); 1989 Tamara McKinney (US)

	Downhill	Slalom	Giant Slalom
1950	Trude-Beiser-Jochum (Aut)	Dagmar Rom (Aut)	Dagmar Rom (Aut)
1954	Ida Schopfer (Swi)	Trude Klecker (Aut)	Lucienne Schmitt (Fra)
1958	Lucille Wheeler (Can)	Inger Bjornbakken (Nor)	Lucille Wheeler (Can)
1962	Christl Haas (Aut)	Marianne Jahn (Aut)	Marianne Jahn (Aut)
1966	Erika Schinegger (Aut)	Annie Famose (Fra)	Marielle Goitschel (Fra)
1970	Annerosli Zyrd (Swi)	Ingrid Lafforgue (Fra)	Betsy Clifford (Can)
1974	Annemarie Moser-Proll (Aut)	Hanni Wenzel (Lie)	Fabienne Serrat (Fra)
1978	Annemarie Moser-Proll (Aut)	Lea Solkner (Aut)	Maria Epple (FRG)
1982	Gerry Sorensen (Can)	Erika Hess (Swi)	Erika Hess (Swi)
1985	Michela Figini (Swi)	Perrine Pelen (Fra)	Diann Roffe (US)
1987	Maria Walliser (Swi)	Erika Hess (Swi)	Vreni Schneider (Swi)
1989	Maria Walliser (Swi)	Mateja Svet (Yug)	Vreni Schneider (Swi)

Super-Giant Slalom
(First held 1987)
1987   Maria Walliser (FRG); 1989 Ulrike Maier (Aut)

OLYMPIC GAMES
Men
Alpine Combined
1936   Franz Pfnur (Ger); 1948 Henri Oreiller (Fra); 1988 Hubert Strolz (Aut)

	Downhill	Slalom	Giant Slalom	Super-Giant Slalom
1948	Henri Oreiller (Fra)	Edy Reinalter (Swi)	-	-
1952	Zeno Colo (Ita)	Othmar Schneider (Aut)	Stein Eriksen (Nor)	-
1956	Toni Sailer (Aut)	Toni Sailer (Aut)	Toni Sailer (Aut)	-
1960	Jean Vuarnet (Fra)	Ernst Hinterseer (Aut)	Roger Staub (Swi)	-
1964	Egon Zimmermann (Aut)	Josef Stiegler (Aut)	Francois Boulieu (Fra)	-
1968	Jean-Claude Killy (Fra)	Jean-Claude Killy (Fra)	Jean-Claude Killy (Fra)	-
1972	Bernhard Russi (Swi)	Francisco Fernandez Ochoa (Spa)	Gustavo Theoni (Ita)	-
1976	Franz Klammer (Aut)	Piero Gros (Ita)	Heini Hemmi (Swi)	-
1980	Leonhard Stock (Aut)	Ingemar Stenmark (Swe)	Ingemar Stenmark (Swe)	-
1984	William Johnson (US)	Phil Mahre (US)	Max Julen (Swi)	-
1988	Pirmin Zurbriggen (Swi)	Alberto Tomba (Ita)	Alberto Tomba (Ita)	Franck Picard (Fra)

Women
Combined
1936   Christel Cranz (Ger); 1948 Trude Beiser (Aut); 1988 Anita Wachter (Aut)

	Downhill	Slalom	Giant Slalom
			-
1948	Hedy Schlunegger (Swi)	Gretchen Fraser (US)	
1952	Trude Jochum (née Beiser) (Aut)	Andrea Mead-Lawrence (US)	Andrea Mead-Lawrence (US)
1956	Madeleine Berthod (Swi)	Renee Colliard (Swi)	Ossi Reichert (FRG)
1960	Heidi Biebi (FRG)	Anne Heggtveit (Can)	Yvonne Ruegg (Swi)
1964	Christl Haas (Aut)	Christine Goitschel (Fra)	Marielle Goitschel (Fra)
1968	Olga Pall (Aut)	Marielle Goitschel (Fra)	Nancy Greene (Can)
1972	Marie-Therese Nadig (Swi)	Barbara Cochran (US)	Marie-Therese Nadig (Swi)
1976	Rosi Mittermaier (FRG)	Rosi Mittermaier (FRG)	Kathy Kreiner (Can)
1980	Annemarie Moser-Proll (Aut)	Hanni Wenzel (Lie)	Hanni Wenzel (Lie)
1984	Michela Figini (Swi)	Paoletta Magoni (Ita)	Debbie Armstrong (USA)
1988	Marina Kiehl (FRG)	Vreni Schneider (Swi)	Vreni Schneider (Swi)

Super-Giant Slalom
(First held 1988)
1988   Sigrid Wolf (Aut)

BOBSLEIGHING

WORLD CHAMPIONSHIPS
(Since 1961)

Two-man
1961	Eugenio Monti/Sergio Siorpaes (Ita)
1962	Rinaldo Ruatti/Enrico De Lorenzo (Ita)

1963	Eugenio Monti/Sergio Siorpaes (Ita)
1965	Tony Nash/Robin Dixon (GB)
1966	Eugenio Monti/Sergio Siorpaes (Ita)
1967	Erwin Thaler/Reinhold Durnthaler (Aut)
1969	Nevio de Zordo/Adriano Frassinelli (Ita)
1970	Horst Floth/Pepi Bader (FRG)
1971	Gianfranco Gaspari/Mario Armano (Ita)

1973	Wolfgang Zimmerer/Peter Utzschneider (FRG)
1974	Wolfgang Zimmerer/Peter Utzschneider (FRG)
1975	Giorgio Alvero/Franco Perruquet (Ita)
1977	Hans Hilterbrand/Heinz Meier (Swi)
1978	Erich Scharer/Josef Benz (Swi)
1979	Erich Scharer/Josef Benz (Swi)
1981	Bernhard Germeshausen/
	Hans-Jurgen Gernhardt (GDR)
1982	Erich Scharer/Josef Benz (Swi)
1983	Ralf Pichler/Urs Leuthold (Swi)
1985	Wolfgang Hoppe/Dietmar Schauerhammer (GDR)
1986	Wolfgang Hoppe/Dietmar Schauerhammer (GDR)
1987	Ralf Pichler/Celest Poltera (Swi)
1989	Wolfgang Hoppe/Bogdan Musiol (GDR)

Four-man

1961	Italy
1962	West Germany
1963	Italy
1965	Canada
1966	Not completed
1967	Not held
1969	West Germany
1970	Italy
1971	Switzerland
1973	Switzerland
1974	West Germany
1975	Switzerland
1977	East Germany
1978	East Germany
1979	West Germany
1981	East Germany
1982	Switzerland
1983	Switzerland
1985	East Germany
1986	Switzerland
1987	Switzerland
1989	Switzerland

"Welcome to the great state of California"
Former president Gerald Ford welcoming competitors to the World Championships in Colorado.

"Ingemar is the one man in Sweden capable of bringing the nation to a stop."
Ingvar Carlsson, Prime Minister of Sweden, on Stenmark's retirement.

"I did not do much before skiing. Now I want time to learn about life."
Pirmin Zurbriggen on his decision to retire in 1990.

"I'm going down thinking about my position, making contact, exploding on take-off, keeping my head down, getting into a good flight position. All of that is going through my mind instead of just Ohhh."
Eddie Edwards on not finishing last.

"The jump was so good and I was in such a good flight position I started to panic."
Edwards on getting injured.

"What is winning the ski race beside Armenia's earthquake?"
Vreni Schneider

OLYMPIC GAMES
Two-man

1932	Hubert Stevens/Curtis Stevens (US)
1936	Ivan Brown/Alan Washbond (US)
1948	Felix Endrich/Friedrich Waller (Swi)
1952	Andreas Ostler/Lorenz Nieberl (FRG)
1956	Lamberto Dalla Costa/Giacomo Conti (Ita)
1960	Not held
1964	Tony Nash/Robin Dixon (GB)
1968	Eugenio Monti/Luciano de Paolis (Ita)
1972	Wolfgang Zimmerer/Peter Utzschneider (FRG)
1976	Meinhard Nehmer/
	Bernhard Germeshausen (GDR)
1980	Erich Scharer/Josef Benz (Swi)
1984	Wolfgang Hoppe/Dietmar Schauerhammer (GDR)
1988	Janis Kipours/Vladimir Kozlov (USSR)

Four-man

1924	Switzerland
1928	United States
1932	United States
1936	Switzerland
1948	United States
1952	West Germany
1956	Switzerland
1960	Not held
1964	Canada
1968	Italy
1972	Switzerland
1976	East Germany
1980	East Germany
1984	East Germany
1988	Switzerland

ICE SKATING

OLYMPIC GAMES
Winners since 1960

Men

1960	David Jenkins (US)
1964	Manfred Schnelldorfer (FRG)
1968	Wolfgang Schwarz (Aut)
1972	Ondrej Nepela (Cze)
1976	John Curry (GB)
1980	Robin Cousins (GB)
1984	Scott Hamilton (US)
1988	Brian Boitano (US)

Women

1960	Carol Heiss (US)
1964	Sjoukje Dijkstra (Hol)
1968	Peggy Fleming (US)
1972	Beatrix Schuba (Aut)
1976	Dorothy Hamill (US)
1980	Anett Potzsch (GDR)
1984	Katarina Witt (GDR)
1988	Katarina Witt (GDR)

Pairs

1960	Barbara Wagner/Robert Paul (Can)
1964	Lyudmila Belousova/Oleg Protopopov (USSR)
1968	Lyudmila Belousova/Oleg Protopopov (USSR)
1972	Irina Rodnina/Aleksey Ulanov (USSR)
1976	Irina Rodnina/Aleksandr Zaitsev (USSR)
1980	Irina Rodnina/Aleksandr Zaitsev (USSR)
1984	Yelena Valova/Oleg Vasiliev (USSR)
1988	Yekaterina Gordeyeva/Sergey Grinkov(USSR)

Ice Dance

1976	Lyudmila Pakhomova/
	Alexsandr Gorshkov (USSR)
1980	Natalya Linitschuck/
	Gannadiy Karponosov (USSR)
1984	Jayne Torvill/Christopher Dean (GB)
1988	Natalya Bestemianova/Andre Bukin (USSR)

WORLD CHAMPIONSHIPS
Winners in the 1980s
Men
1980	Jan Hoffmann (GDR)
1981	Scott Hamilton (US)
1982	Scott Hamilton (US)
1983	Scott Hamilton (US)
1984	Scott Hamilton (US)
1985	Alexandre Fadeyev (USSR)
1986	Brian Boitano (US)
1987	Brian Orser (Can)
1988	Brian Boitano (US)
1989	Kurt Browning (Can)

Women
1980	Anett Potzsch (GDR)
1981	Denise Biellmann (Swi)
1982	Elaine Zayak (US)
1983	Rosalynn Sumners (US)
1984	Katarina Witt (GDR)
1985	Katarina Witt (GDR)
1986	Debbie Thomas (US)
1987	Katarina Witt (GDR)
1988	Katarina Witt (GDR)
1989	Midori Ito (Jap)

Pairs
1980	Marina Tcherkassova/Sergey Shakrai (USSR)
1981	Irina Vorobyeva/Igor Lissovsky (USSR)
1982	Sabine Baess/Tassilo Thierbach (GDR)
1983	Yelena Valova/Oleg Vasiliev (USSR)
1984	Barbara Underhill/Paul Martini (Can)
1985	Yelena Valova/Oleg Vasiliev (USSR)
1986	Yekaterina Gordeyeva/Sergey Grinkov (USSR)
1987	Yekaterina Gordeyeva/Sergey Grinkov (USSR)
1988	Yelena Valova/Oleg Vasiliev (USSR)
1989	Yekaterina Gordeyeva/Sergey Grinkov (USSR)

ICE DANCE
1980	Krisztina Regoczy/Andras Sallay (Hun)
1981	Jayne Torvill/Christopher Dean (GB)
1982	Jayne Torvill/Christopher Dean (GB)
1983	Jayne Torvill/Christopher Dean (GB)
1984	Jayne Torvill/Christopher Dean (GB)
1985	Natalya Bestemianova/Andre Bukin (USSR)
1986	Natalya Bestemianova/Andre Bukin (USSR)
1987	Natalya Bestemianova/Andre Bukin (USSR)
1988	Natalya Bestemianova/Andre Bukin (USSR)
1989	Marina Klimova/Sergey Ponomarenko (USSR)

EUROPEAN CHAMPIONSHIPS
Winners in the 1980s
Men
1981	Igor Bobrin (USSR)
1982	Norbert Schramm (GDR)
1983	Norbert Schramm (GDR)
1984	Alexandre Fadeyev (USSR)
1985	Josef Sabovcik (Cze)
1986	Josef Sabovcik (Cze)
1987	Alexandre Fadeyev (USSR)
1988	Alexandre Fadeyev (USSR)
1989	Alexandre Fadeyev (USSR)

Women
1981	Denise Biellmann (Swi)
1982	Claudia Kristofics-Binder (Aut)
1983	Katarina Witt (GDR)
1984	Katarina Witt (GDR)
1985	Katarina Witt (GDR)
1986	Katarina Witt (GDR)
1987	Katarina Witt (GDR)
1988	Katarina Witt (GDR)
1989	Claudia Leistner (FRG)

Pairs
1981	I Lishovski/I Vorobieva (USSR)
1982	Sabine Baess/Tassilo Thierbach (GDR)
1983	Sabine Baess/Tassilo Thierbach (GDR)
1984	Yelena Valova/Oleg Vasiliev (USSR)
1985	Yelena Valova/Oleg Vasiliev (USSR)
1986	Yelena Valova/Oleg Vasiliev (USSR)
1987	Larissa Selezneva/Oleg Makarov (USSR)
1988	Ekaterina Gordeeva/Sergey Grinkov (USSR)
1989	Larissa Selezneva/Oleg Makarov (USSR)

ICE DANCE
1981	Jayne Torvill/Christopher Dean (GB)
1982	Jayne Torvill/Christopher Dean (GB)
1983	Natalya Bestemianova/Andre Bukin (USSR)
1984	Jayne Torvill/Christopher Dean (GB)
1985	Natalya Bestemianova/Andre Bukin (USSR)
1986	Natalya Bestemianova/Andre Bukin (USSR)
1987	Natalya Bestemianova/Andre Bukin (USSR)
1988	Natalya Bestemianova/Andre Bukin (USSR)
1989	Marina Klimova/Sergey Ponomarenko (USSR)

BIATHLON

OLYMPIC GAMES
Winners Since 1960
10 kilometres
1980	Frank Ullrich (GDR)
1984	Eirik Kvalfoss (Nor)
1988	Frank-Peter Roetsch (GDR)

20 kilometres
1960	Klas Lestander (Swe)
1964	Vladimir Melanin (USSR)
1968	Magnar Solberg (Nor)
1972	Magnar Solberg (Nor)
1976	Nikolay Kruglov (USSR)
1980	Anatoliy Alyabev (USSR)
1984	Peter Angerer (FRG)
1988	Frank-Peter Roetsch (GDR)

4 x 7.5km Relay
1968-88 USSR

NORDIC SKIING

OLYMPIC GAMES
Men
15km Cross Country
1960	Haakon Brusveen (Nor)
1964	Eero Mantyranta (Fin)
1968	Harald Gronningen (Nor)
1972	Sven-Ake Lundback (Swe)
1976	Nikolay Bayukov (USSR)
1980	Thomas Wassberg (Swe)
1984	Gunde Svan (Swe)
1988	Mikhail Deviatiarov (USSR)

30km Cross Country
1960	Sixten Jergerg (Swe)
1964	Eero Manyranta (Fin)
1968	Franco Nones (Ita)
1972	Vyacheslav Vedenin (USSR)
1976	Sergey Savelyev (USSR)
1980	Nikolay Zimyatov (USSR)
1984	Nikolay Zimyatov (USSR)
1988	Alexey Prokuorov (USSR)

50km Cross Country
1960	Kalevi Hamalainen (Fin)
1964	Sixten Jernberg (Swe)
1968	Ole Ellefsaeter (Nor)
1972	Pal Tyldum (Nor)
1976	Ivar Formo (Nor)
1980	Nikolay Zimyatov (USSR)
1984	Thomas Wassberg (Swe)
1988	Gunde Svan (Swe)

4 x 10km Cross Country Relay
1960	Finland
1964	Sweden
1968	Norway
1972	USSR

1976	Finland
1980	USSR
1984	Sweden
1988	Sweden

70 Metre Ski Jump

1960	Helmut Recknagel (GDR)
1964	Viekko Kankkonen (Fin)
1968	Jiri Raska (Cze)
1972	Yukio Kasaya (Jap)
1976	Hans-Georg Aschenbach (GDR)
1980	Toni Innauer (Aut)
1984	Jens Weissflog (GDR)
1988	Matti Nykanen (Fin)

90 Metre Ski Jump

1964	Torlaf Engan (Nor)
1968	Vladimir Byeloussov (USSR)
1972	Wojciech Fortuna (Pol)
1976	Karl Schnabl (Aut)
1980	Jouko Tormanen (Fin)
1984	Matti Nykanen (Fin)
1988	Matti Nykanen (Fin)

Combined

1960	Georg Thoma (FRG)
1964	Tormod Knutsen (Nor)
1968	Franz Keller (FRG)
1972	Ulrich Wehling (GDR)
1976	Ulrich Wehling (GDR)
1980	Ulrich Wehling (GDR)
1984	Tom Sandberg (Nor)
1988	Hippolyt Kempf (Swi)

Women

5km Cross Country

1964	Klaudia Boyarskikh (USSR)
1968	Toini Gustafsson (Swe)
1972	Galina Kulakova (USSR)
1976	Helena Takalo (Fin)
1980	Raisa Smetanina (USSR)
1984	Marja-Liisa Hamalainen (Fin)
1988	Marjo Matikainen (Fin)

10km Cross Country

1960	Maria Gusakova (USSR)
1964	Klaudia Boyarskikh (USSR)
1968	Toini Gustafsson (Swe)
1972	Galina Kulakova (USSR)
1976	Raisa Smetanina (USSR)
1980	Barbara Petzold (GDR)

1984	Marja-Liisa Hamalainen (Fin)
1988	Vida Ventsene (USSR)

20km Cross Country

1984	Marja-Liisa Hamalainen (Fin)
1988	Tamara Tikhonova (USSR)

4 x 5km Cross Country Relay

1960	Sweden
1964	USSR
1968	Norway
1972	USSR
1976	USSR
1980	GDR
1984	Norway
1988	USSR

───── 1990 ─────

ALPINE WORLD CUP

Jan 6-7: Men's slalom and giant slalom (Kranjske Gora, Yugoslavia), women's slalom and giant slalom (Piancanvallo, Italy); *Jan 13-14:* Men's downhill (Garmisch Partenkirchen, West Germany), men's slalom (Badwisee, West Germany), women's downhill and slalom (Haus, Austria); *Jan 16:* Women's super G (Kitzbuhel, Austria); *Jan 20-21:* Men's downhill and slalom (Kitzbuhel, Austria; *Jan 23:* Men's giant slalom (Adelboden, Switzerland), women's giant slalom (Berchtesgarden, West Germany); *Jan 27:* Women's downhill (Pfronten, West Germany); *Jan 27-28:* men's downhill and super-G (Wengel, Switzerland); *Jan 28:* Women's super-G (Lenggries, West Germany).

Feb 2-4: Men's downhill and super-G (Chamonix, France); *Feb 3-4:* Women's downhill and giant slalom (Brigels, Switzerland); *Feb 6:* Men's super-G (Coumayeur, Italy); *Feb 10-11:* Women's downhill and super-G (Meribel, France); *Feb 11:* Men's downhill (Laax, Switzerland); *Mar 3-4:* Men's slalom and giant slalom (Jasna, Czechoslovakia), women's slalom and giant slalom (Candanchu, Spain); *Mar 8-10:*Men's slalom (Geilo, Norway); *Mar 10:* Men's super G (Hemsedal, Norway); *Mar 12:* Men's slalom (Salen, Sweden); *Mar 13:* Women's slalom (Vemdalen, Sweden); *Mar 14:* Women's giant slalom (Klovsjo, Sweden); *Mar 16:* Women's super-G (Are, Sweden); *Mar 17:* Men's downhill (Are, Sweden).

WRESTLING

1989

WORLD CHAMPIONSHIPS
Martigny, Aug 31-Sep 3

FREESTYLE
Light-flyweight/Up to 48kg
1 Kim Jong-Shin (SKo)
2 Li Hak-Son (NKo)
3 Gnel Miejlovmian (USSR)

Flyweight/Up to 52kg
1 Valentin Jordanov (Bul)
2 Vladimir Tagovzov (USSR)
3 Majid Torkan (Ira)

Bantamweight/Up to 57kg
1 Yeung Sik-Kim (NKo)
2 Askari Mohammadian (Ira)
3 Roumen Pavlov (Bul)

Featherweight/Up to 62kg
1 John Smith (US)
2 Gary Bohay (Can)
3 Carsten Ploy (GDR)

Lightweight/Up to 68kg
1 Boris Bovdayev (USSR)
2 Kosei Akaishi (Jap)
3 Ahmet Cakici (FRG)

Welterweight/Up to 74kg
1 Ken Monday (US)
2 Arsen Fadzeyev (USSR)
3 Lodoin Enhbayar (Mon)

Middleweight/Up to 82kg
1 Elmadie Jabraylov (USSR)
2 Melvin Douglas (US)
3 Alcide Legrand (Fra)

Light-heavyweight/Up to 90kg
1 Makharbek Khardtzev (USSR)
2 Jim Scherr (US)
3 Gabor Toth (Hun)

Mid-heavyweight/Up to 100kg
1 Akhmed Atavov (USSR)
2 Bill Scherr (US)
3 Uwe Neupert (GDR)

Super-heavyweight/Over 100kg
1 Ali Reza Soleimani (Ira)
2 Bruce Baumgartner (US)
3 Aslan Khadartsev (USSR)

GRECO-ROMAN
Light-flyweight/Up to 48kg
1 Oleg Koucherenko (USSR)
2 Lars Ronningen (Nor)
3 Gooun Duk-Yong (SKo)

Flyweight/Up to 52kg
1 Alexandr Vgnatenko (USSR)
2 Oztruk Remzi (Tur)
3 An Han-Bong (SKo)

Bantamweight/Up to 57kg
1 Emil Ivanov (Bul)
2 Alexandr Schestarov (USSR)
3 Andras Sike (Hun)

Featherweight/Up to 62kg
1 Kamandar Msjidov (USSR)
2 Hur Byung-Ho (SKo)
3 Mario Olivera (Cub)

Lightweight/Up to 68kg
1 Claudio Passarelli (GDR)
2 Ghani Yalouz (Fra)
3 Zevon Djoulfaloucian (USSR)

Welterweight/Up to 74kg
1 Daulet Tourlukhanov (USSR)
2 Anton Arghire (Rom)
3 Peter Tenev (Bul)

Middleweight/Up to 82kg
1 Tibor Komaromi (Hun)
2 Mikhail Mamiachvili (USSR)
3 Magnus Fredriksson (Swe)

Light-heavyweight/Up to 90kg
1 Maik Bullmann (GDR)
2 Mike Foy (US)
3 Roger Gries (FRG)

Mid-heavyweight/Up to 100kg
1 Gerhard Himmel (FRG)
2 Ilia Vasilev (Bul)
3 Anatoliy Fedorenko (USSR)

Super-heavyweight/Over 100kg
1 Alexandr Karelin (USSR)
2 Laszlo Klausz (Hun)
3 Tomas Johansson (Swe)

CHAMPIONS

FREESTYLE

OLYMPIC GAMES
Light-flyweight/Up to 48kg
1904	Robert Curry (US)
1972	Roman Dmitriyev (USSR)
1976	Hassan Issaev (Bul)
1980	Claudio Pollio (Ita)
1984	Robert Weaver (US)
1988	Takashi Kobayashi (Jap)

Flyweight/Up to 52kg
1904	George Mehnert (US)
1948	Lennart Viitala (Fin)
1952	Hasan Gamici (Tur)
1956	Mirian Tsalkalamanidze (USSR)
1960	Ahmet Bilek (Tur)
1964	Yoshikatsu Yoshida (Jap)
1968	Shigeo Nakata (Jap)
1972	Kiyomi Kato (Jap)
1976	Yuji Takada (Jap)
1980	Anatoliy Beloglazov (USSR)
1984	Saban Trstena (Yug)
1988	Mitsuru Sato (Jap)

Bantamweight/Up to 57kg
1904	Isidor Niflot (US)
1908	George Mehnert (US)
1924	Kustaa Pihlajamäki (Fin)
1928	Kaarlo Mäkinen (Fin)
1932	Robert Pearce (US)
1936	Odön Zombori (Hun)
1948	Nasuh Akar (Tur)
1952	Shohachi Ishii (Jap)
1956	Mustafa Dagistanli (Tur)
1960	Terrence McCann (US)
1964	Yojiro Uetake (Jap)

1968	Yojiro Uetake (Jap)
1972	Hideaki Yanagida (Jap)
1976	Vladimir Yumin (USSR)
1980	Sergey Beloglazov (USSR)
1984	Hideaki Tomiyama (Jap)
1988	Sergey Beloglazov (USSR)

Featherweight/Up to 62kg
1904	Benjamin Bradshaw (US)
1908	George Dole (US)
1920	Charles Ackerly (US)
1924	Robin Reed (US)
1928	Allie Morrison (US)
1932	Hermanni Pihlajamaki (Fin)
1936	Kustaa Pihlajamaki (Fin)
1948	Gazanfer Bilge (Tur)
1952	Bayram Sit (Tur)
1956	Shozo Sasahara (Jap)
1960	Mustafa Dagistanli (Tur)
1964	Osamu Watanabe (Jap)
1968	Masaaki Kaneko (Jap)
1972	Zagalav Abdulbekov (USSR)
1976	Jung-Mo Yang (SKo)
1980	Magomedgasan Abushev (USSR)
1984	Randy Lewis (US)
1988	John Smith (US)

Lightweight/Up to 68kg
1904	Otto Roehm (US)
1908	George de Relwyskow (GB)
1920	Kalle Anttila (Fin)
1924	Russell Vis (US)
1928	Osväld Käpp (Est)
1932	Charles Pacôme (Fra)
1936	Károly Kárpáti (Hun)
1948	Celál Atik (Tur)
1952	Olle Anderberg (Swe)
1956	Emamali Habibi (Iran)
1960	Shelby Wilson (US)
1964	Enyu Valchev (Bul)
1968	Abdollah Movahed Ardabili (Iran)
1972	Dan Gable (US)
1976	Pavel Pinigin (USSR)
1980	Saipulla Absaidov (USSR)
1984	In-Tak You (SKo)
1988	Arsen Fadzeyev (USSR)

Welterweight/Up to 74kg
1904	Charles Erickson (US)
1924	Hermann Gehri (Swi)
1928	Arvo Haavisto (Fin)
1932	Jack Van Bebber (US)
1936	Frank Lewis (US)
1948	Yasar Dogu (Tur)
1952	William Smith (US)
1956	Mitsuo Ikeda (Jap)
1960	Douglas Blubaugh (US)
1964	Ismail Ogan (Tur)
1968	Mahmut Atalay (Tur)
1972	Wayne Wells (US)
1976	Jiichiro Date (Jap)
1980	Valentin Raitchev (Bul)
1984	David Schulz (US)
1988	Kenneth Monday (US)

Middleweight/Up to 82kg
1908	Stanley Bacon (GB)
1920	Eino Leino (Fin)
1924	Fritz Hagmann (Swi)
1928	Ernst Kyburz (Swi)
1932	Ivar Johansson (Swe)
1936	Emile Poilvé (Fra)
1948	Glen Brand (US)
1952	David Tsimakuridze (USSR)
1956	Nikola Stanchev (Bul)
1960	Hasan Gungor (Tur)
1964	Prodan Gardschev (Bul)

1968	Boris Gurevich (USSR)
1972	Levan Tediashvili (USSR)
1976	John Peterson (US)
1980	Ismail Abilov (Bul)
1984	Mark Schultz (US)
1988	Han Myung-Woo (SKo)

Light-heavyweight/Up to 90kg
1920	Anders Larsson (Swe)
1924	John Spellman (US)
1928	Thure Sjostedt (Swe)
1932	Peter Mehringer (US)
1936	Knut Fridell (Swe)
1948	Henry Wittenberg (US)
1952	Wiking Palm (Swe)
1956	Gholam Takhti Reza (Iran)
1960	Ismet Atli (Tur)
1964	Aleksandr Medved (USSR)
1968	Ahmet Ayik (Tur)
1972	Ben Peterson (US)
1976	Levan Tediashvili (USSR)
1980	Sanasar Oganesyan (USSR)
1984	Ed Banach (US)
1988	Makharbek Khadartsev (USSR)

Mid-heavyweight/Up to 100kg
1904	Bernhuff Hansen (US)
1908	George O'Kelly (GB)
1920	Robert Roth (Swi)
1924	Harry Steel (US)
1928	Johan Richthoff (Swe)
1932	Johan Richthoff (Swe)
1936	Kristjan Palusalu (Est)
1948	Gyula Bóbis (Hun)
1952	Arsen Mekokishvili (USSR)
1956	Hamit Kaplan (Tur)
1960	Wilfried Dietrich (FRG)
1964	Aleksandr Ivanitskiy (USSR)
1968	Aleksandr Medved (USSR)
1972	Ivan Yarygin (USSR)
1976	Ivan Yarygin (USSR)
1980	Ilya Mate (USSR)
1984	Lou Banach (US)
1988	Vasile Puscasu (Rom)

Super-heavyweight/Over 100 kg
1972	Aleksandr Medved (USSR)
1976	Soslan Andiyev (USSR)
1980	Soslan Andiyev (USSR)
1984	Bruce Baumgartner (US)
1988	David Gobedzhishvilli (USSR)

WORLD CHAMPIONSHIPS
First held 1951. Not held in Olympic years.
Winners since 1980

Light-flyweight/Up to 48kg
1981	Sergey Kornilayev (USSR)
1982	Sergey Kornilayev (USSR)
1983	Hwan Kim-Chol (SKo)
1985	Hwan Kim-Chol (SKo)
1986	Li Yae-Sik (NKo)
1987	Li Yae-Sik (NKo)
1989	Kim Jong-Shin (SKo)

Flyweight/Up to 52kg
1981	Toshio Asakura (Jap)
1982	Hartmut Reich (GDR)
1983	Valentin Jordanov (Bul)
1985	Valentin Jordanov (Bul)
1986	Sik Kim-Yong (NKo)
1987	Valentin Jordanov (Bul)
1989	Valentin Jordanov (Bul)

Bantamweight/Up to 57 kg
1981	Sergey Beloglazov (USSR)
1982	Anatoliy Beloglazov (USSR)
1983	Sergey Beloglazov (USSR)
1985	Sergey Beloglazov (USSR)

1986 Sergey Beloglazov (USSR)
1987 Sergey Beloglazov (USSR)
1989 Yeung Sik-Kim (NKo)

Featherweight/Up to 62kg
1981 Simeon Sterev (Bul)
1982 Sergey Beloglazov (USSR)
1983 Viktor Alekseyev (USSR)
1985 Viktor Alekseyev (USSR)
1986 Hazri Iszayev (USSR)
1987 John Smith (US)
1989 John Smith (US)

Lightweight/Up to 68kg
1981 Saipulla Absaidov (USSR)
1982 Mikhail Kharachura (USSR)
1983 Arsen Fadzeyev (USSR)
1985 Arsen Fadzeyev (USSR)
1986 Arsen Fadzeyev (USSR)
1987 Arsen Fadzeyev (USSR)
1989 Boris Bovdayev (USSR)

Welterweight/Up to 74kg
1981 Martin Knosp (FRG)
1982 Leroy Kemp (US)
1983 Dave Schultz (US)
1985 Raul Cascaret (Cuba)
1986 Raul Cascaret (Cuba)
1987 Adlan Vareyev (USSR)
1989 Ken Monday (US)

Middleweight/Up to 82kg
1981 Chris Campbell (US)
1982 Tejmuraj Dzgoev (USSR)
1983 Tejmuraj Dzgoev (USSR)
1985 Mark Schultz (US)
1986 Vladimir Modosyan (USSR)
1987 Mark Schultz (US)
1989 Elmadie Jabraylov (USSR)

Light-heavyweight/Up to 90kg
1981 Sanasar Oganesyan (USSR)
1982 Uwe Neupert (GDR)
1983 Piotr Naneyev (USSR)
1985 Bill Sherr (US)
1986 Makharbek Khardtsev (USSR)
1987 Makharbek Khardtsev (USSR)
1989 Makharbek Khardtsev (USSR)

Mid-heavyweight/Up to 100kg
1981 Roland Gehrke (GDR)
1982 Ilya Mate (USSR)
1983 Aslan Khadartsev (USSR)
1985 Levy Khabelov (USSR)
1986 Aslan Khadartsev (USSR)
1987 Levy Khabelov (USSR)
1989 Akhmed Atavov (USSR)

Super-heavyweight/Over 100kg
1981 Salman Khasimikov (USSR)
1982 Salman Khasimikov (USSR)
1983 Salman Khasimikov (USSR)
1985 David Gobedyichviliy (USSR)
1986 Bruce Baumgartner (US)
1987 Aslan Khadartsev (USSR)
1989 Ali Reza Soleimani (Ira)

GRECO ROMAN

OLYMPIC GAMES

Light-flyweight/Up to 48kg
1972 Gheorghe Berceanu (Rom)
1976 Aleksey Schumakov (USSR)
1980 Zaksylik Ushkempirov (USSR)
1984 Vincenzo Maenza (Ita)
1988 Vincenzo Maenza (Ita)

Flyweight/Up to 52kg
1948 Pietro Lombardi (Ita)
1952 Boris Gurevich (USSR)
1956 Nikolay Solovyov (USSR)
1960 Dumitru Pirvulescu (Rom)

1964 Tsutomu Hanahara (Jap)
1968 Petar Kirov (Bul)
1972 Petar Kirov (Bul)
1976 Vitaliy Konstantinov (USSR)
1980 Vakhtang Blagidze (USSR)
1984 Atsuji Miyahara (Jap)
1988 Jon Ronningen (Nor)

Bantamweight/Up to 57kg
1924 Eduard Pütsep (Est)
1928 Kurt Leucht (Ger)
1932 Jakob Brendel (Ger)
1936 Màrton Lörincz (Hun)
1948 Kurt Pettersén (Swe)
1952 Imre Hódos (Hun)
1956 Konstantin Vyrupayev (USSR)
1960 Oleg Karaveyev (USSR)
1964 Masamitsu Ichiguchi (Jap)
1968 János Varga (Hun)
1972 Rustem Kazakov (USSR)
1976 Pertti Ukkola (Fin)
1980 Shamil Serikov (USSR)
1984 Pasquale Passarelli (FRG)
1988 Andras Sike (Hun)

Featherweight/Up to 62kg
1912 Kaarlo Koskelo (Fin)
1920 Oskari Friman (Fin)
1924 Kalle Antila (Fin)
1928 Voldemar Väli (Est)
1932 Giovanni Gozzi (Ita)
1936 Yasar Erkan (Tur)
1948 Mehmet Oktav (Tur)
1952 Yakov Punkin (USSR)
1956 Rauno Mäkinen (Fin)
1960 Müzahir Sille (Tur)
1964 Imre Polyák (Hun)
1968 Roman Rurua (USSR)
1972 Gheorghi Markov (Bul)
1976 Kazimierz Lipién (Pol)
1980 Stylianos Migiakis (Gre)
1984 Weon-Kee Kim (SKo)
1988 Kamadar Madjidov (USSR)

Lightweight/Up to 68kg
1908 Enrico Porro (Ita)
1912 Eemil Väre (Fin)
1920 Eemil Väre (Fin)
1924 Oskari Friman (Fin)
1928 Lajos Keresztes (Hun)
1932 Erik Malmberg (Swe)
1936 Lauri Koskela (Fin)
1948 Gustaf Freij (Swe)
1952 Schazam Safin (USSR)
1956 Kyösti Lehtonen (Fin)
1960 Avtandil Koridze (USSR)
1964 Kazim Ayvaz (Tur)
1968 Munji Mumemura (Jap)
1972 Shamil Khisamutdinov (USSR)
1976 Suren Nalbandyan (USSR)
1980 Stefan Rusu (Rom)
1984 Vlado Lisjak (Yug)
1988 Levon Dzhulfalakyan (USSR)

Welterweight/Up to 74kg
1932 Ivar Johansson (Swe)
1936 Rudolf Svedberg (Swe)
1948 Gösta Andersson (Swe)
1952 Miklós Szilvási (Hun)
1956 Mithat Bayrak (Tur)
1960 Mithat Bayrak (Tur)
1964 Anatoliy Kolesov (USSR)
1968 Rudolf Vesper (GDR)
1970 Vitezslav Mácha (Cze)
1976 Anatoliy Bykov (USSR)
1980 Ferenc Kocsis (Hun)
1984 Jouko Salomaki (Fin)
1988 Kim Young-Nam (SKo)

Middleweight/Up to 82kg

1908	Frithiof Mårtensson (Fin)
1912	Claes Johansson (Swe)
1920	Carl Westergren (Swe)
1924	Edvard Westerlund (Fin)
1928	Väinö Kokkinen (Fin)
1932	Väinö Kokkinen (Fin)
1936	Ivar Johansson (Swe)
1948	Axel Grönberg (Swe)
1952	Axel Grönberg (Swe)
1956	Givy Kartoziya (USSR)
1960	Dimiter Dobrev (Bul)
1964	Branislav Simic (Yug)
1968	Lothar Metz (GDR)
1972	Csaba Hegedüs (Hun)
1976	Momir Petkovic (Yug)
1980	Gennadiy Korban (USSR)
1984	Ion Draica (Rom)
1988	Mikhail Mamiachvili (USSR)

Light-heavyweight/Up to 90kg

1908	Verner Weckman (Fin)
1912	No winner declared
1920	Claes Johansson (Swe)
1924	Carl Westergren (Swe)
1928	Ibrahim Moustafa (Egy)
1932	Rudolf Svensson (Swe)
1936	Axel Cadier (Swe)
1948	Karl-Eric Nilsson (Swe)
1952	Koelpo Gröndahl (Fin)
1956	Valentin Nikolayev (USSR)
1960	Tevfik Kis (Tur)
1964	Boyan Radev (Bul)
1968	Boyan Radev (Bul)
1972	Valeriy Rezantsev (USSR)
1976	Valeriy Rezantsev (USSR)
1980	Norbert Növényi (Hun)
1984	Steven Fraser (US)
1988	Atanas Komchev (Bul)

Heavyweight/Up to 100kg

1896	Carl Schuhmann (Ger)
1908	Richárd Weisz (Hun)
1912	Yrjö Saarela (Fin)
1920	Adolf Lindfors (Fin)
1924	Henri Deglane (Fra)
1928	Rudolf Svensson (Swe)
1932	Carl Westergren (Swe)
1936	Kristjan Paluslu (Est)
1948	Ahmet Kirecci (Tur)
1952	Johannes Kotkas (USSR)
1956	Anatoliy Parfenov (USSR)
1960	Ivan Bogdan (USSR)
1964	István Kozma (Hun)
1968	István Kozma (Hun)
1972	Nicolae Martinescu (Rom)
1976	Nikolay Balboshin (USSR)
1980	Gheorghi Raikov (Bul)
1984	Vasile Andrei (Rom)
1988	Andrzej Wronski (Pol)

Heavyweight

1972	Anatoliy Roschin (USSR)
1976	Aleksandr Kolchinsky (USSR)
1980	Aleksandr Kolchinsky (USSR)
1984	Jeffrey Blatnick (US)
1988	Alexandr Karelin (USSR)

WORLD CHAMPIONSHIPS

First held 1921. Not held in Olympic years. Winners since 1980.

Light-flyweight/Up to 48kg

1981	Zaksylik Ushkempirov (USSR)
1982	Temur Karashvili (USSR)
1983	Bratan Tsenov (Bul)
1985	Miagetdin Allakverdiev (USSR)
1986	Miagetdin Allakverdiev (USSR)
1987	Miagetdin Allakverdiev (USSR)
1989	Oleg Koucherenko (USSR)

Flyweight/Up to 52kg

1981	Vakhtang Blagidze (USSR)
1982	Benyur Pashayan (USSR)
1983	Benyur Pashayan (USSR)
1985	Jan Rønningen (Nor)
1986	Sergey Dyudyayev (USSR)
1987	Pedro Roque (Cuba)
1989	Alexandr Vgnatenko (USSR)

Bantamweight/Up to 57kg

1981	Pasquale Passarelli (FRG)
1982	Piotr Mikhalik (Pol)
1983	Eto Masaki (Jap)
1985	Stojan Balov (Bul)
1986	Emil Ivanov (Bul)
1987	Patrice Mourier (Fra)
1989	Emil Ivanov (Bul)

Featherweight/Up to 62kg

1981	Istvan Toth (Hun)
1982	Ryszard Swierad (Pol)
1083	Hnanu Lahtinen (Fin)
1985	Zhivko Vanguelov (Bul)
1986	Kamandar Madyidov (USSR)
1987	Jivko Vanguelov (Bul)
1989	Kamandar Msjidov (USSR)

Lightweight/Up to 68kg

1981	Gennadiy Yermilov (USSR)
1982	Gennadiy Yermilov (USSR)
1983	Tapio Sipilä (Fin)
1985	Stefan Negrisan (Rom)
1986	Levon Yulfalakyan (USSR)
1987	A Abayev (USSR)
1989	Claudio Passarelli (GDR)

Welterweight/Up to 74kg

1981	A Kudryavtsev (USSR)
1982	Stefan Rusu (Rom)
1983	Mikhail Mamiashvili (USSR)
1985	Mikhail Mamiashvili (USSR)
1986	Mikhail Mamiashvili (USSR)
1987	Jouni Ilomaki (Fin)
1989	Daulet Tourlukhanov (USSR)

Middleweight/Up to 82kg

1981	Gennadiy Korban (USSR)
1982	Temur Abkhasava (USSR)
1983	Temur Abkhasava (USSR)
1985	Bogdan Daras (Pol)
1986	Bogdan Daras (Pol) & Tibor Komaromi (Hun)
1987	Tibor Komaromi (Hun)
1989	Tibor Komaromi (Hun)

Light-heavyweight/Up to 90kg

1981	Igor Kanygin (USSR)
1982	Frank Andersson (Swe)
1983	Igor Kanygin (USSR)
1985	Michael Houk (US)
1986	Andrjez Malina (Pol)
1987	Vladimir Popov (USSR)
1989	Maik Bullmann (GDR)

Heavyweight/Up to 100kg

1981	Mikhail Saladze (USSR)
1982	Roman Wroclawski (Pol)
1983	Andrej Dmitrov (Bul)
1985	Andrej Dmitrov (Bul)
1986	Tamas Gaspar (Hun)
1987	Gouram Guedekhaorui (USSR)
1989	Gerhard Himmel (FRG)

Super-heavyweight/Over 100kg

1981	Refik Memisevic (Yug)
1982	Nikolai Denev (Bul)
1983	Jevgeniy Artiochin (USSR)
1985	Igor Rostorotskiy (USSR)
1986	Thomas Johansson (Swe)
1987	Igor Rostorotskiy (USSR)
1989	Alexandr Karelin (USSR)

YACHTING

The America's Cup was won and lost twice in 1989 without a single boat taking to the water. In March, New York Judge Carmen Ciparack reversed the result of the 1988 contest, saying the San Diego Yacht Club, the defenders, had breached the deed of gift governing the event by racing a catamaran against the monohull of the Mercury Bay Yacht Club of New Zealand.

In September, this decision was reversed by a 4-1 vote of the state appeals court. Both sides then had to prepare for a possible further legal battle and – incidentally – for a race, some day, on the water. After New Zealand's court victory, the country had appointed its own America's Cup Minister and begun preparing gleefully for a fiesta in Auckland in 1992. All contestants for 1992 have agreed on a new class of yacht: 75 foot long and lighter and faster than the old 12-metres.

——— 1989 ———

CHAMPAGNE MUMM ADMIRAL'S CUP
Jul 27-Aug 9

Race 1, RYS Trophy Race (27 miles)
Jamarella (GB) Alan Gray, Gordon McGuire, Lawrie Smith

Race 2, RORC Channel Course (200 miles)
Will (Jap) Ryouji Oda, Hirohumi Reraymama, Geoff Stagg

Race 3, Corum Trophy race (28 miles)
Stockbroker's Container (Den) Jens Hoest, Henrik Soderlund, Christian Schmidt

Race 4, Champagne Mumm Trophy race (28 miles)
Corum (Fra) Philippe Briand, Marc Bouet, Philippe Delhumeau

Race 5, Long Inshore race (40 miles)
Stockbroker's Container (Den) Jens Hoest, Henrik Soderlund, Christian Shcmidt

Race 6, RORC Fastnet Race (605 miles)
Great News (US) Randy Short, Tom Blackaller, Dave Hulse

Final Standings
1 Britain (*Jamarella, Juno IV, Indulgence IV*) 748.0 pts
2 Denmark (*4K, Andelsbanken IV, Stockbroker's Container*) 730.5 pts
3 New Zealand (*Librah, Fair Share, Propaganda*) 667.5 pts

Individual Winner
Jamarella (GB) Alan Gray, Gordon McGuire, Lawrie Smith

COWES WEEK
Class 1 race winners
Solent, Jul 29-Aug 6

Queen's Cup
1	Obsession	Barry Rose
2	Jacobite	Stephen James
3	Old Mother Gun	J Mitchell

Sir Walter Preston Cup
1	Tai Wahn	Ulrich Mathiesen
2	Toy for the Boys	M Guscott
3	Bierkaai	Henk Klunder

Camrose Trophy
1	Bullwinkle	Peter Whiteley
2	Summer Pudding	Mike Enderby
3	Somersault	Robert Carrell

Sidewinder (John Oswald) originally placed.first but disqualified after protest

UP FOR THE CUP

"Barely paying lip-service to the significance of the competition, its clear goal was to retain the cup at all costs so that it could host a competition on its own terms. San Diego thus violated the spirit of the deed."
Judge Carmen Ciparack, Mar 28

"A declaration is made that San Diego's catamaran was an eligible yacht...and that San Diego is entitled to the America's Cup."
New York State of Appeal Court, Sep 19

"The 1988 America's Cup races were manifestly unfair in every sense. True sportsmanship demands far more, as does the very Deed of Gift by which this competition has been sponsored for over a century".
Dissenting appeal judge Bentley Kassal

"This rule (about a mismatch) does not appear in the America's Cup Deed of Gift. Nor can it be inferred from any term or combination of terms found in the Deed and it is contradicted by the history of America's Cup competition."
San Diego lawyer Harold Tyler

"We feel good because it has been a long road. We know that providing principles is never easy and rarely popular."
Tom Mitchell of the America's Cup Organising Committee, Sep 9

"It's wrong, plain and simple. The idea that a competitor can fix a contest to win makes a nonsense of any sport...If the ruling is not overturned, sportsmanship and the Cup are out of the window."
Michael Fay, head of the New Zealand syndicate

Britannia Challenge Cup
1	Jacobite	Stephen James
2	Obsession	Barry Rose
3	Bierkaai	Henk Klunder

Rocking Chair Trophy
1	Obsession	Barry Rose
2	Jacobite	Stephen James
3	Ellora Reamet Titanium	Vincent D'Orgeval

New York YC Cup
1	Batteleur 88	G C Bonar
2	Local hero V	Geoffrey Howison

Only two finishers declared

Coronation Bowl
1	Toy for the Boys	M Guscott

Only one finisher declared

Glazebrook Cup
1	Obsession	Barry Rose
2	Old Mother Gun	J Mitchell
3	Toy for the Boys	M Guscott

———— CHAMPIONS ————

OLYMPIC GAMES
Champions in current classes

Soling
1972	United States
1976	Denmark
1980	Denmark
1984	United States
1988	East Germany

Star
1932	Gilbert Gray/Andrew Libano Jnr (US)
1936	Peter Bischoff/Hans-Joachim Weise (Ger)
1948	Hilary Smart/Paul Smart (US)
1952	Nicolo Rode/Agostino Straulino (Ita)
1956	Lawrence Low/Herbert Williams (US)
1960	Timir Pinegin/Fyodor Shutkov (USSR)
1964	Cecil Cooke/Durward Knowles (Bah)
1968	Peter Barrett/Lowell North (US)
1972	John Anderson/David Forbes (Aus)
1980	Valentin Mankin/Aleksandr Muzychenko (USSR)
1984	Bill Buchan/Stephen Erickson (US)
1988	Michael McIntyre/Bryn Vaile (GB)

The Star racer used by McIntyre and Vaile to win gold at Seoul was reported stolen from a sailing club at Datchet, Herts in February 1989.

Flying Dutchman
(Previously known as Sharpie class)
1956	John Cropp/Peter Mander (NZ)
1960	Bjorn Bergvall/Peder Lunde Jnr (Nor)
1964	Helmer Pedersen/Earle Wells (NZ)
1968	Iain Macdonald-Smith/Rodney Pattisson (GB)
1972	Christopher Davies/Rodney Pattisson (GB)
1976	Eckert Diesch/Jorg Diesch (FRG)
1980	Alejandro Abascal/Miguel Noguer (Spa)
1984	William Carl Buchan/Jonathan McKee (US)
1988	Christian Gronborg/Jorgen Bojsen-Moeller (Den)

Tornado
1976	John Osborn/Reg White (GB)
1980	Lars Bjorkstrom/Alexandre Welter (Bra)
1984	Rex Sellers/Christopher Timms (NZ)
1988	Nicholas Henard/Jean-Yves Le Deroff (Fra)

Finn
(Formerly known as Meulan, International 12-foot, Snowbird, International Olympia and Firefly classes)
1920	Franciscus Hin/Johannes Hin (Hol)
1920	Francis Richards/T Hedberg (GB)
1924	Leon Huybrechts (Bel)
1928	Sven Thorell (Swe)
1932	Jacques Lebrun (Fra)
1936	Daniel Kagchelland (Hol)
1948	Paul Elvstrom (Den)
1952	Paul Elvstrom (Den)
1956	Paul Elvstrom (Den)
1960	Paul Elvstrom (Den)
1964	Willi Kuhweide (FRG)
1968	Valentin Mankin (USSR)
1972	Serge Maury (Fra)
1976	Jochen Schümann (GDR)
1980	Esko Rechardt (Fin)
1984	Russell Coutts (NZ)
1988	Jose-Luis Doreste (Spa)

470 Class
1976	Harro Bode/Frank Hubner (FRG)
1980	Eduardo Penido/Marcos Soares (Bra)
1984	Jose-Luis Doreste/Roberto Molina (Spa)
1988	Thierry Peponnet/Luc Pillot (Fra)

Boardsailing
1984	Stephan van den Berg (Hol)
1988	Bruce Kendall (NZ)

Women's 470 Class
1988	Lynne Jewell/Allison Jolly (US)

AMERICA'S CUP
	Winning boat	Winning skipper
1870	Magic (US)	Andrew Comstock
1871	Columbia (US)	Nelson Comstock
	& Sappho (US)	Sam Greenwood
1876	Madeleine (US)	Josephus Williams
1881	Mischief (US)	Nathaniel Clock
1885	Puritan (US)	Aubrey Crocker
1886	Mayflower (US)	Martin Stone
1887	Volunteer (US)	Henry Haff
1893	Vigilant (US)	William Hansen
1895	Defender (US)	Henry Haff
1899	Columbia (US)	Charlie Barr
1901	Columbia (US)	Charlie Barr
1903	Reliance (US)	Charlie Barr
1920	Resolute (US)	Charles Adams
1930	Enterprise (US)	Harold Vanderbilt
1934	Rainbow (US)	Harold Vanderbilt
1937	Ranger (US)	Harold Vanderbilt
1958	Columbia (US)	Briggs Cunningham
1962	Weatherly (US)	Emil Mosbacher Jr
1964	Constellation (US)	Bob Bavier Jr
1967	Intrepid (US)	Emil Mosbacher Jr
1970	Intrepid (US)	Bill Ficker
1974	Courageous (US)	Ted Hood
1977	Courageous (US)	Ted Turner
1980	Freedom (US)	Dennis Conner
1983	Australia II (Aus)	John Bertrand
1987	Stars & Stripes (US)	Dennis Conner
1988	Stars & Stripes (US)	Dennis Conner

ADMIRAL'S CUP
Team
1957	Britain
1959	Britain
1961	United States
1963	Britain
1965	Britain
1967	Australia
1969	United States
1971	Britain
1973	West Germany
1975	Britain
1977	Britain
1979	Australia
1981	Britain
1983	West Germany
1985	West Germany
1987	New Zealand
1989	Britain

Individual (from 1969)

1969	Red Rooster (USA)
1971	Ragamuffin (Aus)
1973	Saudade (FRG)
1975	Noryema (GB)
1977	Imp (USA)
1979	Eclipse (GB)
1981	Victory (GB)
1983	Diva (Fra)
1985	Phoenix (GB)
1987	Propaganda (NZ)
1989	Jamarella (GB)

WHITBREAD ROUND THE WORLD RACE

Winning Skipper/Boat

1973-74	Ramon Carlin (Mex) *Sayula II*
1977-78	Cornelius van Rietschoten (Hol) *Flyer*
1981-82	Cornelius van Rietschoten (Hol) *Flyer II*
1985-86	Pierre Fehlmann (Swi) *UBS Switzerland*

Winning times:
1974 133d 12h 00m; **1978** 119d 01h 00m; **1982** 120d 06h 35m; **1986** 117d 14h 31m

———— 1990 ————

Feb 3 Whitbread Round the World Race, fourth leg start (Auckland, New Zealand);

Mar 17 Whitbread Round the World Race, fifth leg start (Punta de Este, Uruguay);

May 5 Whitbread Round the World Race, sixth leg start (Fort Lauderdale, USA);

May 18 Whitbread Round the World Race - first yacht expected to arrive Portsmouth;

Aug 4-12 Cowes Week (Isle of Wight).

MISCELLANY

BRITISH SPORTS HONOURS, 1989
New Year
CBE – John Kendall-Carpenter, rugby union player and administrator and headmaster of Wellington.

OBE – Frank Dick, athletics coach; Richard Dodds, Olympic hockey captain; Mike Spracklen, rowing coach; David Whitaker, Olympic hockey coach.

MBE – Tony Allcock, bowls; Eric Bristow, darts; Neville Goss, motor cycling administrator; Chris Hallam, disabled sport; Dusty Hare, rugby union; Fred Lindop, rugby league referee; Mike McIntyre, Olympic yachtsman; James Robinson, schools soccer; Graham Salmon, visually handicapped sport; Robin Surgeoner, disabled swimmer; Ernie Walker, secretary, Scottish FA.

Queen's Birthday
CBE – Ted Croker, secretary of the Football Association.

OBE – Penny Chuter, rowing coach; Josh Gifford, racehorse trainer; Courtney Jones, skating; David Oxley, chief executive of the Rugby League; Fred Trueman, cricketer and savant.

MBE – Vic Charles, karate; Mike Kenny, disabled sport; Judy Leden, hang-gliding; Violet McBride, hockey; Steven Moore, water-skiing; Ian Stark, equestrianism; Ann Trotman, disabled sport.

BETTING
% of adults betting on horses

1978	9.4
1985	7.9
1988	8.6

Sports' share of betting turnover

Horse racing	78
Greyhounds	15
Football	3
Others	4

Source: Ladbrokes/*Racing Post*

SPONSORSHIP
Sports' share of sponsorship in Britain

	£m	%
Motor sports	55	34
Football	20	13
Horse racing	10	6
Snooker	5	3

Golf	5	3
Cricket	3	2
Athletics	2.5	2
Tennis	2.5	2
Other sports	57	35

Source: Mintel/Campaign (1987 figures)

TV RATINGS
The top TV sports programmes 1989 (up to Sep 3)

			Viewers in millions
1 Boxing – Tyson v Bruno	BBC1	Feb 26	14.30
2 Racing – Grand National	BBC1	Apr 8	11.90
3 Tennis – Wimbledon men's final	BBC2	Jul 9	11.71
4 The Match – Everton v Liverpool	ITV	May 3	10.70
5 The Match – Liverpool v Arsenal	ITV	May 26	10.30
6 FA Cup final – Everton v Liverpool	BBC1	May 20	10.29
7 Boxing – McGuigan v McDonnell	ITV	May 31	9.59
8 Tennis – Wimbledon ladies' final	BBC2	Jul 9	9.50
9 The Match – Littlewoods Cup final	ITV	Apr 9	8.79
10 The Match – Arsenal v Spurs	ITV	Jan 2	8.70
11 The Match – Man Utd v Liverpool	ITV	Jan 1	8.68
12 Final Score	BBC1	Apr 15	8.53
13 International Snooker	ITV	Jan 15	8.52
14 100 Great Sporting Moments – Torvill and Dean	BBC1	Feb 19	8.34
15 Final Score	BBC1	Jan 2	8.33
16 The Match – Man Utd v Arsenal	ITV	Apr 2	8.23

Source: Barb/AGB

FAVOURITE TV SPORTS

Under 14 Male and Female	15-29 Male and Female	30-44 Male and Female	45-64 Male and Female	Over 65 Male and Female
1 Football	Football	Football	Football	Football
2 Tennis	Athletics	Athletics	Snooker	Snooker
3 Athletics	Boxing	Tennis	Athletics	Tennis
4 Rugby	Rugby	Rugby	Tennis	Bowls
5 Boxing	Tennis	Snooker	Rugby	Athletics
6 Swimming	Snooker	Swimming	Cricket	Rugby
7 Hockey	Swimming	Cricket	Boxing	Cricket
8 Snooker	Ski-ing	Boxing	Golf	Boxing
9 Basketball	US Football	Skiing	Swimming	Darts
10 Gymnastics	Ice Skating	Golf	Ice Skating	Swimming

THE NATION'S TOP 25 TV SPORTS
(All categories combined)

1 Football	55.33%	8 Cricket	18.47%	15 US Football	11.46%	22 Show Jumping	6.50%
2 Tennis	36.70%	9 Ice Skating	13.91%	16 Basketball	9.65%	23 Badminton	5.94%
3 Athletics	36.19%	10 Gymnastics	13.43%	17 Bowls	9.35%	24 Ice Hockey	5.65%
4 Snooker	34.27%	11 Golf	13.19%	18 Horse Racing	8.26%	25 Rugby League	3.54%
5 Rugby Union	31.93%	12 Skiing	12.82%	19 Wrestling	7.84%	*Source:* Survey of 12,800
6 Boxing	25.96%	13 Hockey	12.63%	20 Volleyball	7.36%	people for the BBC TV
7 Swimming	21.16%	14 Darts	11.86%	21 Motor Racing	7.33%	programme "Move It".

OBITUARY, 1989

Bill ANDREWS, 80, January 9. Somerset cricketer, coach and character who completed the double in both 1937 and 1938 and called his autobiography *The Hand That Bowled Bradman*. His did, for 202.

John BASSETT, 83, February. Penarth full-back who captained Wales nine times.

H.N. "Dickie" BIRD, 65, April 4. Football Association official for 49 years, rising from office junior to deputy secretary.

Tom BLACKALLER, 52, September 7, of a heart attack. Champion yachtsman and lively personality who won the Fastnet Race the month before his death. Twice world champion in the Star class, sailed USA, the beaten challenger semi-finalist, in the 1987 America's Cup.

Martin BLACKSHAW, 38, January 24, in a car crash in France. Chantilly-based racehorse trainer and former British jump jockey.

Bill BOWLES, 89, July 19. Retired head groundsman at Eton and founder of the Institute of Groundsmanship.

Phil BULL, 79, June. British horse racing's white-bearded sage and logician. Founder of the Timeform Organisation.

Lee CALHOUN, 56, June 21, after a stroke. American athlete – the first man to win successive Olympic hurdles titles: the 110m in 1956 and 1960.

Tony CHARLTON, 32, January 3, in a car crash near Ayr. Yorkshire-based racehorse trainer and former jump jockey.

Sir Lance CROSS, 76, May. New Zealand member of the IOC.

Sir Guy CUNARD, 77, January. Amateur steeplechase and point-to-point rider known affectionately as The Galloping Major. "No one else I have heard of," wrote Lord Oaksey, "ever dedicated himself more completely to the thrill of riding horses across country, as fast as they can be ridden."

Laurie CUNNINGHAM, 33, July 15, in a car crash near Madrid. The second black footballer (after Viv Anderson) to play for England which he did six times until injuries spoiled a career of enormous potential. Moved from Orient to West Bromwich to Real Madrid then played for several English clubs (he came on as substitute for Wimbledon in the 1988 Cup final) before returning to Spain to help Rayo Vallecano win promotion to the First Division. Ron Atkinson, his former manager, described Cunningham as probably the best talent Britain had produced since George Best.

Leslie DAWSON, 82, January 6. Motor-cycle racer and innovator.

Esteban DEJESUS, 37, May 12, of AIDS. WBC lighweight champion from Puerto Rico, the only man to beat Roberto Duran in the 1970s. He died after sharing needles in jail while serving a life sentence for killing a man in a motoring dispute.

Eddie DEMPSEY, 77, February 7. Rider of Caughoo, the 100 to 1 winner of the Grand National in 1947.

Kazimerz DEYNA, 41, September 1, in a car crash near San Diego. Polish footballer capped 102 times for his country. Team captain in the match when Poland stopped England qualifying for the 1974 World Cup and scorer of a stunning goal in the team's subsequent win over Italy. Between 1979 and 1981 he had a less successful spell with Manchester City before leaving to join San Diego Sockers and retiring there to coach youngsters.

Olivier DOUIEB, 42, June 22, of cancer. French racehorse trainer who saddled Detroit to win the 1980 Prix de l'Arc de Triomphe.

Ken GEE, 72, April. Wigan prop forward from 1933 to 1954 who won 31 caps for England and Great Britain.

A. Bartlett GIAMATTI, 51, September 1, of a heart attack. Giamatti had become commissioner of baseball just five months earlier and died only eight days after banning Pete Rose for life from the game. A scholar first and baseball enthusiast second: he was an expert on comparative literature, the author of books on Dante and Spenser and, at 40, the youngest-ever president of Yale.

Vernon "Lefty" GOMEZ, 80, February 17. Star pitcher and wit with the New York Yankees in the 1930s. Elected to the baseball Hall of Fame in 1972.

Jack GROUT, 79, May 13. American professional golfer. Jack Nicklaus's first teacher and constant mentor: "He was like a second father to me," said Nicklaus.

Freda HAMMERSLEY, (née James), 77, January. Wimbledon women's doubles champion (with Kay Stammers) in 1935 and 1936 and British Wightman Cup player.

Lord HARDING of Petherton, 92, January 20. Former Chief of the Imperial General Staff and first chairman of the Horse Race Betting Levy Board 1961-67.

Joe HARVEY, 70, February 24. Former half-back, manager and chief scout of Newcastle United; captain of the FA Cup winning teams of 1951 and 52 and the epitome of old-fashioned footballing good humour.

Bill HIDE, 81, February. Racehorse trainer for 22 years and father of jockey Edward.

C.L.R.JAMES, 88, May 31. Trinidadian critic, historian and cricket writer; long-standing keeper of the West Indian game's conscience.

William "Judy" JOHNSON, 89, June 14. Baseball star of the Negro Leagues, barred from the major leagues because he was black but elected to the Hall of Fame in 1975.

George KNUDSEN, 51, January 24. Canadian professional golfer renowned for the beauty of his swing.

Sam LONGSON, 88, January 17. Haulage contractor and former chairman of Derby County; original mentor, later sparring-partner, of Brian Clough.

Stan MARTIN, 92, January 15. Trainer of two Greyhound Derby winners. Ballyhennessy Seal (1945) and Ballymac Ball (1950).

John MATUSZAK, 38, June 17, of an accidental overdose of painkiller. Former Oakland Raiders defensive lineman in Super Bowl teams of 1976 and 1980. He specialised as tough guy both in the team known as "the Evil Empire" and, later, as an actor on films and TV.

Rod MORGAN MBE, 59, April 6. A Welsh rugby selector since 1979 and manager of the 1988 tour to New Zealand. Police superintendent and whole-hearted enthusiast for the South Wales Police team.

Don REVIE OBE, 61, May 26, of motor neurone disease. Talented and tactically shrewd footballer (six caps) who became the most dynamic manager of the 60s and 70s, when he transformed Leeds United into the most powerful side in the country. This was followed by his disastrous promotion to England manager which ended, even before England had failed to qualify for the 1978 World Cup, with his decision to work in the United Arab Emirates which brought him widespread condemnation and a 10-year ban (overturned by the courts) from the FA. He was much loved by his players and turned Leeds into the best team in England though they won surprisingly few trophies and, due to their ruggedness, few friends.

Sugar Ray ROBINSON, 67, April 12. A professional boxer for 25 years, the winner of 175 fights out of 202, the world middleweight (five times) and welterweight champion and almost light-heavyweight champion as well, the sport's supreme stylist. Tributes: "He was without question the greatest fighter ever in the history of boxing" – Bob Arum. "I always felt he was the greatest fighter who ever lived. He was a prince of the ring, and out of it he was an absolute charmer." – Mike Barrett. "I fought Sugar Ray six times. He opened everything that was closed and closed everthing that was open." – Jake La Motta.

George ROBLEDO, 62, April 3. The Chilean-cum-Yorkshireman who played inside forward for Newcastle United and Chile. The third member of Newcastle's '51 and '52 Cup-winning teams to die in six months, after Jackie Milburn and Joe Harvey.

Frank ROSTRON, 81, January 7. Sports official (South African manager at the 1936 Olympics) and reporter, mostly for the *Daily Express*. The only journalist to cover both Los Angeles Games – 1932 and 1984.

Jimmy RUFFELL, 89, September 6. West Ham left-winger between 1920 and 1938; believed to have been their last survivor from the "white horse" FA Cup final of 1923.

Gaetano SCIREA, 36, September 3, in a car crash in Poland. Footballer who spent 14 years with Juventus; an effective and innovative sweeper. He won 78 caps for Italy, including the 1982 World Cup final. Latterly assistant manager of Juventus.

Commander K.A. "Monkey" SELLAR, 82, May. Winner of six England RU caps at full-back in 1927 and 1928 and Sussex batsman who later won the DSO for his part in a naval action at the mouth of the River Scheldt in 1944.

Sarah SHEPPARD, 19, April 2. Killed in a fall while riding in the East Essex point-to-point meeting at Marks Tey.

Wilf SLACK, 34, January 15, of a heart attack while batting in a tour game in The Gambia. St Vincent-born left-handed opening bat who scored prolifically for Middlesex through the 1980s and played three Tests for England in 1986 when he flew out to the West Indies as a replacement.

Doug SMITH, 71, April 11, suicide. Five times champion jockey in the 50s and rider of 3,112 winners (a total beaten only by Sir Gordon Richards and Lester Piggott). He later trained Sleeping Partner to win the 1969 Oaks.

Wally ST PIER, 82, January. Former West Ham chief scout who spent 47 years with the club and discovered Moore, Hurst and Peters.

Henry "Milo" STEINBORN, 95, February 9. Legendary American weightlifter and all-round strong man who was still wrestling professionally aged 70.

Jeffrey STOLLMEYER, 68, September 10, of his wounds after being shot in his Trinidad home by burglars. West Indian opening batsman in 32 Tests, captain in 14; a key member of the 1950 side which first asserted the West Indies' cricketing strength. Later he was active in Trinidad life as a landowner, businessman and senator.

Jesse SWEETSER, 87, May 27. First American to win the British Amateur golf championship.

Edward (E.P.) TAYLOR, 90, May 14. Canadian brewery magnate who became the most successful racehorse breeder of modern times. He bred the brilliant stallion Northern Dancer, three Epsom Derby winners (Njinsky, The Minstrel and Secreto) and 21 winners of Canada's premier Classic, the Queen's Plate.

Bill TERRY, 90, January 9. Baseball player and manager with the New York Giants. A left-handed hitter and first baseman who finished after 14 seasons with a career average of .341, the 12th best in history.

Tommy TRINDER, 80, July 10. Comedian and chairman of Fulham FC from 1956 to 1975.

Harry WHARTON, 51, April 20. Well-known Northern racehorse trainer.

John WYER, 79, April 8. Back-room figure in motor racing who managed four winning teams at Le Mans and played a major role in the development of Aston Martin on and off the track.

THE GUIDE TO 1890

JANUARY: The Calcutta Turf Club exonerated Lord William Beresford over the running over his horse Presto in the Walter Locke Cup at Lucknow. The stewards unanimously decided the horse was not deliberately pulled but severely censured the jockey for "ceasing to persevere far too early".

FEBRUARY: At Dewsbury, Wales beat England for the first time under Rugby Union rules, after five defeats and a draw in the previous games. Stadden's try was the only score.

MARCH: Blackburn Rovers won the FA Cup beating Sheffield Wednesday 6-1 at The Oval in front of a crowd of 18,000, many of whom ran on to the field near the end mistaking a free-kick for full-time.

APRIL: A Welsh boxer, John Hopkins, died after being injured in a prize fight for £1 in front of 20 spectators on Llanwonno Mountain, near Mountain Ash in Glamorgan. His opponent, Collins was charged with grievous bodily harm. At Hampden Park, England and Scotland drew 1-1.

MAY: Yorkshire beat the Australian cricketers at Bramall Lane, largely through the all-round play of Peel.

JUNE: Sainfoin, at 100 to 15, won the Derby, the first winner to come from the Royal Stud at Hampton Court. The crowd was small but the race eventful: the 2000 Guineas winner, Surefoot, who started at 95 to 40 on, almost ran out when about to challenge for the lead. Yorkshire beat the Australians, as did MCC, "Dr Grace playing with a great vigour and dash".

JULY: W.J. Hamilton, the challenger, beat the holder W. Renshaw by three sets to two in the Singles Championship at the All-England Club: "Hamilton showed fine form and his win seemed very popular". London Rowing Club beat Brasenose, Oxford in the Grand Challenge Cup by 1¾ lengths: "Henley kept up its reputation as the champion picnic of the season. Pedestrians of both sexes swarmed down the towpath". England beat Australia at Lord's with 75 not out from WG

Grace: Cries of 'Grace' eventually brought the Doctor to the windows; his appearance evoked loud cheers. . .the Australians earned great praise for "the capital way in which they fought their formidable rivals".

AUGUST: England beat Australia again at The Oval and were due to play a third match. However, "two days disappointments were followed by another, and the third of this season's matches between England and Australia, which should have been played at the Old Trafford Ground, Manchester, was yesterday abandoned. The wet weather made cricket impracticable...."

SEPTEMBER: Surrey won the County Championship in the first year it was officially organised rather than decided by journalists. The Duke of Portland's Memoir won the St Leger in front of the largest crowd ever: 160 trains left Doncaster station after the race.

OCTOBER: The Salford Harriers went on a tour of North America. In the International Handicap meeting in Detroit, W.H. Morton, giving his rivals up to three minutes' start, stopped twice to tie up his shoe laces but still won very easily over five miles.

NOVEMBER: Mr Seagar Hunt MP presided over "an influential meeting" at the Eyre Arms Hotel to oppose the scheme by the Manchester, Sheffield and Lincolnshire Railway company to put a line through Hampstead and St John's Wood, passing in an open cutting through Lord's Cricket Ground.

DECEMBER: "Information has been received from Wisbech of an extraordinary scene amongst the skaters there. Some local matches had been arranged on the canal, but the sluice-keeper, named Pogson, broke up the ice by letting in the water from the River Nene. The feeling against the sluice-keeper became intense. A great crowd assembled with threats of vengeance near his house. Pogson was roughly handled, and had to run for his life. He took refuge in his house afterwards and a thousand people assembled and broke windows and did other damage, also burning his effigy."

Source: *The Times*